ISSUES IN AGING

Mark Novak
San Jose State University

Boston New York San Francisco
Mexico City Montreal Toronto London Madrid Munich Paris
Hong Kong Singapore Tokyo Cape Town Sydney

Senior Series Editor: *Jeff Lasser*
Series Editorial Assistant: *Heather McNally*
Senior Marketing Manager: *Kelly May*
Production Editor: *Won McIntosh*
Editorial Production Service: *Publishers' Design and Production Services, Inc.*
Composition Buyer: *Linda Cox*
Manufacturing Buyer: *JoAnne Sweeney*
Electronic Composition: *Publishers' Design and Production Services, Inc.*
Cover Designer: *Joel Gendron*

For related titles and support materials, visit our online catalog at www.ablongman.com

Between the time website information is gathered and then published, it is not unusual for some sites to have closed. Also, the transcription of URLs can result in typographical errors. The publisher would appreciate notification where these errors occur so that they may be corrected in subsequent editions.

Library of Congress Cataloging-in-Publication Data
Novak, Mark W.
Issues in aging : an introduction to gerontology / Mark Novak.
p. cm.
Includes bibliographical references and index.
ISBN 0-205-43918-7 (alk. paper)
1. Gerontology. 2. Aging. 3. Older people—Social conditions. 4. Older people—United States—Social conditions. I. Title.

HQ1061.N883 2006
305.26'0973—dc22 2005048922

Printed in the United States of America

10 9 8 7 6 5 4 RRD-VA 09 08 07

To my sister Lynne
and my mother-in-law Sylvia Kravis

CONTENTS

5 PERSONAL HEALTH AND WELL-BEING *98*

6 LIFE SPAN DEVELOPMENT *131*

7 RACE AND ETHNICITY *163*

PREFACE

Some years ago I attended a sociology department meeting to present my first proposal for a course on aging. After some questions from the committee, the committee chair (a professor of comparative culture) leaned forward and squinted at me. "I have no objection to you teaching this course," he said. "You have an interest in the subject and knowledge of the area. But, tell me, what in the world will you talk about for an entire semester in a course on aging? People get old, then they die. What else is there to say?"

This colleague wouldn't ask these questions today. Today in the United States there are more older people in the population than ever before. Every day newspaper and magazine articles bring us new knowledge about aging and our aging society. Studies report findings on diet, exercise, pensions, family life, and housing. Televised reports suggest ways to stay healthy and live a long life.

Almost everyone knows something about aging today, and the growth in popular books on this subject suggests that people want to know more.

Issues in aging will grow in importance as more people enter middle and later life. Most university and college students today will face these issues in their careers. For example, the Baby Boom generation has entered middle age and will move like a glacier into old age in the next few years. This mass of people will want services from professionals who understand their needs and concerns. Students in gerontology classes, whatever their major or field of study, will need to know about this aging population.

This book presents facts and information about aging today. It covers the issues that most older people and their families will face. And it deals with issues that an aging society will raise for all of us. Whether you are older yourself; have older parents, relatives, and friends; or plan to work with older people; the information in this text will help you understand aging today.

SPECIAL FEATURES

The interaction between personal aging and social institutions creates many of the issues that older people face. For example, our bodies age—reaction time slows, chronic diseases develop, and the body tends to put on weight. These personal changes become issues when society needs to respond. For example,

- Slower reaction time raises the issue of safe driving in later life. Should we require older people to take a driver's test each year after a certain age? Should we approve licenses with restrictions on when and where an older person can drive?
- More chronic disease raises the issue of how our health care system, designed to treat acute illness, cares for older people. Should we create more long-term care facilities like nursing homes? And if we do, who will pay for this expensive form of care?
- Added weight (around the middle for men and the hips for women) raises issues related to our North American life-style, diet, and health promotion practices. Should we invest more money in health promotion programs for older people? Do physicians need more training in health promotion, diet, and the wellness needs of older patients?

Issues related to aging go beyond the basic need for health care. All older people encounter negative stereotyping, minority older people face low incomes, and changes in the economy force many older workers to retire. Students need to understand these and other issues. This calls for knowledge that sorts the myths from the realities of aging.

I have designed this book for easy use and enjoyable reading. Each chapter presents issues around a single theme—for example, housing, health care, and income security. I present the facts on that theme, the issues related to that theme, and creative responses to these issues.

Chapters also include graphs and tables for the display of complex information. In almost every case, these displays have an accompanying explanation. I have also tried to give the meaning of new concepts in the text, so that students can read along without constant reference to the glossaries.

I have included photos and case studies of older people. Some of these people I have met informally or through my research. Other cases come from insightful articles in the popular press. These additions show the human side of aging. The case studies show the diversity of older people and their unique circumstances. Cartoons are also included to show the lighter side of aging.

The end of each chapter includes a summary of main points, questions for discussion or study, suggested readings, and a glossary of terms. These resources will direct students in their study and help in the review of the chapters.

ORGANIZATION

This book first looks at large-scale social issues—social attitudes, the study of aging, and demographic issues. It then explores how these conditions affect individuals and social institutions. The book concludes with a look at political responses to aging and how individuals can create a better old age for themselves and the people they know.

Chapters 1 and 2 introduce students to aging in the United States and to the study of aging. Chapter 1 looks at people's attitudes toward older people and corrects many of the myths people believe about aging. It also looks at the origins of negative attitudes toward older people and at ways to change these attitudes. Chapter 2 looks at how best to study aging. It reviews the theories and methods gerontologists use in their research.

Chapters 3 and 4 discuss the treatment of older people in various societies and the aging of the U.S. population. Chapter 3 looks at the issue of older people's status in societies past and present. Chapter 4 looks at the issue of population aging in the United States, the increase in the number and proportion of older people in the population. This is the foundation for the chapters that follow.

Chapters 5, 6, and 7 discuss how individuals age. Chapter 5 covers the issue of biological aging and its causes and effects including the changes that take place in personal health and illness. In Chapter 6, psychological and developmental issues related to aging are discussed. This chapter reviews changes in memory and intelligence and the influence of social context on a person's well-being in later life. Chapter 7 looks at race, ethnicity, and culture. It looks at discrimination and societal barriers to good aging. This chapter traces many of the issues that older minority people face to inequality throughout their lives in our society.

Chapters 8 through 14 explore current issues related to health care, income security, retirement, housing, the family, and death and dying. These chapters show that problems related to population aging and to individual aging exist in all these institutions. These chapters propose responses to some of the most serious problems caused by population aging. Chapter 13 looks at intimacy and our relations with those we love. Chapter 14 raises questions and issues related to the treatment of older people at the end of life, prolonging life through technology, and physician-assisted suicide.

The final two chapters, 15 and 16, provide information on politics, social policy, and the need for education related to aging. Chapter 15 deals with the current political system and how it might address the issues raised in earlier chapters. This chapter shows the potential and limits of public response. Chapter 16 encourages students to learn more about aging and discusses potential career opportunities in the field of aging. Taken together, these chapters give an overview of aging in American society.

ACKNOWLEDGMENTS

Authors often say that a book takes a team effort. It's most true for a complex work like this. The team at Allyn & Bacon has given me support and encouragement from the first day. They also supplied expertise in fields that an author can never master. My colleagues include copy editors, photo archivists, marketing specialists, and designers. Some of these people I got to know well. Others worked behind the scenes to produce this work. These people have all earned my gratitude and thanks. A few people deserve special mention.

First, thanks to Jeff Lasser, Acquisitions Editor at Allyn & Bacon. Jeff saw the potential in this book from the start. He believed in the project and gave me sound advice as I went along. Heather McNally, Editorial Assistant, worked to see the manuscript through to printing. We talked often about schedules, permissions, and dozens of other details. Through all the business (*busy-ness*) of producing a book, her enthusiasm for the subject came through. Her good humor and good advice never failed. Thanks, Heather.

Heather also organized the review process, in which academic colleagues comment on an early draft of the manuscript. She chose an outstanding group of reviewers. These reviewers include Esther S. Brannon, West Virginia State Community and Technical College; Betty Hicks, Truckee Meadows Community College; Jennifer Keene, University of Nevada, Las Vegas; Naomi Schlagman, State University of New York, Brockport; Mary Francis Stuck, State University of New York, Oswego; and Diane Zablotsky, University of North Carolina, Charlotte. They spent hours on the review of a text by an anonymous author. This puts the ideal of colleagueship to the test. They passed the test with honors. They raised questions, provided detailed comments, and suggested sources that improved this work. I thank each of them for the time and effort they put into helping me. The students who use this book will benefit from their advice. I alone take responsibility for the book's shortcomings.

Michael Peck, a fellow gerontologist on my own campus, made his personal library available to me. Students in my Sociology of Aging courses told me what they would want to see in a gerontology text. Debra David, a colleague and friend at San Jose State, gave me the opportunity to use material from this text in the classroom. We've had many good conversations about the topics presented here. I appreciate her support and friendship.

I would also like to thank my Canadian colleagues at Nelson/Thomson Canada. I have worked with them on gerontology projects for many years, and they have always given me their support. Cara Yarzab and Joanna Cotton deserve my thanks and praise. My colleague and co-author on other works, Lori Campbell, deserves special thanks. We've worked together on several projects over a number of years. I value her humor, positive outlook on life, and her good wishes for this project.

The librarians at the Martin Luther King Memorial Library at San Jose State helped me with interlibrary requests and database searches. Dean Patricia Breivik supervises an exceptional staff who worked hard to get me the resources I needed to complete this text. I thank them all for their support.

Sharon Cancilla, Zeni Espinosa and Nadia Milukhin from my office helped me to find the time to work on the text. They cleared my calendar, rearranged meetings, and helped me to find days when I could finish the text as the deadline approached. I thank them for their patience and good cheer. Nadia deserves special recognition. She spent hours tracking down obscure sources. I appreciate her help as well as her patience and attention to detail.

A few people serve as my support group every day. Dr. Steve Zlotolow, Associate Dean of International and Extended Studies at San Jose State, works in the next office. We interact throughout the day. His frequent, "No problem. Everything's gonna be OK" helped me keep focused on this work. Steve often held the wheel of the ship on days when I had to give full attention to completing the text. He's a great colleague, friend, and fellow mountain climber. I appreciate his willingness to help me find time for this work.

My mentor and good friend Hans Mohr inspires all of my work. I can never repay him, only thank him for his support and friendship.

My wife, Mona, helped prepare the study material for students at the end of each chapter. All of this took time from her already busy schedule. Some of this work went late into the night in order to meet publication deadlines. She worked as a colleague and scholar to make this a better book.

My son Daniel helped at points along the way. He helped gather sources from the library and the Internet and generally encouraged the work. He's watched me work on this book for several years. Now he has become a scholar himself and plans an academic career. Someday I hope I will help him with one of his books.

I dedicate this book to my sister Lynne and my mother-in-law Sylvia Kravis. For several years Lynne looked after our mother near the end of her life. I lived half a continent away. She did this while she cared for her own young family. She knows too well the meaning of the term *woman in the middle*. No dedication can fully thank her for her devotion. Let this be a small token of my love and esteem.

My mother-in-law, Sylvia Kravis, now in her 80s, is a great-grandmother many times over. She still drives her own car, and she just returned from a Hawaiian cruise with one of her granddaughters. She has raised a happy and productive family. And she's done it through her dedication and devotion to us all. A recent photo shows her surrounded by her children, their spouses, her grandchildren, their spouses, and her great grandchildren. She beams with pride at the camera, her youngest great-grandchild in her lap. She's a role model of successful aging for all of us.

chapter 1
AGING TODAY

Jessie Taylor called for a cab and headed downtown for her last appointment of the day. She works for the state office on aging. She monitors nursing home standards and teaches staff ways to improve patient care. Jessie is 63 years old. She has a Barbara Bush figure, a pixie grin, and a mop of gray hair. As she got out of the cab, the driver got out too. He grabbed her elbow, ushered her across the street, and deposited her on the sidewalk. "You can't be too careful crossing the street these days," he said, then smiled and waved goodbye. Jessie says that when she goes to her local supermarket, the check-out clerk often asks other customers to wait a moment while she checks Jessie's things through. Then, one of the workers helps her to her car with her groceries.

All of this used to surprise Jessie. After all, she works at a job like everyone else, drives her own car when she travels out of town, and serves as a leader in her profession. Yet sometimes people treat her like a frail old woman. People see her kind face, gray hair, and wrinkles and they want to help her. They imagine that she needs help doing simple things because of her age. I asked Jessie whether she ever told people that she didn't need their help. She said that sometimes she does, but she doesn't want to discourage these people from helping someone in the future who may need their help, so often she goes along and grins to herself.

Jessie knows about **stereotyping** and **prejudice** toward older people.[1] She knows about it firsthand, and she observes it every day in her work. She also knows that stereotypes can be useful. They help us get along in a complex world where we know only a fraction of the people we see and meet every day. But stereotypes can lead to problems.

Stereotypes can lead us to misjudge people, to treat them inappropriately, and in the case of older people to assume that they need help. Stereotyping can also lead to prejudice, a negative attitude toward a person, and to **discrimination**, unfair treatment based on prejudice rather than merit. **Gerontology**, the systematic study of aging, attempts to counteract stereotyping and prejudice. It presents a more balanced view of later life. This chapter looks at (1) the benefits to studying aging; (2) the social basis of age stereotyping; and (3) changes in society that will lead to new images of later life.

WHY STUDY AGING?

Everyone can benefit from the study of aging. First, gerontology can help you understand current social issues. A society with an increasingly older population, for example, will experience changes in **social institutions**. Consider the following changes that will occur in three institutions: the family, the health care system, and recreation programs.

- More people than ever before will live in what some gerontologists call *beanpole* families. These families have three, four, or more generations alive at the same time. Each generation has relatively few members due to smaller numbers of children being born. Older people in these families will live into late old age. Some of them will need caregiving help from their younger family members.
- Older people will get more of their health care services in the community. Programs like visiting nurse services, meals-on-wheels, and foot clinics at senior centers will keep older people in their homes longer.
- Older people will take part in more active recreation programs, including fitness programs, adventure travel, and university courses.

These changes will lead to different social service needs, and this will require a shift in economic resources. Should the government give more money to older people? Will this mean less money for other age groups? Will it lead to tensions between the generations? Answers to these questions will decide public policy in the future. The study of aging

[1] The terms *old, elderly,* and *aged* in this book refer to people 65 and over unless another age is given. This fits the definition of the elderly used by the U.S. Census Bureau, the Social Security Administration, and many pension plans. Be aware, however, that many differences exist among people in this age group. Older people differ by race, gender, and region of the country. Older people also differ by age. Some older people today were 40 years old when other older people were children. The term *old people* and other related terms refer at best to a typical older person, not all older people.

allows you to understand and respond sensibly to these and other issues.

Second, you may plan to work in a field that serves older people. Students in nursing, social work, or physiotherapy will almost certainly work with older people. Students in recreation studies, architecture, or family studies will also benefit from understanding aging. Even students in business programs need to know about aging. Companies, from banks to travel agencies, now see older customers as an important part of their clientele. You will find yourself working with older people in almost any field. Knowledge of aging will give you a better understanding of your clients and their needs.

Third, all of us live in families with older members. Between now and when the youngest people who read this book reach old age, your parents and grandparents will face many of the issues discussed here. You can help them deal with the issues of later life by studying aging.

Jeanne, a student in one of my classes, used her knowledge of aging to help her grandmother stay involved in family life. She noticed that her grandmother had begun to avoid Sunday family dinners. She found out that her mother had told her grandmother not to bother making the potato salad for dinners anymore. The mother wanted to make life easier for the grandmother, whose arthritis had gotten worse. The grandmother felt that she had lost an important role in family life. If she couldn't cook for family dinners, she wouldn't come. Jeanne explained the situation to her mother, and they arranged for Jeanne to work with her grandmother in preparing the potato salad. The grandmother enjoyed teaching Jeanne her recipe, Jeanne got to know her grandmother in a new way, and the grandmother started coming to Sunday dinners again. Greater awareness of aging issues can make you a resource to your community, your family, and yourself.

Most people know something about aging before they study the subject. They know about aging from their personal experiences, from their contact with older people in their families and neighborhoods, and from the media. Still, this gives a limited view of aging, one that sometimes mixes truth with bias and myth. A person who has watched a relative or friend die of Alzheimer's disease, for example, may fear aging. But relatively few people suffer from this disease. Most older people are healthy into late old age. Likewise, the media present many negative images of older people. But older people form a diverse group. Some people have problems, while others report high life satisfaction.

Gerontologists work to replace myths and stereotypes with facts and knowledge. They have conducted many studies that look at current images of aging and attitudes toward old age.

AGEISM

Some years ago Robert Butler (1969) coined the term **ageism** to describe these negative attitudes toward aging. He defined ageism as "a process of systematic stereotyping and discrimination against people because they are old" (Butler, 1987, p. 22). He said that ageism "reflects a deep seated uneasiness on the part of the young and middle-aged—a personal revulsion to and distaste for growing old, disease, disability; and fear of powerlessness, 'uselessness,' and death" (Butler, 1969, p. 243). Palmore (2001) reports that, in one sample of older people, 77 percent said they experienced more than one incident of ageism. They most often reported disrespect or the assumption that they had an illness.

Older people may even try to distance themselves from being old. Palmore says that some of the people in his study themselves express ageism. And Cohen (2001) says that some older adults buy into the negative stereotypes, reject aging, and try to stay middle-aged forever. A national study of perceptions of aging in the United States found that less than one-half of older people reported "very serious" or "somewhat serious" problems with health, crime, income, and loneliness. But this same group of older people thought that nearly all older people had "very serious" or "somewhat serious" health, safety, income, or relationship problems (Cutler, Whitelaw, & Beattie, 2002) (see Table 1.1).

Some older people, for example, refuse to use bus passes that give discounts to older people. They

TABLE 1.1
"Very Serious" or "Somewhat Serious" Problems Facing Older People, 2000: A Survey of American Older People

	A Problem for Me (%)		*A Problem for Other Older People (%)*	
	1974	*2000*	*1974*	*2000*
Health	54	42	96	92
Fear of crime	50	36	84	82
Not having enough money to live on	46	36	92	88
Loneliness	36	21	94	84

This nationwide study found that, compared with 1974, in 2000 a smaller proportion of older people reported very or somewhat serious problems. Older peoples' subjective sense of well-being improved over the twenty-five years. But older people's view of other older people stayed roughly the same. Older people continue to think that nearly all other people their age suffer from health, crime, money, and personal relationship problems. Older people have a stereotyped view of other older people. Further analysis of the data in this study found that middle-aged people (aged 35–53) had an even more negative view of older people. Over 90 percent of the Baby Boom group thought that older people today had serious problems with the items on this list.

How do your friends feel about aging? How do you think they would answer if asked about the "very serious" or "somewhat serious" problems that older people face?

Source: Adapted from Cutler, N. E., Whitelaw, N. A., & Beattie, B. L. (2002). *American Perceptions of Aging in the 21st Century: A Myths and Realities of Aging Chartbook.* National Council on the Aging: Washington, DC, Figure 1-1, p. 2 and Figure 1-2, p. 4. Used with permission of the National Council on the Aging.

would rather pay the higher fares than admit their age. A 72-year-old man I met on a bus last December told me he was going to visit the "old folks" at a local nursing home for Christmas. He does not see himself as an old person. Most people, it seems, feel that *old* is five years older than they are.

Some years ago Kalish (1979) and Estes (1979) described a **new ageism.** This refers to the desire to help older people. This view assumes that older people need special treatment due to poor health, poverty, or lack of social supports. Although this positive form of ageism tries to do good, it supports the stereotype of old age as a time of decline and loss. Binstock (1983) called this a **compassionate stereotype**. This stereotype attempts to create sympathy for older people, but it doesn't give a true picture of later life.

Estes found that a federal bureaucracy to care for older people, what she calls the **aging enterprise**, grew out of compassionate stereotyping. Supporters of older people created the stereotype of older people as poor, frail, and dependent. This image created sympathy for older people and led to programs like **Medicare**, the **Older Americans Act**, and improved **Social Security**. These programs did improve older people's lives, but they also set the stage for the current round of **scapegoating**. People now question whether the old deserve such apparently lavish treatment. Some policy analysts and the press declare that older people have plenty of money and political power and they cost too much. Stereotyping, whether negative or compassionate, in the end decreases public support for older people who really need help.

One study found that older people themselves don't support compassionate stereotyping. One older person said, "Some people confound aging with illness." Another said, "People confuse the 90% of older people who are able with the 10% that are not." Finally, "I get tired of the 'good for you' attitude, as if it were surprising that someone 65+ can be involved in a number of physical, intellectual and volunteer pursuits" (National Advisory Council on Aging, 1993, pp. 10–11).

SOURCES OF AGEISM

At a conference a few years ago, a sales representative gave me a complimentary page of comments about getting older. The page had his name and phone number in the outside margins. I suppose he thought that people would pass this page along to colleagues. They would share this bit of humor and his name as well. The page said: "You know you're getting old when . . .

- Everything hurts and what doesn't hurt doesn't work.

BOX 1.1
WHAT'S IN A NAME?

Every group has its preferred referrent. Do we call someone an American Indian, an Aboriginal Person, a Native American? Groups generally adopt and promote a term that presents them in a positive way. However, no acceptable term has evolved to refer to the older population, and anyone who writes about older people or speaks to groups about aging faces a dilemma. What should we call people aged 65 and over? Writer Melinda Beck tackles this question and comes up with a disturbing answer: Ageism, a feeling of discomfort with aging, makes any term unacceptable to older people. Until we tackle and overcome this problem, expect to offend someone no matter what term you choose.

What should we call people *of a certain age*?

That question bedevils not only advertisers and publishers but even advocates for those persons. Elderly? Seniors? Golden agers? "Mature people don't like any of those words," says Gerald Hotchkiss, former publisher of *New Choices for the Best Years.* That magazine started life as *Harvest Years,* then became *Retirement Living,* then *50 Plus* before adopting its verbose current title. "At one point, I asked readers to give us a new name," says Hotchkiss. "They couldn't come up with a good term, either."

Some older people so detest "senior" that they forgo discounts. "If a cute young thing says, 'Do you want your senior citizen's special?' I want to hit her," says Treesa Drury, 52, of the American Association of Retired Persons. Even that group's name isn't quite apt; 40 percent of AARP's members are still working. Other acronyms have been offered: Whoopies (Well-Heeled Older People), OPALS (Older Persons with Active Lifestyles) and Grumpies (Grown-up Mature People). None has taken hold.

The real problem is that any term associated with *old* is still considered derogatory. "We've got to change that from something terrible to something wonderful," says Drury. Until then, she suggests, "How about just *people*?"

Source: From "What Do We Call . . . Them?" by M. Beck. From *Newsweek,* April 23

- Your pacemaker makes the garage door go up every time a pretty girl walks by.
- Your back goes out more often than you do.
- The last time you helped a little old lady across the street it was your wife."

I've read these lines to many audiences and classes of students, and people find them funny. But at the risk of ruining the fun, I suggest that all of these jokes foster ageism. For one thing, they all make older people seem physically and psychologically weak. They also make older people seem less able to do things or imply that they cannot control their bodily functions.

The man who gave me this list saw no harm in the humor, and since then I have received copies of this list from other sources. One copy of this list appeared in *Reader's Digest.* Imagine that a similar list had a racial or ethnic bias. Would you pass it along to your customers or show it to your professor? Would it be published in a national magazine? Few people see these jokes as ageist at first. All of us have grown up with the stereotype of older people as rundown and decrepit. Jokes like these and many other sources in our culture support ageist beliefs.

Great writings from the past, for example, present many ageist images of older people. Aristotle's (1941, Bk. II: Ch. 13, pp. 1405–1406) image of aging shows many of the biases people express today. Old men, he says,

> "are sure about nothing and *under-do* everything. . . . They are small-minded, because they have been humbled by life: their desires are set upon nothing more ex-

alted or unusual than what will help them to keep alive. . . . They live by memory rather than by hope . . . This, again, is the cause of their loquacity; they are continually talking of the past, because they enjoy remembering it. . . . Their sensual passions have either altogether gone or have lost their vigour."

Machiavelli presents the old man in his play *La Clizia* as a lecher. Shakespeare, at the start of *King Lear,* presents the king as a fool. Children's stories throughout history feature rag men, bogey men, and wicked witches, all caricatures of old people. Couper (1994) reviewed the presentation of old age in the current school curriculum. She found that the curriculum often ignores old age and omits references to older people.

One photo from an elementary school book on the human body, for example, showed three pairs of people: a 12-year-old boy and girl, a 15-year-old boy and girl, and a 21-year-old man and woman. This picture omitted human physical development past age 21. Couper found that most social studies books discussed the Civil Rights Act, but few mention the Older Americans Act. She found little mention of Social Security, Medicare, and **Medicaid** in school books. Lucchino, Lane, and Ferguson (1997) trace the shortage of students interested in aging-related fields to a lack of aging content in the schools.

The Media as a Source of Ageism

Popular culture provides more up-to-date examples of ageist treatment. The cartoon show *The Simpsons* depicts Grandpa Simpson as ignorant, forgetful, and timid. In one episode he and his nursing home friends break out of the home to freedom. They make it to the sidewalk, look around, get scared, and shuffle back inside. Studies of prime-time television shows, television commercials, and children's shows have generally found that television underrepresents older people (Signorielli, 2001). When television does portray older people, as in commercials, it often puts them in stereotyped roles (Bradley & Longino, 2001). Older people express concern about these negative stereotypes (Healey & Ross, 2002; Robinson, Popovich, Gustafson, & Fraser, 2003).

Most studies show that the print media also underrepresent older people. A study of pictures in magazines and newspapers in the United Kingdom (Whitfield, 2001), for example, found that they included relatively few pictures of older people. Older people make up 16 percent of that society. But pictures of older people made up 3 percent or less of pictures in newspapers and magazines. The study found that even magazines for seniors showed relatively few pictures of older people.

De Luce (2001, p. 40) reviewed advertising and articles in American popular magazines like *Time* and *Newsweek.* She found that a number of magazines (e.g., *The New Yorker, The New York Times Magazine*) had no ads targeted at people aged fifty and over. Nineteen publications in her study had only one to five ads. De Luce says that these findings reveal the "invisibility" of older consumers.

Krueger (2001) says that only about fifty newspapers in the United States have a reporter dedicated to reporting on aging issues. He says that the

BOX 1.2
INSTITUTIONAL AGEISM

Look around your own social world. Is the university or college environment ageist? An ageist institution would be one in which, subtly or overtly, intentionally or not, an older person would find it difficult to make use of the institution's resources.

Think about your school or campus. Does it show signs of ageism? Consider the following items: (1) the times classes are held; (2) the location of your school; (3) the location of the classrooms; (4) the design of the seats in the classrooms; (5) the lounges (would an older person feel comfortable there?); (6) the music played on campus; and (7) transportation to campus and on campus.

lack of stories on older adults supports stereotyping. It also limits the amount of useful information that the public needs to understand aging. Kleyman (2002) says that, even though few newspapers put resources into reports on aging, the topic will grow in interest. The aging of the baby boom generation, the aging of senior news managers, and a growing interest in topics related to aging will lead to more stories on older people.

Studies have found signs of ageism in magazine articles (Whitfield, 2001), country music (Aday & Austin, 2000), and jokes. Bowd (2003) reviewed 4,200 jokes and found eight categories of negative stereotypes, including the impotent male, the unattractive female, the sick older person, and the forgetful older person. Some studies report the invisibility of older people in television programming and advertising. De Luce (2001) studied ads in thirty-one popular magazines. She found that that some magazines had no ads directed at older readers. Others had very few. Ads with older people in them included ads for cancer survivors, sufferers of memory loss, and loss of sexual vigor.

Ageism even influences retail sales. One student, as part of an assignment to study ageism, entered a woman's clothing store with her mother and grandmother. The store sold moderately priced clothes for women of all ages. The three women walked around the store separately to see whom the sales staff would approach first. The staff approached the student first to offer help and the grandmother last. One woman, in a study of attitudes toward older people, said, "salespersons can be impatient if you are choosing something and are not swift enough." Another woman said, "salespeople will talk to me rather than to my mother who is 85" (NACA, 1993, p. 20).

Lack of Knowledge as a Source of Ageism

Some of what looks like ageism comes from ignorance. Few people know much about aging today except what they see and hear in the media and popular culture. Gerontologist Erdman Palmore (1977) created a Facts on Aging Quiz (FAQ) to explore people's knowledge about aging. Palmore designed the quiz to test physical, mental, and social knowledge as well as common misconceptions about old age. The FAQ has led to a small explosion of studies as researchers from around the world criticized, validated, and modified the original quiz (Pennington, Pachana, & Coyle, 2001; Seufert & Carrozza, 2002; Palmore, 1998).

Palmore himself published Part Two of the quiz in 1981. He later developed a multiple choice quiz (Harris, Changas, & Palmore, 1996). Below you will find a brief FAQ that draws on Palmore's quizzes. Read the questions and answer them either true or false. The answers appear on page 9.

1. All five senses tend to decline in old age.
2. Over 20 percent of the U.S. population is now age 65 or over.
3. The life expectancy of African Americans at age 75 is about the same as that of whites.
4. The majority of older people have incomes below the poverty level (as defined by the federal government).
5. Older workers have fewer accidents than younger workers.
6. People tend to become more religious as they age.
7. Lung capacity tends to decline in old age.
8. At least 10 percent of the aged are living in longstay institutions (i.e., nursing homes, mental hospitals, homes for the aged).
9. Over three-fourths of older people can carry out their daily activities without help.
10. The aged have higher rates of criminal victimization than persons under age 65.[2]

How did you score? Palmore (1998, p. 43) reports a "most disturbing general finding" from the use of the FAQs. "Most people know little about aging and have many misconceptions . . . the average person appears to have almost as many misconceptions about aging as correct conceptions." He found that people scored better on some questions than on others. The questions most often missed included

[2]*Source:* Adapted from "Facts on Aging: A short quiz," by E. B. Palmore, 1977, *The Gerontologist, 17,* 315–320, and "The Facts on Aging Quiz: Part two," E. B. Palmore, 1981, *The Gerontologist, 21,* 431–437.

BOX 1.3
DISGUISED
The Story of Patricia Moore: A Woman Who Disguised Herself as Old

How does it feel to be an older person? Most of us will have to wait many years to find out, but knowing what it feels like might give us each new insights into aging. Patricia Moore, a 26-year-old industrial designer, decided to turn herself into an 85-year-old woman.

Her journey into old age began with a custom-made latex mask and a white wig. She dressed for the part with her mother's purse, canvas shoes, and a cane. She wore bandages on her legs, support stockings, and a cinch to flatten her chest. Old glasses and a pillbox hat completed the disguise.

Pat put her disguise on almost every week for three years. She played the role of an old woman in 116 cities in fourteen states and two provinces in Canada. She says that geography made little difference in how people treated her as an older person. Some people offered her help and treated her kindly. Other people ignored her. Sometimes she faced overt ageism. Below, Pat Moore relates some of her experiences.

When I did my grocery shopping while in character, I learned quickly that the *Old* Pat Moore behaved—and was treated differently—from the Young Pat Moore. When I was eighty-five, people were more likely to jockey ahead of me in the checkout line. And, even more interesting, I found that when it happened, I didn't say anything to the offender, as I

Pat Moore in her disguise as an old woman and as she looks today. (right, © 1983 Helen Marcus)

BOX 1.3
(Continued)

certainly would at age twenty-seven. It seemed somehow, even to me, that it was okay for them to do this to the *Old* Pat Moore, since they were undoubtedly busier than I was anyway. And further, *they* apparently thought it was okay, too! After all, little *old* ladies have plenty of time, don't they?

And then when I did get to the checkout counter, the clerk might start yelling, assuming I was deaf, or become immediately testy, assuming I would take a long time to get my money out, or would ask to have the price repeated, or somehow become confused about the transaction.

What it all added up to was that people feared I would be trouble, so they tried to have as little to do with me as possible. And the amazing thing is that I began almost to believe it myself! Psychologists call it "identification with the aggressor." Even though I wasn't genuinely *old,* I became so intimidated by the attitudes of others, by the fear that they would become exasperated with me, that I absorbed some of their tacitly negative judgement about people of my age.

It was as if, unconsciously, I was saying, in reaction to being ignored and avoided, "You're right. I'm just a lot of trouble. I'm really not as valuable as all these other people, so I'll just get out of your way as soon as possible so you won't be angry with me."

I think perhaps the worst thing about aging may be the overwhelming sense that everything around you is letting you know that you are not terribly important anymore. Walking along a crowded sidewalk, someone bumps into you and, unless you are knocked literally sprawling, keeps going, as if to say you don't count anymore.

I was coming to identify so fully with the *Old* Pat Moore that I felt more like her than like the real me, and as I did, I began to resent the young, healthy, carefree members of my own generation. Psychologically, as far as my own internal well-being was concerned, it was not a good situation.

I would walk down the street and see the faces of young people like myself, and frustration and anger would well up inside me. I felt like grabbing them and shaking them and saying, "You have no idea what's going on out there, in this very city, with so many precious *old* people who just want you to take a little time with them!"

Pat gave up her disguise after three years, but not before she got mugged, met poor and abused older people, and also met kind strangers who helped her on her way. She counts older people among the kindest strangers she met during her time as an old woman.

Does Pat Moore, the young one with the smooth skin and the pretty eyes, ever miss the "*old* lady"?

"Oh, I miss her," Pat answers without hesitation. "She was a good friend. We meant a great deal to each other, but for now we've said good-bye."

"It's not a sad parting, though," she adds with a mischievous smile, "I expect to see her again—in the mirror—in about fifty years!"

Source: From *Disguised* (pp. 75–76, 135, 174), by P. A. Moore with C. P. Conn, 1985, Waco, TX: Word Books. Reprinted with permission of P. A. Moore.

the proportion of older people in long-term stay institutions, the older person's inability to change, and the proportion of older people below the poverty line.

Answers to the FAQ on page 7: Odd-numbered items are true. Even-numbered items are false.

A study by the American Association of Retired Persons (AARP) and the University of Southern California (2004) found similar results. This national study of almost 1,500 Americans found that people answered about half the items on a twenty-five-point quiz correctly. Sixty-four percent of respondents mistakenly thought that a majority of older people lived in poverty. Seventy-three percent mistakenly thought older people were lonely. And 85 percent mistakenly thought that 10 percent of older people live in nursing homes.

Palmore (1998) found that test-takers tended to assume a negative view of older people. He also found that even people with expertise in aging missed many of the FAQs questions. Graduate students and professionals who worked with older people missed about one-third of the true/false questions. Gerontology students and faculty members missed from 10 to 30 percent of the items. These findings suggest that most people have an uneven knowledge about aging. In general, people seemed to have more knowledge of physical changes that come with age and less knowledge of social facts about aging.

Both the Palmore (1998) research and the study by the AARP and University of Southern California (2004) show that the most frequent misconceptions about aging come from negative views of old age. Palmore found that people with more education scored better on the FAQ. People with a high school education averaged between 52 and 60 percent correct. Undergraduates averaged between 55 and 69 percent. Graduate students scored 65 to 76 percent correct. And gerontology students and faculty scored 66 to 92 percent correct. Specialists in the

BOX 1.4

CONAN THE SEPTUAGENARIAN FOR THE AGES: ARNOLD, SLY, CLINT AND OTHERS ARE SHOWING THAT GETTING OLDER MEANS GETTING BETTER. WRINKLES ROCK.

These days, not only does wisdom come with age, so do sex appeal and confidence. The media and pop culture—hand in hand, like king and queen—have ruled that aging ain't so bad.

And with millions of baby boomers chiming in, images of older adults on television, in movies and in advertisements promise to blend getting older with getting better.

"While historically the definition of the old has been made by the young, this media-savvy generation will not feed their own identities to the aristocracy of youth," said Robert Thompson, professor of television, radio and film at Syracuse University. "The image of a baby boomer driving in the fast lane with his left turn signal on will be portrayed in the future by Stallone and Schwarzenegger—and it will be a cool thing to be doing."

By the way, Sylvester Stallone and Arnold Schwarzenegger—Rocky and the Terminator of film fame—are both in their 50s.

Neville Strumpf, professor of gerontologic nursing at the University of Pennsylvania, said medical advances and changing attitudes among older adults about fitness are pushing the old-age threshold forward.

"It's a group of people who are going to reshape their world by virtue of who they are and what they understand themselves to be," said Strumpf, 53. "Old age doesn't look the way it did when my grandparents were around."

It sure doesn't.

This year, in the movies, on television and anywhere else image is cultivated, what's sexy and cool hasn't been exclusively the domain of the young.

On television, Regis Philbin, 66 and sleek with his shimmery jackets and matching ties, is hotter than ever, dramatically prodding contestants on ABC's "Who Wants to Be a Millionaire," and 76-year-old Bob Barker is still spinning the money wheel with style on CBS' "Price is Right" after 28 seasons.

In CBS' outrageously popular summer series, "Survivor," retired Navy SEAL Rudy Boesch outlasted many of his younger tribal rivals to make it to the final four at age 72. On the TNT cable net-

BOX 1.4
(Continued)

work in August, Faye Dunaway, 59, played a stylish and outspoken senator's wife in "Running Mates."

Music has long cherished its classic rockers. Carlos Santana, 53, resumes touring in September to promote his "Supernatural" album, a blend of Latin rhythm, rock and hip-hop that grabbed nine Grammys last year. Another Grammy winner, leggy Tina Turner, 61, is shaking her groove thing on tour in tight capri pants and dresses cut above the knee.

In the world of beauty, women in their 40s and beyond have maintained their sex-symbol status. The long and elegant Iman, 45, who oversees IMAN Cosmetics for women of all shades of brown, recently announced the Aug. 15 birth of her daughter with husband and rock legend David Bowie, 53.

Husky-voiced Lauren Hutton, 55, exercises barefoot along the beach in commercials targeted at menopausal women considering drug therapy. And Barbara Eden, 66, looks as though she probably could still fit into her racy, hot-pink "I Dream of Jeannie" costume as she hawks baked goods for Entenmann's on television.

Given the statistics, the potential for changing reflections of age is astounding, said Bill Burkart, president and chief executive officer of the San Francisco-area Age Wave IMPACT, which advises companies on how to advertise to the 50-and-older audience.

He said Baby Boomers make up "the smartest generation in the history of the world, the best-educated, the wealthiest." And if they want to see hotter, stronger versions of themselves in the popular media, they'll get them, because they won't deal with companies that don't understand what they want, he said.

"They essentially have transformed everything they've touched," from divorce to credit cards, Burkart said. "What you're going to see in the next 10 years is a total redefinition, a total transformation of what it's going to be like to be old."

. . . A cavalcade of sexy seniors in pop culture doesn't prove that the public is upgrading its regard for older adults, said Sheldon Steinhauser, sociology professor at the Metropolitan State College of Denver.

"There is still a great amount of ageism in this society," said the 70-year-old, who runs a consulting firm that helps companies recruit and hold on to older workers. "We may talk about it differently. We may not use some of the nastier terms. At the same time, that doesn't mean the attitudes have disintegrated."

To Steinhauser, however, media depictions of aging seem promising. He said the media and pop culture, bolstered by demands from older people for accurate portrayals and fair treatment, can help sway attitudes.

Take, for instance, John Glenn, the former astronaut and senator from Ohio who returned to space in 1998 at age 77. The press was all over it.

But Steinhauser said ordinary folks accomplish the extraordinary as well.

"What we should begin to realize," Steinhauser said, "it's not just selected exceptions and it's not just the selected celebrities who are out there doing substantial things."

In August, for instance, an 83-year-old woman survived for three days in her car after being run off a highway overpass above a Florida swamp. Doctors say she kept herself alive by drinking rainwater.

And more bold expressions of aging are likely on the way.

"We are no longer going to be defined as little old ladies and doddering old men," said Thompson, the Syracuse professor. "We hold the cultural cards, and we're dealing them accordingly."

Source: Melendez, Michele M. (2000, September 28). Conan the septuagenarian: For the ages: Arnold, Sly, Clint and others are showing that getting older means getting better. *The Seattle Times.* Reprinted with permission from Newhouse News Service.

field of aging scored 90 percent or better (Palmore, 1998). People with more knowledge about aging have a more positive view of old age.

SOME FACTS ON AGING TODAY

Consider some of the correct answers to questions on the FAQ. You will find more details on these questions and the other questions on the FAQ in later chapters. For now, consider the facts presented here and think about why people might have missed these items.

True or False: Over 15 percent of the U.S. population is now aged 65 or over.

False. The proportion of older people in the United States has grown over the past one hundred years. In 1900 about 4 percent of the population was aged 65 or over. By 2000, the proportion of older people had more than tripled to 12.4 percent (U.S. Census Bureau, 2004a; 2004b). The proportion of older people in the population will continue to grow into the next century. By the year 2050, when the last Baby Boomers reach late old age, the U.S. Census Bureau projects that older people will make up 20.3 percent of the population (Federal Interagency, 2000). This aging of the population will transform American society. It will transform policies and programs for older people, open new opportunities for people of all ages, and change our view of later life.

True or False: The majority of older people have incomes below the poverty level (as defined by the federal government).

False. In 2001, 10.1 percent of people aged 65 and over had incomes below the government's poverty line (Smith, 2003). This proportion has dropped from the early 1960s when over 30 percent of older people had incomes below the poverty line. Older people today get more of their income from work or pensions than in the past. In addition, a number of government programs provide a stronger economic safety net than ever before.

This net consists of better pensions, improved Social Security, yearly cost of living increases in Social Security, and a Supplemental Security Income program. Some groups of older people still suffer from high rates of poverty as we will see. But Schulz (2001, p. 2) concludes that overall, "older people today are *economically much better off than they were a little more than two decades ago"* [emphasis in the original].

True or False: At least 10 percent of the aged are living in long-stay institutions (i.e., nursing homes, mental hospitals, homes for the aged).

False. On any given day about 5 percent of people aged 65 and over live in an institution. Zedlewski and colleagues (1990) say that this proportion could rise to over 7 percent by the year 2010 as the older population grows in size. But most older people today and in the future will live on their own or with family members in the community. Most have reasonably good health and manage to care for themselves.

Those who have physical problems and need help use community care programs that range from meals-on-wheels to visiting nurse services. Older people who need help rely mostly on family and friends. People who live in institutions, in most cases, are very old, have poor health, and few informal supports to help them stay in the community.

True or False: The life expectancy of African Americans at age 75 is about the same as that of whites.

True. African Americans have a lower **life expectancy** *at birth* than do whites. An African American child born in 2002 could expect to live to age 72.4. A white child born in that year could expect to live to age 77.9, a difference of 5.5 fewer years of life expectancy for the African American child (National Center for Health Statistics, 2004c). But this question asks about life expectancy *at age 75*. In 2002, the life expectancy for African American men and women at age 75 was 86 years. The life expectancy for white men and women aged 75 in that year was 86.6 years, a difference of only six-tenths of a year.

These figures show the effects of high African American **mortality** in childhood and young adulthood. Poverty, poor health care, and unhealthy living conditions put many African American infants and children at greater risk than whites. Once African Americans reach age 75 they have survived most of the conditions that put them at greater risk than whites.

TABLE 1.2

Estimated Personal Victimization Rates* *by Type of Victimization at Selected Ages, United States, 2002*

	Age of Victim						
Type of Crime	*12–15*	*16–19*	*20–24*	*25–34*	*35–49*	*50–64*	*65 and over*
All personal crime	45.3	58.8	49.0	26.8	18.8	11.0	4.0
Crimes of violence	44.4	58.2	47.4	26.3	18.1	10.7	3.4
Completed violence	12.8	20.7	16.4	9.0	5.5	3.5	1.2
Attempted violence	31.7	37.6	31.0	17.3	12.6	7.2	2.2
Robbery	3.0	4.0	4.7	2.8	1.5	1.6	1.0
Completed	1.8**	3.1	3.6	2.1	1.2	1.2	0.8**
Attempted	1.2**	0.9**	1.1**	0.7**	0.3**	0.4**	0.2**
Assault	39.3	48.6	39.8	22.8	16.1	8.9	2.2
Aggravated	5.0	11.9	10.1	5.2	3.5	1.7	0.7
Simple	34.3	36.7	29.7	17.6	12.7	7.2	1.5
Purse snatching/pocket picking	0.9**	0.6**	1.6**	0.5**	0.7	0.3**	0.6**

*Victimization rate: The annual average number of victimizations per 1,000 persons in each age group.

**Estimate based on about ten or fewer sample cases.

The rate of criminal victimization drops with age. People aged 65 and over, compared to younger people, have much lower victimization rates for all categories of crime listed here (except for purse snatching/pocket picking in which low numbers make the estimates unreliable).

Source: From *Criminal Victimization in the United States, 2002.* Washington, DC: U.S. Department of Justice. Office of Justice Programs, Bureau of Justice Statistics. Table 3. Retrieved: December 20, 2004, *www.ojp.usdoj.gov/bjs/pub/pdf/cvus0201.pdf.*

True or False: The aged have higher rates of criminal victimization than persons under age 65.

False. Older people have the lowest rates of criminal victimization across almost all crime categories. (See Table 1.2.) Older people, compared with younger people, have a much lower risk of violent crime or property crime. And rates have fallen by one-third since the 1970s (Federal Interagency, 2004). However, they do have a high risk for certain types of crime—for example, larceny with personal contact, like purse snatching and pocket picking. Older people show some of the highest rates for these types of crimes in urban settings.

Doyle (1990) uses an opportunity framework to explain patterns of crime against older people. Opportunity refers to the attractiveness of a target, the exposure of the target, and the guardianship or protection of the target. Older people have less exposure to criminals. They tend to stay at home at night and to live in relatively safe neighborhoods. Retired people spend more time at home and so protect their property more. At the same time they do offer an attractive target for purse snatchers and pickpockets on the street.

Other studies support this framework. African American men, for example, showed high rates of assault and intimidation. Many minority older people live in high-crime neighborhoods and have more exposure to criminals. Older men in these neighborhoods may offer attractive targets to criminals (McCabe & Gregory, 1998).

Victimization by Fraud

Older people seem more susceptible to certain types of crime than others. Con artists and swindlers, for example, tend to target older people. Older people have savings that make them attractive targets. They also may have fewer social supports to help them steer clear of a bogus deal (Davis, 1993). Schemes include home repair, medical, and insurance deals.

A study of older people in rural Ohio, for example, found that more than one-third of the sample

(37.3 percent) reported contact with someone engaging in fraud (Shields, King, Fulks, & Fallon, 2002). The AARP (2003c) conducted a survey of 2,000 members aged 50 and over who lived in Montana. Nearly 40 percent of the members believed they had been a victim of consumer fraud or a swindle. About one-third of the respondents said they experienced auto-related fraud or fraud related to their telephone service. Two-thirds of the respondents said that the AARP should make telemarketing fraud a top priority.

Cons and swindles take many forms. Con artists often use the bank examiner swindle on older people. In that case, a con artist calls an older person, often a woman who lives alone, and says that someone is embezzling money from her bank. The caller asks if she will help catch the thief. The caller tells her to withdraw money from her account and give the money to a bank messenger who will arrive at her door. The caller explains that the bank needs to check the serial numbers to catch the crooked teller. The messenger works for the con artist and gets away with the money.

"'Once you hand over your money, there is no recovery,' says Melvin L. Jeter, southern regional security director for NationsBank. 'There's no way any money's going to get back'" (McLeod, 1995, p. 14). Home repair con artists also target older people. They look for homes that need repairs—loose shingles or a broken eaves trough. The swindler then knocks on the older person's door and offers to estimate the cost of repairs. He or she gives a low estimate and says that the older person will have to pay for the work right away to get this deal. The con artist usually asks for cash payment before any work gets done.

Some crooks even drive the older person to the bank to withdraw the money. Once the swindler has the money, the work may never get done or it is done poorly with cheap material. Con artists of this type may come back again and again to do more repairs. They may even try to borrow money from the older person once they have a relationship.

Swindlers have increased their use of technology to bilk older people. *Slamming,* for example, switches a person's phone to another provider without the owner's permission. *Cramming* occurs when a person gets charged for phone services that the owner never ordered. *Nigerian money offers* often come as email messages. They promise to transfer funds to a person's bank account. But, once the person has agreed, further letters demand money for transfer fees, and so forth. These and other electronic schemes use technology to play on a person's ignorance or greed. Older people who have little experience with electronic media serve as easy targets for thieves.

Effects of Victimization

Barbara Barer, an anthropologist at the University of California, San Francisco, found that fraud can lower an older person's self-image. She reports the case of a 96-year-old woman cheated out of money for an emergency alert system. The woman felt so embarrassed about losing the money that she never reported the crime. She felt that if her friends or family knew, they might question her competence.

Barer says that older people also feel that if they report crimes, they may face further victimization. One man arranged for car repairs with a neighbor. The neighbor never did the repairs. The man feared that the neighbor's children would smash his car's windows and slash his tires if he reported the crime.

Barer says that crimes like these against older people can lead to feelings of inferiority and loss of self-esteem. Crimes against very old people can lead to a loss of independence and possibly institutionalization. Barer says that with most crimes, society sees the criminal at fault, but "when a crime is committed against an elderly individual, the victim is implicated for being at fault for allowing it to happen. The mistake is unforgivable. Thus it is preferable to conceal the shame" (Unreported Crime, 1994, p. 4).

The AARP (1999) conducted a study of consumers aged 18 and over. The study found that compared with younger people, older people were more vulnerable to unfair or deceptive business practices. And the oldest age group, 75 and over, had the highest proportion of vulnerable people. Older people with low education levels and low incomes had the highest rates of vulnerability. These people also can least afford the cost of unfair business practices.

Older people, compared with younger people, had less knowledge of consumer rights. And younger people, compared with older people, also tended to take a less trusting attitude toward businesses. These differences between older and younger consumers may make older people more susceptible to con artists. Police often have special pamphlets prepared to alert older people to schemes directed at them. Twenty states share information to foil fraud schemes. Other states sponsor consumer hotlines for older people, training for police, and scanning junk mail for current scams.

Fear of Crime

Some studies find no relation between age and fear of crime (Ferraro, LaGrange, & McCready, 1990; Maguire, Pastore, & Flanagan, 1993). Other studies find that a high proportion of older people fear crime. Bazargan (1994), for example, studied fear of crime in 372 urban African Americans in New Orleans. Women made up 80 percent of the sample. Over 70 percent of the people in the study rated their health as fair or poor. More than half (53.2 percent) of the sample reported fear of crime as a serious or very serious problem for them. More than half (51 percent) felt very or somewhat afraid to walk alone in their neighborhoods during the day. Women felt the most fear of crime outside the home.

A national study in 2000 by the National Council on Aging (Cutler, Whitelaw, & Beattie, 2002) found that 36 percent of older people felt that fear of crime was a "very" or "somewhat" serious problem for them. This figure dropped from 50 percent in 1974. But it still means that more than one older person in three considers crime a serious problem.

Some fear of crime may have a sound basis. Older people who live in high-crime-rate urban areas, for example, report a greater fear of crime than those in rural areas. And they do face a greater risk of victimization than rural older people. Likewise, older people may fear crime because a purse snatching can lead to personal injury. Older people, who live on fixed incomes, may fear the effects of petty theft on their ability to pay their bills. The topic of fear of crime and ways to reduce this fear need more careful study.

RESPONSES TO AGEISM

A recent study (Cutler, Whitelaw, & Beattie, 2002) found that 45 percent of older people felt that their later years were "the best years of my life." Sixty-one percent of the people in this survey said they would feel "very happy" if they knew they could live another ten years. People in this survey said that the key to a meaningful old age lies in having close family and friendships, good health, and a rich spiritual life. Middle-aged people in this sample agreed that these three items held the keys to a good old age.

In this same survey, 68 percent of the older people said that as they grew older "things seem better than I thought they would be." And 89 percent of the older people said that as they looked back on their lives they felt "fairly well satisfied." This survey shows that nearly all older people feel satisfied with life in general and they look forward to the years ahead. This view from old age contradicts many of the stereotypes of aging.

Research shows that stereotypes exist because of ignorance about later life and fear of aging. Even positive stereotypes can lead to prejudice and discrimination against older people. Authors suggest a number of ways to produce a more balanced view of aging. These include more thoughtful use of the media, education programs, intergenerational programs, and legislation that prohibits discrimination based on age.

The Media

Some improvement in attitudes toward older people may be taking place. Janelli and Sorge (2001) reviewed sixty-one children's storybooks published between 1991 and 1999. They found that most authors presented realistic stories. These stories showed both grandmothers and grandfathers as affectionate toward their grandchildren. But stories tended to stereotype the roles of grandmothers and

"Fred got his second wind at eighty."

grandfathers. Grandmothers gave care to others and engaged in household tasks. Grandfathers were often involved in teaching activities.

Magazines and television ads now feature famous seniors. Hall of Fame football player and coach Mike Ditka and former U.S. Senator Bob Dole promote drugs to correct erectile dysfunction. Jack Nicklaus promotes a ceramic and titanium hip replacement option. Fashion model Lauren Hutton, now over 60 years old, wears a low-cut gown to promote a soy-based cereal that "may reduce the risk of heart disease." They send the message that they've taken control of their lives. They actively respond to the physical changes that come with aging.

Luttropp (1995) reports that Oil of Olay skin lotion launched an ad campaign that presented healthy, happy women in their 40s. The campaign also responded to the diversity of the older population. It depicted African American as well as white women who feel content with their age. An African American woman in the ads says she is "looking forward to being the best-looking grandmother on the block" (Luttropp, 1995, p. 5). Other cosmetics companies, such as Clinique, have removed ageist language from their ads, and companies like Nike target some of their ads to a middle-aged audience (Darling, 1994).

Kaufert and Lock (1997) looked at the visual image of menopausal women portrayed in pharmaceutical ads. They found a shift from a negative image in the 1970s to a positive image in the 1990s. The new ads portray women with healthy teeth, hair, and skin. The ads show them playing with grandchildren and socializing with friends. The researchers say that the ads portray fit and sexually active women.

Today the mass media also present an image of healthier, more active older people than in the past. *Time* magazine recently ran a story (complete with an ad for Levitra, the newest erectile dysfunction drug) titled "Still Sexy After Sixty" (Golden, 2004). The article presented vignettes that described the happy sex lives of seniors. Some years ago the comedy series *The Golden Girls* broke ground when it featured four older women. The series portrayed the women as active, engaged, and involved in complex relationships with men. It gained a wide audience and ran for several seasons. Movies such as *Something's Gotta Give,* with Jack Nicholson and Diane Keaton, promote love and sex in later life. So do the afternoon soaps (Darling, 1994).

Astronaut John Glenn returned to space flight at age 77. David Bowie, at age 57, performed through a 112-date tour in 2004. Bob Dylan, now in his 60s, spends as many as twenty weeks touring on the road and continues to produce new music. So do the Rolling Stones. Frere-Jones (2005, p. 94) says that "in 2004, many of the best shows came from older groups who—perhaps owing to experience, new sobriety, humility, or all three—improved their repertory through performance, in ways that their juniors can't."

Architect Frank Gehry, in his 70s, recently designed and oversaw construction of the Disney Concert Hall in Los Angeles. The concert hall has gotten critical raves. Gehry's Guggenheim Museum in Bilbao, Spain, and now the Disney Concert Hall mark him as one of the most creative men of our time. Pulitzer Prize–winning author Toni Morrison, also in her 70s, continues to write, teach, and influence our culture. The mass media have begun to present more varied images of older people.

The Senior Market: A New Image of Aging

A few years ago a young market researcher sat down with three senior executives: one from a cosmetics firm, one from an egg-producing plant, and one from a panty hose company. She explained that

BOX 1.5
SOME MODELS OF GOOD AGING

Do people lose their abilities with age? Is aging a constant downhill course? Some well-known people should cause us to question our beliefs about old age. They show that people can continue to excel long past the normal retirement age. Social scientist Elizabeth Vierck submits the following cases that show the potential of later life.

Leroy "Satchel" Paige was the oldest baseball player, age 59. He pitched three scoreless innings in 1965 for the Kansas City Athletics. When asked about the secret of a good age, Paige gave six rules for staying young.

1. Avoid fried meats which angry up the blood.
2. If your stomach disputes you, lie down and pacify it with cool thoughts.
3. Keep the juices flowing by jangling around gently as you move.
4. Go very lightly on the vices, such as carrying on in society. The social ramble ain't restful.
5. Avoid running at all times.
6. Don't look back. Something might be gaining on you.

- U.S. Supreme Court Justices have an average age of over 70.
- Nearly one-third of U.S. senators and one-quarter of representatives are over age 60.
- Pianist Arthur Rubenstein gave one of his greatest performances at Carnegie Hall at age 89.
- Grandma Moses illustrated *'Twas the Night Before Christmas* at age 100.
- Former Senator John Glenn, the first American to orbit Earth, in 1962, returned to space at age 77 as a payload specialist.
- The current Federal Reserve chairman, Alan Greenspan, is in his 70s and oversees the American economy.

Source: Adapted from *Fact Book on Aging,* by E. Vierck, 1990, Santa Barbara, CA: ABC-CLIO. Also, *Growing Old in America,* by E. Vierck, 2002, Detroit, MI: Gale Group, Thomson Learning, p. 43. Reprinted with permission.

she wanted to study the spending patterns of older people. The executives laughed at her idea. None of them could understand why she wanted to do this. They each explained that they couldn't see this as relevant to their companies' future.

Some marketing directors still hold these views (Lippert & Scott, 2003). But the growing aging market has changed many advertisers' minds and will soon change many more. **Demographers** trumpet the aging of society, and economists tell us that older people today make up the richest generation of older people in history. As a group they sit on a pile of wealth that includes their homes, pensions, savings, investments, and in some cases income from work. Garfield (2004) reports that about 39 million households headed by adults aged 55 and older have $1.6 trillion in annual income. This group controls the large majority of the country's financial assets (Lippert & Scott, 2003). This fact has led some retail companies to target the older consumer. For example, Ikea, the furniture company, has begun to offer delivery and assembly to attract older customers. Some companies now market services and products to the needs and desires of seniors (Foot & Stoffman, 1998).

Business has a sense that the older market will grow in the future, but few companies have an idea of how to attract this older consumer. So far, attempts to target this market have had mixed results. Beck (1990) says that Kellogg's, for example, changed the name of "Bran Flakes" to "40+Bran Flakes" to capture the older market. She says that Kellogg's dropped the "40+" six months later when the name change failed to help sales. Marketing experts say that people do not want a cereal that reminds them of their age. Other products, like a line of gourmet foods called "Singles" (for people who live alone), have also failed to attract older consumers. In this case, experts say that people don't want to be reminded that they eat alone. Bradley and Longino (2001) report that pureed foods for seniors and shampoo for people with gray hair both failed to sell.

Products that play on disabilities or problems turn people off. George Moschis, a researcher at the Center for Mature Consumer Studies at Georgia State University, found that older people will avoid a product if they think the company negatively stereotypes their age group (cited in Beck, 1990). Success in attracting older consumers demands a knowledge of what motivates them. Ambrosius (1994), for example, says that younger and older consumers want different things. Younger people focus on building families, careers, and success in their social roles. Older people want psychological fulfillment (rather than social-role fulfillment) and want to achieve life satisfaction. He says, "We need to be more concerned with personal development . . . and deeper values . . . Remember, no one buys anything merely because of age" (Ambrosius, 1994, p. 11).

One marketing strategy takes the diversity of the older population into account. This approach segments the senior market. It puts older adults into categories like "intense individualist," "liberal loner," or "woeful worrier." Marketers then develop advertisements that they hope will influence these different groups (Leinweber, 2001).

The Ageless Self: Another Form of Ageism

Aging celebrities may serve as role models for Baby Boomers. They make aging look glamorous and challenge negative stereotypes. But they may create a new stereotype of the sophisticated, successful, beautiful senior. These new images of aging may lead to a new form of ageism, the *ageless self.*

Katz and Marshall (2003), for example, note that our consumer society pressures older people to use drugs and products to remain sexually and physically youthful. They say that this promotes an impossible ideal, one that ignores other ways to age. Many of the new images of aging, they say, marginalize the very old, older people with disabilities, and older people with a different view of aging.

Some authors see the current interest in longevity, increases in surgery to alter the effects of aging, and the desire to act young into old age as a rejection of aging. Holstein (2001–2002) says that throughout life women get social approval for their looks. Antiaging medicine plays on women's fears about aging and rejection. Butler (2001–2002) says that antiaging medicine promotes the belief that normal aging is a disease. And this attempt to overcome aging stigmatizes and marginalizes people who look their age. The antiaging trend excludes poor older people who can't afford the cost of antiaging medicines and treatments.

Katz (2001–2002; see also McHugh, 2000) finds that advertisements for retirement communities focus on active life-styles and make life seem problem free. Older people appear to live in a paradise of mature adulthood. These ads promote a life-style for healthy ageless older people. He says that these images can make the problems of aging, like poverty, poor health, or the frailty of late old age, seem deviant. Stoller and Gibson (2000, p. 76) say that "recommendations to join an exercise class, learn ballroom dancing, or take up lap swimming imply sufficient discretionary income to purchase lessons or gain access to appropriate facilities."

Likewise, the move to a retirement paradise implies that the person has enough money to live in one of these communities. These models of aging create new problems for older people. "We find ourselves yearning to be like people in these pictures," one older woman writes, "and belabor ourselves for failing these role models" (Preston quoted in Stoller and Gibson, 2000). This image of the ageless self ignores the diversity among older people and the fact that the body declines with age.

Andrews (2000) challenges the idea of a youthful self within an aging body. This mind/body split, she says, rejects the aging body. She says that older people and society should embrace aging in all its forms. Cruikshank (2003, p. 168) proposes that older people and American society show "frankness about decline and loss of capacity." She argues against the "false cheerfulness" of the ageless self.

This critique of popular images shows a healthy concern for how we think about old age. It also captures the diverse experiences of aging in the twenty-first century. And it shows the need for older people to work out new ways to age. Clarke (2002), for example, studied the attitudes of older women toward beauty in later life. The women in this study felt pressure from the fashion industry to stay thin. But they rejected the current ideal of extreme thinness. They preferred a more rounded body shape for themselves.

These women emphasized the importance of inner beauty. They found beauty in a person's personality, their relations to others, and their inner happiness. Clarke (2002, p. 440) concludes that social ideals shape an older woman's view of herself. And "ageist norms . . . denigrate older women and older women's bodies." But, she says, older women can and do challenge these norms. "Many of the women in my study," she says, "provide an important example of how oppressive social values can be resisted and how individuals may . . . offer alternatives to ageist interpretations of later life" (Clarke, 2002, p. 440).

More changes are needed in society and in our attitudes to have a more balanced view of later life. Researcher David Gutmann reported that at a major annual gerontology conference, papers on incurable disorders (such as Alzheimer's disease) outnumbered papers on treatable problems two to one. He counted seven papers on incontinence for every paper on life span development (cited in Friedan, 1993).

We need to allow for many ways to grow old. Some people want to engage in energetic activities that we associate with youth. Other older people define later life as a time to use their wisdom, share their memories, and offer community leadership. Some people live vibrant healthy lives into late old age. Others live with chronic illnesses. Some seem youthful to us, others look old. No single right way to grow old exists. And none of these ways should meet with social rejection.

Education Programs

A cartoon shows a preteenage boy looking over his grandfather's shoulder at a scrapbook. "Boy, Grandpa," the grandson says, "you looked just like me when you were young. Now I know what my teacher means about how we disintegrate after we're 21" (Montoya in Couper, 1994). Couper

(1994) uses this cartoon to suggest that schools need to do more to educate young people about aging. Curricula and texts have begun to include information about later life.

New educational programs have sprung up in settings from elementary school to medical school. A set of teaching materials called *Positively Aging,* for example, improves middle school students' images of older people. The materials include case studies of older people to teach about aging. A controlled study of this program in Texas found that, compared with the control group, students who took the program drew more positive or neutral images of older people (Lichtenstein et al., 2001).

Lee (2002) studied graduate schools of social work in the United States. The study found that 81.6 percent of schools offered courses on aging (an increase from 74 percent in 1992). About one-quarter of the schools offered a concentration in aging. The field of social work recognizes the need to train more geriatric social workers. A grant from the John A. Hartford Foundation has funded a major effort to strengthen social workers' competencies in gerontology. The projects developed competencies and guidelines for generalist social workers and specialists in geriatrics. Schools will have the option of adopting and implementing these guidelines (Greene & Galambos, 2002).

A review of medical school curricula (Austin, 2000) found that schools offer required and elective geriatric clerkships. Some schools include geriatrics information throughout the four-year undergraduate medical program. Other schools offer geriatrics training in separate clerkships. Many schools offer these programs as electives. The authors say that, given the aging of the population, too few medical students take these programs. They call for mandatory programs to ensure that doctors have some training in geriatrics.

Those who work directly with frail older people (e.g., nurses aides) may have less factual knowledge about aging than supervisors and administrators (e.g., registered nurses). Direct care workers often get the least gerontology education. Their heavy work loads and low pay make continuing their education more difficult. They rarely have professional development funds they can use for courses or conferences. In-service gerontology programs for these workers can increase their knowledge and give them a more balanced view of their patients.

Studies show that fact-based programs alone will not change ageist stereotypes (Stuart-Hamilton & Mahoney, 2003; Scott, Minichiello, & Browning, 1998). A study of medical school students (MacKnight & Powell, 2001), for example, found that home visits had little positive effect on attitudes toward older people. And on some measures the students showed a less positive attitude toward aging. Students in the health sciences who see only ill and institutionalized older people may have a negative attitude toward aging at the end of their studies. A study of college students (Ragan & Bowen, 2001) found that only groups that got reinforcement for their knowledge showed a change in attitude after one month. Gerontology curricula for health professionals need to balance a problems focus with information about successful aging. Health care workers like doctors, nurses, and physiotherapists especially need to learn about successful aging. They need to understand the possibilities for wellness and growth in their patients.

Intergenerational Programs

Social contact between older and younger people can reduce stereotyping. My first contact with older people outside my family, for example, led to my career in gerontology. In 1973, a colleague asked me to speak to a group of older people in a university-sponsored discussion group. I decided to speak on school reform (my main interest at that time).

Thinking I would shock the group with a criticism of traditional schooling, I told them about open classroom structures, new concepts of learning, and the new role of the teacher as facilitator. After I finished, the group looked at me in silence. Then one woman said, "You know, I was the principal at Pine Ridge Elementary School until two years ago when I retired. I brought in most of the changes you've just told us about." She then went on to tell me how she worked to put these kinds of programs in place. Many of the other group members also had taught in the public schools until they retired. They spoke about the administrative and day-to-day problems that these kinds of programs posed for teachers.

I left the room stunned. These people had calmly shattered my stereotype of old age. They knew as much or more about my topic as I did. They were articulate and had great senses of humor. They had just taken me through one of the most enjoyable seminars I had ever led. I resolved to learn more about older people and spend more time with them. This seminar launched me into the next thirty years of my career.

My own experience convinces me that contact between older and younger people can remove ageist stereotypes. But, contact alone does not guarantee more knowledge about older people or less bias against them. Certain types of interaction have a better effect than others. Positive attitudes seem to arise from balanced contact. Hooyman and Kiyak (1993, p. 33) say that stereotyping decreases when older and younger people see each other as individuals with good and bad traits.

Bringle and Kremer (1993) studied undergraduates in a service learning program. Students learned both positive and negative facts about aging. They also took part in a senior companion program. Students visited with an older person twice a week for eight weeks. The researchers found that the program improved students' views of older people and improved their attitudes toward their own aging. An innovative program in Cleveland, Ohio, called "The Intergenerational School" offers mentorship and apprenticeship for students as part of the curriculum. The curriculum involves contact between learners of all ages, including children, middle-aged adults, and older people (Whitehouse, Bendeza, Fallcreek, & Whitehouse, 2000).

"One antidote to ageism," Butler (1993, p. 77) says, "is knowledge, the primary intervention." He reports that knowledge and satisfying contact with older people lead to a more positive view of aging.

Legislation and Social Action

Education can help reduce ageism. But discrimination can also be fought directly through legislation. Past success includes passage of the Age Discrimination in Employment Act of 1967 and the Age Discrimination Act of 1975. Under the 1967 Employment Act (amended in 1974 and 1978) an employer cannot fire someone because of age, cannot refuse to hire someone between ages 40 and 70 due to age, and cannot discriminate in pay because of age.

This kind of legislation, like other kinds of antidiscriminatory legislation, will not end discriminatory acts. Gregory (2001), for example, says that most middle-aged and older workers face discrimination at work sometime in their work lives. Nevertheless, antidiscrimination laws clearly state society's values and the intent to allow workers to stay at work if they choose.

An end to ageism, prejudice, and discrimination will require all of the strategies proposed here: more positive images of older people in the media, education, balanced contact, and social action. It will require that we develop what Neugarten (1980) called an **age-irrelevant society**, a society that judges people by who they are and what they can do, rather than by their ages. The seeds of this kind of society may already exist. Some years ago, Sharon Curtin (1972, p. 50) said that "Almost everyone has someone they know, they love, who is also old. But they regard these loved ones as rather special cases. They may be the rule rather than the exception."

AGING TODAY

George Burns (1896–1996) worked as a comedian into his late 90s. He smoked, drank, and stayed out late. Someone once asked him, "What do your doctors say about all this?" Burns answered, "They don't say anything; they're all dead." George Burns presented a new model of old age: active, purposeful, joyful, enviable.

Each year new people enter the ranks of the old. These people have better education, better financial resources, and better health than past generations of older people. They lead active, engaged lives until late old age, and they will reshape our ideas about aging.

BOX 1.6
TOWARD AN AGE-IRRELEVANT SOCIETY

Historian Andrew Achenbaum says that we may go too far in giving preferred treatment to older people. This amounts to a reverse form of discrimination. It gives one group access to special programs and services based on their age. In an age-irrelevant society, should older people get special benefits? Achenbaum says that we need to look at whether age should serve as the basis for a policy or practice. Mandatory retirement, for example, discriminates against older people because age alone cannot predict ability on the job. On the other hand, he says, shelter allowances should be based not on age, but on need. Many age groups need help with housing costs.

This logic could apply to seniors' discounts as well. A young family of four may have as much need for a discount at a restaurant as a senior couple. A review of age-based policies would sometimes benefit older people and other times not. "Programs that unduly favor or disfavor people because they happen to be 'old,'" Achenbaum says, "should be reconsidered, and then either scrapped or reformulated." The cry of ageism can play on our guilt about our negative feelings toward aging. Achenbaum asks us to use a rational basis for deciding how we treat all people.

Source: W. A. Achenbaum, 1983, *Shades of Gray: Old Age, American Values, and Federal Policies Since 1920* (p. 171), Boston: Little, Brown.

Historian W. Andrew Achenbaum says:

> Nowadays, it seems that older Americans' ability to make more out of less and to come to grips with diminishing expectations as they grapple with the finitude of life actually may point the way to the future posture of everybody else in society. I am not prepared to claim that the elderly are at the vanguard of society, blazing the next frontier of America's revolution. But I am convinced that they will play a key role in that transformation. (1983, p. 170)

CONCLUSION

Ageism can lead to stereotyping, prejudice, and discrimination against older people. It can lead us to misjudge them, to treat them inappropriately, and to assume that they have less ability than they do. Alex Comfort said:

> We can't take the pain out of the facts that humans aren't immortal or indefinitely disease-proof, or that illnesses accumulate as we age. We can, however, wholly abolish the mischievous idea that after a fixed age we become different, impaired or nonpeople. The start of this demystification has to be in our own rejection of it for ourselves, and then in our refusal to impose it on others. (1976, pp. 32–33)

Novelist and travel writer Paul Theroux (2003) says this about aging and old age:

> What all older people know, what had taken me almost sixty years to learn, is that an aged face is misleading. . . . I now knew: the old are not as frail as you think, and they are insulted to be regarded as feeble. They are full of ideas, hidden powers, even sexual energy. Don't be fooled by the thin hair and battered features and skepticism. The older traveler knows it best: in our hearts we are youthful, and we are insulted to be treated as old men and burdens, for we have come to know that the years have made us more powerful and streetwise. Years are not an affliction. Old age is strength enough.

These writers point the way to the future, toward a fuller understanding of age and aging. One that includes the reality of physical change. But one that also includes the potential for wisdom and continued engagement with the world.

Gerontology focuses on older people, but it also asks us to look at ourselves. It asks us to look at our beliefs, values, and actions. Some people want to study aging for the joy of learning something new, but many people have a practical or professional interest in aging. We are all aging and we have friends, relatives, and neighbors who are now or will soon enter old age. Alex Comfort gave one of the best reasons for studying aging: self-interest. After all, he said, old age is a minority group nearly all of us will join one day. The more we know about aging, the more we can create a good old age for ourselves and the people we love.

SUMMARY

- Gerontology is the systematic study of aging. This chapter explains the benefits of studying aging, the social basis of age stereotyping, and the changes that will lead to new images of aging.
- Robert Butler uses the term *ageism* to describe negative attitudes toward aging. New ageism tries to do good by advocating for policies and programs to help older people. But it also supports the stereotype of old age as a time of decline and loss.
- Ageism leads to stereotyping, prejudice, and discrimination against older people.
- The media, advertising, literature, and popular culture are the most common sources of ageism in our society.
- Ageism results from ignorance about aging and misconceptions about old age. The FAQ suggests that people with more education have fewer misconceptions about aging.
- Gerontologists gather and teach facts about aging. This creates a better understanding of later life and a better quality of life for people of all ages.
- Gerontologists suggest that education, the media, intergenerational programs, legislation, and social action can produce a more positive and balanced view of aging.
- These strategies may help end ageism in the future and to develop a more age-irrelevant society. This type of society judges people by who they are and what they can do, rather than by their age.

DISCUSSION QUESTIONS

1. Define *ageism* according to Robert Butler. Explain how it can lead to social and personal problems.
2. Discuss the effects of ageism on older people and propose several strategies to discourage (or end) ageism in our society. How does compassionate stereotyping lead to scapegoating older people?
3. What are some common sources of ageism? Can you list several examples of ageism in your environment?
4. List some common misconceptions about old age today. Did you believe some of these misconceptions yourself, or did you have a more accurate view of aging?
5. What industries, besides those listed in this chapter, could target the older market?
6. How can younger people and university or college students increase their social interactions with older people? How would this benefit society?
7. Do you think an age-irrelevant society will provide a better opportunity for successful aging than our present society? Explain your answer.

SUGGESTED READING

Cohen, Gene D. (2000). *Creative age: Awakening human potential in the second half of life.* New York: Avon Books.

This book counteracts the myth of decline in later life. The author refers to historical examples, scientific research, and case studies to support the idea that older people can live creative lives. The book shows that age, experience, and creativity can lead to inner growth and new potential in later life. The book also suggests ways that older people can enhance their creativity in everyday life.

Morrow-Howell, Nancy, Hinterlong, James, & Sherraden, Michael (Eds.). (2001). *Productive aging: Concepts and challenges.* Baltimore, MD: Johns Hopkins University Press.

This collection of essays by well-known gerontologists advances the concept of *productive aging*. The essays explore the personal, psychological, social, and economic meaning of productive aging in America today. Race, gender, age, and education all influence productive aging. Several of the essays describe programs that provide opportunities for productive aging.

Martz, S. H. (1994). *If I had my life to live over I would pick more daisies.* Wastonsville, CA: Papier Mache.

A collection of fiction, poetry, and photos on what it means to age as an older woman. Provides insight into the experience of older women from their own perspectives. The book offers a dose of reality to combat the myths that lead to ageism.

GLOSSARY OF TERMS

age-irrelevant society A society that judges people by who they are and what they can do, rather than by their age.

aging enterprise The complex of professional services (many of them government sponsored) that serve the older population.

ageism "A process of systematic stereotyping and discrimination against people because they are old."

compassionate stereotype A stereotype that attempts to arouse sympathy or pity for older people.

demographer A person who studies population dynamics. The study of population dynamics is *demography.*

discrimination Unfair treatment based on prejudice rather than on merit.

gerontology The social or natural scientific study of aging. *Geriatrics* refers to the medical practice of care for older people.

life expectancy The number of additional years a person can expect to live at a given age (e.g., life expectancy at birth, or life expectancy at age 65).

Medicare The U.S. medical care program for people who receive Social Security.

Medicaid The U.S. supplementary medical care program for low-income older people.

mortality A measure of the number of deaths per 1,000 members of a population (e.g., people aged 85 to 89) in a year.

new ageism Stereotyping old age as a time of loss and decline to justify help for older people. *See* **compassionate stereotype.**

Older Americans Act The government act passed in 1965 (and amended since then) that established programs and services for older people nationwide.

prejudice A negative judgment made about someone based on a trait or on their membership in a particular group.

scapegoating Blaming a person or group (such as older people) for a complex and hard-to-solve social problem (such as the national debt).

social institutions Sociologists define social institutions as organized patterns of social behavior.

Social Security The United States' retirement income system. Workers pay into this system throughout their lives and collect a pension when they retire.

sociogenic aging Modern society's treatment of older people as if they were "unintelligent, unemployable, crazy and asexual" (Comfort, 1976, pp. 9–10).

stereotyping A stereotype usually has some basis in reality, but it represents an overgeneralization about a person or group. A stereotype leads us to treat older people in terms of a general pattern or characteristic, rather than as unique individuals.

chapter **2**

THEORIES AND METHODS

I visited Frances Kennedy, 68 years old, in her apartment on a cool autumn afternoon. I had just begun a study of how people make transitions in later life. She agreed to take part in the study, and I arranged to visit her home. She had lived alone since her youngest son moved out several years ago. I wanted to understand how she had adapted to living by herself.

"Oh, I love it," she said. "At first I had to adjust. For instance, I couldn't understand how the toothpaste spray got on the bathroom mirror now that I lived alone. I had always blamed that on Jimmy, my son. Finally, I had to admit that it must have been at least partly me all along.

"I love the idea that I can leave a chicken leg or a half container of milk in the refrigerator and find it still there the next day. I can sleep late on Saturdays if I want to, and I can have quiet suppers alone after work.

"I've also developed some tricks to make life interesting. You know, it's not much fun every night coming home and making your own supper. There's no surprise in it. So I found a way to surprise myself. One Sunday a month I prepare a batch of dinners—things like eggplant parmigiana, beef stew, lasagna. Then I put them in containers, seal the lids, and put them in the freezer. I don't label them.

"In the morning, before I go out, I take out two containers and put them on the counter to defrost. When I come home at night I open the containers, pop them in the microwave, and surprise myself with whatever's for dinner.

"I have other ways to make living alone more fun. For instance, I hate to clean house. But there's no one to share the work with now. So I put on a 20- or 25-minute piece of fast music. I have to clean the whole house before the music ends. I've got a whole lot of these games (like putting a label on the window cleaner bottle with the date when I think it will be used up) to make life interesting."

Frances has a creative streak that makes play out of the simplest jobs. Living alone allows her to express this creativity. My afternoon with her showed me why she enjoys living alone. It also gave me insight into why many older women prefer to live on their own.

Research on aging can take many forms. My meeting with Frances took the form of an in-depth interview. I used a few leading questions to guide our discussion, but mostly I wanted her to talk about her life in her own words. The open-ended interview method allowed Frances to reveal her private world to me.

Other research methods help to answer different research questions. And they produce different results. Research methods provide guides on how to collect information, ways to analyze research findings, and ways to report findings so other researchers can verify the results. Some researchers, for example, use survey methods. They mail questionnaires to hundreds or even thousands of people, then analyze the results on a computer. Other researchers conduct controlled studies in laboratories. They ask people to take a paper and pencil test or test a person's reaction time. Historical researchers study diaries and letters. Researchers who want to understand a group's culture or everyday life spend many hours doing field research.

No single method can answer all research questions. Gerontologists choose the methods and theories that best suit their research questions. Sociologists define a theory as a "conceptual model of some aspect of life" (Online, 2004). Theories try to make sense out of a complex reality. They link concepts and ideas into a single pattern. Scientists use theories to develop hypotheses about the way the world works. They then test these hypotheses through their research.

Gerontologists use many theories to guide their research. Some theories apply to individuals and their personal relationships. A gerontologist, for example, might want to understand whom older people turn to for help. The researcher might theorize that older people turn to family members for help before they turn to government services. This theory of social support says that people use informal supports before they turn to formal helpers.

Other theories apply to whole societies. Modernization theory, for example, says that the status of older people decreases as societies modernize. This theory links the treatment of older people to broad social and cultural changes. Other theories describe the effects of a person's economic status on health in later life. "No single theory explains all social phenomena; each focuses on particular aspects of social behavior" (Passuth & Bengtson, 1988, p. 334).

Each theory and method has its limits and its strengths. This chapter looks at (1) theories that guide gerontologists in their research; (2) methods that gerontologists use to gather their data; and (3) future trends in aging research in the United States.

THE STUDY OF AGING: PAST AND PRESENT

Early Developments in Research

Historians trace the study of aging to the ancient scriptures of the Far East, the Bible, and the work of Greek philosophers like Plato and Aristotle. Before the seventeenth century, authors based their writings on their own experiences. The writings reflected writers' fears and the biases of the time.

In the seventeenth century, writers began to base their studies on scientific methods and systematic observations. Most of the early researchers who studied aging were trained in the natural sciences and medicine. By the eighteenth century, scientists began to use mathematical techniques to study aging. Sir Edmund Halley, the discoverer of the comet named after him, created the first table of life expectancy. Benjamin Rush, in 1793, published the first American geriatrics work, *Account of the State of the Body and Mind in Old Age.* This started a modern period in which researchers saw aging as something other than disease. It also marked the start of the medical study of aging.

Quetelet in the mid-nineteenth century proposed a "social physics"—a science that would study human facts and events, express them in numbers, and locate cause and effect relationships. Quetelet, for example, collected physical and social data on people of different ages. He studied birth and death rates and looked at how crime and suicide varied by age. His study, *On the Nature of Man and the Development of His Faculties* (1835), described how human strength and weight varied by age. By the late nineteenth century, the social sciences—sociology and psychology—had also begun to study aging.

Historians credit Elie Metchnikoff of the Pasteur Institute in Paris with the first use of the term *gerontology* in 1905 (Freeman, 1979). Metchnikoff wrote the first gerontology text, *The Problem of Age, Growth, and Death,* in 1908. A short time later, in 1912, the Society of Geriatry—one of the first groups to study aging in North America—was formed in New York. G. Stanley Hall wrote *Senescence, the Last Half of Life* in 1922, one of the first scientific studies of aging in the United States. Hall used survey data to understand religious beliefs and attitudes toward death among older people. He and other writers at this time focused on the problems of old age (Achenbaum, 1987).

GERONTOLOGY RESEARCH TODAY

Research output on aging grew rapidly after World War II. Research on aging in the 1960s moved beyond a study of problems to include studies of normal aging. This included studies of positive developments in later life. Major journals in the United States began to be published between 1946 and 1970. Today, dozens of academic journals around the world publish research on aging, and new ones start all the time. Journals like *The Journal of Gerontology, The Gerontologist,* and *The International Journal of Human Development* serve a wide audience. Other journals target specific groups like nurses, social workers, or recreation professionals. A series of handbooks in biology, psychology, and the social sciences synthesize knowledge on key topics.

A bibliography of sources on aging for the years 1954 to 1974 listed 50,000 entries (Woodruff & Birren, 1975). This list contained more sources than all the writings on aging in the past century. Today, a complete bibliography would contain many times this number of sources. Computerized bibliographies like *AGELINE,* sponsored by the AARP (American Association of Retired Persons), attempt to keep track of the thousands of sources published on aging each year. A search for even one key word in this database can turn up thousands of sources published in the past twenty years.

IS GERONTOLOGY A DISCIPLINE?

The varied approaches that researchers take to aging (biological, psychological, social) raise some questions: Is gerontology a discipline, or is it a subfield within existing disciplines (like sociology or biology)?

Some years ago the Gerontological Society of America (GSA) sponsored the Foundations Project (Foundations Project, 1980). This project asked experts to reflect on the status of gerontology as a discipline. A discipline, the project said, has "a distinct body of knowledge, requiring the establishment of a separate academic unit" (Foundations Project, 1980, p. 6). A number of leaders in the field of aging at that time thought that gerontology met this criterion. They proposed that universities and colleges develop gerontology departments with their own faculty members and with administrative status.

Few schools, however, have taken this route. Gerontologists almost always belong to traditional disciplines like sociology, psychology, or biology. In most cases gerontology programs exist within a social science department, although some schools offer an interdisciplinary option that spans more than one field.

The status of gerontology as a discipline rests on whether gerontology has claim to a "distinct body of knowledge." The GSA put this to a test. The GSA asked 111 experts on aging from fields as varied as biomedicine and economics whether gerontology has a distinct body of knowledge (Foundations Project, 1980). The study asked them to define the core and scope of the field. Although the experts differed on the exact content and boundaries of the field, they did agree that three areas made up the core of aging studies: biomedicine, psychosocial studies, and socioeconomic-environmental studies.

Biomedicine studies look at the changes in the body that come with age, including studies of DNA, the cells, the body's systems, stress, and dementia. The experts showed the most agreement on the content of this subfield. This may be due to the long history of biomedical research on aging. Geriatrics, the medical specialty that deals with older people, draws heavily on biomedical knowledge of aging. Geriatricians, physicians who treat older people, also contribute to this body of knowledge through clinical research.

Psychosocial studies look at the changes that take place inside the individual and between individuals and groups. Researchers study memory, creativity, and learning. They also study personality, relationships, and death and dying.

Socioeconomic-environmental studies look at the effects of aging on social institutions. Sociologists define a social institution as a pattern of social interaction that has a relatively stable structure and persists over time (Online, 2004). Institutions include the economy, the family, and the health care system. Socioeconomic-environmental studies ask, for example, how an aging society will affect the health care system or the economy. These studies also look at the effect of social institutions on aging individuals. For example, how does the U.S. retirement income system (pension plans and retirement policies) affect the experience of aging.

Social gerontology makes up a part of the total body of gerontological knowledge. It includes the psychosocial, the socioeconomic-environmental, and practice-related studies of aging. Clark Tibbitts first introduced the idea of social gerontology in 1954. Social gerontology views aging from the perspective of the individual and the social system. When social gerontologists look at biomedical issues, they focus on the social effects of physical aging. For example, they ask how changes in a person's ability to walk affect their needs for social services. Or they ask how physical aging differs by race and ethnicity. Do older African Americans and whites have the same diseases at the same rates and from the same causes? Social gerontologists also look at changes throughout the life course. They study changes in family life, relationships, and activities. Social gerontology has grown in importance in the past twenty years.

THEORIES OF AGING

My grandmother used to keep her eyeglasses pushed up onto her head. I remember one day watching her walk around the house with a puzzled look on her face.

"Grandma," I said, "what are you looking for?"

"My glasses. I can't find them anywhere."

"They're on your head," I said with a laugh.

"Oh," she said, as she patted her head. "I must be getting old."

In that moment my grandmother expressed a theory of aging: When you get old, you forget things, like where you put your eyeglasses. She didn't think of this as a theory; she didn't know anything about theories. But she had one. When she forgot where she put her glasses, it confirmed her belief that you forget things when you age.

Many psychologists use this same theory in their research. They suspect that memory declines with age, and they have produced volumes of literature to test this theory. In this way my grandmother differs from research psychologists. She believed that memory decreased with age, but she never tried to prove or disprove the idea.

Theories often start with beliefs, common sense ideas, or hunches. But scientific theories differ from everyday theories in that scientists try to state a theory clearly. A theory may contain formal propositions linked to one another. The theory will also produce testable hypotheses that can guide research. Social scientists then study their research findings to see whether they support, reject, or modify the theory.

Bengtson and his colleagues (1999, p. 5) see the primary value of theory as providing "a set of lenses through which we can view and make sense of what we observe in research." Theories help researchers to organize and give focus to their work. Researchers have begun to give added attention to gerontological theory (Bengtson, Rice, & Johnson, 1999; Bengtson, Burgess, & Parrott, 1997).

Gerontologists have developed many theories to explain aging. These range from biological theories of why the skin wrinkles, to theories of why some societies kill their elders. Some gerontologists borrow theories from sociology and psychology and apply them to the study of aging. For example, psychologists have applied theories of mental function to the study of memory (Dixon, Backman, & Nilsson, 2004). Social psychologists have applied Lazarus's (1966) theory of stress and coping to the study of nursing assistants (Novak & Chappell, 1994). Sociologists have applied political economy theory to the study of pensions (Quadagno & Reid, 1999).

Gerontologists create theories to help them explain a set of facts. For example, research shows that older people may need housing with more physical and social supports as they age. The theory of person–environment fit, first advanced by Lawton and Nahemow (1973), explains this trend. This theory says that the supports a person needs depend on two things: a person's ability and the demands of the environment. As ability decreases, demand increases and a person needs more support. This theory interprets the facts and puts them in a framework. It allows researchers to test the relationship between different forces that shape housing needs. It also allows service providers to offer supports that improve an older person's quality of life.

Each theory contains a set of assumptions about people and the world. For example, exchange theory focuses on what people give and get from one another. It helps explain caregivers' service to their spouses or parents. But it has its limits. For example, it says nothing about the impact of modern industrial society on the family. Or about state policies that limit home care benefits to older people. Gerontologists need other theories, like modernization theory or political economy theory, to understand social change and social policy. No single theory in gerontology can explain all the facts about aging (Bengtson, Burgess, & Parrott, 1997). Sometimes gerontologists apply more than one theory to understand a set of facts.

Gerontologists differ in the kinds of theories they favor. The choice of a theory depends on a researcher's training, the subject under study, and even personal preference. The study of gerontological theories shows the scope of gerontological research and the ways that gerontologists think about aging.

TWO LEVELS OF THEORIES

Social gerontologists use theories to explain everything from child–parent relations to the treatment of older people by the government. The following discussion arranges some of the major theories in a framework and gives examples of how gerontologists have applied them in their work. Gerontologists use at least two types of theory: micro-level theories and macro-level theories.

Micro-level theories describe people and their relationships. They focus on small-scale events like interactions between staff and patients in a nursing home, changes in personality with age, and choice of leisure activities. These theories encompass studies of how individuals change as they age. They include the study of memory and intelligence, as well as the study of adjustments to retirement or widowhood.

Macro-level theories look at social institutions (like the family), social systems (like health care or housing), and whole societies. These theories examine the way social institutions shape experiences and behavior (Bengtson, Burgess, & Parrott, 1997, p. S76). These theories focus on large-scale events such as historical changes in family size and structure, health care policies, and how industrial or agricultural societies treat their older people. Modernization theory serves as an example of a macro-level theory.

THREE THEORETICAL PERSPECTIVES

Micro-level and macro-level theories look at different phenomena. Taken together, they show the scope of

BOX 2.1
THEORIES OF AGING
Theories for the Study of Aging

Levels of Theory

Micro	*Macro*
(individual social interaction)	(social structures, social processes)

Theoretical Perspectives

Interpretive	*Functionalist*	*Conflict*
(how individuals define and create social world)	(social order based on cooperation and consensus)	(society based on conflict between social groups)

Theories

social constructionism	structural functionalism	political economy
symbolic interactionism	modernization	moral economy
social phenomenology	disengagement	feminist theories
ethnomethodology	continuity	
social exchange	activity	
	age stratification	
	life course	

This chart presents the most influential theories in the study of aging. It summarizes the discussion in the text.

Source: Aging and Society, A Canadian Perspective, Fifth Edition by NOVAK/CAMPBELL. © 2006. Reprinted with permission of Nelson, a division of Thomson Learning: www.thomsonrights.com. Fax 800-730-2215.

gerontological study. Researchers can choose from three major theoretical perspectives within these levels of study: the interpretive perspective, the functionalist perspective, and the conflict perspective.

Interpretive Perspective

The interpretive perspective most often focuses on the micro-level of social life. It looks at how people relate to one another, how they define situations, and how they create social order. Theories within this perspective include social constructionism (Bengtson, Burgess, & Parrott, 1997), social exchange theory (Homans, 1961), the symbolic-interactionist perspective, social phenomenology, and ethnomethodology (Garfinkel, 1967), as well as an even earlier tradition pioneered by Max Weber (1905/1955). A relatively small number of gerontologists have used this perspective.

Symbolic interaction, based on the work of George Herbert Mead (1934), and social phenomenology, based on the work of Alfred Schutz (1967), fit this perspective. Symbolic interactionists study how symbols like clothing, body language, and written words shape social relations. For example, an older man in a derby hat, a pipe, and an umbrella gives one impression. A young woman in jeans, a bustier, and platinum-colored hair gives another. We would address each of these people differently and make different assumptions about their backgrounds and interests. People learn to read and respond to the symbols around them.

Social phenomenologists take a more extreme view. They speak of "the social construction of reality" (Berger & Luckmann, 1967). They view social order as a creation of everyday interaction. Social phenomenologists often look at conversation to find the methods people use to maintain social relations. For example, if I ask, "How are you?" you understand that I don't want to hear about your athlete's foot. You answer, "Fine." We smile and move on.

A doctor who asks this same question wants to know about your health. You give a different answer to this question in a doctor's office. If you answer, "Fine," the doctor may probe and ask some very personal questions. You will play along and assume that this is part of the doctor's job. A social phenomenologist studies the way that doctor–patient conversations build and create a social reality that we call the medical exam.

The interactionist perspective sees the person as an actor and a creator of social life. People do more than live in social groups and organizations. They play a part in creating and maintaining them. They do this every day and in every interaction. People negotiate who goes through a door first, who sits where at the dinner table, and what kind of clothes to wear to a job interview. All of these actions have meaning, and people learn to read and interpret these meanings from childhood. People also take them for granted and rarely notice what they do.

Symbols also have meaning. I once asked a graphic designer to create a brochure for a gerontology program that I planned to offer. I explained that I would send the brochure to health care professionals. The designer came back with a brochure that had an abstract image on it. The image looked like a bent and crooked figure leaning on a cane. This image reflected the designer's idea of aging. It presented an image that he felt the public shared. I could have used this brochure cover in the program as a case study in ageism.

Gray hair, wrinkles, a walker, all symbolize aging. Symbols or images can have a strong influence on us. The wheelchair symbolizes sickness, weakness, and dependence. Wheelchair designers have worked to change this image. Some wheelchairs now have angled wheels, high-performance tires, and special seats for athletic use. Some physically challenged older people prefer indoor scooters to wheelchairs.

One older woman I know, who used to own a wheelchair, says that her scooter changed her self-image. She felt helpless and stigmatized in her wheelchair. She now rides around her local shopping mall with confidence and self-esteem. Why does the image of a scooter differ from that of a wheelchair? The wheelchair symbolizes illness. The scooter symbolizes freedom and an active lifestyle. People attach different meanings to each. Sociologist W. I. Thomas summed this up in what sociologists call the **Thomas theorem**. "If people define situations as real, they are real in their consequences" (Thomas & Thomas, 1928, p. 572).

The interpretive perspective can give a good understanding of how people interpret their social world, how they interact with one another, and why they do what they do. Gerontologists have used this approach to study how people adapt to retirement, loss of a spouse, and changes in health (Koch, 2000).

Gubrium (1993) studied Alzheimer's disease from an interactionist perspective. Biomedical researchers describe Alzheimer's disease as a series of plaques and tangles in the brain. Gubrium takes the biological fact of Alzheimer's disease as a starting point for his study. He treats the biological findings as social constructions and studies how these concepts and facts form the basis of community life.

Gubrium found that much of the interaction between members of the Alzheimer's community goes on in caregiver support groups. He found that support groups develop a "local culture." Some groups teach and inform members. Other groups focus on emotional issues. "The local cultures of the groups," he says, "were not simply given" (Gubrium, 1993, p. 52). Each member added to the group's pool of experience.

One member's confusion would serve as a chance for other members to speak more about their own experiences. These conversations and examples became resources that members referred to and used to define their own experiences. Members' experiences "entered the exemplary background for further comparison" (Gubrium, 1993, p. 52). Conversations built up a culture of knowledge, examples, norms, and values that support group members shared. Support group members created their culture at the same time that they used it to solve their problems.

One caregiver in a support group said, "I'm really frightened . . . of not knowing how to feel. Should I be feeling something that I'm not? Or not feeling the way I seem to be?" (Gubrium, 1989, p. 261, cited in Gubrium, 1993). Her group helped her to understand that many people feel confused and that the feeling would pass. Support group members often begin with only vague notions about the disease and a vague knowledge about how to behave in the face of the illness. Members help one another create understanding and sensible responses to the disease through their meetings, writings, and interactions.

Kaufman (1993) used an interactionist theory to guide her study of stroke patients because she thought "the voices of individual old people were deemphasized or lost in the conduct of . . . [scientific] research" (Kaufman, 1993, p. 13). She wanted to explore the meaning older people gave to their lives. She found that stroke patients experience a sharp break with past life patterns. She also found that people try to maintian continuity in their lives. They interpret the past and link it to the present. She found that stroke patients worked hard to build links from their past to their future. People who completed this task recovered, even if they still had physical disability. Stroke patients needed to show that they were the same people after their illness as before.

Kaufman places her work within a phenomenological framework. "Phenomenology," she says, "attends to the reality of experience" (Kaufman, 1993, p. 15). It studies a phenomenon—sickness, rehabilitation, health—from the subject's point of view. This type of research requires a close collaboration between the researcher and the subject. The subject's story and the way the subject comes to create that story become the research finding. This approach to research opens the researcher to the world of the subject. The researcher in a well-crafted study learns to see the world through the eyes of the subject and to understand the meaning the subject gives to the world.

Gubrium points to a growing interest in the interpretive perspective. He reports a "decided surge of interest in the place of personal meaning, the unstandardized, and the emergent in everyday life" (Gubrium, 1993, p. 60; Gubrium & Holstein, 1999). But Gubrium cautions against romanticizing this experience. The interactionist perspective, he says, must include an awareness of culture and history. This allows the researcher to see how people create and maintain the meaning of old age in a specific social setting.

BOX 2.2
A QUESTION OF METHOD
"Treasure" by Deidre Scherer

Deidre Scherer of Williamsville, Vermont, has created "images of aging." She cut, pieced, layered, and sewed cloth to create her work. This study in fabric and thread she called "Treasure." Does Scherer's work count as a "research study" of aging? If not, why not? If so, why do you consider it a research study? How does it differ from studies done by social scientists? What do artists discover through their "research"? What can an artist's work teach us about aging?

Source: "Treasure," by Deidre Scherer, *The Gerontologist, 33*(6), 1993.

Deidre Scherer's "Treasure," created from fabric and thread.

Critique of the Interpretive Perspective

Like every perspective, the interactionist perspective gives only one view of social life. Critics of this perspective say, first, that it overlooks the links between the individual and larger social institutions. For example, an interactionist view of stroke patients' self-understanding misses the impact of the hospital bureaucracy on patients' lives. Second, the interactionist perspective does not look at the impact of social policies on people or groups. Third, the interactionist perspective does not discuss power and conflict between social groups. The interactionist perspective would not, for example, study the effects of race on health care services to stroke patients. The functionalist and conflict perspectives focus on these issues.

Functionalist Perspective

The functionalist perspective includes structural-functionalist theory (or functionalism) in sociology. Emile Durkheim promoted this theory at the turn of the last century in *The Division of Labor in Society* (1893). Talcott Parsons developed this theory further in *The Social System* (1951). Functionalism views society as a system made up of many parts. These include religion, the family, education, and politics. Changes to one part of the system lead to changes in the whole system.

Functionalism sees society as an organism that tries to stay in equilibrium. Biologists refer to this as *homeostasis.* Society regulates itself in the same way your body keeps a steady temperature. When you exercise, you overheat your body. Sweat cools you down. A change in one part of the system brings mechanisms into play that reestablish order. An increase in the number of older people, for example, leads to more government money directed to programs for the elderly. More support to older people can create a dysfunction (e.g., a fear that too little money exists for other age groups). This may lead to political backlash and reduced support. The system tries to stay in balance through changes in policies and programs.

Functionalism can explain large-scale political change as well as the way small groups maintain their structure. Functionalism says that norms (shared rules of behavior) and roles (expectations for behavior in a certain social status) shape behavior. People learn these norms and learn to play social roles as they grow older. People conform to these norms through social pressure, but also through belief in society's underlying value system. The values expressed in the commandment "Honor thy father and mother" show up in everyday behavior and in social policies. Failure to honor a parent may lead to informal sanctions, such as criticism from a sister or brother. Extreme neglect may lead to the charge of abuse and legal sanctions.

Informal and formal sanctions create a smooth-running society. People know what to do and what others expect of them. Functionalism focuses on consensus and social order. It assumes that society changes or evolves in a positive direction. It explains social problems as dysfunctions, and it proposes to correct these dysfunctions through the use of experts in planning and the helping professions.

Historically, gerontologists used the functionalist perspective more than any other perspective in their study of aging. Gerontology's most influential early theories are disengagement theory (Cumming & Henry, 1961), activity theory (Neugarten, Havighurst, & Tobin, 1968) (both discussed in Chapter 7), and modernization theory (Cowgill & Holmes, 1972). All three rely on structural-functionalist assumptions. Riley and her colleagues (Riley, 1987; Riley, Foner, & Waring, 1988) also produced a dominant theory based on structural-functionalist principles: age stratification theory.

Age Stratification Theory: An Example of the Functionalist Perspective

Age stratification theory or its more recent identification as the "aging and society paradigm" (Riley, Foner, & Riley, Jr., 1999) links individual aging to social institutions. The theory discusses individual aging, societal aging, and **cohort flow** (Riley, Foner, & Waring, 1988). Age stratification theory describes a "*dynamic interplay* between two interdependent processes: individual aging and social change" (Riley, 1985, p. 371).

Individual Aging

Age stratification theory views aging as a life-long process. People experience biological changes with age. They also experience changes in roles and social positions. Each society sets out a series of roles that people enter and leave as they age. These include the role of child, student, spouse, parent, worker, retiree, and grandparent. These roles and the norms that go with them change over time. Many older people, for example, learned that a person should not have sex outside of marriage. Some of these people now find themselves widowed. They would like to have an active sex life without marrying again. They have to rethink their childhood beliefs about marriage, sex, and old age.

Societal Change

Every society has a set of age grades that stratifies its members. Societies attach certain rights and responsibilities to each age grade. Age grades in the United States include childhood, adolescence, young adulthood, middle age, and old age. These age grades may change over time. Today, for example, French society includes the Third Age of retirees and the Fourth Age of the very old. More people now live in the Third and Fourth age grades than ever before.

The U.S. Census Bureau often divides statistics on older people into two or more groups (e.g., ages 65 to 74; 75 to 84; and 85 and over). This division recognizes that people move through different stages in later life (e.g., many people have to cope with increased frailty after age 85). Gerontologists can learn about a society by studying its age stratification system.

Cohort flow describes the dynamics of the age stratification system. People belong to an **age cohort**, a group of people born at about the same time. People born between 1950 and 1959, for example, form an age cohort. Cohorts move through society's age grade system together. They go through the same age grades and transitions at about the same time.

People in their 80s today experienced the end of World War II in their early adult years. Many of them married just after the war, and they produced the Baby Boom generation. These people share memories of the postwar years as young parents. They also share the memory of the Big Band era, the first television shows, and early commercial air travel.

The Baby Boom generation will remember some of these events, but they may recall more about the first cartoon shows than anything else on television. The Baby Boomers will recall little of the McCarthy hearings or Eisenhower's presidency in the 1950s. Historical events affect each cohort, but each cohort experiences these events differently because they go through the event at a different time in the life cycle.

Each age cohort moves through life as if on an escalator. One group leaves an age grade and the next group enters it. Each age grade places expectations on its members and offers members new roles to play. At the same time, each cohort brings into an age grade a new set of norms and values that lead to changes in social life.

New cohorts and historical events can lead to changes in the age grade system itself. For example, today older people as a group enter old age with more income than older people in the past. The Social Security system, corporate pension plans, and good nutrition allow them to live more active lifestyles and to engage in new activities. The current generation of older people has begun to change our notion of old age. They travel, take courses, and exercise. These new seniors have given rise to new ed-

s
tc
fl
rel
fee
coh
char
parts
see sc
functi ... same
way.

Age ...ication theory has a number of strengths. First, it has helped to separate age differences (between cohorts) from age changes over the life course (aging). Second, it highlights the impact of historical and social changes on individuals and cohorts (Bengtson, Burgess, & Parrott, 1997). Third, it highlights the relationship between aging and social structures. Bengtson and his colleagues (1997, p. S82) say that age stratification theory "provides new ways to explore differences related to time, period, and cohort."

Critique of the Functionalist Perspective

Criticisms of age stratification theory show the limits of the functionalist perspective. First, age stratification theory tends to see society as a homogeneous set of structures and functions that all people in an age cohort experience the same way. This approach focuses on the differences between cohorts, but misses the diversity within them. For example, people in the same cohort differ by gender, race, and ethnicity.

Age stratification theory puts little focus on how gender, social class, race, and ethnicity create inequalities within age cohorts. For example, it says little about the differences between growing old as a lower class woman compared with growing old as [illegible] ences within a [illegible] ence on a person's [illegible] s related to their age [illegible] gender leads to different [illegible] rent responses to sociohistor- [illegible] son's race or gender also deter- [illegible] oices available as the person ages [illegible] Gibson, 1997). For example, the pro- [illegible] privatization of Social Security and the [illegible] nce to invest money for the future will benefit a wealthy older man more than a poor older woman.

Second, the age stratification theory overlooks the person's interpretation of the social world. It emphasizes the impact of society and history on the individual but says little about how the individual makes sense of these conditions and responds to them. People in the same age cohort interpret the world and respond to events in unique ways. A war may turn one person into a patriot and another into a pacifist. An elderly Chinese woman who has just arrived in California from Hong Kong will see the world differently from a retired New England farmer. Age stratification theory overlooks how each of these people interpret the world. It makes little reference to individual control or action.

Third, functionalist theories have a conservative bias. Functionalism sees equilibrium and social order as preferred social conditions. Age stratification theory, for example, focuses on cohorts, norms, and social order, but it fails to account for conflicts and tensions between social groups in society or to issues of power. These conflicts often shape a person's life. Race, gender, social class, and ethnicity create unequal access to a good life in society. Older African Americans today, for example, have poorer health than whites. Racial inequality may explain more about African Americans' life chances than do the norms and values of their age cohort.

Functionalist theories, like the age stratification theory, have their shortcomings. Still, they order the complex changes that take place over the life span.

The life course approach, also a functionalist approach, bridges both the micro-level and macro-levels of analysis. It incorporates social interaction and social structure within its framework (Bengtson, Burgess, & Parrott, 1997). Researchers use this approach to explain (1) the changes that take place over time, (2) age-related and socially recognized life transitions, and (3) the interaction of social life, history, culture, and personal biography (Bengtson, Burgess, & Parrott, 1997; George, 1996). At the micro-level or individual level, the life course approach looks at how events and conditions early in life affect later life. At the macro-level or societal level, the life course approach shows how social change and historical events can create differences between cohorts (Elder, 2000).

The life course approach overcomes some of the limitations of age stratification theory. Some researchers say that no unified, systematic approach to the life course exists. Rather, the life course approach merges theoretical approaches from many disciplines, including sociology and psychology (George, 1996). The life course approach recognizes variety in life course patterns and differences between age cohorts.

It also recognizes differences within age cohorts due to differences in race, ethnicity, social class, and gender (Stoller & Gibson, 1997). This approach takes into account the diversity of roles and role changes across the life course. It recognizes aging as a lifelong, dynamic, interactive, and multidirectional process. For example, an older woman may maintain good relations with her children, she may have trouble walking up stairs, but she may take up a new hobby like painting. Aging involves stability in some areas of life, decline in others, and improvement in others.

The life course approach looks at **transitions** and **trajectories**. Transitions refer to changes in social status or social roles (in particular, when transitions occur, how long they last, how people get through the transitions). Transitions include marriage, divorce, remarriage, widowhood, and parenthood. Work-related transitions also occur, for example, getting a first job or retiring.

Trajectories refer to long-term patterns of stability and change. They may include many transitions. One marital status trajectory may involve the transition to marriage, a subsequent divorce, then a remarriage, and finally a transition to widowhood. Another marital status trajectory may involve only one marriage for life. This involves only the transition to a first marriage and, for one of the couple, the transition to widowhood.

The life course approach has made a number of contributions to the study of aging. First, it bridges the macro-level and the micro-level of analysis by recognizing the importance of social structures and historical context, as well as individual experiences and meanings. It helps us understand the diversity within and between cohorts. Second, the approach brings together sociological, psychological, anthropological, and historical approaches to the study of aging. Third, the life course approach understands aging as a dynamic process that takes place throughout life.

This approach has some limitations. Its broad focus on society, culture, and the individual makes it hard to define as a single theory. Furthermore, as Bengtson and his colleagues (1997, p. S80) say, "it is very difficult to incorporate into a single analysis the many contextual variables . . . that this approach identifies." Still, the life course approach encourages us to think about the many individual and social forces that affect aging.

Conflict Perspective

Conflict theory looks at the tensions that exist between groups in society. It grows out of the work of Karl Marx (1967), who viewed society as a struggle between social classes. Conflict theorists look at the ways socially powerful groups or the government (as a tool of these groups) shape the lives of others. Few gerontologists have used the conflict perspective in their work. Those that do often look at how the economy or state policies influence old age.

In the early twentieth century, for example, new machines demanded faster work. Older workers faced greater stresses than ever before. They often found it hard to keep up with the pace of the new machines. Many companies at this time replaced slower older workers with younger workers. The conflict perspective views these social tensions as part of a class struggle. The owners of factories exploited workers to increase their profits. Older people became victims of the system.

Gerontologists also make use of political economy theory, a type of conflict theory that looks at the state, the economy, social class, and their impact on people (Minkler & Estes, 1999; Quadagno & Reid, 1999). The political economy approach traces the origins of older people's problems to the political and economic structure of capitalist society (Minkler, 1999b). It also looks at how social programs and policies for older people serve the interests of middle-aged, middle-class professionals and can reinforce class, gender, and racial inequalities in later life. The political economy of aging framework sees old age as social construction that mirrors the unequal distribution of resources in youth and middle age.

For example, compared with men, women are more likely to earn less income, work part-time, or have disrupted work histories due to child care or care for other family members. Public and private pension programs tend to reward those with higher incomes and stable work histories. This means that, compared with older men, older women find themselves with fewer pension benefits and less savings. Researchers have begun to study the causes of poverty in later life, women and gender discrimination, the ideology of aging as a social problem, and pensions and policies. Gerontologists have looked at the impact of retirement and pensions on aging (Phillipson, 1999), the structural situation of women and retirement (Zimmerman et al., 2000), and social policy in an aging society (Estes, 1999; Hudson, 1999).

Early work by Estes (1979) took a political economy approach to study welfare programs in the United States. She found that these programs tended to stigmatize older people. They defined the needs of older people as a need for services. This justified the expansion of the social service bureaucracy. Within the social welfare system, older people have little control over the services they can get or the ones they receive. Control lies in the hands of middle-class service workers. These workers define the older person's needs (e.g., for homemaker services, meals-on-wheels, etc.) and dole out services based on their assessment of need.

This system sees service to individuals as the answer to older peoples' problems. But the political economy perspective says that these services lower the status of older people by treating them as social problems. Estes (1979) concluded that those who run the welfare state gain more than those served by it. Quadagno and Reid (1999, p. 344), speaking from within the political economy perspective, say that "the challenge for social gerontology is not simply to understand how people interpret their private troubles but rather to consider also how these private troubles become public issues, thereby generating a societal response."

Estes' work shows the strength of the political economy approach. First, it places the study of aging in the context of large political, historical, economic, and social forces. Second, it views public pensions and income in later life as the outcome of a struggle between competing groups. Third, it predicts that economic and political forces will shape future changes in public pensions.

The political economy approach emphasizes the impact of history and economics on individuals. It shows how the state and social policies can increase or decrease social inequalities (Quadagno & Reid, 1999). But, the political economy approach tends to overemphasize the poverty and problems older people face. It also tends to view the individual as the product of political and economic forces. It pays little attention to individuals' interpretations of social life. It says little about the ways that individuals shape their world through interactions with others. As Bengtson and his colleagues (1997, p. S83) say, this perspective too often "paints a picture of all elders as powerless, forced to exist under oppressive structural arrangements with no control over their own lives."

Feminist theories, within the conflict perspective, bridge both the micro-level and macro-level of analysis. They recognize the importance of social interaction and social structure in the study of aging (Bengtson, Burgess, & Parrott, 1997). Feminist theories hold that society is gendered by nature. Feminist social gerontologists believe that gender defines social interaction and life experiences, including the experience of aging. Furthermore, within a patriarchal system (such as North American society), gender-based inequalities are created and perpetuated. This results in social advantages for men (for instance, higher wages and better pensions) and disadvantages for women (higher rates of poverty in old age).

Feminist theorists criticize other theories of aging and aging research for not focusing enough on gender relations or on women's experiences. Hooyman and her colleagues (2002) state that researchers and practitioners need to find new approaches to address gender, race, and class inequalities that exist across the life course.

Feminist research in aging has focused on many issues: mother–daughter conflict (Ray, 2003), the impact of domestic violence on older women (Vinton, 1999), women and retirement (Richardson, 1999), and the social invisibility of older lesbians (Fullmer, Shenk, & Eastland, 1999).

Feminist theories make an important contribution to the study of aging. First, feminist theories, like the life course approach, recognize the importance of social structure, social interaction, and individual characteristics (primarily gender, but also race, ethnicity, and social class) (Bengtson, Burgess, & Parrott, 1997). Second, they present a more inclusive picture of aging and older adults, by focusing on the majority of the older population—women—and on issues that are relevant to women's lives. Third, feminist theories of aging challenge the traditional focus on men in research (Calasanti, 1996) and the ageist biases in *mainstream* feminist theories that ignore issues of age (Calasanti & Slevin, 2001).

Feminist theories have some limitations. For example, some gerontologists see gender as too narrow a focus for the study of aging. They say that feminist theories attempt to *feminize* the study of aging, and that they overlook the experiences important to older men (Bengtson, Burgess, & Parrott, 1997). Critics also say that feminist theories dwell too much on social problems. They overlook the positive experience many women have in later life and they overlook women's contributions to society (Gibson, 1996). Still, feminist theories of aging contribute to our understanding of aging. They have made gender an explicit theme in the study of aging and later life.[1]

[1]I thank my colleague, Professor Lori Campbell, McMaster University, for developing this review of feminist gerontology.

Critique of the Conflict Perspective

Conflict theories ask questions neither of the other perspectives can. Conflict theories link individual problems to larger social issues of the economy and the state. Still, conflict theories have their limits. First, they overemphasize the poverty and problems that older people face. Second, they overemphasize the effect of social structures on individual aging. Third, they tend to see the person as the product of social and political forces. Conflict theories pay little attention to the responses older people make to social pressures.

Gerontologists need theories to make sense of the mass of detailed information that researchers gather (Bengtson, Rice, & Johnson, 1999). As Bengtson and his colleagues (1997, p. S84) say, "theory is not a marginal, meaningless 'tacked-on' exercise to presenting results in an empirical paper. Rather, cumulative theory-building represents the core of the foundation of scientific inquiry and knowledge."

Gerontological theories offer many explanations of aging. Their variety reflects the many dimensions of gerontological research. Gerontologists have borrowed theoretical perspectives from most of the social sciences. They have modified these theories to fit the study of aging. In some cases, they have developed new theories (like age stratification theory and the life course approach) to fit the issues that gerontologists study. Gerontologists can select from the theories presented here and from many more specific theories in their attempts to understand aging. Each of these theories and perspectives gives us a different insight into what it means to age.

RESEARCH ISSUES AND METHODS

Gerontologists use many different methods to study aging. Methods vary by discipline, by subfields within a discipline, and by the question under study. Methods range from the laboratory work of biomedical scientists to the intelligence tests of psychologists, from studies of diaries and literature, to surveys like the U.S. Census. Some studies use more than one method. The U.S. Health and Retirement Study (U.S. Department of Health and Human Services, 2004), for example, used face-to-face interviews in peoples' homes, telephone interviews, and physiological measurements to study the retirement process. The proper use of research methods ensures that gerontologists end up with reliable and valid results. The following discussion looks at some of the methodological issues that gerontologists face.

Experimental Designs

Social gerontologists want to understand the changes that take place in individuals over time. For example, a gerontologist might want to know how drinking milk in childhood affects bone density in old age. An experiment could answer this question. A researcher could divide a group of children into two groups in childhood. One group would drink milk. The other would not. After sixty years, the researchers would measure the effects of milk drinking on bone density. Of course, gerontologists cannot conduct this kind of experiment. They could not risk the health of a group of children. Even if they could do the experiment, they would have to wait nearly a lifetime to get the results.

Instead, social gerontologists more often work with groups that already exist. For example, a gerontologist might study bone density in two groups of women born at different times. These groups might differ naturally in the diet they ate. Women who grew up during the Great Depression, for example, may have had a poorer diet than women born ten years later. A gerontologist could compare the bone density in these two groups of women in old age.

Gerontologists often conduct this kind of study. These studies take the place of formal experiments and often serve as the quickest, least expensive way to gather information. But this type of study presents problems for the researcher. For example, imagine a researcher who conducts a study of diet and bone density in older women in 2005. She looks at bone density in two groups of women—one group born in 1940 (65 years old) and the other born in 1930 (75 years old and born during the Great Depression). The researcher finds that women born during the Depression (who had poor diets) have less bone density than women born after the Depression.

Does this mean that poor diet in childhood leads to less bone density in old age? Not necessarily. The researchers want to know whether one variable (diet) causes a change in another variable (bone density). They have found a **correlation** or regular relationship between these two variables, but a high correlation between two variables (like childhood diet and bone density in old age) does not prove that one caused the other. Consider some other possibilities.

First, the 1930 group is ten years older than the 1940 group at the time of the study. Bone density may decrease with age. The two groups may differ because bone density decreases between ages 65 and 75. Diet in childhood may have little or nothing to do with this.

Second, the two groups may have begun life with different bone densities due to differences in their mothers' diets. Children born during the Depression may suffer throughout their lives from the effects of their mothers' poor nutrition.

Third, historical events may have influenced these two groups differently. For example, older women from both the 1930 and 1940 groups have begun to exercise in the past few years. This increase in activity will increase bone density, but it may have less effect on older women. This effect makes it unclear whether childhood diet led to the differences in bone density that the researcher found.

These examples show the kinds of problems gerontologists face when they search for the causes of change in later life. Gerontologists generally place changes in old age into one of three categories: age effects, cohort effects, or period effects.

Age effects, due to physical decline, appear with the passage of time. They include an increase in the body's fat-to-muscle ratio, a decrease in lung elasticity, and decreases in bone density. They also include environmentally caused changes like wrinkled skin and cataracts caused by the sun.

Cohort effects are related to the time of a person's birth. A cohort refers to a group of people born around the same time (usually within a five-year period). People born in a certain cohort often share a common background and view of the world. People born just after World War II, for example, were the first cohorts exposed to large doses of television. This shaped their entertainment habits, values, and life-styles.

Period effects are due to the time of measurement. This would include historical effects on measurement like an ongoing war or changes in health habits like increased exercise. These effects have different influences on different age cohorts.

Gerontologists try to disentangle these effects to understand the causes of aging. Maddox and Campbell (1985, p. 20) called this the "age/period/cohort (APC) problem." Gerontologists use a number of research designs to look at these three effects and understand change in later life.

Cross-Sectional Designs

A cross-sectional study takes place when a researcher studies several age groups at one point in time. Many studies use this approach. Brach and her colleagues (2004), for example, used data from a questionnaire study to compare the physical functioning of older people who exercised or stayed active with those who were inactive. The researchers found that people in the exercise group had significantly better physical functioning than the active group and the inactive group. They conclude that twenty to thirty minutes of exercise most days leads to better physical functioning. Bond and her colleagues (2003) studied the relationship between alcohol consumption and depression among Japanese and Caucasian Americans between the ages of 65 and 101. The study analyzed data from over 4,000 people. The study found that the younger people in the study consumed more alcohol and had lower depression scores.

Researchers use cross-sectional designs for a number of reasons. First, cross-sectional sets of data may already exist. This saves time and money. The cross-sectional exercise and activity data used by

Brach and her colleagues (2004), for example, came from a larger longitudinal study, the Aging and Body Composition (Health ABC) study. This information cost thousands of dollars and many weeks to collect. The researchers wanted to compare the responses of several age groups at one point in time, and the data from this already completed study could answer this question.

Second, cross-sectional designs control for environmental events that might affect the study. For example, if the season of the year affects answers on a housing study, then a one-time study can get responses from everyone in the same season. Third, cross-sectional designs allow the researcher to gather data about many age groups in one study.

Cross-sectional studies show differences between age groups. However, they may confuse differences *between age groups* (differences due to when a person was born) with *changes due to aging*. For example, many cross-sectional studies done in psychology until the 1960s found that older age groups had lower intelligence scores than younger age groups. This led to the conclusion that intelligence decreases with age.

Schaie and Labouvie-Vief (1974) said that other things could explain this apparent decline in intelligence with age. They found, for example, that educational differences between the older and younger groups accounted, at least in part, for cross-sectional findings of intelligence decline (*see also* Baltes & Schaie, 1982). Older cohorts with less education tended to do less well on paper and pencil tests and felt more test anxiety. This led to lower intelligence scores.

Most researchers who study aging still use cross-sectional designs. They often do this for practical reasons. Cross-sectional studies cost less to conduct and researchers can analyze the data immediately. But cross-sectional studies can lead to errors in interpretation. They confound aging and cohort effects. Researchers try to overcome this problem. They can combine results from a number of cross-sectional studies. This gives a picture of change over time. This allows gerontologists to study social trends and to assess the impact of social policies. The use of more than one cross-sectional study creates a longitudinal design. Longitudinal studies correct for some of the problems that cross-sectional studies face.

Longitudinal Designs

Longitudinal studies look at age cohorts or individuals over time. Longitudinal studies of intelligence, for example, help untangle the effects of background and environment (cohort effects) from changes due to age. A longitudinal study, for example, can compare a person's test scores at age 45, 50, and 55. This provides a record of how a person's mental ability changes over the years.

The Health and Retirement Study conducted in the United States offers a good example of a longitudinal study. The study collected a first round of data from 12,600 people aged 51 to 61 in 1992. The study also drew an oversample of people from Florida, people of African American descent, and of people with Hispanic background (Health and Retirement Study, 2004). The study collected two follow-up waves of data, one in 1994 and one in 1996. A second study, the Study of Assets and Health Dynamics Among the Oldest Old began in 1998, and the data from the two studies were merged into a single study. The study, using the combined data and sample had conducted seven waves of research by 2004 (Health and Retirement Study, 2004).

This study looks at the retirement experience, savings, health insurance coverage, and economic condition of older Americans. The study focuses on health and economic transitions in later life. It also looks at the role that families play in the economic support of older people. The longitudinal design follows the same people over many years (at two-year intervals). Researchers can use these findings to see what events influence retirement decisions and how people manage the challenges of later life.

One study based on these findings, for example, found that over time education level best predicted a person's retirement decision. People with high levels of education and good emotional health tended to stay on the job. The researchers say that the current trend toward early retirement could end as more educated cohorts enter the retirement years

(Boeri & Baunach, 2002). These and other findings will help policy makers plan for an aging society.

Longitudinal studies pose practical problems. First, they take many years to complete. The researcher, the funding agency, or the public may want faster results. Second, they cost more money than cross-sectional studies. A longitudinal study requires a number of tests or surveys. Third, fewer grants exist for longitudinal studies than for cross-sectional studies.

Longitudinal studies depend on a stream of funding over many years that granting bodies and the government find hard to promise. Fourth, longitudinal studies lose members over time (through dropouts or death). This may lead to confusing findings. For example, if lower intelligence leads to shorter life, then over time, as less intelligent people die off, the average intelligence score for a group may improve. This confounds the study results. Some longitudinal studies try to overcome this problem. They bring new people into the study as people die off or drop out.

Longitudinal studies also have other drawbacks. They confound age effects (due to aging) with period effects (due to the time of testing). For example, intelligence test results reflect economic, social, and political conditions at the time of the test. A war or other stressful social event may affect results on the test. Also, people may improve their test scores with practice as they get tested many times. This reflects a change unrelated to aging.

A third method, time-lag comparison design, tries to overcome the problems raised by simple cross-sectional and simple longitudinal designs. Time-lag studies look at different groups of people of the same age at different points in time (e.g., 70 year olds in 1985, 1995, and 2005). This type of study tries to measure differences between cohorts. Like cross-sectional and longitudinal methods, the time-lag method also presents problems. It confounds cohort effects with environmental effects. If a research study finds that 70 year olds in 2005 visited doctors less often than 70 year olds did in 1985, this difference may be due to the better health of 70 year olds in 2005 (a cohort effect). Or it may be due to a change in the health care system, perhaps higher costs to users that discourage visits to doctors (an environmental effect).

Each of these designs attempts to understand the effects of aging on individuals, and each has its place in the researcher's tool kit. (See Figure 2.1.) Gerontologists must use these methods to get a clearer picture of how people change over time. Complex methods like time-lag designs help sort out the effects of age, cohort, and period. But these results still leave unanswered questions.

For example, a longitudinal design may clearly show that lung elasticity decreases with age. And it may show that this holds true for all age cohorts and at different points in time. But this study says nothing about why the lung changes. Botwinick (1984) says that after studies sort out these effects, the gerontologist's work has only begun. "Separating the confounds," Botwinick (1984, p. 400) says, "is not the end of the line, it is but the beginning." Whatever method the researcher chooses, "common sense and logic must accompany the analysis separating the confounded variables" (Botwinick, 1984, p. 403). Researchers must look closely to find the causes of the change.

Quantitative and Qualitative Methods

Paradigms are frameworks used to think about and organize an understanding of natural or social phenomena (Online, 2004). They define what questions scientists ask and how they conduct their studies. Gerontology has a long history of using a natural science paradigm. This began with studies of physiology and disease. Later, social scientists followed biomedical science in using mathematical measurement. Today, gerontologists often apply the methods of natural science—mathematical measurement, statistical methods, cause-and-effect models—to the study of aging. Philosophers refer to this type of science as **positivism**. Positivism seeks to control natural events like aging. It underlies the work in the biology and physiology of aging. Positivist science has led to many of the breakthroughs in medicine in the past century. It has also led to a more detailed understanding of the aging process.

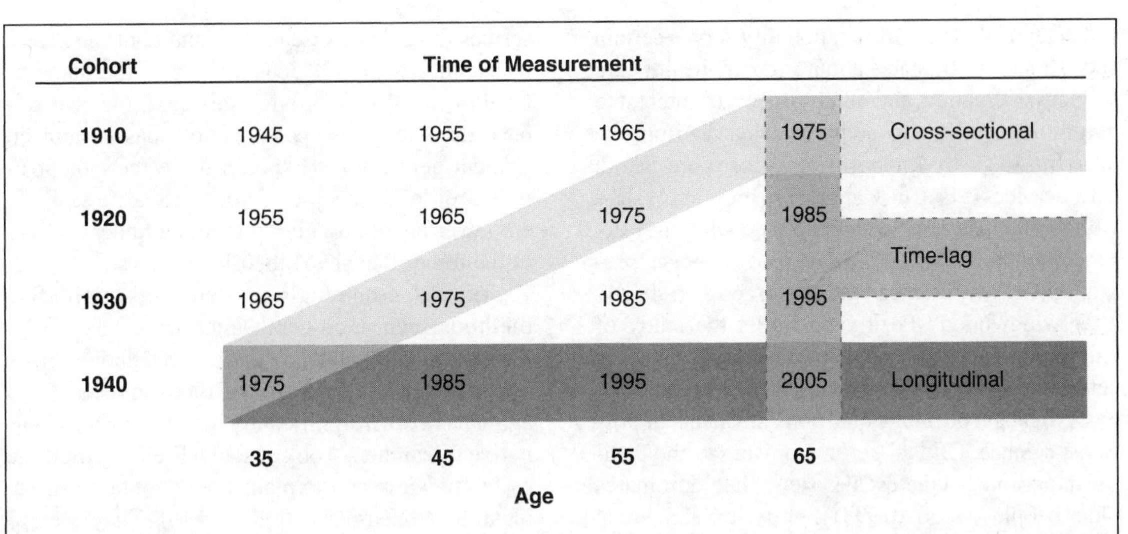

This chart shows the different approaches used in three types of study design.

The cross-sectional study took place in 1975 and studied four age groups (35, 45, 55, and 65) in that year. It compared findings across age groups. This study took a snapshot of age differences at one point in time.

The longitudinal study also began in 1975, but it went on for thirty years. It measured the 1940 cohort four times (in 1975, 1985, 1995, and 2005) at four different ages (35, 45, 55, and 65). The study would have fewer people in it at each time of measurement due to dropouts and deaths. (Some research studies of this type replace people who die or leave the study.) This study could follow age changes in the 1940 cohort.

The time-lag study measured 65 year olds at four times (1965, 1975, 1985, and 1995). This study would have different people in the sample at each time of measurement. It would show how 65 year olds differed at each time of measurement.

FIGURE 2.1

Cross-Sectional, Longitudinal, and Time-Lag Designs

Source: Adapted from *Life-span developmental psychology: Introduction to research methods,* by P. B. Baltes, H. W. Reese, & J. R. Nesselroade, 1977, Monterey, CA: Brooks/Cole.

Positivism assumes a nonreflexive object of study. Hormones, muscles, and vitamins fit this picture. The successes of positivist study in biology and physiology have led to its application to other fields—recreation, family life, and creativity. Positivism has become the main approach to *scientific* study in gerontology and other social sciences (Achenbaum, 2000a; Cole & Ray, 2000).

Positivist scientific study typically uses **quantitative methods**. Quantitative methods emphasize relationships between and among variables through numerical measurement (quantity, amount, frequency) (Neuman, 2003). "Quantitative research refers to counts and measures of things" (Berg, 1998, p. 3). Quantitative methods range from pharmaceutical research on the effects of drugs on older people to census reports on income or marital status.

Quantitative studies can take the form of attitude surveys or studies of caregiver burden. Social gerontologists most often gather data through surveys or questionnaires. Researchers then summarize responses into numerical values for statistical analysis.

This model of scientific rationality serves certain ends. It studies the facts about income, health care services, recreation, and other subjects of interest to gerontologists. It also suggests ways to improve later life (e.g., by finding a need for more health care services). But this approach may apply less well to understanding why people do what they do. For example, why do people quit exercise programs? Or, why do men tend to marry again shortly after widowhood? Positivism limits the study of aging to certain topics and approaches. It rules out certain questions and methods as unscientific.

Critical gerontology questions the ideals of positivist science. Critical gerontologists say the positivist approach creates a system that dominates older people (Moody, 1993). For example, medical science turns the older person into a patient. It prescribes drugs, plans treatment, and controls access to health services. It does all this in the name of health care. But to provide this care, medical science turns the older person into a passive object. Critical gerontology exposes the effects of positivism on older people. Critical research seeks to empower people by giving them an understanding of the forces that shape their lives.

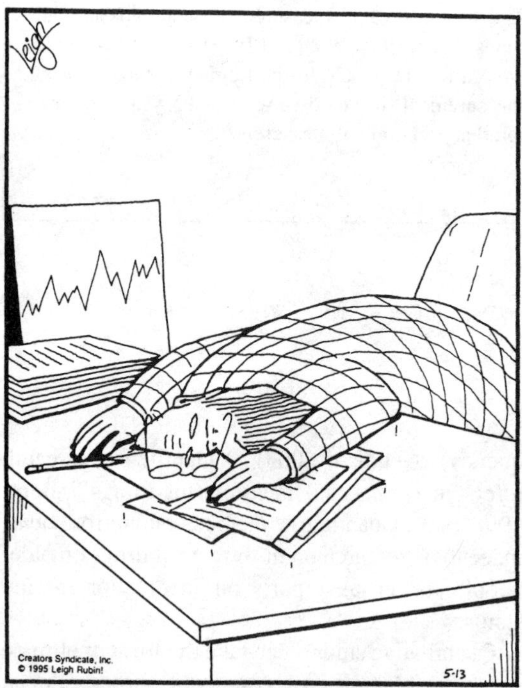

At long last, after a lifetime of research, Dr. Gruber discovered the leading cause of death among the elderly, but before he could release his findings, he died of old age.

Source: By permission of Leigh Rubin and Creators Syndicate, Inc.

Critical gerontologists often use **qualitative methods** such as in-depth interviews, analysis of the content of documents or artifacts, and observation. The use of qualitative methods in research on aging has grown significantly in recent years. Qualitative researchers "look at social life from multiple points of view and explain how people construct identities" (Neuman, 2003, p. 146). They seek to understand the social world and social experience of individuals from the subjects' own perspectives.

Qualitative research does not use statistical procedures or quantification of the data to obtain findings. Qualitative research uses many methods including interviews, life histories, field observation, case studies, and content analysis. It uses an interpretive theoretical approach to understand these data (Berg, 1998).

Qualitative methods include participant observation. Participant observers spend time with group members and observe what they do. Researchers want to learn as much as possible about social life from the participant's point of view. Participant observation studies include studies of national identity formation among minority older people (Tammeveski, 2003), studies of older people in a residential facility (Corbin, 2002), and studies of older people in assisted living facilities (Ball et al., 2004).

Beard (2004) conducted a participant observation study of people diagnosed with Alzheimer's disease. She also used in-depth interviews and focus group discussions to study the experience of memory loss. The study took place over six months. Like many researchers who use this method, Beard used unstructured interviews and accounts of the participants' experiences. She found that, in spite of memory loss, participants found ways to manage the effects of the illness and preserve their sense of self.

Diamond (1992) took a critical approach to the study of nursing assistants (sometimes called *nursing aides*) in nursing homes. At first, he thought he might interview nursing assistants and collect their stories. He envisioned talking with them on their breaks or before and after work. But then, he says, he decided on a more intense method of study—participant observation. "I decided . . . I would go inside to experience the work for myself. I became a nursing assistant" (Diamond, 1992, p. 5).

Diamond, a university professor, had to prepare to enter the field. He went to school for six months to get certified as a nurse's aide. Then he began work in nursing homes. He found that nursing assistants do most of the hands-on work. They lift, bathe, dress, and feed the patients. They get satisfaction from helping patients, but they also get low pay and sit at the bottom of the health care hierarchy. His study turned into a critical report on poor food, understaffing, and corporations that profit from caring for older people. He showed how this translates into a system that exploits low-wage workers and produces low-quality care.

Diamond presents careful descriptions of rational, bureaucratic health care practice. He also offers insight into the unmet needs of patients. Critical gerontology looks for those places and moments where alternative models of aging would improve the lives of older people. The interests of critical gerontology and positivist gerontology differ.

Positivist gerontology wants prediction and control over aging. Positivist studies produce knowledge that the state or experts in the field of aging can use to cure disease, improve housing, or develop effective fitness programs. This takes the form of control by professionals, government agencies, and policies (Moody, 1988b). Critical gerontology, on the other hand, has a different political agenda. It works to "open up possibilities of communication, mutual understanding, and coordinated social action" (Moody, 1993, p. xxiii). It aims to empower older people and enhance their freedom (Moody, 1988b).

Quantitative and qualitative methods each have their strengths and limitations. Quantitative methods, for example, allow researchers to gather a great deal of information on a wide range of issues. Moreover, they can analyze a large sample and generalize their results to a larger population. But quantitative researchers structure their research questions and give respondents limited choices. This kind of research offers little opportunity to capture the rich description of individuals' subjective experiences or perceptions of their social world (Lincoln & Guba, 2000; Neuman, 2003).

Qualitative methods allow researchers to appreciate the complexity of social interactions and behaviors. These methods study how individuals understand and give meaning to their lives. Qualitative research also has its limits. Researchers often use small sample sizes, a practice that limits generalization to a larger population. Some researchers combine both quantitative and qualitative methods in one study (Neuman, 2003).

THE HUMANITIES

The study of aging has grown to include the humanities (e.g., literature, philosophy, fine arts) as well as biomedicine and social science (Cole & Ray, 2000). Frankel says, "The humanities are that form of knowledge in which the knower is revealed . . . when we are asked to contemplate not only the proposition but the proposer, when we hear the human voice behind what is said" (cited in Moody, 1988b).

Scholars in the humanities use many methods to study aging. Vesperi (2002) shows how literary interpretation opens up new ways of thinking about aging. Yahnke (2000), for example, studied the portrayal of aging in films and videos. He looked at how these media presented the themes of intergenerational relations and regeneration in later life. He found that most films give a positive view of aging by showing satisfying relationships and fulfillment in old age.

Shenk and Schmid (2002) list the use of photo archives, self-portraits, photocollage, and photography as resources and methods for studying aging. Winkler (1992) studied pictures of aging by great artists, selecting examples from Ghirlandaio (fifteenth century) to Käthe Kollwitz (twentieth century). These pictures guide us, she says, to reflect on

BOX 2.3
THE BALTIMORE LONGITUDINAL STUDY OF AGING

Longitudinal studies take time, money, and management skill. A lack of any of these will cause a study to fizzle and die. Studies that have lasted many years stand as a tribute to the planning and dedication of their creators and current researchers.

The Baltimore Longitudinal Study of Aging (BLSA), begun in 1958, celebrated its fortieth anniversary in 1998. It is the longest-running scientific study of aging in the United States. The study aims to (1) measure biological and behavioral changes as people age; (2) relate these measures to one another; and (3) separate universal aging processes from disease and the effects of the environment. Researchers have produced over 800 articles and reports using the data from this study. These findings have shaped scientists' and practitioners' thinking about the aging process.

People in the study come to Baltimore every two years for a battery of tests and measurements. In 2004, the BLSA included 1,400 men and women (women first entered the study in 1978). People range in age from their 20s to their 90s. Many people have taken part in the study for most of their adult lives. The study has included over 2,500 people in its history, and it adds new people every year. Some people are fourth-generation BLSA volunteers.

All longitudinal studies face the problem of dropouts. How does the BLSA manage to keep so many of its volunteers in the study over so many years? The BLSA, from the start, treated the people in the study as coworkers. One volunteer said the study "made me feel not like a guinea pig, but like a human being who is part of a great scientific enterprise."

Louise Capone, a 47-year-old woman in the study, who has been tested seven times so far, says:

> This is really what keeps me coming back. . . . We get the results of our own tests, which are nice to have, but also we learn what the study is learning, overall. There is a real sense of being a partner in the study, of working with the researchers toward a goal.

Alice Brands, 83, says she and her husband "felt strongly about making a contribution" and now "look forward to seeing the staff. It's like going home."

The BLSA has produced many breakthroughs and supports for our understanding of aging. Consider the following findings:

- Differences between individuals increase with age.
- People can reduce the decline in oxygen use that comes with age, if they stay active.
- Disease-free older people at rest have cardiac output similar to that of younger people.
- Until at least age 70, problem-solving ability shows little or no decline.
- Personality remains stable through most of life. A cheerful person in youth will stay that way in old age.

These longitudinal findings present a clearer picture of the changes that come with time, and they suggest how people can improve functions that decline through neglect or misuse.

Paul Costa, a personality psychologist, says that the BLSA gives us a new view of aging. "We need not worry that we will become crotchety with age or that only firm resignation can save us from despair and fear of death. . . . We need not dread our future."

Source: From *With the Passage of Time: The Baltimore Longitudinal Study of Aging,* NIH Pub. No. 93-3685, Baltimore Longitudinal Study of Aging, 1993, Washington, DC: U.S. Department of Health and Human Services; *Baltimore Longitudinal study of aging.* Retrieved: January 4, 2005, *www.grc.nia.nih.gov/branches/blsa/blsa.htm.*

the end of life. Historians have studied population trends, church records, and diaries (Haber, 2000). These studies allow us to compare aging today with old age at other times and in other places.

Achenbaum (1993) suggests that gerontologists write autobiographies to expand their own understanding of aging. He admits that this goes against the positivist bias of gerontology research, but he says this will make researchers more aware of the human face of aging.

Aging studies in the humanities stand on the margins of gerontology today, but interest in this approach continues to grow (Achenbaum, 2000a). The GSA at its annual meetings, for example, sponsors an interest group in the humanities, and the second edition of the *Handbook of the Humanities and Aging* (Cole & Ray, 2000) appeared in 2000. Studies in the humanities reflect on the universal experience of aging. They show us the value that great writers, artists, and scholars place on old age. They expose us to new ways of thinking about aging and offer us new ways to explore our own lives.

ETHICAL ISSUES IN RESEARCH

Research studies on human subjects face ethical challenges. And studies of certain frail or vulnerable groups pose unique problems. Researchers need to consider the ethical implications of studying institutionalized older people, those living in poverty (Kayser-Jones & Koenig, 1994), the socially isolated (Russell, 1999), and people with Alzheimer's disease or other cognitive impairments (Karlawish, 2004). They also need to consider the ethics of doing undercover research where the researcher engages in participant observation.

Diamond (1992), for example, says that in some cases he carried on his nursing assistant research in secret. He says he could not have done his work without hiding his purposes from some administrators and supervisors. "I had initially hoped to disclose at every phase of the project my dual objective of working as a nursing assistant and writing about these experiences. . . . [But] it was not possible to tell everyone and proceed with the project" (Diamond, 1992, p. 8).

Diamond says he wondered about the ethics of his study and turned to his university colleagues for support. They reviewed his work and granted their approval. This, he says, gave him some reassurance as he carried on his research. Researchers routinely seek ethical approval for their research.

Most professional associations have a code of ethics for their members to follow. Universities also have ethical guidelines and standards for research. They often have a research ethics committee that reviews proposed projects. The ethics review board must approve each study, weigh the potential risks and benefits, and then give permission for research to proceed.

Universities do this for several reasons: to protect themselves from lawsuits, to ensure that subjects understand the studies they take part in, and to protect subjects from harm. My own university requires ethical review for all faculty and student projects that involve an older person. This includes class projects like interviewing an older person or observing activities at a senior center.

Researchers want to safeguard their subjects, but they also have a selfish reason for keeping high ethical standards. Unethical studies sour the public on research. A few years ago, I visited some senior centers to speak about a study I had begun. A woman raised her hand at the end of my talk.

"You're not the fellow that went around a little while ago asking people about sex, are you?" she asked.

"No, I'm not," I said.

"Well," she said, "that guy asked a lot of questions he had no business asking."

A number of other people in the audience nodded agreement. I met the same question in two or three other groups I visited. I learned that someone had done a questionnaire study on sexuality several years before. This person had not explained the study to the subjects and had left questions unanswered in their minds. I never found out who did this research, but I know that the study upset older people in the community and made it harder for me to gain their trust and support.

Researchers need to consider at least three ethical issues: (1) the need for informed consent, (2) the need to guard subjects against harm or injury, and (3) the need to protect individuals' privacy (Neuman, 2003).

Informed consent means that the researcher tells the subjects the facts about the research and gets written permission from the subjects before they take part in a study. Individuals must freely give their consent, without any coercion. They need to understand that they can decide not to answer any questions without explanation. And they need to know that they can withdraw from the study at any time. Older people who live in long-term care facil-

BOX 2.4
ETHICAL PRINCIPLES OF PSYCHOLOGISTS AND CODE OF CONDUCT

Most professional associations have a code of ethics that guides members' conduct. The American Psychological Association, for example, has an ethics code titled "Ethical Principles of Psychologists and Code of Conduct." This ethics code sets standards of practice for members and states penalties for violating the code.

Section 8, entitled "Research and Publication," discusses the need for institutional approval, informed consent from participants, and the use of deception in research.

8.01 Institutional Approval

When institutional approval is required, psychologists provide accurate information about their research proposals and obtain approval prior to conducting the research. They conduct the research in accordance with the approved research protocol.

8.02 Informed Consent to Research

(a) When obtaining informed consent as required in Standard *3.10, Informed Consent,* psychologists inform participants about (1) the purpose of the research, expected duration, and procedures; (2) their right to decline to participate and to withdraw from the research once participation has begun; (3) the foreseeable consequences of declining or withdrawing; (4) reasonably foreseeable factors that may be expected to influence their willingness to participate such as potential risks, discomfort, or adverse effects; (5) any prospective research benefits; (6) limits of confidentiality; (7) incentives for participation; and (8) whom to contact for questions about the research and research participants' rights. They provide opportunity for the prospective participants to ask questions and receive answers. (See also Standards *8.03, Informed Consent for Recording Voices and Images in Research*; *8.05, Dispensing With Informed Consent for Research*; and *8.07, Deception in Research.*)

(b) Psychologists conducting intervention research involving the use of experimental treatments clarify to participants at the outset of the research (1) the experimental nature of the treatment; (2) the services that will or will not be available to the control group(s) if appropriate; (3) the means by which assignment to treatment and control groups will be made; (4) available treatment alternatives if an individual does not wish to participate in the research or wishes to withdraw once a study has begun; and (5) compensation for or monetary costs of participating including, if appropriate, whether reimbursement from the participant or a third-party payor will be sought. (See also Standard *8.02a, Informed Consent to Research.*)

Other subsections of the ethics code include guidelines on deception in research, debriefing subjects, offering inducements to take part in studies, and maintaining confidentiality. The ethics code requires psychologists to pay special attention to the rights of their subjects. Ethical issues arise, in particular, when researchers study cognitively impaired older people. These people cannot understand the meaning of the research or their role in the studies. Researchers need to take special care to protect the rights of these participants. They need to get consent from family members, institution officials, or other responsible parties before proceeding with their research.

Source: APA Online. (2004). Ethical Principles of Psychologists and Code of Conduct Retrieved: January 6, 2005, *www.apa.org/ethics/code.html*.

ities and socially isolated people may feel some pressure to take part in a study (Kayser-Jones & Koenig, 1994; Russell, 1999).

Researchers must also guard against doing harm or injury to study participants. This includes physical harm and psychological harm. A person might feel embarrassed or upset at some questions they feel they have to answer. Researchers need to minimize risk to participants throughout the research process (Neuman, 2003).

Researchers also seek to protect participants from potential harm by keeping the participants' identity private. Researchers can do this by making sure that data analysis cannot reveal an individual's identity. The researcher should also promise to keep personal information private.

Older people with Alzheimer's disease or other types of dementia present special challenges in research. For example, they may not be able to give true voluntary informed consent (Neuman, 2003). If the mental competency of an individual is in question, the researchers must get written permission from someone who has the legal authority to make such decisions. A family member or staff member in a nursing home may have this authority. Permission from a substitute decision maker allows for research at all stages of the disease (Karlawish, 2004).

THE FUTURE OF GERONTOLOGICAL THEORY AND METHODS

What theories and methods will gerontologists use in the future? Some or all of the following trends will create new theories and methods in the years to come.

- Gerontologists will create new and more sophisticated quantitative methods. These include structural equation models, longitudinal factor analysis, and multivariate effects models. These methods will emerge as computer power increases and as gerontologists apply methods used in other social sciences. These methods will allow gerontologists to test new and more complex theories.
- Hendricks (1997; *also* Gavrilov & Gavrilova, 2001) proposes the use of recent models from natural science—chaos theory and catastrophe theory—to explain aging. These theories and models question the assumptions of linear, probabilistic analyses that gerontologists use today. Hendricks challenges gerontology "to develop mind-sets and measures that address the possibility of non-linear processes" (p. 205). This approach would include the study of unpredictable and dramatic changes in individuals' lives and in their families, work, and neighborhoods. It would also include a study of how people modify their life course through their own interpretations of their lives.
- Gerontologists would like to link the micro-levels and macro-levels of theory. The age stratification theory, the life course approach, and feminist theories comes closest to doing this now, though each has its limits. Researchers support the further development of political economy and phenomenological theories, as well as feminist theories, life course approaches, and exchange theory (Bengtson, Burgess, & Parrott, 1997). These approaches reveal hidden sides of aging. They challenge the myths of aging and explore ways to create a good old age.
- Qualitative methods will continue to play a role in gerontological research. Qualitative methods can explore the experience of aging at a time when more and more people will want to know about that experience (Gubrium & Holstein, 1997). Qualitative methods can also reveal the diversity of later life. Probably only a small number of researchers will use these methods. The positivist paradigm that dominates gerontology continues to give less value to qualitative study. This makes it riskier for researchers to build a career on qualitative work.
- Studies in the humanities will add new methods to gerontological research, such as linguistic analysis, the study of paintings and photos, and autobiographical analysis. New topics of interest in the future will lead to new approaches to the study of aging. Achenbaum (2000a) says that cross-disciplinary studies show promise. These studies blend social science with the studies of art or history.
- Technology will expand research opportunities. Connell (1998) points out that laptop computers allow researchers to enter interview data in the field. She also describes the use of video-based technology to study behavior problems in long-term care settings. Video recording technology allows researchers to observe behavior without a researcher present. This method allows researchers to gather data throughout the day, and a number of researchers can observe and analyze the same data. Researchers have used this technology to study wandering behavior and the causes of falls in nursing homes.

Researchers will use all of these approaches and more as they explore new topics in the study of aging. Chappell (1995, p. 26) says that "the research question . . . should drive our methodological approach and not vice versa." Methods (and theories) will develop as gerontologists ask new questions about aging and society.

CONCLUSION

Gerontologists use a variety of theories and methods to study aging. Theories range from micro-level studies of individuals and interaction to macro-level studies of whole societies. Researchers use interactionist, functionalist, and conflict theories. Methods range from laboratory studies in the biological sciences to surveys and observation studies in the social sciences. Researchers choose the theories and methods that best help them answer their questions.

The range of theories and methods reflects the varied interests of gerontologists. Gerontologists traditionally came from the biological and social sciences. In the past few years, scholars from the humanities have turned to the study of aging. These scholars have added the study of art, literature, and history to the tradition of gerontological research.

The increase in the older population will lead to greater interest in aging and more research in the future. Researchers will come from ever more varied disciplines. They will create new methods and develop new theories as they explore new questions in the field of aging.

SUMMARY

- Gerontology has three subfields: biomedicine, psychosocial studies, and socioeconomic-environmental studies.
- Gerontologists create theories to help explain sets of facts. They use micro-level theories to describe people and their relationships. They use macro-level theories to describe social institutions.
- The micro-level and macro-level of theory can each take an interactionist, functionalist, or conflict perspective.
- Gerontologists use a variety of research methods to study aging. These include mailed surveys, face-to-face interviews, participant observation, and studies of historical documents. The proper use of these methods ensures reliable and valid results.
- Age, period, and cohort effects influence people as they age. Researchers use a variety of methods to disentangle these effects.
- Cross-sectional, longitudinal, and time-lag designs each have strengths and weaknesses. Researchers try to use the approach that best answers their questions, given the resources they have available.
- Critical gerontology tries to understand the forces that shape peoples' lives. Researchers often use qualitative methods, such as in-depth interviews and participant observation, in their studies.
- Historians and researchers in the humanities, such as classicists and English scholars, bring new theories and methods to the study of aging. The multidisciplinary study of aging brings richness to gerontology and to our understanding of later life.

DISCUSSION QUESTIONS

1. List the three areas that make up the field of gerontology. Describe the kinds of questions each area asks and the kinds of things each area studies.
2. Explain the difference between micro-level and macro-level theories. Give examples of each. State the benefits and limits of each type of theory.
3. What are the three theoretical perspectives that gerontologists use in their studies? Explain the advantages and disadvantages of each perspective. Give at least one example of a study that uses each perspective.
4. What is the age/period/cohort problem? How can it influence research results? How do gerontologists try to overcome this problem?

5. Why do gerontologists use cross-sectional, longitudinal, and time-lag designs? Explain the advantages and disadvantages of each type of design.
6. Define the term *critical gerontology*. What methods do critical gerontologists use in their studies? Give an example of a study done using this approach.

SUGGESTED READING

Gubrium, J. F., & Holstein, J. A. (Eds.). (2000). *Aging and everyday life.* Malden, MA: Blackwell.

This book contains essays by thirty gerontologists on the subject of the aging experience. The essays span a range of topics including the cultural construction of aging, changing age consciousness as a person ages, and grief among daughters who have lost a parent. Other essays present examples of aging experiences including the management of aging among exotic dancers, life in a single room occupancy hotel, and the experience of the body through autobiography. The essays show the variety of studies that qualitative researchers have conducted.

Cole, T. R., Kastenbaum, R., & Ray, R. E., (Eds.). 2000. *Handbook of the humanities and aging* (2d ed.). New York: Springer.

This book presents studies of aging from the perspective of history, literature, philosophy, and religion. The studies show the richness that the humanities bring to the study of aging. A final essay by historian W. Andrew Achenbaum raises some disturbing questions about the future of humanistic studies in aging. In particular, Achenbaum sees a lack of young scholars in the humanities who have chosen aging as a topic for study and research.

Biggs, S., Lowenstain, A., & Hendricks, J. (Eds.). (2003). *Need for theory: Critical approaches to a social gerontology.* Amityville, NY: Baywood.

The editors have collected a series of essays on the applications of critical theory to the study of aging. Studies look at personal meaning in gerontology theory, the ways that people negotiate identity in later life, and the family in the context of modernization. A student new to the field may find these essays difficult. But they show how some gerontologists think about aging outside the positivist or functionalist perspective.

GLOSSARY OF TERMS

age cohort A group of people born at about the same time.

age effects The effect of the passage of time on the body and the self.

cohort effects Effects of the time of their birth on a person's life. People born around the same time have many of the same experiences in life.

cohort flow The movement of age cohorts one after another into societal age grades.

correlation A relationship between two things (like age and intelligence scores). It does not show that one thing causes another. For example, age only partly accounts for low intelligence scores among older people. Education differences between young and older people also influence these scores.

critical gerontology The theory attempts to expose the effects of positivism on older people. Critical researchers attempt to empower people by giving them an understanding of the forces that shape their lives.

macro-level theories Theories of large-scale social phenomena like the impact of the government or social policy on older people.

micro-level theories Studies of small-scale social phenomena like personal interactions and small groups.

paradigms Frameworks used to think about and organize an understanding of natural or social phenomena. They define what questions scientists ask and how they conduct their studies.

period effects Effects on a person in a study due to the period in which the study takes place. An economic downturn during a study of retirement, for example, will influence people's decision to retire.

positivism Employs the methods of natural science—mathematical measurement, statistical methods, cause and effect models.

qualitative methods "Look at social life from multiple points of view and explain how people construct identities" (Neuman, 2003, p. 146).

quantitative methods Relationships between and among factors (variables) are emphasized through numerical measurement (quantity, amount, frequency).

social gerontology Psychosocial, socioeconomic-environmental, and practice-related studies of aging are included. It views aging from the perspective of the individual and the social system.

Thomas theorem Sociologist W. I. Thomas said, "If people define situations as real, they are real in their consequences."

transitions Changes in social status or social roles (in particular, when those changes occur, how long they last, etc.).

trajectories Long-term patterns of stability and change.

chapter 3

AGING AT OTHER TIMES, IN OTHER PLACES

Historian David Hackett Fischer says that in a seventeenth century Massachusetts meetinghouse the elders sat in a place of honor, the first bench below the pulpit. Fischer mentions that in one meetinghouse, the three elders in that bench were aged 73, 86, and 92. Among the many ways to get a choice seat, "none was more important than age" (Fischer, 1978, p. 39).

This meetinghouse, with the elders gathered at the front in "the bench of highest dignity," fits our image of aging in the past (Fischer, 1978, p. 39). We imagine a time when older people got respect from the young and esteem from the community. Younger people sought advice from the old, and the old dispensed wisdom to the young. As people got older in this kind of society, their status increased. Today, old age seems to have declined in status. Older people get little respect. They may even serve as the butt of jokes. People deny old age and try to hide it with hair color and skin creams.

The image of old age today, as a time of decline, clashes with the idea we have of old age in the past. But how much of what we imagine about aging in the past fits the facts. Did societies in the past revere and value older people? Do older people in simpler societies today get respect and special treatment? How does the status and treatment of older people in the United States today compare with aging at other times and in other places? Historians and social scientists have tried to answer these questions. They have looked at our society and other societies in the past and present. Their answers may surprise you.

This chapter looks at (1) the influence of social institutions (e.g., the economy, the family, and technology) on the experience of aging and the treatment of older people in three types of society; (2) the issues raised by **demographic change**, **urbanization**, and **modernization**; and (3) how social institutions shape aging today in **developed nations** and **developing nations**.

FOUR TYPES OF SOCIETIES

Sociologists Gerhard and Jean Lenski (1974) described four stages of sociocultural evolution. These stages correspond to four [illegible] and gathering, horticultural [illegible] and industrial. Recently, [illegible] scribed a new sociocultural [illegible] **society**. This chapter looks at [illegible] types: hunting and gathering, [illegible] trial, and postindustrial societies.

Each type of society has a unique [illegible]ization. All these types of society exist [illegible]ay. But they also represent a historical evolution from the simplest to more complex forms of social life. A look at these societies shows the impact of social organization on the status and treatment of older people.

Hunting and Gathering

Hunting and gathering societies consist of small nomadic bands. They may have as few as twenty people, and they live as an extended family. These societies use simple technologies that include fire, small tools, and in some cases domesticated animals. These societies also have a simple division of labor. In most cases, men hunt game and women gather vegetables. The family provides education, health care, and all other social needs. These groups have no permanent settlement. They move from place to place in search of food.

Most simpler societies have undergone rapid change in the past few years. Industry has destroyed many of their habitats. Some groups find themselves confined to reservations. Other groups have adapted to new technologies and opportunities. They now work for the large companies and government projects that use their land. These contacts have led to changes in traditional nomad life. The following discussion refers to traditional hunting and gathering life as it existed in the past and in the present.

Hunting and gathering societies in the past had few older people. A normal life expectancy at birth was about eighteen years, and these societies defined a person as old at age 45 to 60 (Cowgill & Holmes, 1972). Simmons (1960, 1970) says that these societies in the past may have had as few as 3 percent age 65 and over. The terms *old* and *elderly* in this kind of society most often referred to people 50 to 60 years old.

...eneral, older people in a hunting and gather-...g society have high status if their contributions to the group outweigh their cost (Brogden, 2001). This depends in part on an older person's health and strength. It also depends on a culture's ability to provide for people as they age. Some cultures do better at this than others.

Hunting and gathering societies care for older people for many reasons, including love, tradition, and fear of parental witchcraft (Foner, 1993). At least four conditions lead to support for older people in hunting and gathering societies (Cowgill, 1972; Sokolovsky, 1990):

1. The person must play an important role in the society.
2. The person must live near and fit into the extended family.
3. The person must control some important material resource or knowledge.
4. The group must value group well-being over personal development.

Older people in few societies meet all of these conditions, so the treatment of older people varies among hunting and gathering societies. Most simpler societies have two stages of old age. In the first, older people reduce their activity. A man would hunt or fish less. He might share this work with a younger man and provide other services like net mending. A woman might take on more child care or housekeeping work and leave the heavier work to younger women. Keith (1990, p. 93) reports that, compared with men, women have fewer problems with aging. Men often work at more strenuous jobs and may have to give these up as they age. Older women can carry on many of their household and caregiving chores.

Keith says that men build up less support for their old age, but women tend to build "emotional ties that encourage care beyond the call of duty." Cool and McCabe (2002) studied gender roles and aging among the pastoral Niolo of Corsica. They found that older men lose status as their health declines. Men turn their work over to their sons and become dependent on them. But older women gain status with age. They serve as family advisors and problem solvers. Some societies value older men and women as storytellers and keepers of tribal wisdom. Service to the community helps older people maintain their status even as their strength declines.

In the second stage of old age, the person can no longer contribute to the group. Simmons (1960) refers to this stage as **overaged**. Frailty or mental decline makes the person dependent on others for food and shelter. The older person may have too little strength to follow the group. Holmberg (1969, pp. 224–225) says that among the Siriono of the Brazilian rain forest, the overaged become a burden and get treated as "excess baggage." "They eat but are unable to hunt, fish, or collect food; they sometimes hoard a young spouse, but are unable to beget children; they move at a snail's pace and hinder the mobility of the group."

Hunting and gathering societies that move from place to place may abandon or kill their older members. Watson and Maxwell (1977) report on five societies that kill their older members. In at least three of these cases, they say, this only occurs if the older person asks. The Inuit (Eskimo), for example, respect their elders for their wisdom. Collings (2000; 2001) found that successful aging among the Inuit required the ability to manage decreased health and a good attitude. Successfully aging older men and women find their own ways to adapt to decreases in their strength.

Older men start to hunt early in the spring to stockpile food for the winter. They may also strike a bargain with young hunters—for example, the older man may fix the gear while the younger man hunts. Older women sometimes adopt children. An older person gives something to the group when he or she recalls and passes on the knowledge of Inuit lore. This social role makes the old person useful to the group and improves his or her status and treatment in the community (Holmes & Holmes, 1995).

But, a time may come when the older person no longer has the health or strength to contribute to the group. When this occurs, Inuit prefer that the older person make the choice to leave the group and die. But, Holmes and Holmes (1995) say, the Inuit abandon their older people if necessary. Before this happens, the Inuit give the frail older person the worst food and little support. They speed a person's death. The overaged person leaves younger people little choice. The group must survive.

Sokolovsky (1993, p. 52) says that the Mbuti (the Pygmies of the Ituri forest) "have created a potent, positive, but *nonhierarchical image* of the aged, who as a category of person are called *mangese*—'the great ones.'" However, Turnbull (1962, pp. 35–36) says, "old and infirm people, amongst the Pygmies, are regarded . . . with apprehension." The Pygmies must move from place to place and "cripples and infirm people can be a great handicap and may even endanger the safety of the group." The Pygmies, he says, tell stories of older people who, when they cannot keep up with the group, get left behind to die. He describes an old woman, Sau, who knew the legends of abandoned older people. "She made sure everyone knew [she was healthy] by taking the most vigorous and unexpected part in any dispute" (Turnbull, 1962, p. 36).

Glascock and Feinman (1981) report ambivalence toward older people in simple societies. People often gain respect with age, and older people may have a high status. But once frailty sets in, the group withdraws its support (Brogden 2001). Glascock and Feinman studied fifty-seven simple societies and found that in 35 percent of these societies young people treated old people well. In 80 percent of these societies young people showed respect for the aged. Many of these same societies, however, abandoned and killed their elderly. Glascock and Feinman (1981) found nonsupportive treatment (abandonment or killing of older people) in some form in 84 percent of the simple societies they studied.

Keith (1990) helps to resolve these contradictory findings. She says that in simpler societies without much property, older people generally get good treatment. This changes if the group faces a squeeze on its resources. Keith says that these societies may not see killing as bad treatment. They may see it as "a regretted necessity, and often as a shift to another stage of existence in which active social participation will continue" (Keith, 1990, p. 92). Foner (1993) says that in the past the aged Yakut of Siberia asked their relatives to bury them. The group held a three-day feast, then led the older person to a grave in the woods.

These findings question the ideal of a golden age in the past when older people received only love and respect (Warren, 2002; Brogden, 2001). Simpler societies vary in their treatment of older people. Treatment of the older person often depends on how much the older person gives to or takes from the group. These findings also point to a link between a group's resources and its ability to care for infirm older members.

Agricultural Society

Agricultural societies emerged 10,000 years ago at the end of the last ice age, when humans were able to settle in one place, accumulate a surplus of food, and develop more complex societies. Early agricultural societies contained as many as several thousand people. A surplus of food led to a complex division of labor. Because farmers could support more than their own families, some people could work at crafts, business, trade, religion, and warfare. This type of society had social classes as well as complex religious, political, and economic institutions.

These societies had a greater proportion of older people than did hunting and gathering societies. Holmes and Holmes (1995) estimate that in frontier and colonial America people aged 65 and over made up about 2 percent of the population. Scott (1997), in a study of Hartford, Connecticut, and its surroundings in the late eighteenth and early nineteenth centuries, estimates 3 to 4 percent over age 60. In general, older people in agricultural societies worked as long as they could. In the case of farmers, when their strength decreased, they passed the harder work to their sons and took on less-demanding jobs. The younger family members accepted this arrangement because they expected to inherit the land when their parents died.

"Thus," Amoss and Harrell (1981, p. 10) say, "old people who control property . . . can use their rights over it to compel others to support them or provide them goods and services." The old in this kind of society keep their status by owning the land.

"Property rights," Simmons says, "have been lifesavers for the aged. . . . The person who controlled property was able to get more out of life and to get it much longer. Indeed, the importance of property for old age security can hardly be overrated" (Simmons, 1970, p. 36). A strong hand on a fat purse, he says, ensures good treatment for the older person.

Agricultural societies all over the world show this pattern. The Gwembe Tonga of Zambia today, for example, own land and livestock as a hedge against old age. A wealthy man will have many wives and children who will work for him in his old age. The Etal Islanders of Micronesia also attempt to control land, but their customs encourage them to keep only as much as they need for their well-being in old age. They give away as much as they dare and keep the rest as an inheritance for the young who help them in old age (Amoss & Harrell, 1981).

Agricultural America in the Past

The United States began as an agricultural society. Until the nineteenth century, about 90 percent of people lived and worked on farms. Older people in this society had high status. In part, this status came from a belief in the moral authority of the old. "If a man is favored with long life," Increase Mather, a leader in Puritan society, said, "it is God that has lengthened his days" (cited in Haber, 1983, p. 8). According to Benjamin Wadsworth, in *The Well-Ordered Family, or, Relative Duties* (Boston, 1712, pp. 90–102, cited in Scott & Wishy, 1982), "*Children should be very willing and ready to support and Maintain their Indigent Parents.* If our Parents are Poor, Aged, Weak, Sickly, and not able to maintain themselves; we are bound in duty and conscience to do what we can, to provide for them, nourish, support and comfort them."

Wadsworth goes on to say that children who do not care for their parents are "*not Pious,* they neglect what's *Good & acceptable to God.*" Wadsworth bases the status of older people on moral and religious principles. *An Explanation of the Ten Commandments,* published in 1794, said that "children should be ready to nourish and support their parents, if they are able, and there is occasion for it" (New Hampshire, 1794, p. 31, cited in Scott, 1997, p. 39). Care for aged parents repaid the debt that adult children owed to them. It also paved the way for the adult child's future, when they might need care from their own children.

Status also came to older people from ownership of land. Scott (1997) says that a typical farmer's life cycle included passing on his farm to his sons late in his life. But this rarely happened in cases in which land was scarce. Ruggles (2000) says that in one study of multigenerational households between 1850 and 1870, the father held the property in 80 percent of the cases. Sons often had to wait for their father's death before they would own the land and could marry. Land, Fischer (1978) says, was "an instrument of generational politics—a way of preserving both the power and the authority of the elderly. Sons were bound to their fathers by ties of economic dependency; youth was the hostage of age" (Fischer, 1978, p. 52).

Haber (1983) gives the example of Joseph Abbott, who received the family homestead after his father's death. Joseph lived as a bachelor with his parents until his father died at age 73 in 1731. Joseph became head of his own household at age 45. One year later, he married and began his own family.

In the American colonies, some older people gave their land to their children before they died. The father went into semiretirement after passing major responsibilities to his sons. But the economic ties remained. This gave rise to intergenerational tensions. A study of deeds shows that parents used legal means to ensure their good treatment in old age. Fischer (1978), for example, reports that a deed of gift from father to son often stated that the son had to provide for his parents for life. Deeds often specified exactly how many candles and how much cider a mother would receive for the rest of her life after the father's death. If the son failed to fulfill this agreement, he would have to give up the land.

The case of Nicholas Gillison shows that sometimes the law had to take up the older person's case. Gillison gave his estate to his three sons before his death, but found himself in poverty some time later.

In a plea to the county court of York, Maine, in July 1715, he wrote:

> . . . considering my infirmity and weakness in these my advanced years, that your Worships would please to cause Such Suitable maintenance out of my Said Estate from my respective Sons, both for me and my wife, as you in your prudence Shall See meet—and your petitioner Shall Ever pray act." (Court Records of York County, Maine [Portland, 1964], V, p. 167, cited in Scott & Wishy, 1982)

The court, agreeing that he had, "Through his great Imprudence & Ignorence without any manner or Reserve," left himself destitute, ordered the sons to pay for the care of their mother and father from the estate. This case and others suggest the need to shore up the bond of love with legal force.

Fischer (1978) says that older people received respect and veneration in early America, but respect often came at a price. "Running beneath the surface of respect," he says, "was an undercurrent of resentment which rose to the surface from time to time" (Fischer, 1978, pp. 223–224). The young resented their relatively powerless and subordinate position. As a result, "old people received respect without affection, honor without devotion, veneration without love" (Fischer, 1978, pp. 223–224). Over time, the position of the old grew stronger, but they were "more honored, and . . . less loved" (Fischer, 1978, p. 224).

Haber (1983) says that some older people, even those with land and money, felt useless and left out. Joseph Lathrop, in 1805, said, "Once we were men; now we feel ourselves to be but babes. . . . Once we were of some importance in society; now we are sunk into insignificance. Once our advice was sought and regarded; now we are passed by with neglect and younger men take our place" (Haber, 1983, p. 3).

Inequality in Old Age in Early American Society

Agricultural societies based status in old age on land ownership. This meant that older people with land had resources and stood a good chance of receiving respect from the young. But, what about older people without land? Fischer says that "to be old and poor and outcast in early America was certainly not to be venerated, but rather to be despised" (Fischer, 1978, p. 60). People who had retired from work, people without children, widows, and the poor all had little status (Haber, 2000). Many older poor people received awful treatment.

Fischer (1978) describes a New Jersey law of 1720 that ordered searches of ships for old people. The goal: to send them away in order to prevent an increase in the poor. Fischer describes an old man on a coastal ship, "Sick and penniless, ignored by his fellow passengers and finally picked up by the crew and put ashore on a barren and uninhabited island, where he was left to die by himself" (Fischer, 1978, p. 61). Poor old people in Boston in the early 1700s "were often escorted out of town, admonished to return to their original towns of settlement" (Haber, 2000, p. 34).

Scott (1997) reports that many veterans who applied for pensions in the early 1800s "owned nothing but the clothes on their back and perhaps some bedding." She gives some examples of how these poor older people lived:

> Sharp Camp, a seventy-five-year-old black man from Granby, could count up his property easily—he had a walking cane, a 'testament' and a hoe valued together at 96 cents. Ira Clarke, aged sixty-four, was a little better off—with a half acre of land, two small hogs, two tables, and some kitchenware he was worth about $54. . . . Men with resources as meager and dilapidated as these did not live comfortably. (Scott, 1997, pp. 124–125)

Poor older people often had little or no savings. And their families offered little support. In some cases, family members added to their elders' poverty. Children often had less than their parents and depended on the older person for support. Poor health or mental problems could drive a person to peddling, begging, or public charity. If a person "withdrew from labor," Haber (2000, p. 31) writes, "they had to rely upon their own savings, the contributions of their children, or the town's benevolence."

A Boston census of 1743 found that most older widows lived in poverty. Widows often could not inherit property. The land went to their sons or other male relatives. The widow's well-being depended on the treatment she received from others. Smith (1995) found a similar pattern in rural New Hampshire in 1790. Widows without families and resources had no status and no protection in society. Society often placed them in asylums along with "infants, maimed, and lunaticks" (Haber, 1983, p. 25). Fischer (1978, p. 61) says that "if the aged poor were only a small minority, their misery was great."

Haber (1983, p. 5) says that, "clearly, there was never a golden age of senescence in which the old were treated with veneration. For many individuals, even in colonial America, gray hair and wrinkles seemed reason for contempt instead of honor; their age alone was not deemed worthy of respect."

Early American society shows an ambivalence toward older people and old age. Historians have begun to look closely at colonial and postcolonial America. They have found general trends—such as the use of land as a way to maintain status—but they have also found great diversity in status and treatment based on race, gender, and social class.

Modern Industrial Society

Human beings lived in either hunting and gathering or agricultural societies until the mideighteenth century. Three interrelated changes shook the basis of agricultural society at that time: (1) **industrialization**, (2) **urbanization**, and (3) the **demographic transition**.

These changes took place first in Europe and then, in the midnineteenth century, the United States. They still affect American society today. They began at various times in various places. Sometimes an economic change, a demographic change, or a change in values had more influence than other changes. Historians argue about the timing of these changes and where they took place first (Achenbaum & Stearns, 1978; Fisher, 1978; Haber, 1983). But taken together, these three changes transformed European and North American society and created a new age for older people.

Industrialization

Ruggles (2000) says that the United States remained rural and preindustrial from the first arrival of Europeans to possibly as late as 1850. On and near the American frontier (e.g., Texas) farming as a way of life continued up to the twentieth century (Gutmann, 1995). Most older men continued their work into later life. Older women, the never married, or widowed, might work as housekeepers or take in boarders. People worked and saved for their later years and relied on family and friends for support. Older people played an active part in agriculture, politics, and the professions in the early nineteenth century.

Achenbaum and Stearns (1978) say that the Civil War in the early 1860s led to a turning point in the status of older people. He finds that in general before 1860, American society held older people in high esteem. The public considered older people useful and valued their wisdom, experience, and expertise. Before 1830, Achenbaum and Stearns (1978) say, Americans chose "Uncle Sam," an old man with white hair and a beard, as one of their favorite symbols.

A number of historians (Haber, 2000; Haber & Gratton, 1992) disagree with this neat division. They say that this image of respect for older people before 1860 and decline afterward ignores the varied experiences of older people. Still, historians generally agree that by the end of the 1800s, Americans held a less positive view of old age than at the start.

By the end of the nineteenth century, for example, older people had lost many of the social roles they held in the past. For one thing, rapid social change led to a decline in the value of older people's experience. "Gray hair," one writer in 1913 says, "has come to be recognized as an unforgivable witness of industrial imbecility" (cited in Achenbaum & Stearns, 1978). Also, older people often held jobs in marginal fields (Gratton & Haber, 1993). For example, 60 percent of older men in 1890 worked in farming, fishing, and mining. A relatively small proportion of older men worked in manufacturing and mechanical jobs (Haber, 1983). The rise of industry made older peoples' expertise less relevant.

Doctors, planners, and welfare experts began to define older people as weak and incompetent. Their "conception of old age uniformly emphasized its infirmities and limits" (Haber, 1983, p. 4). These and other experts began to define old age as a social problem.

Urbanization

The United States became more urban as it industrialized. Achenbaum (1983) says that the U.S. population grew twelvefold from 1800 to 1890. Cities grew eighty-sevenfold in this same time. From 1920 on, more than one-half the population lived in urban centers (with 2,500 people or more). Mass markets and the mass media shaped peoples' tastes and preferences.

The rise of industry, factories, and wage labor changed social life and aging in the nineteenth century. Factories pulled young people off the land to the cities. This changed the social relations between the generations and led to new intergenerational conflicts. Young people no longer had to wait to inherit the farm in order to enter adulthood. Factory jobs provided independence from a father's decision to give over the land. This meant that parents could no longer control the young through the promise of the family's land. Older people lost the source of their power and veneration (Ruggles, 2000).

Also, people in cities chose to have fewer children than rural people. This meant that people now lived long enough to see their youngest children grow up and marry. By 1910 nearly one in four women experienced the empty nest (Haber, 1983). Older people, with no children to care for, began to seem unnecessary. They also lost the benefit of an income from the adult child who lived at home (Gratton & Haber, 1993). This threw many older families into poverty. More than three-quarters of workers in an 1879 survey said they did not expect to have enough to exist in old age (Haber, 1983).

Older immigrants in cities lived in some of the worst poverty. The wealth of older immigrants in Milwaukee in the nineteenth century, for example, dropped sharply in old age (Haber, 1983). Reform agencies in the cities in the late 1800s often excluded older people from their client list because they thought physical decline put older people beyond reform. This attitude, Haber (1983) says, mirrors the views of colonial Americans who rejected the poor in their day. But now all older people fell into the category of the *overaged.*

These changes took place over time, and not all older people felt their impact. Historians have yet to fully describe the effects of social class, gender, race, and geographical region on the experience of aging. Work by Gratton and Haber (1993; *also* Haber, 2000) shows that the well-being of older people in early industrial society differed by social class. For example, the lives of many working class older people improved with industrialization. They often lived in extended families and pooled their income with their working children. These households had more money for luxuries than did families with younger household heads.

The Age Barrier

(The American Labor Legislation Review, 19 December, 1929)

At the same time, a poor underclass existed among older people. The poorest fifth of American society, for example, had little or no income (Gratton & Haber, 1993; Scott 1997). Single women and widows, immigrants, and African Americans often suffered from extreme poverty. Also, future ideas and concepts about old age—a belief in physical decline, mandatory retirement, and the need for formal social support—took root in this early industrial era.

The Demographic Transition

The demographic transition describes a pattern of population change that took place in western nations over the past 250 years. The developing nations will probably go through this transition, and some of these nations have already started the process. Figure 3.1 shows the population trends over time that create the transition. Myers (1990) divides the process into four stages.

Stage I: The 1600s to Early 1700s. The demographic transition in the United States led to a larger number and proportion of older people than in the past. The data that exist on the United States in the seventeenth and eighteenth centuries show that it was a young country at that time, with between 1.5 percent and 2.2 percent of the population age 65 and over before the first census in 1790. On average, a man or woman could expect to live 50 years. Fischer (1978) reports a **median age** (half the population is over and half under the median age) for various regions in the early and mideighteenth century of between 15.6 and 17.6 years. He says that median age stayed roughly stable from 1625 to 1810.

High **fertility** and high **mortality** kept the United States a young society. Early American families, Fischer (1978, p. 28) says, "produced great swarms of children." At the same time, life expectancy at birth was only 38 in Massachusetts, the colony with the highest life expectancy. It was only 25 in Chesapeake (Fischer, 1978). Many children died in childhood, but even people who lived to age 20 had only about a 40 percent chance of survival to age 60.

The first census in 1790 reported about 50,000 older people, who made up about 2 percent of the population. More than one-half the population was under the age of 16. Achenbaum (1983, p. 13) calls the United States a new nation and "a young republic."

Stage II: The mid-1700s to 1820. In the late 1700s, death rates began to fall and life expectancy began to rise. Better public health, diet, and a decrease in the virulence of disease led to decreases in infant and childhood mortality. Fischer (1978) says that more than one-third of people born in America in 1830 lived to age 60 (compared with as low as 12 percent in the late 1700s). The middle-aged population also survived longer. In 1840 almost 40 percent of white men survived from age 20 to age 70.

Stage III: 1820 to 1960. In the early 1800s, the birth rate began to drop. (This occurred at the start of the 1800s for native-born white women. It occurred later and at different rates for immigrant and minority women.) The average number of children in a marriage dropped from 7.04 in 1800 to 3.56 in 1900. The declining birth rate shaped population aging in the United States for the next 150 years. This coincided with a decline in farming and an increase in industrial work. Women had begun to work in clerical and domestic jobs, which further influenced the decrease in birth rates.

In the 1820 census, the median age of the population increased for the first time in more than 150 years (Fischer, 1978). Fischer reports that median age for the total population rose steadily from 16.7 years in 1820 to 25.3 years in 1920. This increase occurred less steadily and more slowly for the nonwhite population. For nonwhites, the median age rose from 17.2 years in 1820 to 22.4 years in 1920. By the 1920s every group in American society began to have fewer children, and all children could expect to live longer than their parents (Achenbaum, 1983). Fischer (1978) says that the fall in the birth rate in the early part of this century accounts for about 80 percent of population aging at that time.

Stage IV: 1960 to the Present. The United States has a much larger population today than it did at stage I of this process. The United States has a much lower birth rate and a lower death rate than at any time in the past. It also has an older population that

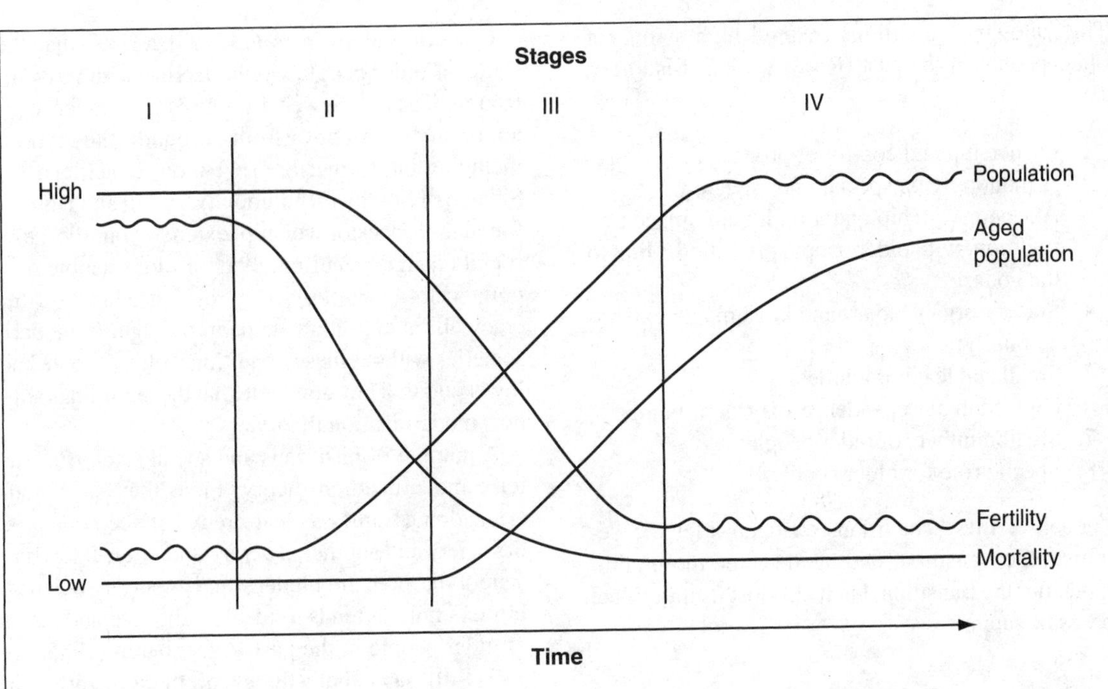

FIGURE 3.1
Stages of the Demographic Transition

Source: Reprinted from "Demography of Aging" by G. C. Myers, in R. H. Binstock & L. K. George, Eds., *Handbook of Aging and the Social Sciences,* 3d ed. (p. 25). Copyright (1990), with permission from Elsevier.

is larger than ever before. In 2000 the U.S. median age was 35.3 years (U.S. Census Bureau, 2000a; 2000b). The population will continue to age as the Baby Boom cohorts move through the life cycle. The first Baby Boom cohorts will reach old age in the early decades of this century, and barring any rapid change in the birth or death rates, the United States will have one of the older populations in the world.

Societies that have gone through the demographic transition—from high to low birth and death rates—face new issues related to a large older population. For one thing, the demographic transition leads to a new perspective on the life cycle. Nearly all children can now expect to live to old age. Most middle-aged people can expect to live a decade or more in retirement, and many older people will live to late old age. A larger population than ever before will live more than 100 years.

The three trends mentioned previously—industrialization, urbanization, and the demographic transition—undermined the status of older people.

The following conditions ensured high status for older people in the past (Rosow, 1965; Eisdorfer, 1981):

1. Ownership and control of property;
2. A monopoly on special knowledge;
3. Ancestor worship and a high value placed on tradition, with older people providing a link to the gods;
4. Society organized around kinship and extended family;
5. Small stable communities;
6. High mutual dependence of group members;
7. Small numbers of older people;
8. Special role for older people.

Each of these conditions changed after the demographic transition. Old age became more common after the transition, but it also lost its traditional bases of support.

Modernization Theory

Modernization theory describes the transformation from preindustrial to industrial society. Simmons (1970), in *The Role of the Aged in Primitive Societies,* first reported a link between the older person's status and technology in a society. He found that the more advanced the technology, the lower the older person's status. Cowgill and Holmes (1972) took this a step further. They said that technology made up only one part of the change from premodern to modern society. Cowgill (1974, p. 127) said that modernization includes the transformation from:

1. A rural to an urban style of life;
2. The use of animals for power to the use of machines;
3. Limited technology to high technology and science;
4. General institutions to specific institutions;
5. General roles to segmented roles;
6. A traditional outlook to a more cosmopolitan outlook;
7. An emphasis on social stability to an emphasis on change.

Cowgill and Holmes (1972) theorized that the status of older people would decline with modernization. They reviewed findings on fourteen contemporary societies from around the world, including the former Soviet Union, Israel, and the Sidamo of Southwest Ethiopia. Cowgill and Holmes found that ancestor worship, extended families, low social change, small numbers of older people, importance of the group, stable residence, and low literacy all favored high status in old age. In modern societies without these conditions, older people had lower status. They conclude that these findings support modernization theory.

A number of historians and social scientists criticize modernization theory. First, they say, modernization assumes a clear break between one type of society and another, a *before* and *after.* It tends to stereotype both premodern and modern societies. For example, it tends to idealize the role and status of older people in the past. Achenbaum (1985, pp. 139–140) says that studies of modernization in western societies show "the persistence from earlier times of favorable, disparaging, conflicting, ambiguous, and ambivalent attitudes toward the aged." He says that this wide range of views has changed little over time.

Second, it remains uncertain whether every nation must follow the western path of modernization. Will societies like Iran, China, or Japan develop in the same way as the West? Will economic change in these countries lead to lower status for older people? The belief systems and values in these countries differ from those in the West. These countries and other nonwestern countries will adapt to individual and population in their own ways.

Third, Achenbaum (1983) reminds us that discontinuities and contradictions exist within a historical period. Today, for example, we believe in individual initiative, but we recognize the need to provide people with health care and other social supports. Also, different racial, ethnic, economic, and regional groups within society will feel different effects of social change. This was as true in the past as it is today.

Fourth, modernization theory overlooks the diversity among premodern and modern societies.

BOX 3.1
OVER THE HILL TO THE POOR HOUSE

The poorhouse has stood as a symbol of humiliation and degradation for centuries. The poorest and most hopeless people lived in the poorhouse, those without family or the means to support themselves. By the midnineteenth century, experts on welfare believed that alms or help to the poor made people lazy. The government turned to poorhouses as a way to look after the most needy and punish immigrants, the poor, and the helpless at the same time. This in theory would discourage people from asking for help.

The number of older people in poorhouses increased as the number of older people in society increased (though the proportion of older people in poorhouses stayed at around 2 percent from 1880 to 1920). In Charleston, South Carolina, for example, old people made up most of the poorhouse inmates. In San Francisco, the average age of people in the poorhouse rose from 37 years in 1870 to 59 years in 1894. In 1903, New York's charity board renamed its public almshouse the Home for the Aged and Infirm.

The nineteenth-century poorhouse stands as a powerful symbol of aging in America's past. It stands at the junction point between agricultural America and the rise of industry. For many of the reformers of the day, it showed the sad state of the older person in the new industrial society.

The following song expresses the fear, shame, and disgrace linked to the poorhouse in the past. The existence of this song suggests that Americans in the past feared mistreatment in old age.

Over the Hill to the Poor House

What no! it can't be that they've driven
Their father, so helpless and old,
Oh, God, may their crime be forgiven,
To perish out here in the cold.
Oh, Heav'ns, I am sadden'd and weary,
See the tears how they course down my cheeks!
Oh, this world it is lonely and dreary,
And my heart for relief vainly seeks.
Ah me! on that old doorstep yonder,
I've sat with my babes on my knee,
No father was happier or fonder,
Than I of my little ones three.
The boys, both so rosy and chubby,
And Lilly with prattle so sweet!

This sheet music cover for "Over the Hill to the Poor House" is from the collection of Elias S. Cohen.

Oh, God knows how their father has loved them,
But they've driven him out in the street.
REFRAIN
For I'm old and I'm helpless and feeble,
The days of my youth have gone by,
Then over the hill to the poor house,
I wander alone there to die.

The sheet music cover for "Over the Hill to the Poor House" is from the collection of gerontologist Elias S. Cohen, who collected sheet music on aging themes. His collection reflects popular concerns about aging in the last hundred years or so. Popular music often dealt with themes like the loss of beauty, love, and the fear of growing old.

Sources: " 'And the Fear of the Poorhouse': Perceptions of Old Age Impoverishment in Early Twentieth-Century America," by C. Haber, 1993, *Generations,* Spring/Summer, pp. 46–50. "Over the Hill to the Poor House," music by David Braham, lyrics by George L. Catlin, 1874, cited in *America's Families: A Documentary History* (p. 282), by D. M. Scott and B. Wishy, Eds., 1982, New York: Harper & Row. Sheet music cover, cover photo of *The Gerontologist, 30*(3), 1990.

It also overlooks variations in the treatment and status of older people by social class, gender, and minority group. Cherry and Magnuson-Martinson (1981) say, for example, that developing nations differ in their political economy. This influences the status and treatment of older people.

Cherry and Magnuson-Martinson (1981) studied the status of older people in modern China. They did find that the status of older people had declined. But they did not find a link between this decline and industrialization, urbanization, education, and other signs of modernization. Instead, their research traced a decline in status to government economic and social policies. The Chinese government outlawed land ownership and the practice of arranging marriages—two sources of status for older people.

These changes took place rapidly and influenced older women more than older men. The researchers say that modernization theory needs to take into account social policies that shape age-group relations. Societies can alter the status of older people directly through political action. Modernization theory proposes that change has a general effect on all older people. But government policies, like those in China, can affect specific groups, like men and women, differently.

Some research suggests a middle ground between the promodernization and antimodernization camps. Haber (2000) reports that some conditions improved while others declined with modernization. Cohn (1982) found that status drops at the start of modernization but improves over time. Maddox (1988, p. 3) says that the modern welfare state has "tended to treat older adults rather generously." Better pensions, continuing education, and better health care have led to higher status for older people.

Postindustrial Society: The United States Today

Postindustrial society refers to societies like those of western Europe, Canada, Japan, and the United States today. These societies have relatively few people who work in manufacturing and food production. Instead, most people work in the service sector. This includes nurses, teachers, and investment counselors. These people sell their technical expertise. People in a postindustrial society generally have a high standard of living. These societies have high social mobility, a concern for equality and individual rights, and long life expectancies.

Older people in postindustrial societies benefit from a number of social conditions. For example, a high standard of living means more social and economic support for older people. Many retirees today receive good pensions, and the poverty rate for older people has declined in recent years.

Older people can find new roles for themselves in this kind of society. The complex economy in a country like the United States allows people to find second careers or to work as volunteers in the service sector. The commitment to equality and minority rights supports older peoples' claim to fair treatment in the workplace. The varied lifestyles and the commitment to self-fulfillment in these societies have allowed older people to discover new roles for themselves. Many older people discover new purpose and meaning in retirement.

As a group, older people live materially better lives today than at any time in U.S. history. Private and public pensions, health care, and social service programs have all improved the quality of life in old age. Schulz (2001, pp. 1–2) says that the following "major breakthroughs" have taken place in programs to help older people:

1. An almost 300 percent increase in Social Security benefits from 1950 to 2000;
2. The development of Medicare and Medicaid benefits;
3. The development of a national Supplementary Security Income program;
4. The indexation to inflation of supports like Social Security and the Food Stamp program.

These programs and others, like senior centers, home nursing care, and assisted living apartments, give older people more freedom and choice.

Some writers say that postindustrial society will make age irrelevant in the future as a source of status (Neugarten, 1980). Society will judge people by what they can do, rather than by their age. Eisdorfer (1981, p. xxi) says that: "The challenge to longevity [today] should be to maximize a person's potential for contributing to himself and to society throughout life."

THE CHALLENGE OF POPULATION AGING

The world grows older every day. In 2000 the world had 418 million people aged 65 years and over. The U.N. projects that by 2050 this figure will more than triple and the world will have almost one and a half billion people aged 65 and over (United Nations, 2002a; 2002b). In 2050 the population of older persons will be larger than the population of children (0–14 years) for the first time in human history.

But population aging will affect different societies in different ways. For example, some countries have relatively high proportions of older people in their populations. In the developed nations of the West, like France, Sweden, and the United States, the proportion of older people in their populations

BOX 3.2

THE COAST SALISH PEOPLE

A Challenge to Modernization Theory

Modernization theory describes a single path from premodern to modern society. It also describes a single outcome for older people: a drop in status. The Coast Salish people of the Pacific coast of North America show an alternative to modernization theory. They show how people can respond to events and shape their future.

Miller (1999) researched the role of older women, grandmothers, in Coast Salish tribes in the 1980s and 1990s. He found that some grandmothers did lose status as they aged. Tribal custom speaks of respect for elders. But elders who did not control resources or who did not make a contribution to the group lost status.

But Miller also found that some grandmothers gained status with age. These women play an important role in tribal culture. Their status comes, in part, from recent changes in tribal life. And their status questions the universality of modernization theory.

Miller calls these women "political grandmothers." They hold office and play a role in the political life of the community. They also preserve traditional practices and the right to tribal membership. This gives them control of fishing rights (the key to material well-being in the tribe). All of these roles give these grandmothers power and prestige in their community.

Also, young people show a new interest in Indian identity and tribal culture. This has led to higher status for certain elders. Miller says that grandmothers "who have ritual knowledge and control (i.e., knowledge of Indian names, shamanistic abilities, or influence over the process of initiation into dancing societies) are in demand and are valued in their communities" (1999, pp. 106–107).

Political grandmothers who hold office link their political role to traditional roles held by women in Coast Salish society. They emphasize their work as teachers and mentors of children and grandchildren in the tribe. These grandmothers also speak out in public. They remind tribal members of their genealogy, traditional values, and cultural practices. These women remain active in public life until late old age. The tribe admires them for the care they gave their families, for providing income to the family, and for their knowledge of tribal customs (Miller, 1999).

Amoss (1981) says that respect for Coast Salish tradition translates into respect for older people. "Every public occasion where the elders appear . . . is punctuated by speeches that reiterate the necessity of respecting them and heeding their advice." The Coast Salish elders have managed to regain status in their changed society. "Far from being the helpless victims of change," Amoss writes, ". . . given the right conditions, elders can not only profit from it, but may even become active agents of change themselves."

Sources: Amoss, P. T. (1981). "Coast Salish elders." In P. T. Amoss and S. Harrell (Eds.), *Other ways of growing old: Anthropological perspectives* (pp. 227–247), Stanford, CA: Stanford University Press; and Miller, B. G. (1999). Discontinuities in the statuses of Puget Sound grandmothers. In M. M. Schweitzer (Ed.), *American Indian grandmothers: Traditions and transitions* (pp. 103–124). Albuquerque: University of New Mexico Press.

BOX 3.3
STATUS OF THE ELDERLY IN SOCIETY

Type of Society	*Proportion of Elderly*	*Source of Status*	*Status of Elderly*
Hunting and gathering	Low 2%	Strength, wisdom, contribution to group	High if healthy, low if "overaged"
Agricultural	Low 4–6%	Tradition, own land	High if landowner, low if no property
Industrial	High 7–12%	Job, income, economic status	Low at start of industrial period, better today
Postindustrial	Highest 12–25%	Job, income, economic status	Moderate if good health and income; could increase in future for young–old group

This chart compares the status of the elderly in four different types of society. Can you describe the life of an older person in each type of society? Can you link the points listed here to the different experiences older people have in each of these societies? For example, how does a high proportion of older people in society affect an older person's experience of aging?

has increased gradually over many decades. And their populations will get older in the future. Some developed countries, like Japan, had relatively young populations until recently. They will see rapid population aging in the years ahead. (See Figures 3.2 and 3.3 on pages 69 and 70, respectively.)

The developing nations (of Africa, Asia, and South America) already have large numbers of older people. In 2000, for example, the majority of the world's older persons (54 percent) lived in Asia (Kinsella & Velkoff, 2001). These countries also have large numbers of young people (due to high birth rates). For this reason, compared with the developed nations, they will have lower proportions of older people in their populations. Still, the large numbers of older people will put new demands on these societies. Developed and developing countries will face unique challenges as their populations age. Each country will make unique responses to population aging. (See Table 3.1.)

THE DEVELOPED NATIONS

The United Nations (2002a) reports that the developed nations of the world will all experience increases in their proportions of older people. The U.N. projects that these countries on average will have more than one-quarter of their populations aged 65 and over by 2025. And they will have one-third of their populations over age 60 in that year. Population aging will extend a trend that, for some of these countries, began in the nineteenth century. Increased population aging will create challenges for the developed nations. For example, all of these countries will face the issue of rising health care and pension costs. These societies may need to shift funds from other types of programs to serve older people. Or they may develop new programs that better fit an older population.

THE DEVELOPING NATIONS

The less-developed nations make up three-quarters of the world's population, and most of them have young populations. In some cases they have as few as 2 percent of their populations aged 65 and over. These countries will age in the years ahead, although they will still have relatively small proportions of older people. African nations will average only a little over 4 percent aged 65 and over in the

BOX 3.4
JAPAN: A CASE STUDY OF POPULATION AGING IN A DEVELOPED NATION

Japan had a population of 84 million people in 1950. By 2000, the population had increased to 127 million (United Nations, 2002b). Over these same fifty years the population aged 65 and over increased more than five times. The Japanese today have one of the longest average life expectancies in the world. According to the United Nations (2002b), at birth a Japanese female can expect to live 85 years, a Japanese male, 77.8 years.

In the year 2000, Japan had 17.2 percent of its population aged 65 and over. But a decrease in fertility and lower death rates will lead to rapid population aging in the future. Projections to the year 2050 show that in that year Japan will have 36.4 percent of its population aged 65 and over (United Nations, 2002b). Myers (1990, p. 26) calls this "a spectacular growth" in the proportion of older people.

The Japanese call this *koreika,* societal aging. A 1995 survey conducted by the Ministry of Health and Welfare in Japan (National Institute, 2004) found that 57.3 percent of the respondents considered population aging "a trouble" or "a serious trouble." And 68 percent of the respondents said that Japan should increase its birth rate to slow population aging. Knight and Traphagan (2003, p.13) say people in rural communities use low birth rates and population aging to explain all kinds of problems. They use this "depopulation consciousness" to explain poor treatment of older people, problems at work, and the inability to find a bride.

Japan has a history of providing social security and health care to its older people. The government has provided a national pension plan and a universal health insurance program since the 1960s. A report by the National Institute of Population and Social Security Research (2002 to 2003) says that these two programs "have become the two main pillars of Japanese social security system." Populations aging will strain the capacity of these systems in the years ahead. This will create new challenges in Japan and will demand new responses from individuals and the government.

Japan faces challenges similar to those of other developed nations. These challenges include higher costs for pensions, more chronic disease, and the need to rethink health care services for an older population. Japan differs from other developed nations in the speed of its transition to an aging society. In only twenty-six years (1970 to 1996) the Japanese older population grew from 7 to 14 percent of the population. By contrast, some European societies took as long as 115 years to see this kind of change (Kinsella & Velkoff, 2001). Japan will have to make changes quickly to meet the needs of its aging population.

year 2025. The developing nations overall will average only about 8 percent in that year (United Nations, 2002a). High birth rates will keep the *proportion* of older people relatively low in these countries, but these nations will see explosive growth in the *number* of older people.

"By the year 2025," Myers (1990, p. 27) says, "over two-thirds of the world's older population will be found in the developing countries." Asia will gain over a quarter of a billion older people. China alone will have 194 million people aged 65 and over by 2025. (By comparison, the entire U.S. population will be about 346 million people in that year [United Nations, 2002b]). High fertility in the past and greater survival of older people in the present will produce this explosive growth.

Developing nations face unique challenges due to population aging. Older people in Africa, for example, often face hardships because urban life, wage labor, and national political movements have lowered their status. Cattell (1994), in a study of older people in Kenya, says that "delocalization," the shift of power outside the community and family, has occurred. This leads to loose family bonds and loss of authority for older people. A study of groups near Lake Victoria found that, in the past, grandmothers played a vital role in raising granddaughters. Today, granddaughters spend most of their day at school, and some live away during the school term. School teachers and more worldly ideas now replace grandmothers and their teachings (Cattell, 1994).

BOX 3.5

CHINA: A CASE STUDY OF POPULATION AGING IN A DEVELOPING NATION

China began its one-child-per-family policy in 1979. This policy aimed to decrease population growth. The government has relaxed the policy somewhat in recent years. But due to this policy, China will age sooner and more quickly than other developing nations.

China had a total population of 1.3 billion people in 2000. Demographers expect the population to grow to almost 1.5 billion people by 2050. Over these same thirty years the population aged 65 will grow from 88 million in 2000 to 341 million in 2050 (United Nations, 2002b).

Between the year 2000 and 2030 the older population will increase by 170 percent (compared with a 102 percent increase for the United States). China's older population will grow from 7 percent of the population (a *young* society) in 2000 to 14 percent of the population (a *mature* society) between 2000 and 2007. The median age in China will grow from 30 to 41 between 2000 and 2003. Researchers trace this rapid increase in population aging to a decrease in China's fertility rate. The one-child policy begun in 1979 accounts for much of this decline in fertility. Due to this fertility decline (a rate of 1.8 in 2000) China will age sooner and more rapidly than other developing nations (Kinsella & Velkoff, 2001). Zhang (2001, p. 12) says that "China has a population that is aging . . . so fast that it has outpaced industrialization and modernization."

China today has the largest population of older people in the world. It also has the largest share of the world's oldest old (aged 80+). These figures raise questions about China's ability to respond to its rapidly aging population. For example, the elderly support ratio (the number of people aged 65 and over per 100 people aged 20 to 64 years old) between 2000 and 2030 will double from twelve to twenty-six. And its parent support ratio (the number of people aged 80 and over per 100 people aged 50 to 64) during those same years will more than quadruple from three to fourteen. For women this ratio will grow nearly six times from five to twenty-eight. These crude figures suggest that Chinese society and its members will need to provide more support for its older population in the years ahead. Most of these older people (about 76 percent of all older Chinese) live in rural areas.

Rural older people depend almost entirely on family support. This provides a support system for older people throughout most of their later years. But illness and frailty can place a burden on family caregivers. This leads to stress and sometimes to family breakdown. Also, younger people often move away from their families. And more older people than ever before live on their own, especially in cities. The Chinese Association of Senior Citizens reports that more than 25 percent of older people in China live alone or with only their spouse (Zhang, 2001). These people face poverty, and they may lack a family support network.

Chinese tradition puts the responsibility for care on the family. But in urban centers, this can also lead to burden and burnout. A study in Beijing found that 50 percent of families report financial, emotional, or other hardship in caring for their older relatives. This pressure will grow in the future as small young families care for four to eight older relatives.

China, like other developing nations, will find it hard to meet the needs of its growing older population. The high cost of building and running long-term care institutions will limit their growth. Also, older people in China prefer to stay at home and get support from their families. China has begun to develop home care options that fit its culture and that meet the needs of its aging population.

The increased number and proportion of older people in China and their need for support will lead to social change. Kinsella and Velkoff (2001, p. 79) say that in the near future China "may anticipate a social and economic fabric radically different from that of today."

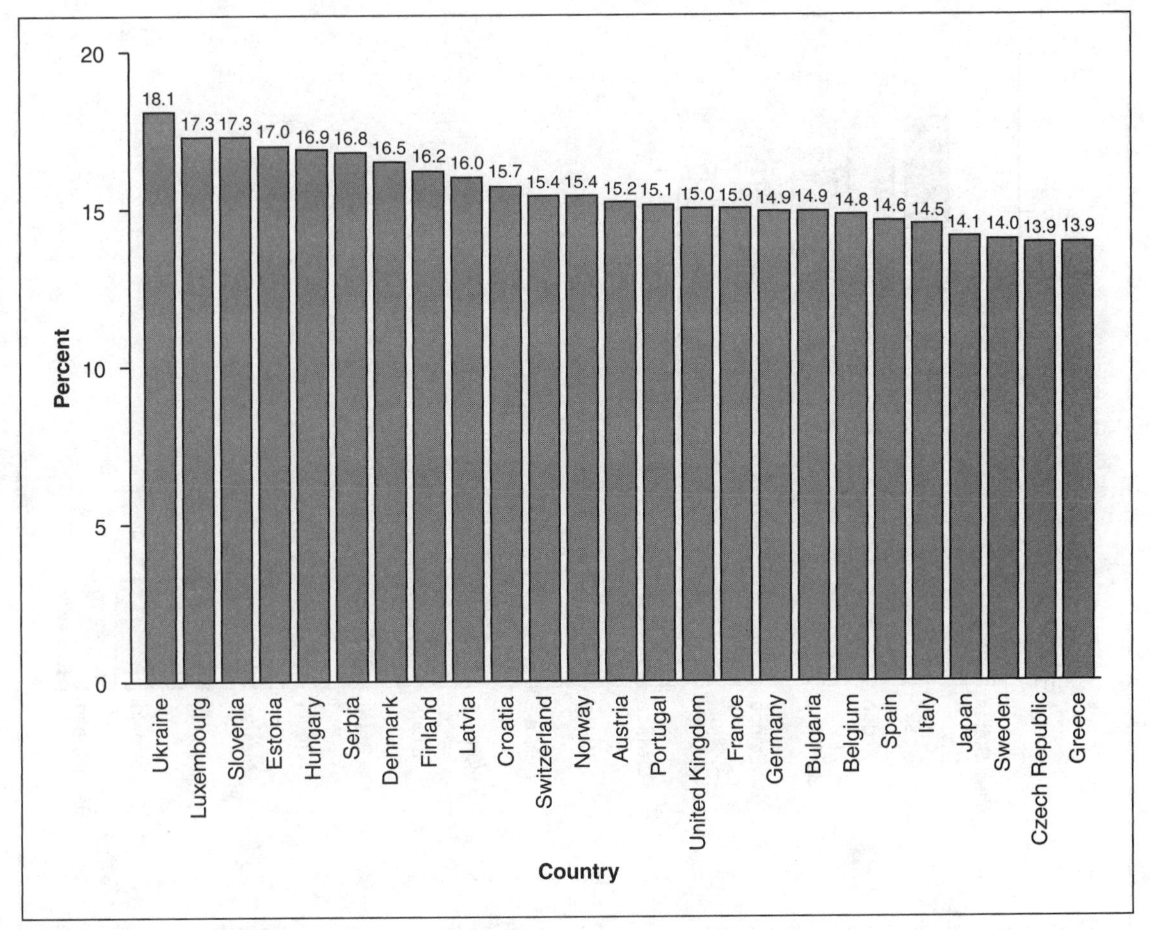

FIGURE 3.2

Elder Populations in Selected Countries, Aged 65 and Over

Source: Kinsella, K., & V. A. Velkoff. (2001). U.S. Census Bureau, Series P95/01-1, *An Aging World: 2001,* U.S. Government Printing Office, Washington, DC. Figure 2-3. Retrieved: January 26, 2005, *www.census.gov/prod/2001pubs/p95-01-1.pdf.*

Older people in African countries often lack basic services. A study of South Africa found that only 47 percent of urban black older people and 15 percent of rural black older people had access to conveniences like running water, sanitation, and electricity. A study of Southern Africa found that in Botswana, Lesotho, Namibia, Swaziland, and Zimbabwe, few older people get a pension. Most work into their 70s and 80s (Gist, 1994; Martin & Kinsella, 1994). Many of these older people still give support to their families. Some give direct financial support to younger people. Others provide services (like babysitting) that allow younger people to work outside the home (Martin & Kinsella, 1994).

Older people in these countries rely on family support for their well-being, but lower fertility, the movement of young people to find jobs, and deaths due to AIDS among the young may reduce the

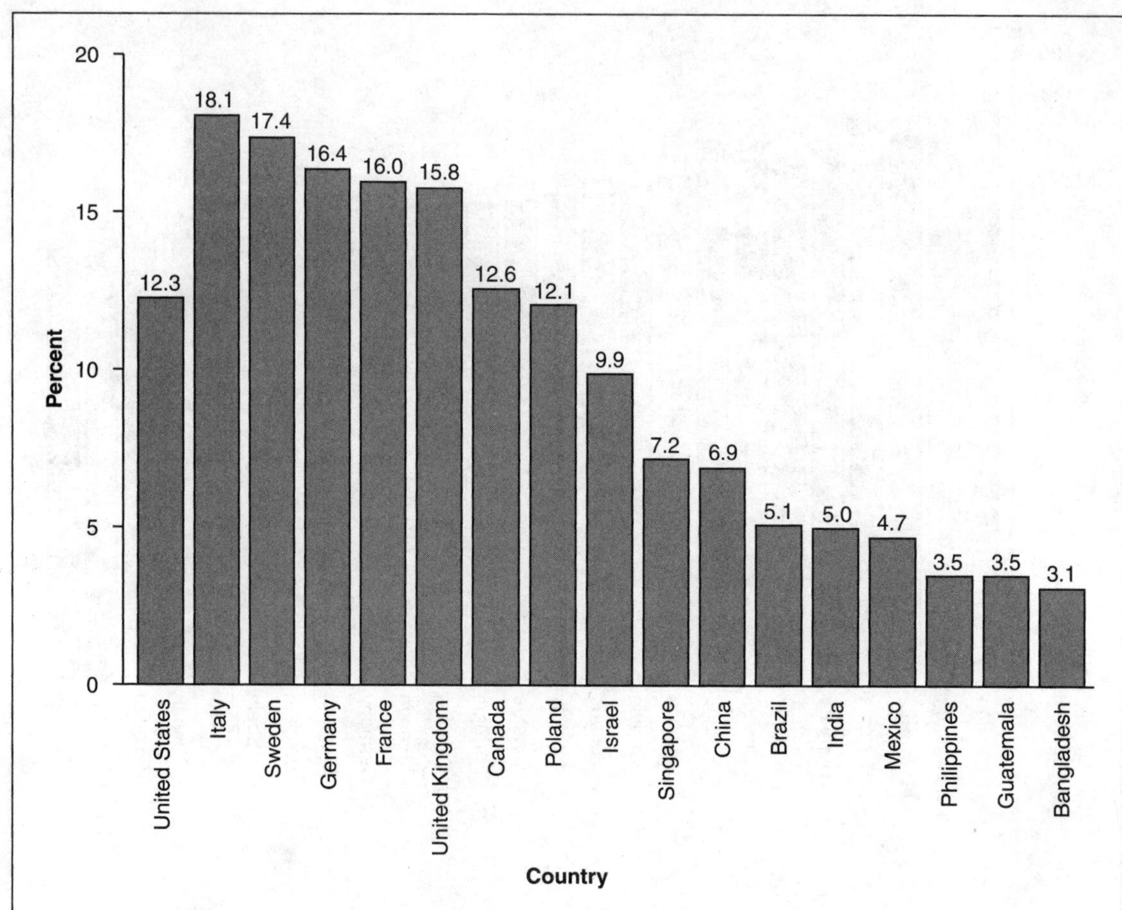

This chart reveals that the developed countries of Europe and North America have the largest proportions of older people. The developing nations (e.g., Singapore and China) have smaller proportions of older people. These proportions will increase if their birth rates decline and life expectancy increases. The least developed nations have the smallest proportions of older people, the highest birth rates, and the highest death rates.

FIGURE 3.3

Elder Populations in Selected Countries, 2000, Aged 65 and Over

Source: Data from Population Division, DESA, United Nations. (2002). *World Population Ageing 1950–2050.* Retrieved: January 4, 2005, *www.un.org/esa/population/publications/worldageing19502050/countriesorareas.htm.*

amount of family support older people can count on. This occurs at a time when the older population in Southern Africa will triple from 3.3 million to 9.4 million people (Gist, 1994).

Studies of Latin America report that older people have an unclear status in these countries today (Sennott-Miller, 1994). Traditional values have weakened, and families find it hard to care for older members. Poor economies in these countries mean that older people have little work and few support services. Young people often have to leave their homes to find work in other countries (Sokolovsky,

2000). Sennott-Miller (1994) says that these countries face a demographic pinch. Some of the poorest countries will see the most rapid increases in older people, but they have the least ability to respond to older people's needs.

More older people will strain current social, health, and economic programs for older people. Sennott-Miller (1994) says that developing nations need more information about their older populations, and they need to plan for an aging society. Countries with social programs and pension plans in place will need to adapt these programs to serve more older people.

The Future of Aging in Developing Nations

On April 12, 2002, the World Assembly on Ageing adopted the International Plan of Action on Ageing 2002 (Nizammudin, 2002). This plan says that older people in every society should take part in social life with full rights as citizens and should age with security and dignity. Older people should take part in the development process, they should have support for their health and well-being, and they should have a supportive environment. The plan recognizes that older women have special needs, that older people want to stay active and engaged, and that societies should foster intergenerational cooperation.

These ideals face challenges in developing nations. The ability of a country to help its older people largely depends on its economy. A country with a strong economy can make more resources available to its older people. But few developing nations have strong economies. Responses that fit western industrialized societies will not necessarily fit developing nations.

The developing nations need solutions that fit their cultures and current economic conditions. For example, developing nations cannot afford expensive pension programs. Krishnan (1990) says that

BOX 3.6
REFLECTIONS ON AGING IN AFRICA

Novelist and travel writer Paul Theroux traveled by land from Cairo to Cape Town. He detailed his journey in his book *Dark Star Safari: Overland from Cairo to Cape Town.* During his travels he passed his sixtieth birthday. This caused him to examine the meaning of age and aging—for him and for the people he met. In the excerpt below Theroux reflects on what aging means in the African context.

"I decided to avoid any birthday celebration. I was so self-conscious of my age that I often asked Africans to guess how old I was, hoping—perhaps knowing in advance—they would give me a low figure. They always did. Few people see elderly in Africa. Forty was considered old, a man of fifty was at death's door, sixty year olds were just crocks or crones. Despite my years I was healthy, and being agile and resilient I found traveling in Africa a pleasure. I did not seem old here, did not feel it, did not look it to Africans, and so it was a great place to be, another African fantasy, an adventure in rejuvenation.

"You are forty-something," Kamal had guessed in Addis. The highest number I got was fifty-two. Little did they know how much they flattered my vanity. But no one was vain about longevity in Africa, because the notion of longevity hardly existed. No one lived long and so age didn't matter, and perhaps that accounted for the casual way Africans regarded time. In Africa no one's lifetime was long enough to accomplish anything substantial, or to see any task of value completed. Two generations in the West equaled three generations in African time, telescoped by early marriage, early childbearing, and early death.

"In southeastern Uganda I wrote in my diary: *I do not want to be young again. I am happy being what I am. This contentment is very helpful on a trip as long and difficult as this.*"

Source: Theroux, P. (2003). *Dark Star Safari: Overland from Cairo to Cape Town.* Boston: Houghton Mifflin, pp. 197–198.

TABLE 3.1
Elder Population Increases, Aged 65 and Over from World and Major Regions, 2000 to 2050

	Population (in millions)			*Increase (2000 as base = 100)*	
	2000	*2025*	*2050*	*2025*	*2050*
World	421.4	832.2	1,464.9	197	348
More developed*	171.0	260.3	320.7	152	188
Less developed**	250.3	571.8	1,144.2	228	457
Africa	26.6	56.9	128.8	214	484
Latin America	29.1	70.1	143.7	241	494
North America	39.0	70.0	92.6	179	237
Asia	216.2	480.6	910.5	222	421
Europe	107.4	148.5	180.1	138	168
Oceania	3.0	6.1	9.2	203	307

*More developed: Europe, Japan, North America, Australia, and New Zealand.

**Less developed: Africa, Asia (excluding Japan), Latin America/ Caribbean, Melanesia, Micronesia, and Polynesia.

The absolute number of older people (1) shows the distribution of older people worldwide; (2) allows for a comparison of the size of older populations that each country and region will have to deal with; and (3) shows the growth rate of the older population in each region. This growth rate gives an idea of how much demographic change each society will undergo.

This table shows that, worldwide, the less-developed countries have a larger number of older people than the more developed countries (although they have smaller percentages of older people). It also shows that the older population will increase in the less developed countries at a faster rate than in the more developed countries.

In 2000, for example, Asia had five and a half times more older people than North America. This reflects the larger size of the total Asian population. Projections show that the Asian older population will increase at a faster rate than the North American older population. This reflects increased life expectancies in Asian countries. By the year 2050, compared to North America, Asia will have more than nine and a half times more older people.

Source: Medium variant data. In Population Division of the Department of Economic and Social Affairs of the United Nations Secretariat, *World Population Prospects: The 2004 Revision* and *World Urbanization Prospects: The 2003 Revision.* Retrieved April 14, 2005, *http://esa.un.org/unpp.*

for a population as large as India's, a basic pension of 100 rupees for older people would cost about $3 billion a year. The Indian states cannot afford this cost.

Government pensions vary by country, but relatively few people in developing nations get a pension. In most developing nations older people have to rely on domestic labor and piece work to survive. In larger urban centers, older people survive by scavenging food and clothing (Sennott-Miller, 1994).

Sokolovsky (2000) reviewed the living arrangements of older people throughout the world. He concludes that the family remains the primary source of support for older people. Where public supports exist, especially in developing nations,

Korea has modernized rapidly in the past few years. This Korean shopkeeper from Seoul runs a boutique at a local market. Many older people in Korea keep shops. Others sew and sell their goods. They help their extended families with the income and stay active in the community.

they can, at their best, support traditional family commitments to the old. He cites Nana Apt, an African sociologist to support this point.

"It is not enough," Apt says, "to talk about the bind of tradition, and it's not enough to talk about its disintegration. We must find ways and means of transforming it into a modern form that will make multigenerational relationships much more viable" (Apt, 1998, p. 14, cited in Sokolovsky, 2000). Sokolovsky (2000, p. 44) goes on to say that traditional systems work best when they fit into local economic and cultural systems. "These systems need to give both youth and elders reason to support each other."

Population aging affects nations and people throughout the world. The developed nations will have greater proportions of older people in their populations in the future. The developing nations will have larger numbers of older people than ever before. These changes will take place in the context of rapid urbanization, industrialization, globalization, and changes to the environment. We cannot look back. New conditions call for new responses. The large number of older people in the world today "remains irreducibly novel," Laslett (1976, p. 96) says, and "it calls for invention rather than imitation."

CONCLUSION

Was there a time when society held older people in esteem and valued their presence? Can we return to a golden age of aging? Will aging in the future be better than aging today?

Historical research shows that the treatment of older people varied from time to time and place to place. Some societies treated older people well and some treated older people badly. Also, the treatment of older people varied by gender, social class, and region even within one society. All past societies have one thing in common—none of them had the number of older people present in society today. None of them had to respond to the rapid population aging that we will see in the next fifty years.

Aging in the future will differ from society to society as it did in the past. The developed and developing nations, for example, will encounter and respond to different challenges. The wealthier nations will need to use resources wisely to serve a growing older population. The poorer nations will struggle to provide a decent life for their larger populations, both young and old. In every case, aging populations will influence politics, economics, the family, and other social institutions.

The United States cannot copy any other society as it moves into the future. It cannot look back to recover a golden age of the past. However, it can look at the past and learn about the source of a good old age. Older people do best when they give to their society. They get the highest esteem when they contribute to society and express themselves. Some societies make this possible. Older people served as matchmakers in China and Japan; they served as spiritual and community leaders in early America. They still serve as ritual leaders among the Coast Salish Indians. When older people played useful roles, they contributed to society and received respect. The United States can create policies with this in mind.

SUMMARY

- This chapter describes four types of societies: hunting and gathering, agricultural, industrial, and postindustrial. Each has a unique social organization that affects the status and treatment of older people in that society.
- The treatment of older people varied from time to time and place to place. In general, society treated older people well if they had land, knowledge, or an ability to give to the group. Society treated older people poorly if they had no resources and could not give to the group.
- Modernization theory describes the transformation from preindustrial to industrial society. This entailed a complete transformation that included change from a rural to an urban style of life. It also included changes

in social roles, beliefs, and the status of older people. Gerontologists report, for example, that as technology increased, the status of older people declined.

- The United States went through the demographic transition in the early 1800s. The country began to industrialize a short time later. This coincided with greater urbanization. These three changes led to more older people in the population, a loss of roles for older people, and a decrease in older peoples' status.
- The developed nations of the world report population aging. They have increasing proportions of older people in their populations. They also have growing proportions of very old people (aged 85 and over). Societal population aging, and the aging of the older population, will create new economic and social challenges for these nations.
- The developing nations still have relatively young populations. They will have increased numbers of older people in the years ahead due to decreased death rates. An increase in the number of older people in these societies will strain current social, health, and economic programs for older people.
- Population aging will influence both developed and developing nations in the future. History cannot give answers to the new challenges that each type of society will face. But history can teach us one thing. When older people have a useful role to play in society, they live a good old age. And society benefits from their contributions and their wisdom.

DISCUSSION QUESTIONS

1. List the four major types of societies discussed in the text. Explain the source of status for older people in each type of society, the positive roles that older people can play in each type of society, and how each type of society treats its older people.
2. Give the stages of the demographic transition. Describe the changes in birth and death rates at each stage. What impact do birth and death rates at each stage have on social institutions? What impact do they have on everyday life? Do you know of any societies at different stages of the demographic transition than the United States? Have you ever visited one of these societies? What did you observe with respect to birth rates, death rates, and population aging?
3. Describe the effects of industrialization and urbanization on older people in the United States from the early 1800s to the present. How have these processes influenced the treatment of older people? Compare the status of older people in the United States today with the status of older people one hundred years ago.
4. What evidence exists for an improvement in the status of older people in postindustrial society? Give specific examples from your everyday life.
5. Compare and contrast the challenges facing the developed and developing nations as a result of the increase in the proportion and number of older people in their societies. Discuss some responses each type of society can make to these challenges.

SUGGESTED READING

Infeld, D. L. (Ed.). (2002). *Anthropology of aging.* New York: Routledge.

The authors in this collection look at aging in North America and in other cultures. The volume contains twenty-six papers that report on the cultural meaning of aging, the role of older people, and aging as portrayed in literature and art. These studies show the many ways that people age around the world and the many interpretations of aging that exist in other cultures.

Ruggles, S., & United Nations. (2000). *Living arrangements and well-being of older persons in the past.* New York: Population Division, Department of Economic and Social Affairs, United Nations Secretariat.

This study examines an issue—living arrangements in the past—that interests historians today. For example, did older people in the past live alone or in multi-generational households? And if they lived alone (or with others) did they do so by choice or out of necessity? Ruggles uses census data from 1850 to 1990 to find answers to these questions.

GLOSSARY OF TERMS

demographic change Change in the structure and dynamics of the population. This includes changes in birth, death, and migration rates.

demographic transition The transition from a society that has high birth and death rates to one with low birth and death rates.

developed nations Countries that have industrial economies and modernized social institutions and have gone through the demographic transition. The developed nations are the nations of North America and Europe, including the former Soviet Union, as well as Japan, Australia, and New Zealand.

developing nations Nations that have begun to industrialize, have begun to develop modern social institutions (like schools and hospitals), and have begun to go through the demographic transition. The developing nations are all nations not listed under *developed nations.*

fertility As defined by demographers, the fertility rate is the number of live births per 1,000 women aged 15–44.

industrialization A social process leading from a rural economy based on animal power and relatively low productivity to a market economy based on steam and electrical power with high productivity.

median age One-half the population is above and one-half below the median age.

modernization The transformation from a preindustrial to an industrial society.

mortality The death rate generally measured as the number of deaths per 1,000 population for a given age group. For infants it is measured as the number of deaths per 1,000 live births.

overaged A life stage in simpler societies when an older person can no longer contribute to the group.

postindustrial society A society that has a large service sector, many complex social institutions, and a high standard of living. Contemporary U.S. society is postindustrial.

urbanization An increase in the size of cities and in the concentration of people in cities. Urbanization often goes along with modernization and industrialization.

chapter **4**

DEMOGRAPHY

Cohen (1994) found that the term *greedy geezers* appeared sixty-eight times in the national media between January 1991 and May 1993. Some of these articles defended older people's rights to services and pensions. Other articles claimed that older people eat up national resources and create a "fiscal black hole" for the country. One television segment on health care quoted an expert as saying to older people: "Look, you can't compromise the lives of your children and your grandchildren by demanding unreasonable things" (Cohen, 1994).

News articles and media reports link the high cost of social and health care services to the rising numbers of older people in the United States, and they propose that a large older population will burden young people with crushing debt. They describe the growth of the older population as a "tidal wave," a burden, or a source of intergenerational conflict. Some writers use population projections to warn about a coming crisis in American society.

The facts about population aging for the past century or so question this image of crisis and conflict. A government report on population aging commissioned by President Herbert Hoover in 1929, for example, looks like yesterday's front-page story. The "aging of the population," the report says, "is not a new process but one that has gone on for more than a century. What is new is the greater speed in recent years and the extent of the changes which have resulted" (cited in Gerber, Wolff, Klores, & Brown, 1989, p. 3).

Figures show that the U.S. population aged steadily for 130 years until 1950 (when the Baby Boom temporarily halted the trend). The trend continued again after the Baby Boom to the present. The growth of the older population in the past and in the future looks more like a steady swell than a tidal wave.

McDaniel (1986) says that crisis thinking comes from a belief in **demographic determinism**. This refers to the belief that changes in population size and structure, like population aging, will inevitably lead to crisis. McDaniel (1986) says that crisis mongers assume that (1) population aging is new, (2) the proportion of older people will be overwhelming, (3) population aging will lead to an increased dependency burden on society, and (4) this will have negative economic consequences. But demographic doomsayers deemphasize society's ability to respond to population change.

True, the rate of growth of the older population will increase in this century. True, the population will age faster than in the past. But popular reports often assume that all older people place demands on society for pensions, health care, or housing. The diversity of the older population alone argues against this. Some older people will draw government pensions and will need health care support. Others will work into late old age and will pay taxes on their salaries and pension income.

Also, American society can adapt to population change. The United States can adopt policies that respond to an aging society. Policies related to health care, occupational health and safety, and public health education can all reduce the cost of societal aging. They can improve the quality of life for people at all ages and create a healthier older population (Korczyk, 2002). Most experts agree that population aging will lead to social change, but they do not agree that it will lead to a crisis or more social problems.

This chapter (1) looks at the facts on population aging in the United States, (2) describes some creative responses to population aging, and (3) considers the future of population aging and its impact on American society.

THE DEMOGRAPHICS OF POPULATION AGING

The dictionary defines **demography** as the statistical study of human populations, especially with reference to size and density, distribution, and vital statistics. The demography of aging looks at older people in the population and at the impact of population aging on society. Population change affects the family, the economy, and social policies. Demographers, experts in the study of population change, use at least three measures to describe **population aging**: (1) the absolute number of older people in a population, (2) the median age of the population, and (3) the increased proportion of older people.

Increased Numbers of Older People

Change in the absolute number of older people in a population gives a crude but useful understanding of the impact of population aging on a society. Demographers use the absolute number of older people in a population to study population change within a society. Figure 4.1 shows the actual and projected increase in the number of older people in the United States from 1900 to 2050.

The older population has grown more than ten times in size from 1900 to 2000, from 3.1 million to 35 million people. Projections show that it will almost double again from the year 2000 to 2050, from 35 million to 68.5 million people.

This growth will take place unevenly over the forty-year period from 1990 to 2030. From 1990 to 2010, the older population will grow relatively slowly by about 1.3 percent per year. This reflects the relatively small number of births during the 1930s. But from 2010 to 2030, when the large Baby Boom cohorts enter old age, the older population will grow by as much as 2.8 percent per year. The U.S. Census Bureau (1996, pp. 2–5) says this will lead to a "massive increase" in the number of older people.

Demographers rarely use the absolute number of older people in a society alone to analyze population aging. They rarely use it to compare aging in different societies. This figure, if used alone, can mislead a researcher. For example, a doubling or tripling of the older population can seem like an overwhelming change to a society, but its effect will depend on many things, including the society's economy, its policies, and its total rate of population growth.

Increased Median Age of the Population

Demographers use the **median age** of the population as a second measure of population aging. This measure gives a rough estimate of a population's age structure. Half the population is older and half younger than the median age. It offers a sensitive measure of increases or decreases in population aging.

Figure 4.2 shows the changes in the median age of the U.S. population from 1820 to 2050. An increase in the median age means that the population has gotten older. Note that the median age has more than doubled over the years, from seventeen years in 1820 to a projected thirty-nine years in 2050. Note also that the increase halted during the 1960s and 1970s. This signals a reversal in the process of population aging for those years.

Why did this occur? These declines in median age mark the effects of the Baby Boom that took place after World War II. The median age increased again between 1970 and 1990 from twenty-eight to thirty-three years. Demographers rarely use the median age alone as a measure of population aging. The median age says little about the relative size of age groups within the population, or about changes in the size of age groups relative to one another.

INCREASED PROPORTION OF OLDER PEOPLE

Gerontologists most often use the proportion of people aged 65 and over in the population as a measure of population aging. This measure shows the relationship between the older group and the rest of society. An increase in the proportion of older people, for example, means a decrease in the proportion of other age groups. It gives an indication of how much influence the older group will have on social life. Figure 4.1 shows the proportion of people aged 65 and over in the United States for the years 1900 to 2050. Note that the proportion increases from 4 percent in 1900 to 20 percent in 2050 when the last of the Baby Boom generation reaches late old age.

Measuring Trends

Each of these measures of population aging shows the same trend: the aging of the U.S. population. Each measure gives a unique perspective on this phenomenon. For example, the **absolute number of older people** gives an idea of how many people will enter retirement at a certain time. It also gives some idea of the number of customers who might want to invest in condominiums or buy cars. The median age points to shifts in the political interests of the population. A higher median age means more people interested in programs and policies for later middle-aged and older adults.

The **proportion of older people** shows the relationship between older and younger age groups. For example, in 1900 older people made up 4 percent of the population, but people under age 18 made up 40 percent of the population. In 1980 older people made up 11 percent and young people made up 28 percent of the population. By the year 2050, older people (aged 60 and over) will make up 26.9 percent and younger people (aged 0 to 14) will make up only 18.5 percent of the population (United Nations, 2002). These figures suggest the need to shift resources to serve older people in the future. Gerontologists use these measures to assess various impacts of population aging on social life and to project social changes due to population aging.

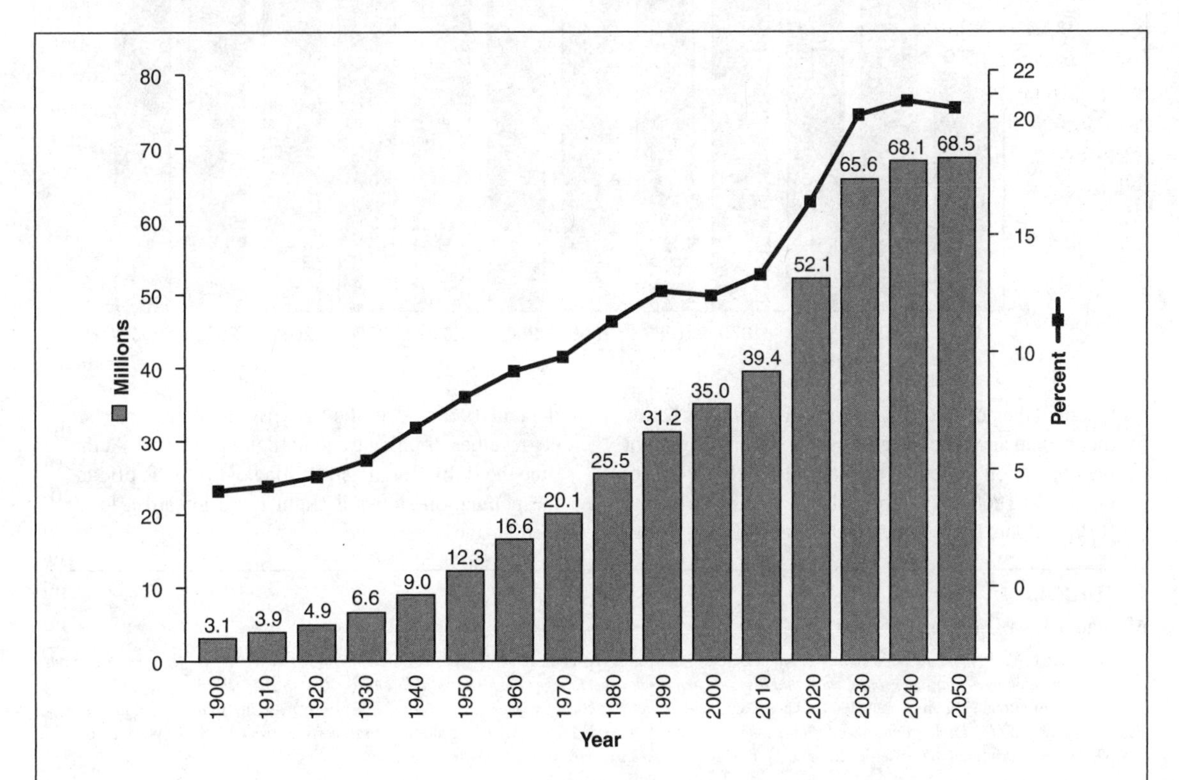

*The projections presented here reflect the U.S. Census Bureau's "middle series" projections. The U.S. Census Bureau makes a number of projections based on a number of fertility, mortality, and migration assumptions. The middle series assumes a fertility rate in 2050 of 2,150 births per 1,000 women, life expectancy at birth in 2050 of 79.7 years for men and 85.6 years for women, and an ultimate net migration of 880,000 per year.

The 1900 to 1980 data are tabulated from the Decennial Censuses of the Population and exclude Armed Forces overseas. Projections (1990 onward) are middle series projections and include Armed Forces overseas.

FIGURE 4.1

U.S. Elder Population, Aged 65 and over, 1900–2050*

Sources: Adapted from Hetzel, L., & Smith, A. (2001). *The 65 Years and Over Population: 2000—Census 2000 Brief.* Retrieved: March 21, 2004, *www.census.gov/prod/2001pubs/c2kbr01-10.pdf*; Hobbs, F., & Stoops, N. (2002). *Demographic trends in the 20th century.* U.S. Census Bureau, Census 2000 Special Reports, Series CENSR-4. Washington, DC: U.S. Government Printing Office. Retrieved: January 19, 2004, *www.census.gov/prod/2002pubs/censr-4.pdf*; U.S. Census Bureau. (1996). *65+ in the United States.* Current Population Reports, Special Studies, P23-190. Washington, DC: U.S. Government Printing Office. Retrieved: March 21, 2004, *www.census.gov/prod/1/pop/p23-190/p23-190.html.* Middle series projections from 2010 on.

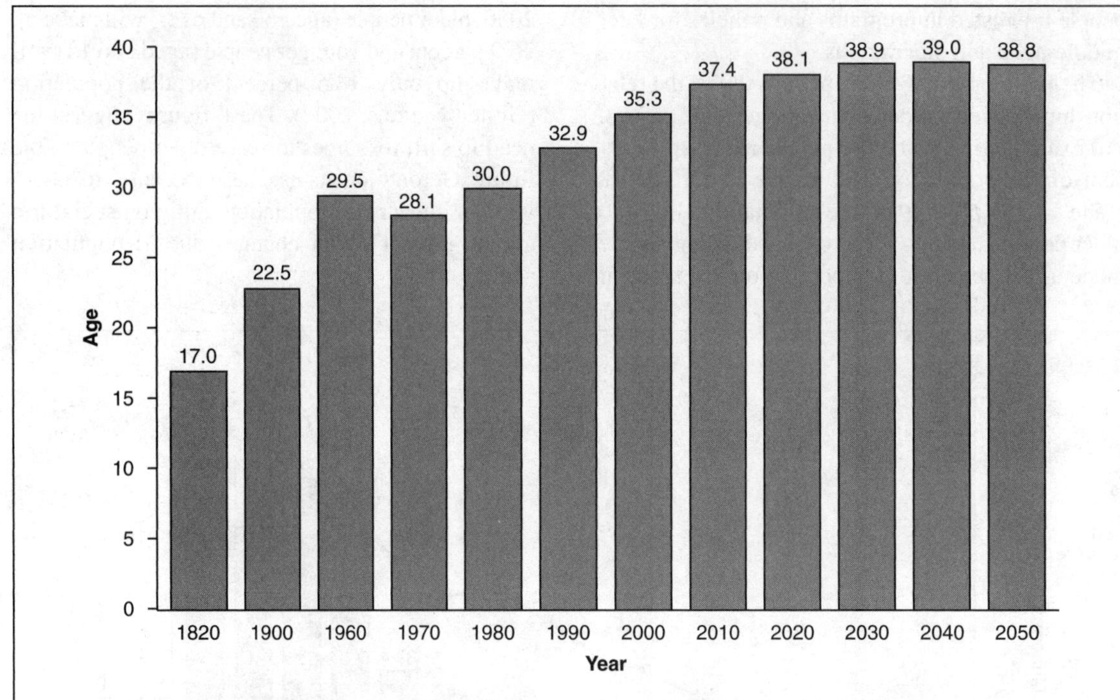

One-half the population is above and one-half is below the median age. These figures show a steady aging of the population (based on median age) with the exception of the 1960 to 1970 period. The post–World War II Baby Boom led to a decrease in the median age until the mid-1960s. After the Baby Boom, American society resumes its aging trend until the year 2050. At that time the Baby Boom generation begins to die off, and the population shows a slight trend toward a lower median age.

FIGURE 4.2

Median Age of U.S. Population, 1820–2050

Sources: Vierck, E. (1990). *Fact book on aging.* Santa Barbara, California: ABC-CLIO; U.S. Census Bureau. (2000). *(NP-T4-G) Projections of the total resident population by 5-year age groups, race, and hispanic origin with special age categories: Middle series, 2000 to 2050.* Washington, DC: Population Projections Program, Population Division, Retrieved: March 21, 2004, *www.census.gov/population/www/projections/natsum-T3.html*; Hobbs, F., & Stoops, N. (2002). *Demographic trends in the 20th century.* U.S. Census Bureau, Census 2000 Special Reports, Series CENSR-4. Washington, DC: U.S. Government Printing Office. Retrieved: January 19, 2004, *www.census.gov/prod/2002pubs/censr-4.pdf.*

THE CAUSES OF POPULATION CHANGE

A population can change in three ways: people move into or out of a society, people die, and people are born. Demographers study **migration**, **death rates**, and **birth rates** to understand population aging.

Migration

Migration has played a relatively small role in population aging in the United States and will likely play a smaller role in the future. Because immigrants typically arrive in the United States as young adults, their presence tends to lower the country's median age. They also tend to have children, which further lowers the median age.

Migrants who come of age in the United States have an impact on population aging forty-five or fifty years later. This delayed effect accounts for some of the increase in the older population until 1960. Many of the people who came of age before 1960 immigrated to the United States between 1905 and 1914. Between 1901 and 1910, for example, nearly 9 million immigrants arrived in the United States, by far the highest rate of immigration in the past one hundred years (U.S. Census Bureau, 2002a).

Immigrants have less impact on population aging today than at certain times in the past. First, the immigrants from earlier in this century have died off. Second, more restrictive immigration laws have kept the group of foreign-born older people relatively small. (Immigration averaged around 700,000 people per year of all ages in the 1980s.) This has relaxed somewhat. In 1990 the government lifted quotas on family reunification, which led to larger numbers of immigrants (some of them older people) than in the 1980s.

Still, the numbers remain relatively small, on average about 900,000 immigrants in total in each year during the 1990s (U.S. Census Bureau, 2000a). Third, low immigration levels in the future will mean small proportions of foreign-born older people. The U.S. Census Bureau middle series projections put immigration in the year 2050 at about 880,000. A number similar to the recent past, but a relatively small proportion of the total U.S. population.

Changes in immigration laws, the quality of border control, and the flow of immigrants make future migration figures uncertain. Illegal immigration, mostly by young people, would slow population aging in the short run, but demographers find it hard to assess the impact of this illegal group. Zopf (1986, p. 5) concludes that "the largest impact of immigration on the aging of the population has probably passed." For this reason, death rates and birth rates will have the greatest impact on population aging.

Death Rates

Death rates fell throughout this century for whites and nonwhites and for men and women (see Table 4.1). This means that more people survived into old age than ever before. Life expectancy at birth in 1900 was 47.3 years. It reached a record high of 77.2 years in 2001, a two-year increase over 1990.

These gains in life expectancy largely reflect decreases in infant mortality. The National Center for Health Statistics (2003) reports that from 1960 to 2001 infant mortality fell steadily. The rate decreased from 26.0 (per 1,000 live births) in 1960 to 6.8 in 2001. This is the lowest rate ever recorded in the United States. Both African Americans and whites showed a decline in infant mortality from 1960 to 2001. African Americans showed a decline from 44.3 in 1960 to 14.0 in 2001 for both sexes. Whites showed a decline from 22.9 in 1960 to 5.7 in 2001 (National Center for Health Statistics, 2003). Still, the 2001 figures show that African Americans have an infant mortality almost two and a half times the rate of whites. This reflects lower incomes, poverty, and less access to high-quality medical care for African Americans.

The United States could see further decreases in infant mortality. Countries such as Hong Kong, Japan, and Singapore have rates below 4 per 100,000. But, these countries have small, homogeneous populations. Serow, Sly, and Wrigley (1990) project little further increase in life expectancy in the United States for ages under 60 in the future.

Instead, demographers project increases in life expectancy for people over age 65. They project these gains for both whites and nonwhites, men and women (Day, 1996). Myers (1990, citing Preston, Himes, & Eggers, 1988) reports that decreased mortality at older ages plays a big role in increased life expectancy today. Between 1980 and 1985, for example, mortality declines in later life accounted for about two-thirds of increases in the U.S. population's mean age.

These changes in life expectancy will shape the size and structure of the older population. By the year 2050, men at age 65 can expect on average to live another 20.3 years, and women can expect to live another 22.4 years (Day, 1996). The conquest of cancer or further declines in stroke and heart disease death rates, could increase life expectancy still further in old age. This will mean, among other things, further increases in the number and proportion of the oldest old people in the population. In the past, population aging took place because of decreased infant mortality. Today and in the future, population aging will occur mostly because of increased longevity.

Birth Rates

The decline in the **fertility rate** and the birth rate, more than any other cause, explains population aging during the past century. This may surprise you. Why should the rate of children born influence aging?

Demographers define the *fertility rate* as the number of live births per 1,000 women aged 15 to 44; they define the *birth rate* as the number of live births per 1,000 population. A high fertility rate (many births) will increase the proportion of younger people in society. This will keep the population relatively young. A low fertility rate will mean a proportionately greater number of older people. Couple a low fertility rate (fewer children) with a low death rate (people living longer) and you get population aging in the United States today.

At least three specific changes in birth rate influenced population aging in the United States. First, an increase in births took place before 1920 (Easterlin, 1987). The end of World War I in part accounts for this increase. So does the large number of young immigrants in the early 1900s who began having children at this time. These people (the children born around 1920) entered old age in the mid-1980s. They will make up the very old population in the United States in the early years of this century.

Second, an explosion in births, the Baby Boom, took place after World War II, between 1945 and 1960. This generation has shaped U.S. society and culture ever since. The education system built schools for them in their childhood; the housing industry built homes for them as young adults; and the travel, leisure, and health care industries await their arrival into old age. This group, compared with past generations, has greater expectations for its living standards in later life (Dychtwald, 1999).

The Baby Boom generation will begin to enter old age around the year 2010. Nearly all of this group will have entered old age by the year 2030. By the year 2050, the United States will have an estimated 80 million older people. This will come to more than twice the number of older people alive in 2000 (U.S. Census Bureau, 1996). Dychtwald (1999, p. 2) says that the size of the older Baby Boom generation will create an "astonishing 'age wave' " that will reshape the marketplace, social services, and politics in the next century.

TABLE 4.1
U.S. Life Expectancy at Birth (in Years)

	White		*African American*	
	Male	*Female*	*Male*	*Female*
1970	68.0	75.6	60.0	68.3
1980	70.7	78.1	63.8	72.5
1990	72.7	79.4	64.5	73.6
2001	75.0	80.2	68.6	75.5
2010	76.1	81.8	70.9	77.8

This table shows the increase in life expectancy at birth for whites and African Americans in the United States for selected years from 1970 to 2010. All four groups show an increase in life expectancy. African American men and women, from 1970 to 2001, have narrowed the gap in life expectancy with their white counterparts. Whites of either sex continue to have longer life expectancies than African Americans. But the projection to 2010 shows an increase for all groups and a narrower gap between whites and African Americans.

Sources: Adapted from U.S. Census Bureau. (2002b). *Statistical abstract of the United States.* Washington, DC: U.S. Government Printing Office. Retrieved: March 21, 2004, *www.census.gov/prod/www/statistical-abstract-02.html*; Arias. (2004). *United States life tables, 2001. National vital statistics reports*, Vol. 52(14). Hyattsville, MD: National Center for Health Statistics. Retrieved: March 21, 2004, *www.cdc.gov/nchs/data/nvsr/nvsr52/nvsr52_14.pdf.*

Third, fertility has declined from the mid-1960s to the present. The U.S. birth and fertility rates began to fall after 1960 (with a rate of 118) and hit an all-time low of sixty-one in 2002 (Downs, 2003). This has led to a sharp increase in the median age and an increase in the proportion of older people. Zopf (1986, p. 24) says that declining birth rates dominate the news of population aging in the United States. "The birth rate has fallen so significantly in virtually all parts of the nation," he says, "that the aging of the population is one of [America's] universal demographic phenomena [*sic*]."

Will birth rates stay low in the future? Will the population keep getting older? No one can say for sure. But worldwide trends suggest that U.S. birth rates will continue to fall. Other developed nations have seen similar sharp decreases in fertility rates. Sweden, Japan, and Italy have birth rates far below the rate needed to replace their populations. Some countries, like Sweden, have tried to reverse this trend. But they have had little success.

Birth rates reflect changing social and demographic conditions. Consider the following social forces that lead to a decreased birth rate: (1) New methods of birth control allow couples to choose how many children they will have. Gee (1982, p. 61) says that "population aging is the unplanned by-product of planned parenthood." (2) Young people in developed nations spend more years in school and in starting their careers than ever before. (3) Most young women today, compared with the past, work outside the home. They start families later and want fewer children. (4) "The current low birth rate," a government report says, "primarily reflects the smaller proportion of women of childbearing age in the U.S. population, as baby boomers age and Americans are living longer" (National Center for Health Statistics, 2003). All of these trends lead to lower birth rates.

THE CHALLENGES OF AN AGING POPULATION

On average, a man aged 65 today can expect to spend 16.4 years in old age. A woman can expect to spend 19.4 years as a senior (Arias & Smith, 2003). Myers (1990, p. 32) calls this the "metabolism of the population." The older group will grow over the next fifty years or so, but it will not grow steadily. For example, population aging will slow and in some years will reverse itself between 1996 and 2011 (U.S. Census Bureau, 1996).

Between 1990 and 2000, for instance, the proportion of older people in the population decreased. The slow growth in the 65- to 74-year-old group accounts for this trend. But this will change in the early to middle years of the twenty-first century when the Baby Boom cohorts enter old age. These new cohorts will bring with them better health, new life-styles, and new concerns. At the same time, a larger number of people than ever before will live into late old age. These people, some of them over 100 years old, will have unique health and social service needs. The composition of the older population (the number of younger and the number of older seniors) can tell us about the challenges the United States will face as the population ages.

The Aging of the Older Population

Demographers divide the older group into subgroups. In the past, gerontologists defined the group aged 55 to 74 as the young-old and those aged 75 and over as the old-old. But population aging has led to a refinement of this scheme. Research reports now often divide the older population into three groups: 65 to 74, 75 to 84, and 85 and over. All of these groups have grown in size during the past century.

The U.S. Census Bureau (1996) reports that the 65- to 74-age group in 1990 was eight times larger than in 1900, the 75 to 84 group was thirteen times larger, and the 85 and over group was twenty-five times larger. These groups will all grow in size into the next century. But the oldest age group will be among the fastest growing groups in the population. For example, between 1990 and 2000 the oldest age group increased by over one-third (from 3.1 million to 4.2 million) (Hetzel & Smith, 2001). (See Figures 4.3 and 4.4 on pages 85 and 86, respectively.)

People aged 85 and over form a unique group within the older population. This group will grow more than four times in size from 1990 to 2030. It will grow more than six times in size from 1990 to 2050 (U.S. Census Bureau, 1996). By 2050, nearly a quarter of the older population (aged 65 and over) will be 85 years old or over. This makes the oldest old population one of the fastest growing age groups in the country. Better health care and disease prevention have led to longer life in old age, and they will extend the lives of more people in the future.

The oldest old population (aged 85 and over) looks very different demographically from the young-old population (aged 65 to 74). Dunkle, Roberts, and Haug (2001) analyzed data from a longitudinal study of people in their 80s and 90s who lived in the midwestern United States. They found that many of these people had small social networks. Although more than one-half the men in their study (52.2 percent) had spouses, only 11 percent of women were married. One-third of the people in this study had no living children. The researchers found that the social networks of these people declined over time.

The oldest old people have multiple chronic conditions and high rates of disability. They also consume large amounts of services compared with their numbers. Freedman and his colleagues (2004) studied the amount of care services people aged 75 and over used each month during a three-year period. The researchers found that over the three years this group increased its care hours by 38 percent.

Wang (2004) reports that the 85 and over population accounts for 1.5 percent of the population, but used 16.1 percent of Medicare fee-for-service payments. This group also uses the most nursing home services. Hetzel and Smith (2001) report that 18.2 percent of people aged 85 and over live in institutions compared with only 1.1 percent of people aged 65 and over. Feder and her colleagues (2001) predict an increase in the use of long-term care services in the future. Increases in the oldest old population will have a large impact on national health care costs and policies.

Ethnic and Racial Variations

The racial and ethnic composition of the older population changes as new people enter old age. Today, for example, the nonwhite population of the United States is younger than the white population. Older

BOX 4.1
CENTENARIANS

The Census Bureau reports that in 2000 the United States had 50,454 people aged 100 and over. This represents one out of every 5,578 people in the United States and an increase of about 35 percent over the number of centenarians in 1990 (Hetzel & Smith, 2001). The Census Bureau predicts that by the year 2080, the United States will have over 1 million people aged 100 or over. This will be a twentyfold increase over current figures. Vierck (2002, p. 2) calls this a "centenarian boom." And Beard (1991, p. 4) calls these centenarians "the new generation." Never before have so many people reached 100 years old. "If one counted all the people in the world who had ever reached 100 years before the birth of the present centenarian generation," she says, "they would not equal the number now alive."

What is it like to live to 100 years old? Will more centenarians mean more chronic health problems like Alzheimer's disease? Will it mean more years of suffering for more people? Perls, who conducted the New England Centenarian Study, thinks that people who live to age 100 as a group will have better health than people twenty years younger. His pilot work found low proportions of centenarians with Alzheimer's disease. These people had better cognitive ability and health than expected.

Perls also found that men in their 90s have better mental functioning than men in their 80s. Also, he has found what he calls a "gender crossover." Women tend to outlive men, but men who live beyond age 80 live healthier, more independent lives than women. Men who survive to late old age have greater physical and mental resources than expected.

Alfred Benedetti, 101, serves as a model for the old age Perls describes. Benedetti performed in the Senior Olympics for the past eleven years, entering the javelin, shot put, and basketball free throw events, and he bowled twice a week. He said that his health and long life came from avoiding tobacco and alcohol—except for the shot of port wine he drank every day. He stayed busy reading, writing, and working with his hands.

Genetics may explain part of the reason for long life and well-being in late old age. Those who live long may have genes that protect them from routine physical decline. They may also have genes that increase their ability to overcome disease and keep organs functioning well. Good health and a strong physical system lead to survival into late old age.

Sources: From *Centenarians: The new generation,* by B. B. Beard, 1991, New York: Greenwood Press; "The Oldest Old," by T. T. Perls, January 1995, *Scientific America,* pp. 70–75; Vierck, E. (2002). *Growing old in America.* Detroit, MI: Gale Group; and Hetzel, L., & Smith, A. (2001). *The 65 years and over population: 2000—Census 2000 brief.* U.S. Census Bureau. Retrieved: March 21, 2004, *www.census.gov/prod/2001pubs/c2kbr01-10.pdf* or *www.census .gov/population/www/cen2000/briefs.html.*

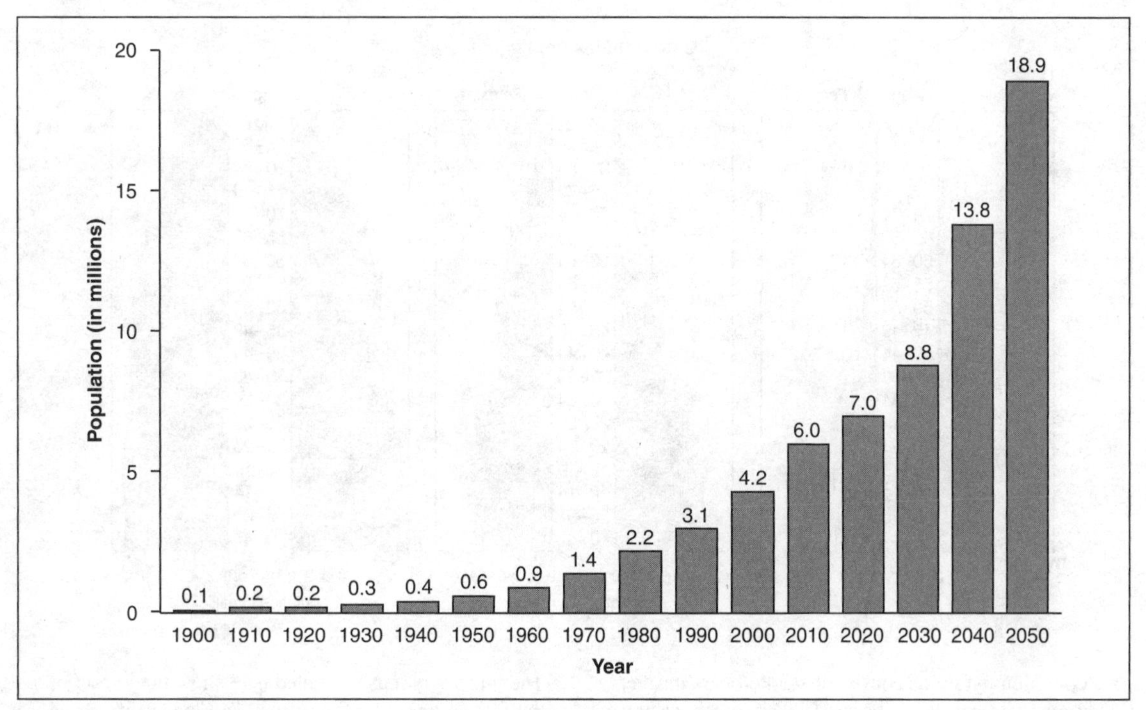

FIGURE 4.3
Population 85 Years and over, 1900 to 2050
Source: U.S. Census Bureau. (1993). Decennial Censuses for specified years and *Population Projections of the United States by Age, Sex, Race, and Hispanic Origin, 1993 to 2050.* Current Population Reports, P25-1104. Washington, DC: U.S. Government Printing Office. Data for 1990 from *1990 Census of Population and Housing,* CPH-L-74, *Modified and Actual Age, Sex, Race, and Hispanic Origin Data.*

people make up only 8 percent of the African American and 5 percent of the Hispanic populations compared with 13.4 percent of the white population (National Center for Health Statistics, 2003). This difference reflects higher fertility rates and higher mortality among nonwhites. However, these rates will change in the years ahead, and they will lead to changes in the older population.

Myers (1990) says that by the year 2050, 15.6 percent of the Spanish-origin population will be aged 65 and over. This will lead to greater ethnic and racial diversity in the older population. "In the future," Serow, Sly, and Wrigley say, "the racial structure of the older population [60+] is likely to become increasingly Nonwhite" (doubling from 14 percent of the age 60 and over population in 1980 to 27 percent in 2080) (Myers, 1990; Serow, Sly, & Wrigley, 1990, pp. 9–10).

Regional Distribution

Internal migration (**in-migration**) in the United States in the past several decades has led to decreases in the proportion of older people in the northeast, increases in the proportion of older people in the midwest, and increases in the proportions of older people in the south and west. These findings reflect three trends that lead to an older population: accumulation, recomposition, and congregation (Longino, 2001).

Accumulation

This takes place when older people stay behind and young people move out of an area. Midwestern states (Iowa, Missouri, North Dakota, and South Dakota) made up four of the fourteen states with the highest concentrations of older people in 2000. The **out-migration** of younger people accounts for this.

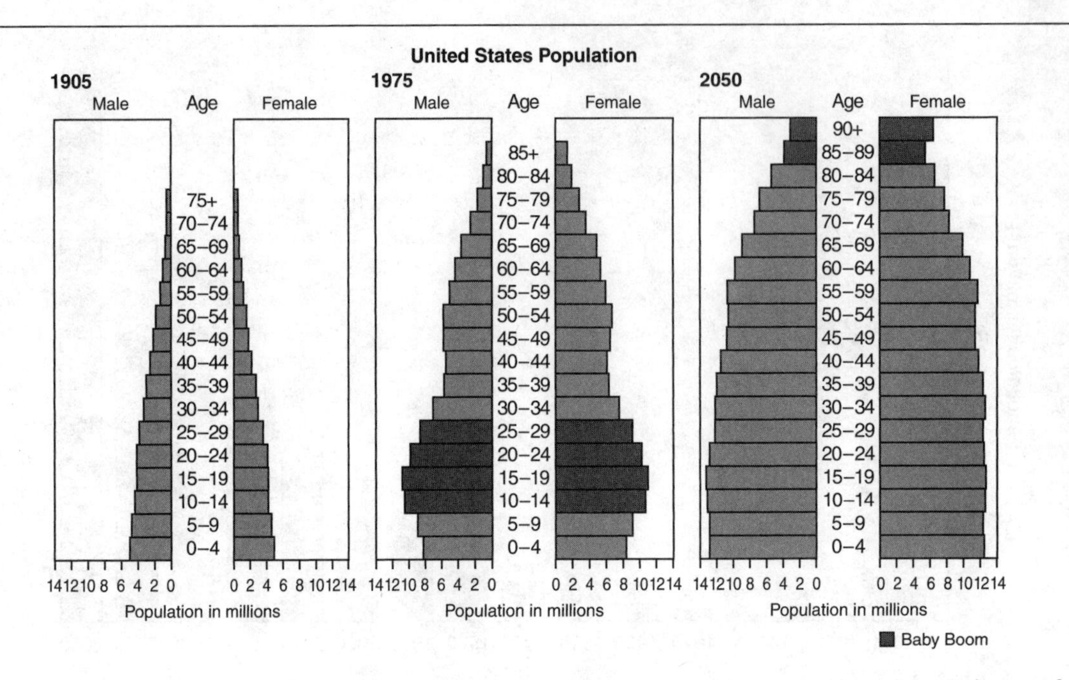

Population pyramids consist of stacked bars that represent five-year age cohorts. The bottom bar shows the youngest age group (0 to 4 years), the top bar the oldest group (90 and over). The left side of the bar contains the data for men, the right side for women.

A population pyramid gives a graphic profile of a society's age structure. Pyramids allow demographers to compare the age structures of two countries. They allow a viewer to compare male and female age structures in one society. And they allow a viewer to compare segments of the population (e.g., the size of the 5- to 9-age group with the 0- to 4-age group).

The three pyramids presented here show the impact of the Baby Boom, the Baby Bust, and longer life at the oldest ages. These three influences lead to the square-shaped pyramid of 2050. The movement of the Baby Boom generation can be seen through the life cycle by comparing the pyramids from 1975 and 2050. The Baby Boom appears as the 10- to 29-year-old age groups in 1975. It shows up as the 85 and over age group in 2050. At this point, many of the Baby Boom generation has died. Note the large size of the 85 and over age groups in 2050 compared with 1975. Longer life expectancies and the continued large size of the Baby Boom generation lead to this large group of very old people.

FIGURE 4.4

Images of Aging: Population Pyramids for the United States, 1905, 1975, 2050

Sources: U.S. Census Bureau. *Estimates of the Population of the United States, by Single Years of Age, Color, and Sex: 1900 to 1959.* Current Population Reports, Series P-25, No. 311. U.S. Government Printing Office: Washington, DC, 1965; U.S. Census Bureau. *Preliminary Estimates of the Population of the United States, Age, Sex, and Race: 1970 to 1981.* Current Population Reports, Series P-25, No. 917. U.S. Government Printing Office: Washington, DC, 1982; Jennifer C. Day. U.S. Census Bureau. *Population Projections of the United States, Age, Sex, Race, and Hispanic Origin: 1993 to 2050.* Current Population Reports, Series P2-1104. U.S. Government Printing Office: Washington, DC, 1993 (middle series projections).

Young people leave this region to find work, often in the sunbelt states. Projections show that northeastern states like Maine, Pennsylvania, and Rhode Island will age in the future in part because of outmigration. If present trends continue, they will rank among the ten oldest states in the year 2020 (U.S. Census Bureau, 1996).

Recomposition

This takes place when older people move into an area that younger people leave. For example, some older people move to rural areas to retire. These areas may offer little opportunity for young workers. But they offer a low cost of living and beautiful scenery that suits older people (Hunt, Marshall, & Merrill, 2002). Arkansas and Missouri fit this pattern. They had large numbers of older people in 2000. And projections show that they will have some of the highest proportions of older people in the country in 2020 (19.3 and 17.5 percent of the population, respectively).

Congregation

This takes place when people of all ages move to an area, but older people arrive at the fastest pace. Florida, Arizona, and North Carolina fit this pattern. The large numbers of older people who have moved to Florida make this the oldest state in the country in 2000 (with 19.6 percent of its population aged 65 or over). Only Arkansas and Arizona will reach this level in the year 2020. By that time, Florida will have over one-quarter of its population aged 65 and over.

Other sunbelt states (like California and Nevada) with large numbers of older people also attract large numbers of young people. This keeps the proportion of older people relatively low. The movement of many Baby Boomers to the sunbelt, for example, has delayed population aging in that region until later in this century. But, Longino (2001, citing Frey, 1999) says, "this pattern should continue to fuel the aging of the Sunbelt in the early decades of the 21st century." Only Florida has both large numbers and a large proportion of older people. Florida in 2000 had six of the ten cities in the United States with the highest proportions of older people. Clearwater, Florida, in that year had 21.5 percent of its population aged 65 and over (Hetzel & Smith, 2001).

Interstate Migration

Willa Reich lived in Manhattan all of her adult life. When she was in her 60s, her son and his family moved to Florida, but her daughter and her daughter's family remained in the city, a few minutes away by car. Willa's apartment was a short subway ride from her job, and with her daughter nearby, she felt content where she was.

Nevertheless, when Willa retired at age 65, she began to consider a move. She had a good pension from the city, Social Security, and some savings. The neighborhood had gotten worse, the winters felt more severe, and her son in Florida kept asking her to move south. She went to look at a condominium apartment north of Miami during one visit to her son. The complex had a clubhouse, swimming pools, a lake, a transportation system, and recreation activities. Her son lived only an hour away by car. She decided to move. Two years later her daughter and family moved to a town a few miles away. Willa now has both her children and grandchildren nearby, and she enjoys the life-style she wants. Willa will probably live in her new community for the rest of her life.

Willa's decision to move to a southern small town fits a pattern similar to that of many older people today. Demographers find that migration patterns follow the life course. Studies done in the 1980s found a stable pattern that has lasted for decades. The tendency to move peaks at around age 20 to 24. This coincides with students leaving school and with marriage. Younger people move to find jobs and set up their own families. From age 35 on, the tendency to move declines slowly until retirement. Children, a job, and community ties all limit the tendency to move during the middle years. Migration picks up again for some people between ages 60 and 70 after people retire. An increase in migration occurs again at the end of life due to declines in health (Longino, 2004).

Longino (2001) says that people tend to move for three reasons in old age: retirement, moderate disability, and major chronic disability.

Retirement

The first type of move, at retirement, Longino (1990; 1992) calls **amenity migration**. People move to enjoy a new life-style, to be with friends who have moved, or to establish a new identity as a retiree. He also describes another kind of amenity move: a move back to a person's childhood home state. People who do this often moved in their youth to find work. They then return to their roots in retirement. African Americans have a relatively high rate of this type of migration.

Moderate Disability

The second type of move is what Wiseman and Roseman (1979) call "kinship migration," or what

Meyer and Speare (1985) call "assistance moves." This takes place when the older retiree moves back near his or, more often, her children. Illness, disability, or widowhood lead to this move. People who live in rural areas will move to more urban centers at this time so they can get the health care and support they need from their children and from social services.

Major Chronic Disability

The third move comes near the end of life. Meyer and Speare (1985) call this a move in "preparation for aging." Older people move from a community setting (their own home, an apartment, or living with their children) to an institution. These moves often take place within the person's local community. This move coincides with increased disability and the need for institutional health care.

Amenity Migration

Longino (1990, p. 52) says that people who make their first move after retirement look for "places of natural beauty and more pleasant climates." Studies in Canada, Great Britain, and the United States report the same results. Older people tend to migrate to specific areas. Mobile older people tend to move to places with a mild climate often by the coast. They also look for places with a reasonable cost of living (Walters, 2002). "The pattern is never random," Longino (1990, p. 52) says, "nor are migrants randomly selected from among all older people." For example, Hazelrigg and Hardy (1995) found that most migrants are retired, married, and generally have higher incomes than their peers in their new location. They also have more education and better health than older people who stay put. Migrants are also "overwhelmingly Anglo" (Longino, 1990, p. 53).

Research shows that destination characteristics tend to determine the place people choose, more than nearness or distance from the preretirement home. Some states in the United States have a great attraction for retirees. Ten states received 56.3 percent of out-of-state migrants aged 60 and over in 1990. Longino (2001) notes some changing trends in interstate migration. First, the top receiving states lost some share of interstate migrants between 1980 and 1990.

Also, California slid from 13.6 percent of all older migrants in 1960 to 6.9 percent in 1990. The high cost of living and relatively high taxes in California help explain this decrease in migration. Still,

"The kids are grown before you know it, aren't they?"

the sunbelt states get the largest share of migrating retirees. Florida, California, Arizona, Texas, and North Carolina get the largest streams of older migrants from states outside their regions. Longino (2001, p. 111) calls these "national destination states."

Longino (2001, 2004) notes some counterintuitive trends. For example, many retirees migrate to attractive places in neighboring states. New Yorkers and people from Pennsylvania often migrate to the New Jersey shore. Cape Cod, the Wisconsin Dells, and the Pocono Mountains of Pennsylvania attract retirees. Also, older people move out of sunbelt states. Florida, for example, contains the one hundred top counties that send migrants out of state. Disability and the need to live near their children motivates these moves. Los Angeles county seniors often move to Arizona, Nevada, or Oregon. Relief from the high cost of living and a more relaxed life-style draws them to these locations.

Often, migrants have visited a place before. Some have even lived in the place for part of the year in the years before they move. Some never move permanently. They live in a sunbelt location until the weather turns hot. Then, they head back north to their homes. Longino (2001) refers to these people as "seasonal" or "cyclical" migrants. These people live a life-style different from that of permanent migrants.

Some permanent migrants take part in community life. Others remain aloof and bond with other migrants. They never become part of the community. Longino (1992) says that migrants should think about their social needs as well as the climate before they make a move. The charm of golf or fishing, he says, will wear off in a year. People need to think about the community life, the culture, and the kinds of services they use (e.g., a library or a theater). "Long-term satisfaction," he says, "is more strongly determined by whether or not they can do the things they want to do and be the person they want to be in retirement" (Longino, 1992, p. 30).

The migration of older people to sunbelt states after retirement sometimes creates tension between the migrants and the long-time residents. Some Sunbelt communities fear that older migrants will lead to increased health and social service costs. But when Longino (1990) reviewed the data on health, transportation, and service use in host communities, he found no evidence for the supposed high costs of older people.

In 1995, when Sidney Amber was 109, he worked as a weekend host for Sears' restaurant near Union Square in San Francisco. Sidney wore out three birth certificates, paid Social Security past the age of 100, and attributed his long life to a shot of Lea & Perrins Worcestershire Sauce several times a week.

In the south, for example, except for Florida, most older migrants came from the region or were returning to their native states. Local residents saw them as natives. Longino (2001) reports that Florida's income from older migrants came to $8.3 billion between 1985 and 1990 (up from $4 billion in 1975 to 1980). Sastry (1992) found that retiree migrants had large positive economic effects on the Florida economy. Retirees contribute by spending their pension funds and paying taxes. This benefits older and younger people The migration of older people also creates jobs in host communities.

Experts still disagree on the benefits of older peoples' migration to an area. Research shows that older people create economic growth in smaller towns and retirement settings. But as these older people age, they may place new demands on their communities.

The long-term cost may outweigh the short-term benefit of migration to a community. Continued migration by younger retirees will offset this cost. So will out-migration that often takes place late in life. The complexity of migration decisions and trends makes it difficult to predict future costs or benefits.

Urban–Rural Distribution

In the United States, about three-quarters of older people live in metropolitan counties (with a city of 50,000 or more people) (Longino, 2001). Longino (2001) says that from the 1950s onward, older people have tended to live in suburbs of these cities. Central cities have attracted more young people. And older populations in suburbs have increased proportionately as children move out and older people age in place.

Two trends explain the presence of older people in cities. First, many older people in the city centers have always lived there and will age in place. They have close friends in the neighborhood. They see

BOX 4.2
LIFE IN A RETIREMENT COMMUNITY
Pro and Con

I recently visited a friend who lives in a retirement community near Fort Lauderdale, Florida. At the main entrance, a line of cars waited to get in. A security guard walked up to my car with a clipboard and asked whom I was visiting. I told him and said that my host had called ahead to clear my arrival. He went into a guardhouse to check the guest list. When he returned, he asked to see my driver's license, then walked around the car to check the license plate and jot down the number. Finally, he waved me through. By this time I felt hot, bothered, and ready to turn around.

I have had an easier time crossing national borders than getting into this community. The delay may have annoyed me as a visitor, but the person I visited loves living here. She has made new friends and keeps busy with exercise classes, mah jong, and movies. She also likes the sense of security she gets from the high fence and the guardhouse at the entrance.

Many other older people feel the same way about their retirement communities. These enclaves attract more people every year. They offer a life-style that many older people want in retirement. Sun City in Arizona, one of the largest retirement communities in the United States, has 50,000 residents and its own banks, shopping plazas, golf courses, and restaurants. Retirement communities offer a self-contained world. They offer convenience, social activity, and security.

Critics see a downside to retirement communities. Kastenbaum says these communities can create a "fortress mentality." They often cut themselves off from the local community and from local social issues. Some communities refuse to pay taxes for the local school system. People in these settings may even cut themselves off from their families. "An old man and woman move down here and build a mansion," Jim Martin, retiree and social activist says. "Then he dies and she's left living in his mausoleum. Then what? They cut all their lifelines to everybody!" (cited in Crispell & Frey, 1994).

Some communities limit the length of stay of anyone under eighteen. Some communities discourage visits by families with young children. Gerber, Wolff, Klores, and Brown (1989) quote one of the rules at a retirement community in Florida: "Children require the constant supervision of those responsible for them. They must be kept from interfering in any way with the quiet and comfort of residents."

How would you feel about living in a community like this? What are the pros and cons of retirement community living? Would you want your parents or grandparents to move to one? Would you like to visit them there?

Sources: "American Maturity," by D. Crispell & W. H. Frey, 1995, in H. Cox, Ed., *Aging* (10th ed.), Guilford, CT: Dushkin. *Lifetrends: The Future of Baby Boomers and Other Aging Americans,* J. Gerber, J. Wolff, W. Klores, & G. Brown, 1989, New York: Macmillan. "Encrusted Elders: Arizona and the Political Spirit of Postmodern Aging," by R. Kastenbaum, 1993, in T. R. Cole, W. A. Achenbaum, P. L. Jakobi, & R. Kastenbaum, Eds., *Voices and Visions of Aging: Toward a Critical Gerontology,* New York: Springer.

neighbors and friends when they shop or go to church. Those who live in cities outside institutions tend to be non-white, have the least money, have low mobility, and live alone.

In 1990, for example, elderly Hispanics had an eight times greater likelihood of living inside than outside a metropolitan area. Elderly African Americans had a four times greater likelihood of living in a city than outside one. Whites had only a three times greater likelihood of living in a city than outside one. Older minority group members in cities sometimes have problems getting to and using social and health care services. Barriers like language, poverty, poor transportation, and lack of knowledge about services may keep people from using programs.

Second, Smith (2004) describes a tendency for educated former suburbanites to move back to the city in later life. She reports that this group of older people enjoy the culture and services that big cities offer. One couple that moved from the Washington suburbs to a downtown neighborhood said that the museums and cultural events only partly explain their move. "It's the restaurants, it's the stores, it's the sense of vitality on the streets, the diversity of age and ethnic groups. It's a lively atmosphere to live in."

This trend may grow as the Baby Boom ages, and some of its members choose the excitement of city living. Smith reports that Del Webb, the company that pioneered the Sun City life-style in the southwest, has begun to develop city-oriented properties. They have considered developing an urban high-rise retirement community for active people who want to live downtown.

Suburban communities also show an increase in older people and in the proportion of older people. At least three trends account for this increase. First, suburbs attracted young couples after World War II. As these people age in place, they increase the number and proportion of older people in the suburbs. This trend accounts for most of the increase in older people in suburbs today.

Second, the children of these older people grow up and move away. This leads to a greater proportion of older people in certain suburbs. Third, some older people move to the suburbs when they retire (Longino, 2001). These people tend to be married, have more money, and live in their own homes. They may move into suburban or small-town retirement communities. Preston (1993) projects an increase in the size of smaller centers when Baby Boomers retire.

Changes in the Sex Ratio

The sex ratio shows the proportion of men to women in the population. The formula for the sex ratio looks like this:

$$\text{Sex ratio} = \frac{\text{Number of men} \times 100}{\text{Number of women}}$$

A ratio of one hundred for people aged 65 and over would mean an older population with one man for every woman. The lower the ratio, the smaller the proportion of men in the older population.

In 1900, men aged 60 and over in the United States outnumbered women in that age group 105 to 100 (Hobbs & Stoop, 2002). These figures reflect the high rates of female deaths due to childbirth at the turn of the century. This ratio has declined throughout most of the twentieth century. In 2000, the older population had a ratio of 96.3 men for every 100 women (Hobbs & Stoop, 2002).

At least two trends account for the increase of women over men in later life: (1) better health care for women during their childbearing and middle years, and (2) increases in cigarette smoking and work-related diseases among men in this century. But recently, this trend has begun to reverse itself. Between 1980 and 2002, the gap in life expectancy between men and women narrowed. A girl born in 1980 could expect to live 7.4 years longer than a boy born in that year. But a girl born in 2002 could expect to live only 5.2 years longer than her male counterpart (National Center for Health Statistics, 2004b).

These figures show a convergence of life expectancies for men and women. This may be due to increased cigarette use by women. Also, large numbers of women have entered the work force, and they now face the same working conditions as men.

Table 4.2 shows the sex ratio at various ages. Notice that the ratio declines with each older age group. In 2001, the group aged 95 to 99 has a ratio about one-third that of the 65- to 69-age group. This

TABLE 4.2
U.S. Sex Ratios by Age for Selected Years

	Year			
Age	*2001*	*2030*	*2050*	*2070*
65–69	85.2	89.1	90.2	91.7
70–74	80.1	85.9	87.5	89.9
75–79	72.1	80.6	83.4	87.7
80–84	62.2	72.9	77.9	82.9
85–89	49.5	63.2	70.2	75.9
90–94	37.5	52.8	60.6	67.5
95–99	28.9	43.0	51.0	58.7
100+	22.0	33.1	40.9	49.4

The sex ratio is the proportion of men to women in the population. The figures in the table represent the number of men for every one hundred women. In any given year, compared with younger age groups, older age groups show lower sex ratios. This occurs because the proportion of men in an age cohort decreases over time. Note that demographers expect more men to survive in each age group in the future. This leads to higher sex ratios. Demographers predict that the life expectancy of men and women will come closer together in the future. This will mean a decrease in the rates of widowhood and more married couples in the older population.

Source: U.S. Census Bureau. (2000). Projections of the Total Resident Population by 5-Year Age Groups, and Sex with Special Age Categories: Middle Series, 2001 to 2005, 2025 to 2045, 2050 to 2070. Population Projections Program. Population Division. Washington, D.C. Retrieved: April 26, 2004, *www.census.gov/population/projections/nation/summary/np-t3-b.pdf* and *np-t3-f.pdf*, and *np-t3-g.pdf*.

reflects the greater life expectancy of older women compared with older men.

This low sex ratio points to another characteristic of the older population today. Women stand a greater chance of widowhood than men. Several factors account for this. First, women tend to marry older men. Second, men have a shorter life expectancy than women in later life. Third, whereas men tend to remarry, women tend to stay single. In 2002, for example, only 13.9 percent of men aged 65 and over were widowed; in that same year and age group, 45.5 percent of women were widowed (U.S. Census Bureau, 2004b).

The higher proportion of women in later life and their greater chance of widowhood makes old age a different experience for women and men today. Women, more than men, have to adapt to a singles' life-style. They need to create social supports outside of marriage. And they have a greater stake in the quality and availability of services and supports in later life.

The future of aging for men and women may look different due to the increases in the life expectancy of men. Happily married couples will live more years together. And women who experience widowhood will typically do so at a later age. This will provide women as well as men with more in-home support in later life.

THE IMPACT OF POPULATION AGING

Dependency Ratios

The aging of the older population will lead to change in what demographers call the **total dependency ratio**. This is the ratio of the 0 to 14 and 65 and older age groups to the rest of the population (aged 15 to 64). This ratio gives a crude measure of how many middle-aged (working) people exist to support younger and older people in the population.

Demographers express the total dependency ratio in the following formula:

$$\text{Total dependency ratio} = \frac{\text{Population 0 to 14 plus population 65+} \times 100}{\text{Population 15 to 64}}$$

Table 4.3 introduces the concept of the elderly and youth dependency ratios. The **elderly dependency ratio** refers to the number of people aged 65 and over divided by the population aged 15 to 64, multiplied by one hundred. The **youth dependency ratio** refers to the number of people aged 0 to 14 divided by the population aged 15 to 64, multiplied by one hundred. These ratios show how these two subgroups contribute to the total dependency ratio.

Table 4.3 gives a good summary of recent demographic change in the United States. The total dependency ratio decreased from 1990 to 2000 and picks up again into the middle of the next century. In 2050 it reaches a level similar to that of 1930.

TABLE 4.3
U.S. Dependency Ratios

Year	*Old Age Ratio*	*Youth Ratio*	*Total Ratio*
1990	19.0	32.9	51.9
1995	19.6	33.5	53.1
1998	19.4	32.7	52.1
2000	19.1	32.2	51.3
2025	30.1	32.2	62.3
2050	33.9	33.0	66.9

The measurement of dependency ratios differs from one source to another. This source uses ages 0 to 14 as the measure of youth, ages 65 and over as the measure of old age, and ages 15 to 64 as the measure of the general population (neither youth nor aged).

The old age dependency ratio measures the relationship between the population aged 65 and over and the general population (aged 15 to 64). The youth dependency ratio measures the relationship between the population under age 15 and the general population (aged 15 to 64). Addition of these two ratios gives the total dependency ratio. These figures provide an indication of how many people in the general population exist to support younger and older people in the population.

Note that the composition of the total ratio changes over time. In 1990 young people made up 37 percent of the total ratio. By the middle of this century (2050), older people will make up more than one-half of the total dependency ratio. The traditional view of the old age dependency ratio holds that older people make large demands on society's resources. But as healthier, better educated, and active older people enter old age, they may not follow this traditional pattern.

Source: U.S. Census Bureau. (2000). Population and Dependency Ratios per 100 Persons, Four Series, 1990 to 2100. Washington, D.C. (Middle series projections). Retrieved: January 6, 2005, *www.census.gov/population/documentation/twps0038/tabF.txt.*

Several considerations are worth noting.

- First, the elderly and youth dependency ratios make up different proportions of the total dependency ratio at different points in time. Until 1950, for example, the youth dependency ratio made up almost the entire total dependency ratio. In 2050, older people account for half the total dependency ratio.
- Second, the elderly dependency ratio increases throughout this period. But, it makes a sudden jump after the year 2000.
- Third, the youth dependency ratio stays roughly the same from 1990 to 2050.
- Fourth, the ratio of working people aged 15 to 64 to those aged 65 and over decreases dramatically into the next century. By 2050, the United States will have only 2.5 younger adults for each older person.

This table shows that the increase in total dependency ratio is due to an increase in older people in the population. Some see this as a sign of trouble in the future. They see this as a shift from lower cost programs for younger people to high-cost programs for older people. Kotlikoff (1993), for example, warns about increased costs for health care and potentially less investment in long-term programs like care for the environment, infrastructure improvements (roads and bridges), and education.

A smaller number of children may reduce the costs for schooling. This could allow local and state governments to meet the higher costs of an aging population. But, not counting the costs for public schools, children rely mostly on private support from their parents. An older population depends more on public sources of support. This means that the same total dependency ratio, but with a higher elderly dependency ratio, may mean greater social cost in the future.

Programs such as Medicare and Social Security depend on intergenerational support. They assume that society will transfer some funds from the younger generation to the older generation. This works well today with a large working-age population and a relatively small older population. The future will see a large group of older people depend on a smaller group of younger people. Peterson (1999, cited in Korczyk, 2002) takes a gloomy view of the future. He calls the increase in older people a "global hazard" that "may actually do more to shape our collective future than deadly superviruses, extreme climate change or the proliferation of nuclear, biological and chemical weapons."

Not everyone agrees with this conclusion. A look at other countries with populations older than the United States suggests how the United States can adapt to an aging population. Many societies have

Friends from a Salado, Texas, retirement community share a hot tub. One of them, Liz Carpenter, says, "Aging has become very stylish." She notes that "All the best people are doing it."

greater elderly dependency ratios than the United States. Countries like Sweden and Austria already have dependency ratios similar to those projected for the United States in the next century. These countries have not faced a crisis due to their aging populations. They have well-developed social welfare systems and some of the highest standards of living in the world. This suggests that the United States can adapt to an older population in the future without crisis or social upheaval.

Easterlin (1991) reports similar findings. He studied the demographic patterns in ten European countries and the United States from 1870 to the present and projected to 2050. He found that in 2040 these countries have greater total dependency ratios than at present, but "overall dependency levels as projected for the first half of the 21st century are not out of line with what has been experienced in the past century" (Easterlin, 1991, pp. S302, S305).

Jackson and colleagues (2003) studied old age dependency ratios in twelve countries. The study assessed, among other things, the public burden of an aging population. The study placed the United States (along with Australia and the United Kingdom) in a low-vulnerability category. The authors say that the modest dependency ratio in the future and a pension system balanced between public and private sources will allow the United States to adapt to its aging population. These authors and others (Korczyk, 2002) take a close look at dependency ratios and fail to see an economic crisis due to population aging.

Critique of Dependency Ratios

The conclusions drawn from dependency ratios seem self-evident. The word *dependency* itself leads to the conclusion that more older people will place a greater burden on society. A closer look at this measure, however, raises questions about its ability to predict the future. For example, this formula assumes that all people in an age group behave the same and have the same needs. Dependency ratios assume that all people aged 20 to 64 work, support themselves, and support the older and younger populations. But many people aged 20 to 64 (college students, for example, and unemployed people) depend on others or public funds for their income.

Dependency ratios also assume that all people aged 65 and over depend on younger people (or public support). But many older people work part-time or have private pensions and savings that make them independent of public support. Some Baby Boomers in their preretirement years have opted for new careers rather than retirement. These people prefer new career opportunities and income to government pensions (Reynolds, 2004). If this trend continues, these people will stay at work long past the current retirement age of 65.

The dependency ratio may serve as a handy way to look at the cost of an aging society, but it creates a fiction based on weak assumptions. The dependency ratio assumes that an older population will only increase societal costs. But more older people in society may lead to a better use of resources. An older society, for example, will have a lower crime rate, lower auto accident rate, and increased concern for fitness and disease prevention. Older people, many with good incomes, will spend their savings on travel, restaurants, and professional services. Many older people will help support their younger family members and will give to their communities as volunteers. These trends will make better use of social resources and create a better quality of life for all age groups.

Korczyk (2002) says that the characteristics of older people (e.g., their health) and social policies have the greatest effect on the cost of an older population. Retirement policies today, for example, encourage retirement at age 65. Ironically, countries with the highest elderly dependency ratios encourage older people to leave the work force early. They appear to demand economic dependency by the older population.

In the future, these countries may rethink these policies. The United States has already taken action. Over the next few years, it will gradually raise the age of eligibility for full Social Security payments. Marmor (2001) says that the government can also control Medicare and other health care costs. He shows that practices like the use of Diagnosis Related Groups begun in the 1980s can control and reduce hospital fees. Koitz and his colleagues (2002; *also* Thau & Roszak, 2001) say that government planning for an older population should start immediately.

A stronger economy and improved private pension plans would reduce the impact of an older population on public funds. Korczyk (2002) says that society's economic stablity and growth would expand the job market. It would allow people to save for retirement, and it would provide young people with good salaries. This will help them pay for services that will support an older population. Better private pension plans would help people stay financially independent in later life.

Friedland and Summer (1999, p. 5) say that "society can and will adjust [to an aging population] as it has done before. But adjustment will be easier if the challenges are addressed in a rational manner today." How well the United States manages this shift will depend on how well people understand population aging and how well our society prepares for change. Much of this planning has begun, but more will have to take place in the years ahead. Preparation for the future will take planning, thought, and creative social action, and all of us will play a part in this societal transformation.

CONCLUSION

I worked for some years at a university campus in a northern city. I headed home one day in January and noticed my wife about a block ahead of me, pushing one of our children in a baby carriage. She reached the corner of the busiest intersection in town and began to cross when the light changed. The slush from the cars slowed the wheels of the carriage in the street and she only made it to the center island. There she climbed the snow bank and hauled the carriage (and our child) up to safety.

As she caught her breath, she noticed that an elderly woman had just reached the bottom of the snow bank and was trying to climb up. The traffic had started and the woman looked scared. My wife reached down and helped the woman to safety. They stood breathing hard in the cold air with a look of weary triumph. They had both braved the city streets and won a small victory.

People imagine that more social services, longer traffic lights, or new architectural designs to serve an older population will inhibit social life. The demographic doomsayers imagine that an older population will bring only higher costs. But an older society can benefit all of us. In the previous story, the older woman needed a longer red light to cross the street, but so did my wife and our baby. And I wouldn't mind if I didn't have to climb over snow mountains to get on the bus or risk a concussion when the bus whips into traffic just as I move toward my seat. An older society might be a more humane society. And a more enjoyable place for all of us.

SUMMARY

- The United States population aged steadily for the past century and will continue to age in the future. Social scientists believe that population aging will lead to social change, but they do not think that it will lead to conflict, crisis, and more social problems.
- Demographers study the aging of society and the impact of societal aging on social institutions. Demographers use three measures of population aging: the absolute number of older people in a society, the median age of the population, and the increased proportion of older people.
- Population change occurs due to migration, deaths, and births. The decline in the fertility rate is the major cause of population aging in the United States today.
- Demographers divide the older population into subgroups. They refer to young-, middle-, and old-old. Each of these groups have unique needs.
- Internal migration has led to a shift in the proportions of the older population in different parts of the United States. It has led to decreases in the proportion of older people in the northeast and to increases in the proportion of older people in the south, midwest, and west.
- People tend to move for three reasons in old age. Gerontologists call the first type of move a retirement move, the second type, a moderate disability move, and the third type, a major chronic disability move.
- Two things account for the greater number of women to men at every age in later life. First, better health care for women during their childbearing and middle years. Second, increases in cigarette smoking and work-related diseases for men. Current trends show an improvement for life expectancy for men. This may lead to more similar numbers of men and women in old age in the future.
- Demographic studies show an increase in the elderly dependency ratio. Some researchers believe that this increase will lead to a future crisis in the cost of services for older people. Other researchers believe that the older population will lead society to a better use of resources. Most gerontologists agree that U.S. society needs to prepare for an aging population. New policies and new approaches to services can meet the challenges of population aging.
- U.S. society will need to change to meet the needs of older people. Many of these changes will lead to a better quality of life for all age groups.

DISCUSSION QUESTIONS

1. List the measures that demographers use to describe population aging. Give the strengths and weaknesses of each measure.
2. State three changes in social institutions that will come about due to population aging.
3. What are the three causes of population change in the United States today? What effect does a declining birth rate have on population aging? Why does it have this effect?
4. List some of the pros and cons of having children today. Do you think that young people in the United States today want to have many or few children? Think for a moment about how many children you would like to have. What about your friends and other people your age? What effect will today's decisions about having children have on the future age structure of the U.S. population?
5. How long do you expect to live? How does that influence your decisions with respect to diet, exercise, relationships, career, and any other important component of your life? What if life expectancy was 120 years or 150 years? How would you think differently about your life? What differences would it make in planning your future?
6. Describe the migration patterns of older people in the past twenty years or so. Do you know anyone who has migrated within the United States after retirement? Where did they move from? Where did they move to? Why did they move? Were they satisfied with their move?
7. Look at the three population pyramids presented in this chapter. Compare the size of the older population (65 and older) with the younger population (age 14 and under). What do you see? Compare the ratio of men and women in the three oldest age groups. Now compare one pyramid with another and look at the total size of the three oldest age groups. What accounts for the different shapes of these pyramids?

8. Give three reasons why an older
greater chance than an older man o
a spouse? What social changes may
hood for women less common in the fu

SUGGESTED READING

Korczyk, S. M., AARP. Public Policy Insitute, & AARP. (
Back to which future: The U.S. aging crisis revisited. W
ington, D.C.: Public Policy Institute, AARP. Available on
at *http://research.aarp.org/econ/2002_18_aging.pdf.*

This paper looks at many of the issues presented in thi chapter. It also assesses the impact of population aging on health and income in later life as well as the cost of health care. The paper concludes that demography is not destiny. The effect of population aging on society will depend on the health and abilities of the older population as well as on public policy.

Frey, W. H., DeVol, R. C., & Milken Institute. (2000). *America's demography in the new century: Aging baby boomers and new immigrants as major players.* Santa Monica, CA: Milken Institute.

This policy paper looks at two demographic trends: the aging of the Baby Boom and the immigration of Asians and Hispanics to the U.S. It looks at the impact of the Baby Boom

a ... ations be-
tw ... an upbeat, optimistic
loo ... ng in America. It lays out the chal-
leng ... pportunities that lie ahead.

GLOSSARY OF TERMS

absolute number of older people The total number of older people in a society.

amenity migration A move in retirement in order to enjoy the life-style in a new location. People in the colder northern United States might make amenity migrations to the sunbelt.

birth rate The number of live births per 1,000 population.

death rate The number of deaths per 1,000 people of a given age. Demographers translate this into life expectancy at a given age.

demography The study of the size, structure, and development of human populations.

demographic determinism The belief that a specific population change leads to a specific social change (e.g., that an aging population will lead to higher costs to society).

elderly dependency ratio The ratio of people aged 65 and over to the population aged 15 to 64.

fertility rate The number of live births regardless of age of mother per 1,000 women aged 15 to 44.

in-migration Migration into a country, region, or state.

median age One-half the population is above and one-half below the median age.

migration Movement into or out of a country or other area. Internal migration can take place from one region of a country to another.

out-migration Movement out of a country, region, or state.

population aging An increase in the number of older people in a society, an increase in a society's median age, or an increase in the proportion of older people in a society.

proportion of older people The number of people aged 65 and over divided by the total population, multiplied by one hundred (to give a percent).

sex ratio The ratio of men to women in the older population.

total dependency ratio The ratio of the population 0 to 14 years plus the population aged 65 and older to the population aged 15 to 64.

youth dependency ratio The ratio of the population 0 to 14 to the population aged 15 to 64.

chapter 5

L HEALTH AND WELL-BEING

Jeanne Calment of Arles, France, died in 1997 at the age of 122 years and 164 days. She lived the longest reliably documented life in human history. Ms. Calment claimed to have met Vincent Van Gogh in her father's store and to have attended Victor Hugo's funeral. For her 121st birthday she released a four-song CD and videotape entitled "Maitresse du Temps" (Time's Mistress). The songs include rap and techno numbers that back up stories from her life. In 2004, Ramona Trinidad Iglesias-Jordan (de Soler) (114 years old) claimed the title of the world's oldest person. She replaced Charlotte Benkner, the oldest woman in the United States who was also 114, but a few months younger than Ms. Iglesias-Jordan (de Soler).

How did these women live so long? For one thing, Ms. Calment stayed active throughout her life. She lived on her own in a second-floor apartment until age 110 and she rode a bicycle until age 100. Other centenarians also attribute their long life to an active life-style. Some say they like regular sex, never worry, or drink a shot of whisky before bed. One 100-year-old man claimed that he lived so long because he ate a pound of peanuts a day. Someone once said that to live 100 years, you should eat a hot bowl of oatmeal every morning for 1,200 months. The United States today has more 100 year olds than ever before. As biologists and physiologists work to extend **life expectancy** even further, more and more people will live close to the maximum human **life span** of about 120 years.

This chapter looks at the biology of aging and health in later life. It describes (1) biological theories of aging; (2) how aging affects health, activity, and life satisfaction; and (3) how people can respond to physical changes that come with age.

BIOLOGICAL AGING

Biologists and physiologists study aging in everything from one-celled animals to human populations. Austad (2001) defines biological aging as "a process of intrinsic, progresive, and generalized physical deterioration that occurs over time. . . ." **Intrinsic aging** includes decreases in lung capacity, loss of brain cells, and hardened arteries. **Extrinsic aging** includes changes in the body due to sunlight, smoking, or noise. Scientists try to separate out the effects of these two causes of aging (Austad, 2001).

Strehler (1977; *see also* Williams, 1992) lists four criteria for intrinsic (or true) aging. First, true aging is universal. It occurs in all members of a species if they live long enough. Wrinkled skin in humans fits this definition. Second, true aging is basic to the organism. A person cannot undo it or stop it. Decreased lung elasticity falls into this category. Third, true aging is progressive. Debris accumulates in the cell over time until the cell stops working. Fourth, true aging is deleterious. It leads to decline in physical function. This puts the person at risk of illness and leads to death.

These criteria describe **senescence**, normal functional decline that takes place in the human body over time. If you have any doubt what senescence means, do a simple test. Gently pinch the skin on the back of a baby's hand, then pinch the skin on your own hand and the skin on a 70 year old's hand. Notice that you can hardly get a grip on the chubby skin of a baby. Your skin and the older person's skin will feel thinner and less elastic. Notice that the baby's skin pops back into place immediately. The older person's skin may form a slight peak that remains after you take your hand away. The effects of senescence will differ from person to person (due to genetics and variation in body functions), but in general, skin elasticity declines with age.

Scientists want to know why this and other intrinsic changes take place over time. They want to know what causes intrinsic aging. Why, for example, does skin become less elastic? Why don't cells in the human body live forever? Scientists have developed a number of theories to explain intrinsic aging.

THEORIES OF BIOLOGICAL AGING

Aldwin and Gilmer (2004) say that over a dozen biological theories of aging exist. Biological theories of aging often reflect the methods and models of researchers and their disciplines as much as the basic processes of aging. This chapter presents a variety of theories. Each gives some insight into how the body ages.

Schneider (1992) places these theories in one of two groups: (1) Programmed theories locate the cause of aging in the action of inherited genes; and (2) error theories locate the cause of aging in the normal function of the body over time. Probably both of these causes play some role in aging. These two causes, working together, lead to decreased ability of the body to fight off internal and external threats. This in turn leads to an increased chance of death as the body ages.

Programmed Theories

Programmed theories say that the same processes that cause animals to grow and thrive also lead to senescence and death. Scientists have found the strongest evidence for programmed senescence in the body's cells.

Programmed Senescence

Human life begins with a single fertilized cell. This cell divides many times to form the human body. Some cells—such as those in the brain and spinal cord—stop dividing in youth. Other cells—such as intestinal cells and blood cells—divide throughout life. Until the 1960s, scientists thought that cells could divide an unlimited number of times, but Hayflick and Moorehead (1961) found that cell division had a limit, and that this limit differed for each species. Scientists refer to this as the **Hayflick Limit**.

Tortoise cells, for example, divide 90 to 125 times before they die. Chicken cells divide fifteen to thirty-five times, and human embryo cells forty to sixty times. Hayflick and Moorehead found that the older the cell donor, the fewer times the cell could divide before death. Cells from young people, for example, could divide about fifty times before they stopped. Cells from adults could divide only about twenty times more before they died. Based on these findings Hayflick and Moorehead estimated the human life span at 110 to 120 years.

Hayflick and Moorhead took their research a step further and looked inside the cell to see why cell division stopped. They found that before cells die, their structure and function change. They found that cells showed signs of aging after a year of active division in the lab. These cells took a longer time to double, gradually stopped dividing, accumulated debris, and in the end totally degenerated. Cells produce less energy, make enzymes more slowly, and allow waste to fill up inside them. Eventually cells stop dividing. Biologists call this the **phase III phenomenon**.

These results show that (1) cells undergo programmed decline, (2) the rate of decline differs for each organism, and (3) genetic differences play a role in determining an organism's life span (Hayflick, 1996). To understand these changes at the cellular and systemic level, some scientists look to the molecular and genetic structure of the cell.

Aldwin and Gilmer (2004; *also* Wang, Autexier, & Chen, 2001) describe the process of apoptosis. *Apoptosis* is a genetic process that switches off the cell's ability to divide. This process controls growth and produces normal development. But it also leads to cell death and breakdown in the body over time.

Crews (1993) describes another genetic process that leads to physical aging. Researchers find that some genes serve a positive function early in life, but damage the system later. Scientists call these **pleiotropic genes**. A gene, for example, might order calcium production in a 10 year old. A young person's body needs calcium to build bones and teeth. This same gene might lead to too much calcium in a 60 year old. This could produce calcium deposits in the person's arteries. Apoptosis and pleiotropy suggest that aging occurs as a by-product of normal human development (Gerhard & Cristofalo, 1992). More knowledge of genes' actions might allow scientists to turn genes on and off as needed. This could prevent or reverse aging.

Endocrine and Immunological Theory

Some scientists have looked at entire systems of the body to understand aging. For example, researchers have known for some time that the production of the sex hormones estrogen and testosterone tends to decrease as we age (Harman et al., 2000). Other studies show that the timing of hormonal release and the responsiveness of tissues to hormones also decline with age (Bartke & Lane, 2001). The age-related decline in hormones may trigger the aging process in humans.

BOX 5.1

THE LONGEVITY TEST

No one yet has found the secret to longevity, but modern science offers some clues about how to live a longer and probably a healthier life. Dr. Elliott Howard, a New York City cardiologist, has created a longevity test based on government research and his own patients. The test asks you to review your health history, family background, and life-style. Although it cannot predict your exact length of life, it allows you to compare yourself to average Americans who live into their 70s. The test also serves as a good survey of the topics that gerontologists study in order to understand physical aging.

For each category below, circle the appropriate numerical factor in the lefthand column and enter the total score for that category. Add the total scores for all categories to arrive at your life style risk level.

Personal History

Choose all that apply:

–2 No cancer or heart disease in parents who live beyond age 75
–1 No cancer or heart disease in one parent who lived beyond age 75
+2 Coronary heart disease before age 50 in one or both parents
+3 Coronary heart disease before age 40 in one or both parents
+2 High blood pressure before age 50 in one parent
+3 High blood pressure before age 50 in both parents
+1 Diabetes mellitus before age 60 in one or both parents
+2 Cancer in a parent or sibling
+2 Stroke before age 60 in one parent

Total:

Weight

Your weight is:

0 Always at or near ideal weight
+1 Now 10% over ideal weight
+2 Now 20 to 29% over ideal weight
+3 Now 30 to 39% over ideal weight
+4 More than 40% over ideal weight

Total:

Blood Pressure

Your blood pressure is:

–2 Below 121/71
0 121/71 to 140/85
+2 141/86 to 170/100
+4 171/101 to 190/110
+6 Above 190/110

Total:

Cholesterol

Your blood cholesterol level is:

–2 150 to 170
–1 171 to 190
0 191 to 210
+1 211 to 240
+2 241 to 280
+3 281 to 320
+4 Over 320

Your high-density lipoprotein (HDL) cholesterol level is:

–2 66 to 80
–1 51 to 65
0 41 to 50
+1 31 to 40
+2 25 to 30
+3 Below 25

Total:

Smoking

You don't smoke now. In the past, you:

–1 Never did, or quit over 5 years ago
0 Quit 1 to 5 years ago
+1 Quit within the past year

You now smoke:

+1 Pipe or cigars
+2 Less than a pack of cigarettes a day
+3 A pack a day
+4 1 to 1½ packs a day
+5 2 packs a day
+5 And drink alcohol 5 or more times a week
+3 And take birth control pills

(continued)

BOX 5.1
(Continued)

You have smoked:
+3 for at least 10 years
+5 For more than 20 years
Total:

Alcohol

You drink:
−1 Never or rarely
0 No more than 5 oz. of wine, 12 oz. of beer, or 1½ oz. of hard liquor 5 times a week
+1 Two glasses of alcohol a day
+2 More than two glasses a day
Total:

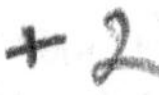

Exercise

To keep fit, you:
−2 Exercise vigorously more than 45 minutes 4 or 5 times a week
−1 Exercise vigorously at least 30 minutes 3 times a week
0 Exercise moderately at least 30 minutes 3 to 5 times a week
+1 Exercise moderately at least twice a week
+2 Exercise usually on weekends or less than twice a week
+3 Rarely or never exercise
Total:

Diet

Your eating habits include (choose all that apply):
+2 Using salt freely without tasting food first
+2 Eating cabbage, broccoli, or cauliflower less than 3 times a week
+3 Eating high-fiber grains, such as whole-wheat bread, brown rice, and bran cereal, less than once a day
+3 Eating fruits and vegetables less than 3 times a day
+1 Following fad crash diets once or twice a year

You eat beef, bacon, or processed meats:
+3 5 to 6 times a week
+2 4 times a week
+1 2 times a week

You eat eggs:
+3 2 every day
+2 6 to 8 eggs a week
+1 4 to 6 eggs a week

You eat ice cream, cake, or rich desserts:
+2 Almost daily
+1 Several times a week

You eat butter, cream, cream cheese, and cheese:
+3 Every day
+2 Almost daily
+1 2 to 3 times a week
Total:

Stress

Describe your personality:
+1 Intense desire to get ahead
+2 Constant driving for success
+2 Easily frustrated, annoyed, or irritated
+2 Angry and hostile if losing in competition
+3 Angry and hostile even if successful
+2 Don't express anger or feelings
+2 Frequent knots in stomach, poor sleep, or headaches
+2 Hardly laugh, depressed often
+2 Constantly strive to please others rather than yourself
+2 Rarely discuss problems or feelings with others
−1 None of the above
Total:

Motor Vehicle Safety

When you travel, you (choose all that apply):
−1 Usually use mass transit
0 Travel by car less than 200 miles per week
+1 Travel by car 200 to 400 miles per week
+2 Travel by car over 400 miles per week
+2 Rarely use a seat belt
+2 Often exceed the speed limit
+2 Ride a motorcycle
+4 Ride a motorcycle without a helmet
+4 Sometimes drink and drive or ride with a driver who has been drinking
+6 Often drink and drive or ride with a driver who has been drinking
Total:

BOX 5.1
(Continued)

Interpreting Your Score

Add the totals for all categories and find the result below.

–14 to 3

Low risk. Odds are you will live a long and healthful life if you continue to limit risks.

4 to 30

Moderate risk. You can expect to live a long life but risk ill health. Like most Americans, you can change a few habits and greatly reduce your risk of cancer, stroke, heart disease, and motor vehicle accidents and perhaps add years to your life.

31 to 70

High risk. You are at considerable risk of developing a serious illness and shortened life. But you can improve your life expectancy by changing some of the habits that earned you scores of 2, 3, 4, or higher.

Over 70

Very high risk. Based on your life-style and personal history, you are at dangerous risk for serious illness and premature death unless you see a physician and eliminate as many risk factors as possible.

The items in this test give you some idea of the factors that lead to a longer (or shorter) life. How did you do? What would you need to change to improve your score? Are items missing here that you think should be included in this kind of test?

Source: "The Longevity Test," *U.S. News & World Report,* January 28, 1991, pp. 62–63. Adapted from *Health Risks,* by E. J. Howard (1986). Foundation for Study of Exercise, Stress, and the Heart.

Studies show that replacement of hormones in both men and women can help prevent some signs of aging (National Institutes of Health, 1993). Harman and colleagues (2000), for example, say that a decrease in testosterone in older men can lead to osteoporosis and broken bones. They report that in some studies of older men, testosterone replacement therapy improved lean body mass, muscle strength, and grip strength. They propose further research to explore the benefits of this treatment.

The immune system also ages. It goes into a decline as early as age 20 as the thymus gland begins to shrink. By age 50 this gland has almost ceased to exist. The decline in T cells from the thymus gland and their decline in function lead to a reduced ability to fight infection and disease. This kind of programmed change in the body may lead to age-related problems such as a higher risk of Alzheimer's disease, increased risk of cancer, and hardening of the arteries (Effros, 2001). Even in cases where the number of antibodies stays high, their quality decreases and they lose their effectiveness. Effros (2001) reports that infections cause most of the deaths in people over 80.

Programmed theories view aging as a normal part of growth and development. They link senescence to growth, development, and the body's normal functions. Any attempt to slow or stop these processes will require more knowledge of the body's cellular and genetic functions.

Error Theories

Error theories view aging as a by-product of errors or mistakes within the body. Some of these errors come from inside the cell, others from outside the cell. In both cases, they lead to declines in cellular and physical function.

Somatic Mutation Theory

Mutation theories link aging to mistakes that take place in the synthesis of proteins. The cell nucleus contains deoxyribonucleic acid (DNA) and ribonucleic acid (RNA). These chemicals help maintain the body's structure and function. To do this, DNA gets transcribed to messenger RNA (mRNA), and mRNA in turn oversees the creation of proteins that structure the cell, fight disease, and keep the body in balance. Scientists suspect that some of what we call aging comes about due to mutations or changes in DNA (Stearns & Partridge, 2001; Vijg, 2000).

DNA, RNA, and proteins face constant attack from inside and outside the body. Radiation from x-rays, for example, can damage DNA. So can chemicals in the body. Schneider (1992) says that the cell has to cope with 100,000 oxidative lesions (due to chemical attack) each day, in each cell. Damage to DNA can lead to mutations when the cell divides. This can lead to changes in mRNA and in turn to damaged proteins. Because mRNA and proteins help produce more proteins, errors compound. A large number of defective proteins would lead to cell and tissue death. Some studies have found increased DNA lesions and increased somatic mutations with age (Vijg, 2000).

Cross-linking Theory

The long-term exposure of proteins to glucose (sugar) molecules leads to a process called **glycation**. Glucose molecules attach themselves to proteins. This results in proteins binding together, or **cross-linking** (Gafni, 2001). This process increases with age. Cross-links toughen tissue and cause some of the damage associated with aging, including stiffened connective tissue, hardened arteries, and loss of nerve and kidney function. Foreign chemicals (like glucose) can set up links between the DNA strands. This may stop the strands from dividing. Pollutants like lead and smoke can also cause cross-link damage.

The body does have a way to combat cross-links. Immune system cells called **macrophages** seek out glucose molecules, engulf them, destroy them, and send them to the kidneys for elimination. However, this defense breaks down with age as kidney function declines and macrophages become less active (Effros, 2001). As a result, cross-links increase over time. The accumulation of cross-links in the body ultimately leads to physical system breakdown.

Researchers have experimented with methods to delay or prevent cross-linking. These methods include tests of a drug called amino-guanidine to inhibit cross-links and enhance the body's repair system. Cross-links may cause only a part of aging, but the study of how to prevent them means that one day medicine may be able to prevent this process.

Free Radicals Theory

Grune and Davies (2001, p. 25) describe the "oxygen paradox." Human beings need oxygen to live. Oxygen allows us to take energy from our foods. But oxygen can also damage cells and their contents.

Free radicals due to oxygen production in the body serve as one source of damage that leads to aging. Free radicals are molecules that have an unpaired electron, a large amount of free energy, and a tendency to bond with other molecules. Normal cell metabolism produces free radicals. These molecules can damage tissues and other molecules (like DNA, RNA, and cell proteins) (Austad, 2001; Sohal & Weindruch, 1996). Grune and Davies (2001, p. 41) say that some "respected scientists declare that the free radical theory of aging is the only aging theory to have stood the test of time."

Free radicals act in three phases. First, the body produces free radicals. It does this when, in the course of metabolism, an extra electron gets attached to molecular oxygen. Second, the free radical roams through the body and takes an electron from another molecule. This creates a new free radical. This chain reaction produces harmful chemicals in the body. Third, free radicals react with molecules like DNA or RNA. This ends the process but damages the cell (National Institutes of Health, 1993).

Free radicals damage many sites in the cell. The DNA in mitochondria (where oxidation takes place) face a high risk of damage (Stearns & Partridge, 2001). Studies show that free radical damage to

BOX 5.2
THE SEVEN DEADLY THINGS THAT REALLY DO US IN

Genetic researcher Aubrey de Grey thinks humans could live for as long as 5,000 years if we could overcome the following list of biological challenges to long life. The list below also serves as a good summary of biological effects on the body that lead to aging.

From Alzheimer's to wrinkles, the woeful litany of symptoms that come with aging is virtually endless. But de Grey has boiled it down to seven underlying processes. Almost all of these contribute to the major killers heart disease and stroke; cancer is an effect of no. 3.

1. **Too few new cells.** Cells of the skin, digestive tract, blood, and other systems lose the ability to renew themselves. Result: loss of muscle mass, brain cells, and bone.
2. **Too many old, harmful cells.** Cells can no longer divide as they should, refuse to die, and secrete toxic proteins, causing muscles to become fatty and skin to deteriorate.
3. **Mutations in the cell nucleus.** The nucleus is the central control area that houses DNA in trillions of our cells. Mutations in the DNA underlie cancer, and make it diabolically hard to treat.
4. **Mutations in mitochondria.** These ancient structures in the cells are the body's energy generators and have their own DNA. Mutations cause loss of vigor and may underlie diseases like Parkinson's.
5. **Junk within cells.** Cells lose the ability to break down their own waste and gradually fill up with it, causing lumps in artery walls, macular degeneration, neurodegeneration, and other ills.
6. **Junk between cells.** Proteins that are normally part of cells break away and form globs of gunk, causing Alzheimer's and some kinds of liver disease.
7. **Proteins sticking together.** Structural molecules needed for ligaments, artery walls, lenses of eyes, etc., gum together. Result: hardening of arteries, high blood pressure.

Source: "This man would have you live a really, really, really, really, long time." *Fortune Magazine,* June 14, 2004, pp. 137–142. Reprinted with permission.

DNA increases rapidly with age. It can lead to diseases like late onset diabetes, arthritis, cataracts, hypertension, and atherosclerosis (Levine & Stadtman, 1992; National Institutes of Health, 1993). Cells in the heart, brain, and skeleton also face a high risk of free radical damage because of the oxygen in their environments. Free radical attack can damage proteins. This causes a change in the protein's structure and makes it unable to perform its function. Repair systems in older cells become less efficient and older cells produce fewer antioxidants (Aldwin & Gilmer, 2004).

Free radicals also lead to an accumulation of chemical by-products in the cell. Gordon, Ronsen, and Brown (1974) report that free radicals create large fatty molecules in the cells, called **lipofuscin**. These molecules show up as brown *liver spots* on the skin. Lipofuscin makes up about 6 to 7 percent of the human heart muscle and nearly 75 percent of the volume of nerve cells by age 90 (Strehler, 1977). As lipofuscin takes up more room in the cell, it may interfere with the cell's ability to create enzymes, release energy, and get rid of wastes. This leads to more sluggish performance—a sign of aging. Researchers find that lipofuscin blocks cell reproduction and leads to cell death (von Zglinicki, Nilsson, Docke, & Brunk, 1995, cited in Aldwin & Gilmer, 2004).

The body must repair free radical damage or replace damaged cells. Fortunately, chemicals in the body, called antioxidants, bind and neutralize free radicals. Antioxidants include such nutrients as vitamins C and E and beta carotene, as well as enzymes in the body like superoxide dismutase (SOD) (Grune & Davies, 2001; Beckman & Ames, 1998). Research on food supplements suggest that certain foods (like green tea, broccoli, and cauliflower) may have an antioxidant effect. These antioxidants prevent most, but not all, oxidative damage. Some damage still accumulates with time and contributes to the deterioration of tissues and organs.

Other Theories

Programmed and error theories describe only some of the explanations of why aging takes place. Other approaches explain aging through population dynamics (Gavrilov & Gavrilova, 1991), the life history of the organism (Arking, 1991), and the theory of natural selection (Crews, 1993). Darwin, for example, said that natural selection selects genes that support the survival of an animal up to the age of reproduction. For example, animals that survive to the age of reproduction pass their genes on to the next generation. Animals that have characteristics that work against survival do not live long enough to pass on their genes. These genes get selected out of the gene pool. In other words, the fittest animals survive and pass on their traits to the next generation. This ensures the survival of the species.

But genes that have an effect after the reproductive age (genes that might cause arthritis or cancer) don't get selected out. Animals that have these genes lived to reproductive age and passed them on to the next generation. The next generation will also suffer from these later life problems. Michael Rose at the University of California at Irvine put this simply. "We are genetic garbage cans," he says, "for genes that produce bad effects at later ages" (Schmidt, 1993, pp. 72–73). Rose tested this theory. He delayed reproduction in seventy generations of fruit flies. His older flies could then pass on longevity genes to the next generation. His research extended the flies' life expectancy by 80 percent and produced healthier flies.

Rose (1993) believes that a theory of aging based on natural selection will eventually replace other theories of aging. But right now gerontologists have many theories of aging to choose from. Each tells us something about aging, but no single theory accounts for all the changes that occur with age. Scientists currently view aging as the result of many interactive and interdependent processes. These ultimately determine life span and health in the individual.

THE EFFECTS OF AGING ON BODY SYSTEMS

Intrinsic changes take place in the cells as we age. Over time these changes compound and lead to changes in the body's systems. All of the body's systems decline or lose reserve capacity with age, but each system, and the organs and structures in the system, decline and deteriorate at different rates after maturity.

This section looks at how some of the body's systems change with age. The limits of space make it impossible to give a full picture of physical changes due to aging. You can find more complete discussions of physical change in reference books like *The Handbook of the Biology of Aging* (Masoro & Austad, 2001). The discussion here focuses on three systems that change with age and influence an older person's ability to function in everyday life: the musculoskeletal system, the endocrine system, and the senses.

Musculoskeletal System

Muscle and bone content decrease with age. Flanigan and his colleagues (1998) say that with age the number of muscle fibers declines and the remaining neurons become less efficient. This leads to muscle weakness. A person has to make more effort to carry out a task. Some studies report that muscles begin to lose strength by age 20 or 30. Other studies show more stable strength until 50 or 60. Muscle mass can decrease by 50 percent by age 80 (Digiovanna, 2000). Also, the incidence of muscular diseases (like amyotrophic lateral sclerosis [Lou Gerig's disease]) increase with age. Flanigan and his colleagues (1998) say that exercise training can reduce muscle loss due to normal aging.

The skeletal system also changes with age. Bones replace about 10 percent of their content each year; but, from about age 20 on, the bones lose more cells than they replace. They also lose hardness and density. This makes them less able to twist and bend without breaking. Murray (1996) says that loss of bone mass increases the older person's risk of a fracture. Murray reports that women lose between 20 and 25 percent of their bone mass during the ten years after menopause. Men also lose bone mass, but at a slower rate than women.

Compared with men, this puts women at higher risk of a fracture in later life. More than 10 million men and women suffer from osteoporosis—porous bones. This disease increases the risk of fracture. Aldwin and Gilmer (2004) say that 60 percent of women aged 65 and over have some amount of osteoporosis. And 90 percent of women past the age of 80 have serious amounts of bone loss. The Osteoporosis and Related Bone Diseases National Resource Center (cited in Aldwin & Gilmer, 2004) reports that half the women aged 50 or over will suffer from a fracture (often of the wrist or hip) due to osteoporosis.

Research shows that exercise can slow the rate of bone loss (Koncelik, 2003). Weight-bearing exercise—like lifting weights—increases bone density. Exercise builds muscle, helps a person maintain the appropriate weight, and improves balance. Exercise also lubricates the joints and reduces the risk of arthritis. All of these outcomes improve bone strength, improve health, and help prevent fractures.

Researchers find that even the oldest-old people improve their muscle mass and strength with weight training (Rowe & Kahn, 1998; Haber, 2003). One study of older men reports that after three months of weight training their muscles grew in size and strength. In some cases, the men doubled and tripled the strength of their leg muscles. Because muscle burns more calories than fat, weight training can also help a person lose weight.

Researchers at Tufts University studied two groups of older women. One group received no training. The other group followed an intensive training program on exercise machines for forty minutes twice a week. At the end of one year, the women who did not exercise had lost bone density. The women who had exercised gained bone density in their legs and back. They also had stronger leg and back muscles and better balance. Researcher Miriam Nelson says, "The study shows for the first time that a single treatment can improve several risk factors for spine and hip fractures in older women" (Pumping Iron, 1994).

Studies of very old people show similar results. Rowe and Kahn (1998; *also* Haber, 2003) report on a study of frail older people in a nursing home. People who took part in a strength training program (some as old as 98) showed an average strength increase of 174 percent. Some disabled people began to walk without the help of a cane.

Nearly 1.5 million older women each year in the United States suffer bone fractures due to falls. These injuries cause hospitalization, reduce a person's social contacts, and often lead to further illness. Training to produce stronger muscles and bones and better balance could reduce the rate of falls and fractures among older women.

The Endocrine System

Glandular tissues make up the endocrine system. They include the hypothalamus, pituitary gland, adrenal glands, ovaries, and testes. These glands secrete hormones into the bloodstream. The hormones then act on specific sites in the body. The endocrine system responds to both internal and external changes in the body and controls growth, metabolism, reproduction, and responses to stress.

The endocrine system changes with age. The hypothalamus, a gland that regulates water treatment by the kidney, can produce water imbalance in an older person's body in times of acute illness. A number of endocrine glands affect sexual function, and these functions decline with age. The adrenal glands, for example, secrete hormones, including androgens and estrogens, that produce secondary sexual characteristics. These hormones decline with age. Likewise, the pituitary gland in women at around age 55 stops producing hormones to stimulate the ovaries. Men experience a 35 percent decrease in testosterone levels between ages 21 and 85. Harman and his colleagues (2000) report low levels of testosterone in 20 percent of men over age 60, 30 percent of men over age 70, and 50 percent of men over age 80. This leads to a gradual decrease in sexual activity from the teens to old age.

Menopause usually begins between ages 45 and 55. A woman experiences longer menstrual cycles and then stops menstruating. Estrogen and progesterone levels decline after menopause, and a woman may feel physical changes like hot flashes and emotional upsets (MedlinePlus, 2004b). A number of current authors claim that medical science has turned this normal process into a disease.

BOX 5.3
MENOPAUSE
The Social Construction of Biological Change

Bones, muscles, and blood change as we age. Most people accept this as a natural process. But physical change takes place in a social context. How we view a physical change like menopause—as a loss, as illness, as something to treat or overcome, or as a sign of normal aging—depends on the meaning we attach to the change. Menopause offers a case study in the interpretation and reinterpretation of physical change.

Feminist writer Germaine Greer (1991) calls it *The Change.* Popular author Gail Sheehy (1992) calls it *The Silent Passage.* Whatever it is called, menopause has played a role in the mythology of female aging for centuries, and much of this mythology created fear and shame. Today, writers present a more balanced view of this change.

Menopause means the end of regular menstrual bleeding. It comes about as estrogen decreases in a woman's body around the age of 50. This marks the end of a woman's childbearing years. Menopause has two common symptoms—hot flashes and vaginal dryness. Some women complain of other symptoms such as insomnia, headaches, irritability, and depression. These symptoms cause physical discomfort and may cause psychological distress.

The Boston Women's Health Collective describes hot flashes as "feeling heat and sweat flooding one's head without warning." Tulandi and Lal note that between 50 and 85 percent of menopausal women feel some sort of hot flash. The decrease in estrogen in the body or changes in blood vessel size may cause this feeling. These problems decrease as a woman's body adjusts to new hormonal levels.

Some studies show that hormone replacement therapy, treatment with both estrogen and progesterone, can reduce the symptoms of menopause. Controversy exists, however, about the effectiveness of treating menopause with estrogen. Some studies show harmful side effects of estrogen treatment, like increased rates of uterine and breast cancer.

Weg says that medical science too often uses the disease model to describe menopause. Clinical descriptions create a picture of the *sick* woman at this time of life. This view led in the past to many unnecessary hysterectomies and to removal of women's ovaries in order to *cure* the illness. It also led to the mass prescription of hormone replacement drugs. The disease model of menopause may change in the future. Studies show that most women cope well with menopausal symptoms.

The National Institute on Aging suggests simple methods to cope with problems like hot flashes—wear layered clothing, sleep in a cool room, drink cool liquids. About 20 to 40 percent of women have few or no problems due to menopause. Women in societies that value youth over age tend to report more menopausal symptoms. So do women whose lives focus on child rearing and the family. Weg says that women with more than one role report the best response to menopause.

Kaufert (cited by Markson) says that only 2 percent of women in a large study said they regretted that their periods had ended. Almost 40 percent expressed relief, and only 11 percent saw menopause as a major life event. Society and culture play an important role in shaping a woman's feelings about menopause.

Sources: "Menopause," by the Boston Women's Health Collective (1982), in S. H. Zarit (Ed.), *Readings in aging and death: Contemporary perspectives, 2d ed.,* New York: Harper & Row; "Estrogen replacement therapy: A time to be cautious," by M. Freedman, July/August, 1995, *Aging Today,* pp. 12–13; "Menopause: Psychological aspects," by E. Markson (1987) in G. L. Maddox (Ed.), *The encyclopedia of aging,* pp. 437–438. New York: Springer; "Menopausal hot flash," by T. Tulandi and S. Lal (1985). *Obstetrics Gynecology Survey, 40,* pp. 553–563; "Menopause: Biomedical aspects," by R. Weg (1987), in G. L. Maddox (Ed.), *The encyclopedia of aging,* pp. 433–437. New York: Springer; National Institute on Aging. (2004). Menopause. *Age page. Health information.* Retrieved on April 25, 2004, *www.niapublications.org/engagepages/menopause.asp.*

Sensory Changes

All five senses—smell, taste, touch, hearing, and sight—change with age. Some senses show more dramatic changes than others. Even with one sense, like smell, sensitivity decreases for some smells earlier than for others.

Taste, Smell, and Touch

Scientists call taste and smell the *chemical senses.* A person has about 9,000 taste buds. They sense sweet, salty, sour, and bitter. By age 40 to 50 in women and age 50 to 60 in men, the number of taste buds declines. Also, the taste buds decrease in size. Still, studies find only a small decline in the sense of taste with age. The taste sensitivity to salty and sweet foods tend to decrease first.

Taste and smell go together. Aldwin and Gilmer (2004, p. 164) say that "most of what we consider taste is actually a function of smell." Studies show some loss in the sense of smell with age, especially after age 70. Sensitivity to some smells, like the smell put in natural gas, declines earlier than sensitivity to others, like the smell of roses (Bartoshuk & Weiffenbach, 1990). A decrease in the sense of smell can lead to a loss of interest in food. This can lead to weight loss and poor health. Poor smell can also put a person at risk if they can't smell a gas leak or rotten food.

The sense of touch also declines with age. Receptors for touch, temperature, and vibration decrease in sensitivity. Controversy exists about whether sensitivity to pain decreases or increases with age. Decreased blood circulation to the skin and degeneration of receptors to the brain may account for the loss of the sense of touch. A decreased ability to feel sensation can lead to injury from burns and slower reaction time to pain.

Sight

Changes in sight and hearing have the greatest effect on a person's ability to function in later life. Changes in vision can begin as early as age 30. By age 55, most people need glasses for reading.

The eye structure and function change with age. Eyes produce fewer tears, and older people may feel discomfort due to dry eyes. Also, the eye's pupil, compared with its size at age 20, decreases by about two-thirds by age 60. The eye's lens yellows and turns cloudy. Eye muscles weaken and limit the eye's rotation. This reduces the older person's visual field.

Some older people lose sensitivity to light and some also report a loss of color sensitivity. Older people also have a harder time seeing a contrast between light and dark as they age. Changes in vision also include slower adaptation when moving from a brightly lit to a dark area, decreased ability to see fine detail, problems adapting due to glare, and a decline in peripheral vision (Schieber, 2003). These changes can limit how well a person can see under certain conditions. For example, drivers encounter many of these conditions, mostly at night. Drivers' tests for older people, for example, could use measures of contrast sensitivity to assess how well a person can cope with glare and night driving.

Most people adapt to changes in sight as they age and have good eyesight beyond their 80s (National Institute on Aging, 1991). They correct for normal

changes by wearing glasses, using large-print books, and using better lighting (Schieber, 2003). Surgery can correct more extreme problems like cataracts or a detached retina. Some people cut back on the amount of night driving they do (Medline-Plus, 2004a). Better lighting and better road signs would help older drivers.

Hearing

A person loses some hearing each year after age 50. Most people don't notice the change, but by age 60 about 30 percent of people suffer from some hearing loss. This figure increases to 50 percent for people age 85 and older (National Institute on Aging, 2004). Men lose hearing at twice the rate of women after age 30. Most people notice hearing loss when they have trouble hearing low frequency tones—the kind common to speech. This starts to occur on average between ages 60 and 70.

A hearing problem can lead a person to withdraw from social contacts. It can lead friends and family to label the older person as confused or unhelpful. Older people may come to distrust others who won't speak up or who seem to whisper in their presence. Hearing problems can lead to isolation and depression.

Hearing loss can take several forms:

- Presbycusis, for example, develops as a person ages. A person may find it hard to hear conversations or callers on the phone. Work-related damage, heredity, loud noise, or prescription drugs can all lead to this form of hearing loss. A doctor can diagnose and treat this problem.
- Tinnitus, another type of hearing problem, is a ringing or roaring in the ear. Loud noises, medicines, or other health problems can lead to tinnitus. People with tinnitus should avoid loud noises. Music can soothe this problem.
- Conductive hearing loss comes from a blockage in the ear canal. Wax buildup can cause this problem. A doctor can clean out the ear and solve this problem.

The National Institute on Aging (2004) gives the following advice to people who work with or know someone with a hearing problem.

- Speak *low and slow*. Take your time when you talk to someone with a hearing loss. Do not speed up your speech or shout.
- Stand or sit in front of the person. Speak at a distance of three to six feet so the person can see you clearly. Have the light on your face (not behind you).
- Let the person see you before you start speaking. Use facial and hand gestures to emphasize what you say.
- Do not cover your mouth or chew while speaking.
- Rephrase what you say. Use different words if the person did not understand you.
- Have presenters at large events use a public address system.
- Include the person in all discussions about him or her. This will reduce feelings of isolation.

No medical cure exists for loss of hearing due to deterioration of the hearing mechanism (Fozard & Gordon-Salant, 2001). But, technology today can help older people deal with hearing loss. Hearing aids, telephone-amplifying devices, adapters to televisions and radios (so that the person can hear more clearly without disturbing others), and even electrical implants under the skin can help a person deal with hearing loss.

PERSONAL HEALTH AND ILLNESS

Changes in Health Status

Today older Americans have a longer life expectancy and live more years in good health than ever before. They live more active lives than seniors in the past, and they have more opportunities to enjoy recreation and leisure activities. But a longer life expectancy has also meant more people who suffer from the chronic diseases in old age.

The shift from a young to an older population in the United States has led to a change in the pattern of disease. The rate of acute illness (like diphtheria, typhoid, and measles) has decreased during this century. More children now live, grow to adulthood, and enter old age. This leads to an increase in the rate of chronic illness (like arthritis, diabetes,

BOX 5.4
LEADING CAUSES OF DEATH IN THE UNITED STATES

In 1900, acute diseases of childhood and youth led to most deaths in the United States. Today, chronic diseases of old age lead the causes of death. Gerontologists refer to such a shift in the leading causes as an epidemiological transition. This refers to the transition a society makes from having a high proportion of deaths due to acute diseases to having a high proportion of deaths from chronic diseases. This change in the causes of death brings about corresponding changes in the health care system. Different types of illness require different types of treatment and can change the organization of health care service. Chronic diseases most often occur in later life. They require long-term treatment and the development of long-term care resources (e.g., nursing homes, home care, respite care programs).

1900	*2001*
Pneumonia-influenza-bronchitis	Heart disease Cancer
Tuberculosis	Stroke
Diarrhea and enteritis	Chronic lower respiratory disease
Heart disease	

Sources: Chronic disease epidemiology and control, by R. C. Brownson, P. L. Remington, and J. R. Davis (Eds.), (1993), Washington, D.C.: American Public Health Association, and *Health, United States, 1993,* National Center for Health Statistics (1994). Hyattsville, MD: Public Health Service; Arias, E., Anderson, R. N., Hsiang-Ching, K., Murphy, S. L., & Kochanek, K. D. (2003). *Deaths: Final data for 2001.* National vital statistics reports; Vol. 52, No. 3. Retrieved: April 25, 2004, *www.cdc.gov/nchs/data/nvsr/nvsr52/nvsr52_03.pdf.*

and heart disease). Scientists refer to this as the *epidemiological transition* (Gribble & Preston, 1993).

Today chronic disease accounts for 70 percent of all deaths in the United States. They lead to activity limitations and cost us 70 percent of our $1 trillion health bill (U.S. Department of Health, 2004). Nearly every major chronic disease (except certain cancer) increases in frequency and severity with age. The leading chronic illnesses include (in order of prevalence) heart disease, cancer, stroke, chronic lower respiratory disease, influenza and pneumonia, and diabetes (Freid, Prager, MacKay, & Xia, 2003). Heart disease, cancer, and stroke alone accounted for more than 60 percent of all deaths among people aged 65 and over in the year 2000 (Freid, Prager, MacKay, & Xia, 2003). (See Figure 5.1.)

Older people also suffer from a variety of nonlethal chronic diseases. These include arthritis, hearing impairment, and cataracts. This means that a decrease in death rates due to the major killers in old age—heart disease, cancer, and stroke—would have a paradoxical effect. It would lead to longer life, but possibly also to more years of life with nonlethal chronic illness. A number of gerontologists have debated this possibility. You will read about this later in a discussion on the **compression of morbidity hypothesis**.

Some rates of chronic illness differ by race and gender. African Americans age 65 and over, compared with whites, for example, have only about two-thirds the rate of emphysema and about two-thirds the rate of heart disease. But older African Americans, compared with whites in 2001, had about a 30 percent higher rate of hypertension and more than one and a half times the rate of diabetes.

Older women, compared with older men, have higher rates of diabetes, hypertension, asthma, and arthritis. Older men, compared with older women, have higher rates of stroke, heart disease, and deafness (National Center for Health Statistics, 2004a; 2004c). Older women live longer than older men, but they have poorer health. Differences in income, work-related stress, and habits like smoking and drinking account for most of this these differences in illness rates.

Limits on Activity Due to Physical Decline

National studies in the United States show that chronic conditions lead to functional loss. And this leads to disability and activity limitations in older people (Molla, Madans, Wagener, & Crimmins, 2003). Twenty-six percent of older people in 2001

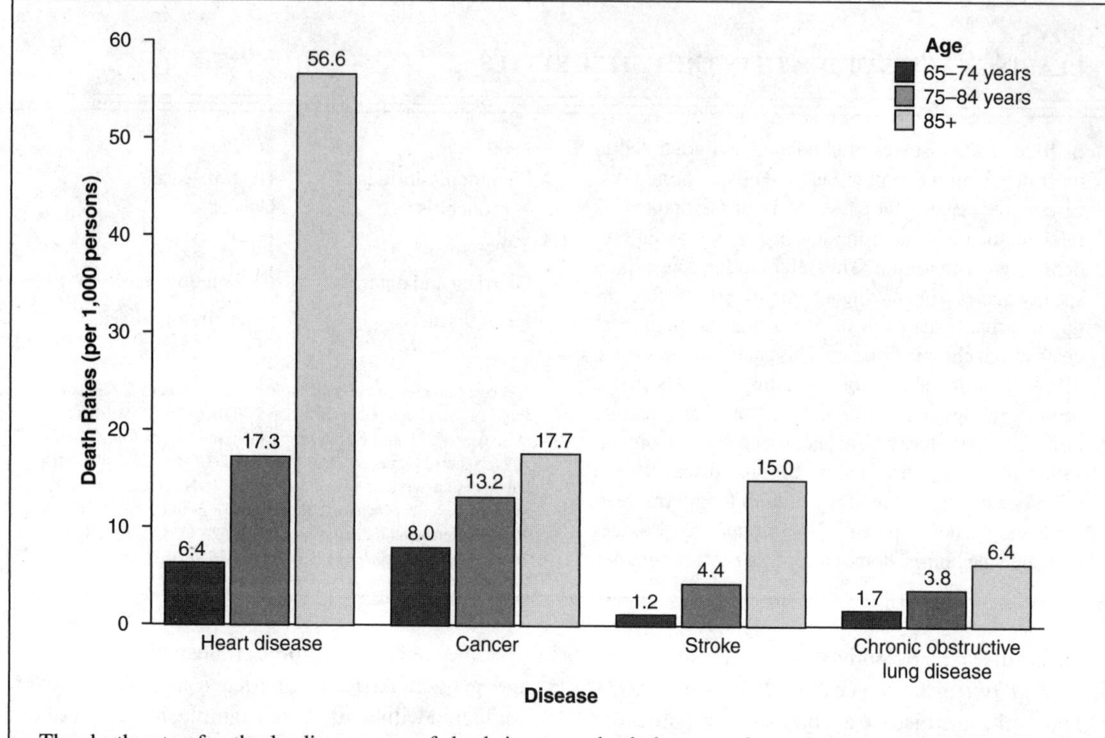

The death rates for the leading causes of death increase dramatically with age. For example, the 85+ group, compared with 65 to 74 year olds, shows more than a ninefold increase in the rate of death due to heart disease, more than a doubling of the death rate due to cancer, a twelvefold increase in the rate of death due to stroke, and almost a fourfold increase in the rate of death due to respiratory disease. Longer life and the growth in the very old population will see an increase in the number of deaths and in the death rate due to these chronic diseases.

FIGURE 5.1

The Four Leading Causes of Death by Age, 2001

Source: Arias, E., Anderson, R. N., Hsiang-Ching, K., Murphy, S. L., & Kochanek, K. D. (2003). Deaths: Final data for 2001. National vital statistics reports; Vol. 52, No. 3. Retrieved April 25, 2004, *www.cdc.gov/nchs/data/nvsr/nvsr52/nvsr52_03.pdf.*

reported some activity limitation due to a chronic condition (Freid, Prager, MacKay, & Xia, 2003). Ten percent of older Medicare beneficiaries reported a limitation in at least one **activity of daily living** (ADL) (Freid, Prager, MacKay, & Xia, 2003). For the purposes of this discussion, an ADL limitation includes a physical, mental, or emotional problem that causes a person to need help with "bathing or showering, dressing, eating, getting in or out of bed or chairs, walking, and using the toilet" (Freid, Prager, MacKay, & Xia, 2003, p. 77).

Older people also report limitations in an **instrumental activity of daily living (IADL)**. Nine percent of older men and 15 percent of older women report limitations in their instrumental activities of daily living (U.S. Department of Health and Human Services, 2003). IADLs refer to home management activities like using the phone, shopping, and doing light housework. Limitations may range from a mild problem such as trouble dialing the phone to more serious problems such as the inability to eat or use the toilet. A decrease in the ability to care for oneself signals a drop in quality of life and in the number of active years a person will live (Prohaska, Mermelstein, Miller, & Jack, 1993).

ADL and IADL problems increase with age (see Figures 5.2 to 5.4). The U.S. Senate Special Committee on Aging and the American Association of Retired Persons (U.S. Senate, 1991, p. 108) said that:

> The majority of elderly people in their younger retirement years are relatively healthy and are not as limited in activity as frequently assumed—even if they have chronic illnesses. However, health and mobility do decline with advancing age. By the eighth and ninth decades of life, the chance of being limited in activity and in need of health and social services increases significantly.

Data from the National Center for Health Statistics (2004c) supports this view. The National Center for Health Statistics reports that in the year 2000,

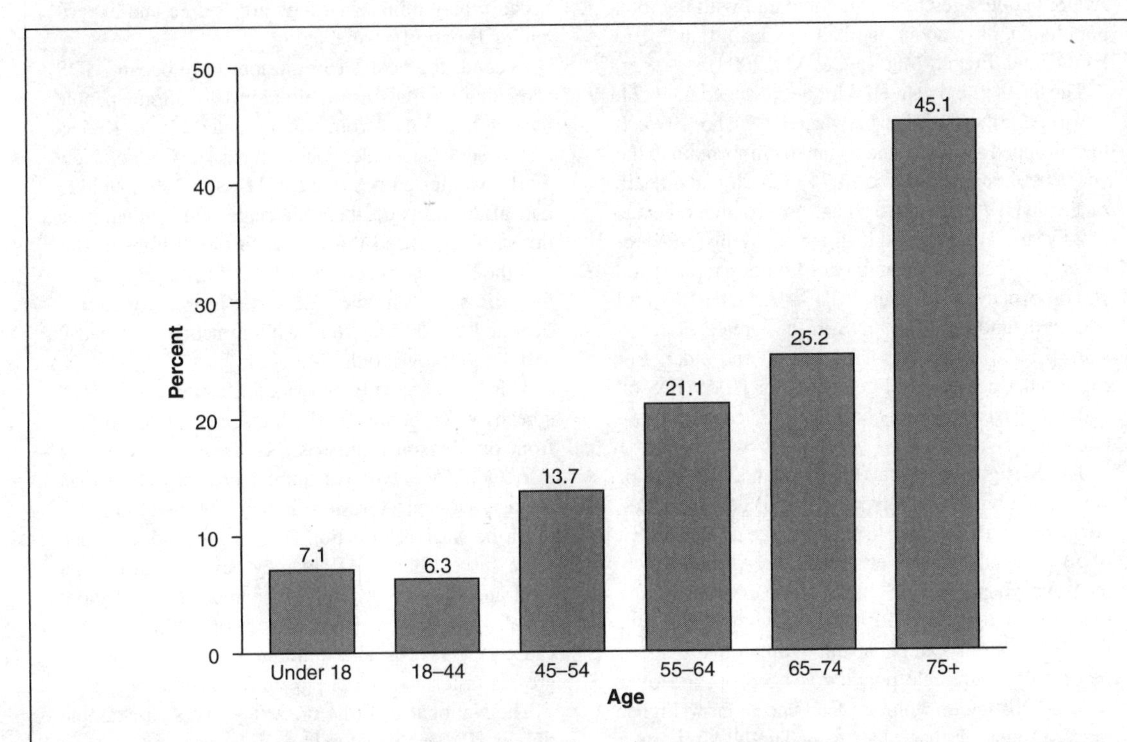

The proportion of the population with activity limitation due to chronic conditions increases with age. The older age groups show sharp increases in activity limitation. One in four people aged 65 to 74 report at least one activity limitation due to chronic conditions. Nearly one-half of the population aged 75 and over report some activity limitation. Older age groups may need assistance with ADL. As these older age groups increase in size, the number of people needing help with daily activities will increase.

FIGURE 5.2
Activity Limitation from Chronic Conditions, 2002
(Percent of persons with any activity limitation)

Source: Health, United States (2004). Table 56, p. 214. Hyattsville, MD: National Center for Health Statistics.

BOX 5.5
FACTS ON AIDS AND OLDER PEOPLE

Few people think of the elderly when they hear the words human immunodeficiency virus (HIV) or acquired immune deficiency syndrome (AIDS). AIDS occurs when HIV has weakened the immune system to the point at which a person can get life-threatening infections and cancers. The media have linked HIV to gays, intravenous drug users, and sexually active young people. The data support this view. Young people aged 25 to 54 have the highest death rate from AIDS. People aged 65 to 74, compared with the total population, have about one-half the death rate due to HIV (Freid, Prager, MacKay, & Xia, 2003).

The death rate due to HIV for people aged 65 to 74, however, almost tripled between 1987 and 1995. It then dropped suddenly and began to climb again to the year 2000. People aged 65 to 74 in 2000 had a death rate from HIV higher than all age groups under the age of 24 years. The National Institute on Aging (NIA) reports an increase in the number of older people (aged 50 and over) with HIV and AIDS. "About 10% of all people diagnosed with AIDS in the United States—some 75,000 Americans—are age 50 and older. Because older people don't get tested for HIV/AIDS on a regular basis, there may be even more cases than we know."

The NIA goes on to say that women and people of color run a higher than average risk of getting AIDS. African Americans and Hispanics make up 52 percent of people aged 50 and over with AIDS. African American and Hispanic men make up 49 percent of the male population aged 50 and over with AIDS. But African American and Hispanic women make up 70 percent of the female population aged 50 and over with AIDS. Older women of all races show higher rates of infection than older men. The NIA reports a 40 percent increase in AIDS cases among women aged 50 and over. Two-thirds of these women got the virus from having sex with an infected partner or by sharing a needle. The NIA reports that HIV and AIDS cases continue to grow in number in communities of color and among women. The NIA encourages older people at risk to get tested.

The older population in the future may show an increase in deaths and illness from HIV and AIDS. Why is there a projected increase in AIDS among older people? First, a person can have HIV ten years or more before the body's immune system breaks down and AIDS appears. Intravenous drug users, for example, may become infected with HIV in their younger years but may not show signs of the disease until old age. More people in the future will enter old age with the HIV virus. The NIA says that "people age 50 and older may not recognize HIV symptoms in themselves because they think what they are feeling and experiencing is part of normal aging."

Second, the health care system only began AIDS screening for transfusion blood in 1985. Some people have gotten AIDS from contaminated blood. Kellerman describes an older couple in Nassau County, New York, who tested positive for AIDS in 1993. Neither had affairs outside their marriage and neither used drugs. They traced the illness to blood transfusions that the husband received in 1982. "If I could get it," the wife said, "anyone who had a husband who was operated on, or who slept with someone who had it and didn't know, could also get it."

Third, any sexually active adult can get HIV. HIV spreads when bodily fluids like semen or blood pass from one person (who has the disease) to someone else. Older women have thinner uterine linings than younger women. Abrasions in their uterine linings can open the way for infection. This makes older women more susceptible to HIV if they have sexual contact with an HIV carrier. Kellerman indicates that older people may stand a greater chance of getting HIV because they have weaker immune systems. AIDS progresses faster in an older person for this reason.

The National Institute on Aging gives an example of how HIV can develop in an older person:

> Grace was a happily married woman with a family and a career. After more than 20 years of marriage, her husband left her. After her divorce, she began dating George, a close family friend she had known for years. They became lovers. Because she was beyond childbearing years, she wasn't worried about getting pregnant and didn't think about using condoms. And because she had known George for

BOX 5.5
(Continued)

years, it didn't occur to her to ask about his sexual history or if he had been tested for HIV.

At age 55 she had a routine medical checkup. Her blood tested positive for HIV. George had infected her. She will spend the rest of her life worrying that the virus will develop into life-threatening AIDS—that any cough, sneeze, rash or flu would, in fact, indicate AIDS and perhaps the beginning of the end of her life (The National Institute on Aging, 2004b).

Kellerman reports that a 53-year-old man who has HIV says he probably got the virus through sexual contact. People might feel uncomfortable about speaking about AIDS, the man says, but "they have to be able to say, 'If you don't wear a condom, we won't have sexual intercourse.' It's not worth dying for."

The NIA proposes that older people use condoms when having sex, avoid sharing needles, ensure that their partners do not have HIV, and get tested if they or their partners have had a blood transfusion between 1978 and 1985 or a transfusion in a developing nation. Early detection and treatment offers the best hope of keeping the virus in check. Older people who do not get the disease may still find their lives affected by it. Older people may serve as caregivers to adult children with AIDS. Some older people have to play the role of parent to grandchildren whose parents have AIDS. Also, as more AIDS patients enter the long-term care system, they will compete with older people for services, such as home care. The AIDS epidemic in the years ahead will affect older people by affecting policies for health care delivery.

Sources: "HIV transmission risks of older heterosexuals and gays," by J. A. Catania, H. Turner, S. M. Kegeles, R. Stall, L. Pollack, S. E. Spitzer, & T. J. Coates (1989), in M. W. Riley, M. G. Ory, & D. Zablotsky (Eds.), *AIDS in an aging society,* pp. 77–95. New York: Springer; "Other end of spectrum: AIDS strikes elderly," by V. Kellerman, April 24, 1994, *New York Times*; "HIV, AIDS, and older adults," National Institute on Aging (1994), *Age Page,* Washington, DC: U.S. Department of Health and Human Services; "AIDS and older people: The overlooked segment of the population," by M. Riley (1989), in M. W. Riley, M. G. Ory, and D. Zablotsky (Eds.), *AIDS in an aging society,* pp. 3–26. New York: Springer; Freid, V. M., Prager, K., MacKay, A. P., & Xia, H. (2003). *Chartbook on trends in health of Americans.* Health, United States. Hyattsville, MD: National Center for Health Statistics; National Institute on Aging (2004). HIV, AIDS, and older people. *Age page. Health information.* Retrieved on April 25, 2004, *www.niapublications.org/engagepages/aids.asp.*

71.5 percent of Medicare beneficiaries aged 65 to 74 lived without limits on ADL or IADL. But in that same year, only 24.9 percent of Medicare beneficiaries aged 85 and over lived without a limitation.

Some groups more than others face higher rates of disability in old age. African Americans, compared with whites or Hispanics, for example, report a higher proportion of ADL and IADL limitation (U.S. Department of Health and Human Services, 2003) (see Figures 5.2 and 5.4). Women at every age, compared with men, report a higher proportion of ADL and IADL limitations. A third of older people with a disability (most of them women) live alone. They face the greatest risk of institutionalization. Miller and her colleagues (1993) found that people aged 80 and over had the most ADL problems and faced the greatest risk of institutionalization (Miller, Prohaska, Mermelstein, & Van Nostrand, 1993).

An increase in the older population and in the very old population could lead to more people with disabilities in later life. But recent research offers some hope against this possibility. Studies show a steady decline in disability rates among older people in the past few years (Manton & Gu, 2001).

The National Long Term Care Survey, for example, reports that disability rates fell by 2.6 percent each year between 1994 and 1999. In total, from 1982 to 1999, the disability rate fell from 26.2 to 19.7 percent of older people. During this same time the population of older people increased by 30 percent. By 1999, the United States had fewer disabled older people than it did in 1982. This decrease applies to African American as well as whites. Researchers

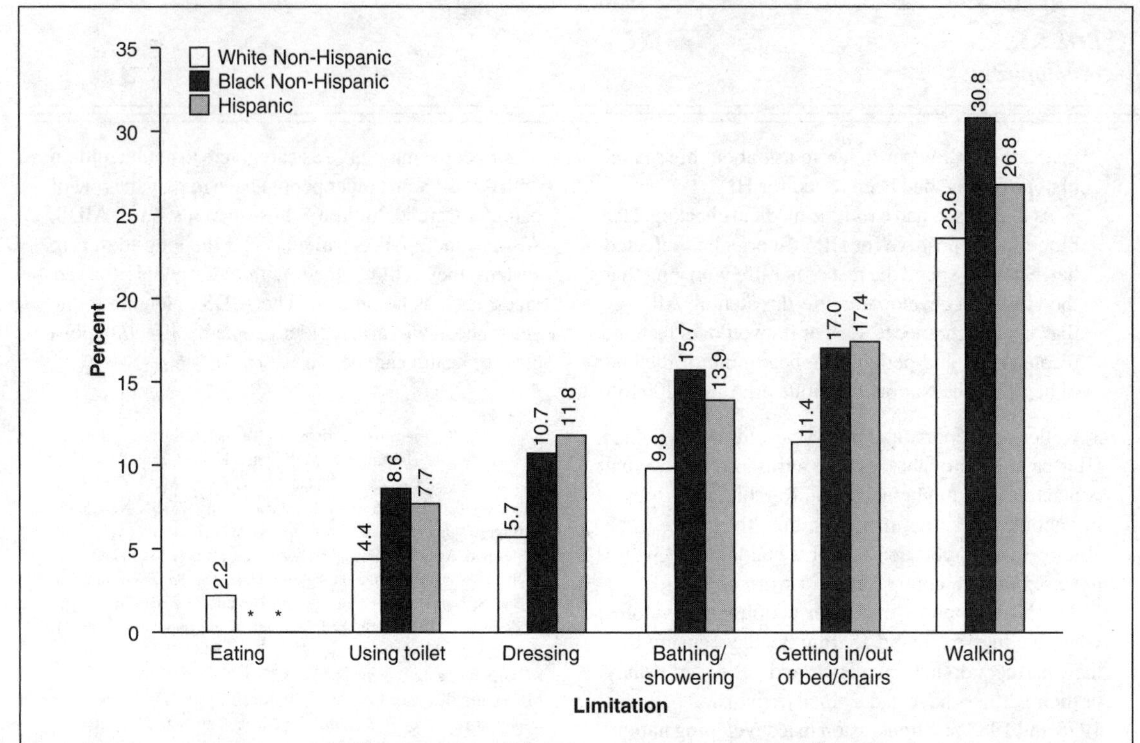

These figures show that older people have the greatest problems with mobility, transferring in and out of chairs or bed and walking. The proportion of people who experience ADL limitations differs by race/ethnicity. Whites, for example, have the lowest proportion of people with any ADL limitations. Blacks and Hispanics, compared with whites, have one and one-half to two times the proportion of older people with ADL limitations. These figures show the effects of poverty, health care treatment, and life-style choices over a lifetime.

These figures also show that the large majority of older people in the community live without ADL limitations. But, people with limitations in ADLs need support to live on their own in the community. The lack of this support can lead to institutionalization. Compared with whites, a higher proportion of older blacks and Hispanics will need assistance in order to stay in the community.

*Sample size under 50, too small to report results.

FIGURE 5.3

Activity of Daily Living Limitations, Community Dwelling People, Aged 65 and over, 2002

Source: National Center for Health Statistics. (2004). Trends in health and aging. Functional status and disability. Retrieved January 9, 2005, *http://209.217.72.34/aging/TableViewer/tableView.aspx* and *http://209.217.72.34/aging/ReportFolders/reportfolders.aspx.*

could not pinpoint the cause of these declines. They propose that better public health, improved treatment of diseases in later life, fewer smokers, and better education all play a role in decreasing disability.

These findings suggest older people lead healthier lives today than in the past. Other studies show that disability can decrease (as well as increase) in later life. A study in Canada (Statistics Canada, 2000) reports that about 20 percent of older people developed a long-term activity limitation between 1994 to 1995 and 1998 to 1999. But about one-third of older people with long-term activity limitations

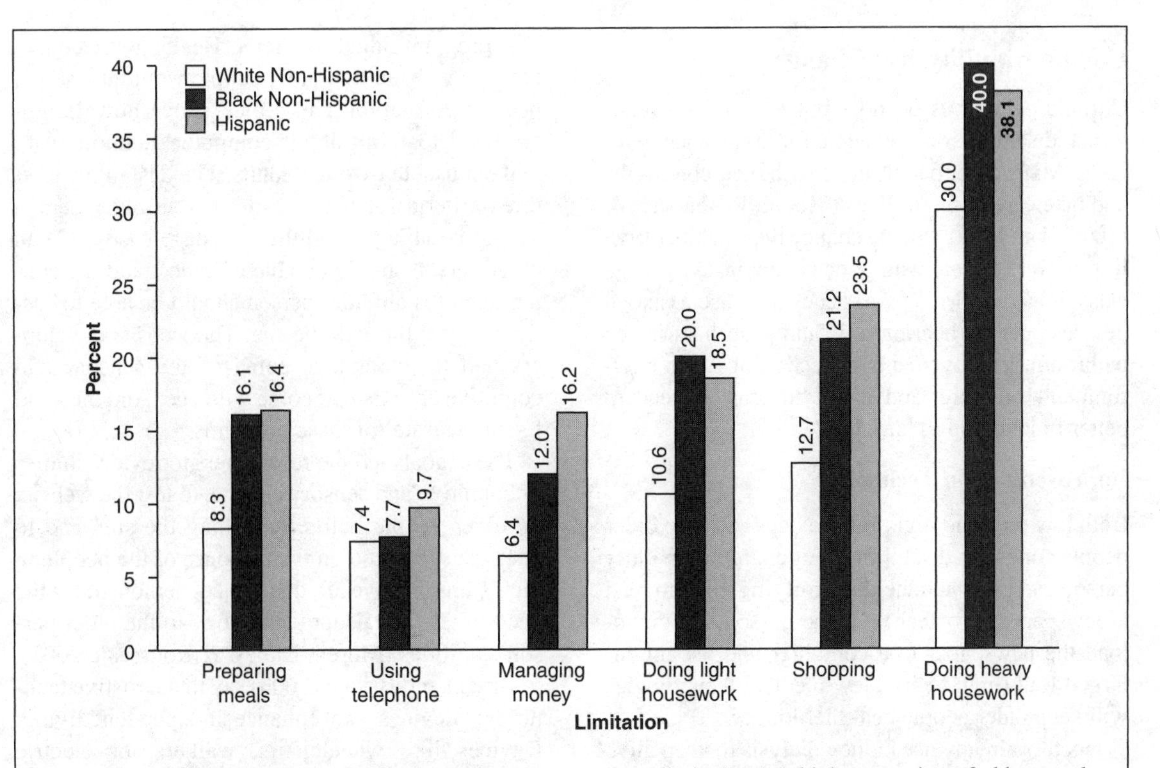

The inability to perform IADLs leads to a decrease in the quality of life. These figures show that most older people who live in the community have no limitations on their primary (IADL) activities. People need the most help with strenuous activities like light housework, shopping, and heavy housework. Homemaker supports (like help with shopping or cleaning) will improve the quality of life for people who have these limitations. A high proportion of older people in all groups need help with heavy housework. But, compared with whites, black and Hispanics have higher rates of limitations in all categories. This points to a need for support for minority elders with specific activities for them to maintain a high quality of life.

FIGURE 5.4

Instrumental Activity of Daily Living (IADL) Limitations, Community Dwelling People, Aged 65 and over, 2002

Source: National Center for Health Statistics. (2004). Trends in health and aging. Functional status and disability. Retrieved January 9, 2005, *http://209.217.72.34/aging/TableViewer/tableView.aspx,* also *http://209.217.72.34/aging/ReportFolders/reportfolders.aspx.*

(31 percent of men and 37 percent of women) overcame their limitations during this time.

An eight-year longitudinal study in the United States found that nearly a quarter of people who aged successfully improved their physical function during the study (Rowe & Kahn, 1998). "Activity limitations and dependency are not necessarily long-lasting. . . . This may reflect the natural resolution of some conditions (back problems, for example) and effective treatment of others (such as arthritis), resulting in improvements in functional ability" (Statistics Canada, 2000, p. 29). Health promotion, disease prevention, and effective management of disability can reduce the need for health services. They can even lead to rehabilitation and restored good health.

Coping with Physical Change

Chronic conditions do not always turn into functional disability or the need for assistance with ADL. Many older people cope with their conditions and take care of themselves (Moore, Rosenberg, & Fitzgibbon, 1999). People change their habits (drive less at night to deal with poor vision or take a yoga class to ease arthritis pain). They also use assistive devices such as hearing aids and grab bars in the bathroom. Improvements in technology, the environment, self-care, and life-styles can all lead to better functioning in later life.

Improvements in Technology

Both low-tech and high-tech devices can help older people cope with disabilities. For example, an older person can use a handheld magnifying glass to read a newspaper (low tech). Or the person can download the newspaper to a computer and use an enlarged font (high tech). New medical technologies will keep older people healthier longer.

Doctors already use kidney dialysis to keep alive many older people with kidney failure. Insulin pumps dispense a steady dose of insulin to improve the length and quality of diabetics' lives. New drugs for care after a stroke reduce vascular spasms and increase survival rates. Other technologies include rehabilitation programs, simple devices like large rubber grips for spoons, and prosthetics like hip replacements.

Computers also benefit people with disabilities. Already computers allow people to order groceries online, use email to keep in touch with friends, and play chess with a grandchild across the country (Kaplan, 1997). Likewise, online banking allows disabled people to manage their accounts, pay bills, and organize their funds from home. Computer databases and websites provide information on disabilities, coping methods, and even support groups online. All these resources will increase in the future. Today, the older population falls into two groups. Those who feel comfortable using the latest technologies, and those who don't (Liu & Park, 2003). But future cohorts of older people will have a lifetime of experience with computers and will feel comfortable using these tools.

A program called NIHSeniorHealth.gov set out to create a website that older people would use to get health information. This project shows how designers need to think about computer technology to make it usable by older adults. The design team set three criteria for the website: (1) an older person should be able to read the web page easily; (2) an older person should be able to understand the content; and (3) an older person should be able to easily navigate through the site. The website developers had to understand some of the sensory and cognitive deficits that come with age. And they had to compensate for these problems.

These goals led the researchers to review studies of cognitive and sensory change, to test the website on older people before launching the site, and to alter the site based on the response of the people in their study. Above all, this project demonstrates the need to test and adapt technology to the older person's abilities (Morell, Dailey, & Rousseau, 2003).

Bryant and Bryant (2003) say that assistive technology devices can enhance independent living. Devices like wheelchairs, walkers, or electric scooters all increase a person's mobility. People who use assistive devices say they rely less on others and an assistive device can help a person stay out of a nursing home (National Council on Disability, 1993). But some people refuse to use an assistive device. A cane, for example, may make a person feel *old.* Cott and Gignac (1999) say that older people reject devices that make them look different or dependent.

Sometimes a shift in design can overcome this resistance (Gitlin, 2003b). One woman rejected the use of a motorized wheelchair because it made her feel helpless. But she accepted and even bragged about a motorized scooter that served the same purpose. She enjoyed driving around her local mall and felt empowered by the technology. Designers of devices need to understand how the older person sees the world. Researchers say that for people to accept technological aids, first, they need to know about them, second, the aids need to be affordable, and third, people need to know how to use them.

Older people benefit from training on all devices. Training programs need to focus on specific needs (e.g., how to use a computer or a DVD player)

(Charness, 2003; Rogers & Fisk, 2003). Effective training increases the older person's confidence and increases the use of assistive devices.

Gene therapy in the future may have a profound effect on health and illness in later life. Genes make up a part of the DNA in every cell and hold the code for over 100,000 proteins that keep the body working. Gene therapy will allow a researcher to replace a defective gene and reverse a state of illness or physical decline. Researchers would use recombinant DNA methods to (1) multiply the gene in a bacterial culture, (2) use a benign virus to place the gene in the host's cell, and (3) allow the gene to produce a needed protein. Scientists may use this technology to cure immune system breakdown, Parkinson's disease, and cancer.

Improvements in the Environment

Changes in the environment can also improve the quality of life for older people. Improved lighting, for example, can create safer and more enjoyable living spaces. Older people take more time to adapt to changes in lighting, their eyes grow more sensitive to glare, and their color perception weakens. Koncelik (2003) says that, compared with the eye of someone aged 25, the eye of a person aged 70 takes three times longer to adapt to a change in light level. Also, compared with a younger person's eye, the older person's eye needs more light to perform the same task. Designers have created lighting that eases the transition from bright to dimly lit rooms, reduces glare in hallways, and provides more light in dining rooms (Calkins, 2003).

Architects can also use materials that cut down on glare or reduce the echo in hallways and rooms. Koncelik (2003, p. 127) says that the technique of "redundant cueing" can improve the environment. A sound like a beep can go along with a change in color to signal a change in floor level. Designers now routinely include devices like grab bars in the tub or a ramp outside a home to increase the safety and mobility of older people.

Computers can now control hearing aids so that the aid adjusts the sound to the environment. The user can filter out high- or low-pitched sounds or reduce background noise (Koncelik, 2003). New technologies can also allow families to visit with and watch television with a relative in a nursing home thousands of miles away. Technology can allow families to monitor older relatives at risk of falling. These technologies help older people age in place (Hutlock, 2003). Pentland (2003) says that in the future a pair of eyeglasses may display the name of the person the wearer meets or may relay health care information to a caregiver.

Technology can create a safer environment and can enhance the user's quality of life. Hoenig and her colleagues (2003) found that technology aids decreased the number of hours of personal help a person needed. But they found that poorer people made the least use of technology devices. More financial support is needed for poorer people who need technological help.

Improvements in Self-Care

Self-care refers to exercise, good eating habits, rest, stress release, and medical checkups. People can choose from a variety of health promotion and health maintenance methods. These include exercise programs like T'ai chi, acupuncture, chiropractic treatment, and relaxation therapies. Haber (2003) reviewed these methods and found that a market exists for alternative therapies. He reports that in 1997, 40 percent of Americans use some form of alternative therapy. Relaxation techniques and chiropractic treatment had the largest following. These techniques appeal to people with chronic illnesses that do not respond to conventional medical therapy.

Trombley and her colleagues (2003) report on a massage therapy program offered to people in two long-term care facilities. They find that massage therapy relieved tension from pain. The study combined massage with music therapy and reminiscence therapy to improve. These methods improved residents' general well-being.

Technology can also enhance self-care. This can take the form of diet and medication checklists, computerized self-assessment programs, and communication systems for sensory-impaired older people. Wagner and Wagner (2003) found that older people use self-care information if they have it at hand. They studied the use of a self-care handbook and a telephone advice line in one community. They found that, compared with younger people, people aged 65 and over made more use of the self-care handbook. And that the handbook got the most use among all age groups. This shows that low-tech interventions like information sources can encourage self-care.

Some studies show that self-care lowers health care costs. Wheeler (2003) conducted a controlled study of women aged 60 and over with heart disease. The study taught the women how to manage their health care. Women chose a health behavior to improve, for example, exercise. A health educator then taught the women how to assess their chosen behavior, develop a plan to improve this behavior, and monitor their response. Women in the program got a workbook, videotape, and self-monitoring tools (a log book).

The control group continued with their usual health practices. The self-care group, compared with the control group, used about one-half the number of inpatient hospital days and had about one-half the inpatient hospital costs. Wheeler says that the program saved five dollars in hospital costs for every dollar spent on the program. Easom (2003) says that older people in self-care programs benefit from encouragement, contact with role models of good self-care, and a supportive environment.

Social support plays an important role in self-care programs. Miller and Iris (2002) studied members of a wellness center to understand members' views of health promotion. They found that older people want social contact and social support along with a wellness program. People wanted to interact with others during their program. The researchers say that program designers need to keep these preferences in mind when designing programs for older adults.

Changes in Life-Style

Chrenoff (2002) says that a program of life-style change should include a smoking cessation program, better nutrition, and increased exercise.

Decreased Smoking. Older men and women in 1999 through 2001 reported the lowest rates of smoking among the adult population. They also reported the highest rates of former smokers. Research shows that the benefits of quitting begin almost immediately (Rowe & Kahn, 1998). And the benefits of quitting last into late old age. Ostbye and Taylor (2004) found that people who had quit smoking at least fifteen years before their study began had the same life expectancy as people who had never smoked. The benefits of quitting smoking seem obvious by now.

Smoking leads to a long list of physical problems. Research links smoking to heart disease, lung cancer, emphysema, high blood pressure, stroke, and other major diseases that debilitate and kill people in later life. Cataldo (2003) calls smoking the number one preventable cause of disability and death among older people. Unfortunately, among adults over age 18, older smokers showed the lowest proportion of those who intended to quit (Schoenbom et al., 2004). And older smokers, who want to quit, have the hardest time quitting. Lantz and Giambanco (2001) report that people who try to quit have a relapse rate of 70 percent after three months and 90 percent after one year. Cataldo (2003) says that, compared with younger smokers, older smokers get less guidance and less support for quitting.

Health promotion programs for older adults often include sessions on smoking cessation (Cheong et al., 2003). Lantz and Giambanco (2001) say that programs need to include education about the benefits of quitting, nicotine substitutes, and in some cases antidepressants. Programs sometimes require intensive intervention. Lantz and Giambanco describe a case where interventions included education, nicotine substitutes, antidepressants, as well as group support and regular contact with a psychiatrist. The researchers show the challenge that smokers and their supporters face when a person has an addiction to cigarettes. But they urge professionals who work with smokers not to give up and to use all of the methods available to help smokers quit.

Better Nutrition. Scientists have studied changes in diet that could slow the aging process. They agree that good nutrition can support health and limit the progress of disease (Bates et al., 2002). Research on free radicals, for example, has led to the hope that eating antioxidant-rich food could hold back or reverse aging. Antioxidants (found in foods like carrots, broccoli, blueberries, and in green tea) may halt the effects of free radical damage in the body.

Studies suggest that vitamins C and E also have antioxidant effects on the body (National Institutes of Health, 1999). But studies of antioxidants report mixed results. A study of a diet rich in superoxide dismutase, a common antioxidant in the body, found that digestion broke down superoxide dismutase's structure. Other studies show that when cells detect added antioxidant vitamins, they lower their own production of antioxidants. This leaves free radical levels the same.

Vitamins and minerals can have good effects on the older body apart from their effect on free radicals. Vitamin C may reduce heart disease by blocking the formation of fatty proteins. Increased vitamin E may reduce the risk of Alzheimer's disease (National Institute on Aging, 2002). Research shows that calcium and vitamin D in the diet increase bone density. This may help prevent osteoporosis in older women.

What do these results mean for the older person's diet? What should older people eat to stay well and delay the aging process? First, metabolic rate decreases with age. An older person either has to eat less or exercise more to maintain an ideal weight. Second, older people need to make sure that they get at least minimum adult requirements of basic nutrients. They should also follow general guidelines that apply to people of all ages (e.g., avoid refined sugars and fats).

Third, vitamin supplements may help older people stay in good health (Rowe & Kahn, 1998). Some older people lose their appetite or find it difficult to chew food. This can lead to vitamin and mineral deficiencies. A vitamin supplement can help ensure that a person gets the nutrients needed. Jeffrey Blumberg of Tufts University says "proper nutrition won't abolish the aging process, but it could slow the decline and postpone the onset of disease" (Schmidt, 1993, p. 69).

Exercise. Exercise, along with a good diet, leads to better physical functioning in later life. Studies show that exercise can slow the aging process, improve health, and improve physical function. Research finds dozens of benefits from exercise in later life. They include reduced body fat, greater muscle mass, greater strength, improved cardiac output, improved endocrine-metabolic function, lower blood pressure, decreased hypertension, decreased heart disease, and decreased osteoporosis.

But older people tend to exercise less than younger people. More than one-third of men aged 65 and over reported either low physical activity levels or inactivity. By comparison only 15 percent of men aged 18 to 24 reported these low levels of activity. Women, compared with men, show higher rates of inactivity at all ages. Over 40 percent of older women reported low levels of activity or inactivity. About 22 percent of younger women (aged 18 to 24) reported these low levels of activity (Freid, Prager, MacKay, & Xia, 2003).

People aged 75 and over, compared with those aged 18 to 24, reported about one-half the rate of engagement in leisure-time physical activity. The more vigorous the activity, the greater the gap between the participation rate of younger and older groups. Younger people compared with older people showed almost six times the rate of participation in vigorous activity. Few people aged 65 and over (less than one-quarter of those aged 65 to 74 and 11 percent of those aged 75 and over) engage in vigorous physical activity (Schoenbom et al., 2004). Only 15.6 percent of people aged 75 and over engaged in *any* regular physical activity (compared with 39.7 percent of people aged 18 to 24).

Inactivity among older people increases their risk of illness and disability. Studies show that the more often a person exercises, the better the person's health. Exercise can even buffer other risks created by smoking or by having high blood pressure (Rowe & Kahn, 1998). Sobczak (2002) reports that exercise can stop and in some cases reverse the trend toward loss of mobility and dependence that sometimes come with age.

Kahana and her colleagues (2003) say that among the many things older people can do to improve their well-being, "physical activity most consistently yields benefits for physical health and quality of life." Rowe and Kahn (1998, p. 98) call physical

BOX 5.6

STUDY LINKS VIGOROUS EXERCISE AND LONGEVITY

Sweating It Out Beats Moderation

Moderate exercise may well be the route to a healthier life, but if living longer is your goal, you will have to sweat.

A new Harvard study that followed the fates of 17,300 middle-aged men for more than 20 years has found that only vigorous activities, and not nonvigorous ones, reduced their risk of dying during the study period. The beneficial effects of vigorous exercise on longevity have long been assumed but were not firmly established.

Men who reported at least 1,500 calories worth of vigorous activity each week had a 25 percent lower death rate during the study period than those who expended less than 150 calories a week.

To achieve the level of exercise associated with longevity, a person would have to do the equivalent of jogging or walking briskly for about 25 kilometres [15 miles] a week.

In general, the more active the men were, the longer they were likely to live. This effect of vigorous exercise was seen even in men who smoked or were overweight, although those with neither of these health-robbing factors did better.

However, no consistent beneficial effect on longevity was found among the men who pursued only nonvigorous activities such as golf.

The enhanced longevity associated with vigorous exercise mainly resulted from a reduced number of deaths from cardiovascular disease, said Dr. I-Min Lee, an epidemiologist at the Harvard School of Public Health, who directed the study.

Source: Jane Brody, *New York Times* Service to *The Globe and Mail,* April 19, 1995, p. 1.

fitness "perhaps the single most important thing an older person can do to remain healthy. Physical activity is at the crux of successful aging, regardless of other factors." Chapter 12 discusses exercise programs for older people in more detail.

COMPRESSION OF MORBIDITY HYPOTHESIS

Controversy exists over the benefits of longer life expectancy. Some researchers believe that longer life will lead to more years of good health. They say that longer life will push disease and loss of function to the last years of life. Other researchers believe that we will live longer, but with more years of chronic illness.

Some years ago, Fries (1980, 1987a) predicted that as life expectancy increased, people would have fewer years of disability, suffer less from chronic disease, and need less medical care. He predicted that death would come for most people around the age of 85 after a short illness. This, he said, would create a **rectangularization of the life curve** as more people live out the full human life span. Longer life, he said, would lead to a **compression of morbidity** (illness) at the end of life. (See Figure 5.5 on page 124.)

This hypothesis produced controversy during the 1980s and early 1990s. Some results at that time suggested that people would live more years with disabilities as life expectancy increased (Crimmins, Saito, & Ingegneri, 1989). Researchers reasoned that we cannot control nonfatal diseases like arthritis and Alzheimer's. So, they said, the prevalence of these diseases would increase as more people lived longer. They predicted that the total number of disabled people in society would increase in the future (Olshansky et al., 1991).

But, recent research supports Fries' predictions of morbidity compression (Laditka & Laditka, 2000; Vita, Terry, Hubert, & Fries, 1998; Crimmins, Saito, & Ingegneri, 1997). Between 1985 and

1995, for example, life expectancy increased at age 65. Likewise, at age 65 the percent of **disability-free life expectancy** also increased. White men at age 65 in 1995, compared with 1985, increased their disability-free life expectancy by nine percent. White women gained 2 percent, black men gained 6 percent, and black women gained 3 percent (Molla, Madans, Wagener, & Crimmins, 2003). This means that long life led to more years free of the illnesses that cause disability.

More detailed studies show that some groups gain more disability-free years than other groups. Crimmins and Saito (2001), for example, found that people with higher educational status showed a compression of morbidity, but those with less education showed an expansion of morbidity. This suggests that illness in later life is not an inevitable outcome of longer life. Instead, these findings point to the plasticity of the body as it ages. The morbidity compression hypothesis supports attempts to improve health and well-being in later life by prevention and life-style changes.

Fries (1990) said that healthier life-styles, exercise, and good public health would lead to healthier life into late old age. Recent research supports this view. Studies find that higher socioeconomic status (Melzer et al., 2000), smoking reduction (Bronnum-Hansen & Juel, 2001), and regular physical activity (Ferrucci et al., 1999) all lead to a relative compression of morbidity. Vita and colleagues (1998) found that people at lower risk of illness (those who exercised, did not smoke, and had low or normal weight) faced disability at later ages (*see also* Hubert, Block, Oehleth, & Fries, 2002). These people, compared with those at high risk, also have fewer disabilities, less serious disabilities, and face disability for a shorter time at the end of life.

Fries also said that the variation in ability among seniors shows room for further compression of morbidity (*see also* Vita, Terry, Hubert, & Fries, 1998). In other words, if some people live morbidity-free lives into late old age, other people can follow this pattern. Laditka and Laditka (2000) say that women can benefit most from this view. Women live longer than men and have a higher risk of disability due to chronic illness. Compression of morbidity would lead to more active lives for older women. The potential for further improvement in well-being among older people has led to the study of successful aging.

Banana George was born January 22, 1915. He learned to water-ski at age 40 and to barefoot water-ski at age 46. In 2003, Water Ski Magazine named him a water-ski "Icon," the International Waterskiing Federation awarded him the Order of Merit, and he was inducted into the Florida Sports Hall of Fame. His motto is, "Do It."

SUCCESSFUL AGING

Cross-sectional studies show declines in most body functions with age. The older the person on average, the poorer their physical function. This holds for kidney, lung, and heart function, among others. These findings led to the idea that aging takes a steady downhill course, and that the body wears out on a set schedule. But researchers have begun to question this view. Studies have looked at the effects of exercise, nutrition, and healthy life-styles on aging (Chernoff, 2002). They find that people can maintain good health and physical function into

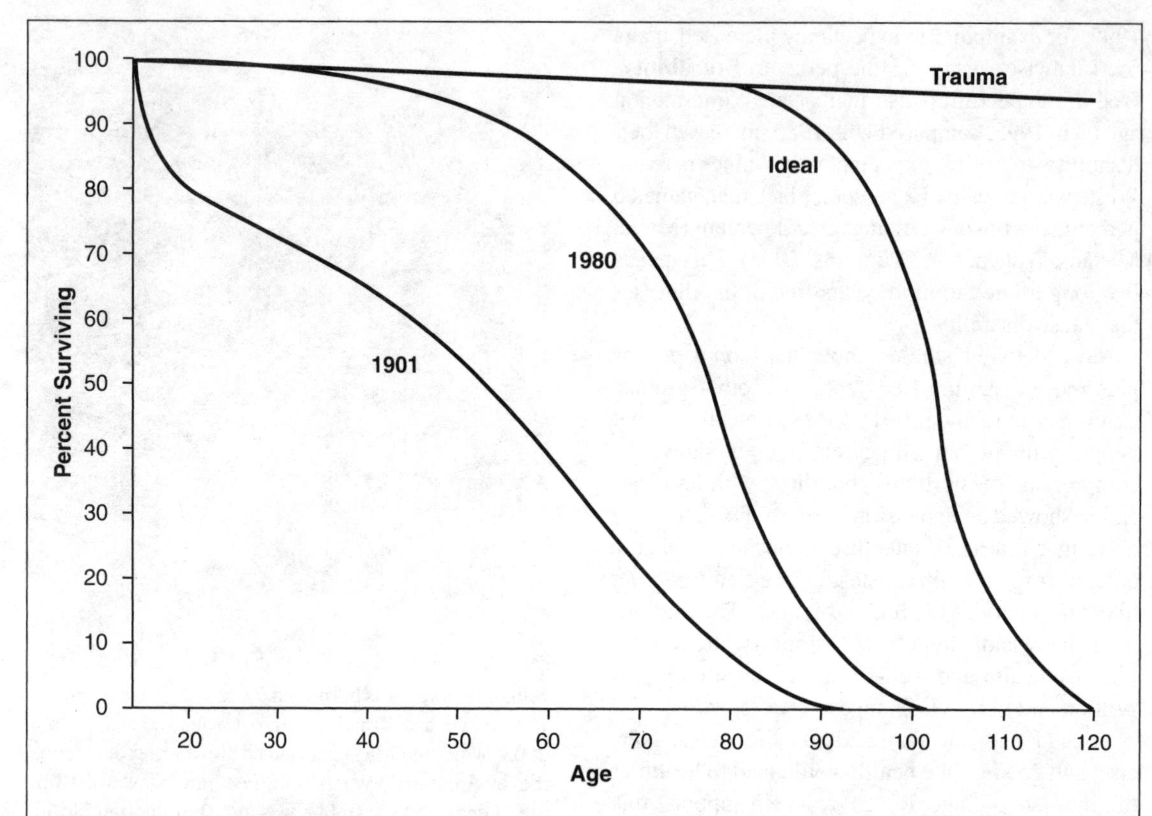

The chart shows the rectangularization of the life curve that has taken place over the past century. The curve gradually assumes the shape of a rectangle as more and more people live out a complete life span (of 100 to 120 years). Fries assumes a finite life span that populations like that of the United States will soon reach. Fries predicts that medical science will delay the onset of chronic disease, and people consequently will live more years with less disability. Scientists call this the compression of morbidity hypothesis. A number of studies raise questions about this prediction.

FIGURE 5.5

Compression of Morbidity

Sources: Adapted from 1901—James Glover, United States Lifetables, 1890, 1901, 1910 and 1901–1910, U.S. Department of Health and Human Services, National Center for Health Statistics, 1980; and 1980—U.S. Decennial Lifetables for 1979–1981, Vol. 1, No. 1, in United States Lifetables, U.S. Department of Health and Human Services, National Center for Health Statistics, 1985. Also, Compression of morbidity, by J. F. Fries, 1983, *Milbank Memorial Fund Quarterly, 61*(3), pp. 397–419, and Compression of morbidity: Miscellaneous comments about a theme, by J. F. Fries, 1984, *The Gerontologist, 24*(4), pp. 354–359.

late old age. Kahana and her colleagues (2003), for example, describe a variety of activities that can buffer physical decline and lead to successful aging. Activities include consumer awareness, self-improvement, access to technology, and engagement in physical activity.

Rowe and Kahn (1998, p. xi) say that gerontologists have spent too much time on the study of *normal aging* (the study of illness and disability). Instead they) propose that gerontologists study people who age well. Today, for example, the large majority of older people (about three-quarters of men

BOX 5.7
BASIC NUTRITION IN LATER LIFE

Nutrition can lead to a longer, healthier life. But many older people eat barely enough to stay healthy. Podolsky reports that almost one person in four over age 70 had a high risk of poor nutrition. Another 38 percent had a moderate risk of poor nutrition. This includes people with a good education and good income.

Podolsky presents a test that researchers at the Boston University School of Public Health have used to assess an older person's dietary habits. It lays out the basics of a healthy diet and good eating habits in old age.

A Nutrition Self-Test
Here's a nutrition check for anyone over 65. Circle the number for all statements that apply. Then check the total against the nutritional score.

1. An ongoing illness or current condition has made me change the kind or amount of food I eat. (**2 points**)
2. I eat fewer than two full meals per day. (**3 points**)
3. I eat few fruits, vegetables, or milk products. (**2 points**)
4. I have three or more drinks of beer, liquor, or wine almost every day. (**2 points**)
5. I have tooth or mouth problems that make eating hard for me. (**2 points**)
6. I don't always have enough money for the food I need. (**4 points**)
7. I eat alone most of the time. (**1 point**)
8. I take three or more different prescription or over-the-counter drugs a day. (**1 point**)
9. Without meaning to, I have lost or gained ten pounds in the past six months. (**2 points**)
10. I can't always shop, cook, or feed myself. (**2 points**)

Nutritional Score
0–2: Good. Recheck in six months.
3–5: Marginal. Your local office on aging has information on nutrition programs. Recheck in three months.
6 or more: High risk. A doctor, registered dietitian, or local social worker should see this test and suggest how to improve your nutrition.

This nutrition self-test places nutrition in the context of the older person's health and environment. A look at the questions shows some of the sources of poor nutrition in older people. Questions 1 and 5 focus on illness. Questions 2, 3, and 4 focus on unhealthy choices. Questions 6 and 9 focus on poverty. Questions 7 and 10 focus on living alone. Question 8 focuses on medication problems. The questions provide a checklist for reducing an older person's risk of poor health. Are there other questions a checklist like this ought to contain?

Source: From "Health: Is Grandpa Malnourished?" by D. Podolsky, December 21, 1992, *U.S. News & World Report,* pp. 99–100. Reprinted with permission.

and women) rate their health as good to excellent (U.S. Department of Health and Human Services, 2003).

Rowe and Kahn urge gerontologists to study this new generation of healthy older people. "There was a persistent preoccupation," they say, "with disability, disease, and chronological age, rather than with the positive aspects of aging." Researchers also underestimated the effects of lifestyle choices and other social and psychological conditions on the well-being of older people."

Rowe and Kahn (1998, p. xii) set out to create the basis for a "new gerontology," a study of successful aging. Successful aging refers to "people who

BOX 5.8
CALORIE-RESTRICTED DIET
The Secret to Longevity?

The study of caloric restriction has grown into one of the most active areas of aging research. Walford (1983; Weindruch & Walford, 1988) conducted some of the earliest research into the effects of calorie restriction on aging. He fed lab mice a diet with all needed nutrients, but with 30 to 60 percent fewer calories than normal. He found that a calorie-restricted diet in lab mice led to longer life and better health. Bartke and Lane (2001, p. 301) say that calorie restriction of 60 to 70 percent of normal led to "impressive extension of life in laboratory rodents." Barzilai and Gabriely (2001, p. 903S) call calorie restriction "one of the most robust observations in the biology of aging."

The National Institutes of Health (1993, p. 27) report that "undernutrition has increased the life spans of nearly every species studied—protozoa, fruit flies, mice, rats, and other laboratory animals." Yu, Masoro, and McMahan (1985) found that calorie restriction led to longer life even for rats who began the diet in early middle age. Many studies now exist to support the effects of calorie restriction on longer life and a healthier old age (Masoro, 2001). Sprott and Roth (1992) report that undernutrition produces healthier, more active animals with less disease than animals half their age. Bronson and Lipman (1991) report that a low-calorie diet delays the start of all tumors and almost all other damage to the body. Masoro (2001) says that calorie restriction leads to youthfulness in a long list of biological and physical functions. And Austad (2001) says that in studies of laboratory rodents, calorie restriction lengthens life and leads to more vigor in later life.

How does calorie restriction affect longevity? Masoro (2001, p. 401) concludes that "the reduction in energy intake . . . is the major dietary factor underlying the life-prolonging and anticarcinogenic action of calorie restriction." This, in turn, influences all of the body's systems.

Researchers have found that calorie restriction retards age-related declines in DNA repair. Calorie restriction also decreases the accumulation of mutations in the cells. Researchers have found that low-calorie diets may cut down the number of free radicals in the system (Masoro, 2001). Finally, calorie restriction lowers fat in the body and this keeps blood sugar levels in balance (Barzilai & Gariely, 2001).

Will people take up low-calorie diets in the future? Probably not. Walford spent two years in Biosphere 2, a futuristic experiment in an artificial environment in Arizona. While there, he put himself on a calorie-restricted diet and lived on two-thirds the average calories of a man his age.* Other members of the Biosphere team refused to follow Walford's diet. A spokesperson for the project observed, "They're not lab rats."

Calorie restriction may not gain wide adoption among humans. But studies of calorie restriction reveal some of the mechanisms that lead to aging and disease in later life. These studies could lead to treatments or cures for chronic disease.

*Walford died of cancer at age 80 in 2004.

Sources: "Concepts and theories of aging," by S. N. Austad, 2001, in E. J. Masoro and S. N. Austad (Eds.), *Handbook of the biology of aging* (5th ed.) (pp. 3–22). San Diego: Academic Press; "Reduction in rate of occurrence of age-related lesions in dietary restricted laboratory mice," by R. T. Bronson and R. D. Lipman, 1991, *Growth Development and Aging, 55,* pp. 169–184; "Health: hold the cheese," by C. Crabb, October 14, 1991, *U.S. News & World Report,* p. 18; *In search of the secrets of aging,* p. 27. National Institutes of Health, 1993, Washington, DC: Department of Health and Human Services; "Biomarkers of aging: Can we predict individual life span?" by R. L. Sprott and G. S. Roth (1992). *Generations,* Fall/Winter, pp. 11–14; "Nutritional influences on aging of Fischer 344 Rats: I. Physical, metabolic, and longevity characteristics," by B. P. Yu, E. D. Masoro and A. McMahan (1985). *Journal of Gerontology, 40,* pp. 657–670; R. L. Walford and L. Walford (1994). *The anti-aging plan: Strategies and recipes for extending your healthy years.* New York: Four Walls Eight Windows.

demonstrate little or no loss in a constellation of physiologic functions" and who therefore "would be regarded as more broadly successful in physiologic terms" (Rowe & Kahn, 1991, p. 21). Successful aging means more than aging without disease. Rowe and Kahn (1998, p. 38) define successful aging as the ability to maintain (1) a "low risk of disease and disease-related disability"; (2) "high mental and physical function"; and (3) "active engagement with life."

The concept of successful aging begins with the idea that people differ in rates of aging. Research from the Baltimore Longitudinal Study of Aging (BLSA), for example, found that some older people showed rapid decline in kidney function over a short time, but about 35 percent of the subjects showed no decline in kidney function over many years (Williams, 1992). Studies of people with healthy hearts found that some people in their 60s and 70s have cardiac output similar to that of 20 year olds (Williams, 1992).

BLSA researchers report two conclusions related to successful aging. First, chronological age "cannot be linked to a general or universal decline in all physical and mental functions," and second, "there is no single, simple, pattern to human aging" (National Institute on Aging, 1993). According to Rowe and Kahn (1998), many studies show that changes in diet, exercise, and social relations inhibit and in some cases reverse physical decline. One study looked at the effects of a weight loss program on health. The study found that a low-calorie diet "improved or reversed every single risk factor" (Rowe & Kahn, 1998, p. 57).

Studies show that diet, exercise, and healthy life-styles can reverse the risk of hypertension, heart attack, and stroke. The study of successful aging shows that people can modify the risk of illness and live more years in good health. Rowe and Kahn (1998, p. 58) say that "to a much greater degree than previously recognized, we are responsible for our own health status in old age."

Some researchers see a contradiction in this view of successful aging (Thompson & Forbes, 1990). If a person can avoid decline through life-style or environmental changes, then this decline must not be intrinsic or true aging. The biologist who wants to know the causes of true aging may find little value in the concept of successful aging, but physiologists and practitioners who work to improve well-being in later life find the concept useful. Studies of people who have adapted well to change over time can serve as models of aging for the rest of us.

Foofie Harlan, age 76 when this photo was taken, worked as a postal clerk in Sun City, Arizona. She has four great-grandchildren. A good advertisement for the benefits of exercise in later life, she attends two aerobic classes each week to keep fit. This picture shows her stretching during her regular exercise routine.

CONCLUSION

Some years ago Hayflick (1981, p. 176) said that a short-range goal of gerontology "would simply be to reduce the physiological decrements associated with biological aging so that vigorous, productive, non-dependent lives would be led up until the mean maximum life span of, say, 80 years." This he considered a feasible and worthwhile goal. And studies in the biology and physiology of aging show that more people than ever before have begun to achieve this goal.

But what of the future? Some scientists propose an optimistic scenario. Crews (1993, p. 288), for example, says that "the possibility of human life span extension is real and interventions that postpone human aging are a likely prospect." Rose (1993, p. 72) says that:

> Given enough time and resources, there is no reason to doubt that eventually we will be able to postpone human aging, at least to some extent. . . . [T]here is the further possibility that increases in the human "health span" could likewise be open-ended. . . . [E]volutionarily postponed aging involves an enhancement in performance at later ages, not an extended period of debility. The long-term prospect, then, is more of an extension of youth than an increase in longevity, though the latter does occur.

People live longer today and stay healthier than ever before. The technical ability to extend life and improve the quality of life in old age now exists. And the future may see more life extension. But we may arrive at that point before we have worked out the social effects of this change. For example, how would personal and social life differ if people on average lived for 120 years? How would this change our ideas about youth, middle-age, and old age? Would retirement at age 65 make any sense? Would people and society adjust their life cycles and careers to meet this new schedule?

Studies of people aged 100 years or more throughout the world give some clue about what a long lived society will look like. These studies report that a long lived people have good genes, a purpose in life, physical activity, independence, close family ties, friends, good hygiene, a simple balanced diet, low stress, good self-esteem, and a belief in God (Palmore, 1987). In other words, centenarians live balanced lives in supportive social settings.

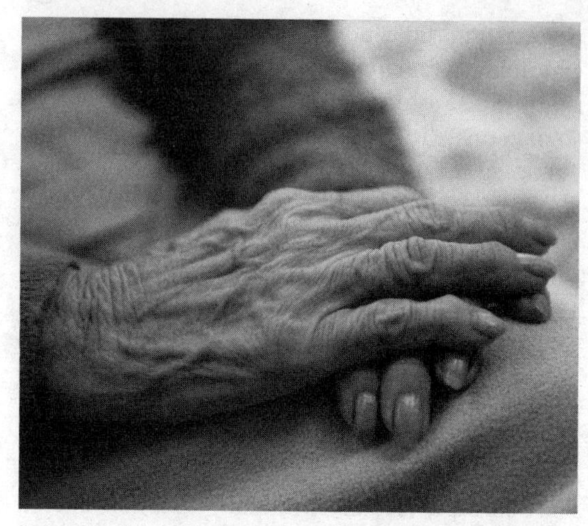

These hands of an older person show some of the changes in the skin that come with age. Note the leathery look, age spots, and wrinkles. Everyone's skin shows similar objective changes with age. How we see these changes (for example, as ugly, beautiful, or tragic) depends on us. I recall my grandmother's hands. I saw a lifetime of service in her weathered skin.

These findings suggest that we take the quest for a long life out of the realm of science fiction. Instead, we should place the search for a long and full life where it belongs: within the power of each of us and the society we live in. We can and will extend life through scientific research and improvements in the quality of life. But life extension will only put off the deeper question. Can we give meaning and purpose to those added years?

SUMMARY

- Gerontologists distinguish between two causes of aging: intrinsic aging due to normal physical decline and extrinsic aging due to life-style, the environment, and disease.

- Scientists have developed two different classes of theory to explain the cause of aging. Programmed theories locate the cause of aging in programmed actions by the genes. Error theories locate the cause of aging in external and internal assaults on the body over time. Research suggests that both of these causes play a role in physical aging.
- Bones, muscles, blood, and hormones change as we age. The five senses also decline as a person grows older, although the senses decline at different rates.
- The rate of chronic illnesses like arthritis, diabetes, and heart disease increases as the population ages. The rate of acute illness decreases with population aging. Chronic illnesses tend not to cause death (as do heart disease, cancer, and stroke), but they lead to long-term illness and the need for help with everyday activities.
- Most older people report no problems in performing ADLs, but the proportion of people who report limitations increases with age. By late old age (aged 85 and over), people often need help in order to live on their own in the community.
- The Baltimore Longitudinal Study of Aging (BLSA) reports that physical and mental functions do not uniformly decline with age. No single pattern of human aging exists. Studies show that changes in diet, exercise, life-style, and social relations may inhibit or reverse physical decline. Technological innovations can improve a person's ability to function even with a disability.
- Some researchers propose that the study of normal aging limits our understanding of health and well-being in later life. They propose the study of successfully aging older people. Studies of people who live in good health into late old age may give scientists clues about how to improve aging for everyone.
- Compression of morbidity occurs when chronic disease comes later in life and when it approaches a population's life expectancy. The late onset of chronic disease compresses illness into fewer years at the end of life. This could result in decreased use of medical care and services in the future.
- Scientists in the future may be able to extend the human life span. This will likely increase the number of healthy years people will live. These changes will raise the question of how to make the best use of the added years people will have available to them.

DISCUSSION QUESTIONS

1. Distinguish between intrinsic and extrinsic aging. List the four criteria for intrinsic (true) aging. Can you give examples of each type of aging in your own life? In the lives of older people you know?
2. Name the two classes of theories that gerontologists have developed to explain the causes of aging. What perspective does each type of theory take on the process of aging?
3. How do our senses change with age? What problems does this present to the older person? Suggest some things that older people, their friends, and relatives can do to compensate for declines in each of the senses.
4. What changes in the pattern of disease took place as American society aged? Why did this change take place? What implications does this have for the health care system?
5. What are ADLs and IADLs? What do they tell us about older people? What causes limitations in ADLs and IADLs? How do other people help an older person cope with ADL and IADL problems? What types of people provide this help? Do you know of any people or groups in your area who provide ADL or IADL help? Who are they and what do they do?
6. What are some of the responses older people can make to the effects of aging? For example, what can older people with arthritis do to maintain the quality of their life?
7. Explain the term "rectangularization of the life curve." Link this term to the "compression of morbidity hypothesis." What do these two concepts suggest about aging in the future?
8. How would personal and social life differ if people on average lived for 120 years? How would this change our ideas about youth, middle-age, and old age? How would retirement be affected? What would society need to do to adjust to a longer life span?
9. What long-term goal do scientists propose for the study of biological and physical aging? Do you think science will reach this goal? Why or why not? How will this change social life as we know it?

SUGGESTED READING

Wykle, M. L., Whitehouse, P. J., & Morris, D. L. (2005). *Successful aging through the lifespan: Intergenerational issues in health.* New York: Springer.

This collection of readings applies the concept of successful aging to issues related to intergenerational relations. Articles look at a wide range of topics, including how older people can engage in productive aging, exercise and diet to maximize well-being, and the opportunities to build family relations through caregiving. The book suggests ways to make aging a positive experience and later life a time of challenge and personal growth.

Charness, N., & Schaie, K. W. (2003). *Impact of technology on successful aging.* New York: Springer.

This series of articles looks in depth at many of the issues and themes raised in this chapter. Articles examine how technology can help older people deal with sensory changes, the impact of computers and the Internet on older people, and the use of assistive devices. The articles describe ways that technology can reduce dangers and provide people with the support they need to live independently in the community.

Walford, R. (2000). *Beyond the 120 year diet.* New York: Four Walls, Eight Windows.

A readable and practical guide to understanding Walford's view of aging, caloric restriction, and life extension. The book reviews technical topics like biomarkers, free radical theory, and metabolic efficiency. It shows how Walford's 120-year diet would reduce cancer, hypertension, stroke, diabetes, and other illnesses that plague old age. In the later chapters of the book, Walford turns his scientific understanding of caloric restriction into a practical program for life extension.

GLOSSARY OF TERMS

ADL Activities of daily living, a way to measure a person's ability to care for him- or herself.

compression of morbidity hypothesis The idea that modern science can push chronic illness and disability to a time shortly before death.

cross-linking Damage to the DNA and proteins due to free radical attack and other types of chemical attack (such as glycation).

disability-free life expectancy The number of years a person will live without a severe or moderate disability.

extrinsic aging Changes in the body due to the impact of the environment or lifestyle choices such as sunlight, smoking, or noise.

free radicals Oxygen radicals that bond with chemicals in the body and cause damage to cell and body functions.

glycation A process that occurs due to the long-term exposure of proteins to glucose (sugar) molecules. This leads to cross-linking and chemical malfunctions in the body.

Hayflick limit The maximum number of times a cell can divide. This differs for each organism.

IADL Instrumental activities of daily living, such as banking and cooking.

intrinsic aging Physical decline due to the normal working of the body (such as the Hayflick limit).

life expectancy The number of years that people of a given age can expect to live.

life span The maximum number of years a specific organism can live.

lipofuscin A fatty deposit that builds up in the cells with age.

macrophage Immune system cells that seek out invading or noxious molecules, engulf them, destroy them, and send them to the kidneys for elimination. This protects the body from processes such as glycation and crosslinking.

phase III phenomenon The buildup of debris in the cell and the decline in cell function.

pleiotropic genes Genes that have a positive function at one point in life but that may harm the body through their action later in life.

rectangularization of the life curve The idea that more and more people will live the full, natural life span. This idea also assumes that humans have a fixed and unchangeable life span.

senescence Physical decline, aging.

chapter 6

LIFE SPAN DEVELOPMENT

What is a good old age? Consider these three cases. Each person shows a different response to the challenge of aging.

Sarah Foote, 89, won the Successful Aging Award in Middlebury, Connecticut, in 1993. Sarah worked as a nurse for twenty-seven years. Now she spends her time on a variety of activities. She eats lunch each day at a nearby senior center, attends exercise classes there on Tuesday and Thursday mornings, and on Tuesday afternoons she attends a Merry Menders sewing program.

On Tuesday evening she attends a bell choir practice in nearby Naugatuck. On Thursday and Friday she goes to a prayer group at her church. On Wednesday she plays the piano at a nearby convalescent home, and Thursday afternoons she teaches macrame at the library. She attends her garden club meetings once a month, and she lectures five times a month on the history of Middlebury. Sarah does all of this and still finds time for her family of three children, five grandchildren, and three great-grandchildren (Robinson, 1993).

Becky Reitman, 73, reports high life satisfaction, but at a slower pace. She lives alone in a seniors housing complex in central New Jersey. She has arthritis in her legs and an unstable walk due to a broken hip that healed poorly. These problems limit her activity, but Becky takes the complex's bus to a local shopping center twice a week. The bus driver helps her with her packages. She watches television, knits, and talks to friends on the phone most mornings. After lunch she sits in the lobby with a group of other tenants. Once a month she goes to a movie in the lounge.

Pasquale Ianni, 66, has followed a third path to a satisfying old age. He lives in his own home with two of his unmarried adult children. Seven years ago Pasquale had a heart attack that nearly killed him. His illness left him depressed and without a purpose in life. To pull himself out of his depression, he enrolled in a leadership program for seniors. The program required a community service project, so he offered to set up a meal program for the Italian community through Villa Rosa, a seniors housing complex. The program delivered meals to people who could not come to the complex for lunch. Pasquale now runs this program. His role as a community leader gives his life meaning and purpose.

Three people, three cases of high life satisfaction, yet each person shows a different pattern of aging. Sarah Foote has stayed active in many of the things she did during her younger years. Becky Reitman has withdrawn from most of her middle-aged activities. She lives a quiet life, content to see only a few people and limit her activity. Pasquale Ianni has found new roles to replace those of middle age. He feels good about what he has done, and he looks forward to future community service.

Each of these people takes part in activities and relationships that they find meaningful. They have each met and overcome challenges to achieve a good old age for themselves. Good aging in this chapter refers to the mastery of inner and outer challenges in later life. These challenges include changes in mental ability, changes in social relations, and changes in social status. These challenges and the older person's response take place in a social context. This chapter looks at (1) mental function and self-development in later life; (2) issues raised by changes in a person's psychosocial condition; and (3) creative responses to change in old age.

MEMORY AND INTELLIGENCE

Ruth and Ray, both in their 80s, take ballroom dance lessons on Friday evenings. I met Ruth one Friday after their class. She looked worried. I asked her what was wrong.

"Is there something the matter with Ray?" she asked. "Tonight, after dinner at our favorite restaurant he couldn't remember where he'd parked the car."

I said I didn't think she had to worry much about this. Ray, a former scientist, has a keen mind. He can learn and remember a complex series of dance steps in an hour and dance them a week later. I said she could put this memory lapse in the category of *benign forgetfulness.* A physician I know tells older patients, "You don't have to worry if you can't recall where you put your eyeglasses. You should start to worry if you don't remember that you wear eyeglasses."

Like Ruth, many older people worry about the loss of memory as they age. They assume that memory loss will take place as a part of the normal aging process. They also fear the loss of their mental abilities. But, Pearman and Storandt (2004) say that these worries often have little basis in fact. Recent research questions the idea that memory and other mental abilities decline radically with age.

Scheibel (1996), for example, says that the stability and adaptability of the brain allows for continuity and growth in mental potential throughout life. Research on memory and intelligence shows that varied changes occur in mental ability. In some cases, mental ability improves. In most cases, older people adapt well to changes in mental function.

Memory

Memory refers to recall after learning has taken place. Psychologists in the field of aging have spent more time on the study of memory than on any other subject. Smith (1996, p. 236) says that studies of memory and aging made up "34% of all the published papers in the two journals *Psychology and Aging* and *Journal of Gerontology: Psychological Sciences*." Psychologists have developed a number of theories about how memory works (and how it changes) in later life.

Researchers break the process of remembering into a series of steps. Most researchers use an information-processing model to guide their work (Schieber, 2003). This model includes the following steps: (1) a person perceives information—psychologists call this sensory memory; (2) the person acts on this information, transforms it in some way, while the information sits in short-term memory; and (3) the person stores the information in long-term memory, the storehouse of knowledge that also includes the rules for applying knowledge.

Take the example of looking up and remembering a phone number. You open the phone book and see the number (sensory memory). You repeat it to yourself a few times as your eye moves from the phone book to the dial (short-term memory). You make a rhyme of the number so you can remember it later (long-term memory). The greatest mental work goes on when a person stores information in long-term memory.

Most psychological studies test memory in the laboratory. This allows the researcher to control outside influences and to compare performance between age groups. These studies often use a cross-sectional design. For example, the researcher gives subjects of different ages a list of words to remember. The researcher then tests the subjects' recall and compares the performance of young and old people. In general, older people perform less well than younger people on this kind of test. This suggests a general decline in memory with age. But further research shows that results differ when researchers study different parts of the memory model.

For example, studies find little difference between younger and older people in sensory memory or primary memory. Young and old people perceive information (such as a phone number) about equally well. And both young and old people hold this information in consciousness about equally well.

A number of studies report a decrease in episodic memory, including **working memory**. This type of memory selects, manipulates, and stores recent information (Backman, Small, & Wahlin, 2001). In addition, working memory processes new information while it stores other information temporarily (Schieber, 2003). A decline in working memory takes place in older people when irrelevant information comes between two things to be remembered. Older adults, compared with younger people, also have a harder time remembering information in a scrambled order. This requires that they hold all information in memory and then make sense of it.

Topic changes also place a greater load on working memory and older people forget relevant information when topics change rapidly. Brown and Park (2003), for example, found that decreases in working memory lead to poor comprehension and recall of novel medical information. Craik (2000, p. 82) says, "it is clear that older adults have particular problems in situations where they must hold, manipulate, and integrate moderate amounts of information over short time spans."

Studies have also found differences in function between young and old people in long-term memory. Researchers have looked in detail at the process of long-term memory to understand this difference. Long-term memory requires **encoding** (learning information), **storage** (putting information away), and **retrieval** (getting information back out). Psychologists believe that how someone retrieves information (how they search for it and find it in memory) depends on how they acquired it (how they organized and stored it). Studies shows that encoding and retrieval account for most of the memory performance differences between younger and older people.

Researchers find that, compared with younger people, older people use less efficient strategies to encode (or learn) information. Perfect and Dasgupta (1997) found that older adults could not think of encoding strategies or used less elaborate methods of encoding. The researchers believe that encoding, rather than retrieval, accounts for the lower recall rate in older adults (Schieber, 2003). Annon and Lee (1994) found that it takes older people longer to get information into memory.

Ska and Nespoulous (1988, p. 408) found that "elderly subjects reproduced less during the encoding phase and retrieved fewer elements during the recall phase." Speeded tasks increase the gap between young and old subjects. Older people take in less information and fail to encode some items. They miss items presented rapidly, miss items late in a list, and encode some items at the expense of others. Older people may do worse on speed trials because they do not have time to encode effectively.

Older people, compared with younger people, also have more trouble with retrieval. It takes older people longer to get information out. Cerella (1990), for example, found that latency (the time a person takes to process or retrieve information) increases with age. This occurs regardless of the content of the task (Nettelbeck & Rabbitt, 1992). Cerella says this shows a "generalized slowing" in the nervous system, and he considers this a classical finding in the field of cognitive psychology.

More recent research supports this conclusion. Madden (2001, p. 289) says that "slowing is a fundamental dimension of age-related change in cognitive function . . . ." Birren and Schroots (1996) say that these findings show the link between decreased brain integrity and mental ability. Park (2000) likens the older mind to a computer. The computer has a large store of memory in the hard drive. But it has limited RAM (random access memory). This computer will process information slowly. The processor cannot efficiently use the large store of memory in the hard drive. "The computer works, but perhaps a little less efficiently than one would like" (Park, 2000, p. 5).

Some years ago Cerella (1990, p. 201) traced the slowing of mental functioning to breakdown in the physiology with age. Mental functioning (such as memory), he says, may be "distributed throughout the information-processing system rather than being localized in particular stages." He proposed that breakdown in the older person's neural network accounts for the slowing of information processing. Breakdowns in the network lead to more travel time within the brain before a message registers. This explains the generalized slowing of response, and it accounts for why older people do less well on speed trials.

Lindenberger and Baltes (1997, cited in Park, 2000) propose that sensory decline serves as a measure of brain integrity and has a strong impact on all cognitive abilities. They found that visual and auditory ability explained nearly all age-related declines on a series of psychological tests. Further research by this team controlled for education, social class, and income. They still found declines in cognition based on sensory decline. They say that this points to "a common factor or ensemble of factors," the decrease in the brain's structural and functional integrity.

Recent work supports this view. Raz (2000) reviewed the literature on the relationship between mental performance and neural activity in the brain. Studies of encoding found that, compared with younger people, older people showed less activation or no activation in certain parts of the brain during these tests. The studies also found differences in how older and younger people's brains functioned when they worked on harder verbal recall tasks. Researchers have begun to describe the neural sources of memory changes in later life.

Research on the link between brain function and mental performance has just begun (Prull, Gabrieli,

& Bunge, 2000). The most recent edition of the *Handbook of Aging and Cognition* (Craik & Salthouse, 2000) contains several reviews of the literature on brain function and mental performance. Psychologists have also studied genetics, cellular function, and brain physiology to understand the effects of aging on mental ability. These studies show a growing interest among psychologists in the biology and physiology of mental functioning.

Laboratory studies reveal a systematic decline in memory with age. But differences in educational background, test conditions, and lack of experience at encoding can all influence performance. Barnes and her colleagues (2004) studied literacy and mental ability in a group of white, well-educated, older people (mean age, 76). They found a strong relationship between literacy and all measures of mental ability in their study. The higher the rate of literacy, the higher the test scores on mental functioning.

Studies show that a supportive test environment leads to improvements in older subjects' ability to learn paired words. Supports can include guidance in how to encode information, testing people on familiar topics, giving people control over the speed of learning, and external cues to help learning (Zacks, Hasher, & Li, 2000). All of these supports lead to better performance.

Memory and Everyday Life

Laboratory studies raise an important question: How well do these findings describe how an older person functions in everyday life? The answer is not very well. We know that in the laboratory older people, compared with younger people, do less well under time pressure or when they have to learn information that they see as irrelevant (Hess, Rosenberg, & Waters, 2001). But memory studies have poor ecological validity (they do not translate well from laboratory to life) (Park & Gutchess, 2000; Rendell & Thomson, 2002).

Studies of familiar problem-solving tasks show older people can do as well as younger people. Mireles and Charness (2002) used a neural network model to measure chess-playing performance in the laboratory. They found older people, who often had a larger knowledge base, recalled more accurately than did younger people. Preexisting knowledge overcame some of the effects of the slowing due to neural breakdown.

Craik (2000) found that semantic memory, our store of factual information, shows little decline with age. On IQ tests, for example, older and younger people show little difference in their knowledge. Older people also have a good memory for past personal events (Zacks, Hasher, & Li, 2000). The more automatic the recall (e.g., driving a car in the person's own neighborhood), the better the older person will perform (Park & Gutchess, 2000). Poon (1985, p. 435) says that "in general, evidence to date shows minimal differences in memory for familiar discourse materials that may be found in the everyday environment."

Liu and Park (2003) say that older people who keep up their mental abilities can compensate for losses in mental functioning. They may put more effort into a task, they may draw on experience and skill, or they may develop new skills. Willis (1996) says that experts use strategies that decrease their need to search for information. They skillfully select the information they need. People with a high level of skill tend to use these methods.

Dixon and Cohen (2001) say that **competence** (a person's skill at real world tasks) can improve with age. Research shows that a simple practice like note taking reduces the pressure on working memory and leads to better comprehension and better recall (Morrow, 2003). They go on to say that older people often show more competence in daily life than psychological tests suggest.

Older people appear to have more mental ability than tests measure. Adams and her colleagues (2002) studied how well older and younger women recalled a story that the researchers asked them to tell. They found that younger storytellers showed better recall than older storytellers when they told their stories to an experimenter. But they found no differences in recall when the older and younger storytellers told their stories to children. Also, the older storytellers, more than younger storytellers, adjusted the complexity of their retelling to suit their listeners. The researchers say that memory research needs to take social context into account when comparing older and younger subjects.

Backman and his colleagues (2000, p. 501) summarize the literature on memory and aging:

> no form of memory appears to be fully resistant to the negative influence of human aging. Thus, age-related deficits may be observed in tasks assessing implicit memory . . . semantic memory . . . primary memory . . . working memory . . . and episodic memory. . . . However it is important to note that the size of age-related deficits and the consistency with which such deficits are observed varies systematically across different forms of memory. Specifically, age deficits tend to be *large and robust for measures of episodic memory and working memory, smaller and more contingent on demand characteristics in tasks assessing implicit and semantic memory, and even smaller in primary memory tasks*" [italics added].

Studies show that memory in old age varies by individual (education and gender), life-style (social activity), and health. Some people show greater decreases in memory than do others. Also, research shows that older people have a reserve mental capacity. They can improve memory performance by using memory cues and by training. Salthouse and Craik (2000, p. 701) say that researchers should look at ways that older people can put off the declines that come with age and "optimize [their] mental capacities."

Intelligence

Intelligence refers to the mind's ability to function. Psychologists have developed tests to measure intelligence, and studies of intelligence mirror the research on memory. According to Woodruff-Pak (1989), the study of adult intelligence went through four phases. In phase I (1920 to 1950), researchers believed that intelligence declined steeply with age. In phase II (late 1950s to mid-1960s), researchers placed more emphasis on stability in intelligence in later life. In phase III (late 1960s to mid-1970s), research on improving intelligence test scores met with some success. In phase IV (late 1970s to present), researchers developed a new understanding of intelligence. This includes the study of wisdom and new methods used to explore this concept.

Most intelligence studies take place in a laboratory and compare performance of younger and older people on intelligence tests. Berg and Sternberg (2003, p. 104) call this the "psychometric perspective." This perspective has dominated the field. Studies up to the 1960s used cross-sectional methods. They showed a peak in intelligence around age 30 and a steady decline after that. Later longitudinal studies showed a decline as well, but only after age 60 (Schaie, 1990a).

Intelligence tests assess a number of mental skills. These include skill in vocabulary, comprehension, and performance (e.g., the mental rotation of a figure). Studies showed that older people do less well on performance scale scores than on verbal scale scores. Botwinick (1984, p. 254) says this "classic aging pattern, relative maintenance of function in verbal skills as compared to performance skills, has been seen many times with a variety of different populations." These findings show that when tests measure more than one dimension, results show both decline and stability with age.

In the 1960s, Horn and Cattell (1966; 1967; Cattell, 1963) proposed a multidimensional model of intelligence. They described two types of mental abilities: **fluid intelligence** and **crystallized intelligence**. Their model proposed that these two types of intelligence differ in their rate of decline with age.

Fluid intelligence refers to activities like creative design, quick response to a question, or mental rearrangement of facts. This type of intelligence relies on how well the central nervous system works. Crystallized intelligence refers to abilities like vocabulary, association of past and present ideas, and technical ability. It depends on a person's education or store of information.

Researchers suggest that fluid intelligence declines after age 14. Fluid intelligence includes many of the processes linked to memory, like organizing and storing information. Crystallized intelligence, on the other hand, refers to information already learned. This increases throughout adulthood as a person gains more knowledge and skill. Studies found declines in crystallized intelligence only after age 70 (Horn, 1982).

This model explains the differences between older peoples' verbal and performance scores. Verbal scales measure crystallized intelligence; performance questions measure fluid intelligence. Fluid intelligence may follow the decline of the biological system from the teen years on. Crystallized intelligence shows stable intelligence scores and even increased scores with age (Park, 2000).

Longitudinal and Cross-Sectional Methods

Some researchers have criticized the methods used to conduct research on memory and intelligence. Most of this research uses cross-sectional designs (Schaie & Hofer, 2001). Studies test young and old people at one point in time and compare their scores. These findings confound differences between age cohorts with changes that take place due to aging. For example, young and old people in these studies differ in test-taking ability, language skill, health, and other conditions. These differences account for some of the differences found in memory and intelligence scores. Cross-sectional studies cannot say whether memory changes in an individual over time. Schaie and Hofer (2001) say that cross-sectional studies "provide a very poor basis for inference" about how age affects changes in an individual's mental functioning.

Longitudinal studies attempt to overcome this problem. These studies look at changes in individuals' scores over time (Schaie & Hofer, 2001). They separate the effects of **age differences** from **age changes**. Longitudinal studies find that some individuals show little decline with age, others show more. They also show that some older people have scores that equal those of some younger people. These findings point to differences between individuals within an age group and to similarities in ability between age groups.

Schaie (1990b, p. 114) studied one group of older people over time. He found that "virtually none of the individuals . . . showed universal decline in all abilities monitored, even by the eighties." This finding suggests that people experience unique changes in their mental abilities as they age—some people show decline, but others show stability or even improvement (Birren & Schroots, 1996).

Some research explores the older person's ability to improve intellectual functioning. Schaie (1996), for example, conducted a seven-year longitudinal study. He found that, compared with a control group, trained older subjects showed less decline in intelligence over time. He proposes refresher courses to help older people retain the benefits of training. Older people who live in good health and in a challenging environment score better on intelligence tests than those who do not (Gold et al., 1995). People who read books and newspapers, who travel and talk with friends, keep their minds fresh.

Researchers now think that individuals can modify their intellectual functioning as they age. Baltes (1997, cited in Norris 1998, p. ii), has developed a model of mental development in later life that he calls "selective optimization and compensation." He says that people who age well select tasks that will likely lead to success. They keep up the skills they have and they compensate for losses by gaining new skills and knowledge.

This model recognizes that aging can bring loss. But it also shows that people can adapt to changes and improve their mental ability as they age. Berg and Sternberg (2003) say that greater use of selective optimization may lead to more successful aging and greater life satisfaction.

Baltes and Willis (1982, pp. 120–121) say that "people can learn to make better use of their minds at any age. The logical approach [to observed decrements in mental functioning in late life] might be the development of compensatory education programs at about the time of retirement." Chapter 12 discusses some of these programs in detail.

NEW MODELS OF MENTAL ABILITY IN LATER LIFE

Schroots (1995) says that psychologists tend to view life as a hill: mental ability increases, reaches a plateau, then declines. But, Schroots says, this view has begun to change. Researchers have begun to study wisdom. And this offers a different view of psychological change in later life.

Paul B. Baltes, Director of Berlin's Max Planck Institute for Human Development and Education, has conducted some of the most respected research on intelligence. He says that two concepts have led to changes in his thinking about mental ability in later life (Baltes & Baltes, 1990). First, research

BOX 6.1
FIVE CRITERIA OF WISDOM

Paul Baltes, the head of the Berlin Wisdom Project, prepared a list of five criteria for wisdom. He based the list on research findings from cognitive psychology and life span development theory. A person who had wisdom, he says, would have "exceptional insight into life matters and good judgment and advice about difficult life problems."

1. Rich factual knowledge about life matters.
2. Rich procedural knowledge about life problems.
3. Life span contextualism: Knowledge about the contexts of life and their temporal (developmental) relationships.
4. Relativism: Knowledge about differences in values and priorities.
5. Uncertainty: Knowledge about the relative indeterminacy and unpredictability of life and ways to manage it.

Source: P. B. Baltes, J. Smith, U. M. Staudinger, & D. Sowarka. (1990). "Wisdom: One facet of successful aging?" In M. Perlmutter, (Ed.). *Late life potential,* 63–81 Washington, DC: Gerontological Society of America. Reprinted with permission of the author.

shows variability between individuals. In general, younger people outperform older people on intelligence tests, but on a given measure, some older people perform better than younger people.

Morse (1993), for example, found the greatest variability among older people on fluid intelligence tasks. Second, research shows **plasticity** in brain function, personality change, and skill development for each individual. Each person has a reserve mental capacity. Each person can change and adapt. Training, practice, and education can enhance the ability to grow in later life. Dixon and Cohen (2001, p. 138) say that these findings offer a "cautiously optimistic perspective, with emphases on resilience and adaptation in late life . . . ."

Baltes (1992; 1993) concludes that past research has taken too narrow a view of mental ability in later life. He says that certain types of cognitive processes, what he calls **cognitive mechanics** (similar to fluid intelligence), decline with age. Other types of cognitive processes, what he calls **cognitive pragmatics** (similar to crystallized intelligence), improve with age. Baltes says that knowledge and culture can enrich cognitive pragmatics throughout life.

Baltes set out to explore the "new domain" of cognitive pragmatics in old age. To do this he set up the *Berlin wisdom project.* This project defines wisdom as "expert knowledge about the important and fundamental matters of life, their interpretation and management" (Featherman, Smith, & Peterson, 1990). The project studies wisdom by asking older people to solve real-life problems. One problem, for example, asked people to respond to a suicidal call from a friend. Another asked people to give advice to a 15-year-old girl who wants to get married (White, 1993).

A person who displays wisdom has insight into life's conditions and shows good judgment. This person gives good advice. Rybash, Hoyer, and Roodin (1986) say that younger people may do better than older people in problem solving in a laboratory or classroom. They can answer clearly structured problems faster than older people. But older people may do better at *problem finding.* Older people have a greater ability to shape and solve a problem in a less-defined situation (Shedlock & Cornelius, 2003). Baltes (1992) reports that older people get higher scores than younger people on problems related to real-life dilemmas. More than half of the top responses, he says, come from people over age 60.

Montgomery and her colleagues (2002) studied wisdom in a group of people aged 60 to 88. They found that wise people guided others, had knowledge and experience, and applied moral principles. Ardelt (2000) found that wisdom in older women led to greater life satisfaction, better health, and better family relationships. McKee and Barber (1999) say that wisdom allows a person to critically view cultural illusions and to act on the basis of universal

BOX 6.2
WISDOM IN LATER LIFE

Socrates, in *The Republic,* says that he likes to talk to older people. They have gone along a path that all of us will one day follow. Their years have given them knowledge about life and aging. Some might call it wisdom. Consider the following thoughts on aging by some thoughtful older people.

Art Blake, a retired judge from Jamaica, says that recently he attended the funeral of a friend. He flew back to Jamaica and went directly to the church from the airport. His plane landed early, so he arrived at the church before anyone else. "I watched as the people arrived," he says. "Many of them I knew from my childhood; we went to school and grew up together. These are all old people, I thought. Then I thought, I too must look like this. But I couldn't see it in myself. I shave every day and I don't see my age. But I could see it in them. . . . The mind plays tricks on you."

Art serves as the legal advisor to an education program for older people and sits on the advisory board of a university certification program. "We want to be young," Art says. "We use creams to smooth out the wrinkles. But this is the most natural process. We cannot help but get old."

Bertrand Russell developed new interests as he aged. He began his career as a mathematician, moved on to philosophy, then in late old age turned to political and social issues. At age 80 he said that the best way to overcome old age "is to make your interests gradually wider and more impersonal, until bit by bit the walls of the ego recede, and your life becomes increasingly merged in the universal life. An individual human existence should be like a river—small at first, narrowly contained within its banks, and rushing passionately past boulders and over waterfalls. Gradually the river grows wider, the banks recede, the waters flow more quietly, and in the end, without any visible break, they become merged in the sea and painlessly lose their individual being."

John Holt, an educator who wrote about children and their untapped potential, reflected on education for adults later in his career. Holt took up the cello in late middle age. In his book *Never Too Late,* he wrote about his experience learning the instrument and about his own potential as a person: "If I could learn to play the cello well, as I thought I could, I could show by my own example that we all have greater powers than we think; that whatever we want to learn or learn to do, we probably can learn; that our lives and our possibilities are not determined and fixed by what happened to us when we were little, or by what experts say we can or cannot do."

Sources: From *Vital maturity,* by M. Puner (1979). New York: Universe Books; and *Never too late: My musical life story,* by J. Holt (1978). New York: Delacorte Press.

principles. Kramer (2003, p. 132) that a wise person has an "awareness of the relativistic, uncertain, and paradoxical nature of reality." This person interacts with others "in a way that does not put those others on the defensive" (Kramer, 2003, p. 133).

Wisdom makes older people more skilled at working in everyday life. This could allow older people to play a unique role in modern society. Baltes and his colleagues suggest that a society with more older people will have a greater storehouse of wisdom. Society could use that wisdom to redefine problems that escape rational and technical solutions (Featherman, Smith, & Peterson, 1990).

More older people thinking and advising about practical problems could enhance the quality of life for everyone. But for this to occur, society first has to recognize wisdom in its older people (Baltes, 1993). Then it has to have the good sense to make use of it. Baltes's work takes the first step by expanding our view of mental potential in later life.

PERSONALITY DEVELOPMENT AND THE SELF

Some psychologists and social psychologists have focused on personality growth in later life. Erik Erikson (1963) developed one of the best-known models of human development. McCrae and Costa (1990, pp. 11–12) call it "the single most important theory of adult personality development." Erikson based his model of the life course on Freud's psychosexual stages. The model assumes that:

1. A fixed set of stages for the life course exists.
2. These stages unfold over time just as the physiology develops over time.
3. At each stage the person faces a challenge with a positive and a negative pole.
4. A healthy personality will achieve the goal of the positive pole and then have the resources to tackle the challenge of the next stage.

Erikson's model of the life course has eight stages. The eighth stage corresponds to old age. Erikson says that in this stage a person either achieves a sense of "integrity" or falls into "despair and doubt." This stage demands that a person "be, through having been, to face not being" (Erikson, 1959, Appendix). Erikson describes this last stage as a time of inwardness and reflection. One reviews the past and accepts one's life as a product of one's actions within one's culture. This last stage sums up the other stages. A person who achieves integrity faces death without despair. This person serves as a model for the young, who learn to trust their culture and follow its prescriptions (Erikson, 1963; 1982).

A number of gerontologists have criticized the final stage of Erikson's model (Butler, 1975; Novak, 1985–1986). This stage describes old age as a time to disengage from life and look back. It ignores the fact that older people go on living. Butler, for example, takes issue with the idea that people in old age can only accept who they are and what they have been. "People are locked in by such a theory," he says. They may look healthy from Erikson's point of view, but they suffer because they are trapped by their work, marriage, or life-style. "Excessive or exaggerated identity seems clearly to be an obstacle to continued growth and development through life and to appreciation of the future. . . . Human beings need the freedom to live with change, to invent themselves a number of times throughout their lives" (Butler, 1975, pp. 400–401).

Other researchers have expanded or modified on Erikson's model. Antonovsky and Sagy (1990) studied people of retirement age in Israel. They re-

"You're still the King of the Apes as far as I'm concerned, dear."

port four developmental tasks around the time of retirement—active involvement, reevaluation of life satisfaction, reevaluation of world outlook, and development of a sense of health maintenance. Boegeman (1989) taught a creative writing class to people aged 60 to 80. She reported that the women in her classes saw themselves as still growing and learning. Boegeman said that women at this age have more time to devote to creative work than earlier in their lives. This raises the question of gender differences in personality development. Do men and women follow the same stages at the same time?

Research findings point to varied patterns of development that depend on social context as well as inner unfolding (Hendricks, 1999). This contextual view of life span development takes into account a person's culture, social class, educational level, and gender. It also looks at a person's sociohistorical context (Lamme & Barrs, 1993).

Moody (1993), for example, links the life course described by Erikson and others to life structured by mass education and industrialism. Fry (2003, p. 284) calls this the " 'institutionalized' life course." The structure of this life course emerged in the late nineteenth and early twentieth centuries. This may have been a limited moment in the history of western societies. This life course fits a society where a child goes to school, a young person takes one job for life, and an older person retires with a pension.

Fry (2003, p. 284) finds other life course structures in other societies. Small-scale societies, for example, often refer to a "generational life course." "Within generational life courses, the life plan is to mature into adulthood, have a family, work in subsistence, and simply live."

Eyetsemitan and Gire (2003) studied the life course in seven nations. They found that Erikson's stages did not fit the timing of life events or the roles of older people in developing nations. They found that stages occurred at much lower ages than in the developed world. For example, the stage of late adulthood could occur as early as age 44 or less. They also found that older people in developed nations often played a "generative" role that Erikson's theory puts in middle adulthood.

Moody (1993, p. xix) says that old age "is becoming less determinate, less role-governed, and other life stages are moving in that direction as well." Today, people divorce, remarry, have children, start businesses, leave careers, return to careers, and return to school at all ages in adulthood. Studies find many stages in the life cycle and different stages and patterns for men and women. These findings reflect the diversity of the life course in a time of social change (Ryff, Kwan, & Singer, 2001).

Self-Development in Later Life

Critics of stage models call for a more flexible model of the self in later life. Some social psychologists put this dynamic model of the self at the center of their studies (Ruth & Coleman, 1996).

Breytspraak (1995, p. 93) defines the self as "the ability to be aware of one's own boundaries and individuality and to reflect upon these." Ritzer (1992, p. 202) says the self has "the ability to take oneself as an object." It can act as both subject and object. Sociologist George Herbert Mead (1934) theorized that the self had two parts: the *I* and the *me*. The *I* referred to the inner world of the person, to impulses, motives, hopes, and fears. The *me* referred to the self constructed through social interaction. The *me* responds to social norms and values. It arises and is maintained through social contact. Through the self we can take the role of the other person and see ourselves as (we imagine) others see us. The *me* makes a person sensitive to the views of others and to social norms and values in general.

Breytspraak (1995) says that two motives shape behavior as people age. First, people try to view themselves positively and to present a good image of themselves to others. Second, people try to maintain their sense of self in the face of a changing social environment. This makes the self a dynamic process more than a state of being. The self constantly shapes interaction and interprets events to achieve these two goals. Blanchard-Fields and Abeles (1996), for example, found that older and younger people view themselves differently. Older people, compared with younger people, have a more limited view of their future selves. They reported fewer hopes and fears for their future selves. And they tend to define themselves in relation to their current concerns, especially health. This reflects the older person's place in the life course and their realistic view of the future.

McAdams (1996, p. 134) says that identity in later life relies on a "lifestory." And this story, along with the self, changes over time (Tornstam, 1999). Near the end of life, the self may live in the present. Ruth and Coleman (1996, p. 317) reviewed studies that described a "spiritual Me." A person in later life may begin an inward journey. Tornstam (1999) refers to this as "gero-transcendence"—the self begins to expand its boundaries and reflect on the meaning of human life. At this time, a person reviews the connection to childhood, the link to earlier generations, and the meaning of life and death.

Aging poses a number of challenges to the self. These challenges come from at least three sources: social attitudes toward older people, physical decline, and the loss of social roles. Ageism, for example, poses a challenge to everyone in later life. The self's sensitivity to others' perceptions can make ageism a painful experience. It can lower a person's self-esteem. In our society a person must work to combat ageism. A strong social support network makes this easier. For example, friends and family can give a person feelings of worth and importance that combat negative stereotypes.

Physical decline also challenges a person's sense of self. People who get their self-esteem from playing sports may feel let down as their ability decreases with age. Our culture links driving a car with maturity, adulthood, freedom, and self-sufficiency. No longer being able to drive may undermine an older person's self-esteem. Even people with Alzheimer's disease, a radical loss of the self, resist giving up driving.

Sports programs for older people, such as the Seniors Olympics or the Seniors Golf Tour, help people maintain their self-esteem in the face of physical decline. So do programs that refresh older people's driving skills. Tornstam (1999) found that a health crisis can challenge views of the self that are taken for granted. It can lead to an inward journey. A 68-year-old man who learned that he had heart disease says that his illness caused him to read books he would never have otherwise read. "I think there is so much in these new things . . ." he says, "I'm in the middle of a process where I have a lot to learn."

Finally, role loss can rob a person of self-worth. Social roles give a person status, purpose, and a sense of achievement. Loss of roles threatens a person's well-being. Retirement, widowhood, and the empty nest all challenge a person's sense of self. Most people cope with these role losses and find new sources of esteem. A widow may find self-worth in volunteer work counseling other widows. A retired machinist may find self-esteem in a second career as a handyman. Sometimes these new roles lead to a more satisfying sense of self. The challenge of role loss demands that the older person search for new meaning in later life. This search for a good age can take many forms.

Ryff and Keyes (1996, cited in Qualls, 2002, p. 10) report six dimensions of psychological well-being in later life: "autonomy, environmental mastery, personal growth, positive relations with others, purpose in life, and self-acceptance." Ryff and her colleagues (1999) report that wealthier, better educated people feel more purpose in life and report more personal growth in old age. Ryff and Keyes' summary of the literature shows the link between the self and social conditions like income, education, and social class.

A person's culture also plays a role in self-development. How does the culture view old age? What roles does the culture offer older people? Answers to these questions shape a person's sense of self in later life. Singer and Ryff (1999, cited in Ryff, Kwan, & Singer, 2001) found, for example, that people with a history of poverty showed less physical decline if they had strong social relationships. A person with more resources (e.g., education, money, health) has a better chance of achieving psychological health in later life. Ryff and her colleagues (2001) call for more research on the effect of social integration on health and well-being in later life.

Spirituality: The Search for Meaning in Later Life

The search for a good old age can take many forms, including religious faith, service attendance, and nontraditional spiritual beliefs. Some people see spirituality as their personal relationship to God.

Others see God everywhere in the natural world. Moberg (2001, p. 10) defines spirituality as a person's "ultimate concern, the basic value around which all other values are focused, the central philosophy of life."

Spirituality can take place within organized religion or through personal beliefs and rituals. Some people express their spirituality outside traditional religious channels. They may feel oneness with nature or a commitment to the betterment of all life. Benjamin Franklin, for example, expressed his spiritual beliefs through service to his fellow citizens. Some older people turn to eastern and western meditation practices to feel a sense of wholeness. They feel that yoga and T'ai chi exercises create a sense of unity within themselves and with the environment. Studies show that spiritual practices such as these can lead to better health, improved social relations, and high life satisfaction (Chan, 2003).

The diversity of American life today, with its many ethnic and cultural groups, leads to many different religious and spiritual perspectives. Most Americans claim some form of Christianity as their religious belief. Other faiths include Judaism, Islam, Bahai, Buddhism, Hinduism, Sikhism, Confucianism, and Taoism.

American spiritual life in the past often centered on the church or synagogue. Religion gave people a common set of values, involved them in a community of like-minded people, and gave meaning to life. Many older people today still feel a strong connection to their religious communities and have a strong religious faith (McFadden, 1996). And older age groups have kept up their attendance even though younger age groups show a decrease in religious attendance. More than one-third of the older people in one study said they would spend more time on religion if they could change their commitments (DeGenova, 1992, cited in McFadden, 1996).

Seniors also report the largest financial contributions to their place of worship. Moberg (1997, cited in Schulz-Hipp, 2001, p. 87) says that older people show the strongest religious belief "on almost all measures" and that "this has remained the same year after year when similar questions are asked." This commitment to religion partly reflects the past experiences of older people. In the past, religion played a bigger role in people's lives than it does today.

The commitment to religion may also reflect the role that faith can play as way to cope when health, income, and social supports decline in late old age. Coping methods include prayer, faith in God, and support from clergy and the faith community. Religious belief can help a person find meaning in the face of despair.

Religious leaders and caregivers can help older people live their faith. It's important that professionals understand and respect the religious traditions of the people they serve. Professionals can help a religious community provide support to older members, and they can help older members take part in their religious communities. Support can take the form of arranging outreach religious services or carpools to places of worship.

Spiritual practices, whether formal religious services or quiet reflection on the past, can bring fullness to later life. Psychologist Viktor Frankl (1990, pp. 7–10) teaches that later life provides a unique time for inner growth. He says that older people can bring in the "the harvest of their lives." McFadden (1996) says that researchers and practitioners need to learn more about the many expressions of religion and spirituality in later life. They can then apply this understanding to improve the quality of later life.

SOCIAL PSYCHOLOGICAL CHANGE

Social psychologists propose at least three ways for people to adapt to changes as they age—disengagement, activity, and continuity.

Disengagement Theory

The **disengagement theory** of a good age grew out of the Kansas City Studies of Adult Life in the 1960s. The Kansas City project took place in two waves. The second wave interviewed 280 people aged 50 to 90 over a six-year period. Researchers from a number of disciplines, including psychology and sociology, conducted the research, and many publications reported their findings. One discovery was that as people aged, social interaction decreased. This decreased interaction took place, at least in part, because society withdrew from the older person (e.g., through mandatory retirement).

Cumming and Henry (1961) developed the disengagement theory of aging out of these findings. Disengagement theory saw decreased interaction as the outcome of *mutual* withdrawal of society and the older person. Disengagement, they said, allows older people to naturally withdraw from social contacts and roles as their strength declines. It also allows society to remove older people from social roles before the final disengagement—death. This creates a smooth transition from one generation to the next. Disengagement theory sees withdrawal as inevitable, universal, and satisfying to the individual and society.

Critics attacked disengagement theory for at least three reasons. First, it supports the negative stereotype of older people as frail and unable to perform social roles. Second, the theory assumes that younger people perform social roles better than older people. This supports mandatory retirement based on age. Third, it assumes that all older people will (or should) respond to aging in the same way.

Activity Theory

Activity theory serves as an antithesis to disengagement theory. This theory says that activity leads to the highest satisfaction in later life. Activity theory assumes that older people have the same needs as people in middle age. It assumes that disengagement takes place against the older person's will (e.g., through mandatory retirement or the death of age mates). Satisfied older people resist the shrinkage of their social roles. They find substitutes for the roles that they lose over time.

Neugarten, Havighurst, and Tobin (1968) reanalyzed the Kansas City data used by Cumming and Henry. Using different measures, they found "moderate support for the activity theory" (Neugarten, 1987, p. 373). They also found at least three types of active people who report high life satisfaction. One group started new activities to fill in for lost roles. The researchers called this group "reorganizers." A second group stayed active and held on to middle-aged roles. The researchers said these people were "holding-on." A third group narrowed the range of their activities but stayed active. The researchers called these people "focused."

More recent research finds that activity leads to high life satisfaction (Carstensen, 1991; Johnson & Barer, 1992). However, research also suggests that both activity and disengagement theory give too simple an account of aging. Activity alone, for example, cannot ensure satisfaction in later life. Ray and Heppe (1986) found that the number of activities did not predict happiness, but a commitment to activities did. Studies show that people report the greatest satisfaction when they engage in activities that they find meaningful (Singleton, Forbes, & Agwani, 1993).

Continuity Theory

Continuity theory emphasizes continuity over the life course. Atchley (1999b) says that people age best if they can view change in later life within an existing pattern of thought or behavior. People also

Sol Lewinson, a model of continuity, lives in Los Angeles and has been selling vacuum cleaners since the 1930s.

adapt best if they can use strategies from their past experience to cope with current challenges.

Atchley applies continuity theory to internal structures like a person's sense of self. He also applies it to external structures like the environment, relationships, and activities. Continuity theory suggests that mildly active people in their middle years will feel most satisfied with a mildly active old age. Very active people will stay very active.

Quirouette and Pushkar (1999) studied a group of well-educated women. They found that these women planned to continue their activities. The women had a strong core identity, and they expected their abilities to continue into later life. Research by Smale and Dupuis (1993, pp. 298–299) supports "the importance of continued involvement in leisure activity throughout one's lifetime even if some activities are dropped in favour of others." Atchley (1989) says that a person's own preferences and social expectations create continuity in later life.

Atchley (1989) contrasts continuity theory with activity theory. He says that activity theory assumes that for a good age a person needs to balance each loss of activity with a gain, but continuity theory assumes an evolution. People integrate new experiences into their past history and move forward. Atchley uses the model of a drama to describe this process. "Everyday life for most older people," he says, "is like long-running improvisational theater in which the settings, characters, and actions are familiar and in which the changes are mostly in the form of new episodes rather than entirely new plays" (Atchley, 1989, p. 185). Continuity leads to a strong self-image, good mental health, and competence in daily life.

Each of the three theories—disengagement, activity, and continuity—offers insight into how people adapt to change as they age. Some studies suggest that the disengagement theory applies best to people in late old age (Gray & Calsyn, 1989). People in this phase of life may lack the energy to keep up their past activities. They may welcome disengagement and find satisfaction in a less active life-style. Other studies support the activity and continuity theories (Beck & Page, 1988; Singleton, Forbes, & Agwani, 1993). Studies of aging in other countries using the Kansas City measures have found more patterns of good aging. Neugarten concludes that there is "no single pattern of optimum aging" (1987, p. 373).

The Life Course Perspective

The **life course perspective** is a grand view of the life cycle. It includes growth through social roles and stages of life, it takes into account social institutions, and it places all of this in a historical context (Stevens-Long & Michaud, 2003).

The life course perspective contrasts with simpler models of the life cycle. The simplest life cycle model proposes a steady decline in function with age. Shakespeare offers one view of this model, in which life ends "sans teeth, sans eyes, sans taste, sans everything." Biological studies support this model. However, once psychologists move away from a biological model, as they need to do in adult studies, they require new concepts (Stevens-Long & Michaud, 2003). These concepts link the individual to the social environment. The life course perspective offers this view.

First, the life course perspective sees development as a lifelong process. The person changes continually from birth to death. This model differs from stage models. It does not include an end point (such as ego integrity). Instead it sees crisis and change as an ongoing part of life. Riegel (1979, p. 13), an early proponent of the life course perspective, states this simply, ". . . developmental and historical tasks are never completed. At the very moment when completion seems to be achieved, new questions and doubts arise in the individual and society" (Riegel, 1976, p. 697).

Second, this model sees development as a process through which the individual and society change in response to each other. This gives rise to many stages of development and to many patterns of development. People's individual life course development depends on their physical condition, intelligence, personality, coping styles, resources, gender, race and ethnicity, and the social world they live in. This model turns the researcher's attention to the social context to explain the timing, direction, and length of developmental stages (Stevens-Long & Michaud, 2003; Wapner & Demick, 2003).

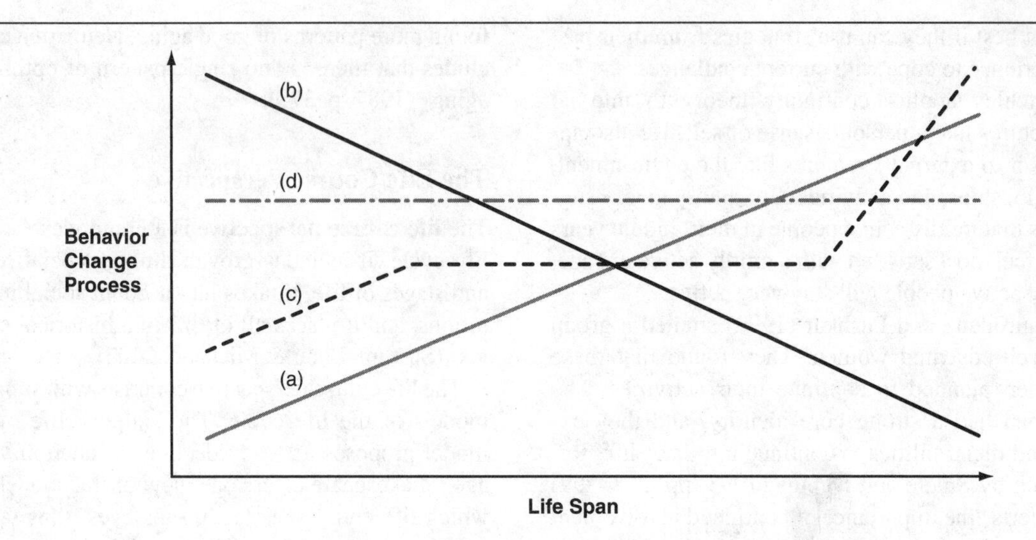

In this chart of life span development, the lines show that multidimensional and multidirectional changes can take place throughout life. A person can experience increases in some abilities (a) and decreases in others (b). Also, some abilities can take a nonlinear pattern (c). For example, a person may learn the piano in childhood, not play for many years, and then begin to play and improve again in later life. Many other patterns occur as well, including stability throughout life (d).

FIGURE 6.1
Life Span Development

Source: Adapted from "Developmental psychology," by P. Baltes, 1987, in G. L. Maddox (Ed.), *The encyclopedia of aging,* pp. 170–175. New York: Springer Publishing Company, Inc., New York 10036. Used by permission.

Third, this model sees development as a normal part of living at every age. The child, for example, grows physically taller and stronger. The adult gains more social influence and status with age. A person, even in late old age, can create wholeness and a sense of continuity out of past experience. This search for meaning in later life can take the form of new roles (as family advisor or confidant to the young) or through reminiscence and life review. Settersten (2003) presents a summary of the life course perspective's main principles (see Figure 6.1):

1. Development is multidimensional and multispheral: People develop biologically, physically, psychologically, and socially. And development in each dimension takes place at different rates. Likewise, development takes place in many spheres of life—in the family, at work, through leisure, etc.
2. Development is multidirectional: People change throughout the life course. They may grow and develop on one dimension and may decline or experience stability on another dimension. For example, a person may grow in knowledge in later life, but may decline physically.
3. Development takes place throughout life: Development goes on from birth through death. But development takes different forms—it occurs at different rates, on different dimensions, and within different spheres—at different times in life. Early views of human development focused on childhood and youth. The life course perspective looks at the whole of life. So, for example, a disabled older person may regain a lost ability through exercise and physiotherapy.
4. Development takes place through continuity and discontinuity: Some development takes place at specific times in life, other developments take place throughout life. Physical

growth or maturation takes place from childhood to young adulthood. But learning and the growth of wisdom go on throughout life.

5. Development takes place in an historical context: Historical, social, and demographic events shape the lives individuals and age cohorts. The Baby Boom generation has lived through a time of prosperity and peace in the United States. Post-WWII prosperity, television, mass advertising, mass education, and the rebellious years of the 1960s all shaped the lives of Baby Boomers. They will bring these unique experiences with them into old age (adapted from Settersten, 2003).

The Structure of the Life Course

Society sets out the structure of the life course. This structure includes life events that mark transitions from one life stage to another.

Life Events

Life events shape personal development and the lives of entire cohorts of people. They present a person with the challenge of change. They often mark a transition between one stage of life and another. Life course researchers look at three types of life events: (1) nonnormative events (unplanned events, like an illness or an accident); (2) normative, history-graded events (like the Great Depression or World War II); and (3) normative, age-graded events (events that occur at a certain time in life, like a first marriage or retirement).

Nonnormative events come as a surprise and can strain our resources and coping methods. Normative, history-graded events link us to our culture and our time. They change the world and can leave a lifelong imprint on us. Normative, age-graded events guide us along a socially accepted path of growth. The study of life events looks at the influence of society on human development. It shows the importance of social patterns and cultural guideposts throughout the life course.

Nonnormative Life Events

Events such as accidents, illness, or a fight with a neighbor take place without warning. Society does not prescribe these events. They do not fit into the normal order of the life cycle and people cannot plan for them. Nonnormative events often come as a shock. An illness such as a stroke, for example, can damage a person's self-image and relationships. In one case, a husband and wife had been married for twenty-seven years. At age 52 the husband had a stroke that paralyzed his right side. He could barely talk and needed a wheelchair to move around. He felt depressed and bitter about his illness. His wife worried about his mood, which put a further strain on their relationship. Neither the husband nor wife had prepared themselves for this event, and society gave them little guidance about how to deal with it.

Normative, History-Graded Life Events

On the afternoon of November 22, 1963, I sat at my desk in the tenth grade in a classroom in Snyder High School in Jersey City, New Jersey. Someone called the teacher to the door. She came back into the room and told us that President John F. Kennedy had been shot in Dallas, Texas. We sat in silence as we heard the news. At the time, we did not know whether he would live. We ran home that day to watch the story unfold on television.

Nearly every American alive at the time of President Kennedy's death remembers where they heard the news. History-graded events such as the death of a president, the Great Depression, or the Vietnam War change the lives of all the people living at that time. These events have different effects on different age cohorts. People in the youngest age cohort, from birth to five years, will not remember an economic recession. People in their early 20s will experience that same recession just as they enter adulthood. They will remember those years as a time when they found it hard to enter the job market and start their careers. A history-graded event can shape the lives of an entire generation.

Demographers label the people born between 1945 and the early 1960s the Baby Boom, because of the increased number of births following World War II. This history-graded event has forced Baby Boomers to compete for grades, jobs, and houses. Easterlin (1987) says that the large size of this group led them to expect only modest economic success, and this in turn led them to have small families.

These same age cohorts may face a shortage of public pensions and services in retirement.

Cohorts that come after the Baby Boom will benefit from the size of the Boomer cohorts. The Baby Boom cohorts will begin to retire in the early years of the twenty-first century. This may cause a labor shortage that will leave younger people with their pick of jobs. Likewise, Boomers will sell their larger homes to move to smaller retirement homes. This may create a market in which younger people can buy these homes at lower prices.

Historical events get filtered through the age stratification system, the system of age grades a society uses (e.g., child, adolescent, young adult). The 1900 to 1910 cohort went through the Great Depression of the 1930s in young adulthood, and the Depression affected their decisions to marry, as it did the early years of their careers. The Depression also affected the cohort born between 1920 and 1930, but it had a different effect on these people. They lived through the Depression as children. Some of them may not remember the Depression at all; others may simply have accepted the hard times as "the way things are."

Gerontologists use the term **generation** to describe people who share an awareness of their common historical or cultural experiences, but who may come from different cohorts. The Baby Boom cohorts born between 1945 and the early 1960s form a generation; they have all lived under the threat of nuclear war, and they have lived in a relatively affluent time in American history. Braun and Sweet (1983–1984) developed a generational event theory of development. **Generational event theory** says that attitudes form for a generation in their teens. People who grow up at the same time in the same society share the same attitudes. And these attitudes shape a generation's worldview throughout life.

Like nonnormative events, history-graded events can happen without warning, and sometimes the changes they bring about do not show up until years later. The destruction of the World Trade Center on September 11, 2001, for example, had an immediate effect on American society. The President declared a war on terrorism, the government set up a new Office of Homeland Security, and everyone had to submit to more careful searches at airports.

The war in Iraq will also influence all Americans. But it will have a different effect on a two year old than on a 52 year old. Young children today will have little or no memory the World Trade Center bombing. They will read about it in their history books. Many young adult national guard personnel have gone to fight in Iraq. And some Baby Boomers protest the war in Iraq. They lived through the Viet Nam war era in their teen years, and they question the wisdom of fighting wars in foreign countries. This example shows how a single historical event can have a different effect on different age cohorts.

Normative, Age-Graded Life Events

Some years ago Riley, Johnson, and Foner (1972; Riley, Foner, & Riley, Jr., 1999) developed a sophisticated model of the life cycle, the age stratification model (later termed the *aging and society paradigm*). This model linked individual development to the social structures that shape personal growth. Riley and her colleagues said that society orders age cohorts into an **age stratification system**, a series of age grades through which people move as they age. They call this "cohort flow."

As cohorts age (and members die), cohorts replace one another in society's age structure. As cohorts flow through the age structure they change the size of particular age groups (e.g., the size of the group twenty to thirty years old will differ in 1940 and 1970 and 2010). New groups of people enter each age grade over time. People aged 20 to 25 today will enter the age grade of old age forty to forty-five years from now.

New cohorts also bring new experiences with them as they age. Older cohorts today, for example, have less education than younger cohorts. Younger, more educated groups will probably demand more educational opportunities when they reach old age.

People experience the age stratification system as a series of life events such as a high school graduation, the birth of a child, or retirement around a certain age. We enter high school, flow through a series of school grades, and leave after a few years. Younger students enter to take our place.

A 93-year-old former vicar and train enthusiast, Reverend Edgar Dowse is reportedly the oldest person in the world to earn a PhD. He received a doctorate in March 2004 from the London School of Theology, whose degrees are validated by Brunel University, UK. This is Doctor Dowse's seventh degree in higher education.

Normative, age-graded life events often fit the physical changes that take place as we age. Society expects a woman to have a child during the most active part of her childbearing years (aged 18 to 35). Likewise, we expect someone to graduate from high school around age 17 or 18. Society helps people make normative age grade transitions. For example, women in the United States hold baby showers to mark a woman's entry into motherhood. A high school graduation marks a passage to a new phase of life. Other events such as marriage or retirement involve **rites of passage** to bring closure to one life phase and help ease people into the next.

This structure of the life course includes the timing of life events such as graduation, marriage, and retirement. A 28-year-old medical school student, for example, may feel too old to be a student. Someone who retires at age 50 due to poor health may feel too young to leave the workforce. A person who gets promoted to vice president of marketing at age 25 may feel lucky to get this job so young. Social norms shape our sense of order and the timing of life events.

Settersten (2003) speaks of being **on time** or **off time** for life events. A person off time—early or late—may feel discomfort or dissatisfaction. Elder and Johnson (2003, p. 65) give the example of retired auto workers in poor health. These workers felt dissatisfied with retirement because they felt they had to leave work too early. A few years ago, a secretary in our office became a grandmother at age 40. She felt proud of her new granddaughter and wanted to tell everyone about her, but she also felt that being a grandmother made her an old woman, something she wanted to avoid. She therefore held back making a big announcement of the event. When she told people about her granddaughter, she would also explain how old this made her feel. By saying this she implied that she was not old, but that she was a grandmother ahead of schedule.

Life events also differ by gender. Society has expectations for when a woman will have a first child. Also, women, compared with men, experience widowhood in later life because in many cases women live longer and marry older men. A widowed woman will tend to stay unmarried. A widowed man will tend to remarry. Men, compared with women, will more likely retire on time (at age 65) due to their unbroken work careers and the likelihood that they will have a pension plan. Women have broken work careers (due to caregiving and child rearing responsibilities). They tend to have smaller pensions or no pension at all of their own. Compared with men, fewer women have the option of a formal retirement at age 65. These differences reflect the different treatment of men and women throughout the life course.

The study of life events can make it seem like people have little influence on their own development. It seems like they can only respond to events that happen to them. But, Kahana and Kahana (2003, p. 235) say that people respond to the world. They call this "proactivity." People adapt and change their behavior and ways of thinking to minimize stress and maximize development.

For example, people can give up one role in order to take on another. A worker may decide to retire early to volunteer at a local youth center. Or a person may decide to take up an exercise program after reading about the effects of obesity on health in later life. Kahana and Kahana (2003) list a number of other proactive responses to the environment, including planning ahead, asking for help, and adapting a home environment in response to physical changes. People can and do respond to history and their environment as they age.

Nonnormative, history-graded, and normative life events shape our lives. They affect each of us differently as our personalities interact with the external environment. Each of us brings a lifetime of personal experience and interaction with society into later life.

PSYCHOLOGICAL DISORDERS: ABNORMAL AGING

Studies of memory, intelligence, and the life course describe normal aging. But some people suffer from psychological problems like loneliness, depression, or thoughts of suicide in later life. Psychologists call these functional disorders because they interfere with a person's ability to function. These problems have no clear organic or biological cause. The older person may have suffered with this problem for many years. Other older people suffer from organic disorders. These include Parkinson's disease, stroke, and Alzheimer's disease. These illnesses arise due to a malfunction in the brain.

Organic Disorders: Cognitive Impairment in Later Life

Studies show that changes in the brain that come with age can lead to cognitive disorders (Vintners, 2001). Writers refer to these disorders as organic brain syndrome, senile dementia, or simply dementia. These general terms describe a variety of or-

BOX 6.3

ALZHEIMER'S DISEASE

Stages and Symptoms

People with Alzheimer's disease (AD) will go through a series of stages as cognitive impairment increases. The following description gives some of the signs that appear at each stage.

Common Changes in Mild AD

- Loses spark or zest for life; does not start anything.
- Loses recent memory without a change in appearance.
- Loses judgment about money.
- Has difficulty with new learning and making new memories.
- Has trouble finding words; may substitute or make up words that sound like or mean something like the forgotten word.
- May stop talking to avoid making mistakes.
- Has shorter attention span and less motivation to stay with an activity.
- Easily loses way going to familiar places.
- Resists change or new things.
- Has trouble organizing and thinking logically.
- Asks repetitive questions.
- Withdraws, loses interest, is irritable, not as sensitive to others' feelings, uncharacteristically angry when frustrated or tired.
- Won't make decisions. For example, when asked what she wants to eat, says, "I'll have what she is having."
- Takes longer to do routine chores and becomes upset if rushed or if something unexpected happens.
- Forgets to pay, pays too much, or forgets how to pay; may hand the checkout person a wallet instead of the correct amount of money.
- Forgets to eat, eats only one kind of food, or eats constantly.

BOX 6.3
(Continued)

- Loses or misplaces things by hiding them in odd places or forgets where things go, such as putting clothes in the dishwasher.
- Constantly checks, searches, or hoards things of no value.

Common Changes in Moderate AD

- Changes in behavior; concern for appearance, hygiene, and sleep become more noticeable.
- Mixes up identity of people, such as thinking a son is a brother or that a wife is a stranger.
- Poor judgment creates safety issues when left alone; may wander and risk exposure, poisoning, falls, self-neglect or exploitation.
- Has trouble recognizing familiar people and own objects; may take things that belong to others.
- Continuously repeats stories, favorite words, statements, or motions like tearing tissues.
- Has restless, repetitive movements in late afternoon or evening, such as pacing, trying doorknobs, fingering draperies.
- Cannot organize thoughts or follow logical explanations.
- Has trouble following written notes or completing tasks.
- Makes up stories to fill in gaps in memory. For example, might say, "Mama will come for me when she gets off work."
- May be able to read but cannot formulate the correct response to a written request.
- May accuse, threaten, curse, fidget, or behave inappropriately, such as kicking, hitting, biting, screaming, or grabbing.
- May become sloppy or forget manners.
- May see, hear, smell, or taste things that are not there.
- May accuse spouse of an affair or family members of stealing.
- Naps frequently or awakens at night believing it is time to go to work.
- Has more difficulty positioning the body to use the toilet or sit in a chair.
- May think mirror image is following him or television story is happening to her.
- Needs help finding the toilet, using the shower, remembering to drink, and dressing for the weather or occasion.
- Exhibits inappropriate sexual behavior, such as mistaking another individual for a spouse. Forgets what is private behavior and may disrobe or masturbate in public.

Common Changes in Severe AD

- Doesn't recognize self or close family.
- Speaks in gibberish, is mute, or is difficult to understand.
- May refuse to eat, chokes, or forgets to swallow.
- May repetitively cry out or pat or touch everything.
- Loses control of bowels and bladder.
- Loses weight and skin becomes thin and tears easily.
- May look uncomfortable or cry out when transferred or touched.
- Forgets how to walk or is too unsteady or weak to stand alone.
- May have seizures, frequent infections, falls.
- May groan, scream, or mumble loudly.
- Sleeps more.
- Needs total assistance for all activities of daily living.

Sources: Adapted from *Caring for people with Alzheimer's disease: A manual for facility staff* (2d ed.), by L. P. Gwyther, 2001. Published by the American Health Care Association (1201 L Street, NW, Washington, DC 20005) and the Alzheimer's Association (919 N. Michigan Ave., Suite 1100, Chicago, IL 60611). Reprinted with permission from the Alzheimer's Association. Retrieved June 26, 2004, *www.alzheimers.org/pubs/stages.*

ganic brain disorders. The development of lesions, neurofibrillary tangles, and amyloid plaques in the brain, for example, lead to dementia—confusion, forgetfulness, and sometimes antisocial behavior (Berg & Sternberg, 2002). Some individuals with these disorders wander, strike out, or resist help from their caregivers. Dementia cases create stress for both professional care providers and family caregivers.

Alzheimer's disease (AD) is the most common form of dementia among older people (National Institute on Aging, 2004). About 3 percent of people aged 65 to 74 have AD. This rate increases to nearly half of people aged 85 and over. In total, as many as 4.5 million Americans have AD.

None of the research so far has produced a method to treat AD (the most common form of dementia). Physicians often cannot make a clear diagnosis of the disease. They first try to rule out other causes of confusion and personality decline such as brain tumors, blood pressure problems, or hyperthyroidism. Dozens of other illnesses must be ruled out before an illness can be diagnosed as AD (Hermann, 1991). Caution prevents doctors from quickly reaching a conclusion of AD because a patient might have a treatable illness or a problem like overmedication or infection.

Tierney and Charles (2002) report on the development of a new Alzheimer Predictive Index. Physicians can use this index to assess people who have some memory loss. Research shows that 89 percent of the time the index can predict the onset of Alzheimer's disease within 2 years. This index and other new methods will lead to earlier diagnosis. Early diagnosis helps families cope with the disease's progress. Researchers who study early treatment hope to develop ways to slow or stop the progress of the disease. Some drugs, such as vitamin E and cholinesterase inhibitors, may slow the progress of the disease in its early stages. Other drugs, such as sleeping pills and antidepressants, can control some of the symptoms. But, at present, nothing can stop the progress of the disease.

Alzheimer's disease patients go through a series of changes over a number of years. On average a person with AD lives eight to ten years after diagnosis. But some people live as long as twenty years with the disease. The progress of the disease differs for each person. But researchers have tried to organize the disease's progress into a series of stages. This helps caregivers assess their current situation and predict what they will have to deal with in the future.

A person in the early stages of the disease, for example, shows signs of forgetfulness. The person asks the same question over and over or repeats the same story word for word. The person may forget how to do simple tasks like cooking or playing cards (National Institute on Aging, 2004). A spouse or family member may not notice these signs at first. But as the disease progresses, it has more obvious effects on behavior and social relations. The person will eventually need full-time care, often in a nursing home.

AD poses problems for family caregivers. Studies of caregiver burden find that caregivers suffer from the demands of care. Caregivers often feel physical exhaustion. A caregiver may have to stay awake at night to prevent a spouse from wandering out of the house. Or the caregiver may face a physical struggle when he or she tries to bathe the person with AD.

Caregivers can also feel anger when a person asks the same question again and again or when the person damages something in the home. One woman woke up to find that her husband had filled the toilet with oranges. Another time her husband wandered into a neighbor's yard with a kitchen knife in his hand. The neighbors called the police and it took hours to calm the neighbors and get her husband back in the house.

Another woman recalls that she first became worried when her husband, a physician, lost his way home from work one night. He planned to stop at a patient's house for a short house call around 5 PM. The patient lived only a few blocks from their house, so his wife expected him home by 6 PM. She began to worry at eight o'clock when she still hadn't heard from him. An hour later he came in exhausted. He had spent the last three hours driving around their neighborhood looking for their house.

As the disease progresses, the demands of care increase. Many caregivers try to keep the relative at home as long as possible (Schulz & Martire, 2004).

This leads to increased stress and can lead to illness for the caregiver. Many books and websites now exist to advise caregivers on how to manage their care receiver. Also, the Alzheimer's Society, local hospitals, and community service agencies offer support groups for family members. Zarit and his colleagues (2004) report on the development of a Memory Club. Care partners meet for ten sessions in groups of eight to ten pairs. A social worker and neuropsychologist supervise the meetings. The meetings provide information about memory loss. They also provide a supportive setting for care partners to discuss their experiences. Other support programs include adult daycare and overnight respite programs that give caregivers temporary relief from the demands of care.

The National Institute on Aging estimates that the direct and indirect cost of AD in the United States reaches $100 billion per year. If science finds no cure for AD and if current trends continue, 13.5 million Americans will have AD by the year 2050. This will increase the cost of caring for people with AD and will increase the burden AD places on families and the health care system. Scientists continue to work on finding a cure for AD. And the President's budget in 2005 contained a $12 million allocation to support innovative programs. These programs demonstrate new and effective ways to care for people with AD.

Functional Disorders

The prevalence of organic mental disorders will increase as the U.S. population ages. But, older people also suffer from functional disorders such as loneliness, depression, and despair that leads to suicide. These problems have their roots in the person's social setting as well as the person's psychology.

Loneliness

Gerontologists distinguish between social isolation and loneliness. Social isolation refers to the decrease in social contacts that often come with age (Hall & Havens, 2002). Widowhood, the deaths of friends, children moving away, these events can lead to social isolation. Loneliness comes about when a person feels a *relational deficit* or a gap between the number of relationships desired and the number the person has (Weiss, 1973). Loneliness refers to a dissatisfaction with the quantity or the quality of social relationships (Hall & Havens, 2002).

Older people who have lost a spouse, another family member, or a friend tend to feel lonely (Dugan & Kivett, 1994; Havens & Hall, 2001). Institutionalized older people with few family supports also feel lonely (Osgood, Brant, & Lipman, 1991). People who live alone tend to report loneliness (Miedema & Tatemichi, 2003). But, a person may feel lonely even if the person has many social contacts. For example, a widow may play an active part in her bridge club, but she may feel lonely because she misses the company of her husband. Hall and Havens (2002, citing Holmen et al., 1992) say that some older people who live with their children or with siblings report high levels of loneliness.

Weeks (1994) estimates that 40 percent of older people feel lonely. Kirk and his colleagues (2001) studied people who attended a daytime meal program in rural Louisiana. They found that while most of these people (53 percent) live alone, only 30 percent said they felt lonely or very lonely. The researchers say that lack of social contact for these people did not necessarily lead to loneliness. Attendance at the meal program and other activities in this senior center may have decreased these participants' sense of loneliness. Participants said they attended the center because they enjoyed the social contact. A study of very old adults (aged 85 and over) found that affection from and for their children reduced loneliness (Long & Martin, 2000).

A program in the United Kingdom offered a *befriending* service to older adults who lived alone. Visitors visited the clients one hour per week. The older people valued the service and the reliability of the visitors. Some of these friendships developed into personal relationships that included social activities and other types of support (Andrews, Gavin, Begley, & Brodie, 2003).

Some institutions have used animal-assisted therapy (visits by a pet to the facility) to combat loneliness (Banks & Banks, 2003). Not all residents enjoyed the visits by these pets. But the researchers found that visits of thirty minutes once a week reduced loneliness for patients who enjoyed the presence of animals. A controlled study found a significant decrease in loneliness among the group that received visits from a pet (Banks & Banks, 2002).

Technology can also help older people combat loneliness. Cell phones and the Internet can help people to stay in touch with relatives and friends. McMellon and Schiffman (2002) studied "cybersenior empowerment." They found that older people can use the Internet to combat loneliness. The researchers asked a sample of older people about their Internet use. They found that nearly all of the people in the study (91 percent) used email to keep in touch with friends. People in the study who had physical limits or those who lived in social isolation felt more in control of their lives. Older people run the risk of loneliness as they age.

Some people adapt to social isolation and enjoy being alone. But other people prefer a more active and engaged social life. Awareness of this preference can help family members and social service providers respond to seniors' needs. Loneliness puts a person at risk for other problems. Research shows that loneliness and poor health often go together. Fees, Morton, and Poon (1999) found that feelings of loneliness led to a poor assessment of physical well-being. Isolation and loneliness can lead to further physical and mental breakdown. This can lead to further problems, such as an increased risk of drug and alcohol abuse and suicide.

Alcohol Abuse

Researchers (Wagenaar, Mickus, & Wilson, 2001; Abrams, 2001) call alcoholism a hidden or invisible epidemic. Studies report that between 1 and 3 percent of older people suffer from the effects of alcohol use (Blondell, 1999). Older people, compared with other adult age groups, have lower rates of alcohol abuse (bingeing and heavy drinking) (SAMHSA, 2003). But the effects of alcohol dependency differ for older and younger people. Older people, compared with younger people, show less tolerance for alcohol, worse damage to health from alcohol use, and an increased chance of alcohol and drug interaction (Blow, Oslin, & Barry, 2002; Spencer & Hutchison, 1999).

Research reports two types of older problem drinkers: early onset and late onset. Early onset drinkers begin alcohol abuse in their middle years. These people make up about two-thirds of older alcoholics (Barnea & Teichman, 1994). Early onset drinkers often have serious emotional problems (Wagenaar, Mickus, & Wilson, 2001). They bring their drinking problems with them into old age.

Schonfeld and Dupree (1990) found that early onset drinkers had higher depression scores than other drinkers. They also had more severe psychological problems. The early onset group reported that they got drunk twice as often as other drinkers. They also showed about twice the rate of leaving treatment as other drinkers.

Late onset drinkers begin to abuse alcohol in their 50s and 60s and tend to have a milder drinking problem (Atkinson, 1994). They begin drinking in response to stresses such as widowhood, retirement, or poor health (Wagenaar, Mickus, & Wilson, 2001). These events threaten a person's self-image and change the person's life-style. Dunlop and her colleagues (1990) say that other stresses such as ageism, low income, and a feeling of uselessness can lead to chemical dependency.

Schonfeld and Dupree (1990) say that older drinkers (regardless of onset) often drink alone and in response to loneliness, boredom, and depression. Both types of drinkers had high rates of widowhood or divorce and weak social support networks. A national survey in the United States surveyed 1,418 people aged 60 and over. The study found that older people who reported stressful losses tended to abuse alcohol. Family, spouse, or friends tend to buffer these losses. Problem drinkers said that drinking increased during times of great stress. At these times, their needs went beyond what their support networks could provide (Jennison, 1992).

The Center for Substance Abuse Treatment (CSAT) recommends that older people drink no more than one standard drink per day or seven drinks in a week. And older adults should drink no more than two standard drinks at any time. The CSAT rates more than two drinks on one occasion as a binge. Blow and his colleagues (2002) say that this recommendation fits with what we know about the effects of alcohol on older people. It also defines a level of drinking that fits with studies on the good health effects of alcohol.

The U.S. Substance Abuse and Mental Health Services Administration (SAMHSA) (2001) projects an increase in the number of older people who will need treatment for substance abuse in the future. Two things account for this: the increase in the older population and, compared with previous generations, the higher rate of alcohol use among the Baby Boom generation. SAMHSA also projects a greater need for rehabilitation and treatment programs.

Older people need unique rehabilitation programs designed for the issues that they face in later life. These age-specific treatment programs focus on rebuilding support networks and coping with common problems older people face. Researchers (Hinrichsen, 1990; Wagenaar, Mickus, & Wilson, 2001) say that older people recover best through group therapy, social support, and Alcoholics Anonymous. Successful programs help older people rebuild social networks and help them cope with depression, grief, and loneliness.

Depression and Suicide

Blazer (2003, p. 1) calls depression "the most frequent cause of emotional suffering in later life." Community studies of major depression find rates of 1 to 4 percent. Researchers propose higher rates of clinical or minor depression. D'Mello (2003, p. 3) estimates that 14 percent of older people in the United States suffer from "significant depressive symptoms." Other studies of clinical depression in community-dwelling older people range from 8 to 16 percent (Blazer, 2003). Symptoms of depression include lack of interest, feelings of worthlessness, poor ability to concentrate, inability to make decisions, insomnia, loss or gain of weight, and suicidal thoughts. Some researchers say that in older people depression can show up as "withdrawal, apathy, and lack of vigor" (Blazer, 2003, p. 2).

Depression can lead to further problems for the older person. Apathy can lead to poor eating habits and loss of weight and strength (D'Mello, 2003). This puts the older person at risk of frailty, falls, and broken bones. The research also links depression to other illnesses like heart disease and inflammation (Blazer, 2003). Depression can also lead to disability. One study found that depression increased the risk of mobility decline by 67 percent and increased the risk of ADL decline by 73 percent (Penninx et al., 1999). Depression may also give a clue to the onset of AD or vascular dementia (Blazer, 2003).

Untreated, depression can lead a person to feel hopeless and to commit suicide (Blazer, 2003). Suicide rates for older people decreased by one-half between 1950 and 2000 (Freid, Prager, MacKay, & Xia, 2003). Still, older people have a higher rate of suicide than other age groups (Conwell, 2001; National Center, 2004). In 2001, one older person in the United States took his or her life every ninety-seven minutes. Younger people made up 13.9 percent of the population and committed 13.4 percent of the suicides. Older people made up 12.7 percent of the population in 1999, but committed 18.8 percent of the suicides (Hoyert et al., 1999).

Suicide rates vary within the older population (see Figure 6.2). The oldest age groups (aged 75 and over) have a suicide rate about 25 percent higher than the rate for 25 to 44 year olds. In 2002 people aged 85 and over had the highest suicide rate of any older age group (18.0 deaths per 100,000 population). Older men (65+) had a rate over eight times that of older women. Among the 85 and over age group, men have a suicide rate over fifteen times that of women in the same age group (National Center, 2004). Men aged 85 and over have the highest suicide rate of any gender group in the United States (Bharucha, 2003). Suicide statistics probably underestimate suicides among older people. The official figures miss people who fail to take medications or who overdose themselves. They miss people who starve themselves or intentionally hurt themselves in accidents.

Older white men (aged 85 and over) have the highest suicide rate of any age, gender, or racial group (Szanto et al., 2002; Conwell, 2001). They had a rate six times the U.S. age-adjusted rate of suicide. And they account for 82 percent of all suicides among older people (Roff, 2001). The age-adjusted suicide rate for white men aged 75 to 84 in 2001 came to 40.11 deaths per 100,000 population. This

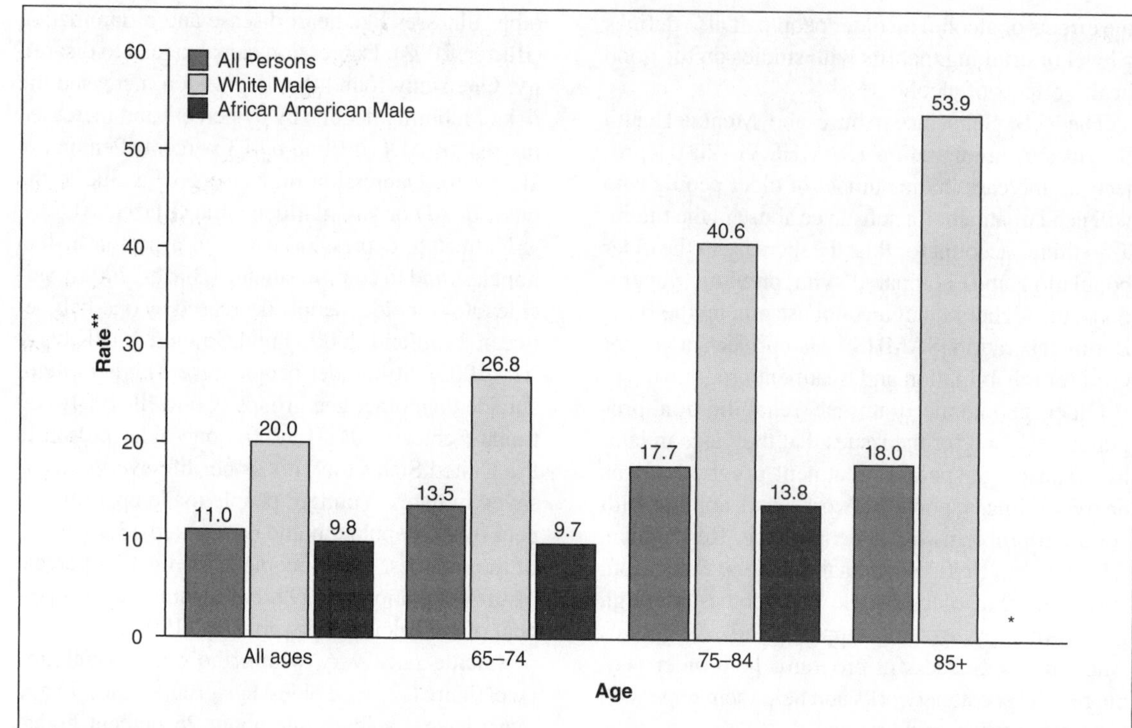

This chart compares the suicide rate for people of all ages and those aged 65 and over. Note that the suicide rate increases with age for all people (regardless of race or gender) and that the oldest age group (85 and over) has a higher rate than any other age group.

Also, note the high rate of suicide for older white males, compared with younger white males and African Americans at any age. The rate for the oldest white males is three times that of the general population, and about three times that of African American males in the oldest comparable group (75–84 years). These figures show that white males run a higher risk of suicide than other age and racial groups. And the older the white male, the higher the suicide risk.

*The low rates for African American males are unreliable and are not shown.

**Deaths per 100,000 resident population

FIGURE 6.2

Death Rates for Suicide, for All People, White Males, and African American Males, Age 65 and over, 2002

Source: Health, United States, 2004. Hyattsville, MD: National Center for Health Statistics. Table 46, pp. 197–198.

was almost ten times the rate for white women aged 75 to 84 (4.28 per 100,000). It was almost three times the rate for African American men in this age group (13.9 per 100,000). African American women had too few suicides in this age group for comparison (National Center, 2004).

Older people not only kill themselves at a higher rate than younger people "but they do it with 'determination and single-mindedness of purpose' not encountered among younger age groups" (Seiden, 1981, cited in Osgood, Brant, & Lipman, 1991). Osgood, Brant, and Lipman (1991) say that in the general population the ratio of attempts to actual suicides stands at 10 or 20 to 1. The ratio in early adulthood may be 200 attempts to every suicide. Older people have a rate of four attempts to every completion.

More older women attempt suicide, but more men succeed. Szanto and her colleagues (2002) report that older people who commit suicide have planned this for a long time. Those who have attempted suicide in the past also show an increased risk of successful suicide in later life. A study of suicide among older people (mean age, 73) in South Carolina found that men made up 85 percent of the cases. They had a suicide rate six times that of older women.

Most of the male suicides in this study used a gun (Bennett & Collins, 2001). Conwell and his colleagues (2002) studied the use of firearms and the risk of suicide. They found that men who kept an unlocked and loaded gun at home showed the greatest tendency to commit suicide. This reflects the preference of men at all ages for more violent forms of suicide.

What accounts for these high rates of suicide among some older people? No single cause or explanation fits all cases of suicide. Researchers find that depression, isolation, loneliness, bereavement, and physical illness all put older people at risk of suicide (Szanto et al., 2002; Bennett & Collins, 2001). These risk factors often build on one another. For example, a widowed person may live alone and feel depressed. Illness may add to feelings of depression. Corr, Nabe, and Corr (1994) speak of "bereavement overload." A person may not have time to grieve for one loss before another one strikes.

Turvey and her colleagues (2002) studied over 14,000 people aged 65 and over over a ten-year period. They found that people who committed suicide reported feelings of depression, poor self-reported health, poor sleep quality, and the absence of a relative to talk to. Older people who want to die have often lost hope. Suicide notes will say the person feels "tired of life" (Osgood, Brant, & Lipman, 1991, p. 5).

Duberstein and colleagues (2000) found that depressed older people (50+) who thought about suicide had long-standing patterns of introversion and closedness to new experiences. Szanto and her colleagues (2002) say that antidepressants may lower the risk of suicide. Fiske and Arbore (2000–2001) propose prevention programs that screen for depression and feelings of hopelessness. They say that even a small increase in feelings of depression should signal the need for support and preventive efforts.

Conwell (2001) says that older suicide victims often have many problems including psychiatric illness, hopelessness, social losses, and physical decline. Professionals need to consider a number of interventions to reduce the risk of suicide.

Durkheim (1951) proposed that a lack of social integration led to high rates of suicide in modern society. Normlessness or *anomie,* a lack of connection between the person and society, puts a person at risk. Current research on suicide in later life supports this view. Older people often lose the contacts and links that prevent suicide. Retirement, the deaths of friends, and a move to a nursing home weaken the older person's social network. As this network shrinks, the person may lose a sense of purpose and meaning. This increases the risk of suicide.

Treatment for depression (and suicide attempts) in older people most often includes antidepressant drugs and psychological therapy (Blazer, 2003). Some studies find that aerobic exercise and even exposure to bright light can decrease depression. Short-term psychotherapy—cognitive behavioral therapy and interpersonal therapy—can reduce depression in less severe cases. Cognitive behavioral therapy helps patients to change their thought patterns away from thoughts about depression or suicide. Interpersonal therapy focuses on improved responses to grief, interpersonal disputes, role transitions, and interpersonal deficits. Both methods show good results with older people.

Blazer (2003, p. 13), in a review of the literature, says that a combination of drugs and therapy "appears to be the optimal clinical strategy in preserving recovery." Still, researchers need to look more closely at the effects of drug therapy on depression and suicide prevention in later life.

Barriers to treatment of depression exist. Isolated older people may not get diagnosed. Some older people may want to avoid the label of depression. They underreport their symptoms. Studies show that more than 70 percent of older suicide completers visited their doctor within the last month of their life (Bharucha, 2003). This suggests that physicians and other health care workers may not detect a desire to commit suicide in the older person. General or family practitioners may lack the experience with psychological disorders or they may lack to time to diagnose the problem.

Finally, the cost of treatment for depression may create a barrier to care. This can include the cost of copayments and drug treatment (Kyomen & Gottlieb, 2003). Blazer (2003) says that social conditions and policies—decreased pension benefits, reduced health care benefits, and the loss of close social ties—can bring on depression. This can set the stage for social breakdown and suicide.

SOCIAL BREAKDOWN AND RECONSTRUCTION

Kuypers and Bengtson (1973; *also* Myers, 1995) said that a link exists between psychological distress—problems such as loneliness, alcohol abuse, depression, and suicide—and the older person's social environment. They describe a **social breakdown syndrome** that shows how social conditions lead to personal problems (see Figure 6.3). The circle refers to changes inside the person; the items outside the circle refer to social forces that shape the person's experience. The syndrome has seven steps:

1. Role loss occurs. This often takes the form of retirement or widowhood. The person at this point loses the normative guidance that came from work or a relationship. Retirement, for example, can cause the sudden loss of reference groups. These groups help us create and maintain a good self-image. These losses make a person susceptible to social breakdown.
2. People who lose social roles expose themselves to external labeling. A social role gives us a part to play in the drama of everyday life. The absence of a role can lead to feelings of normlessness, a lack of purpose or meaning in life.
3. Society may label an older person as useless or incompetent. Middle-aged children sometimes take responsibilities from their parents in the name of care and concern. About ten years ago my oldest son saw me digging at a tree root.

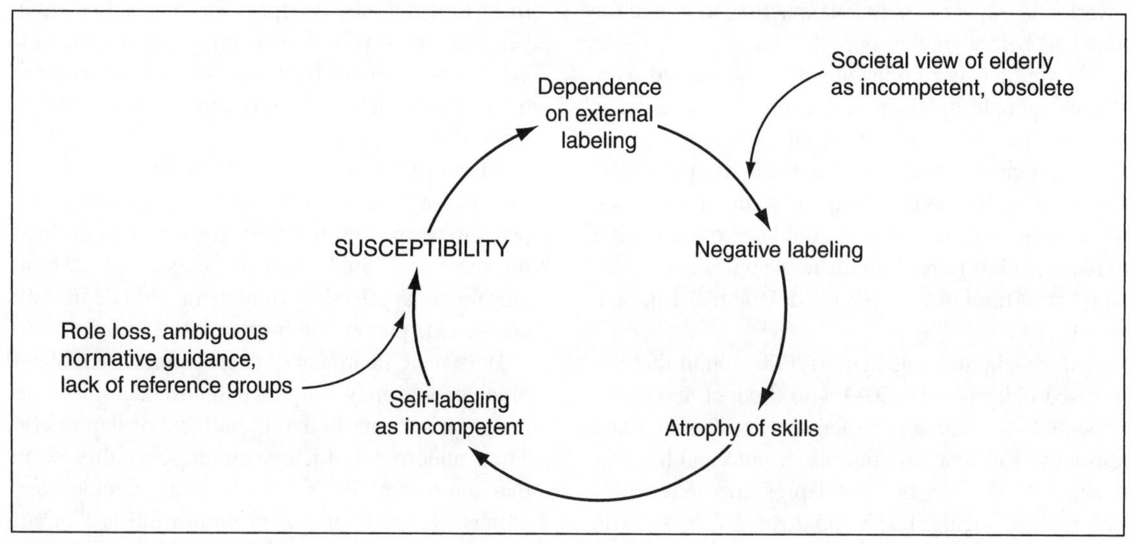

FIGURE 6.3
A Social Breakdown Syndrome

Source: From "Social Breakdown and Competence: A Model of Normal Aging," by J. A. Kuypers and V. L. Bengtson (1973). *Human Development,* 16, p. 190. Reprinted with permission from S. Karger AG, Basel.

"Here let me help you with that, Dad," he said, thinking that I was probably getting too old for that sort of thing (I was in my 30s at the time). I wasn't very susceptible to his labeling then, but thirty years from now I might be. Institutions often create excess dependence by leaving patients nothing to do for themselves.

4. The older person may assume a dependent role in response to being treated as less able. A fine line exists between kindness to an older person and placing them in a dependent role. Malcolm Cowley (1980) gives a good example of this process from his own experience. "We start by growing old in other people's eyes, then slowly we come to share their judgment." He recalls the time he backed out of a parking lot and nearly collided with another car. The driver got out, ready to fight. "Why, you're an old man," he said after seeing Cowley. Then he got back in his car and drove away. Cowley bristles when he remembers the event. Some years later, he says, "a young woman rose and offered me her seat in a Madison Avenue bus. That message was kind and also devastating. 'Can't I even stand up?' I thought as I thanked her and declined the seat. But the same thing happened twice the following year, and the second time I gratefully accepted the offer, though with a sense of having diminished myself. 'People are right about me,' I thought. . . . All the same it was a relief to sit down and relax" (Cowley, 1980, pp. 5–6).
5. The older person learns to live down to others' expectations. Cowley, for example, learned to accept the seat from the young woman. The next time he might gaze around the bus looking for someone to offer him a seat. He will have learned a new skill that fits the dependent role.
6. The person loses past skills. One woman I met in a nursing home made her bed the first week after she arrived. One day she went out without making the bed. When she got back, the staff had made the bed for her. "Oh," she thought, "isn't that nice." She never made the bed again. In time the arthritis in her hand got so bad from lack of movement that she couldn't have made the bed if she wanted to.
7. People label themselves as sick and inadequate. This supports the definition of older people as incompetent and obsolete. The older person goes out less, has fewer social contacts, and has fewer roles to play. The loss of social roles and contacts with others can create despair and a loss of meaning in life. This leaves the older person with no resources to combat negative labeling and a feeling of uselessness. This decreases social supports further and increases role loss.

Kuypers and Bengtson (1973) proposed a way to reverse this cycle. They call this the **social reconstruction syndrome**. Figure 6.4 shows this model. They suggest changes to the social system to support the older person. This approach includes (1) a new value system based on a person's worth as a human being rather than as a source of production; (2) greater self-reliance; (3) a strong internal sense of control; (4) learning new problem solving methods; (5) better supports such as housing, transportation, and pensions; (6) maintaining coping skills; and (7) a reduced susceptibility to external judgments.

Social supports (including group and personal counseling) hold a key to social reconstruction (Antonucci & Akiyama, 1993). The type of support differs for each person (Rathbone-McCuan, 1996). Some people benefit from senior housing that encourages socializing among residents. Some people need better education and counseling programs for substance abuse. Other people benefit from caregivers' support groups. Bartels and Smyer (2002) call for more community-based rehabilitation and support programs.

De Leo and colleagues (1992 and 1995, cited in Bharucha, 2003) provide one model. They developed a Tele-Help/Tele-Check service. This program offers telephone help to older isolated people and a twice-weekly visit to clients to offer emotional support. This program appears to reduce suicide, improve mood scores, and decrease hospitalizations. Almost any process around the circle in

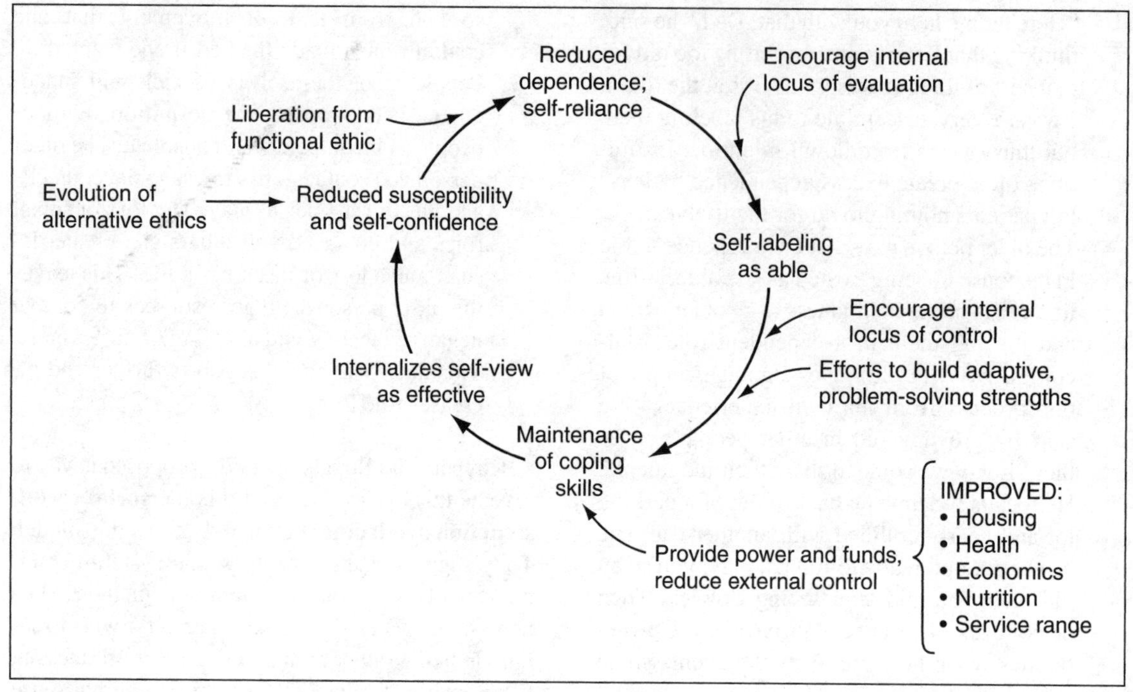

FIGURE 6.4

A Social Reconstruction Syndrome

Source: From "Social breakdown and competence: A model of normal aging," by J. A. Kuypers and V. L. Bengtson (1973). *Human Development, 16,* p. 197. Reprinted with permission from S. Karger AG, Basel.

the reconstruction diagram (Figure 6.4) strengthens the older person's internal and external support system. The reconstruction syndrome sees social supports as a path to a strong sense of self and a high quality of life.

CONCLUSION

New models of aging and new images of old age have begun to emerge. Researchers for years based their studies of memory and intelligence on laboratory studies and on a model of age as decline. Studies confirmed this decline when they compared the mental function of older and younger people. New models of aging study the talents that develop in later life. These include the older person's heightened ability to use practical knowledge and the expression of wisdom.

Likewise, stage models of human development have given way to multidimensional models of development. These models include many more ways to live well in old age. They better fit the diverse older population and the complex lives of people in postindustrial society. They also recognize the potential for further growth and development in later life.

Finally, terms such as *multidimensionality, plasticity,* and *variability* describe the many life-styles that older people live today. At the least, modern society can provide supports that keep people from social breakdown. But society can do more. It can create the conditions for a good old age. This includes supportive housing, good transportation, adequate income, and meaningful roles to play. Society can take into account the individual and the cultural diversity of the older population. It can recognize the potential in older people, and it can accept and encourage many versions of a good old age.

SUMMARY

- As people age, they experience changes in mental ability, social relations, and social status.
- Memory refers to recall after learning has taken place. Studies find little difference between younger and older people in sensory and short-term memory. Researchers find the greatest difference in function between younger and older people in long-term memory.
- Longitudinal research on intelligence (the measure of mental capacity) shows a difference in intellectual performance between younger and older people. But intelligence differs less on some measures than on others. Fluid intelligence tends to decrease with age; crystallized intelligence can increase with age.
- Aging poses challenges to a person's sense of self. These challenges result from social attitudes toward older people, physical decline, and loss of social roles. Social psychologists propose that people adapt well to aging through disengagement, activity, or continuity.
- Spiritual belief and membership in a religious community brings fulfillment and meaning to many older people. Some people hold traditional religious beliefs based on faith in God and church doctrine. Other people see God in the order of the natural world. Older American's today hold many spiritual beliefs, engage in diverse spiritual practices, and belong to many different faiths. This diversity will increase in the future. Traditional religious communities can help older people take part in community life by providing supports like transportation and outreach.
- The life course perspective proposes that development is a lifelong process. A person's individual life course development depends on their physical condition, intelligence, personality, coping styles, resources, gender, and the social world they live in.
- Life course researchers propose that three types of events shape a person's life: nonnormative or unplanned events; normative, history-graded events; and normative, age-graded events.
- Organic brain disorders (like AD), loneliness, alcohol abuse, depression, and suicide are potential problems in old age. Experiences such as illness, widowhood, and retirement can lead to social breakdown. The social reconstruction process gives the older person support to cope with these problems.

DISCUSSION QUESTIONS

1. Describe the process of remembering something. How does this process differ for older and younger people?
2. What effect does age have on a person's intelligence? Why do some studies confound cohort and age effects? What research method do researchers use to separate cohort effects and age effects?
3. What challenges to the self does a person face with age? Give some examples of what people can do to maintain self-esteem as they age.
4. Define the terms *on time* and *off time* in relation to life events. Have you ever found yourself in this situation? Why did this occur? What did it feel like? How did you deal with the experience?
5. List and explain the three types of events that shape a person's life. Which type of life event has affected you most so far in your life? Give examples of each type from your own life. How did you cope with these life events?
6. What life events can lead to psychological problems in later life? What events will more likely affect women than men? How do men and women differ in their ways of coping with personal problems? Give examples of the different responses for each gender (e.g., suicide or alcohol abuse).
7. What can society do to prevent or buffer problems older people face in later life? Do you know of any prevention or support programs for older people in your community? Describe them. What prevention programs are needed in your community but don't exist at this time?
8. Do all ethnic, racial, and income groups have equal access to social supports in later life? What might inhibit someone from a minority group from seeking and using community supports?

SUGGESTED READING

Jung, C. G. (1976). The stages of life. In J. Campbell (Ed.), *The portable Jung.* Harmondsworth, England: Penguin.

A classic short essay that takes a profound look at healthy aging. Jung describes the unique task of later life as a recovery of culture, a time for reflection and inner development. He says that we may need to learn how to make the most of this time of life.

Atchley, R. C. (2000). Spirituality. In Cole, T. R., R. Kastenbaum, & R. E. Ray (Eds.), pp. 324–341. *Handbook of the humanities and aging, 2nd Ed.* New York: Springer.

Atchley, a gerontologist known for his insights into retirement and the meaning of later life, reflects on the meaning of spirituality in old age. Atchley shares the sources of his own spiritual beliefs and practices. He discusses the value that a study of spirituality adds to a gerontological literature that focuses on scientific studies of aging. The study of spirituality, Atchley says, opens the discussion of non-scientific dimensions of aging including transcendence, the search for meaning, and increased self-knowledge.

McFadden, S. H., Brennan, M., & Patrick, J. H. (Eds.). (2003). *New directions in the study of late life religiousness and spirituality.* Binghamton, NY: Haworth Pastoral Press.

A series of essays on religious activity and spirituality in old age. The articles discuss the role of spirituality in providing quality health care to older people, the meaning of religion and spirituality to different racial and ethnic groups, and the role of religion in helping people cope with problems like dementia, caregiving, and bereavement.

GLOSSARY OF TERMS

activity theory The belief that activity leads to the highest satisfaction in later life.

age changes Changes in a person due to the aging process (e.g., the slowing of reaction time).

age differences Differences between age groups due to their different experiences (and not due to aging). This would include differences in intelligence scores due to differences in education level between older and younger age groups.

age stratification system The system of age grades that every society has. People move through these grades as they age.

cognitive mechanics Similar to fluid intelligence. The ability of the mind to work quickly and respond to demands.

cognitive pragmatics Similar to crystallized intelligence. The ability of the mind to store and use information over a lifetime.

competence A person's skill at real world tasks.

continuity theory The belief that people adapt to change by integrating new experience with past history and moving forward.

crystallized intelligence Abilities such as vocabulary, association of past and present ideas, and technical ability, which depend on a person's education or store of information.

disengagement theory The belief that as people age, social interaction naturally decreases.

encoding Learning information, preparing it for storage in the mind.

fluid intelligence Activities such as creative design, quick response to a question, or mental rearrangement of facts, which rely on how well the central nervous system works.

generation People who share an awareness of their common historical or cultural experiences, but who may come from different age cohorts.

generational event theory Attitudes form for a generation in their teens. People who grow up at the same time in the same society share the same attitudes.

life course perspective A grand view of the life cycle. It includes growth through social roles and stages of life, it takes into account social institutions, and it places all of this in a historical context.

off time Refers to life events that occur at a time other than when society has programmed them to occur (e.g., a first birth for a woman at age 50).

on time Refers to life events that occur when society has programmed them to occur (e.g., a high school graduation in the mid-teen years).

plasticity The ability to change and adapt with age.

retrieval The recall of information from mental storage.

rite of passage An event that marks a passage from one life stage to another (e.g., a retirement party).

semantic memory Our store of factual information.

social breakdown syndrome A process of decline for the older person that begins with a loss of social status or social role.

social reconstruction syndrome A process of rebuilding the older person's self by providing social supports.

storage Saving learned information for retrieval at a later time.

working memory This type of memory selects, manipulates, and stores recent information.

chapter 7

RACE AND ETHNICITY

Bart Hircus runs exercise classes for older people at seniors housing complexes and recreation centers. A few years ago, a Native American senior center invited him to hold some fitness classes. They assigned him a room and announced the class in advance. He came to the center eager to work with this new group of people.

About ten people, men and women, showed up for his session. He began with warm-up stretches and then put on some peppy music. He launched into his routine and his usual patter. But he noticed that after a few minutes his students began to drift out to a nearby patio for a smoke and some talk. People would wander in and out to see how the class was going or to watch Bart do the exercises.

This went on for about thirty minutes. Finally, Bart gave up the exercising and began talking with the center members. He found that they didn't get the point of all this jumping around. They had worked hard all their lives. Some of them had trapped, hunted, and lived in the bush. They associated exercise with hard work. They couldn't understand why anyone would get sweated up and not get paid for it. To them this looked like work, and they wanted no part of it.

After he gave up trying to get them to exercise, Bart enjoyed his experience. He says he learned a lot from listening to these people and from coming to understand their points of view. He does things differently today when he has to present a program to a minority group audience. For one thing, he gets to know something about the culture and background of the group before he begins. For another, he explains the purpose of the program and its benefits in advance. Finally, he tailors the program to the background and experience of his students.

Today, gerontologists know that culture and life events shape an older person's worldview. For example, many older minority members face disadvantages today due to discrimination they have faced throughout their lives. Other minority members have just arrived in the United States and have little knowledge of American society, its language, and customs.

Gerontologists have learned that cultural and economic barriers can keep minority older people from living a good old age. They also know some of the things that can bring down these barriers: offering a service in a minority language, using minority staff to deliver the service, or locating services in settings that will attract minority members. The study of minority aging expands our understanding of aging today and suggests ways to improve older minority members' lives.

This chapter looks at (1) the size, composition, and socioeconomic status of minority groups; (2) the experience of aging as a minority group member; and (3) creative responses to the challenge of minority aging.

WHO ARE THE MINORITY ELDERLY?[1]

The term **dominant group** in the United States applies to the white population. Whites make up a numerical majority of the population in the United States. More importantly, this group has the most power and controls most of the social and economic resources in the country. The encyclopedia defines a *minority* as a culturally, ethnically, or racially distinct group living within a larger society. Social scientists add that a minority group faces "subordination and discrimination within society" (Markides, 1987b).

Sociologists include women and gays in this definition, but here we focus on minorities based on race, ethnicity, and national origin. The term *minority* as we use it here applies to the four largest groups recognized by the U.S. Census: African Americans, Latinos, Asian American/Pacific Islanders (APIs), and American Indians/Alaskan Natives (Figure 7.1).

Many people think of the United States as a **melting pot**. It takes in people from around the world and turns them into *Americans*. This image arose in the early years of this century when European immigrants poured into this country. Many of them settled in cities on the East Coast and adapted to American customs to survive. The melting pot ideal encouraged children to leave behind their parents'

[1]Minority groups do not agree on a single term to describe their groups. And government reports differ in their designation of each group. Here I use the most preferred terms at this time to respect the preferences of these groups. I use the terms African American or black; Hispanic, Latino, or Latina; and American Indian or Native American to describe each of these groups.

language and customs. Assimilation opened the way for these people to enter middle-class American life.

This view now seems naive. Large numbers of Jews, for example, emigrated to the United States early in the 1900s. They adopted the customs and culture of the dominant population, but they hold onto a strong group identity. The same can be said for Asian Americans and Hispanic Americans. People understand the need to assimilate in their public lives. But they often maintain their culture through religious practices, festivals, and food. Ethnic identity survives for many generations and may even grow stronger as later generations celebrate their ethnicity.

The United States today looks more like a **pluralistic society** where many racial and ethnic groups exist side by side. Even third- or fourth-generation Americans today show pride in their Italian, Polish, Chinese, or other ancestry. More recent immigrants show even closer ties to their original language and culture. People adopt a civic mask for public relations, but for many people "ethnicity is kept and used to solidify one's psyche and organize resources to meet challenges" (Educating, 1992, p. 30).

Ramon Valle, a sociologist at San Diego State University, says that an **assimilation continuum** exists. The continuum runs from very traditional to bicultural to very assimilated. People can fit in different places on this continuum for different parts of their lives. A minority group member may be very assimilated in the office, but adopt a traditional worldview at home (Culture, 1992).

An example will make this clear. A colleague of mine from India wears a suit and tie to the office every day. He speaks English with only a mild accent, and he shows few outward signs of his ethnic background. But at home he carries on many traditional Indian practices. He eats a vegetarian diet, he reads his tradition's scriptures, and he performs a *puja,* or religious ritual, every morning before work. He fits in the bicultural category of Valle's continuum. He scores high on assimilation in the workplace, but he also scores high on tradition at home.

An African American friend would score high on assimilation at the office and in his personal life, but he does not want to be completely assimilated either at home or at work. At work, he stands up for the interests of African Americans and expresses views that highlight his racial identity. He also owns a cottage in rural Virginia near his birthplace. He drives

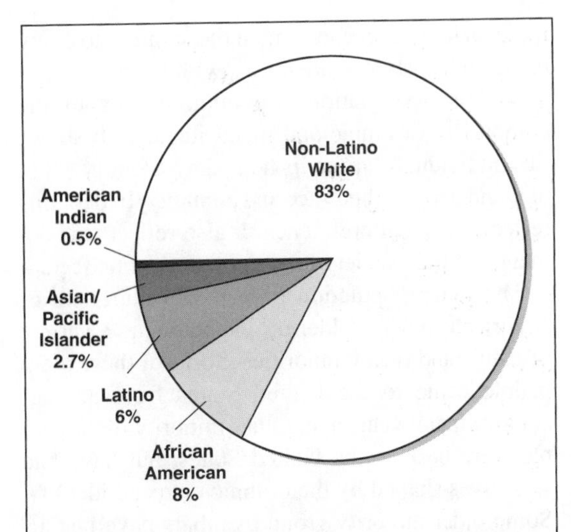

Non-Latino whites make up the large majority (83 percent) of the older population. Some groups, such as Asian Americans and American Indians, make up a relatively small portion of the older population. Other groups, such as Latinos and African Americans, make up larger proportions of the older population. All of these minority groups will grow in size and will make up a greater proportion of the older population in the future.

By the year 2010, for example, the U.S. Census Bureau projects that the minority older population will grow to about 20 percent of the total older population (up from 17 percent in 2002). This increase in the minority older population will require new policies and programs to meet minority elders' needs.

The figures in the chart total more than 100 percent because Latino Americans can also appear in the white and the African American racial category.

FIGURE 7.1

Population of the U.S. by Racial and Ethnic Group, 2002

Source: U.S. Census Bureau. (2003). Statistical Abstract of the United States. No. 13. Resident population by race, Hispanic origin, and age: 2000 and 2002. Retrieved July 13, 2004, *www.census.gov/prod/2004pubs/03statab/pop.pdf;* also *www.census.gov/prod/www/statistical-abstract-03.html.*

there on long weekends and in the summer to enjoy the rural life-style he identifies with his roots.

Valle's assimilation continuum points to the complexity of ethnic and racial identity. It shows that individuals differ in how they identify with, use, and express their race and ethnicity. In part, this reflects personal preference. It also reflects the demands of U.S. society for a common public face.

The older population reflects the pluralism of American society. Older people belong to a variety of ethnic and racial minorities. Some of these older people came to the United States from another country many years ago. Other minority older people were born in the United States, but have had their lives shaped by their ethnic or racial identity. Some older minority group members have just arrived in the United States. They came by choice, to follow their middle-aged children, or as refugees. These new immigrants face culture shock as well as issues related to aging.

Researchers find that diversity exists even within a single minority group (Williams & Wilson, 2001). Latino Americans, for example, have come to the United States from Cuba, Puerto Rico, South America, and Mexico. Each subgroup has a different culture and worldview, although research reports often refer to them all as Latino. Even within a minority subgroup (such as the Mexican American group), older people differ by age, gender, personality, how long they have lived in the United States, and whether they live in an urban or rural setting. This great diversity among the minority population makes the study of minority aging fascinating. It also makes generalization risky.

"We are all of the same opinion, Ms. Beckwith. What's more, we look like America."

WHY STUDY MINORITY AGING?

"Until recently," a Gerontological Society of America report (GSA Task Force, 1994, p. vii) says, "the study of aging in America has been principally the study of the older Whites." But gerontologists have begun to show a greater interest in minority aging.

Why this interest? First, minority older populations have begun to grow in size and grow in proportion to the dominant older population. This growth will continue in the future. Second, minority older people often have lower incomes, poorer health, and shorter lives than other older people. The study of minorities can lead to more responsive programs for older people and a better quality of life for minority elders. Third, studies show that minority group members experience aging differently than do whites. Leisure (Wilcox, 2002) and retirement (Calasanti, 2002), for example, can mean something different for minority elders than for the dominant culture. Fourth, minority groups can teach us other ways of growing old. They show the strength and resourcefulness that older people bring to their communities and to our society.

Finally, older populations express the diversity of American society. They keep and pass on many of the traditions of their cultures and add to the richness of American life. Minority Native American elders, for example, often keep up the traditions of their society (Penman, 2000; Schweitzer, 1999). Some of these elders have lived through their culture's change from a hunting and gathering to a modern society. Some African American elders keep alive family stories, recipes, and values. They provide models of strength and stability in a changing world. Japanese elders recall key moments in the history of their group's life in North America. Some remember the deportations that took place during World War II. They know firsthand the pain of prejudice and discrimination. These elders serve as valuable resources for younger generations.

DEMOGRAPHIC CHARACTERISTICS OF DOMINANT AND MINORITY GROUP ELDERS

Non-Latino Whites: The Dominant Group Older Population

The elderly non-Latino white population includes a variety of ethnic groups of European origin. The non-Latino white subgroups with the largest numbers of people—mostly of European origin—have a long history of settlement in the United States. Compared with the national average, they also have greater proportions of their populations aged 65 and over. And they have more formal education and lower rates of poverty than most older minority group members. For example, elderly whites have twice the high school graduation rate of elderly Latinos and 1.7 times the rate of elderly blacks. API elderly also have a lower rate of high school graduation than whites. But they have a higher rate of university graduation. One in five API elderly have an undergraduate education (Williams & Wilson, 2001).

These differences between the majority and minority groups reflect the historical experiences of the minority elderly. Many older Latino Americans grew up outside the United States and, compared with whites, had fewer educational opportunities. Older blacks experienced racial discrimination, segregated schooling, and, compared with whites, had fewer opportunities to get higher education.

Measures of poverty show results similar to those of education. Older blacks have nearly three times the rate of poverty of older whites (older American Indians have a rate of poverty similar to blacks), older Latinos have two-and-a-half times the rate of poverty of older whites, and API elderly have about a 25 percent higher rate of poverty than do older whites (Williams & Wilson, 2001).

Williams and Wilson (2001) go on to say that when poverty figures include the near poor (those above poverty, but less than twice the poverty level) the gap between whites and minority elderly grows. They report that 16 percent of whites fell into the poor and near poor group. But 45 percent of blacks, 34 percent of Latinos, and 19 percent of API elderly fall into this group. Some subgroups (rural older people, women, the oldest old) within these minority groups have even higher rates of poor and near poor elderly. And women, compared with men, in all racial groups have fewer financial resources.

Members of the non-Latino white group will likely have access to and make the most use of **formal support systems**. These systems include government programs, as well as community centers and ethnic associations. Today, agencies and policies have designed most programs for the older people in the non-Latino white group. But, this relatively large and dominant older population will shrink in size in the years ahead. And this group may decrease to 67 percent of the total older population by 2050 (Williams & Wilson, 2001).

Hayes-Bautista and his colleagues (2002, p. 14) say that the "'browning of the graying of America'" will create new demands for social supports. They report that the Latino and API older population has grown in the past few years. In California, for example, between 1990 and 2000, Latino and API older people account for 70 percent of the growth in the older population. The size of the non-Latino white group in California stayed the same during this period. Researchers have done a relatively small amount of research on older minority group members. But the study of these older people leads to a more complete view of aging in America.

The Minority Older Population

In 2002 minority older people made up about 17 percent of the U.S. population aged 65 and over (U.S. Census Bureau, 2003e). However, by the year 2020, the U.S. Census Bureau says, the proportion

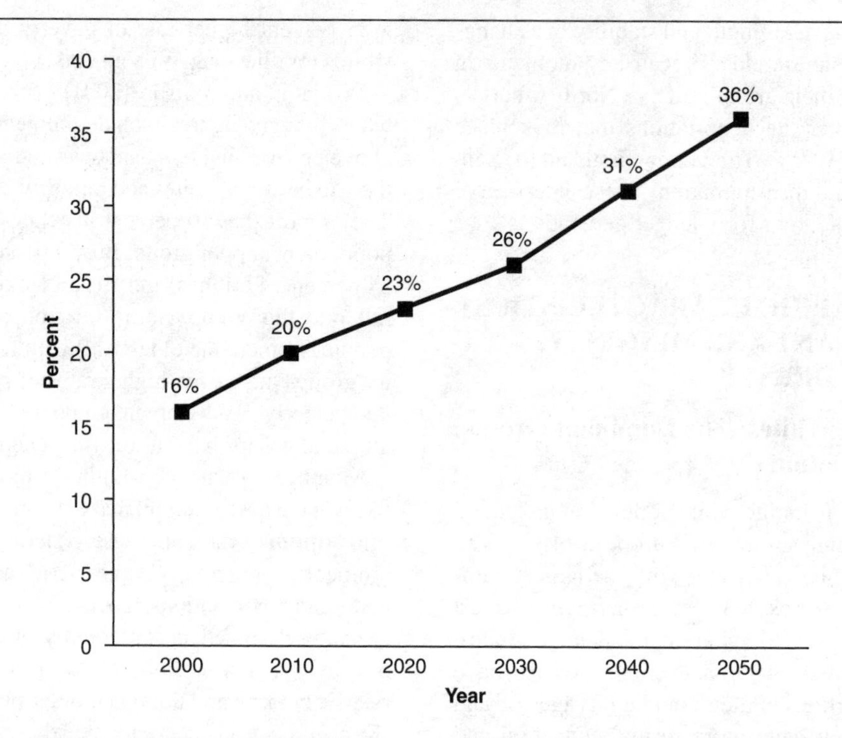

More than a doubling in the proportion of minority members in the older population will take place between 2000 and 2050. Several demographic forces account for the increase. Minority populations have higher fertility rates than the white population. These children will add to the older minority population in the future. Longer life expectancies for minority group members will mean more older minority elders in the future. Also, older immigrants who come to the United States with their families will increase the older minority population. Many of these immigrants will belong to the Latino and Asian minority groups.

The Latino group will see the greatest numerical increase in its older population. The older Latino population is projected to grow sixfold between 2000 and 2050. Older people will make up 16 percent of the Latino population by the year 2050 (up from 6 percent in 2000). This will put more demand on the family and community supports. It will also lead to a shift in public resources toward this group's needs.

FIGURE 7.2
Proportion of Minorities in the U.S. Population Aged 65 and over, 2000–2050

Source: U.S. Census Bureau, National Population Projections, Summary Files. (NP-T4) Projections of the total resident population by 5-year age groups, race, and Latino origin with special age categories: Middle series, 1999–2100. Retrieved July 13, 2004, *www.census.gov/population/www/projections/natsum-T3.html.*

of minority group members in the older population will grow to 23 percent. By the year 2050, it will grow to 36 percent—about double the 2002 proportion (U.S. Census Bureau, 2003e). Each minority group will contribute to this increased proportion of minority older people (see Figure 7.2).

Diversity of the Minority Population

Minority groups differ from the white population in mortality, fertility, and migration. Minority groups also differ from one another. The Latino group, for example, has a young population due to high fertility and high levels of immigration. This group will show

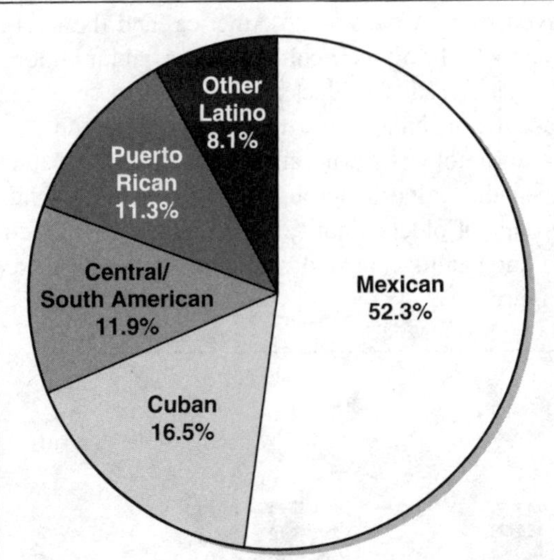

The chart shows the diversity of subgroups within the Latino older population. Mexican Americans, most of whom live in the southern and western parts of the United States, make up one-half the Latino older group. The other subgroups live mostly in the eastern part of the United States. Each of these groups has a unique history, cultural heritage, and experience in the United States. These differences lead to different experiences of aging within each community.

The Cuban population, for example, has the oldest population of the Latino groups. Nearly one-quarter (22.7 percent) of this group is aged 65 or older. Nearly one-half the Cuban group (46.7 percent) is aged 45 or over. The other groups have relatively young populations (between 4.0 and 6.6 percent is aged 65 and over). This reflects the immigration patterns of these groups—the Cubans arrived in a wave in the 1950s and most of them aged in place in Florida. The other groups continue to immigrate to the United States, and for this reason have younger populations. These differences lead to different community support networks and different abilities of the families and communities to support their older members.

FIGURE 7.3

Subgroups within the Latino U.S. Older Population (65+), 2002

Source: U.S. Census Bureau. (2003). Statistical Abstract of the United States. Population, No. 46. Retrieved July 13, 2004, *http://www.census.gov/prod/2004pubs/03statab/pop.pdf.7*

growth in its older population in the years ahead. century. Even within the Latino minority group, subgroups differ in their demography and cultural background (Du Bois, Yavno, & Stanford, 2001).

Some Latino elderly come from Cuba. Others come from Puerto Rico, Latin America, and Europe (see Figure 7.3). Each of these groups has a unique demographic structure. Cuban Americans, for example, make up the second largest group of Latino elderly. Williams and Wilson (2001) say that this is because many of these people came to the United States in middle age in the 1960s as political refugees after the Cuban revolution. Cuban Americans make up only 3.54 percent of the total Latino population but 16 percent of the older Latino population (U.S. Census Bureau, 2003e).

Mexican Latinos make up nearly one-half of the older Latino population. Most of them live in California. Some of these people trace their family origins in the United States to colonial times. Others arrived in the 1950s to do agricultural work. Still others have just arrived as legal and illegal immigrants. This group has many young adults and a high birth rate. They have a young population today, but will add to the older Latino population in the future (Hayes-Bautista, Hsu, Perez, & Gambon, 2002).

Other minority groups show similar diversity. Asians form at least twenty-six subgroups (Williams & Wilson, 2001). Each of these groups has a unique culture, demographic structure, and history in the United States. The Chinese subgroup makes up 30 percent of Asian elderly. Japanese and Filipinos each make up 24 percent of the Asian elderly group. Koreans make up 8 percent of Asian elders, Asian Indians make up 5 percent, and other groups make up the rest of the Asian elderly population.

These subgroups (like those of the Latino population) each have their own history in the United States. Most Chinese older people, for example, were born in the United States. Their parents immigrated to the United States in the early twentieth century (Williams & Wilson, 2001). Japanese American elders also have a long history in the United States. Most Vietnamese and Cambodian elderly immigrants entered the United States recently. Each of these groups has a different relationship with American culture and different access to social and economic resources (Hayes-Bautista, Hsu, Perez, & Gambon, 2002).

Jackson and Jackson (1992, p. 2) caution against seeing all African Americans as similar. Some African Americans came to the United States as slaves before the Civil War. Their descendants make up the largest proportion of African Americans today. But other African Americans have recently arrived from Africa, South America, and the Caribbean who bring their cultural values and traditions. "American Blacks," Jackson and Jackson say, "are a race that includes many different ethnic groups."

Gerontologists who study minority aging must keep this minority group diversity in mind. Subgroups of older minority Americans will have different health care and social service needs (see Figure 7.4).

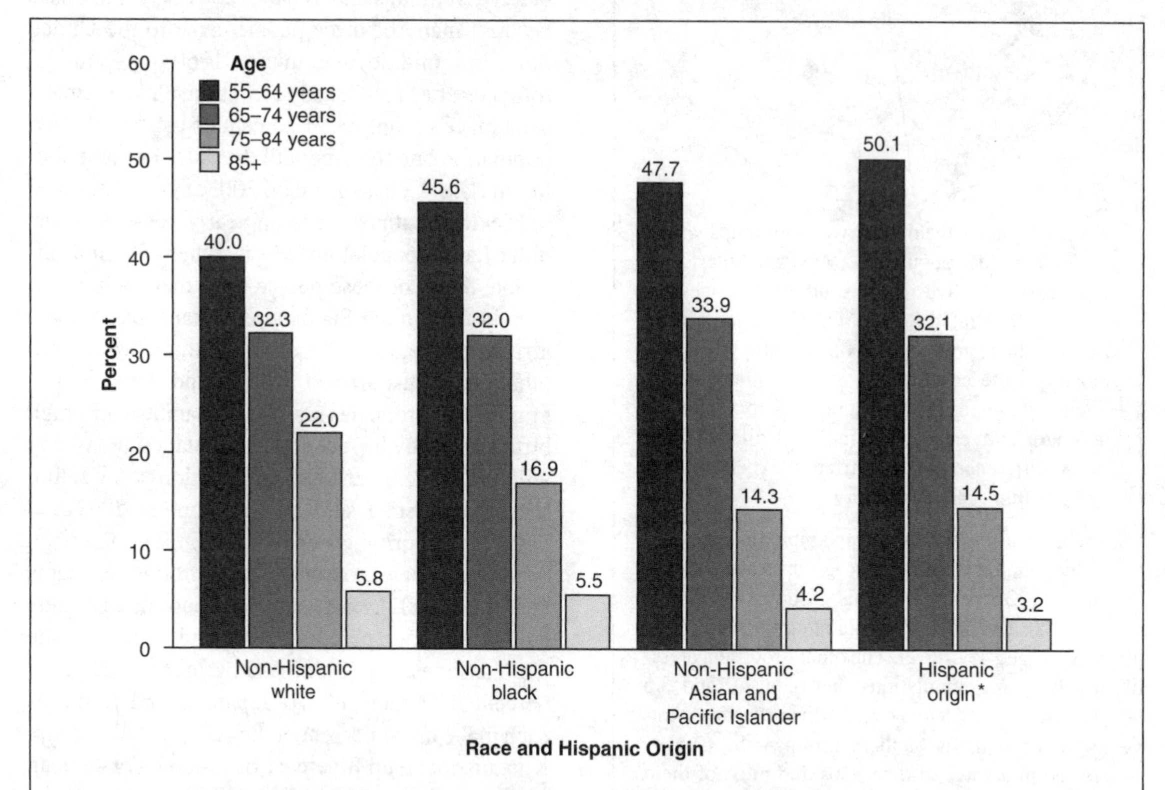

Note that the different racial and ethnic groups have different distributions of their older populations. The non-Hispanic white group has the oldest age distribution—60 percent of the 55 and over population is aged 65 and over. This group has almost 6 percent of its population aged 85 and over. The Hispanic group has the youngest older population with about one-half of the 55 and over population aged 65 or over. It has only about 3 percent of its population aged 85 and over. These differences are due to differences in birth rate, life expectancy, and immigration patterns.

*Hispanics may be of any race.

FIGURE 7.4

Percent of People 55 Years and Older by Race and Hispanic Origin, 1999

Source: Smith, D., & Tillipman, H. (2000). The Older Population in the United States: Population Characteristics. Current Population Reports, Population Characteristics, P20-532. U.S. Department of Commerce, Census Bureau, Washington, DC. Retrieved June 26, 2004, *www.census.gov/prod/2000pubs/p20-532.pdf.*

The Aging of the Minority Population

The minority older population as a whole is aging. In 2002, 4.6 million Americans were aged 85 and over. This will increase to 19.4 million people by the year 2050—a fourfold increase (U.S. Census Bureau, 2003e; 2004a). Over this same time period, the number of oldest old African Americans (85+) will increase sixfold, and the oldest old Latinos will increase twelve times. Other minority groups will also show large increases in their oldest old populations.

These dramatic increases in numbers may put a strain on informal supports. Very old minority elders who rely on family supports today may have to turn to formal supports for help. Right now, minority elders tend to underuse formal supports. These supports may not suit their needs. Formal supports will have to adapt their services and modes of delivery to meet the needs of the growing very old minority population.

THREE THEORIES ON MINORITY GROUP AGING

Gerontologists study the impact of minority group membership on aging. They ask how a minority person's experiences throughout life affect that person's experience of old age. Three theories describe the effects of minority group membership on the older person: **multiple jeopardy**, **leveling**, and the **life course perspective**.

Multiple Jeopardy

Societies use age, gender, social class, and minority group membership to classify people. Young, male, upper middle-class, and white place a person at the upper end of North American society. Old, female, lower class, and minority group membership place a person at the lower end. The multiple jeopardy perspective says that a person with more than one of these characteristics, for example, a minority member age 65 and over, will face multiple jeopardy. According to this view, a person in multiple jeopardy will face an increased risk of death and illness, compared with whites, as they age.

Some gerontologists gave a broad meaning to multiple jeopardy. They viewed the poorer health and income of older minority group members, compared with dominant group members, as evidence of multiple jeopardy (Belgrave & Bradsher, 1994). Markides, Timbers, and Osberg (1984) gave a more precise meaning to multiple jeopardy. They said that multiple jeopardy exists when (1) the minority group has poorer health or lower income than the dominant group; and (2) the minority group, compared with the dominant group, shows greater declines in health and well-being with age.

This means that multiple jeopardy exists when age adds to the disadvantage already experienced by a minority group in middle age. The gap between the two groups must widen with age for multiple jeopardy to exist. Markides (1987b) called multiple jeopardy the "key conceptual model in the field" of minority group studies in gerontology.

Researchers find it hard to measure multiple jeopardy. For one thing, most studies of multiple jeopardy use a cross-sectional method. They look at a minority group at one point in time. This makes it impossible to tell whether things have gotten worse for minority members, compared with dominant group members, as they have aged. It could be that older age cohorts differ in some way from younger cohorts, regardless of race.

For example, African Americans have poorer health than whites in old age, in part because older African Americans had poorer health and nutrition in their youth. This has to do with poverty (and indirectly to discrimination) in American society. It only becomes multiple jeopardy if the gap between African Americans' health relative to whites' widens as they age.

Markides (1987b) says that researchers need to study people over time to test for multiple jeopardy. Longitudinal study could also control for social class differences. Multiple jeopardy may affect only lower class minority group members. If so, then social class rather than minority group membership leads to multiple jeopardy.

Critique of Multiple Jeopardy Theory

A number of researchers find the multiple jeopardy theory limited. First, some recent studies of older

African Americans' health find no evidence of multiple jeopardy. Kelley-Moore and Ferraro (2004), for example, found differences in health between older African Americans and whites. They found that African American older people had poorer health and more disability than whites. Age did not amplify differences based on race (Binstock, 1999). The researchers say that this supports the "persistent-inequality" thesis. They conclude that African Americans have poorer health early in life, and this carries through to old age.

Second, Jackson, Taylor, and Chatters (1993, p. 2) reject the multiple jeopardy perspective. They say, it takes a "victim-centered" approach. It shows the negative effects of discrimination on minority older people. But it fails to study the strengths and coping abilities of minority members. This does an injustice to minority elders.

Third, Hayes-Bautista and his colleagues (2002, p. 39; *also* Williams & Wilson, 2001) report data that fails to support the multiple jeopardy theory. They used California data to look at health risks and mortality among older minority group members. They found that elderly African Americans fit the model of a minority health disparity in later life. But Latino and API elderly showed the opposite of this model.

Compared with non-Latino whites, Latino and API elderly showed *lower* relative risk of death from nearly all of the major diseases of old age. They call this an "epidemiological paradox." In other words, these two minority groups have the risk factors—low income, low English language ability, and low educational achievement—that should lead to multiple jeopardy. But these groups show the opposite of multiple jeopardy in old age—they have a *lower* risk of illness and premature death than non-Latino whites. These findings call into question the general application of multiple jeopardy theory to all racial and ethnic groups.

Still, the multiple jeopardy theory has had some value. It has led researchers to separate the effects of age from lifelong effects of inequality. This perspective offers a framework for longitudinal studies of specific subgroups of older people.

Leveling

Some studies find that multiple jeopardy describes only some characteristics of older minority members' lives. Williams and Wilson (2001) say that ethnic identity can help a person adapt to the stress of living as a minority member. It can also offer people self-esteem and career opportunities.

The leveling perspective says that the health and incomes of minority and dominant group members look more alike as people age. Markides (1983), for example, studied the incomes of African Americans, Latinos, and whites at various ages. This study found that minority and dominant group incomes got closer with increased age. The decrease in white incomes after retirement mostly accounts for this leveling.

For example, a pension rarely replaces a middle-class person's salary. Middle-class workers usually see a decrease in income when they leave their jobs. Minority members with low incomes may see no decrease in income with age. Many of these people work past age 65 because they have no pensions. The lowest earners may even see an increase in income when they receive Social Security payments. These trends lead to a smaller income gap between minority and dominant groups as they age.

Studies of the oldest old lend some of the strongest support to the leveling perspective. Studies of mortality find that minority group members show higher mortality than the rest of the U.S. population until age 65. From age 65 onward, they show lower mortality than the population as a whole. Hayes-Bautista and his colleagues (2002) found this tendency in data on Latino and API elderly in California. Elo and Preston (1997) found this **mortality crossover** among blacks for men between the ages of 85 and 89 and for women aged 90 to 94. Corti and colleagues (1999) found this crossover in blacks after age 80. John (1994) reports this mortality crossover by age 65 in Native Americans.

A study by the National Caucus and Center on Black Aged, Inc. (1998) found a reversal of the crossover effect in 1995 figures that compare life expectancy for whites and blacks aged 85 and over. Still, the oldest blacks in the data show an almost equal life expectancy to whites (the groups differed by only 0.1 years). So, while these data do not show a crossover effect, they do show that the life expectancy gap between whites and blacks closes in late old age.

Studies of leveling, like studies of multiple jeopardy, often look at older minority group members at one point in time. This makes it hard to say exactly why the crossover effect takes place. Gerontologists think that this crossover occurs because whites gain benefits in life expectancy early in life due to better nutrition and medical care. But only the healthiest minority group members survive into late old age (Corti et al., 1999; Gelfand, 2003). Those who do survive show extreme hardiness. They resist common causes of death in later life and so have longer life expectancies than whites.

Both the leveling and the multiple jeopardy perspectives have their place in the study of aging. But they take too simple a view of minority and dominant group differences in later life. For one thing, they miss the differences of experiences within minority groups. They also fail to understand the effects of earlier life on minority older people.

The Life Course Perspective

Gerontologists have begun to take a broader view of minority group aging. The life course perspective begins with the idea that life unfolds from birth to death in a social, cultural, and historical context. This perspective looks at the impact of social institutions, historical periods and events, personal biography, life cycle stage, life events, and resources on the minority older person (Damron-Rodriguez, 1998). This perspective looks at differences between minority groups, cultural subgroups within a minority group, and age cohorts among minority group members. Fry (1990, p. 132) says that the life course perspective "invites us to look for variation."

The life course perspective looks for continuities and discontinuities within minority groups. For example, it links early life experiences to actions and attitudes in later life. The life course perspective also links life experiences to the minority norms for timing life events and entering and leaving social roles.

Jackson, Chatters, and Taylor (1993, p. 307; *also* Williams & Wilson, 2001) used the life course perspective to study African Americans. Their work linked poverty, illness, and higher mortality in middle age and early old age to earlier life experiences. African Americans, they say, form a diverse group. But "the United States from cradle to grave [places African Americans] at disproportionate risk for physical, social, and psychological harm." The life course perspective gives researchers a framework for studying the links between different stages of the life cycle. It places individual development within a social, historical, and cultural context.

Institutional Completeness: An Example of Life Course Differences

The life course perspective proposes that gerontologists study how a group's culture and context affect aging. Each minority group provides a different context for its members. This differs for subgroups within a minority and for regions of the country. A minority group's institutional completeness, for example, can influence members' quality of life. Institutional completeness refers to the number of agencies, programs, family, friendship networks, and religious institutions in an older person's environment. An institutionally complete context provides strong support for the older person.

African Americans in large cities, for example, have a wide array of services and programs available. If they choose, they can attend an African American church, an African American adult day program, and see an African American counselor. African Americans in a large city can meet their social, health care, and personal needs within their minority communities. Service providers in these communities may understand the unique needs, perspectives, and backgrounds of minority older people.

A study of Vietnamese and Chinese older people in California shows the importance of social supports for minority older people. This study found that both the Vietnamese and Chinese groups lacked English language skills. This led to physical, mental, and social problems. However, poor English had less effect on the Vietnamese older people in the study. The researchers (Morton, Stanford, Happersett, & Molgaard, 1992, p. 173) concluded that "the Vietnamese community may act as an effective buffer to the stress associated with the acculturation process. Without a large community structure for support, it is probable that impairment levels would increase."

Many Vietnamese older people even give up government support to live near members of their minority group. The ethnic community provides these people with "a reservoir of collective support for economic and psychological adjustment" (Morton et al., 1992, p. 174).

Tran, Ngo, and Sung (2001) show how the lack of community supports affects Vietnamese elders. The researchers report that many Vietnamese elders without community supports lived in poverty and isolation. And often their children had few resources to share. If the Vietnamese elder lived in a nonethnic neighborhood, the elder had few social contacts. Their isolation increased due to the absence of newspapers, television, or radio in their own language. Their lack of English also created a barrier to the use of health or social services. This report shows the importance of a supportive community to ethnic elders.

Native American elders who live on reservations benefit from the informal supports available there. Elders live close to one another and their kin. They form a small but distinct group within the reservation. Reservations often lack formal supports (such as visiting nurse programs or meals-on-wheels), but elders call on kin, neighbors, and friends for support if needed (University of North Dakota, 2003).

Native American elders who live in a city such as Los Angeles often lack a supportive setting. First, the 11,000 people who make up this population live in a 4,000-square-mile area. Kramer (1992, p. 50) found these people scattered widely over the area. "The largest concentration of elders in one zip code," she says, "was 33 persons."

Second, this area had poor transportation and no intergenerational center. Third, elders came from as many as 200 tribes and spoke at least eighty different languages. Fourth, elders had little contact with one another or with younger Native Americans. City dwellers lived socially isolated lives and got little support.

The concept of institutional completeness shows the importance of the social environment to minority older people. It also shows that members of the same minority group can experience aging differently, depending on their social context. The life course perspective encourages analyses that look at the minority group culture and social life.

Structured Inequality and Personal History

Structured inequality refers to inequalities built into the social system. Personal history refers to a person's passage through life. The life course perspective looks at the links between personal history (youth, middle age, and old age) and a person's social and historical context. For example, early life experiences shape African Americans' status and roles in later life. For many African Americans, for example, low-paying jobs and low income in youth lead to low-paying jobs in middle age and poverty in later life.

African Americans aged 85 today were born around 1920. They lived their teen years during the Great Depression, and their early adult years during World War II. They had children during the Baby Boom and retired during the 1980s. These people faced economic hard times, physical danger, and overt racial discrimination. They can trace some of their health and economic problems today to the historical time they lived through. Jackson, Taylor, and Chatters (1993, p. 6) take a life course perspective when they emphasize the "systemic forces and poor opportunity structure" that work against African Americans throughout life.

THE IMPACT OF MINORITY GROUP MEMBERSHIP ON AGING

A person's experience of aging depends on many things other than simply being a member of a minority group. It depends on whether members assimilate into the wider society, when they emigrated to the United States, the institutional completeness of their community, and the geographic closeness of members. It depends on how much or how little the minority culture values older people, on past and present discrimination against minority group elders, and on many other social conditions. It depends on the older person's life experiences, the historical events they experience, and the resources they have available. It also depends on how they use these resources, their gender, educational background, and marital status. These conditions differ for members of different minority groups, and they differ for subgroups within a minority.

Each perspective—multiple jeopardy, leveling, and the life course—gives some insight into minority aging. The lens of multiple jeopardy highlights poor housing, poor nutrition, and low income among minority older people. The leveling perspective reports on these same issues, but it looks at the way that aging balances inequalities.

Multiple jeopardy and leveling alone miss important details about minority aging. "They do not reveal . . . important issues of group lifestyle and coping mechanisms" (Barresi, 1990, p. 249). This requires the life course perspective. It looks at how minority groups and their members adapt and survive. A full picture of minority aging requires all three perspectives.

A LOOK AT FOUR MINORITY GROUPS

The four largest U.S. minority groups are African Americans, Latinos, API, and Native Americans. These groups differ in size and in their proportion of the population. As noted earlier, they also differ by the proportion of older people in each group. And they each have subgroups. These subgroups, for example, the Vietnamese, Chinese, Korean, and Japanese groups within the Asian group, differ almost as widely from one another as they do from the dominant group. The discussions of these groups point out some of the differences between subgroups of minority elders.

African Americans

Health

African Americans (non-Hispanic blacks) made up 8 percent of the older U.S. population in 2001. Older African Americans make up 8 percent of the total African American population (Anderson et al., 2004). Most studies of older African Americans focus on the differences between African Americans and whites. These studies show the negative effects of race on African American elders.

Studies show, for example, that African American older people lag behind whites on measures of income (see Figure 7.5), education, and health (Williams & Wilson, 2001). Older African Americans will probably show improvement on these measures in the future as younger cohorts move into old age. But, due to continued inequality at all ages, older African Americans may still lag behind non-Latino whites on measures of well-being.

Hayes-Bautista and his colleagues (2002; Burggraf, 2000) report that African Americans have poorer health than non-Latino whites on most measures. They face a greater likelihood of heart disease, cancer, cerebrovascular disease, and diabetes. Compared with non-Latino whites, they have higher rates of disability (Kelley-Moore & Ferraro, 2004), spend less on health care, and see a doctor less often. They also have less access to quality medical care, receive fewer medical procedures than whites, and receive more procedures for illnesses due to delayed diagnosis (Williams & Wilson, 2001).

Dancy and Ralston (2002) studied the barriers to health care for three groups of African Americans—rural blacks, women, and those aged 75 and over. These groups all face a high risk of poor health. The researchers found that all groups faced economic barriers (poverty or low economic resources) and expressed lack of confidence in the health care system. These barriers kept them from getting the formal health care they needed.

The National Caucus and Center on Black Aged (1998) reports that African Americans of all ages have a higher incidence of cancer than white Americans. They also have a higher cancer mortality than whites. The National Caucus (1998, p. 62) also reports that "hypertension affects African Americans with much greater frequency than it does for Whites." The National Health and Nutrition Examination Survey III (Burt et al., 1995, cited in National Caucus, 1998) found that almost three-quarters of African American men and women aged 60 to 74 had high blood pressure (a sign of hypertension).

Gelfand (2003) reports that, compared with elderly non-Latino whites, elderly African Americans have higher rates of arthritis, hypertension, and diabetes. Also, compared with any other racial or ethnic group, older African American women face a higher risk of cancer. A higher percentage of African American older people, compared with white older people (40 compared with 26 percent) rate their health as fair or poor (Gelfand, 2003, citing Ferris, 2000). Poor health early in life carries over into old age. Also, poor health means lower earnings during a person's working years. Poor health among younger people today will likely lead to poor health in old age.

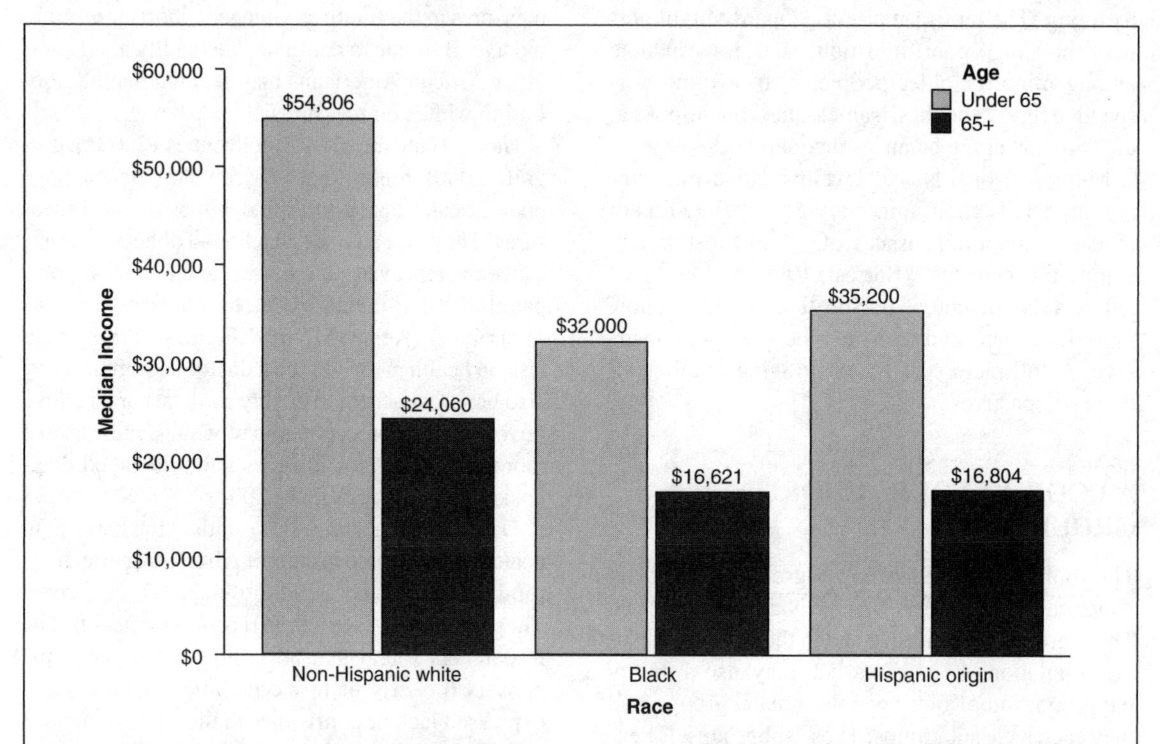

The older population for all races and ethnicities has lower incomes than younger people. Also, for both younger and older age groups, whites have higher incomes than blacks and Latinos. The lower income for minority older people shows the effect of lower minority member incomes earlier in life. Note that the income gap lessens between non-Hispanic whites, blacks, and Hispanics. Social Security helps narrow the gap in incomes in later life. All groups show about a 50 percent decrease in income between the younger and older age groups. But Social Security provides a floor for minority group members that in old age brings their incomes closer to that of non-Hispanic whites. Social Security keeps many minority older people out of poverty.

FIGURE 7.5

Median Income of U.S. Households by Age and Race, 2001

Source: Wu, K. (2003). Income and Poverty of Older Americans in 2001: A Chartbook. Washington, D.C.: AARP Public Policy Institute. Based on U.S. Census Bureau, March 2002. Current Population Survey (machine-readable micro data). Retrieved July 14, 2004, *http://research.aarp.org/econ/ip_cb2001.pdf.7.* Reprinted with permission.

Income

Elderly blacks face economic disadvantage when compared to non-Latino whites. In 1998 elderly whites had an income 1.6 times that of elderly blacks. Elderly whites had a per capita household income twice that of elderly blacks (due to the larger size of black families). Compared with elderly whites, twice the proportion of elderly blacks relied on Social Security for their sole source of income. Elderly blacks on average have only about one-quarter the net worth of their white counterparts. And more than one older African American in five lives in poverty (U.S. Census Bureau, 2002; Williams & Wilson, 2001). (See Table 7.1.)

Honig (1999) studied the expected retirement wealth of 4,371 households. The measure of total wealth included financial wealth, housing wealth, pension benefits, and Social Security benefits. White households in the study had an expected wealth in retirement of $390,950. Black households had about one-half the white household expected retirement total—$189,023. On every measure of financial well-being, compared with whites, elderly blacks show a disadvantage.

The disadvantage that African Americans face in later life reflects career and income disadvantages earlier in their lives. For example, compared with blacks, a higher proportion of white workers have higher paying managerial or professional jobs. A higher proportion of black workers, compared with white workers, work in lower paying service, production, transportation, and material moving jobs (U.S. Census Bureau, 2003d).

Older African American women face unique hardships. African American women, for example, have a lower rate of pension coverage than any other racial or gender group in the United States. They have the lowest annual median pension benefits ($1,908) of any racial or gender group (Chen, 1994). And they have the lowest median income of any racial, ethnic, or gender group (except older Hispanic women). Conway-Turner (1999) says that the number of women of color increases with each decade.

The type of work African American women do and their family responsibilities throughout life account in part for their low income. A lifetime of low pay, time off from paid work to raise children, work in the peripheral sector of the economy, and poor pension plans, all lead to high rates of poverty for older African American women.

African American women aged 65 and over have a higher rate of poverty than any other race or gender group in the United States (except older Hispanic women). African American women's median

TABLE 7.1

Poverty in the Elder Population

People below the Poverty Level by Age and Race/Ethnicity, 1999

	65+	*75+*
All races	9.9	11.5
Non-Latinó white	8.2	10.0
Asian	12.3	13.7
Latino (of any race)	19.6	21.8
American Indian	23.5	26.3
African American	23.5	26.6

Non-Latino whites have the lowest rate of poverty of any racial or ethnic group. Asians have the next lowest rate. In both older age groups (65+ and 75+) Latinos have almost twice the poverty rate of non-Latino whites. American Indians and African Americans aged 65 and over have almost three times the poverty rate of non-Latino whites. For the group aged 75 and over American Indians and African Americans have two and a half times the poverty rate of non-Latino whites.

The life course perspective in part explains the inequalities that show up in these figures. For example, the older age group (75+) shows higher poverty rates for every racial and ethnic group. This reflects lower salaries, the lack of pensions, and fewer years paying into Social Security programs for this oldest group. Also, widowed women in this group have the least likelihood of having a private pension, investments, or savings.

The three groups with the highest poverty rates in old age (Latino, American Indian, and African American) have higher poverty rates than non-Latino whites throughout life. For these groups, poverty carries through into old age. Sources of inequality in minority members' lives include overt and covert discrimination in employment, high unemployment rates, part-time work, seasonal work, low pay, poverty in middle-age, and few pension plans in domestic and service jobs.

Source: U.S. Census Bureau, *Statistical Abstract of the United States.* (2003). No. 697. People below poverty level by race, sex, and age: 1999. Retrieved July 13, 2004, *www.census.gov/prod/2004pubs/03statab/income.pdf;* also *www.census.gov/prod/www/statistical-abstract-03.html.*

income in 2001 came to $16,282. This put them below every other racial, ethnic, and gender group except Hispanic women (U.S. Census Bureau, 2003d). They depend heavily on Social Security and Supplemental Security Income (SSI) for their income (Binstock, 1999). Their low Social Security benefits (the SSI goes to the poorest older people) reflect their low income during their working years. They carry the inequalities of gender, social class, and race into old age (Conway-Turner, 1999).

Social Security and SSI favor married couples. This further hurts older African American women, many of them single. African American women have nearly twice the rate of widowhood of white women at age 65. Three-quarters of African American women are widowed by age 75 (Grambs, 1989, cited in Ovrebo & Minkler, 1993). Ovrebo and Minkler (1993) say that Social Security pays a maximum benefit that equals only 76 percent of the poverty line for single people. And this income level cannot support a decent quality of life (Binstock, 1999). This policy works against older African American women.

Studies of the inequality of African Americans in later life make an important point. They argue for greater opportunity for African Americans throughout life, and they suggest the need for financial and health care resources to help African American older people age well. (See Figure 7.6, page 180).

Family and Community Life

Most studies of African American aging take a multiple jeopardy perspective. These studies compare the minority experience of aging with the experience of aging in the dominant group. They focus on inequality and highlight minority group problems.

Stanford (1990, p. 41) objects to this approach. "Collectively," he says, "African American older persons should be viewed from the perspective of their own history, without having to suffer the indignity of being compared with those older persons who have, for the most part, had entirely different social, political, and economic experiences." A look at the African American family and community should focus on the unique experience of the African American older person and on the diversity of experiences within the African American older population.

Research suggests two views of the African American family and its effect on older people. First, high divorce rates, teen pregnancies, and single-parent households lead to an unstable family. This perspective emphasizes the problems that African Americans face as they age. Second, African American families have adapted to poverty, discrimination, and social problems. These families have flexible structures that allow them to cope with a stressful environment.

This perspective emphasizes the ability of the African American family to care for its aging members. It suggests that older African Americans in many cases have rich family and community supports, even in the face of social problems (Cantor & Brennan, 2000; Williams & Wilson, 2001).

The first National Survey of African Americans studied 581 randomly chosen older people from across the United States. Part of this study looked at African American adult children of older people. The study found that 90 percent of children reported that they helped their parents. One-third of these children said they gave frequent help (Chatters & Taylor, 1993). When adult children face poverty and family breakdown, they may lack the resources to give help. The findings show, however, that most African American adult children give some support to their parents.

Williams and Wilson (2001) say that older African Americans, compared with whites, tend to live in extended families. Fewer of them live alone. And they tend to live with children and grandchildren. They also tend to give and get help across generations. Peek and her colleagues (2000) interviewed 1,200 older people in Northern Florida communities. They found that, compared with whites, older African Americans with disability more often got support from their grandchildren. The researchers say that the large size of African American families and the tendency for older people to live with their children accounts for these findings.

Older African Americans also develop social networks to add to their family supports. More often than whites, they interact with and get support from friends, church members, and associations. The segregation of many African Americans in inner-city neighborhoods has led to a neighborhood focus (especially for poorer people). Older African Americans, more than whites, think of their neighborhoods as centers of personal influence (Jackson, Taylor, & Chatters, 1993). They know and visit their neighbors and use their neighbors as a resource.

Older African Americans have wide networks of friends and neighbors. Compared with other minority groups and whites, they also include **fictive kin** as a part of their informal support networks. Fictive kin are nonrelatives who give social support to the older person and act as confidants (Cantor & Brennan, 2000). Older African Americans refer to fictive kin as just like family.

One national study (Chatters, Taylor, & Jayakody, 1994) found that 45 percent of African Americans had fictive kin. African Americans over age 85 often used fictive kin for social support (Johnson, 1999, cited in Gelfand, 2003). Childless African American older people sometimes adopt **play siblings** to get the support they need (Johnson & Barer, 1990). They bond with a formal care worker and consider them a "best pal" or "like a sister to me."

Friendship provides satisfying relationships for many older African Americans. Taylor, Keith, and Tucker (1993) found that 80 percent of African Americans said they got help from a close friend. Sixty percent got support from church members. Over one-half got support from extended family members (Taylor, 1993). Only a small proportion of people reported social isolation with no close friend or supports. The researchers conclude that older African Americans "are embedded in support networks comprised of both family and friends" (Taylor, Keith, & Tucker, 1993, p. 62). Older African Americans create a satisfying old age for themselves out of limited economic and social resources.

Older African American women give support to their families as well as receive it. Padgett (1989) says that they often play a role as **kintenders** who have authority and respect. Cantor and Brennan (2000) compared the care for grandchildren among different minority groups. They found that African Americans reported more ongoing care for grandchildren. Twenty-two percent of low income African Americans and 39 percent of moderate income African Americans reported day-to-day care of grandchildren. Only 4 percent of moderate income whites reported day-to-day care.

A high proportion of African American grandparents (between 29 and 39 percent) said they gave care because the child's parent could not do so. Gelfand (2003, citing Lugaila, 1998) says that compared with other groups, African American grandparents had twice the likelihood of fully parenting their grandchildren.

Care for grandchildren today extends the historical role that grandparents have played in the African American family (Gelfand, 2003). "The African American grandmother is a heroic archetype, the highest status a woman can attain in the African American community" (Ovrebo & Minkler, 1993, p. 305). Gibson (1986, p. 195) says that "elderly African American women have been a wellspring of support and nurturance over time."

Religious belief, a support network, and a good self-image, all make the older African American woman a source of strength in her family and community (Ovrebo & Minkler, 1993). But Jackson (1972) cautions against stereotyping all older African American women as matriarchs or mother surrogates for grandchildren. Cantor and Brennan (2000, p. 227) say that "for many [African American grandparents] such care involves burdens in terms of time, energy, finances, and emotional strain."

Cantor and Brennan (2000) studied African American older people in New York City. They found that most people use formal supports as a complement to informal supports. The most often used community services included hospital emergency rooms, senior centers, and religious leaders. The church also plays an important role as a social support for African American older people.

African American Men

Most studies of African Americans in the United States have focused on women. Studies of African American men often emphasize the problems they face and their absence from African American family life. Those who are single (never married), separated, or divorced have the highest poverty rates among older African American men: 56 percent of

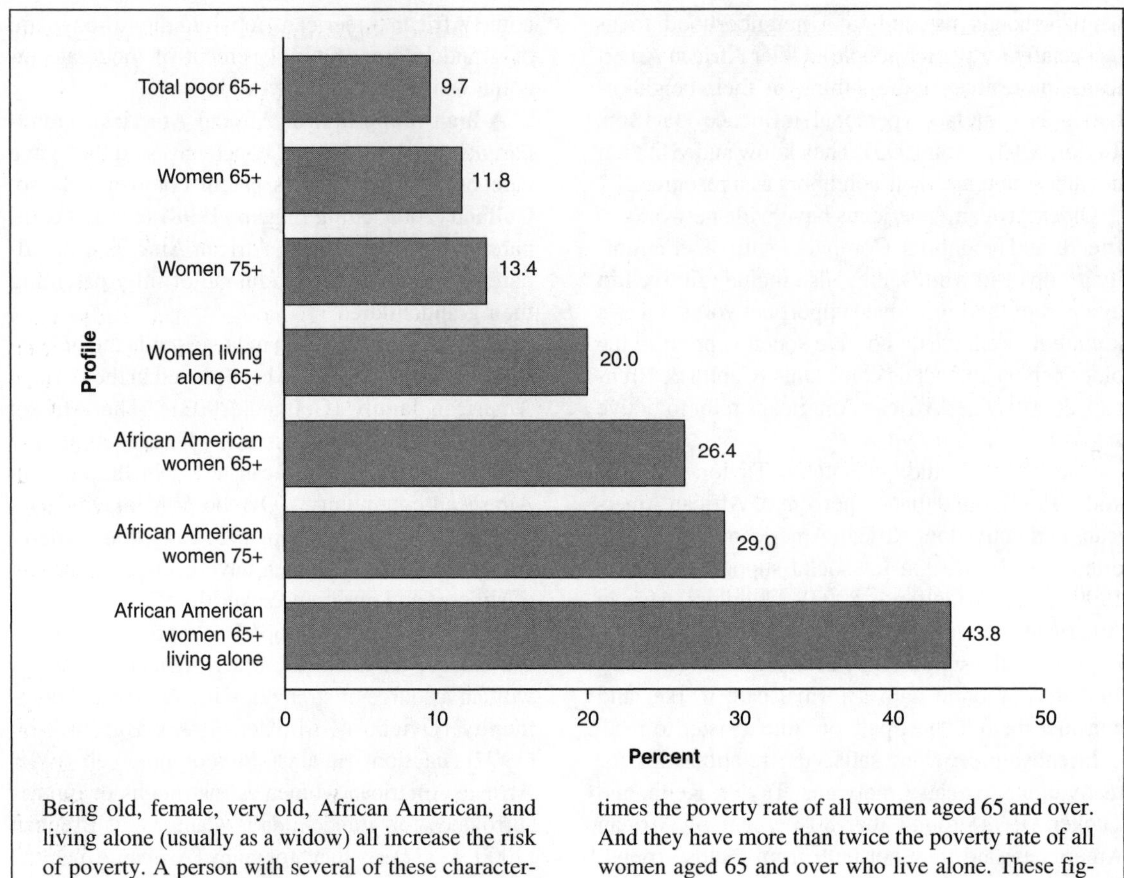

Being old, female, very old, African American, and living alone (usually as a widow) all increase the risk of poverty. A person with several of these characteristics (e.g., an elderly African American woman who lives alone) shows the greatest risk of poverty. Older African American women who live alone have four times the poverty rate of all women aged 65 and over. And they have more than twice the poverty rate of all women aged 65 and over who live alone. These figures show the impact of multiple risk factors (especially race) on income in later life.

FIGURE 7.6

Profile of the Elderly Poor, 1999

Source: Dalaker, J., & Proctor, B. D. (2000). *Poverty in the United States, 1999*. U.S. Census Bureau, Current Population Reports, Series P60-210. Washington, DC: U.S. Government Printing Office. Retrieved July 14, 2004, *www.census.gov/prod/2000pubs/p60-210.pdf.*

single men fell below the poverty line, followed by 48 percent of separated men, and 45 percent of divorced men. These men risk isolation, poor nutrition, and poor health in later life. The extended family offers these men less support than it does older women (Kart, 1990).

Kart (1990) says that this image of the poor and absent older African American man overlooks the majority of older men. He reports, for example, that in 1985, 60 percent of older African American men were married and lived with their spouses. Married men had the lowest poverty rate among African American men (19 percent). Men in these married couples take part in an extended kin network.

Kart (1990) reports that 15 percent of all older African American couples have a child aged 18 or under living with them (about one-half of these are grandchildren). "Presumably," Kart says (1990,

p. 110) "the aged Black males in these families are active in the child-grandchild-rearing activities of the families." And they can serve as role models for their male grandchildren (Hayslip, Shore, & Henderson, 2000).

Burton and DeVries (1992, p. 52) give examples of grandfather caregivers from their research.

- Simon, age 67, has looked after three of his grandchildren since their birth. The children now range from 7 to 13 years. "I had no idea I would be raising these children this long," he says. "I am going to be raising kids all my life, I know it. I just know it."
- Pervis, a 62-year-old grandfather says, "I got a lot on my back. I take care of my wife who has cancer and my two grandbabies. Sometimes, I think that it's a losing battle. But I have faith in the Almighty and I have two good boys who help me."

These men and their family commitments challenge the simple image of the absent older African American man. They also show the conflicting emotions grandfathers face in the caregiving role. Thomas, Sperry, and Yarbrough (2000) say that grandfathers give care and give advice. But, compared with grandmothers, they express less grandparenting satisfaction.

Kart says that discrimination throughout life leaves many older African American men on the margins of society. But a man with a role to play can make a contribution to family and community life. John Jordon worked as a baggage handler. He missed many chances for promotion during his career due to discrimination, but he found self-esteem and status in the church.

There, over twenty-five years, "he had moved from a pew member to a deacon. Now he was also treasurer of the church—a job of enormous responsibility that required banking a thousand dollars weekly. Mr. Jordon's church appreciated his talents, and Mr. Jordon was a faithful man and loved his church. There he was somebody" (Kart, 1990, p. 111, citing Dancy, 1977).

The diversity of African American men should alert policymakers and service providers to their varied needs. Single men in poverty risk poor health and homelessness. Married men, who give care to their wives, children, and grandchildren, may need more home care support. A more accurate view of African American older men can target supports to meet their needs.

The Future of African American Aging

Some demographic and social trends today will influence aging in the African American family in the future. First, older people in the African American family may have fewer resources to draw on. For example, many African American women in their teens and early 20s today already have children. Children born to these young women will be old themselves when these women reach late old age. These children will have to care for frail or chronically ill parents and for themselves, yet they may have limited resources to do so.

William Means leads a weekly Bible study group at Kethley House in Cleveland, Ohio.

This points to the need for more formal supports. Cantor and Brennan (2000) found that in New York City 42 percent of their sample said they needed more formal support in the past year. Formal support can also free the older person from reliance on family or provide support in the absence of family members. Johnson and Barer (1990, p. 732) say that with more formal supports in place for inner-city African Americans, "for the first time in their lives, individuals have autonomy to withdraw from problematic family relationships and concentrate on those relationships that are more rewarding."

Second, high mortality for younger African American men will lead to relatively few men compared with women in later life. This will produce more single older women, many of whom will live alone. Jackson, Chatters, and Taylor (1993, p. 316; *also* Dilworth-Anderson, Williams, & Williams, 2001) say that a growing number of older African American adults "are at severe risk for impoverished conditions and poor social, physical, and psychological health in old age." They base this conclusion on "the inevitable poor prognosis of the life experience paths into older ages of so many African Americans."

Third, current conditions for young people in different parts of the African American community will shape their lives in old age. Research shows more middle-class African Americans than ever before. Cantor and Brennan (2000) noted differences in the economic, health, and social conditions of poor and moderate income older African Americans. In many cases, the moderate income African Americans had an experience of aging more similar to whites than to poorer African Americans. This points to a widening gap in the experiences of poor and middle-class African Americans.

Middle-class African Americans of the future may feel they have little in common with poor African Americans. This could fragment the political power that African Americans can wield as a group. Middle-class older African Americans may feel concerned about different issues (e.g., lower taxes) than poor older African Americans (who may want higher Social Security benefits). These two groups may press for support of their own issues, rather than issues related to poverty and race. Gerontologists, service providers, and policymakers will have to take into account the different experiences of aging within the African American community.

Hispanic Americans

Health and Income

Latino elders made up 5.4 percent of the U.S. population aged 65 and over in 2002 (U.S. Census Bureau, 2003e). Williams and Wilson (2001) say that this proportion will grow to 17.5 percent of the older population by the year 2050. Older Latino Americans make up 5 percent of the total Latino population (Anderson et al., 2004).

A number of subgroups make up the Latino older population. These subgroups differ in size and in their proportion of the older population. The history of each subgroup in the United States accounts for this difference. The Cuban group, for example, arrived in the United States in a wave after the Cuban revolution. Few people have migrated from Cuba since then. And the Cuban community has had a relatively low birth rate. For these reasons, this community, among all the Latino groups, has the largest proportion of older people.

Health

Latino elderly men, compared with whites, have lower death rates from cardiovascular disease and certain types of cancer (Markides & Coreil, 1988). Latino elderly women show about the same rates as other groups. But Latino older people have greater rates of diabetes, infections, and parasitic diseases (Markides, 1987a). Their many years of hard work under poor conditions can lead to poor health in later life.

Cantor and Brennan (2000) studied 337 Latino elderly persons in New York City. They found that over one-half of the people in the study reported fair or poor health. Only 7 percent said they had excellent health. Older Latinos also had a higher rate of impairment than white or African American older people. Harsh working conditions also lead to "accelerated aging," shorter careers, and shorter life expectancy (Gallegos, 1991, p. 182).

Poor health has an effect on older Latinos' lifestyles and mood. Older Latinos, compared with whites, had more trouble with household activities and advanced activities of daily living (Lum, Chang, & Ozawa, 1999). Eighty-five percent of older Latino women say they have a chronic illness and 45 percent say they have trouble with activities of daily living (Burggraf, 2000).

Older Latinos tend to use hospitals and nursing homes less often than do whites (Mui & Burnette, 1994). They give lack of funds and fear of hospitals as the reasons for underuse. Lack of private

BOX 7.1
THE OLD ONES OF NEW MEXICO

Gerontological studies of Latino elders often emphasize the differences between them and the non-Latino white population. The Latino older person usually comes out second best. They look poor, uneducated, and needy. Gerontologists have begun to call for a more complete study of racial and cultural differences in later life. They suggest more study of the uniqueness of each group. This uniqueness comes through when we hear the voices of older people themselves.

Psychologist Robert Coles studied older Latinos in New Mexico. In his work he captures the voices of the Spanish-speaking people he met. We get a glimpse of the world through their eyes.

An old woman says:

> I won't let my family celebrate my birthdays anymore; and when I look at myself in the mirror a feeling of sadness comes over me. I pull at my skin and try to erase the lines, but no luck. I think back: all those years when my husband and I were young, and never worried about our health, our strength, our appearance. I don't say we always do now; but there are times when we look like ghosts of ourselves. I will see my husband noticing how weak and tired I have become, how hunched over. I pretend not to see, but once the eyes have caught something, one cannot shake the picture off. And I look at him, too; he will straighten up when he feels my glance strike him, and I quickly move away. Too late, though; he has been told by me, without a word spoken, that he is old, and I am old, and that is our fate, to live through these last years.
>
> But it is not only pity we feel for ourselves. A few drops of rain and I feel grateful; the air is so fresh afterwards. I love to sit in the sun. We have the sun so often here, a regular visitor, a friend one can expect to see often and trust. I like to make teas for my husband and me. At midday we take our tea outside and sit on our bench, our backs against the wall of the house. Neither of us wants pillows; I tell my daughters and sons that they are soft—those beach chairs of theirs. Imagine beach chairs here in New Mexico, so far from any ocean! The bench feels strong to us, not uncomfortable. The tea warms us inside, the sun on the outside. I joke with my husband; I say we are part of the house: the adobe gets baked, and so do we. For the most part we say nothing, though. It is enough to sit and be part of God's world. We hear the birds talking to each other, and are grateful they come as close to us as they do; all the more reason to keep our tongues still and hold ourselves in one place. . . .
>
> A man is lucky; it is his nature to fight or preach. A woman should be peaceful. My mother used to say all begins the day we are born: some are born on a clear, warm day; some when it is cloudy and stormy. So, it is a consolation to find myself easy to live with these days. And I have found an answer to the few moods I still get. When I have come back from giving the horses each a cube or two of sugar, I give myself the same. I am an old horse who needs something sweet to give her more faith in life!

Source: From Coles, R. (1973). *The Old Ones of New Mexico,* pp. 6–7. Albuquerque: University of New Mexico Press.

health insurance (sometimes called *Medigap*) may also keep older Latinos from using formal services. Latinos, compared with whites and other minority groups, have the highest proportion of uninsured people. About one-third of older Latinos have insurance only through Medicare. They use Medicaid to cover basic expenses (Villa & Arnda, 2000). And many older Latinos lack even this basic coverage. Gelfand (2003) reports that the poorest older people (the lowest 20 percent in income) spend 32 percent of their income on health care.

This lack of health insurance in old age reflects a lifelong lack of health insurance. Schur and Feldman (2001) found that, compared with non-Latino whites, Latino workers had four times the rate of chronic uninsurance. They often work in industries that offer no health insurance. But even in industries with insurance, Latino workers had lower coverage rates than whites. One-half of Latino workers born outside the United States had no health insurance in 1997. Long waits, impersonal service, and poor communication also create barriers to health care use.

Burggraf (2000) says that health care providers often do not understand the culture and family lives of Latino elders. This leads to low service use by Latinos and to poor health. Researchers for years reported that older Latinos tend to rely on informal supports to look after their health care needs (Mui & Burnette, 1994). This research has created an ideal of the supportive Latino family. But families do not always provide the care an older person needs. In some cases, the family steps in because the community lacks formal resources to help the older Latino person. Researchers call for more complete formal services for Latino elders (Gelfand, 2003).

Income

Latinos generally have lower incomes than African Americans or whites. Latinos had an average income in 2002 of $13,003 per year. About one-half the white average income of $24,127. Latinos also had almost two and a half times the rate of poverty of the white older group (19.6 percent compared with 8.2 percent) (U.S. Census Bureau, 2003d). In a study of expected retirement wealth, Honig (1999) found that Latino households, compared with whites and blacks, had the lowest expected net wealth.

Cantor and Brennan (2000, p. 143) summarize these findings when they say that Latino elders (in New York City) "whether in terms of social class, occupational history, income, extent of poverty, or perceived economic well-being reveal a consistent picture of low socioeconomic status and inadequate financial resources."

Many older Latinos have spent their lives working in low-paying jobs. They will get low Social Security benefits and they have little chance of a private pension. Cantor and Brennan (2000) found in their New York City sample that between 91 percent (Puerto Ricans) and 62 percent (other Latino origins) received Social Security. But for one in five members of their sample, Supplemental Security Income (paid to the poorest older people) served as their main source of income.

Differences in income exist among the Latino older population. In general, Puerto Ricans have the most income (in part due to their lifelong U.S. citizenship), followed by Cubans, and then Dominicans and others. Younger Cubans, more than any other Latino group, tend to work in technical, sales, and clerical work. Nearly one person in five (18.6 percent) with a Cuban background has a Bachelor's degree (U.S. Census Bureau, 2003d). Compared with other Latino subgroups, they have a better chance of a good income in later life. Their higher incomes during their working years give them the chance to save and invest for their retirement.

Puerto Ricans, on the other hand, show the greatest tendency to work in low-paying service jobs. They tend to have lower incomes and higher poverty rates than Mexican Americans and Cubans (U.S. Census Bureau, 2003d). Andrews (1989) says that low-income Latino elders would benefit from SSI. But in her study, few people who could get SSI knew about this program.

Poverty rates differ within the Latino population. One-fifth (21.4 percent) of all Latino older people lived below the poverty line in 2001. Again, rates differ by subgroup. The rate for Mexican Americans was 23 percent, the rate for Puerto Ricans was 26 percent, and the rate for Cubans was 17 percent (U.S. Census, 2003b).

Family and Community Life

Latinos show a clear disadvantage on economic measures, but they seem less disadvantaged on measures of family relations and informal supports. Goodman and Silverstein (2002) report that Mexican American elders, compared with non-Latino whites, tend to live in multigenerational families. Most often the older person lives in the adult child's home.

Latino migrants, compared with non-Latino migrants, show more than double the rate of living with their children (21.0 to 8.2 percent). Recent Latino migrants show triple the non-Latino rate (Biafora & Longino, 1990). Latino women aged 65 to 74 had four times the rate of living with their children compared with whites (Bastida & Juarez, 1991). Burr and Mutchler (2003) say that among Mexican American families, this tendency increases if the older person has poor English language skills and if the person lives in a non-Spanish speaking community.

Wilmoth (2001) says that the tendency for older Latinos to live with their children reflects their cultural background. A national survey of 2,352 middle-aged adults (aged 45 to 55) asked about family relationships. The survey found that, compared with whites and African Americans, Latinos showed the most family focus. The report calls Latino adult children "engaged caregivers." They reported that they did more for their parents and felt guilty for not doing enough (Belden, Russonello, & Stewart, 2001, p. 89).

Support in the Puerto Rican family flows in two directions—to the older person and from the older person to others (Sanchez, 2001). For example, older Puerto Ricans expect their children to look after them in old age. They expect their children to visit and call often. But they also give support to younger family members. Freidenberg (2000, pp. 102–103) studied Puerto Rican elders in El Barrio, Spanish Harlem in New York City. Eiliana, one of her respondents, describes her commitment to her family. She says:

"Yes, I continued being here with them [the grandchildren]. I rose early and I took them to school, at fourteen! Don't believe that because I saw them big I abandoned them! . . . I would take the kids to school and would leave them, and at ten in the morning I was already calling to see if they were at school. . . ."

Older Mexican Americans give advice to younger relatives and pass on cultural history. They also get health care and social support from family members (Du Bois, Yauno, & Stanford, 2001). The family often acts as a bridge between the older Latino person and the wider society. Children of older migrants who have close contacts with their parents often help them make use of formal social services.

Belden and associates (2001) found that adult children talk to medical personnel on behalf of their parents. And a high proportion of adult children provide personal care such as bathing, dressing, and eating (21 percent, almost double the rate of the total group studied). Forty percent of Latino adult children provide financial support to their parents (compared with only 27 percent of the sample as a whole). Beyene, Becker, and Mayen (2002) found that close family relations buffered the effects of aging among Latino elderly. People in strong family relationships reported good to excellent health and thought of aging as a blessing.

Some studies caution against stereotyping all Latino families as close and supportive. Studies of Mexican Americans in the southwest, for example, have found that city life has weakened family ties. Also, caregiving responsibilities often fall to women. These women show a strong commitment to care for their aging relatives, but caregiving can create a burden for them (Kolb, 2000). If a family cannot give care to an older person, living together can lead to poor treatment and abuse (Gallegos, 1991).

Cantor and Brennan (2000) say that the family focus of Latino elders leaves them with fewer options if the family cannot give support. Compared with whites and African Americans, they have fewer friends, confidants, and neighbors to call on in an emergency. Their lack of English skills makes it harder for them to turn to formal community supports.

A study of U.S. Census data found that, compared with other Latino groups, Cuban immigrants showed the highest rate of independent living.

A Hispanic grandfather helps his granddaughter with her homework. Hispanic grandparents often play an active role in their children's and grandchildren's lives.

Among older Cubans, married people with the most financial resources tended to live on their own (Wilmoth, 2001). Martinez (2002) interviewed seventy-nine older Cubans immigrants in Miami. More than one-half (53.2 percent) of these people lived alone. Only 7.6 percent lived in multigenerational households.

These older Cubans idealized the large family that includes the old and the young. But they resigned themselves to the reality of the nuclear family. Many of these people said that they preferred to live alone. They felt that younger people thought of older people as a nuisance. The demand of jobs and the pressure to succeed in the United States leads many Cuban young people to spend less time with their families (Gelfand, 2003).

The Future of Hispanic American Aging

Latinos form a diverse group. Some immigrated many years ago, some only yesterday. In addition, Latino subgroups come from different cultures. Puerto Rican elders, for example, may have a support system in Puerto Rico that they can call on if needed. They can return to Puerto Rico for support whenever they choose because they have U.S. citizenship. Other groups, such as the Cubans, have to make the best of conditions in the United States. This may mean learning to live a more independent life in old age. Finally, older Latinos in urban centers have access to more formal supports. Those in rural areas may rely almost entirely on informal supports.

Every Latino community could use more accessible and available support services. Differences within the Latino group mean that service providers need to shape programs to fit individuals' and subgroups' specific needs. The growing size and importance of the older Latino population calls for more knowledge about this group's service needs. This will include studies of functional ability, the impact of poverty on health, and the use of formal and informal social supports.

Asian Americans

Asian Americans make up 2.6 percent of all people aged 65 and over in the United States. Older Asian Americans made up 8 percent of the total Asian American population (U.S. Census Bureau, 2003e). Asian Americans include people from the Far East (China, Japan, Taiwan, etc.), and Southeast Asia (Malaysia, Singapore, Thailand, etc.). Morioka-Douglas and Yeo (1990) say that this group contains more than twenty different ethnicities. A list of major subgroups of older Asian Americans includes Chinese, Filipino, Asian Indians, Vietnamese, and Koreans. All of these groups number more than one million people in the United States (Gelfand, 2003). Smaller groups include Japanese, Afghans, Pakistanis, Thais, Laotians, and Cambodians. More than two-thirds of Asian Americans live in California. Each subgroup has a unique history in the United States.

Health

Asian Americans in general have good health. Gelfand (2003, citing Hahn & Eberhardt, 1995) says that elderly Asian men and women have an average life expectancy five years longer than whites. Certain illnesses affect subgroups of the Asian elderly population. For example, older Asians, compared with whites, have a higher incidence of liver, stomach, and pancreatic cancer. Japanese and Filipino older people also have an increased incidence of diabetes (Gelfand, 2003).

Few studies have looked at the health care needs of Asian Americans. Lee and her colleagues (Lee, Yeo, & Gallagher-Thompson, 1993) report that Korean American older people need more information about illness and prevention. The researchers suggest that education programs need to offer this information in Korean. Research on Asian Americans needs to include enough people in a sample so that researchers can study different subgroups' use of services. This will make it easier to know what help specific minority group members need.

Studies show that Asian Americans are underserved by social service agencies that do not specifically serve Asian Americans. Lee (1992) found that in Chicago, for example, only three of twenty-two agencies served Asian American clients. Even agencies that focus on Asian Americans' needs overlook some Asian groups. Lee reports that these agencies served 3,000 people, but only thirteen clients had Vietnamese background. All agencies could improve their service through a better understanding of Asian American older people and their needs. For example, Lee (1992) says that beliefs in the similarity of all Asian people lead agencies to miss the needs of subgroups. Also, agencies need to serve clients in the client's preferred language.

Income

In general, Asian American elders have the highest economic status of any minority group. Compared with African Americans or Latinos, they have a poverty rate closer to whites. However, economic status differs by subgroup within the Asian American population.

For example, some older people within the Chinese subgroup speak only their native language. They recently arrived in the United States. They often have low incomes and rely on family members for support. Other members of the Chinese community come from families that have lived in the United States for many generations. These people live middle-class and upper middle-class lives. They work as professionals or own their own businesses.

Nearly all older people in the Filipino subgroup came to the United States as immigrants. Earlier Filipino immigrants have Social Security or pensions. More recent immigrants have to rely on their children for support. Older people in the Korean and Vietnamese subgroups live mostly on the west coast, have high rates of poverty, and rely on family members for social and economic support.

Older people in the Japanese subgroup have higher incomes and longer life expectancy than other Asian American elders. The Issei (first generation) arrived in the United States between 1870 and 1924, when laws cut off immigration. They brought traditional Japanese customs and values. The Issei celebrated Japanese holidays, honored the first-born son, and had a strong family-centered (versus individual-centered) view of the world. They committed themselves to the upward mobility of their children, the Nisei, through education.

The Nisei, who were born in the United States between 1910 and 1940, are aged 55 to 85 today. This generation has mixed Japanese and American values. They value education, respect for authority, and investment for the future. The Sansei, the third generation, serve as caregivers to their parents either in their parents' homes or as visitors to their parents in institutions. The Nisei and Sansei vary in their commitments to traditional Japanese values and culture.

Family and Community Life

Most Asian Americans come from traditions that respect older people. Belden and associates (2001) found that, compared with members of other groups, more middle-aged people of Asian background expected to care for elderly parents. Seventy-three percent of the Asian adults in their sample said they felt responsible for parent care (compared with only 49 percent of Americans in general). Almost this same proportion of Asian adults (72 percent) said they felt guilty and that they should do more for their parents (compared with 48 percent of the total sample).

Asian adults often give a lot of care to their parents. This includes working with health care professionals to arrange care and giving personal care themselves. Asian adults also have made adjustments in their work and personal lives to support their elderly parents. The demands of caring for an elderly parent sometimes clash with the demands of work and other activities. Asian American adults, more often than other groups, report stress due to the demands of care.

Kendis (1989) studied Japanese American elders (aged 60 and over) in Gardena, California. The elders in this study said they felt financially and socially secure. They also saw their children as a support system in case they needed help. One woman said, "If you get sick, you need someone to hold onto. Good friends are okay for one or two weeks, but not for longer" (Kendis, 1989, p. 103). This woman looks to her family for long-term support.

Shibusawa, Lubben, and Kitano (2001) report that adult children in the Japanese subgroup express obligation and gratitude toward their parents. For example, a high proportion of unmarried Japanese elders live with their adult children. Still, these researchers say, Japanese elders today prefer to live on their own near their children. Elders today have accepted the American values of independence.

Sung (2000, p. 235) suggests that "sensible elderly persons" in Asian communities adapt to American life by changing their expectations. They treat younger people as equals, they share their ideas with younger relatives, and they use social service agencies to meet their needs. In some cases, the demands of life in the United States and the adoption of U.S. values have weakened family support for older people.

Older people in the Chinese subgroup sometimes choose to live apart from their children, preferring to live in *Chinatowns* where they have access to other elders of Chinese heritage. They also have access to the foods and cultural life they enjoy (Gelfand, 2003). These people often live with little income and in poor housing conditions. They risk illness and isolation from their families. But they live in the community of their choice.

The Future of Asian American Aging

The Asian American group has grown faster than any other minority since 1970 (mostly through immigration), and they have a longer life expectancy at age 65 than other minority groups or whites. Although many Asian American elders get support from their families, others lack that support. These people need help from formal social services. Language and cultural barriers keep some of them from getting the help they need. Yee (1999, p. 46) calls for more "culturally competent services and health systems" to meet the needs of older Asian Americans.

Lee (1992) suggests that social service agencies recruit Asian American workers. Also, community agency and health service boards should include Asian American community leaders. This would give agencies a clearer picture of community members' needs. Kim and Kim (1989) say that curricula in universities should sensitize social work students to the needs of Asian Americans. Client education programs can also help Asian Americans learn to stay healthy and to use the health care system (Roberts et al., 1989).

Native Americans

Health and Income

The term *Native American* refers here to American Indians and Alaska Natives (Eskimo and Aleut). The U.S. Census Bureau (2003e) reports that, in 2002, 163,000 Native Americans aged 65 or over lived in the United States. Native Americans made up about one-half of 1 percent of the older U.S. population. They made up about 6 percent of the total American Indian and Alaska Native population (Anderson et al., 2004).

Like other minority groups in American society, the Native American population has many subgroups. John (1994) says that 278 reservations exist; 500 tribes, bands, or Native villages; and as many as one-hundred unrecognized tribes. They speak as many as 150 languages. Many live on reservations, but 62 percent of all Native Americans live off reservations in cities and towns. Two-fifths of Native Americans live in the western United States (Gelfand, 2003).

This variety reflects the politics and economics of the United States, and the history and social structure of Native American society. It makes generalizations about this group difficult. Studies of Native Americans often make reference to the high status of Native elders. But Baldridge (2002, p. 256) says that "the fact that elders are so highly regarded in Indian political rhetoric contrasts dramatically with their poor health and socioeconomic status and with tribes' frequent failure to provide adequate senior programs for them.

Health

Older Native Americans suffer from poor health. They report high rates of heart disease, cancer, diabetes, and chronic liver disease and cirrhosis (related to alcohol abuse) (Baldridge, 2002). Native Americans show increasing rates of diabetes. Twenty-four percent of Native Americans over age 65 had this disease—a 25 percent increase between 1990 and 1997 (Gelfand, 2003, citing Burrows et al., 2000). In some communities, Baldridge (2002) says, more than one-half the people aged 50 and over have diabetes. Some reservations have the highest rates of diabetes reported anywhere in the world.

A needs assessment of eighty-three tribes (Walker, 2002) found that "a greater percentage of Indian elders consider their health to be fair or poor (48%) than elders in the general population (34%)." Also, "many more Indian elders are overweight or obese (75%) than their non-Indian counterparts (53%)." Baldridge (2002) says that Indians have a life expectancy 3.3 years less than that of whites. Indians also die of alcoholism at 4.6 times the rate of whites, of tuberculosis 4.2 times the rate of whites, and of diabetes 1.6 times the rate of whites. These high rates of chronic illness lead to high rates of disability.

John and Baldridge (1996) report that 73 percent of Native Americans aged 55 and over report limitations in activities of daily living. John and his colleagues (1999, p. 57) say that compared with non-Hispanic whites, "twice as many Native Americans between the ages of 65 to 74 experience some type of functional impairment." Native Americans have some of the highest rates of disability of any ethnic group in the nation.

Income

Native Americans have lower incomes than other U.S. older populations (Schweitzer, 1999). In a study of Native American elders in rural and reservation settings, John (1994) found that Native Americans had only two-thirds of the overall median household income in the United States. Native Americans also had very low personal income. More than one-half (57 percent) of rural and reservation elders lived in a household with income below 125 percent of the poverty line. The U.S. Census Bureau reports that between 1998 and 2000 Native Americans had a poverty rate of 26 percent. A rate higher than whites or any other minority group (Gelfand, 2003, citing U.S. Census Bureau, 2001). John (1994, p. 53) concludes that "poverty is a significant problem among American Indian elders."

These conditions prompted the federal government's Administration on Aging to identify Native Americans as a priority group. This means that Native American elders should get special attention because they have many health, social, and economic problems. They also tend to have less access to formal support programs. For example, the Indian Health Service targets only a few programs (like transportation) to older Native Americans (Bane, 1991), and it offers few services to urban Native Americans.

Also, few community-based programs such as home care or respite care exist for Native elders (Polacca, 2001). Only twelve nursing homes exist for Native Americans in the entire nation (Baldridge, 2002). This means that many Native American elders who need institutionalization must live in nursing homes off their reservations. This can lead to isolation and culture shock. When asked "if at some point in your life you become unable to meet your own needs," most Indian elders (70 percent) indicated they would be willing to go to an assisted living facility. Only 18 percent of the elders indicated they would be willing to use a nursing home (Walker, 2002).

Even when services exist, Native American elders often choose not to use them. Many Native Americans consider programs insensitive to their culture. Elders mistrust government services, including health care services. They prefer their own traditions of medicine (Wykle & Kaskel, 1994). They go for help only when serious illness threatens their lives. A study of elders in Los Angeles County found that Native American elders see the social service system as "disrespectful at best or outright hostile at worst" (Kramer, 1992, p. 49).

Family and Community Life

Some authors have reported on the important role that older women play in Indian society. And many studies report on the respect that Indians have for their elders. Schweitzer (1999), for example, gathered reports on grandmothers' roles in a number of Indian tribes. She notes that in some cultures, such as the Hopi and Navajo, a child can have many grandmothers. The culture defines grandmotherhood broadly to include many older female relatives.

In other Native American cultures, a person becomes a grandmother by adopting a grandchild. In still other cultures the term *grandmother* applies to any older woman. Grandmothers actively teach the younger generation about tribal customs. They do this by telling stories to their grandchildren (Amoss, 1999), by demonstrating and teaching crafts like weaving (Hedlund, 1999), or by performing traditional ceremonies that include healing or naming children (Jacobs, 1999).

Weibel-Orlando (1990) says that many grandparents take an active role in raising their grandchildren. Schweitzer (1999, p. 8, citing Weibel-Orlando) says that "of all the characteristics we observed [in the research], one trait dominates: Indian grandmothers are almost universally engaged in childcare and childrearing." Elders take part in cultural renewal programs in schools, provide foster care, or actually raise their grandchildren. They may babysit a grandchild for short periods. They may care for a city-raised grandchild during summer vacations. Or they may raise a grandchild if the parents have too few resources or have a drug addiction. These periods of childrearing allow grandmothers to pass Indian culture to their grandchildren.

Older Indian women typically find the grandmother role appealing. But they also feel the burden of caring for a grandchild, especially if they need help themselves (Schweitzer, 1999). Baldridge (2002) says that reports on grandparenting tend to romanticize the elders' place in modern Indian society. Grandparents who get called into the parenting role often feel they have no choice. They have to help because of a breakdown in their adult child's life.

Glass and Huneycutt (2002) refer to this as grandparenting due to the four D's: drugs, divorce, desertion, or death. One survey of Indian elders asked how they felt about caring for grandchildren. Eighty-six percent of respondents said that younger people should not expect elders to care for young children for long periods of time. And 77 percent felt that it was "abusive or wrong" to have elders take on this task. Schweitzer (1999, p. 9) says that Indian elders feel "happiness . . . at the new status . . . sometimes mixed with ambivalence."

Similar issues arise when adult children have to care for an aging parent or grandparent. Elders ranked child, spouse, sibling, other person, grandchild, or other relative in that order as sources of support (John, 1994). Eighty percent of Native elders gave spouse or child as the most likely support. About one-half of Native American elders rely on a child for support. A study of Native American elders in Michigan, conducted by researchers at Wayne State University, found that most elders have family nearby. Only about 5 percent had no living children (Wayne State, 1994).

These findings suggest that the large majority of Native American elders have informal support systems in place if they need them. Shomaker (1990) says that in Navajo culture a reciprocity exists between children brought up by grandmothers and grandmothers in later life. In this society grandmothers often raise their daughters' children. These women raise their grandchildren to believe in lifetime reciprocity. The children owe their grandmothers for the care they get as children. The grandchildren expect to care for their grandmothers in their old age. Older women in this culture often live on their own even in late old age. Children and grandchildren provide the supports that make this possible.

The poverty and social breakdown in some Native American communities lead to problems for older people within the family. Families with good incomes, stable employment, and stable marriages can supply the most support, but some families have few resources to spare. And the stress of caregiving can lead to elder abuse. One study found that 81 percent of elders expressed worry about abuse (Baldridge, 2002). Brown (1989, p. 17, cited in Baldridge, 2002) reported that abuse can occur when a family has "caregiving responsibilities thrust upon them for which they were unprepared." Schweitzer (1999) says that frail elders, who need the most support, face the greatest threat of neglect or abuse.

Conditions on reservations can also lead to financial abuse. The lack of work on reservations, for example, has led older Native Americans' families to rely on their elders' Social Security checks for survival. This may be the only cash income a family gets. Younger people then have to rely on the older person for support. Some studies report abuse of older family members in this situation due to poverty and dependence (John, 1994). Schweitzer (1999, p. 15) says that "economic deprivation where lack of money means lack of food, fuel, and housing, creat[es] hardships for all members of the family. Elder abuse may result."

The Future of Native American Aging

Gerontologists say that elders who have no land get the most support when they control some resource. Navajo women control the value of reciprocity, and they pass this on to their grandchildren. Arapaho elders in Wyoming keep their prestige by controlling religious ritual (Fowler, 1990). The Coast Salish elders gain respect for their role as political leaders (Miller, 1999).

Miller (1999) describes the important role that older women play in cultural renewal among the Coast Salish tribes. Curley (1987, p. 472) reports a renewed interest by the Native American community in its culture and tradition. The community knows that it "cannot survive without the knowledge and wisdom held by the elders—the preservers of the Indian race, culture, and history."

At the same time, Indian elders face poverty, poor health, and sometimes abuse. Schweitzer (1999) calls this the "paradox of aging" in Indian society. Studies, documentaries, and public ceremonies show that elders have respect and support within Indian society. Still, the data on income, health care, and family relations show that elders face hardship. Schweitzer (1999) says that this paradox reflects both the cultural values that give respect to elders and the current problems that Indian communities face today. She calls these two sides of a coin. "Families find themselves encountering both conditions at the same time" (Schweitzer, 1999, p. 19).

John and his colleagues (1999) call for better health screening and prevention. They point to the high rates of preventable diseases such as diabetes, obesity, cancer (due to smoking), and liver disease (due to heavy drinking). They propose improvements in health screening programs by the Indian Health Service. They also call for home safety improvements to cut back on injuries and accidents. Agencies need to tailor their programs and services to the cultural needs of Native Americans (Hendrix, 2003). They say, for example, that older Native Americans see their own health in the context of their communities. The researchers suggest that prevention programs should emphasize the good effects of health promotion on the older person's family.

Baldridge (2002) sums up the condition of aging in Indian society today. He says that improvement of elders' conditions depend on improving the conditions of Indian life in general. "Until tribes can generate sufficient revenues," Baldridge (2002, p. 265) says, "or until federal and state governments provide better funding and access to programs, local improvement of these infrastructures is unlikely." Elders cannot live a high quality of material life if their children and grandchildren suffer from poverty and deprivation. Low incomes, poor quality housing, lack of transportation, and poor health care affect the old as well as the young.

RESPONSES TO MINORITY GROUP AGING

Torres-Gil (1987) says that minority elders will take a more active role in social change in the future. Local senior centers, commissions, committees, and advisory boards now give minority older people a chance to speak up on issues. A number of national associations for minority groups now exist. These include the National Caucus and Center on Black Aged, Inc., National Association for Latino Elderly

(Asociación Nacional Por Personas Mayores), the National Indian Council on Aging, and the National Asian Pacific Center on Aging. These associations speak for their respective minority groups to the government, they sponsor research, and they disperse information about their group. Hayes-Bautista and his colleagues (2002) describe the challenges posed by an ethnically and racially diverse older population.

- First, different groups have different health and social service needs. All groups could benefit from diabetes education and prevention programs. But specific groups, such as African Americans, could benefit from specific programs (in this case targeted heart disease and stroke prevention programs) (Johnson & Smith, 2002).
- Second, diversity exists within ethnic groups. The API group contains American-born older people as well as recent immigrants. This group contains members from many different cultures. These subgroup speak a variety of languages and may need services delivered in their native tongue. Johnson and Smith (2002) report that one-third of Latino patients and one-quarter of Asian Americans have trouble communicating with their doctors. Physicians and health care workers need to overcome communication barriers to deliver treatment. Public health providers need to use local minority media to spread word of health care programs.
- Third, minority members may mix traditional medicine with modern medical treatment. They may prefer traditional medical treatments, and they may prefer a physician from their own group. Physicians need to understand these preferences to gain the older person's trust and compliance. They also need to monitor interactions between western drugs and folk medicines.
- Fourth, the time of a person's immigration influences their eligibility for programs and services. For example, older people who immigrated recently (like some Philippine islanders), may not be eligible for certain government health care and income programs. These people may live in poverty and have unmet health and social service needs.

The unique needs of minority older people means that they often have less access to quality health care. For example, compared with non-Latino whites, minority members less often have health insurance. They may also face discrimination and prejudice when they interact with the health care system. Minority members may distrust the health care system and avoid using health care services (Johnson & Smith, 2002). Takamura (2002) calls for more health care workers with linguistic competence and knowledge of minority cultures.

Some new education programs for Alzheimer's caregivers try to overcome language and cultural barriers. A program for Puerto Rican caregivers includes bilingual and bicultural material (Educating, 1992). The Morehouse School of Medicine in Atlanta, Georgia, has developed a peer education program for inner-city African American caregivers.

Morton and her colleagues (Morton, Stanford, Happersett, & Molgaard, 1992, p. 174) suggest that agencies create "programs designed to reinforce and preserve traditional cultural beliefs and practices, and promote respect for cultural differences." Programs that consult with members of the minority group and include them in the development of programs will have the greatest success.

Gallegos (1991) agrees. He says that social service workers should use a **cultural competence** model of service. This model goes beyond service delivery. It builds competence in older people, strengthening their ability to function in the wider society. Hendrix (2003) likewise calls for an *intercultural collaboration* approach to service. This approach balances the health care worker's formal approach to medical care with the cultural needs of the minority elder. It encourages humility in the health care worker and respect for the older person's culture.

An increase in minority health care workers would also lead to better cooperation between older people and the health care system. Burggraf (2000) reports that only about 7 percent of doctors come from minority backgrounds and fewer than one in five is a woman. Johnson and Smith (2002) say that an increase in minority health care workers would encourage more minority elderly to use the health care system.

Social policy has a role to play here. Studies show that older minority group members tend to underuse social and health care services. Researchers in the past traced this to strong family support systems in minority groups. But more recent writings suggest that programs and services fail to meet the needs of minority elders. Minority elders may fall back on family supports because they cannot or do not want to use existing formal supports.

Native Americans, for example, need more long-term care services such as home care on reservations and in cities. Rural minority older people in general need more services (Bane, 1991). A study of health care for rural African Americans in Arkansas, Tennessee, and Mississippi looked at available services. Forty-seven percent of the people in the study said their community had no doctor (Parks, 1988). Many rural older people lack transportation to services. This ranks as the major barrier to services (Bane, 1991). Service agencies and government programs need to create more available and accessible services for minority elders. These programs need to take into account the diversity of the minority older population and minority members' unique cultural perspectives.

CONCLUSION

Minority members make up about 10 percent of the older population. Researchers divide the minority population into four main groups—African Americans, Latino Americans, API, and Native Americans. Each of these groups contains unique subgroups. These subgroups sometimes differ as much from one another as they do from the dominant population.

Some studies show that minority membership compounds the problems that older people face. Other studies show that minority group membership can level differences in old age.

The life course perspective puts minority aging in the context of personal history, culture, world events, and the conditions in the wider society. This perspective gives the most complete understanding of minority aging. It allows researchers to look at a person's health, income, and social service needs. It also encourages researchers to look at a person's culture, family and social supports, and community life.

The minority older population will increase in the years ahead. Social policies and programs must adapt to meet these older peoples' needs. This will require programs that fit the needs of minority older people from many diverse backgrounds. More research on minority aging will help shape programs and policies that suit minority older people. Health and social service professionals need more education about minority aging. This will increase their awareness of minority elders' needs and improve services to their clients.

SUMMARY

- This chapter examines the size, composition, and socioeconomic status of older minority groups. It discusses the experience of aging as a minority group member, and it describes creative responses to the challenge of minority aging.
- The term *dominant group* in the United States applies to non-Latino white people. This group makes up a numerical majority of the U.S. population and controls most of the social and economic resources in the country. Social scientists define a minority as a group that faces subordination and discrimination within society.
- The United States looks like a pluralistic society in which many social and ethnic groups live together. An assimilation continuum exists that runs from very traditional to bicultural to very assimilated. The older population reflects the pluralism of American society.
- Gerontologists study minority aging because (1) older minority populations have increased in size; (2) the study of older minorities can lead to more responsive programs for older people; (3) minorities experience aging differently than do whites; and (4) minority groups can teach us other ways of growing old.

- The white population makes up about 90 percent of the population aged 65 and over. The proportion of minority people in the older population increased slowly until the year 2000 and then has speeded up.
- Three theories describe the effects of minority group membership on the older person: multiple jeopardy, leveling, and the life course perspective.
- Poverty, discrimination, and social problems such as divorce, high mortality, and teen pregnancies influence aging in African American families. Older African Americans rely on strong informal support networks to deal with these problems.
- Latino Americans demonstrate clear economic disadvantages compared with whites, but they seem less disadvantaged on measures of family relations and informal supports. Studies show that, although industrial and city life weaken family ties, Latino American elders still tend to live in multigenerational families.
- Asian American elders have a higher economic status than any other minority group. They also have longer life expectancies. Many Asian American elders get support from their families. They may also need help from formal supports, but language and cultural barriers sometimes keep them from getting the help they need.
- Native Americans have many health, social, and economic problems. They also tend to underuse formal support programs. The lack of formal supports on reservations and long distances between reservations and support services disadvantage Native Americans. About one-half of Native American elders rely on a child for support.
- Researchers suggest that social service workers use a cultural competence model of service. This model not only delivers service to the minority community, but it also builds competence in the older person.

DISCUSSION QUESTIONS

1. Explain the difference between a dominant group and a minority group. What racial and ethnic groups form the largest minorities in the United States today?
2. What does Ramon Valle mean by the term *assimilation continuum?* How does this continuum apply to a pluralistic society? Give an example of how a person's private and public conduct might fit into different places on this continuum.
3. What are the demographic forces that will account for the increase in the older minority group population in the future? Do the forces differ for different minority groups? If so, how? What effect will this increase have on American society?
4. Define the terms *multiple jeopardy, leveling,* and *life course perspective.* Describe the strengths and weaknesses of each approach to studying minority aging.
5. What problems face aging African American families today? How do they cope with these problems? What future problems will African American older people face due to changes in family life?
6. Explain why diversity within the Hispanic older community leads to different experiences of aging for members of different subgroups. Give specific examples of the diverse responses to aging within the Hispanic minority group.
7. What barriers keep Asian Americans from getting the social supports they need as they age? Do some of these same barriers apply to other minority groups? How can social service agencies overcome these barriers?
8. What unique problems do Native Americans face due to geographic location? What are the pros and cons of reservation living for older Native Americans?
9. What can health care and social service workers do to improve care and service to ethnic elders? Give two examples of specific changes that would improve care and service.

SUGGESTED READING

Freidenberg, J. M. (2000). *Growing old in El Barrio.* New York: New York University Press.

The author interviewed forty-one Puerto Rican elders aged 60 and over in New York's East Harlem (El Barrio). Most of the people in the book arrived in New York in the 1950s. The book provides an ethnographic account, through in-depth interviews, of these people's lives in old age. People describe, in their own words, their everyday lives. They discuss their relations with their families, their health and income, and their use of community resources. The book provides a detailed picture of later life in this unique community.

Gelfand, D. E. (2003). *Aging and ethnicity: Knowledge and services (2nd Ed.).* New York: Springer.

This book provides an overview of aging in the United States. It includes discussions of ethnicity and gerontological theory, immigration patterns, and an overview of major ethnic groups including African American, Latino, and Asian American elders. The later chapters focus on the program and social service needs of older ethnic group members.

Olson, L. K. (Ed.) (2001). *Age through ethnic lenses: Caring for the elderly in a multicultural society.* Lanham, MD: Rowman & Littlefield.

The editor has collected essays that look at older people from diverse backgrounds. Essays discuss long-term care in relation to the racial and ethnic groups discussed in this chapter. Essays also discuss other minority groups including Mormon, Amish, and Jewish older people. The book gives a glimpse at the variety of minority groups (other than racial and ethnic groups) that make up the older population today (including gay and lesbian older people). The essays propose ways to improve care for the wide variety of older people who make up the aging population today.

GLOSSARY OF TERMS

assimilation continuum Ramon Valle's idea that minority assimilation ranges from very traditional (nonassimilation) to bicultural to very assimilated.

cultural competence An older minority person's ability to function in the wider society.

dominant group The racial or ethnic group with the most power in society. This group may or may not have a numerical majority of the population.

fictive kin Friends, neighbors, and service workers that an older person views as a family member.

formal support systems Health care and social service systems, often run by the government or some large institution. The client pays for the service (or someone pays on the client's behalf).

institutional completeness The amount of institutional support available to an older minority person. More complete communities have an array of formal supports available to older people.

kintender An older person who looks after other family members. The older person may care for a spouse, a child, or a grandchild.

leveling A decrease in the gap between minority and dominant group members as they age. For example, the income gap between minority and dominant group members closes with age.

life course perspective The idea that life unfolds from birth to death in a social, cultural, and historical context. This perspective looks at how people are affected by social institutions, historical periods and events, personal biography, life cycle stage, life events, and resources.

melting pot The idea that the United States takes in immigrants and transforms them into *typical* Americans. The melting pot concept assumes that immigrants give up their minority status and ethnic identity over time.

mortality crossover Minority group members show shorter life expectancies than whites until old age, and then in later old age they show greater life expectancies than whites. This is the crossover.

multiple jeopardy The theory that the negative effect of being a member of one risk group is increased if you are also a member of another risk group. For example, gerontologists say that older minority women may suffer the effects of multiple jeopardy.

play siblings A type of fictive kin; nonrelatives (e.g., neighbors or formal care workers) who bond with an older person and are considered a best friend or sibling.

pluralistic society A society in which many racial and ethnic groups exist side by side. People maintain their racial and ethnic heritage and still take part in the wider society. (The contrasts with the concept of U.S. society as a melting pot.)

chapter 8

THE HEALTH CARE SYSTEM

In the spring of 1991 my mother fell as she walked down the steps outside her doctor's office. She had broken her hip many years before and walked with an uneven gait. When she lost her balance on the steps, she feared that she had broken her hip again. An ambulance took her to a nearby hospital for x-rays. The doctors thought she had a hairline fracture in her hip. She couldn't walk well enough to be on her own at her apartment, so the hospital discharged her to a nursing home.

I lived about 2,000 miles away at the time and arrived in town after my mother had settled into the home. My sister and I knew that she could only stay in the nursing home for a short time under **Medicare**. The costs would start to mount after that. So we created a discharge plan that would allow my mother to move back to her own apartment after a short stay with my sister. To carry out this plan, we had to find the health care and social supports she needed to live on her own.

My mother had friends in her apartment building. They would visit and look after her social needs. But we knew she needed help with bathing and meal preparation, and she needed transportation to and from her doctor's office. I spent several mornings on the phone, calling agencies, community groups, religious groups, and government offices in my mother's town. Could someone help me put together a package of services that would allow her to live on her own?

I had not heard about Area Agencies on Aging at the time. They might have helped me find the resources I needed. But on my own I could find no agency or group to coordinate services for my mother. This nearly drove my sister and me crazy. Our mother needed to leave the nursing home—she needed no further medical care and the place depressed her. I had to get back to work and my family. We felt unsure we could get my mother the support she needed.

This prospect raised a number of fears for us. First, we saw that our mother had gotten worse in the nursing home. She felt bored and slept during the days. This kept her awake at night, so the staff gave her sleeping pills to help her sleep. The pills made her groggy and dull during the day, so she dozed all day and completed the vicious circle. Second, we knew that she could afford institutional care for a year or two, at most, before she would spend all her assets. Then she could get **Medicaid**. But this could mean a move to another institution, possibly one further from my sister's home.

In the end, my sister patched together a collection of people to support our mother. She organized friends, neighbors, relatives, a visiting nurse, someone to clean the house, and a person who made and delivered meals. My sister became our mother's **care manager**. She visited at least once a week and spoke on the phone with my mother at least once a day. She did all this while she cared for her own family. The plan worked pretty well. We knew, however, that any decline in my mother's health would send us back to the phones again, and we feared that a further decline in health would send my mother to an institution for good.

Many families in the United States face this problem. The current health care system does best at providing medical care in hospitals, nursing homes, and doctors' offices. It does less well at helping families to keep older people at home. This means that people will find help when they get an **acute illness**. They will probably find financial support to help pay for radiology, x-rays, surgery, and other medical services. But people with some **chronic illness** or disability who want to stay well and live on their own may have trouble finding support, and they will probably have to pay for this support themselves.

The health care system today consists of a mixture of publicly and privately funded programs. These programs hardly form a comprehensive system of care. Schulz (2001, p. 205) calls the United States "very unusual when compared with most other countries in the industrialized world." He reports that twenty-four countries out of twenty-nine provide government health insurance to 99 percent or more of their people. The U.S. government system covers only 33 percent of U.S. citizens. Most people have to rely on private health insurance through their work. But many employers do not offer health insurance. As a result, an estimated 14.8 percent of workers have no insurance coverage at all (Kaiser Commission, 2004).

Problems exist for people of all ages. But older people, who have unique health care needs, face problems in every part of the system. This chapter looks at (1) the structure of the health care system today, (2) the issues that this system creates for an aging society, and (3) how the system has begun to change to meet older people's needs.

THREE MODELS OF HEALTH CARE

Social scientists use three models to describe different approaches to health care in the United States today: the medical model, the social model, and the health promotion model. A model simplifies real life, but it presents a system's basic structure, activity, and values. Each model defines the goal and practice of health care differently. Each one meets different needs of the older population. A review of these models gives a picture of the U.S. health care system today.

The Medical Model

The medical model focuses on diagnosis and cure of illness. It defines health care as sickness treatment. Care most often takes place in a doctor's office, hospital, or nursing home. The medical model uses drugs, surgery, and rehabilitation to treat disease. Chappell and her colleagues (Chappell, Strain, & Blandford, 1986, p. 101) say that within this model, "medical care and treatment are defined primarily as technical problems, and the goals of medicine are viewed in terms of technical criteria, such as validity, diagnosis, precision of disease-related treatment, symptom relief and termination of disease process." Physicians control most of the treatment that takes place within this model. They also control or influence the activities of other health care professionals. Physicians learn this approach in medical school. They get little training in other forms of treatment, like health promotion or community long-term care.

The current system of health care services and government reimbursements supports the medical model (Schulz, 2001). Government financing of health care, through Medicare and Medicaid, mostly pays for doctors' or institutions' services. Schulz (2001, p. 214) says that "most public money for long-term care currently goes for institutional care, and the inadequate availability of community care services . . . encourage[s] overutilization of institutional options."

The Social Model

The social model of health care defines health and care more broadly than does the medical model. Health in this model refers to more than the absence of disease. It refers to a person's ability to function in the social world. A person may need medical care to do this. An older person often needs other kinds of care as well. Family counseling, home health care, and adult daycare all form part of the social model. Health care in this model most often takes place in the community. This model includes health care professionals, but also social workers, counselors, and volunteers. The doctor, in this model, works as part of a health care team.

The social model of health care suits an older population. Today, most older people live on their own in the community. They need little medical help, but they may need social and personal supports to live on their own. **Activities of daily living (ADLs)** and **instrumental activities of daily living (IADLs)** refer to basic activities needed to live alone or to live a good quality of life. Even among the most disabled people (with five or six deficits in ADLs), two-thirds live in the community (Brody & Morrison, 1992). The social model of health care aims to keep them there. Community care involves coordination of services among many health care professionals. It includes formal and informal care, and it involves case management and multidisciplinary assessment of needs and outcomes.

Until the 1990s, the social model got little public or private support. But the rising costs of hospital care led to a shift in Medicare payments. This encouraged early discharges from hospitals and led to more care in the community. Kane and Kane (2001) say that a large portion of Medicare payments began to go toward home health care. Also, the Medicaid program encouraged states to set up community-based health care programs. Medicaid funded these programs as long as states could show reductions in nursing home costs. Kane and Kane (2001) say that a number of states have set up statewide programs to serve people with disabilities at home.

Still, Schaffer (1993) says, the health care payment system puts medical treatment at the center of care. Medicare and Medicaid, for example, support home health care, but they often require nursing or therapy as part of the program. This sometimes leads people to use expensive skilled nursing care in order to get personal care (like help with bathing).

Health care for older people has begun to shift toward the social model. The high cost of institutional care drives this change. But so do the needs of an aging population. **Functional capacity** rather than the presence or absence of illness will measure well-being. Health care providers will judge their success by how well they help people manage on their own. This fits the new reality of an aging society.

The Health Promotion Model

Health promotion includes the concept of disease prevention and reduced disability. Current research shows that many older people can maintain their functioning into late old age. A national study of older people (Cutler, Whitelaw, & Beattie, 2002) found that 72 percent of older people reported good to excellent health.

With proper support, some people can even get back lost abilities. Health care professionals have begun to try new treatment and management strategies. These include public health measures such as flu vaccination, antismoking campaigns, diet education, and yoga classes. Health promotion and disease prevention professionals work to keep older people healthy and even to improve fitness and well-being.

These three models form a continuum of care—from the most intensive acute medical care, to management of health conditions in the community, to activities that prevent disease and promote health. Too often, the system serves the person at the acute care end of this continuum, and the medical model guides the choice of treatment. This leads to high costs for care and sometimes to **overmedicalized service**. Health care professionals and policymakers have begun to explore the social and health promotion models of care. These models may save the system money in the long run, and they provide the kind of care that fits older people's long-term needs.

THE U.S. HEALTH CARE SYSTEM TODAY

Older people had few health care insurance options until the mid-1960s. First, they did not form a group (like a corporation), so they could not get group insurance. Second, most older people could not afford the cost of private insurance premiums in old age. Third, insurance companies could deny coverage to a person with a preexisting illness. Older people needed insurance to protect them from the high cost of medical care.

Congress made a major commitment to health care for older people when it passed the Medicare program in 1965. Until then, only about one-half of older people (compared with 75 percent of people under age 65) had health insurance (National Academy, 1995b). Medicare came into being in part because of an atmosphere more receptive to older people's issues.

Theodore Lowi called this "interest group liberalism" (Pratt, 1976, p. 98). Lowi traces this atmosphere to John F. Kennedy's support for groups that took part in national policymaking. Spokespersons for older people took advantage of this moment. They played on a developing sympathy for older people and their needs. They also allied themselves with the American labor giant, the AFL-CIO.

The American Medical Association opposed Medicare at that time, claiming that it created "socialized medicine." But older people's groups claimed that Medicare simply extended programs like Social Security. They said that it took a "truly American" approach to the solution of a social problem. The American Medical Association in this debate looked selfish and opposed to progress. The new sympathy for older people and their needs, along with strong allies and a shrewd campaign, led to the passage of Medicare (Gluck & Reno, 2001).

Koff and Park (1993) say that older people's groups won only a partial victory. The American Medical Association still managed to stop the passage of a comprehensive health care program. The program that did get passed attempted to please a variety of players. Insurance companies got to manage Medicare claims from health care providers. This brought them income. Hospital associations gained because Medicare featured hospital insurance. Physicians accepted the plan because they got a direct method of payment for services to the poor. Each of these groups saw the chance to get some profit from the system.

The Medicare program, however, created the seeds of its future problems. None of the groups that supported and provided services to Medicare had an interest in containing health care costs. They all benefited from more claims and higher priced services. This, in part, led to spiraling costs and the threatened bankruptcy of the system today.

Medicare

The Medicare program contains two parts: Hospital insurance (part A) and supplementary medical insurance (part B). People eligible for Social Security get part A insurance at no cost when they turn 65. Part A includes four kinds of care: care in a hospital, care in a nursing home after a hospital stay, home health care, and hospice care.

A payroll tax funds the hospital insurance program. Employees pay 1.45 percent of their income; employers match this amount. The money collected goes into a Federal Hospital Insurance Trust Fund. All hospital insurance expenses come from this fund.

The hospital insurance program sets guidelines for standards of care in hospitals and other agencies that take part in the program. The program also reviews costs of services, sets limits on costs, and in the case of most hospitals, pays a set rate for a specific diagnosis. Medical review groups of doctors in each state see that care given under the program meets standards of quality and effectiveness.

Older people make up almost 90 percent of the 40 million Medicare beneficiaries. Women make up 56 percent of all Medicare beneficiaries. Many of these women live alone and have low incomes (Medicare, 2004). In 2001, 39.6 million people aged 65 and over enrolled in Medicare part A. Part A paid out $143.4 billion to older people in that year. This came to an average of $3,621 per older person (Freid et al., 2003).

People may choose to get Supplementary Medical Insurance (also called part B insurance) if they are entitled to part A, are aged 65 or older, and live in the United States. If a person chooses part B, the government deducts a premium for part B from Social Security benefits ($66.60 per month in 2004), and matches these fees from general revenues (taxes). Part B includes benefits for doctors' services, medical equipment, laboratory tests, radiation therapy, and other expenses. Supplementary Medical Insurance requires a yearly **deductible** ($100).

Supplementary medical insurance participants may also have to make **coinsurance** payments (usually 20 percent of charges) and payments for services above Medicare limits. Physicians and other service suppliers may or may not agree to participate in the Medicare program. Those who agree, accept the Medicare limits on charges. They may then get payment directly through Medicare. Patients will pay only the deductible and the coinsurance payment. Patients with a doctor who does not accept assignment to Medicare part B must pay the doctor themselves. They then get paid back for the amount of the bill accepted by Medicare.

Schulz (2001) says that only about 50 percent of doctors accept assignment to Medicare. Doctors who opt out of the Medicare system can charge as much as 115 percent of the Medicare allowable rate. This means that many older people with Medicare insurance still have to pay some costs for a doctor's care out of their own pocket.

Medicare part B enrolled 37.6 million people aged 65 and over in 2001 and paid out $101.4 billion to this age group. This came to $2,697 per person. The amount paid by the two programs (part A and part B) came to $244.8 billion in 2001 (up from $3.3 billion in 1967 and $111 billion in 1990) (Freid, Prager, MacKay, & Xia, 2003; Medicare, 2004). Most of the money paid out through

Medicare (part A and part B) went to pay for inpatient hospital care and doctors' fees (Freid et al., 2003).

Over time, Medicare has covered less and less of older people's medical costs. In 1995, for example, older people paid out on average about 20 percent of their income on uncovered health care costs. The poorest people paid almost one-third of their income for health care treatment (Schulz, 2001). Out-of-pocket expenses include payments for eyeglasses, hearing aids, dental care, and prescription drugs. These costs for everyday items drive up the cost of health care for individuals. (See Figures 8.1 and 8.2.)

The Medicare program now offers a Medicare + Choice (in addition to the original Medicare plan). The Medicare + Choice (pronounced *Medicare plus Choice*) plan offers a Medicare Managed Care Plan and Medicare Private Fee-for-Service Plan. These plans provide services that coordinate care or lower out-of-pocket expenses. Some plans offer prescription drug benefits (Medicare, 2004). These plans

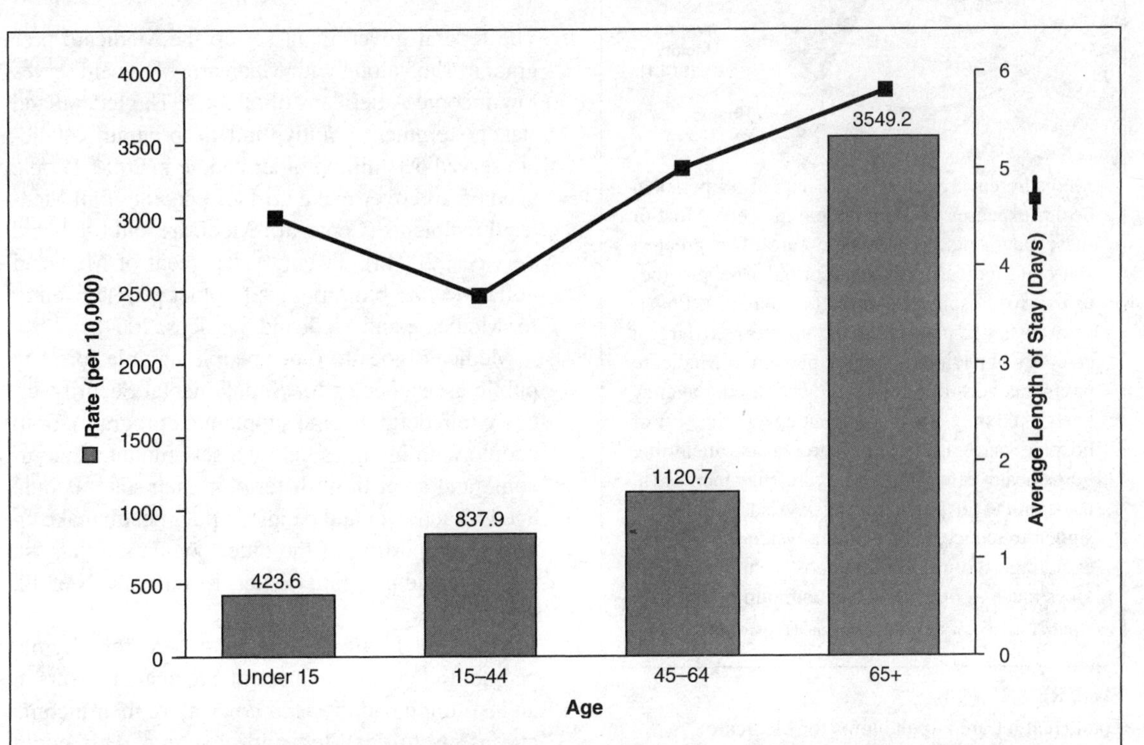

The discharge rate measures the number of hospital discharges in a year (per 10,000 population). This chart shows the hospital discharge rate for four age groups. Note that the discharge rate increases with age. It increases dramatically for people aged 65 and over. The oldest age group has almost nine times the rate of the youngest age group. Also note that from age 15 onward the number of days per stay increases. The oldest group tends to stay in the hospital almost one and one-half times longer per stay than the 15- to 44-age group. These figures show the older population's higher hospital usage rate and (compared with younger age groups) their tendency to use more hospital resources.

FIGURE 8.1

Hospital Discharge Rates, 2001

Source: Hall, M. J., & DeFrances, C. J. (2003). 2001 National hospital discharge survey. Advance data from vital and health statistics, No. 332. Hyattsville, MD: National Center for Health Statistics. Retrieved July 24, 2004, *www.cdc.gov/nchs/data/ad/ad332.pdf.*

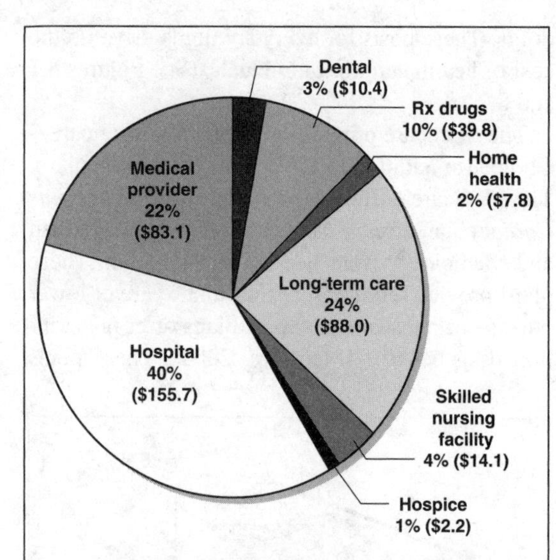

Medicare covered nearly one-half of all personal health expenses of older people in 1999. Most of these payments go for acute care. The greatest share of Medicare payments for older people goes to pay for hospital expenses (40 percent). Physician costs (22 percent) make up the next largest category of payments. Only 2 percent of Medicare payments goes to cover home health care agency costs. And only about 1 percent covers the cost of hospice care. Long-term care costs, including home health care and hospice care, may increase in the future as the population ages. Also, policies designed to reduce hospital and physician costs may encourage the use of lower cost health care services (such as outpatient and community care).

**Note:* Total does not equal 100 percent due to rounding.

FIGURE 8.2

Total Health Care Expenditures for Medicare Beneficiaries, 1999

Source: Centers for Medicare & Medicaid Services. (2004). Total Health Care Expenditures for Medicare Beneficiaries, Section III.B.5, p. 5. Program information on Medicare, Medicaid, SCHIP, and other programs of the Centers for Medicare and Medicaid Services. PowerPoint presentation. June 2002 edition.

operate under contract to Medicare and they differ from state to state. About 14 percent of Medicare beneficiaries have enrolled in these private plans (Feder, Komisar, & Niefeld, 2001). (See Table 8.1.)

The Bush administration in 2003 added a Prescription Drug Discount Card to the Medicare program. This program allows cardholders to get a discount on prescription drugs. The amount of discount depends on a person's income and whether the person has other insurance. The government plans to use the card program until it puts in place a proposed Medicare drug benefit program (slated for 2006).

Medicaid

The federal government set up the Medicaid program in 1965 along with Medicare. Medicaid serves low-income Americans of all ages. The federal and state governments jointly fund this program. Medicaid served 5.1 million older people in 2004. People aged 65 and over make up 11.1 percent of all Medicaid recipients (Center for Medicare and Medicaid Services, 2004a). Twenty-six percent of Medicaid dollars ($44.5 billion) goes to older people (Center for Medicare and Medicaid Services, 2004b).

Medicaid goes to older people eligible for state public assistance or for Supplemental Security Income (a federal income supplement program), or to people with incomes below a set amount. This income and asset limit differs for each state. People aged 85 and over and people in poor health make up a large proportion of the older population that use the Medicaid program (Feder, Komisar, & Niefeld, 2001).

Medicaid finances long-term care for eligible people. In the past, spouses of Medicaid patients in an institution had to *spend down* all of their income and assets to get Medicaid coverage. This could leave the spouse in the community in poverty. The new policy allowed spouses of institutionalized Medicaid patients a living allowance and other resources. Some people get both Medicare and Medicaid benefits.

States may pay for Medicare Supplementary Medical Insurance (part B) for Medicaid clients. The amount of service clients get, how long they get the service, and the types of service covered differ from state to state and even within a state during a year. The federal and state governments give

© Stayskal, *Tampa Tribune.*

matching funds to the Medicaid program. The program offers a number of basic services, including inpatient hospital care, physician services, and skilled nursing home services.

Medicaid pays nursing home expenses for needy older people or for people who have used up most of their own income and assets (Schulz, 2001). Without Medicaid support, most older people who now get Medicaid could not afford nursing home care.

Medigap and Long-term Care Insurance

The Medicare and Medicaid programs cover only a part of older people's medical expenses. Figures for nursing home expenditures, for example, show a gap between Medicaid payments and out-of-pocket expenses. Also, older people will see increases in out-of-pocket home care expenses. This has led many older people to take out private health insurance, called *Medigap insurance.* This covers the difference in cost between government health care plans and the cost of medical treatment. Private insurance companies offer Medigap policies.

Medigap companies offer ten standard policy options. Policies cover charges such as hospital deductibles and physician **copayments**. They also cover services such as preventive screening and outpatient drug costs. Each plan offers a different combination of services. The government sets standards for this kind of insurance. For example, companies that sell this insurance cannot cancel it or refuse to renew it based on a person's health.

These plans offer added protection, but they also have some drawbacks. First, they only cover deductibles and copayments for Medicare services. If Medicare does not cover a service, Medigap insurance will not cover it. For example, general Medigap insurance does not cover long-term care services such as nursing home placement and home health care. Yet older people feel the greatest concern about the costs of a long-term illness.

Special long-term care policies do exist, but they vary widely in the services they cover and in their costs. Some policies set conditions before a person can collect on a policy. For example, a policy may only pay for nursing home care in a **skilled nursing facility**. Or it will pay only if a person enters a nursing home from a hospital.

A survey in the 1990s found that 68 percent of the respondents reported a strong interest in buying long-term care insurance. But, Schulz (2001) notes, a policy for a 65 year old can cost between $2,000 and $4,000 per year. Studies show that only 10 to 20 percent of older people can afford this cost. The high cost of policies, the many conditions on coverage, and people's different circumstances make long-term care insurance unlikely for most older people. This puts a large part of the older population at risk of poverty if they have a long-term illness.

The Cost of Care

The United States since 1960 has led the western nations in health care spending in absolute dollars per person and as a percent of the gross domestic product. In 2001, for example, the United States spent $1.4 trillion on health care or 14.1 percent of its gross domestic product. This came to $5,035 per person in that year. Compared with most other western nations, this comes to about 50 percent more as a proportion of gross domestic product and about twice the per capita expenditure (Freid, Prager, MacKay, & Xia, 2003).

Costs have gone up each decade at an average rate of 10.2 percent from the 1960s to today (Freid et al., 2003). Economy-wide inflation and changes in the

TABLE 8.1
Medicare Payments Original Medicare Plan
Selected Medicare Services, 2004

Service	*Period Covered*	*Medicare Pays*	*You Pay*
*Medicare Part A**			
1. Hospitalization	First 60 days	All but $876	$876
Semiprivate room, general nursing,	61st–90th day	All but $219/day	$219/day
services, and supplies	91st–150th day	All but $438/day	$438/day
	Beyond 150 days	Nothing	All costs
2. Skilled nursing	First 20 days	100% of approved amount	Nothing
Facility care	21st–100th day	All but $109.50/day	Up to $109.50/day
Semiprivate room, general and skilled nursing, services, and supplies	Beyond 100 days	Nothing	All costs
3. Home health care	Unlimited as long as you meet Medicare conditions	100% of approved amount; 80% of equipment	Nothing for services; 20% for equipment
4. Hospice care $5 drug	Unlimited	95% of approved amount for inpatient respite care	5% for respite care; copayment
*Medicare Part B***			
4. Medical expenses deductible once 20% of amount after doctors' services surgery, therapy	Unlimited if medically necessary	80% of approved amount after $100 deductible	100% per year plus approved deductible
5. Home health care services; equipment	Unlimited as long as you meet Medicare conditions	100% of approved amount; 80% of equipment	Nothing for services; 20% for equipment

*2004 Part A monthly premium: None for people who have full Social Security credits. Others can buy Medicare service for $174 and $316 per month (in 2003) depending on the number of Social Security credits they have.

**2004 Part B monthly premium: $66/60.

Source: Medicare and You 2005. Retrieved January 10, 2005, *www.medicare.gov/publications/pubs/pdf/10050.pdf.*

use of health care services account for three-quarters of this cost. Medical inflation and population growth account for the rest (Freid et al., 2003). Costs for health care now make up almost one-quarter of all federal government expenditures and about 15 percent of state and local government expenditures. The Center for Medicare and Medicaid Services (Medicare, 2004c) projects continued increases in health care costs (above 1990s levels) to 2010. This agency projects a 2.5 percent per year increase in health care costs above the gross domestic product. This means that health care will make up 17 percent of the gross domestic product by the year 2011.

Federal, state, and local governments in the United States paid nearly one-half (45.4 percent) of the total health care bill in 2001. Private sources (e.g., insurance and out-of-pocket payments) made up the rest. Of the government's share, most of the money went to pay for Medicare and Medicaid programs. Medicare and Medicaid (and the State Children's Health Insurance Program—SCHIP) account for one-third of the $1.3 trillion spent on health care in the United States (Centers for Medicare, 2004c). And 54 percent of health care spending in 2000 went to pay for hospital and physician costs (Medicare, 2000). (See Figure 8.3.) The U.S. Senate Special Committee on Aging (1991) said that rising health care costs (not pension outlays) explain most of the increase in government spending on older people.

Some people point to the increase in the number of old and very old people in the United States as a

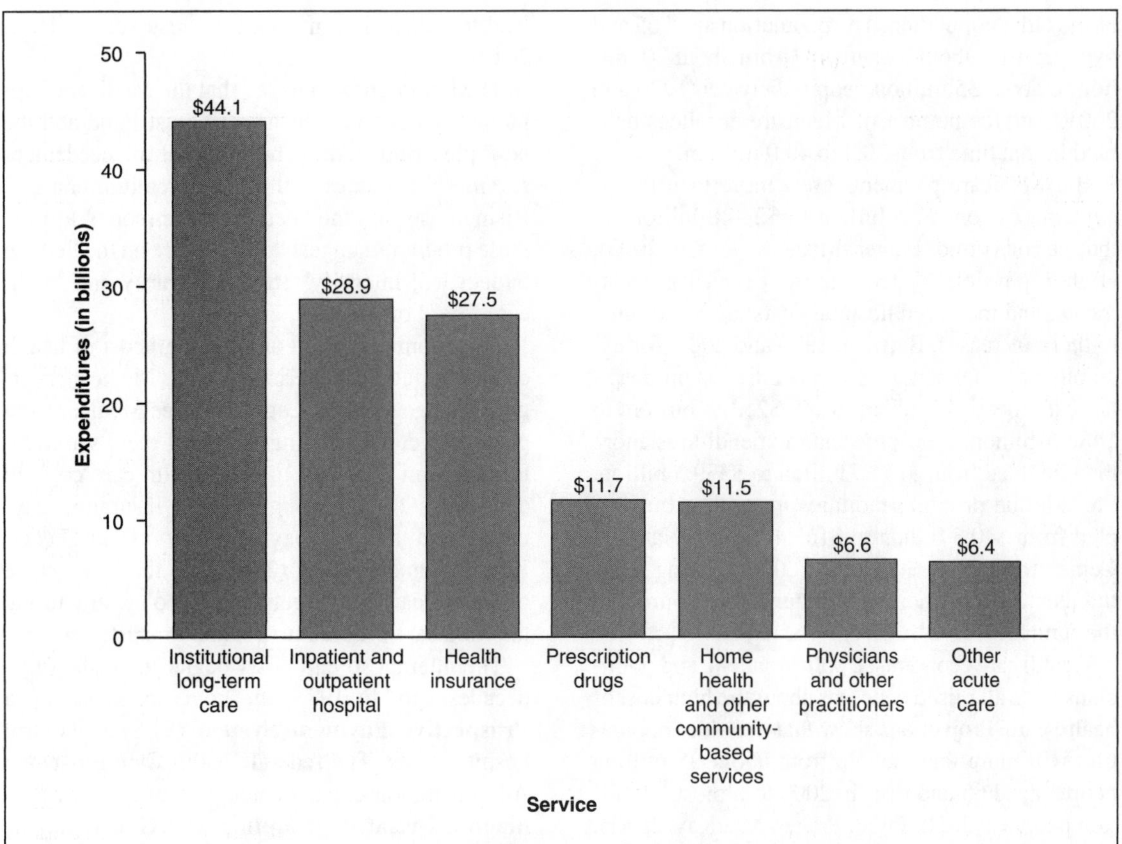

The majority of Medicaid dollars goes to cover nursing home costs ($44.1 billion). Hospitals, health insurance (to private health care providers), drugs, and home health care services make up the bulk of Medicaid expenditures. Medicaid helps the most needy older people. Many of them are the very old. They often need institutional care and home care support. Drug costs have risen sharply in the past few years. Researchers predict a rise in the cost of home health care in the future.

FIGURE 8.3

Where the Medicaid Dollar for the Elderly Goes (Expenditure in Billions of Dollars)

Source: U.S. Department of Health and Human Services. (2000). A chartbook of Medicaid 2000. Retrieved January 10, 2005, *www.cms.hhs.gov/charts/medicaid/2Tchartbk.pdf.*

cause of higher health care costs. This does explain some increase in costs. The very old population (aged 85 and over), for example, has grown faster than other segments of the population. This age group uses more hospital and physician services than any other age group. Still, the increased number of older people cannot account for all the increase in health care costs. Studies show that the system itself has created higher costs.

For one thing, government programs have expanded and now cover more costs of health care for older people. This has led to an expansion of hospital, nursing home care, and community care. The proportion of personal health care expenses covered by government programs, for example, increased from 21.4 percent in 1960 to 43.4 percent in 2001 (Freid, Prager, MacKay, & Xia, 2003). Also, the cost of care has grown faster than the rate of growth of the older population. The population aged 65 and over grew by about 50 percent (from about 20 million to about 35 million people) between 1970 and 2001. And the number of Medicare enrollees doubled in that time from 20.4 to 40.0 million.

But Medicare payments grew more than thirty-two times (from $7.5 billion to $244.8 billion) in that period (Freid, Prager, MacKay, & Xia, 2003). Higher physicians' fees, more expensive treatments, and increased hospital costs all contributed to these increases. Between 1990 and 2002, for example, personal health care expenditures on hospital care nearly doubled from $253.9 billion to $486.5 billion. And physician expenditures more than doubled from $157.5 billion to $339.5 billion. Prescription drug expenditures more than quadrupled from $40.3 billion to $162.4 billion (National Center for Health Statistics, 2004c). Rising costs threaten to eat up more of the country's resources in the future.

Health care economists, policymakers, and politicians have all raised concerns about the high cost of health care. Projections show that the older population will more than double from about 35 million people aged 65 and over in 2000 to almost 82 million people in 2050 (Freid, Prager, MacKay, & Xia, 2003). One person in five will be aged 65 or over at that time. The health care system will need to change in the years ahead to control costs and meet the needs of this older population. Each part of the system needs reform. (See Figure 8.4.)

Cost of Care and the Older Population

Medicare Costs. Rising health care costs threaten the Medicare program. The 2004 Annual Report of the Medicare Board of Trustees contains dire warnings about the financial state of the Medicare program. "The fundamentals of the financial status of . . . Medicare," a summary of the report says, "remain problematic under the intermediate economic and demographic assumptions. . . . The financial outlook for the Medicare Hospital Insurance (HI) Trust Fund that pays hospital benefits has deteriorated significantly from last year, with annual cash flow deficits beginning this year and expected to grow rapidly after 2010 as baby boomers begin to retire. The growing annual cash deficits . . . will lead to exhaustion in trust fund reserves for HI in 2019."

The report goes on to say that the Medicare Supplementary Medical Insurance Trust Fund and the new prescription drug benefit will all need more revenue from taxes and higher premium charges. Rising costs and the need for more money to fund these programs suggest "the pressure on the Federal budget will intensify" (Social Security and Medicare Board of Trustees, 2004).

This looming deficit and the high cost of health care to the federal government make Medicare a target of budget cutting. Legislators see Medicare as a place to reduce spending. Some of them see Medicare reform as a way to shift health care costs to consumers (e.g., through higher insurance payments and more copayments by users). Feder, Komisar, and Niefeld (2001) say that the debate over Medicare has largely focused on restructuring the Medicare program to contain or shift costs.

The attempt to cap costs began more than two decades ago. In 1983, the government set up a **Prospective Payment System (PPS)** to control hospital costs. The federal Health Care Financing Administration created categories of illness called **diagnosis-related groupings (DRGs)**. Hospitals then categorized patients by their medical condition. Medicare reimbursed hospitals for a fixed number of days of care according to the patient's DRG. If a hospital kept a person longer, the hospital paid the extra cost.

The PPS replaced an open-ended system in which hospitals got paid according to how long they kept a patient and what they did for the patient. The PPS encouraged hospitals to discharge patients on schedule or sooner. Hospitals that discharged patients early got to keep the extra money allowed by the patient's DRG.

The PPS accounts in part for a decrease in the number of hospital stays by older people between 1980 and 2001, and for the continued low number of days per stay today (relative to the 1980s) (Medicare, 2004; Kozak, Owings, & Hall, 2004). Some studies report lower hospital costs and better care under the PPS (Fillit, 1994).

The PPS system also led to increased use of outpatient services and community hospital use. Out-

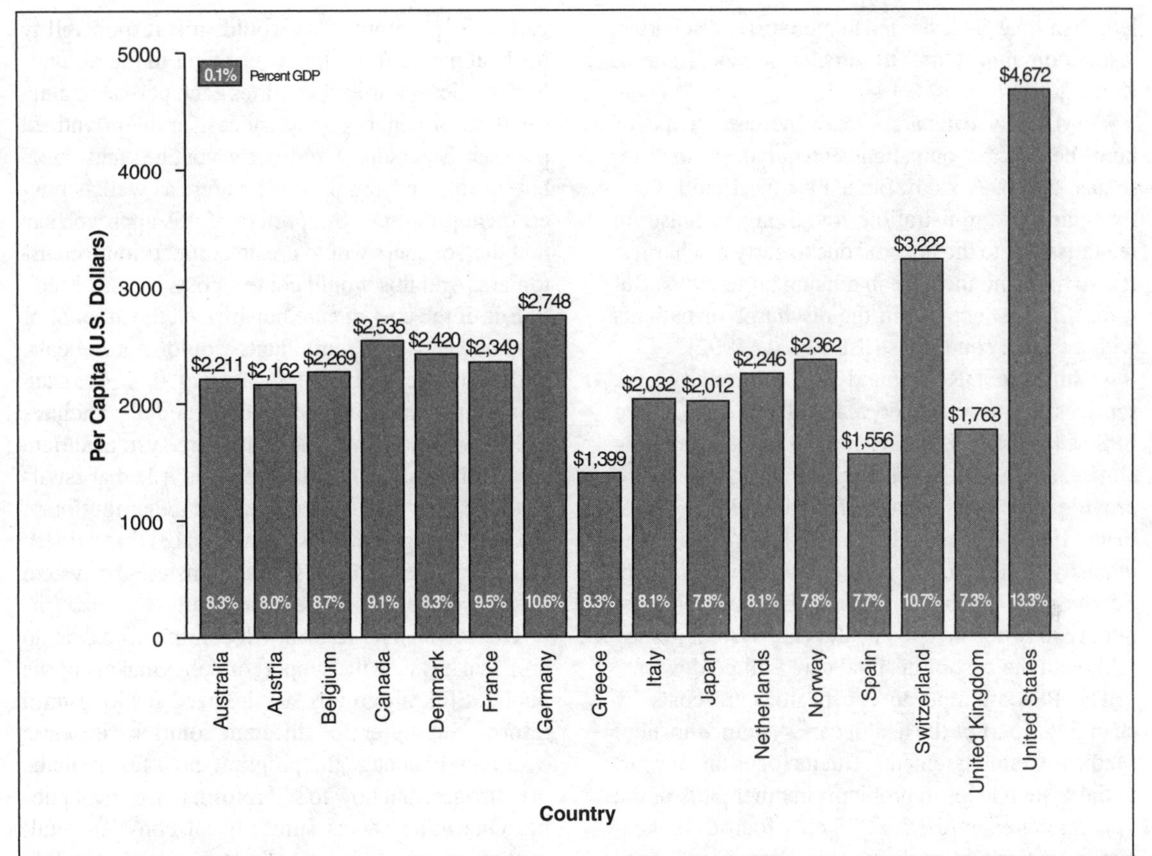

The United States spends more money on health care as a proportion of its GDP than any other developed nation. Some countries spend little on health care as a proportion of GDP because they offer less formal health care service to their people. But even among countries with a full network of formal services (like Canada or Switzerland), the United States ranks highest in cost. Physician fees, costly intensive daily hospital service, administration costs in hospitals, the use of high technology, and high insurance administration costs all add to the high cost of U.S. health care.

FIGURE 8.4

Health Expenditures, Per Capita and Proportion of the Gross Domestic Product of Selected Developed Nations, 2000

Source: Adapted from Freid, V. M., Prager, K., MacKay, A. P., & Xia, H. (2003). *Chartbook on trends in the health of Americans. Health, United States, 2003*, Hyattsville, MD: National Center for Health Statistics, Table 111, p. 305.8.

patient use tripled from 13 percent of hospital service use in 1980 to 37 percent in 2000. Managed care programs also contributed to decreased hospital use. They encourage alternative types of treatment to control costs (Medicare, 2004).

The PPS poses problems for older people on Medicare. First, the system encourages hospitals to release Medicare patients early, and it may restrict the treatment a person gets. It also encourages hospitals to have more private-pay patients. These patients have no DRG limits attached to their stay.

Second, the DRG system takes no account of the person's general health or the severity of the illness. A healthy 65-year-old man and a frail 85-year-old woman who both need a hip replacement fall into the same DRG. But the 85-year-old woman may need more hospital days to recover. The hospital has an incentive to get both patients out in the same length of time. This has led to more early discharges to the community and to nursing homes (Kane & Kane, 2001).

Third, early discharges may increase costs for home health care, outpatient, and nursing home care (Estes, 2000). A study funded by the Health Care Financing Administration found no increase in readmissions to the hospital due to early discharges. It also found no increase in nursing home stays. But it did find an increase in the discharge of patients with unstable conditions (Kahn et al., 1992).

A study of DRGs found that community care services had more heavy care clients due to the PPS (Clifford, 1989). Discharge planners, nursing homes, and home health agencies said they had to provide more units of care due to the PPS (Wood & Estes, 1990). Kane and Kane (2001) note that as the intensity of care increases, the cost of care goes up. So, the early discharge to a nursing home or community may not save the health care system money (although the cost of hospital care will go down).

The PPS attempts to cap health care costs by changing a part of the health care system—hospital Medicare reimbursements. But its focus on one part of the system leads to problems in other parts of the system. For example, the PPS only focuses on hospital care. Early or unplanned discharges can lead to further illness and greater need for medical care. Also, decreased hospital days lead to increased need for home care and this can end up costing as much as hospital care (Kane & Kane, 2001). The PPS system shifts more of the cost of health care to the nursing home or the community. This may also shift some of the costs to the patient.

Further attempts to reform the health care system took place in 1994 and 1995. President Clinton planned a major reform of the health care system including Medicare. His plan (and several similar plans proposed by others) moved toward coverage for all Americans. It also included some prescription drug and long-term care benefits for older people. This met with political opposition and failed in Congress. Both parties claimed that the public did not back broad reform.

Feder and her colleagues (2001) report that proposals to restructure Medicare include a plan to privatize the program. This would shift responsibility for health care from the government to the individual. Medicare currently entitles each person to a defined set of benefits and services. In the privatized plan, each person would get a voucher and could buy insurance from private insurers as well as government programs. Supporters of this approach say that the vouchers would create competition for customers. And this would control costs.

But, if the cost of care outstripped the amount of the vouchers, then individuals would bear the cost. Feder and her colleagues say that this approach would move away from the fundamental principles of Medicare: (1) that the health care system should spread the risk of health care costs; (2) that an affordable, universal system requires redistribution of income through the tax system; and (3) that the federal government does best at administering a system to serve older people, rich and poor.

The debate over reform will continue. To date no proposal has won the support of policymakers or the public. Still, all groups see the need for long-term reform. Supporters of different solutions disagree over how to change the program, how fast to make the changes, and how to sell reform to a critical public. One thing seems sure: "fiscal constraint will continue to plague future policy initiatives" (Mueller, 1993, p. 119). This means that the Medicare program will at best maintain its current benefits in the years ahead.

Medicaid Costs. The Medicaid program pays for a variety of services for the poorest older people. Services include inpatient hospital care, care in a skilled nursing facility, doctors' fees, and insurance premiums (e.g., for Medicare).

Medicaid payments rose from $6.3 billion in 1972 to $168.3 billion in 2000. The growth rate of cost has decreased in recent years. But in 2003 costs increased an average of 9.3 percent. Part of this increased cost over time came from increased services. The Medicaid program pays two-fifths (42 percent) of the cost of nursing home expenses.

Medicaid has expanded to provide more home and community-based services. These include **respite care**, **personal care**, and **chore services**.

Home health services covered by Medicaid rose from $229 per person on average in 1972 to $3,135 per person on average in 2000 (Freid, Prager, MacKay, & Xia, 2003). These services meet the needs of older people in the community who have limitations on ADL.

But part of the cost increase in Medicaid comes from increased doctor and hospital fees along with higher administrative costs. The system, for example, lets physicians and hospitals set their own fees. This leads to increases in health care costs over time and to fragmented reforms that try to control costs.

Again, as with Medicare, legislators propose cuts in Medicaid spending. Smith and his colleagues (2003) report that all fifty states and the District of Columbia put in place cost-containment measures in 2003. And in 2004, forty-nine states reduced or froze payments to providers. Forty-four states put in place methods to reduce prescription drug spending.

The researchers say that in many states the year 2004 marked the third year in a row that the state took action to reduce Medicaid costs. Legislators who support cuts also call for increased user payments, options to Medicare/Medicaid payments (such as employer-sponsored plans), and more enrollment in managed care programs such as **health maintenance organizations (HMOs)**.

Critics of these proposed cuts say that they will increase private insurance costs to individuals, increase costs for home care, and put limits on nursing home care to the poorest older people (Hey, 1995). This debate will lead to some reform, but it will probably raise new issues related to accessibility of health care for poor and very old people. A look at the personal cost of health care will show why cutbacks in government support will hurt the poorest people.

The Rising Personal Cost of Health Care

Even with increased federal health care payments in the past few years, the amount paid by individuals for health care increased. Vierck (2002) says that, compared with younger people, health care costs take a larger proportion of older people's budgets. She reports that health care accounts for between 10 and 14 percent of the average older person's expenses. Much of this goes to pay for insurance.

This comes to more than double the proportion of income that younger people spend on health care. Medicare and Medicaid cover some health care costs. But older people had to pay out of their own pockets a high proportion of costs for long-term care, prescription drugs, physician care, dental care, hospitals, and home health services. For poorer older people this creates a burden. And some people fail to visit a doctor or take medications because of the cost.

Even with the risk of high long-term care costs in the future, very few people have long-term care insurance outside of the Medicaid program. This leaves older people and their families with little protection against the cost of a long nursing home stay. It puts many people at risk of losing all their assets if they have a catastrophic illness. A catastrophic illness or long-term care can wipe out a lifetime of savings and throw the older person into poverty. (See Figure 8.5.)

Public Dissatisfaction

Future increases in health care costs will place an added burden on the government and on older people. These increases might make sense if the U.S. public got more for its dollar. But the National Center for Health Statistics (1994, p. 42) says that "despite high levels of health expenditures in the United States, health outcomes lag behind those in many other developed countries."

The high cost of care and the weak return in outcomes from the U.S. health care system accounts in part for the public's lack of satisfaction. Schulz (2001) reports that in an international study 40 percent of people in Canada, the Netherlands, Germany, and France thought their health care system worked "pretty well." Thirty percent of people in Australia, Sweden, Japan, and the United Kingdom felt this way. But only 10 percent of Americans thought the U.S. health care system works "pretty well." Mueller (1993, p. 165) says that "a national survey in 1990 found that 29 percent of the American public favored completely rebuilding the health care system and 60 percent favored fundamental changes."

A picture of the U.S. health care system emerges from these findings. First, taxpayers and individuals

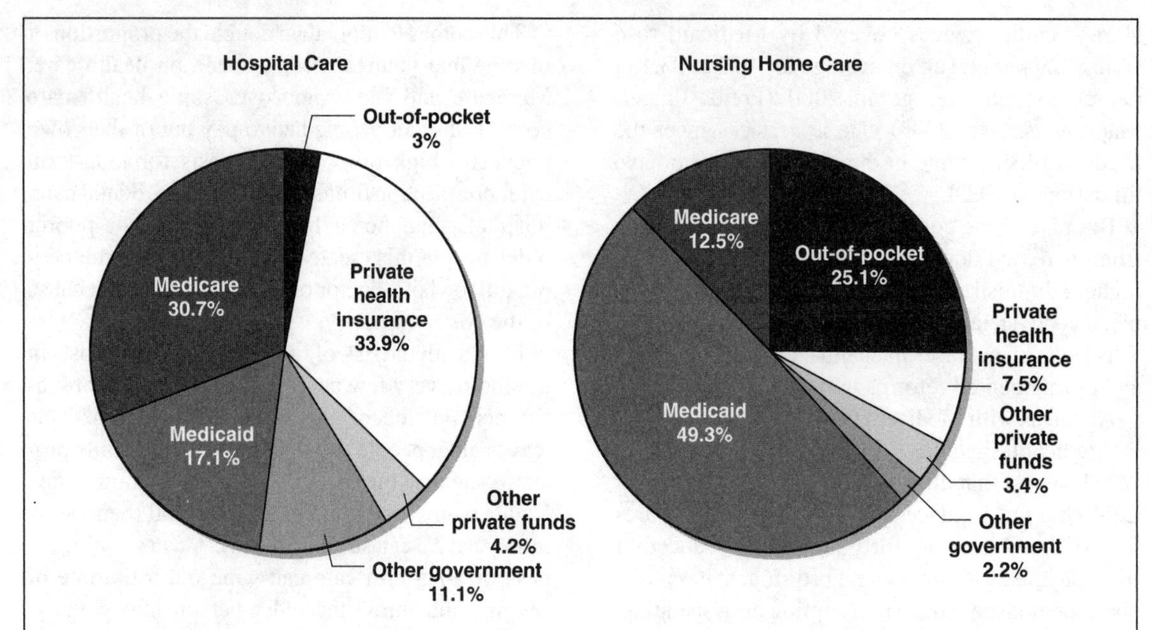

These charts show how health care costs affect individual and government health expenses. The charts show a clear difference in government and private support for hospital and nursing home care. A combination of government and private insurance plans covers 97 percent of hospital costs. This provides a safety net for most people who need hospital care.

Medicare funds, however, cover only 12.5 percent of nursing home care. Individuals pay more than one-third (36 percent) of nursing home costs (including health insurance) out of their own resources. Medicaid pays for 49 percent of nursing home costs, but only 60 percent of all nursing home patients get Medicaid payments. This leaves 40 percent of nursing home patients with little or no protection. Middle income families fear the cost of a long-term nursing home care. The health care system provides them with little protection from the ruinous effects of a catastrophic illness.

FIGURE 8.5

Funding for Long-Term Care, 2002

Source: National Center for Health Statistics. (2004). *Health, United States, 2004*. Hyattsville, MD. Table 119, p. 330.

pay a lot for health care; second, Americans get less for their money than people in other countries; and third, young and old people feel dissatisfied with the current system.

Structural Flaws

As costs rise in the future and as more people enter old age, concerns about health care will grow. Some of these concerns will focus on the high cost of caring for an aging population. But a focus on population aging creates a misleading view of the increasing cost of health care. Population aging will have some effect on health care use and costs in the future, but this will occur slowly and over many decades.

Binstock (1993) looked at the relationship between population aging and health care costs in twelve industrial countries. He found little relationship between health care costs and the proportion of people aged 65 and over or 80 and over. He found that many nations with high proportions of older people do not have runaway health care costs.

Cohen (1994, p. 401) says that "it is simplistic to frame the health care debate entirely in terms of age." Many economic and social forces create increases in health care costs. These include inflation, rising costs of professional services, and increased costs for medications and equipment. Schulz (2001) lists the causes of rising costs in order of importance:

1. Expanded use of medical technology and services;
2. A lack of spending limits on physicians and hospitals;
3. Inflation and especially inflation in medical care costs;
4. Increased numbers of people (especially the elderly) who use services; and
5. High administrative costs due to a decentralized insurance system.

Nedde (1993) goes on to include "excess capital investment, the performance of unnecessary procedures, and administrative waste" as primary reasons for increased costs. She concludes that "the importance of demographics . . . has been exaggerated."

Lazenby and Letsch (1990) say that an increase in the older population accounts for less than one-quarter of increased health care costs. Rising health care costs have more to do with the organization of the health care system than with population aging. Medicare and Medicaid are complicated programs. Each program makes exceptions and applies rules to different cases in different ways. In addition, Medicaid rules vary by state. This makes access to services a problem for some people.

BOX 8.1
SETTING LIMITS

Daniel Callahan, ethicist and health care critic, proposed rationing as a way to deal with increased health care costs. His book *Setting Limits* focused on the increased numbers of older people in society and on the heavy use of health care resources by older people as a group. He predicted that an older population would draw health care resources away from younger people who need them. Callahan presented three principles that the health care system could use to cut treatment for older people.

1. Medical care should not prolong life after people have passed their natural life expectancy (somewhere between 70 and 80 years).
2. After people have passed their natural life expectancy, medical care should only relieve suffering. It should no longer attempt to extend life.
3. Medical technology should not be used to extend life beyond the natural life expectancy.

Callahan said that these policies would reduce the cost of health care for older people and their families, lead to a high quality of life until late old age, and keep society's health care costs down.

Binstock and Kahana (1988) took issue with Callahan's proposal. Callahan, for example, said that physically strong and mentally alert older people could get treatment if they come down with a sudden illness. He would apply his plan only to frail older people in need of long-term care.

But Binstock and Kahana asked who would decide what care a person should get. Would a second illness lead to a withdrawal of care? A third? What about a frail older person who could live well with medical support? Why should this person get no treatment? Binstock and Kahana asked why Callahan used age as a criterion at all in deciding who should get medical treatment.

Callahan made little reference to the social, moral, and ethical changes that his proposal would bring about. He also remained vague about who would put this policy of rationing into place. Many people disagree with rationing as a solution to the rising cost of health care, but Callahan's work expresses a concern, shared by many, about health care costs in an aging society.

Sources: Setting limits: Medical goals in an aging society, by D. Callahan (1987). New York: Simon & Schuster; also, "An essay on *setting limits: Medical goals in an aging society,*" by R. H. Binstock & J. Kahana, 1988, *The Gerontologist, 28,* pp. 424–426.

Smith (1992, p. 244) says that U.S. health insurance looks the way it does because of "professional dominance and institutional weakness." The government lacked a clear national health care policy when it set up Medicare. At the same time, the medical profession blocked changes that would lessen its power or its income. The program we have today came about in order to reduce conflict and get some program in place. The result Smith (1992, p. 244) says,

> was fragmented, in the sense that it was both a national and a state program and that it began with two schemes of payment, one for hospitals and another for the physicians. It contained, as well, numerous subsidies for and concessions to providers, designed to secure their support for the program or at least, to buy a grudging acquiescence.

So, from the start the medical model shaped the U.S. health care system. Medicare, the program that pays for most of the health care services in the United States, leans toward support for doctor and institution services. Although Medicare will pay for home health care services, it pays primarily for medical services such as skilled nursing care, physical or speech therapy, home health aides, and medical supplies. Medicare will not pay for homemaker services or meals delivered at home. All of this gives Medicare-supported home health care a medical slant and raises costs.

Doctors, hospitals, drug companies, and other health care providers benefit from a growing health care system. These interest groups resist drastic changes. The American Medical Association, for example, discourages doctors from taking part in the Medicare program (Schulz, 2001). Medical care interest groups (like drug companies and health care providers) lobby against changes that will reduce their revenue or power.

Also, the U.S. health care system has high administrative costs. A study that compared the Canadian and U.S. health care systems found that the U.S. system had higher costs for doctors and hospitals, but the two systems differed most on administrative costs (Barer, Hertzman, Miller, & Pascali, 1992). The U.S. system has a web of government, private insurance, and individual sources of payment. The administration of this complex system drives health care costs up. Ball (1987, cited in Schulz, 2001), for example, reports that between 15 and 35 percent of a person's Medigap insurance premium goes to pay for administrative costs.

Finally, only a relatively small proportion of older people use high proportions of medical care (Kane & Kane, 1987). Figures show that *as a group* older people go to the hospital more often, stay in the hospital for more days, and visit physicians more often than younger people. The use of services rises steadily with age.

But these figures hide the variation in use within the older population. For example, 9 percent of older people will use 5 years or more of nursing home care in their lifetime. This small group will account for 64 percent of the cost of care. The large majority of older people (68 percent) will use less than 3 months of care in a lifetime and will account for about 1 percent of costs (Kemper, Spillman, & Murtaugh, 1991).

Cohen (1994, p. 401) says that "it is time to turn the public debate away from its increasingly myopic and misleading focus on older people and back to an examination of real issues." This will turn attention to the system itself. The current system lacks sensitivity to the needs of older people. Older people with chronic illnesses and disabilities need different kinds of care than acute care patients. Chronic care patients need long-term care.

Kane and Kane (2001, p. 406) say that chronic care "represents the equivalent of a movie as opposed to a series of [acute care] snapshots." Care for patients with chronic illnesses requires that caregivers monitor patients over time, assess their needs, and adjust care to suit the individual. This type of care typically takes place outside the acute care setting (e.g., the hospital or doctor's office). It most often takes place in the community, in a person's home.

This type of care requires case management, a coordinated system of services, and an ongoing assessment of service outcomes. Some programs have shown that they can provide this coordinated care in a community at a reasonable cost. The On Lok

BOX 8.2
DRUG ABUSE
The Limits of the Medical Model

Drug use increases with age. Older people take more drugs than younger people and more kinds of drugs. They often have multiple health problems and take many drugs at once. Semla and his colleagues (1993) say that older people make up 12 percent of the U.S. population but account for 31 percent of the prescription drugs sold in the United States.

Sometimes drug use can turn to abuse. Older people who abuse drugs often use tranquilizers or narcotic analgesics (pain relievers). Some people get these drugs by *doctor shopping* and collecting prescriptions. Other people become addicted to drugs through many years of use.

Lois Reynolds began taking tranquilizers after a nervous collapse when two of her children moved out on their own. The drugs worked well in the short run and allowed her to go back to work. But here is the rest of the story in her own words.

It was about a month before I began to feel somewhat normal, and six months to a year before I could say I was, for sure. I did not need the drugs, *but* if I did not take them, I would begin to feel nervous and would become afraid I was going to have a relapse. Time marches on, and so did my ulcers and headaches. About one year after this, the doctor and I decided that it was necessary for me to have surgery for the ulcers, which consisted of removal of 75 percent of my stomach. Thus another crisis, and continuation of drugs. Now I ask some of you, does this sound familiar? I think this is the story of most prescription drug dependency.

. . . During the next few years, I became sedated to the point that my blood pressure and pulse were so low, my headaches so severe, that I had to do something. To relieve the headaches, I started taking a stimulant (Dexedrine), which is a controlled substance, but was also prescribed by the doctor. Now I was 12 to 15 years down the drug road—still taking 4 tranquilizers, 4 Dexedrine, plus 8 Tylenol a day, and feeling great. I continued a normal, happy life for another 10 years until I retired from work at age 62.

So began the "Golden Years," until boom, all of a sudden I had been home for a couple of years and had begun to get bored and depressed because my husband was still working, as were all my friends, and I was pretty much alone.

Now I needed something for my depression, and the doctor gave it to me. So I had three drugs to cope with. By this time, I had slowly increased the dosage of tranquilizers and Dexedrine, each to eight a day, and the trouble really began. The drugs no longer had the same effect and I wasn't feeling as well.

I began to give more thought to making a serious effort to get off drugs, and I decided to enter the hospital. This was a good start, but not quite a success. I managed in a week's stay in the hospital to cut the amount considerably, but did not follow up on the treatment.

The doctor told me he doubted if I would ever be able to do without drugs completely due to the length of time I had been taking them. So I accepted that as a fact and did nothing more for five years. At that point, I began hearing news reports that made me decide that if I were really serious about wanting to get off drugs, then I could. There were so many people going through these programs that were successful. If they could, so could I.

Reynolds finally signed up for a program for drug-dependent older people. The program offered medical care and counseling for one year. At the time she wrote her story she had quit drug use for fifteen months and vowed to stay drug free. She concludes with advice to other older people.

I have no qualms about discussing this with anyone, as I feel no guilt about what happened. After all, I was only following the doctor's orders at all times. . . .

Sources: From "Drug free after 30 years of dependency," by L. Reynolds (1990). *Aging Magazine, 361,* pp. 26–27; also, "Patterns of drug prescribing," by T. P. Semla, A. Schwartz, H. Koch, & C. Nelson, in J. F. Van Norstrand, S. E. Furner, & R. Suzman (Eds.), *Health data on older Americans: United States, 1992,* pp. 187–193. Hyattsville, MD: National Center for Health Statistics.

program in San Francisco (described in the following section on Managed Care with a Community Focus) serves as a model for community-based long-term care.

LONG-TERM CARE: A RESPONSE TO OLDER PEOPLE'S NEEDS

The image most people have of long-term care is of a nursing home, but long-term care also refers to help with shopping, bathing, or chores around the house. Long-term care includes in-home services and community-based services, as well as institutional care.

Institutional Care

In 1999, the United States had 18,000 nursing homes and housed 1.6 million people (91 percent of them over the age of 65) (National Center for Health Statistics, 2004a). On any day, 4 percent of the older population in the United States lives in a nursing home. However, at age 65, a person has about a 40 percent chance of entering a nursing home at some point in their lifetime (Schulz, 2001).

Some people stay only a short time, for example, as a stopping point from hospital to home. About one-third of the people who spend time in a nursing home will stay for less than three months. Others spend the last years of their lives in nursing homes. About 20 percent spend five years or more (Rich, 1991, cited in Schulz, 2001). Schulz (2001) says that about 13 percent of all older people account for 90 percent of all nursing home costs.

People differ in their risk of entering a nursing home. For example, the older the person, the greater the chance of living in a nursing home. Schulz (2001) reports that the proportion of people aged 85 and over in nursing homes will increase from 42 percent in 1986 to 1990 to 51 percent in 2016 to 2020. Women also run a greater risk than men of entering a nursing home. In 1999, for example, women aged 65 and over outnumbered older men in nursing homes by three to one. This difference reflects the fact that older men more often than older women have a spouse at home to care for them.

Race also influences nursing home admission. Older whites outnumber older African Americans in nursing homes by almost nine to one (National Center for Health Statistics, 2004a). This difference may reflect cultural differences like more family and community supports. Or it may reflect the fact that African American older people feel alienated from the health care system. They avoid moving to a nursing home, an essentially white environment.

Coughlin and her colleagues (Coughlin, McBride, & Liu, 1990) found other risk factors including cognitive impairment, functional impairment, nonhomeowner, recent hospital release, and living in an area with many nursing home beds. A person without community supports also faces an increased likelihood of living in a nursing home.

The U.S. government in the late 1980s attempted to improve the quality of nursing homes through legislation. The Omnibus Budget Reconciliation Act of 1987 set strict standards for nursing home quality. This act required clear care plans for patients, a declaration to patients of their rights, and a minimum number of nurses on duty each day. The legislation met problems in the field. Nursing homes got the regulations late, surveyors had little training, and nursing homes got little extra funding to cover improvements in service. But once implemented, these regulations led to improvements in nursing home quality.

Most older people prefer to stay in their own homes. They choose this option for at least two reasons: (1) they prefer the independence of living on their own, and (2) they may not be able to afford a nursing home. On average, a one-year stay in a nursing home in 1999 cost $51,000. Costs varied by the services needed and the part of the country. Nursing home care in a large city can cost as much as $60,000 per year.

"Many people believe that Medicare, Medicaid, and private supplemental health insurance provide substantial nursing home benefits. Unfortunately, due to restrictions on reimbursements, this is not the case" (AARP, 1992, p. 16; Schulz, 2001). For example, Medicare only covers skilled nursing care in a skilled nursing facility, and most facilities in the United States do not offer this level of care. Medicaid pays for long-term care. But this program requires that a person spend down all their personal assets (they may keep only about $2,000) before Medicaid will pay the bills. Medical insurance generally pays only part of the costs of nursing home care for older people. Users of nursing home services pay over 45 percent of costs (AARP, 1992). This can deplete a person's assets and leave them with few resources when they return home. It can often leave a spouse with little money to live on.

Community-Based Services

Leutz and his colleagues (1993) say that community long-term care programs have four goals: (1) keep potential patients out of nursing homes; (2) meet the social and personal care needs of older people; (3) meet health needs not covered by Medicare; and (4) link medical care and social support to keep the older person in the community. Community care services range from **adult daycare**, to respite services, to home health care.

Adult daycare programs may follow either the medical model, social model, or a combination of the two models of care. Medical model programs offer rehabilitation, nursing care, and health assessment. Social model programs offer exercise, crafts, and social contacts. Adult daycare programs have increased in the United States from 300 in 1975 to over 4,000 in 2000. Nearly 90 percent of these program are nonprofit. Programs typically have about forty members and attract people with an average age of 78 years. A typical program member is white, unmarried, and female. About one-half of all clients in adult daycare have a cognitive impairment (Gaugler & Zarit, 2001).

Medicare does not cover adult daycare, but nearly one-half the people in these programs get Medicaid. Studies disagree on whether these programs keep people out of nursing homes longer or save money. This may be because these programs attract people close to institutionalization already. A Veterans Affairs study of adult daycare found little evidence for improved health of patients, but the study did find greater patient and caregiver satisfaction compared with people in nursing homes (Hedrick et al., 1993; Rothman et al., 1993). Kirwin (1991) says adult daycare serves as a mild intervention. It will probably not delay institutionalization, but it does support caregivers' attempts to keep an older person in the community.

Respite services also give family caregivers a break from the demands of care. These programs take many forms. Some nursing homes, for example, offer one- or two-week respite stays for care receivers. Other programs send someone into a caregiver's home to sit with a care receiver and give the caregiver a day off. Medicaid will cover respite costs for people at risk of institutionalization. Some states help fund respite programs. In some cases, families pay for respite on their own.

Home health care programs deliver services to a person at home. Vierck (2002) reports that 13,300 agencies in 1998 offered home care services. Medicare and Medicaid certified the large majority of these programs (84 percent and 85 percent, respectively). The programs served almost 2 million patients in 1998. People aged 65 and over made up 69 percent of home care patients. Home care programs minimize the effects of illness and give the older person as much independence as possible. Services most frequently used include bathing and showering, dressing, moving a person from bed to chair, and using the toilet. Home care programs also offer help with shopping (for food or clothes), light housework, medications, and meal preparation (Vierck, 2002).

Home health care can have many goals. Some home care programs aim to rehabilitate an older person after an injury. Others aim to help a person get well without complications after a hospital stay (Kane & Kane, 2001). Still others aim for a comfortable death (Kane, 1995).

Costs vary for home care services. An Oregon home care program, for example, will pay up to $1,950 per month for in-home services. Costs for services range from $2.85 per hour for live-in care providers to about $8.50 per hour for someone to deliver personal care. The program requires people with higher incomes to pay something for the services (Heumann, 2004). Public funding for home health care boomed when the government put limits on hospital stays. Because home care services appear to cost less than institutional placement, home health care looked like an answer to rising costs.

Recent research questions this idea. Kane and Kane (2001, p. 414) say that "the debate about whether community-based long-term care is actually cheaper than nursing homes has raged for some time." They note community care may cost less per unit to deliver. But as the amount of service to a person increases, the cost of community care can equal or go beyond the cost of institutional care. Also, community care may attract more people to use health care services. This increases the number of people served and raises the total cost of health care. The Medicaid program allowed states to pay for home care as long as the states could show comparable savings in institutional care.

The 1981–1982 National Long-Term Care Channeling Demonstration Project, a study still cited in the literature (Kane & Kane, 2001), looked at the costs of home care services for disabled and frail older people (Kemper, 1990). The study involved 6,000 older people with severe disabilities. These people lived in the community. The project substituted case-managed long-term care for nursing home care. Case-managed care provides care designed for the individual. A case manager assesses a person's needs, arranges for care, and monitors outcomes.

This project studied the cost of community care and satisfaction with this type of service (Kemper, Brown, Carcagno, et al., 1988). The project found that the cost of care went up by about 18 percent due to added services, and nursing home use fell very little (Wiener & Harris, 1990). However, people in the project said they had fewer unmet needs, felt increased satisfaction with the care they got, and had higher overall life satisfaction (Carcagno & Kemper, 1988).

Polich (1989) reviewed several community care programs in the United States and found that the projects met client needs, increased client satisfaction, and led to coordinated service. The programs did less well at controlling costs and use. Weissert and Hedrick (1994) reviewed thirty-two studies of community-based programs. Almost all studies found that programs did not keep clients from declines in health, and they saved money only through careful program management.

Still, users of the programs report increased life satisfaction, and they prefer these programs to institutionalization. Home health care may not save the system money, but it provides older people with the kind of care they want and need. Weissert and Hedrick (1994) say clients' preferences for these programs make the strongest argument for offering them.

The government has tried to control home care costs. The Balanced Budget Act of 1997, for example, changed the way Medicare reimburses for home care. Medicare shifted away from a cost-based reimbursement system to a PPS. This meant that providers got paid a set amount for a specific client need (rather than an amount based on the company's cost to deliver the service). This led to large declines in the use of home health services by Medicare/Medicaid beneficiaries. The National Center for Health Statistics (Bernstein et al., 2003) reports that the rate of home care use by older people rose from 29.6 per 1,000 persons in 1992 to 52.5 per 1,000 persons in 1996. The rate then fell back to 27.7 per 1,000 in 2000.

This decrease in home care service after 1996 reflects the impact of the BBA's prospective payment system on care delivery. An evaluation of the PPS "found that prospectively paid home health agencies significantly reduced the length of time patients remained in home health care as well as the average number of visits" (Bernstein et al., 2003, p. 40).

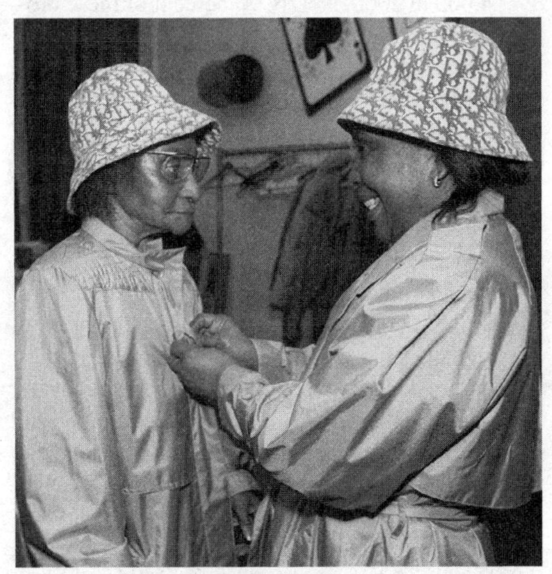

A daughter takes her mother home at the end of the day from the Central Harlem Senior Citizens Coalition Center in New York. Her mother spent the day in an activity program designed to give respite to family caregivers.

One study (Murtaugh, McCall, Moore, & Meadow, 2003) reported a 60 percent decline in average annual home health visits. Another study (McCall, Peterson, Moon, & Korb, 2003) found a 22 percent decrease in the percent of Medicare beneficiaries using home health services after the change to a PPS. They also found a 39 percent decrease in the number of visits per year.

These researchers say that this reduction in services put vulnerable groups, such as nonwhites, women, and people aged 85 and over, at risk. Pagan (2002) says that under the PPS many companies that delivered home care either sold out or closed down. Schulmerich (2000) estimates that 30 percent of home health agencies closed their Medicare services when they could not operate within the new guidelines (Schulmerich, 2000).

The new prospective payment system may lead to better control of expenses. But it may also reduce the amount of home care available to older people. The government and care providers will need to find a balance between the cost of home care and the growing need among older people for home care services.

Managed Care: Alternative Delivery Methods

Managed Care with a Medical Focus

Managed care plans promise some control of health care costs and usage rates. These plans are based on **capitated payments**. This means that a payer (Medicare, Medicaid, or a private insurer) prepays a set amount per person per month for care. The organization then has to manage care to stay within this budget and earn a profit. Most managed care programs take the form of HMOs or **competitive medical plans (CMPs)**. These programs have expanded in the past few years. An HMO contracts with Medicare to provide services. People join the plan and pay a monthly premium. They also make small copayments for services.

HMOs offer some advantages over regular Medicare. They take an interdisciplinary approach to care and coordinate all services to a client. This allows them to keep track of a person's health record, past contacts with specialists and therapists, and use of prescription drugs. HMOs can also help with early long-term care planning and can provide community care after hospital discharge. Some of these plans focus on rehabilitation and even have rehabilitation teams that provide services in a person's home. Some HMOs offer preventive care, items like eyeglasses and hearing aids, and dental care.

Wetle (1993) says that HMOs have not developed programs well suited to older people. **Social health maintenance organizations (SHMOs)** have done better at putting together an array of services for this group. The staff of Brandeis University started the first SHMOs in 1985 as part of a National Demonstration program (Van Ellett, 1993). Like HMOs, SHMOs assume the total cost of care for a person for a set monthly fee. The agency bears the risk of high costs. SHMOs combine medical care with social supports. They use case management to arrange services and control costs. This kind of program targets people who need help with ADLs, but do not need skilled nursing care or therapy.

Van Ellett (1993) reviewed four SHMO demonstration projects in the United States. These SHMOs met older people's acute and chronic care needs, and they held costs and use within limits. Leutz and colleagues (1991) say that SHMOs could give millions of people access to catastrophic care protection and community long-term care services. HMOs could add SHMO benefits to their services for an added fee. This would give people the insurance they need at no added cost to Medicare.

Kane (1991) cautions that some people may not want to pay for these extra benefits and some people cannot afford to pay. Also, some SHMOs limit enrollment to low-risk clients. These two conditions protect the SHMOs from heavy costs, but limit the program to select, relatively healthy people.

Managed Care with a Community Focus

The On Lok SeniorHealth of San Francisco, a community long-term care program, has served as a model for community care programs throughout the United States. *On Lok* means "peaceful, happy abode" in Chinese. The program began in 1972 as a drop-in center that served warm meals. About three-

BOX 8.3

CASE MANAGEMENT: MEETING THE CHRONIC CARE NEEDS OF OLDER PEOPLE

Older people often have more than one chronic condition. They may need more than one kind of health care service. This can lead to a lack of coordination of service and to high health care costs. Case management offers one of the most flexible responses to this problem. The case manager assesses need, plans and arranges for care, and monitors outcomes on a case-by-case basis.

White lists six characteristics of case management. Case management:

1. Designs a program to fit the needs of each person;
2. Looks at the person and the environment, including social, psychological, and economic resources;
3. Enhances self-care and involves clients in decision making;
4. Aims to maintain or expand a client's abilities and increase the person's independence;
5. Uses varied (informal and formal) resources and services;
6. Coordinates existing services.

Hospitals, community health care agencies, and private companies have applied case management to care for older people. Community agencies use case management to screen and coordinate client care. Screening and assessment can often lead to community placement instead of institutionalization.

Sources: From "Case management," by M. White (1987), in G. L. Maddox, (Ed.), *The encyclopedia of aging,* pp. 92–96. New York: Springer; also, "Long-term care," by H. Richardson (1990), in A. R. Kooner (Ed.), *Health care delivery in the United States (4th Ed.),* pp. 175–208. New York: Springer.

quarters of On Lok's participants (On Lok's term for clients) have Chinese ancestry. Many of On Lok's workers speak Chinese. The program also serves other minorities including Filipino, Italian, and Hispanic older people.

On Lok combines medical services with adult daycare, home care, and transportation. On Lok receives monthly capitated payments from Medicare, Medicaid, and individuals. In 1983 Congress allowed On Lok to get a set fee from Medicare and Medicaid for each person in the program. On Lok took 100 percent of the risk of paying for all of the client's services out of this amount. The program now serves 950 mentally and physically frail older people, a high-risk, high-cost group (On Lok SeniorHealth, 2004). Without On Lok, most of these people would live in an institution.

On Lok contracts with health care professionals and institutions for services. It also runs On Lok House, a fifty-four-apartment complex for frail older people, and a respite unit. The program also arranges for groups of participants to live with companions in private apartments (Miller, 1991).

Der-McLeod and Hansen (1992) say that care usually lasts until a person's death. On Lok tailors its services to each family's needs and to its ethnicity. It assesses a family's ability to give care and discusses family members' roles in the caregiving process. This assessment provides families with services to relieve their stress.

The program also builds caregivers' knowledge and skills at managing the older person's disabilities. On Lok workers teach caregivers to notice signs of decline in a frail older person. Social workers in the program help families cope with changes like institutionalization and death. The program also includes the participant in care planning. Professionals help patients express their "health wishes" or preferences for treatment (Der-McLeod & Hansen, 1992, p. 72). This includes decisions about resuscitation and tube feeding. A study of the program found lower costs for hospital and nursing home services and more use of community services (Zawadski & Eng, 1988).

On Lok has inspired the start of programs in other states. It now belongs to the national long-term care demonstration project called Program of All-Inclusive Care for the Elderly (PACE). On Lok advised on the creation of the PACE project. This project serves nursing home–eligible people aged 55 who live in the community.

PACE began by serving frail older people at eight sites in eight states. Today, twenty-five PACE sites exist in fourteen states under Medicaid (Medicare, 2004). Each site has about 200 enrollees. A person who wants to take part in PACE voluntarily enrolls. They must be 55 years old or older, live in the PACE service area, have a screening by a team of health professionals, and agree to terms of enrollment.

The PACE programs follow the original On Lok method of payment. The programs get a fixed amount each month per enrollee from Medicare and Medicaid. The PACE programs include all Medicare and Medicaid services in that state. The programs also include at least sixteen other services, including social work support and nursing facility care. PACE day centers provide meals, transportation, recreational therapy, and other support services. The programs provide many of these services 24 hours a day, 7 days a week, 365 days a year.

Enrollees can get services at day centers, at referral services, or in their own homes. This includes hospital care, nursing home care, and treatment by a medical specialist. A medical team decides on a person's need. Today more than seventy organizations in thirty states are in various stages of the PACE model, from start-up to full operation (On Lok SeniorHealth, 2004).

Rich (1999) says that PACE programs lead to more community care, fewer hospital days, and a low rate of nursing home use. Also, people in the PACE programs report high satisfaction and excellent care ratings. Chatterji et al. (1998; *also* Eng et al., 1997) found that PACE programs led to less use of hospitals and nursing homes. They provided community care at a cost comparable with other approaches. And they showed improvements in health and functional ability similar to other approaches (cited in Kane & Kane, 2001). These programs serve as models of community care. However, Kane and Kane (2001, p. 419) say, "We know much more about how to deliver good chronic care for older persons than we are willing to put into practice."

Today, relatively few older people in the United States have access to this type of coordinated service. Huttman (1987, p. 146) says that barriers exist throughout the country to the use of community services. Services "are scattered, limited in the number of people they can serve, and are often exclusively for the poor, or for the rich, and seldom for the large middle income group."

A system of community-based long-term care does not exist in the United States at present. Community care programs such as On Lok and PACE offer promise for the future. These pilot programs show that managed community care can control costs and provide quality care to an older population. Kane and Kane (2001, p. 419) say that "we know much about how to provide better care, but we lack the will to implement that knowledge."

DISEASE PREVENTION AND HEALTH PROMOTION

Disease prevention and health promotion programs provide other ways to control illness in an aging society. Some of these methods have caught on in the United States. For example, restaurants have no-smoking sections, and some airlines brag about smoke-free flights worldwide. Magazines on fitness, running, and dieting appear on every newsstand. Even fast-food restaurants offer salads and low-fat dishes to a health-conscious public. Disease prevention and health promotion extend to include things we take for granted, like water and air quality standards, vaccinations, and regular medical checkups.

Researchers describe three types of disease or disability prevention: primary, secondary, and tertiary (Kane & Kane, 2001). Primary prevention refers to stopping new problems from arising. For example, warnings on cigarette packs try to discourage smoking to prevent heart disease. Secondary prevention refers to screening to detect problems. Doctors do this when they check patients for hypertension. Tertiary prevention refers to stopping current problems from getting worse. For example, doctors use surgery or drug therapy to treat cancer.

Some studies of health promotion programs show promising outcomes. Wheeler (2003) describes a program for older women with cardiac disease titled, Women Take PRIDE. This program encouraged a group of 233 women to engage in self-management of their heart conditions (219 women served as a control group and received usual care for their conditions). Each woman in the experi-

This exercise-swim program takes place in Cerritos, California. The program promotes health and attempts to prevent illness through exercise.

mental group selected a behavior to focus on (based on their physician's suggestions). Behaviors included exercise, medicine taking, diet, etc. The women met in groups with an educator to learn a process for monitoring and managing their behaviors. The women got instructional material, diaries to keep notes, and a number to call with questions they might have. The study found that, compared with the control group, women in the program made significantly less use of hospital inpatient services. This led to significant cost savings and better health for these women.

One large study of primary prevention gives some idea of the potential for prevention programs. Richardson and Harrington (1993) studied a program called Healthtrac. This program offered health risk assessments, education on healthy life-styles, and tracking the progress of over 1 million workers.

Researchers found, in a controlled study, that after two years, people in the program showed significant improvement in blood pressure, weight, and general health. People in the program also reported fewer visits to their doctors and fewer hospital stays. The study found that people who did not smoke, who did not drink excessively, who had moderate weight, who used seatbelts, and who exercised, saved health care dollars.

Health promotion programs go beyond preventing illness; they attempt to improve health. Health promotion includes programs that improve nutrition, life-styles, and fitness. People can take part in health promotion even though some of their physical functions decline. For example, a person with arthritis can improve health with a low-fat diet.

The best health promotion programs allow older people to play a role in program design. These programs enhance the older person's well-being. (A person develops a sense of self-efficacy, a sense that they can control events in their lives (Easom, 2003; Thornton & Tuck, 2000). Many studies now support the value of active life-styles. Iso-Ahola (1993) reports that an "active leisure lifestyle" does at least two things. It directly benefits health, and it helps to buffer the influence of life events and illness.

Other studies support this view. Swinburn and Sager (2003) report that physical activity reduces the incidence of diabetes and hypertension, and increases bone density. Orsega-Smith, Payne, and Godbey (2003) note that improved fitness leads to greater endurance and flexibility.

Disease prevention and health promotion should play an increasing role in health care in the future. Young (1994) says that health promotion and disease prevention can decrease three of the major chronic conditions of old age (arthritis, high blood pressure, and heart disease). They can also reduce the incidence of the three major causes of death in old age (heart disease, cancer, and stroke).

Antismoking publicity, for example, explains much of the significant decrease in cigarette smoking in the United States between 1965 and 2002. The proportion of male smokers aged 65 and over dropped by almost two-thirds from 28.5 percent to 10.1 percent during this period. The proportion of female smokers aged 65 and over during this period began at 9.6 percent in 1965, rose to 13.5 percent in 1985, and dropped to a low of 8.6 percent in 2002 (National Center for Health Statistics, 2004b). Decreases in smoking among older people will lead to longer life expectancies and better health as they age.

Some barriers exist to an increase in health-promoting behavior. First, middle-aged and older people expect less benefit from exercise than do younger people (Searle, 1987). They may carry this attitude into later life and may resist health promotion programs. Second, older people tend to live sedentary lives, and relatively few show a desire to be more active. Health promotion programs may have to overcome lifelong habits and negative attitudes toward exercise. Young (1994) says many programs and professionals offer advice to older people about health promotion, but relatively few older people change their habits.

Third, many older people who join exercise or fitness programs drop out. And many people who could benefit most from these programs never join. Programs face information barriers, beliefs about the causes and cures of illness, and economic barriers. Poor older people have less money and time than middle-class people for health promotion activities. Health promotion programs must find ways to attract older people and keep them coming back.

Chapter 12 discusses fitness and exercise programs in more detail. It describes the benefits of these programs, the challenges they have to meet, and some ways to overcome these challenges. In the case of poor people, this means designing programs that take their social context into account.

A health promotion program in rural North Florida shows what a program needs to do to meet the needs of older minority members. This program first enlisted the help of African American community leaders through local churches. These leaders set up a health advisory council and committees at four churches. The council members identified problems, set priorities, and helped design the program. The result was an effective program. One-half the people in the program had lower weight and lower blood pressure after eighteen months. They all reported feeling better.

This program shows the need for local leadership, local control, and integrating a program into community life (Cowart, Sutherland, & Harris, 1995). Another challenge faces health promotion and disease prevention efforts. Much of the research on health promotion focuses on individuals' behaviors and life-styles. But McKinlay uses a political economy perspective to show how the economic system produces illness.

He calls health promotion programs "downstream endeavors" (McKinlay, (1985, p. 485). They ignore the social context that leads people to get sick. For example, air pollution, solvents in water and food, and pesticides all do greater damage to older people than to people in middle age. Also, drug companies encourage the use of drugs such as estrogen to reduce menopause symptoms, but research questions the wisdom of estrogen use. This drug may increase a person's risk of cancer.

McKinlay (1985, p. 485) says that business and industry often profit at the expense of people's health. The health promotion focus on the individual overlooks the economic forces that lead to ill health. McKinlay admits the value of individual health promotion and disease prevention activity. But too often, he says, the "*beginning point* in the process [the marketing and production of products that create illness] remains unaffected by most preventive endeavors, even though it is at this point that the greatest potential for change, and perhaps even ultimate victory, lies" (McKinlay, 1985, p. 493). Health promotion and disease prevention must have an impact on the production of illness to have their greatest effect.

Watson and Hall (2001) also look at the social environment as a source of health risk. They say that a person's social class, employment status, and level of education all influence health and well-being. Likewise, poverty leads to anxiety, insecurity, stress, and poor social networks. These conditions threaten good health. These findings show that a healthy older population depends on a supportive social environment. Models of a quality health care system need to include improvements in the environment and decreases in social inequality.

FUTURE ISSUES IN HEALTH CARE

Availability

Availability refers to the existence of services. Some parts of the country have many services for older people. Other regions have few. Wallace (1990a) studied the lack of services in two metropolitan areas in Missouri. He called these gaps "no-care zones." He found that 49 percent of state case managers in these regions said that people could not get respite care though they needed it. Thirty-nine percent of the case managers said people needed, but could not get, transportation help. A third of the case managers said older people needed skin care but could not get it.

Bull and Bane (1993) say that rural areas offer fewer services to older people than do metropolitan areas. They give three reasons for this lack of service. First, rural hospitals have fewer patients, make smaller profits, and get lower reimbursement from Medicare. Second, rural hospitals have fewer high-tech services. This means younger old people go to urban centers for care. Third, rural settings have fewer health care professionals like doctors, nurses, and pharmacists. Still, older people in these areas need medical help as much as or more than their urban peers.

Bull and Bane (1993) suggest a number of ways to improve access to health care in rural and nonmetro settings. First, create programs that encourage health professionals such as doctors and nurses to move to rural settings. The National Health Service Corps has had some success at this. It offers medical school scholarships in return for two or more years' work in "Health Professional Shortage Areas" (Bull & Bane, 1993).[1]

Second, offer incentives to encourage current health professionals to move to rural areas. Incentives can take the form of start-up grants for rural practices, tax credits, and subsidies to help health professionals avoid burnout.

Third, technology can enrich health care in rural settings. It cannot overcome the absence of health professionals or hospitals, but it can overcome some barriers due to distance. For example, people can get health screenings and can do home shopping by phone. Fax machines can send prescriptions to a distant pharmacy and arrange for delivery of the medicine.

Accessibility

Accessibility refers to whether a person can get the services that exist. Barriers to services can include lack of knowledge, eligibility, money, transportation, bad weather, or geography. People in rural settings often face more than one barrier to access. So do minority group members.

Distance and isolation present barriers to access for rural older people. Better roads and transportation would make it easier for older people to get to services and vice versa. Attempts to improve access must overcome the effects of blizzards, floods, and heat waves on health care delivery.

The Kaiser Family Foundation (2003) conducted a study of health care access in Washington, DC. The study found that 19 percent of poor or near poor older people said they had not visited a doctor in the past twelve months (compared with 4 percent of higher income older people). Yet the poorer people reported poorer health. The report also found that 22 percent of poor or near poor older people failed to fill a drug prescription in the past twelve months because of the cost. Only 7 percent of higher income seniors report these practices.

Takamura (2002) notes that a gap in health care access exists between non-Hispanic whites and minority older people. Latino and African American people (of all ages), compared with whites, gave the lowest ratings to the health care service they received (Kaiser Family Foundation, 2003).

Also, minority older people, compared with non-Hispanic whites have lower rates of health care insurance. Thirty-seven percent of Latinos (of all ages) have no health insurance. Nearly one-quarter (23 percent) of African Americans have no insurance. One in five (21 percent) Asian and Pacific Islanders have no insurance. The cost of copayments, deductibles, and dissatisfaction with service leads poorer and minority old people to underuse health care resources. These findings suggest that poorer and minority group older people have less access than whites to health care.

Changes in service to minority elders could include better office hours, a more convenient location of the doctor's office, more minority physicians, and home care. Health promotion programs could take place in churches and should include older people in program planning (Ralston, 1993).

Coordination

The United States needs better coordination of health care services (Kane & Kane, 2001). Often older people and their families become case man-

[1]The U.S. Office of Management and Budget defines *rural* as an area of low residential density and size (under 2,500 people). The term *nonmetro* refers to counties that lie outside metropolitan areas. The Office of Management and Budget defines metropolitan as an urbanized area of 50,000 or more people and a total population of 100,000 or more that includes adjacent counties.

BOX 8.4
PRIVATE CASE MANAGEMENT SERVICES

Some people have turned to private case managers to coordinate services for themselves or a family member. Children who live far from their parents, for example, may need someone to look in on a parent and coordinate care. They may wonder, "Is Mom taking her pills regularly? Is Dad handling his bills okay? How is she managing her shopping? Does he ever have visitors?"

Reporter Esther Fein describes the use of a case manager by one caregiver who lives many miles from her elderly aunt.

Beverly Wagner has logged hundreds of hours on the telephone, flown regularly from Michigan to New York, and missed dozens of days of work, all trying to arrange care for her 94-year-old aunt, who lives in Manhattan and is losing the ability to care for herself.

After failing to persuade her aunt to move from her apartment of 50 years near Lincoln Center into her lakeside house in Michigan, Mrs. Wagner finally hired Fine and Newcomber Associates, a geriatric guidance and family counseling service in Manhattan. Fine and Newcomber is one of hundreds of companies that have sprung up over the last several years to help people coordinate and monitor the affairs of aging relatives who do not live nearby.

In the past, without local people to look out for them, the elderly have often been forced prematurely into nursing homes or made to move in with relatives in distant cities where people and geography are unfamiliar.

But these days, many who must minister to elderly relatives from a distance are turning to referral services that provide information about care of the elderly, and to geriatric care managers who, for a fee, will shoulder many of the tasks families usually take on.

The company Mrs. Wagner hired has arranged for a daily meal delivery for her aunt, found a housekeeper who comes twice a week to clean, shop and accompany her to doctors' appointments, and sends a social worker weekly to make sure everything is running well. If there is an emergency—a phone that goes unanswered, a middle-of-the-night fall—they respond.

"It has saved my life and my family life," said Mrs. Wagner, a nurse in Onekama, Mich. She paid the company an initial consultation fee of $150, and now pays the company $65 an hour, for a monthly average of about $100, none of which is reimbursed by insurance. The housekeeper is paid by Mrs. Wagner separately.

"I was spending so much time and money between the travel and the day-to-day calling that I finally had to take a leave of absence," she said. "If I wasn't physically there on one of my two-week stretches visiting her, then I was mentally involved. It took up my work days. It made for a bad relationship with my husband. It was really stressful and the distance just made it an awful, impossible situation."

[The] growing elderly population's desire for independence, coupled with the mobility of the American work force, has left millions of people like Mrs. Wagner scrambling to arrange assistance to aging relatives who live far away.

Sources: From "Looking beyond family to aid the elderly," by E. B. Fein, *New York Times,* April 6, 1994, p. A1. Copyright © 1994, The New York Times Co. Reprinted with permission; also, "Home alone: If your parents need help and you're miles away, call a care manager," by F. Leonard, 1993, *Modern Maturity,* December–January, pp. 46–51, 77.

agers. They find and contact specialists, let specialists know about other medical services they use, and follow up on treatment. Kane and Kane call this a "client driven" system. Information about the patient can get lost. Who, for example, will let the home health nurse know about the specialist's findings?

Area Agencies on Aging offer long-term care planning help. So do hospital discharge planners, some senior centers, and some social agencies. A doctor may also help set up a long-term care plan. Some people have turned to private care management services. They help decide what services a person needs, where to find them, and how to coordinate them. Care management within a larger service (like a hospital) may come free of charge. A private care management firm will charge a monthly fee. No public or private insurers will cover the charge of private care management.

The AARP (1992, p. 1) sums up the problems with the long-term care system today. "It's not always easy to find these services, and when found, they often are costly. Some options are not universally available and many forms of care are not covered by insurance."

CONCLUSION

Health care costs have increased in the recent past, and projections suggest that costs will go up in the future. Some writers point to an aging society as the cause of these increases. They say that older people use more health care services and that an increase in the number of older people will drive health care costs through the roof.

A closer look at the health care system shows that the system itself accounts for some of the increase in costs. The current system relies on the medical model to serve an aging population. This model developed and had its greatest successes in response to acute illness. But an older population has more chronic than acute illnesses. The medical model often provides older people with costly care that fails to meet their needs.

Older people have varied needs, complex medical histories, many chronic conditions, and uncertain outcomes from treatment. They need long-term care services. These services help with a variety of supports that range from medical care to help with activities of daily living. Community care and home health supports often suit the older person better than institutional care and expensive medical treatment.

Health promotion may create a healthier older population in the future. This approach fits a society that values activity and engagement in social life. But many reports on programs simply describe the programs or report on positive program outcomes. Researchers need to conduct more controlled studies of health promotion programs. Studies need to look at whether these programs improve health and save health care dollars as they claim.

The current health care system will need to change to serve an aging society. It will have to offer a broader range of services, it will have to provide more community care and offer nonmedical supports to help older people stay in the community, and it will have to recognize the value of prevention and health promotion. It will also have to provide coordinated services with fewer barriers to access.

All this will take place in a time of economic cutbacks, while the system continues to deliver service. Someone said this is like trying to change a tire while driving down the highway at 60 miles per hour. This will take skillful management and public support. But the outcome will be a system that better fits the needs of an aging society.

SUMMARY

- Social scientists use three models to describe the approaches to health care in the United States: the medical model, the social model, and the health promotion model. The medical model focuses on diagnosis and cure of illness. The social model focuses on helping a person function in everyday life. And the health promotion model focuses on prevention and well-being. The health care system in the United States today favors treatment using the medical model. But this model best fits treatment of acute illness. Chronic illnesses, the type most common among older people, can better be served through the social and health promotion models.
- Congress established the Medicare program in 1965. Until then, only about half of older people had health insurance. The Medicare program contains two parts: hospital insurance (or Part A) and medical insurance (or Part B). People who receive Social Security get Part A insurance at age 65. People with Part A can pay extra for Part B insurance.
- The Medicare program now offers a Medicare + Choice (in addition to the Original Medicare Plan). The Medicare + Choice (pronounced Medicare plus Choice) plan offers a Medicare Managed Care Plan and Medicare Private Fee-for-Service Plan. These plans provide services that coordinate care or lower out-of-pocket expenses. Some plans offer prescription

drug benefits. The Bush administration in 2003 added a Prescription Drug Discount Card to the Medicare program. This program allows card holders to get a discount on prescription drugs.

- Congress also set up the Medicaid program in 1965. This program serves low-income Americans of all ages. Older people make up about 12 percent of Medicaid recipients.
- The high cost of the U.S. health care system results from costly intensive-care hospital service, hospital administration costs, high insurance administration costs, and advances in high-cost technology.
- In an attempt to control hospital costs, the federal government set up the PPS. The PPS led to a drop in older persons' length of stay in hospitals, but this method poses problems for older patients. It encourages hospitals to release Medicare patients early (because Medicare pays less for care than private patients do), to restrict their treatment, and to increase the number of private patients they accept.
- Health care expenses have increased and they take up a large part of the older person's budget. Most of this money pays for insurance, medical supplies, and prescription drugs. Catastrophic illness and long-term care in an institution can wipe out a family's savings. Future increases in health care costs will affect government programs and older people.
- Community-based services link medical care and social supports to help keep older people out of institutions. Community services range from adult daycare programs to home care and respite services.
- HMOs take an interdisciplinary approach to care and coordinate all services for a client. An HMO gets a certain amount of money per person (a capitated payment) to provide that person with health care. The HMO has an incentive to stay within its budget and earn a profit. This type of plan promises some control of health care costs. At the same time, it provides comprehensive care to its clients.
- The national PACE demonstration project shows that community health care programs can provide high-quality service and control costs. Research shows that PACE programs reduce hospital and nursing home stays. This kind of program also gets high marks from clients and patients.
- Disease prevention and health promotion can lead to lower health care system costs. People who do not smoke, drink moderately, exercise, and wear seatbelts have lower health care costs than others. Health promotion and disease prevention programs can create a healthier society.
- The health care system needs to improve by making services widely available, removing barriers to access, and coordinating services.

DISCUSSION QUESTIONS

1. List the three different approaches to health care. Define the goals and practices of each.
2. Explain how part A and part B of the Medicare program work and how the government funds each part of this program.
3. Who can receive Medicaid? What services does Medicaid support?
4. The Medicare and Medicaid programs cover only part of an older person's medical expenses. State two ways that older people cover the rest of the costs.
5. List the major reasons for the increase in health care costs for the elderly. What effect does this increase in costs have on the Medicare program?
6. How does the PPS attempt to control hospital costs? What problems does this approach pose for older people?
7. Why are some people dissatisfied with the U.S. health care system? Suggest some approaches the government can use to reduce the cost of health care for older people and their families.
8. What types of services must the medical system develop to respond to the increase in chronic medical conditions? Describe how adult daycare, respite, and home health care programs each work.
9. On Lok serves as a model for other HMOs throughout the United States. Describe how On Lok operates. Discuss the benefits that PACE programs offer to older people.
10. What types of programs do disease prevention and health promotion include? How can these programs benefit older people physically, psychologically, and financially?
11. How must the current health care system change to serve the future needs of an aging society?

SUGGESTED READING

Haber, D. (2003). *Health promotion and aging: practical applications for health professionals (3rd ed.).* New York: Springer.

The author emphasizes the need for older clients or patients to work with health professionals to promote good health. The book encourages older people to take an active role in their well-being. Topics include exercise, nutrition, alternative medicine, and public health. A good overview of how to create a healthy old age by combining the self-knowledge of the older person with the expertise of the health care professional.

Crandall, W. H., & Crandall, R. (1990). *Borders of time: Life in a nursing home.* New York: Springer.

The authors present vignettes of older residents, photos of their everyday lives, and comments in their own words. The combination of photos and comments makes the people they report on come alive.

Tepper, L. M., & Cassidy, T. M. (Eds.). (2005). *Multidisciplinary perspectives on aging.* New York: Springer.

This collection of essays looks at the health care needs of older people and at how the health care system can best meet those needs. The essays cover a range of topics including the impact of an aging society on the health care system, financing health care, and health promotion. A good collection of the latest thinking on these and other topics related to health care for older people.

Dychtwald, K. (Ed.). 1999. *Healthy aging: Challenges and solutions.* Gaithersburg, MD: Aspen.

This collection of readings looks at current trends and future models of health care. The authors explore new concepts of health care quality, consumer demands for service, and health care for the Baby Boom generation. The articles cover a full range of topics from health care financing to exercise, health promotion, and community-wide prevention. A good source for exploring creative approaches to health care for older people.

GLOSSARY OF TERMS

accessibility Can a person get to a health care service or program? If yes, it is accessible.

acute illness Short-term illness or condition; treatment often leads to full recovery. Examples include measles, influenza, and a sprained ankle.

activities of daily living (ADL) Basic activities needed to live alone or to live a good quality of life. Examples include toileting, preparing food, and bathing.

adult daycare A program that provides socializing, recreation, and meals for older people outside their homes in a group setting.

availability Does a health care service or program exist? If yes, it is available.

capitated payments A set amount (usually per month) that a program such as an HMO gets to serve each of its patients. The HMO must use its resources to provide services for this amount or less in order to make a profit.

care manager Someone who coordinates health care for an individual.

chore services Paid household help.

chronic illness Long-term illness or condition, often a lifelong problem; treatment controls symptoms but seldom leads to full recovery. Examples include arthritis, asthma, and hypertension.

coinsurance Payments the patient makes to cover part of a health care bill. For example, a person may pay 20 percent of all health care costs (in addition to paying a yearly deductible).

copayment Like coinsurance; the portion of a medical bill that the patient has to pay.

deductible The amount of money a person has to pay before health care insurance begins to cover health care bills. For example, a person may pay the first $100 per year of health care expenses.

diagnosis-related grouping (DRG) System in which hospitals categorize patients by medical condition. Medicare reimburses hospitals for a fixed number of days of care according to the patient's DRG.

functional capacity People's ability to function on their own.

health maintenance organization (HMO) Health care program that provides members with all or most of their health care needs for a set fee.

instrumental activities of daily living (IADL) Activities that enhance a person's quality of life. Examples include shopping, using the phone, and light housework.

Medicaid The federal government health care program for low-income Americans of all ages.

Medicare The federal government health care program for all people who receive Social Security. Medicare contains two parts: hospital insurance (part A) and medical insurance (part B).

overmedicalized service Use of the medical model to treat chronic illness and functional problems. For example, the use of sleeping pills to help someone sleep when more exercise during the day would do the same thing.

personal care Community services such as help with bathing or toileting.

prospective payment system (PPS) System in which hospitals are paid a predetermined amount for treatment of each patient disorder.

respite care Short-term relief for caregivers of chronically ill patients.

skilled nursing facility A facility that provides medical care by licensed nursing staff.

social health maintenance organization (SHMO) An HMO with social services such as counseling.

chapter 9

FINANCES AND ECONOMICS

A glance through the *Bulletin,* a newsletter published by the AARP, shows the interests of older people today. Articles focus on Medicare and **Social Security** policies and on issues like later life career change. Advertisements describe rental car bargains, investment funds, vacation options, and exercise equipment. The AARP sends the *Bulletin* to about 25 million older people in the United States. Readers include retirees from all parts of the country, from all social classes, and from different racial and ethnic groups. The articles, investment tips, and advertisements for travel suggest that older people today have educated tastes, good health, and sound incomes. A travel section banner for a newspaper aimed at seniors reads: "If you don't go first class, your heirs will."

In the past thirty years or so, older people's finances have improved dramatically. Social Security provides people with a financial safety net and this has decreased poverty in old age (Freid, Prager, MacKay, & Xia, 2003). Retirees have better private pensions than ever before. And older people have assets, such as investments and mortgage-free homes, that increase their net worth. Today, most older people have enough money to cover their basic expenses and still have some left over for recreation and leisure. A national survey found that between 1974 and 2000, the proportion of older people who said money was a "serious personal problem" for them decreased from 44 to 29 percent (Cutler, Whitelaw, & Beattie, 2002).

Things have improved so much in general that some critics wonder whether older people do too well. They call the new generation of seniors "greedy geezers" (Salholz, Clift, Thomas, & Bingham, 1990). These critics ask whether the United States should support this affluent older population through public pension plans. Some writers see a conflict between this high cost of caring for an older population and the needs of children (who have the highest poverty rates in the country). They ask whether support for older people has gone too far.

Critics of public income security programs for older people ignore the fact that government programs have led to the older population's current well-being. Schulz, for example, shows what it would take to save for a comfortable old age. He says that if a person wanted to replace 60 to 70 percent of their preretirement income, they would need to save about 20 percent of their "*earnings each and every year*" (Schulz, 2001, p. 105, emphasis in the original). Most people could not or would not save at this rate. Without public pension plans, a large proportion of older people would live in or near poverty. Public pension plans ensure that everyone will have income security in old age. Private pension plans help people replace the income lost when they retire.

Also, the current system still does not provide an adequate income for everyone. In 2001 almost 6 million older people lived in **poverty** or **near poverty**. Very old people, minorities, and disabled older people face the greatest risk of poverty. Very old women have some of the lowest incomes in the country (Administration on Aging, 2003). Pockets of poverty such as these call for better pension funding, not cutbacks.

Controversy exists about the amount of money that older people get, about the costs of federal pension programs, and about whether the government should reduce the funding to pension programs in the future. To get at the truth of aging and pensions today, we first need to separate fact from myth.

This chapter looks at (1) the structure of the U.S. retirement income system and how it works, (2) the flaws in the system and ideas for reform, and (3) the future of retirement income in the United States.

HISTORICAL DEVELOPMENT OF THE U.S. PENSION SYSTEM

The change from an agricultural to an industrial society caused great upheaval in society wherever this occurred. People moved to the cities and took jobs in industry. This led to new risks for workers and less support from traditional sources. In an agricultural society, people did as much as they could given their health and strength. They relied on younger family members to take up the heavier work.

In the cities, injuries, unemployment, and old age could put a sudden end to a worker's career. This led to discontent among unemployed and retired workers and caused a crisis for many older people who had no means of support. State governments realized that some groups of people, like the old, needed help to survive. Governments often started pension plans and unemployment insurance to win loyalty to the existing government.

Otto von Bismarck, chancellor of Germany, put the first national pension plan in place in 1889. The plan combined old-age and unemployment insurance. Workers and employers paid into the plan. Unemployed workers and older workers at age 65 could draw benefits. Bismarck used these social reform measures to combat socialism and the discontent of the working class (Myles, 1984).

By the early 1900s, Denmark, New Zealand, and Britain all had old-age security programs. The United States was one of the last industrialized nations to create a national old-age insurance plan. Koff and Park (1993) give one reason for this delay. Industrialization came late to the United States. The U.S. frontier allowed people to move out of industrial work if they chose. This meant that a large part of the U.S. workforce in the nineteenth century still lived an agricultural life-style. In 1870, for example, one-half of adult workers in the U.S. worked on farms (Social Security Administration, 1997).

This changed in the early twentieth century as more people moved to the cities and industrialization increased. In 1900, for example, nearly one-third of men said they had retired. Many of them left work due to health problems. These workers had to rely on their own savings, relatives, or charity for survival. By the late 1920s, the number of older people out of work had grown, and local poor laws and families could not care for these needy older people. The state and federal governments responded to this problem with the first U.S. social insurance programs. These programs offered a subsistence income to the neediest people.

The Great Depression of the 1930s created a national economic crisis. The Depression left many older people and people near retirement without any savings for their old age. For example, less than 10 percent of older people who died during this time left any estate at the time of their death (U.S. Department of Health, 1993). Haber (1993) says that at this time older people began to fill the poorhouses. Twenty-eight state welfare programs for older people existed. Also, charities and religious groups provided help to older people. These programs offered mostly food and shelter, but little cash. The Depression spread state funds to the limit and provided too little help for older people. No state had an old-age insurance program and no state had plans for one (Koff & Park, 1993).

The Depression convinced many that people could fall into poverty due to circumstances beyond their control. Healthy younger people as well as the old and disabled needed help. The Great Depression of the 1930s, Schulz (2001, p. 105) says,

> went a long way toward exposing the great political lie of American welfare debates: that poverty was generally the result of the laziness or personal unworthiness of particular individuals. . . . Millions of jobless workers and their families suffered severe financial problems because of an economic catastrophe caused by factors unrelated to their own personal activities.

At the start of 1933, for example, 12 to 14 million people in the United States had no jobs, and 19 million people (about 16 percent of the population) signed up for state relief (U.S. Department of Health, 1993). In 1937 nearly one-half of all people aged 65 and over (47.5 percent) had no income (Social Security Administration, 1997).

These conditions fed workers' discontent. Populist and socialist movements sprang up across the country. "There was even some concern," Koff and Park (1993, p. 149) say, "that the unhappy condition of workers across the country could lead to riot and anarchy." General labor strikes in San Francisco and Minneapolis, for example, created concern for the social order.

The federal government passed the Social Security Act on August 14, 1935, in part as a response to these conditions. Like the program developed in Germany, Social Security responded to social and economic distress. The Social Security Act created a social insurance program that protected workers in business and industry from unemployment and poverty in retirement. It also moved older workers out of the labor force and created jobs for the young (Myles, 1991).

Achenbaum (cited in Oriol, 1987, p. 290) says that Social Security "opened a new chapter in the history of old age in the United States by establishing the first nationwide institutional structure to assist older Americans." Former Senator Moynihan said that Social Security "put an end to what was the great terror of life—growing old and having no income and getting ill" (Rovner, 1995).

Workers paid into the program according to their earnings. Employers matched workers' payments. These payments created a pool of money that workers could draw on when they retired. Workers received benefits linked to the amounts they paid into the system. The poorest older workers got added benefits to boost their income in retirement. The act also included a plan for the federal government to pay one-half the cost of state benefits to the neediest older people.

The system began collecting payments in a reserve account in 1937 and began paying pensions to workers after 1940. The first benefits ranged from $10 to $85 per month (U.S. Department of Health, 1993). The program in those early days covered 56 percent of all workers. It did not cover the self-employed, casual laborers, or domestic workers. The program also excluded railroad workers, who had their own plan.

In 2004, the Social Security program covered 156 million workers or 96 percent of the labor force in the United States. It includes programs for the disabled, for widows and orphans, and for the very poor. Social Security today has the official title of Old-Age, Survivors, and Disability Insurance (OASDI). It forms part of a retirement income system that provides a safety net for the poorest older people and an income replacement system for middle-income retirees.

THE U.S. RETIREMENT INCOME SYSTEM TODAY

The retirement income system in the United States consists of a combination of public and private income sources (see Figure 9.1). These include government pension programs, **employment pensions**, and private savings. Think of these income sources as tiers in a pyramid. Government programs make up the broad base of the pyramid. Ninety percent of people aged 65 and over receive Social Security benefits. And Social Security forms the only income for about 20 percent of older people. Social Security on average makes up the largest part of older people's income. It makes up almost 4 percent of the total income of all older people (Social Security Administration, 2004a).

A large number of people have pensions from their employers. These private (or employment) pensions make up the next largest part of older people's income (about 20 percent of total income). Income from work makes up about another 20 percent of older people's income (Wu, 2003). And finally, a smaller number of people have assets that make up another 20 percent of their income (Federal Interagency Forum, 2000).

Gerontologists often refer to this mix of public pensions, private pensions, and work and assets as the **three-legged stool** of the retirement income system. Most people will need income from each part of the system to maintain their preretirement lifestyles.

Level One: Social Security

The U.S. government offers OASDI pension, better known as Social Security, to retired workers who have paid into the program. In 2003, workers and employers each paid 6.2 percent of the worker's covered earnings (a total of 12.4 percent of earnings) as a Social Security tax (Social Security Administration, 2003b).

Employers withhold this tax from workers' pay and submit it with their own portion to the Internal Revenue Service. This money goes into a trust fund to pay only for these programs. The government never intended for Social Security to create a large reserve fund. Benefits get paid out to people today from payments made by current workers (economists call this a **pay-as-you-go plan**).

In 2004, the Social Security Administration says, more than 47 million people got Social Security benefits. (See Figure 9.2, page 232.) They got a total of $492 billion in payments. Seventy percent

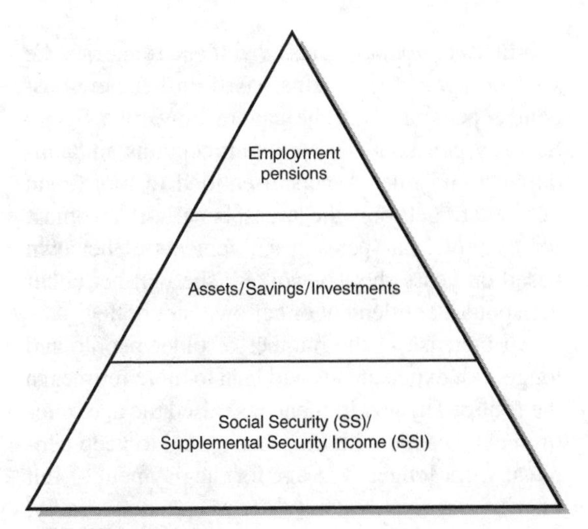

FIGURE 9.1
Three-Tiered Retirement Income System

of these payments went to retired workers and their dependents, another 14 percent went to survivors of workers, and 16 percent went to disabled workers and their dependents (Social Security Administration, 2004a). In 2003, more than 2.2 million new retirees and their dependents received Social Security payments. This makes Social Security the largest income maintenance program in the United States.

At times, money has gathered in the Social Security fund. For example, the federal government increased payroll tax rates in 1977 and 1983 to provide a three-year benefit surplus by 2015. The government increased this tax to build up reserves for the Baby Boomers from the year 2010 on. This led to Social Security surpluses of more than $1 trillion from the year 2000 on. The trust fund came to almost $1.5 trillion at the end of 2003, more than at any time in the fund's history (Social Security Administration, 2003c).

But the Social Security Administration says that $1.5 trillion cannot cover the program's future benefit obligations. Fears that the Social Security system will go bankrupt in the short run have no foundation. But, Social Security's Chief Actuary says that over the longer term—seventy-five years or more—the fund will face a massive and growing shortfall. If current payroll tax rates stay the same, the shortfall will begin in 2018 and the trust fund will be exhausted by 2043. The total shortfall over the seventy-five years (from 2004 to 2078) will amount to $3.7 trillion. The Social Security Advisory Board proposed four ways to deal with this growing problem (Social Security Administration, 2004b). We discuss these later under the topic of pension reform.

Social Security serves as a financial safety net for most retired workers and their families. The government offers this program "to replace, in part, the income that is lost to a worker and his or her family when the worker retires in old age, becomes disabled, or dies" (U.S. Department of Health, 1993, p. 7). Social Security also provides an income floor for the poorest older people. In 2003, for example, about two-thirds of people who got Social Security benefits said that these benefits made up more than one-half of their total income. Twenty percent of people who got Social Security in that year claimed it as their only source of income (Social Security Administration, 2004a).

Who Gets Social Security?

Workers who have paid into the system and were born before 1938 get full Social Security benefits at age 65. (The full-retirement age increases for those born after 1938 because people live longer today than in the past.) Workers can begin to get benefits as early as age 62, but at that age retirees get reduced benefits because they will draw a pension for more years. A person born after 1929 must have at least 40 quarters of earnings (or about ten years of work covered by Social Security) to get benefits (Social Security Administration, 2004b). The Social Security program bases benefits on a person's highest earnings of all years worked after 1950. The program indexes a person's earnings and gives greater weight to people with low incomes (Schulz, 2001). This provides the poorest people with proportionately higher benefits.

Social Security also provides a pension for workers' spouses. A woman who worked as a homemaker, for example, would have made no Social Security payments. She would have no Social Security pension of her own. Instead, she receives 50 percent of her husband's benefits. This gives the couple 150 percent of the husband's pension. A person entitled to Social Security benefits also gets Medicare (part A) hospital insurance and may buy Medicare (part B) medical insurance. A married woman who has worked only in the home gets the same Medicare benefits as her husband.

A widow can get benefits after age 60. The amount of benefit depends on the widow's age and her husband's entitlement. A widow's benefit ranges from 71.5 percent of her husband's benefit amount if she takes the pension at age 60, to 100 percent of his pension if she begins at age 65. A widow will get Medicare coverage if her husband would have. She continues to get payments even if she remarries. Or she can apply for benefits based on her new husband's pension. But she cannot draw two Social Security pensions. The program contains an "anti-duplication" rule. A person entitled to more than one benefit gets only the largest benefit. If a woman, for example, has pension entitlements of her own based on years she has worked, she will get either her spousal entitlement or her own, not both.

An increase in the number of older people and longer life expectancies will lead to more retirees in the future. The government has raised the age of retirement to cope with this change and to keep people at work longer. The age for the payment of full

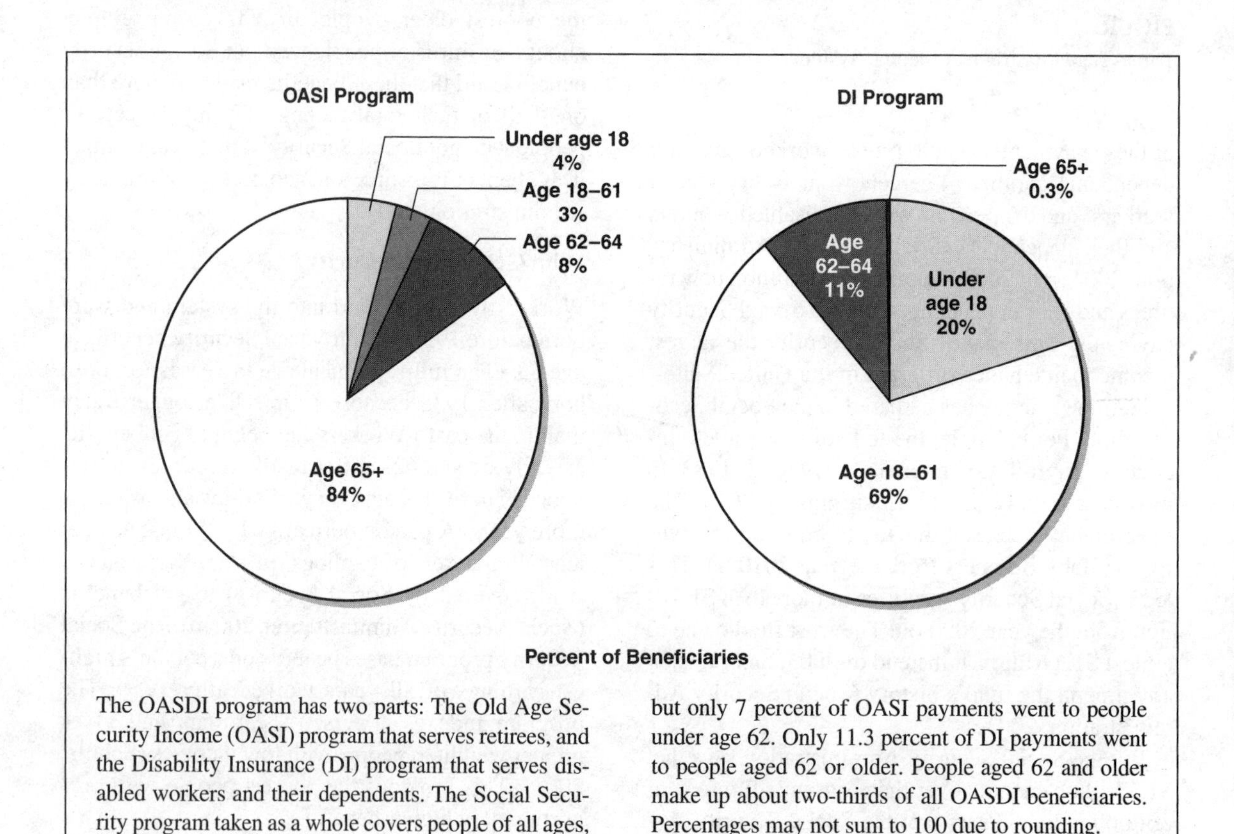

The OASDI program has two parts: The Old Age Security Income (OASI) program that serves retirees, and the Disability Insurance (DI) program that serves disabled workers and their dependents. The Social Security program taken as a whole covers people of all ages, but only 7 percent of OASI payments went to people under age 62. Only 11.3 percent of DI payments went to people aged 62 or older. People aged 62 and older make up about two-thirds of all OASDI beneficiaries. Percentages may not sum to 100 due to rounding.

FIGURE 9.2
OASDI Beneficiaries, 2004

Source: Social Security Administration. (2004). Office of Policy. Office of Research, Evaluation and Statistics. *Fast Facts and Figures About Social Security*, p. 17. Retrieved January 10, 2005, *www.ssa.gov/policy/docs/chartbooks/fast_facts/2003/ff2003.pdf.*

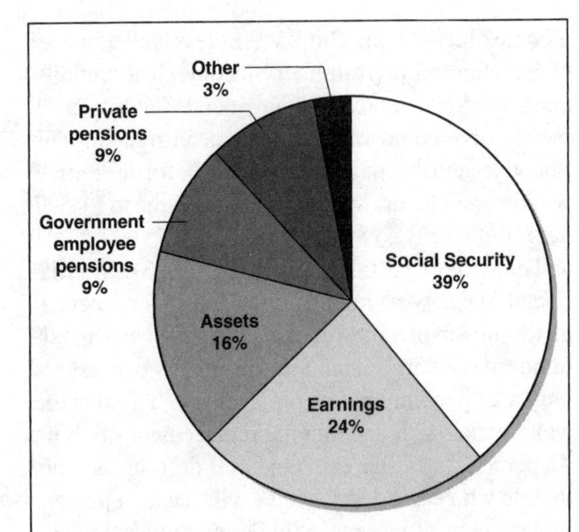

These proportions have remained largely unchanged over the past decade. Compared with 1994, older people now get a larger share of their income from earnings (24 percent in 2001 compared with 17 percent in 1994). During this same time, the share of income from assets decreased (from 21 percent in 1994 to 16 percent today). This reflects the tendency for many workers to continue working after age 65. Some do this because they enjoy their work. Many people work past the normal retirement age because they need the money.

Social Security still makes up the largest share of older people's incomes. Many older people rely on national pension programs to support themselves. Private pensions accounted for only 9 percent of older people's incomes in 2001. But this share tripled from 3 percent in 1962.

FIGURE 9.3

Income Sources of People Aged 65 and over, 2001

Source: Social Security Administration. (2004). Office of Policy. Office of Research, Evaluation and Statistics. *Fast Facts and Figures About Social Security,* p. 6. Retrieved January 10, 2005, *www.ssa.gov/policy/docs/chartbooks/fast_facts/2003/ff2003.pdf.*

Social Security benefits will start to increase in the year 2003 and will reach age 67 in 2027 (Social Security Administration, 2004b). The government also began taxing Social Security benefits in 1984 to reduce the cost of the program. From that year onward, a couple or single person paid tax on their adjusted gross income over a certain amount. The higher a person's total income, the more they pay back to the Social Security system.

The Social Security program accounts for the sharp decrease in poverty rates for older people since the 1950s. Social Security adjusted benefits to reflect increases in the consumer price index. This helped protect retirees' incomes from inflation. But recent changes in the law have put the brakes on Social Security increases. And many older people will feel financially pressed by rising costs. Also, people who did not work, who had low-paying jobs, or who did not pay into the system (e.g., older immigrants) get little or no Social Security benefits. These people need further assistance to bring them at least near the poverty line. (See Figure 9.3.)

Supplemental Security Income

Social scientists use two definitions of poverty: **relative deprivation** and **absolute deprivation.** Relative deprivation refers to people's feelings of poverty in relation to people like themselves.

Absolute deprivation refers to the minimal income needed to survive—to buy food, clothing, shelter, and health care. People who lack this minimum income are defined as poor. The U.S. government sets poverty levels each year based on this minimum. Discussions of poverty in the United States usually refer to a standard of absolute deprivation. The U.S. government in 2001 set a yearly income of $8,494 as the poverty threshhold for an aged individual. The threshhold for families with a head over the age of 65 in that year came to $10,715 (Social Security Administration, 2003a).

Congress approved the **Supplemental Security Income (SSI)** program in 1972 to help older people and others in need, whose incomes fall below the official poverty threshhold. In 2002, 34.6 million people in the United States had income that fell below the official poverty threshhold. This came to 12.1 percent of the population (Proctor & Dalaker, 2003).

Congress kept this program separate from Social Security. People pay into Social Security and it has its own trust fund, but SSI gets paid out of general revenues. SSI provides a safety net to elderly, blind, and disabled people with little or no income. It offers direct and uniform payments to people who meet the program's requirements. The program guarantees an income at 75 percent to 90 percent of the poverty level. This is the largest cash assistance program in the United States for older people in need. Most states supplement the SSI payments. About one-fifth of SSI recipients get a state supplement (Health and Human Services, 2001).

To receive SSI benefits, a person must have an income that falls below the Federal maximum SSI benefit level—$564 per month for an individual and $846 per month for a married couple in 2004. If single, a person must have resources or assets less than $2,000 ($3,000 for a couple). Assets include property but exclude the home a person lives in, a car worth up to $4,500, food stamps, life insurance (up to $1,500), and personal household goods.

A person can earn up to $20 a month from any source without loss of SSI benefits (sources include Social Security, pensions, donations of food and clothing). The program also allows a person to earn $65 per month from work without loss of benefits. After the $20 basic deduction and the first $65 from work income, a person loses 50 cents of SSI for every dollar earned (Schulz, 2001). Fifty-eight percent of SSI recipients in 2002 also got Social Security payments (Social Security Administration, 2003a; 2003b). Many of these people will lose some of their SSI benefits because their Social Security payment comes to more than $20 per month.

The federal government made SSI payments to about 6 million older people in 2002. Overall, women made up 58 percent of people who got benefits. The proportion of older people who get SSI has declined from 60 percent of all SSI recipients in 1974 to 35 percent at the end of 1993, to 29 percent at the end of 2003. This reflects better incomes from Social Security for the poorest older people (Social Security Administration, 2003a).

Level Two: Employment Pensions

The Social Security program has worked well to keep many older people out of poverty. It provides a safety net for the disabled, widowed, and low-income older person. But it works less well as a way of maintaining preretirement income. The middle-class worker cannot rely on Social Security as a means of income replacement in retirement. The Social Security payment in 2004 for a retired worker aged 62 or over and a spouse came to $1,527 per month, only $18,324 per year.

The U.S. Department of Health (1993) says that Social Security payments in the future for a person in the upper-income bracket, who paid the maximum amount in Social Security taxes, can expect only a 27 percent income replacement. The average wage earner will see income replacement of about 41 percent to buffer this potential drop in income. People who earned low wages will see a 55 percent replacement of income. Middle- and upper-income people cannot maintain their preretirement life-styles on Social Security benefits alone. Private pensions supplement Social Security and help middle-income and upper-income earners maintain their life-styles.

Private pension coverage grew after World War II and peaked in the 1980s at 46 percent of employees in a private pension plan. This proportion dropped to 43 percent by the 1990s (EBRI, 2004a). About one-half of all retirees aged 55 and older now get a pension either from their own or from a spouse's employer (EBRI, 2004a). Schulz (1988) says that private pension plans often guarantee a 25 percent replacement of income (higher in industries such as manufacturing). This applies to people with a long service record. In the best case, private pensions and Social Security together provide between 50 and 80 percent of workers' preretirement income. Schulz (1988) cautions that these figures express ideal conditions. Many people will get less than these replacement rates.

The Employee Retirement Income Security Act (ERISA) of 1974 regulates pension plans to protect workers. ERISA sets standard rules for participation in pension plans and rules for the eligibility of workers. Schulz (2001, p. 253, emphasis in the original) says that ERISA's principal focus "*was on expanding the supervision and regulation of private plans.*" For example, ERISA ensures that **vesting** of pension benefits takes place. Vesting means that

BOX 9.1
BASIC PRINCIPLES OF THE SOCIAL SECURITY PROGRAM

The U.S. Department of Health lists five principles of the Social Security program:

1. **Work-related benefits.** Workers pay into the program and receive benefits according to the amount paid in. The higher the income, the greater the amount received. The program weights benefits to help poorer workers.
2. **No means test.** A worker earns credits toward Social Security benefits and receives benefits regardless of other income, pensions, or savings. The program expects workers to save for retirement through other sources such as private pensions. A retirement test does exist that reduces benefits for people with incomes over a certain amount.
3. **Contributory.** A payroll tax for Social Security pays for benefits and at times has built a reserve fund. Payment into the program creates a commitment from workers to the Social Security system.
4. **Compulsory coverage.** Workers (with only a few exceptions) must pay into the program. This spreads the risk of social insurance among the workforce. It also means that workers and their families will have a guaranteed base income in retirement.
5. **Rights defined in law.** The law guarantees the right to Social Security for a worker who has paid into the system. A person may appeal a decision through the courts if necessary.

These principles ensure that nearly all workers and their families in the United States will have at least a basic income in retirement. The Social Security program has removed the threat of poverty from millions of older Americans. The Social Security Administration says that Social Security kept two-fifths of older people out of poverty in 1992. The Administration estimates that without Social Security the poverty rate for older families would have been 52 percent (compared with 14 percent) in that year.

Sources: From Social Security Programs in the United States, U.S. Department of Health and Human Services, Social Security Administration, Office of Research and Statistics, 1993, Washington, DC: U.S. Government Printing Office; Fast Facts and Figures About Social Security, U.S. Department of Health and Human Services, Social Security Administration, Office of Research and Statistics, 1994, Washington, DC: U.S. Government Printing Office.

workers will get all or part of their earned benefit from a company when they leave. They will get this benefit even if they have moved to a different company. Full vesting now takes place after five years for most covered workers (Schulz, 2001). ERISA also guarantees workers the right to choose a joint and survivor option, which provides a pension for a spouse after a worker dies.

Vesting does not guarantee a good pension for workers who change jobs. For example, the value of vested money left in a plan does not increase if a plan improves benefits for continuing workers. Also, some companies link a pension to the person's salary. If a person leaves this type of firm, their benefits will reflect only the salary they had when they left the company. They will have a smaller pension than someone who has stayed with the company until retirement. Inflation will erode the value of this vested pension.

Portability helps solve this problem. Portability allows a person to transfer the money value of their vested pension to another plan (Schulz, 2001). This option requires complex administration. For this reason, few portable pension plans exist. But some multiemployer plans do offer portability. A plan for U.S. university professors, for example, pools pension payments from professors across the country into a single fund. This allows professors to move from one school to another throughout their careers without pension loss.

Schulz (2001) says that the high cost of running pension plans and reporting on them has led some employers to cancel them. Also, many companies now opt for **defined contribution plans** rather than

defined benefit plans. Defined benefit plans promise a set amount to workers when they retire. These plans often base this figure on a person's salary (often the highest three or five years) and their number of years of service. Defined contribution plans say how much workers have to pay into the plan, but they do not guarantee a specific return. The return depends on the investments the plan has made with the money paid in. This type of plan means more risk for the worker.

One-half of all workers in the United States belong to a defined benefit plan. These plans serve both the employee and large employers. These plans encourage workers to stay with one employer and this leads to workforce stability. They also entail little risk for workers and provide workers with a clear picture of their future pension payments.

Many new plans opt for the defined contribution option. These plans appeal to small businesses because they can better predict future pension costs. Mayer (1993) says that three-quarters of new pension plans that start up each year are defined contribution plans.

Pension plans for workers in federal and state government jobs (also the military) often have cost of living increases built in. These plans adjust to inflation automatically, but place caps on the amount of increase. Some private companies adjust pensions periodically. But most private sector pensions (especially defined contribution pensions) drop in value over the years.

Schulz says, "almost no employer-sponsored plan in the private sector *automatically* adjusts the pensions being paid in retirement for increases in the cost of living" (2001, p. 263, emphasis in the original). He reports that during the high inflation period of 1983 through 1988, for example, private pensions increased by only 10 percent of the inflation rate. People with defined contribution plans risk the greatest loss of income due to inflation (Schulz, 2001).

Workers in the future may also get income from Individual Retirement Accounts (IRAs). These accounts allow people without a pension plan to save a defined amount of money tax free each year. The tax-deductible amount came to $3,000 a year in 2004 (and this amount will increase gradually over time). Workers with pension plans can also set up IRAs. They do not get a tax deduction for the amount they put in, but their money gains tax-free interest until they draw it out.

The Employee Benefits Research Institute reports that in 2002 IRA accounts held $2.4 trillion (2004a). IRA accounts encourage personal savings for retirement and give workers control over a part of their retirement income. Lower-income earners make less use of this program than people with higher incomes. This means that a large part of the deferred taxes on IRAs go to support the retirement savings of people with high incomes. For this reason some people argue against this type of program.

Longer life for more workers in the future may mean more years of decreasing pension value due to inflation. Combine this with the choice of early retirement (more years drawing a pension) and some people with private pensions will find that they slip into poverty as they age. (See Figures 9.4 and 9.5.)

Level Three: Personal Assets and Other Income

Financial assets and earnings from work make up the third largest source of income for older people. Schulz (2001) cautions that many people underreport their income and liquid assets (e.g., interest revenue). People with higher incomes tend to underreport the most. This makes it hard to assess the exact incomes of older people from assets and earnings.

Fifty-eight percent of older people claimed some asset income in 2001 (Administration on Aging, 2003). Older people have three major sources of asset income: (1) savings and checking accounts, (2) financial investments (stocks and bonds), and (3) other investments such as bank deposits, art, or rare collections. Asset income makes up about 20 percent of older peoples' incomes.

Twenty-two percent of older people report earnings as part of their total income. Earnings provide older people with another 20 percent of their income (Administration on Aging, 2003), about the same proportion they receive from private pensions (Wu, 2003).

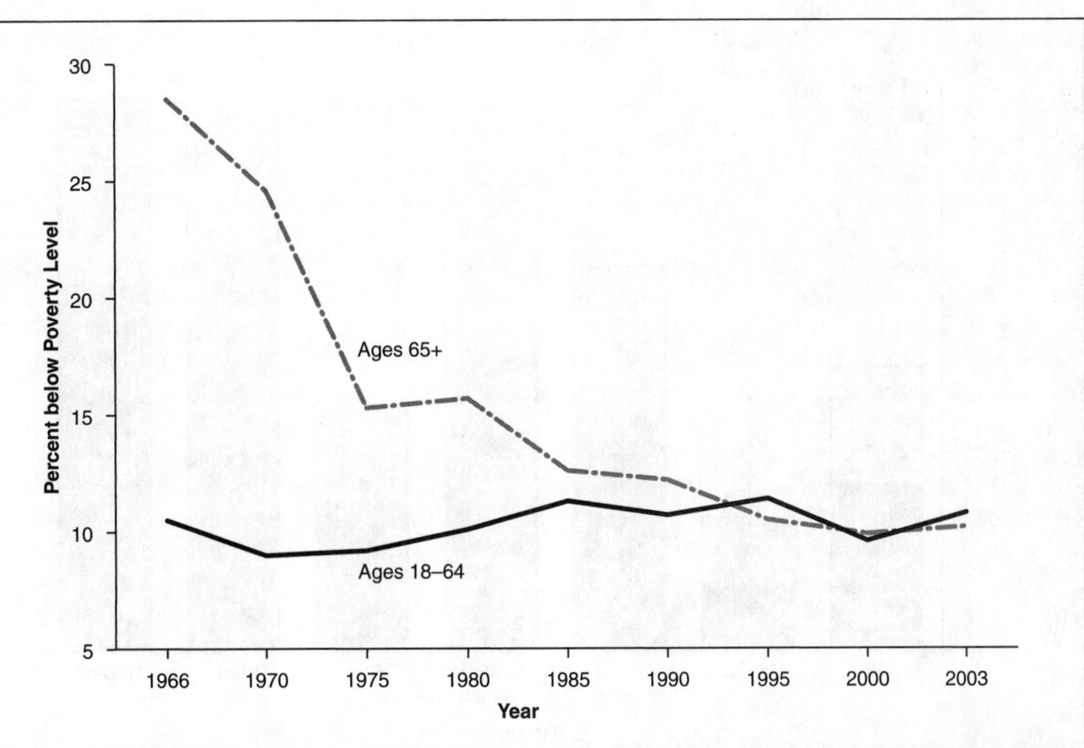

The poverty rate decreased for the younger adult population through the mid-1970s in the United States. It then rose again by 2003 to the same level as the mid-1960s. The poverty rate decreased dramatically for older people from 1966 to the mid-1970s. It then continued to decline to 2003. At that point, the poverty rate had dropped by almost two-thirds from its 1966 level. The rate of poverty among older people about equals that for younger adults today.

This chart excludes the poverty rate for children (under 18 years). That rate came to 17.6 percent in 2003. This high rate of poverty among children raises the nonelderly poverty rate. This gives older people a significantly lower poverty rate than children and a lower rate than the younger population as a whole. Increased Social Security benefits largely account for the decrease in poverty among older people.

FIGURE 9.4

U.S. Poverty Rates

Source: U.S. Census Bureau. (2003). Historical poverty tables. Based on Current Population Survey, Annual Social and Economic Supplements. Poverty and Health Statistics Branch/HHES Division, U.S. Census Bureau, U.S. Department of Commerce, Washington, DC. Retrieved January 10, 2005, *www.census.gov/hhes/poverty/histpov/hstpov3.html*

Younger old people tend to have the most income from earnings. Many younger old people (under age 75) still work part-time. Older old people tend to rely on public pension programs for their income. Older people also have other assets they cannot quickly convert to cash. These provide no income but add to older people's total wealth. For example, much of older people's net worth reflects home ownership. Nearly one-half (49.8 percent) of the total net worth of older households comes from owning a home (Orzechowski & Sepielli, 2003). Older people also get tax breaks on income and other in-kind government transfers (like Medicare benefits). These resources help raise older people's incomes.

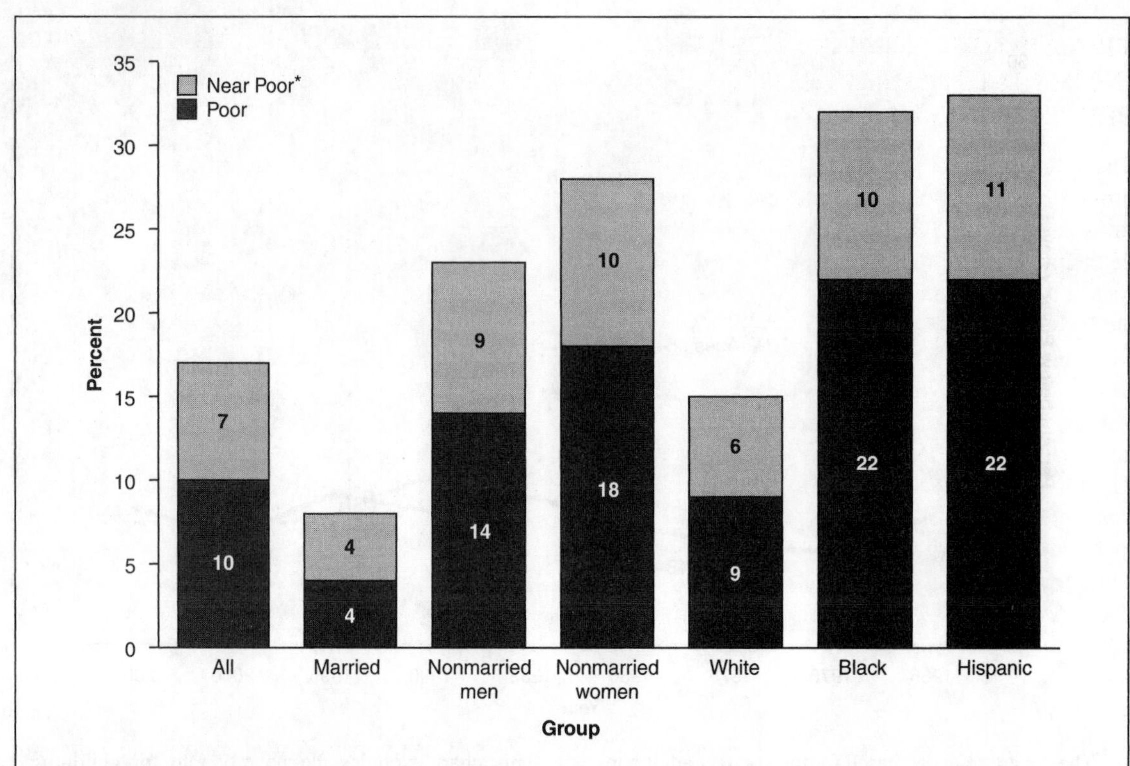

Nonmarried women and minority group members run the greatest risk of living in poverty or near the poverty line. Their poverty and near poverty rates range from 28 to 33 percent. This means that roughly one in three unmarried women and minority group members live in or near poverty. These figures stand in contrast to the 17 percent poverty and near poverty rate for all older people. These figures show that pockets of poverty exist even though the overall poverty rate for older people has decreased. These figures also show the value of looking at near poverty rates. The addition of the near poor to poverty figures shows that a large group of older people live on very low incomes.

*The near poor group lives between the poverty line and 125 percent of the poverty line.

FIGURE 9.5

Income of the Aged Population: Poverty and Near Poverty Rates, 2001

Source: Social Security Administration. (2004). Office of Policy. Office of Research, Evaluation and Statistics. *Fast Facts and Figures About Social Security*, p. 8. Retrieved January 10, 2005, *www.ssa.gov/policy/docs/chartbooks/fast_facts/2003/ff2003.pdf.*

With home equity taken aside, in 2000 the group aged 55 to 64 has the highest net worth in the country ($32,304) followed by the group aged 65 and over ($27,588) (Orzechowski & Sepielli, 2003). This makes sense because older people (55 and over), compared with younger people, have had more time to accumulate wealth and assets. The age group 65 and over, compared with younger age groups, had the highest proportion of their net worth (excluding home ownership) in stocks and mutual fund shares. The group aged 70 to 74 has the highest net worth among all age groups when the figures take home equity into account. These averages, however, hide large differences in net worth within the older population. Many old people have limited financial resources.

THE IMPACT OF THE RETIREMENT INCOME SYSTEM ON OLDER PEOPLE'S INCOMES

The 1960s and early 1970s saw the greatest improvements in income for older people. Poverty rates for older people dropped by one-half from 28.5 percent in 1966 to 14.6 percent in 1974. Families with heads aged 65 or over saw a one-third increase in their incomes during this time (from $14,000 to $19,000). What accounts for this improvement in older people's finances?

First, new retirees had paid into Social Security and pension plans longer than retirees in the past. These retirees get better benefits than older retired workers. Second, Congress added a cost of living increase to Social Security between 1968 and 1971. This increased benefits by 43 percent. Prices during this time rose only 27 percent. Third, in 1972 the government added another 20 percent increase to Social Security benefits.

Older people's finances continued to improve during the late 1970s and 1980s. The poverty rate for older people dropped from 35 percent in 1959 to 10.2 percent in 2000. In 2001 older people had a poverty rate only slightly higher than all other age groups (10.2 percent compared with 9.4 percent) (Dalaker, 2001). Census data also show that older people, compared with people aged 18 to 64, have a smaller proportion of their population deep in poverty (2.2 percent compared with 4 percent) deep in poverty (Dalaker, 2001). Clearly, older people's incomes showed a marked improvement from 1960 to the present.

Still, retirement almost always leads to long-term decline in income, though not necessarily to poverty. Even among relatively well-off older people, Schulz (2001, p. 42) says, "many [find] themselves faced with a sharp decline in income relative to their preretirement levels and a consequent decline in their living standards." Schulz (2001) reports that in retirement a one-worker couple would need between 68 and 82 percent of their preretirement income to maintain their standard of living. And "only 6 percent to 8 percent of new retired workers replaced at least two-thirds of their *highest* earnings" (Schulz, 2001, p. 152, emphasis in the original). Single people, minority group members, and women do less well. A look at inequality in later life will show the impact of retirement on people with different social histories.

INEQUALITY IN LATER LIFE

Overall, older people have better incomes today than in the past. Public pensions, private pensions, cash and noncash assets have all improved for most older people.

Better public pensions account for much of the income security among the older population today. They ensure a good old age for more people than ever before. Still, pockets of poverty exist within the older population. Some groups within the older population have much lower incomes than others. Older people have different work histories and different amounts of past income. They also have different backgrounds that shaped their past and influence their present incomes.

The U.S. Census reports, for example, that almost 16.9 percent of older people had incomes between the poverty level and 1.25 times the poverty level. This is somewhat higher than the proportion of adults aged 18 to 64 in this near poverty category (13.3 percent) (Dalaker, 2001). This means that older people will more likely live near or slightly above the poverty line than the rest of the adult population. Dalaker (2001, p. 10) says that "these differences indicate that people aged 65 and over were more highly concentrated just above the poverty level than they were among the extremely poor."

Reports on income and assets for the total older population hide differences within the older age group. For example, in 2000, the richest fifth of the older population had a median net worth more than ten times that of the poorest fifth. But many older people who have a high net worth have little cash. An increase in the value of an older person's home, for example, will increase their net worth, but they still have little money to spend. They live house rich and cash poor. If the figures exclude home equity, then the richest fifth has a median net worth of almost one hundred times the poorest fifth ($328,432 versus $3,500) (Orzechowski & Sepielli, 2003).

Some groups in American society run a greater risk of poverty than others. Women, compared with men, for example, show higher rates of poverty at every age. But, the greatest disparity between men and women shows up in later life. Older women, compared with older men, had almost twice the rate of poverty (12.4 percent compared with 7.0 percent) (Spraggins, 2003). The oldest old have the lowest incomes of any older people. People with more than one characteristic (e.g., minority women) have an increased chance of poverty. Most poor older people will live in poverty for the rest of their lives.

The economic conditions of older people differ by age, gender, marital status, and race. A closer look at these differences gives a better understanding of how income varies within the older population.

Age Differences and Income

The older the person, the greater the chance of a low income. In 2003, families headed by a person aged 65 or over had a median income of $23,787, about one-half the median income of all households ($50,171) (DeNavas-Walt, Proctor, & Mills, 2004). But in 2003 the older old population, families with heads aged 75 or over, had median incomes of only $19,470, less than one-half the income of people aged 60 to 64 ($41,541), and only about eighty percent of the income of all older people ($23,787) (Bureau of Labor Statistics, 2003).

People aged 75 and over in 2001 had a poverty rate of 11.2 percent. This came to about 20 percent higher than the rate for people aged 65 to 74 (9.2 percent). People aged 75 and over also had a higher proportion of near poor than the 65- to 74-age group (18.8 percent compared with 14.7 percent) (AARP, 2001). These figures show improvement in the rate of poverty among all older people and among the older old population. Still, the figures show that poverty rates increase with age.

Poverty figures do not include people who live in institutions or with other relatives. These *hidden poor* individuals, if counted, would increase the poverty rate of older people. Schulz (2001, p. 17) says that "all evidence to date shows this group (aged 75 to 80 and older) to be economically less well-off than the younger aged." The young-old and old-old also spend their incomes in different ways. The young-old entered adulthood after World War II and lived more affluent life-styles. Compared with the oldest old, for example, the young-old spend more money on travel and restaurant food. This in part reflects their better health, but it also reflects their greater resources. The young-old entered old age with better pensions and have had fewer years to see their pensions decline in value. Also, some new retirees work past the age of 65 to add to their incomes.

Very old people grew up during the Depression and World War II. They have fewer resources than the young-old. Widowhood, poor pensions in the past, and the declining value of fixed pension payments leave the oldest old to rely mostly on Social Security. Very few of them can earn money to raise their incomes. Compared with the young-old, the oldest old spend more money on health care. These expenses can eat up a large share of a very old person's income and savings. This makes the oldest old vulnerable to cuts in public pension plans and decreases in Medicare or Medicaid benefits.

This woman retiree in Amsterdam, New York, delivers a newspaper on her afternoon paper route. She uses the money she earns to meet her expenses.

Gender and Income

A look at income by gender shows that older women have lower incomes than older men. Wu (2003) reports that older women in 2001 had a median income only 57 percent that of older men. And they had a lower income at every age after age 65. Also, women make up 60 percent of the older population, but make up 70 percent of older people in poverty (International Longevity Center, 2003). In 2003, older women had a poverty rate of 12.4 percent. Older men in that year had a rate of 7.0 percent (40 percent of the rate for women) (Spraggins, 2003; Wu, 2003). And few older women (8.6 percent) work outside the home.

Those who did work, often had nontraditional work arrangements—part-time or temporary help. Generally, these jobs offer low pay and no benefits (Muller et al., 2002). Stone (1989) calls this the "feminization of poverty" among older people. Women also report different sources of income than men. A greater proportion of women (44 percent), compared with men (28.7 percent), relied on Social Security for 90 percent or more of their income (Wu, 2003). Fifteen percent of women got spousal benefits and 24 percent got adult survivor benefits.

More men than women (83 to 54 percent) got retired worker benefits (U.S. Department of Health, 1994). Men also got larger Social Security pensions than women. These figures point to past inequities between men and women and their different work histories. Many older women of today worked as homemakers. They relied on their husbands' incomes during their middle years and now they rely on their husbands' pensions in old age. Women whose husbands had no private pension, widows who no longer receive a spousal private pension, women with small spousal pensions, and the oldest women, whose pensions or savings have lost value with time, have the lowest incomes and often find themselves in poverty. Many of these women face poverty for the first time in old age.

Older women often have little experience coping with the financial problems they face. They may also have little knowledge of the social welfare system and the programs that might help them. Some women in poverty, for example, could qualify for SSI benefits. But, often these benefits go unclaimed because people do not know about the program.

This pattern has begun to change as more women work outside the home. In 1998, for example, 51.2 percent of women aged 55 to 64 worked in the labor force, about double the 1930 rate (Muller et al., 2002; Ferber, 1993; Rayman, Allshouse, & Allen, 1993). Likewise more women than ever before claim benefits from their own earnings as well as their husbands' (U.S. Department of Health, 1994). More women in the future will have their own pensions and Social Security benefits. They will have worked for many years and will have better education than women in the past. This will lead to better paying jobs and improved incomes for older women.

More women in the workforce may narrow the income gap between men and women in old age in the future, but this gap will probably still exist. At least four conditions will lead to lower retirement incomes for women in the future.

First, Social Security bases its benefits on yearly earnings over thirty-five years. This suits men who spend all their adult years in the labor force. But women often have shorter work careers than men. In 1999, for example, of people who got pensions for the first time, women had thirty-two years of paid work. Men had forty-four years of paid work (International Longevity Center, 2003).

Many women take time out of the labor force to care for their families. Social Security averages these zero income years into a woman's lifetime earnings to arrive at thirty-five years of earnings. This will give her lower average earnings than if she had worked for thirty-five years or more. Compared with a typical man in the labor force, a woman with these lower earnings will get a smaller pension. Women who care for their families now and in the future will face this same inequity. A projection to the year 2010 found that only 22 percent of women aged 62 to 65 in that year would have at least thirty-five years of work. Even by the year 2030 only one-third of women aged 62 to 69 would have a complete work record (Fierst & Campbell, 1988).

Chen (2001) notes that women who rely on their husbands' pensions may also face problems. Some of these pension plans stop payments on the death of the retiree. And even in cases where the pension continues, it loses buying power over time.

Second, women tend to work part-time and in small businesses. These jobs rarely provide pension plans. Also, a woman who enters and leaves the workforce due to family care will not work long enough to accumulate a large private pension. Women who start their own businesses (a growing trend) seldom have pension plans. This means a woman can work for a lifetime and still have little or no private pension coverage of her own.

Third, lower pension benefits for retired women reflect the fact that women work in the lowest paying jobs. This leads to less income, lower Social Security payments, and lower benefits in retirement. Rayman and her colleagues (1993, p. 137) say that "contrary to the popular myth, the majority of women, young and old, continue to work in traditionally female occupations and receive low earnings."

These writers go on to say that almost three-fifths of working women work in three types of jobs: sales, service, and clerical. Women in service sector jobs often find they have little or no pension or health benefits. Only 27.8 percent of women worked in managerial or professional jobs. Of this group, the majority (56 percent) worked in lower paying professions as teachers or registered nurses. They may get pensions, but pensions based on relatively low pay.

Fourth, discrimination leads to lower pension benefits for women. Rayman and her colleagues (1993) report on a National Academy of Science panel that studied the earnings gap between men and women. The panel traced only one-half of the earnings gap to characteristics of workers (such as differences in education or time out of the labor force) (U.S. Department of Labor, 1982). Instead, the study found that the income gap is due to "sex discrimination, compounded for older women and women of color by race and age discrimination" (Rayman, Allshouse, & Allen, 1993, p. 143).

Perkins (1993) agrees. She sorted out the effects of class, race, gender, and age to explain poverty among women in later life. She found that job segregation by sex and discrimination best explained women's low pay. Employers discriminate in hiring, placement, and promotions.

Perkins' (1993) work challenges other theories of low pay for women, like the human capital theory. This theory says that women lose their skills when they stay home to raise children. For this reason, the theory says, they get lower pay. Perkins (1993) compared African American and white women. She found that African American women spend less time than white women out of the workforce raising children, but they still get low pay due to discrimination at work. Perkins (1993) sees poverty in later life as the outcome of unfair practices in the workplace throughout a woman's career.

Recent work supports this view. In the 1960s, for example, women earned only about 60 percent as much as men. The gap between incomes for men and women has begun to close as more women work full-time in the labor force. But an income gap based on gender still exists. In 2000, women who

A poor older woman reads a grocery store flyer.

"If we take a late retirement and an early death, we'll just squeak by."

worked full-time all year had a median income of $28,823. Men in that year earned $39,020 (International Longevity Center, 2003).

The effects of past inequality will affect the current generation of older people. And the continuing income gap will affect younger women when they reach old age. Malveaux (1993, p. 168) says that "the economic status of older women is a map or mirror of their past lives, reflecting their education, employment history, and marital status. The economic problems that older women face are extensions of the problems and choices they faced earlier in their lives."

Marital Status and Income

Like married people of all ages, older married couples have lower rates of poverty and better incomes than nonmarried people. Husband and wife families had a median income in 2001 of $34,558. In that same year single women aged 65 and over who live alone had a median income of $17,232, single men in this age group who live alone had an average income of $30,900 (Wu, 2003).

These figures show, once again, the income gap between single men and women. They also show the negative effect of widowhood on an older woman's income. Some private pension plans stop when the former employee dies. A widow with only Social Security will get only 71.5 percent of her husband's pension benefits if his benefits began at age 60. Many of these older women live alone. And as the figures show, the median income of older women who live alone came to less than one-half the income of older husband and wife families (Wu, 2003).

Couples have higher incomes than an unmarried person for at least three reasons. First, some couples benefit from having had two incomes for all or part of their married life. This allowed for more savings and in some cases two pensions. Second, a couple can get the highest earner's Social Security benefits. The spouse of the pensioner then gets 50 percent of that benefit as a spousal pension. Third, widows make up a large proportion of single people. They often experience a decrease in income after a spouse's death (Schulz, 2001).

Couples and single older people will have better incomes in the future due to Social Security and better private pension plans today. But differences due to marital status will still exist. In part, this will occur because the married group includes younger old people. They will enter old age with more resources, and some will work in their early retirement years. Older unmarried people will include very old, widowed women who live alone. These women will rely on public sources of income in the future. These sources have improved in recent years but still provide relatively low benefits. (See Figure 9.6.)

Minority Status and Income

Minority older people have lower incomes than non-Hispanic whites. African American and Hispanic men aged 65 and over had median incomes roughly two-thirds that of older non-Hispanic whites. Older African American women had a median income almost the same as older non-Hispanic white women. Hispanic older women had a median income about three-quarters that of older non-Hispanic whites. But women in each group had a median income significantly lower than their male counterparts (Wu, 2003). Wong (2002) says that migration patterns (how long a person has lived in

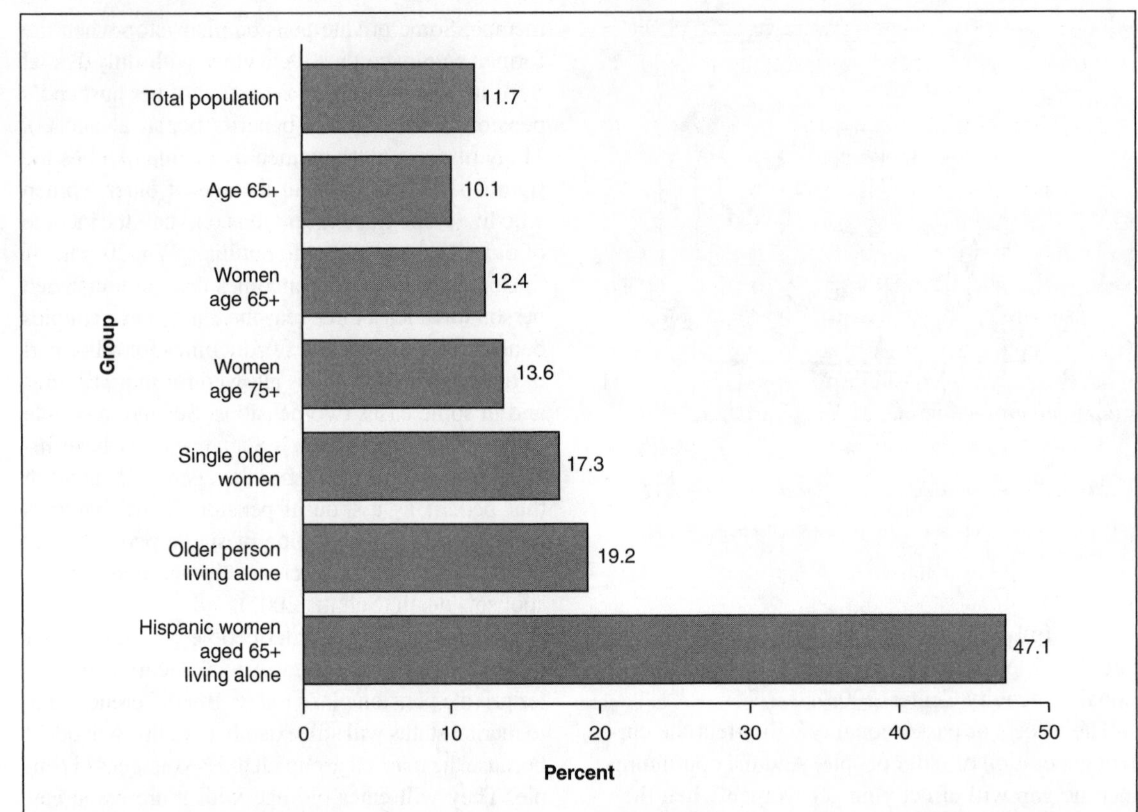

This chart shows that women have higher than average poverty rates in old age. But women with certain characteristics (e.g., living alone) have even higher poverty rates. These characteristics accumulate to create multiple jeopardy for some people. Wu (2003) says that older women had a higher poverty rate (12.4%) than older men (7.7%) in 2002. Older persons living alone were much more likely to be poor (19.2%) than were older persons living with families (6.0%). The highest poverty rates (47.1%) were experienced by older Hispanic women who lived alone.

FIGURE 9.6

Poverty Rates among Selected Vulnerable Groups, Percent of Population in Poverty

Sources: Wu, K. (2003). Income and poverty of older Americans in 2001: A chartbook. Washington, DC: American Association of Retired Persons. Retrieved September 6, 2004, *http://research.aarp.org/econ/ip_cb2001.pdf*; Administration on Aging. (2003). A profile of older Americans: 2003, Washington, DC: U.S. Department of Health and Human Services. Retrieved September 6, 2004, *www.aoa.gov/prof/Statistics/profile/2003/2003profile.pdf*; Anzick, M. A., & Weaver, D. A. (2001). *Reducing poverty among elderly women.* ORES Working Paper Series Number 87. Division of Economic Research. Washington, DC: Social Security Administration. Retrieved September 11, 2004, *www.ssa.gov/policy/docs/workingpapers/wp87.pdf.*

the United States) affect the incomes of Mexican older migrants. She found that those who had lived in the United States longest had the highest individual and household incomes (although they had lower health care coverage).

The Women's Institute for a Secure Retirement (2000) reports that "only 15 percent of older black women and 8 percent of Hispanic older women received [private] pension income in 2000." These figures reflect income inequalities that minority members face throughout life. Honig (1999) reports that the median household income for whites of all ages came to ten times that of African Americans or Hispanics. And the Women's Institute for a Secure Retirement (2000) says that in 2000 only "38 percent of black women, 26 percent of Hispanic women and 38 percent of Asian/Pacific Islander women [were] covered by any sort of pension in the workplace."

The similarity of pension income among these groups of minority older women points to their reliance on Social Security pensions in later life. Wu (2003) reports that 46.9 percent of older Hispanic and 41 percent of older African American Social Security recipients got all of their income from Social Security (compared with 19.6 percent of older white people). Social Security provides minority older people with a basic income and tends to level racial and ethnic income differences in later life.

Minority members bear a higher burden of poverty in old age than do whites. African American and Hispanic older people in 2001 had a poverty rate of 22.1 percent and 21.6 percent, respectively, more than two and a half times the non-Hispanic white rate of 8.1 percent (Wu, 2003). Older minority women who live alone have more than three times the poverty rate of those who live with families. Older Hispanic women who live alone face the highest rates (47.1 percent) (Administration on Aging, 2003). Chapter 7 gives more detail on inequalities in later life due to race and ethnicity.

The U.S. government reports data on poverty rates in later life for African Americans, whites, and Hispanics, but few data exist on Asian older people. Asians have higher median incomes than whites. And they have a poverty rate in old age about the same as non-Hispanic whites (about 10 percent and 8 percent, respectively) (Proctor & Dalaker, 2003). But studies report high poverty rates among some groups within the Asian community.

Bergman (1991), for example, says that Vietnamese Americans may have a poverty rate of 36 percent, and Filipino Americans may have a poverty rate of 25 percent. These high rates will translate into low incomes in later life. Also, Malveaux (1993) says, older Asian women tend to outlive their husbands. These widows often have little education and speak little English. They have trouble applying for programs such as SSI, and few of them have private pensions. This puts them at risk of poverty.

Older African American women worked a double employment ghetto. They worked in typically female jobs and in typically African American female jobs (Women's Institute, 2002). These jobs included dietician, file clerk, lab technician, and cleaning and health service worker. These jobs pay low wages and offer poor pension benefits.

The income gap between older African American and white women may decrease in the future. African American women have begun to take on jobs in administration and management. These jobs offer pension plans and health insurance. Still, discrimination exists and an income gap between older African American and white women will probably remain (Rayman, Allshouse, & Allen, 1993).

A study by the Administration on Aging (2003) summarizes the effect of gender, race, and ethnicity on income in later life. The study found that "older women had a higher poverty rate (12.4 percent) than older men (7.7 percent) in 2002. Older persons living alone were much more likely to be poor (19.2 percent) than were older persons living with families (6.0 percent). The highest poverty rates (47.1 percent) were experienced by older Hispanic women who lived alone." A person with more than one of these characteristics faces a high risk of poverty. These facts and others call for pension reform that focuses on the income needs of poorer older people. (Refer to Figure 9.7.)

PENSION REFORM

"The key to reducing poverty in old age," gerontologist Beth Hess said, "is to eliminate income disabilities at earlier life stages. If *affirmative action* for women, blacks, and Hispanics ensured equal opportunities for education, jobs, and promotions throughout their lives, they would enter old age with a more secure income base and higher pension entitlements than is now the case" (Hess, 1987, p. 532). Reports on income and inequality in later life continue to support Hess's comment. The need for pension reform points to the need for societal reform. Pay equity, an end to segregation of women in low-paying jobs, and an end to racial discrimination would all create better pensions for minority older

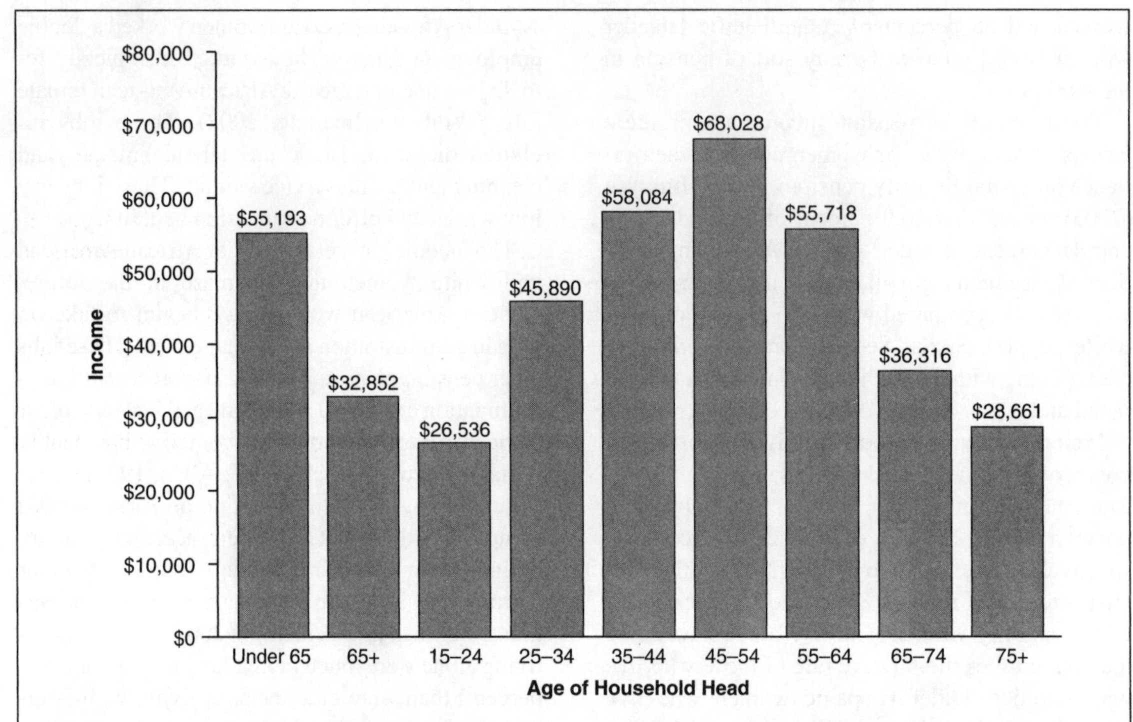

Income rises steadily with each age cohort from age 15 on and peaks between the ages of 45 and 54. From that point on retirement reduces household income. People aged 65 have incomes about 60 percent of those under age 65. Many people aged 65 to 74 will adjust to living on less money than they had during their working years. Those in the oldest age group (75 and over) have household incomes only about one-half that of people under age 65. This makes low income and poverty a particular problem for the very old.

FIGURE 9.7
Median Income of Elder Households

Source: Adapted from U.S. Census Bureau. (2000). Income 2000. Table 4. Median Income of Households by Selected Characteristics, Race, and Hispanic Origin of Householder: 2000, 1999, and 1998. Washington, DC. Retrieved January 10, 2005, *www.census.gov/hhes/income/income00/inctab4.html.*

people. Pension reform can at best try to make up for some of these inequities.

Social Security Reform

Social Security forms the bedrock of income for older people today. People who worked outside the labor force (e.g., homemakers) or people who had low paying jobs rely almost entirely on Social Security payments. Wu (2003, p. 27) says that "nearly 38 percent of Social Security beneficiaries receive 90 percent or more of their income from Social Security."

And Social Security grows in importance as a person ages. Social Security made up more than one-half the median income of people aged 80 and over in 2001 (compared with only 31.6 percent for people aged 65 to 69) (Wu, 2003). Younger old people often continue to work, they have better pensions, and their pensions have not yet lost buying power due to inflation. The oldest group (aged 80 and over) has none of these advantages and may also face widowhood. This will lower their incomes further and increase their reliance on Social Security.

Increases in Social Security benefits and indexing Social Security to the cost of living account for the decrease in poverty among the older population in recent years. Wu (2003, p. 57) estimates that "without Social Security benefits, the poverty rate would increase from 10.1 percent to 46.7 percent for all older persons, and from 11.9 percent to 57.4 percent for those aged 80 and older." This makes Social Security reform a key to ensuring a strong pension system in the future.

The current system assumes that older people fall into two types: single workers or married coupes. And it assumes that married couples consist of a worker (usually the husband) and an unpaid homemaker. Schulz (2001, p. 157) says that "the social security benefit structure reflects a pattern of marital life and family obligations which is no longer typical in the United States." For example, most women now work for at least part of their middle years and many women now enter old age divorced or separated.

Also, women have a widowhood rate in later life five times that of older men. And an older woman married less than ten years and divorced gets no spouse's or widow's Social Security pension (Schulz, 2001). Social Security needs to create a set of policies that reflect the reality of marriage today and women's current work patterns and careers. The following reforms would bring Social Security policies in line with a woman's life course today.

Family Care

The current system gives no credit to homemakers who spend years and sometimes a lifetime out of the labor force. These people, mostly women, either have no Social Security pension in later life or have to depend on their spouse's pension. Women who spend some time as a homemaker and then enter the labor force get a smaller pension because they have smaller lifetime earnings. Some authors (Malveaux, 1993; Rix, 1993) propose a dropout allowance of 10 years. This would allow a homemaker (or other type of family caregiver) to drop these years in the calculation of average yearly earnings. This would recognize a woman's role as family caregiver and would increase her pension in retirement. A lower cost version of this policy could apply this ten-year dropout allowance only to people with low incomes.

A more costly approach to improved pensions for homemakers would provide them with **homemaker credits**. Malveaux (1993) says that estimates of unpaid wages from household work range from $700 billion to $1.4 trillion per year. A person would get credits based on an estimated income for this work. This plan could either pay pensions out of general revenue, or homemakers could pay into the plan.

Countries such as Japan, the United Kingdom, and Germany allow homemakers to contribute to the government pension plan. In the United States, the homemaker credit plan will probably not pass as legislation (Schulz, 2001). Disagreement exists over how to finance this option and how much homemakers should get. Still, this proposal points to the value of women's work and the lack of recognition it receives.

Spousal Pensions

A married woman, who paid into Social Security, but whose benefits come to less than one-half of her husband's, will get benefits based on her husband's pension. She will get 50 percent of her spouse's income (or an amount to bring her pension up to 50 percent of her husband's amount if she has a small pension of her own). A woman who has a pension greater than one-half of her husband's pension will get her own pension amount. The Social Security Administration gives an example of this. If a wife worked and will receive a Social Security pension of $850 per month and her husband worked and will receive a Social Security pension of $1450 per month, they will each get their own pensions (Social Security Administration, 2004e). If she did not work, she would get $725 or one-half of her husband's pension.

Some critics say the system should do away with or reduce benefits for women based on the husband's pension. They say that working women today should get their own Social Security pensions regardless of their husband's pension. This would save money on at least two counts. First, women with lower pensions would not have their pensions topped up to one-half of their husband's pensions. Second, homemaker spouses of wealthier pensioners would not get pensions of their own. Critics of this proposal say that it would also hurt women who had low incomes. The current system protects women in poorer families by ensuring that they will have a pension based on their husband's earnings.

Some authors suggest a pension policy based on shared earnings (Rix, 1993; Schulz, 2001). This method would pool a married couple's benefits into a total benefit. The couple would then split the benefit between them. One-half would go to each spouse in the case of divorce or widowhood. This would give homemakers an earnings record they could draw on regardless of divorce. This policy would cost more than the present policy. Also, it would mostly benefit two-earner couples and divorced women. It might disadvantage some people, like widows and divorced men (Rix, 1993). Some version of this plan might arise in the future as more working women lobby for a change in the current policy. But at present even supporters of the idea worry that it would increase benefits to some, while decreasing benefits to others.

Another proposal, one that would follow the German model, suggests that homemakers get direct coverage and benefits. This would recognize the work of homemaking as a contribution to a family's and society's economic well-being. This proposal would cost more money and Schulz (2001) says that any increase in Social Security costs will get little support in Congress.

Widows' Benefits

When a retired worker dies, the spouse loses spousal benefit and gets only the full worker's benefit. This means that a surviving spouse will continue to get only two-thirds of the pre-death income. But economists say that a single person needs about 80 percent of a couple's income to maintain his or her standard of living. The decrease in income after widowhood can throw a surviving spouse into poverty (Schulz, 2001). Women face the greatest risk of this decrease because they often have no other pension income.

Social Security needs to provide a better pension to widows to help them maintain their standard of living after a spouse's death. The program might fund this policy change by providing smaller spousal benefits with both spouses alive and a higher survivor benefit when one spouse dies.

Income Limits

Social Security puts earnings limits on retirees under age 65 and two months (in 2003). This policy hurts people who had low incomes in the past because it limits the amount they can supplement their pension with work income. In 2003, Social Security allowed a person under age 65 and two months to earn only $11,280. Social Security will reduce benefits for this person $1 for every $2 earned above this amount (Social Security Administration, 2003b).

This policy ignores the fact that women, for example, get 25 percent lower Social Security benefits on average than men. They also have smaller personal savings and less likelihood of a private pension than a man. This policy forces some women to limit their income or to get paid off the books (Rones & Herz, 1989). It amplifies the inequities between women and men. Social Security could raise the earnings limit to help people keep more of their earnings. Or it could allow no limit for people who have low pensions because they did little or no paid work in the past due to family care.

Schulz (2001) says that "the biggest obstacle to social security reform for women is the inability to devise a reform plan at reasonable cost without lowering benefits for some retirees." Ross and Upp (1993, cited in Schulz, 2001), two experienced policy researchers, say that "these conflicts [between different group needs] appear insoluble." Still, the system needs reform. Rayman and her colleagues (1993) call for a new commission to review Social Security policy with women in mind.

Supplemental Security Income Reform

Critics of SSI point to three problems with the program. First, it pays benefits below the poverty line; second, state supplements vary widely; and third, the program enrolls only about one-half the people eligible. This leads to varied levels of support across the country.

Improved Benefits

Federal SSI payments now only ensure an income of about 75 percent to 90 percent of the poverty line for the poorest older people (Social Security Administration, 2003b). A panel created to review the SSI program recommended increased benefits to bring all older people to at least the poverty line. The panel also recommended that the Social Security Administration increase the amount of assets a person can have and still get SSI benefits. Leavitt and Schulz (1988) found that about one-third of people with incomes low enough to get SSI had assets above the SSI minimum. But most of these people received little cash income from these assets (e.g., their home). This left them in poverty and with no SSI help. An increase in the allowance for assets would open SSI to more low-income people (Schulz, 2001).

State Supplements

States differ in the SSI supplements they give. For example, in 1998, California added an average of $461.37 to recipients, Kansas added $333.33, and Arkansas $314.81 (U.S. Census Bureau, 2000c). No simple answer exists for this problem of varying supplements. To some extent, the differences reflect local conditions, like the cost of living in each state. But supplements also reflect the state economy and the local political climate. State benefits can get cut more easily than federal benefits. This puts poor older people, especially minorities, at risk of reduced income (Malveaux, 1993).

Higher Enrollment Rates

All people below the poverty line can receive SSI and Medicaid coverage. Unfortunately, about 40 percent of people eligible for SSI do not take part in the program (Schulz, 2001). Many of these people have never heard of SSI. Others believe they have to give up their homes or stop working to get SSI payments. The paperwork puts off frail older people and those who speak a language other than English. And many people avoid SSI because it links them to poverty.

The Administration on Aging has increased outreach to older people eligible for SSI. It has funded outreach projects including a computerized screening program to match people with programs and a toll-free number to take applications by phone. But even a direct letter from the Social Security Administration encouraging people to apply led to only a 3 percent response (Schulz, 2001).

The asset test associated with SSI keeps many older people from getting SSI benefits. Most poor older people have few assets. But, Schulz (2001, p. 239) says, "the asset test for SSI is so stringent that some people with inadequate incomes are denied assistance because of small amounts of savings and other resources." A less stringent test would allow more poor older people to take advantage of SSI.

Private Pension Reform

Private pensions also need reform. In 2001, for example, only about one-half of all workers in the United States (55.5 percent) had private pension coverage. This means that more than 70 million at that time gained no pension credits other than Social Security (Bigler, 2002). Bigler says that the higher a person's income, the more likelihood that the person had a pension. He notes that 62.4 percent of professionals had a company pension plan, and about 45 percent of blue collar craft and repair workers had company pensions. But in service jobs only about one-quarter of all workers paid into a pension plan.

The data show that poorer people in low-paying jobs tend not to have pensions. Bigler (2002) reports that 38 percent of workers with incomes of less than $40,000 per year in 1998 took part in a pension plan. But 70 percent of workers who made between $40,00 and $74,900 took part in pension plans. Low-income workers tend to work for smaller companies, work part-time, and have less money to pay into a pension plan. This forces them to rely almost solely on Social Security. And the government never intended the Social Security system to serve as a full replacement for preretirement income.

An expansion of private pensions to more workers will provide a better income for more older people. At the least, the government needs to continue its oversight of private pensions (through the ERISA). This helps ensure that those people who pay into pension plans will get a pension when they retire.

Vesting

Vesting refers to an employee's entitlement to his or her pension payments plus the payments of the employer. Pension plans often require five or ten years of employment for full vesting. The federal government, through the ERISA of 1974 ensures that workers will have access to their pensions through vesting. But a long vesting period works against workers who change jobs often, lose their jobs, or who take time out for family care. A worker can work for a lifetime in a variety of jobs and still have no vested pension funds. The federal government could legislate a shorter vesting period. This would ensure that more workers get their full pension entitlements at retirement.

Portability and Indexing

Most private pension plans lack portability, and many do not index pensions to inflation. Lack of portability limits a worker's ability to change jobs and can limit the pension a person gets in retirement. Portability requires cooperation between employers with different pension plans. Given the number of plans and their different policies, portability proves difficult.

Indexing pensions to the cost of living will protect workers from future inflation. This will cost workers more money when they pay into a plan, but it would ensure a better pension in retirement.

Better Private Plan Insurance

Companies often place their retirement funds in the hands of insurance companies, which invest the money and guarantee the company's retirees a pension for life. Most insurance companies take modest risks for stable returns, but some have taken extreme risks with this money. They have invested in junk bonds and unsound real estate deals. Executive Life, a company in California, lost retirement fund money that left thousands of people with smaller pensions than they had expected (Malveaux, 1993).

Underfunded pension plans have too little money in them to pay their workers' pensions in the future. The federal government set up the Pension Benefit Guaranty Corporation (PBGC) under ERISA to insure private defined benefit pension plans. People in these plans would look to the PBGC for help if a pension plan could not pay benefits.

Schulz (2001) says that in the late 1990s the PBGC covered about 42 million workers in 44,000 plans. But the PBGC has faced financial crises since the mid-1980s. Company closures and bankruptcies created deficits that congress acted to cover. Changes in laws and higher insurance rates changed this. But again in 2004 the PBGC declared a deficit as it supported workers in failing companies.

In 2004 the PBGC for the first time paid benefits to over 1 million people—an annual total of $3 billion. The fund's executive director said that the PBGC could cover its costs for several years. But the agency lost $12.1 billion in 2004. And it has long-term obligations of $62 billion and only $39 billion in assets (Kirchoff & Adams, 2004).

People who get pension help from the PBGC may get less than they hoped for. For example, the PBGC pays only up to $38,659 per year if a company fails and cannot pay its pensions. Some people will get much less than this. Underfunded pension plans, even with PBGC insurance to back them up, will lead to pension losses for many people.

The National Committee to Preserve Social Security and Medicare says that pensioners need a "Bill of Rights and government action to defend" pensioners against pension plan abuses (Research and Policy Development, 1994b, p. 2). The PBGC itself wants the law to require employers to have the funds in place to meet workers' future pensions. Too many employers today make promises to workers that they cannot keep. For example, they promise better pensions, but fail to pay more into the employees' pension plan (Mayer, 1993).

ERISA required that companies have enough funds to pay workers' pensions, but it gave companies thirty years to meet this requirement. Some of these companies will close before they can meet their pension obligations. This will leave workers with reduced pensions or no pensions. Some of these companies expect that the government will pick up the bill if they fail to pay workers' pensions. Unless reform takes place, many workers will find themselves with less income than they expect, and the taxpayers will have to bail out pensions through the PBGC.

The U.S. retirement income system provides a decent standard of living for most older people and keeps most of the poorest older people out of poverty. But each part of the retirement income system needs improvement. These improvements will help people in the most need now, and they will ensure a better old age in the future.

THE FUTURE

Weinstein (1988, p. 7) called retirement at the end of the last century the "golden age of the golden years." This golden age in part reflects planning and hard work by older people in the past, but it also reflects economic growth in the years after World War II, a low dependency ratio, and improved pensions. All of this could change in the future. Already politicians and policy analysts project hard times ahead for future generations of older people.

Will the Social Security program go broke as some critics claim? Will today's workers have a pension to count on when they retire? The OASDI trust fund had a surplus of $1.5 trillion in 2004. And the fund receives more than $80 billion in interest each year on this amount. But the system pays out money as it comes in (a pay-as-you-go system). And this system will face problems in the years ahead.

The large size of the Baby Boom generation, a low birth rate with smaller numbers of workers, and people living longer than ever before will all strain the Social Security system. The Social Security Administration (2004b) says that, if income and benefits continue at the current rate, then by the year 2018 Social Security will need to dip into its surplus. And by 2042 the surplus will be gone. The program will be unable to make its payments.

A smaller work force (two workers to each retiree in 2042 versus sixteen workers to each retiree in 1950) will create a funding shortage. The system will collect less money than it needs to pay out. This will lead to a 27 percent reduction in benefits for retirees from 2042 onward. Unless the system brings in more funds, by the year 2079 benefits could be as low as one-third of those today.

The Social Security Administration sums up the problem. "Social Security is not sustainable over the long term at present benefit and tax rates without large infusions of additional revenue. There will be a massive and growing shortfall over the 75-year period [2004–2079]" (Social Security Administration, 2004d). Social Security's Chief Actuary projects a $3.7 trillion shortfall over the next seventy-five years.

The Social Security Trustees and other government experts, such as the Chairman of the Federal Reserve Board, say that we need to make changes now. The independent, bipartisan Social Security Advisory Board has said, "As time goes by, the size of the Social Security problem grows, and the choices available to fix it become more limited" (Social Security Administration, 2004d).

The report of the OASDI Board of Trustees proposes four actions that the system needs to take immediately: (1) the system needs to immediately and permanently increase payroll taxes by 15 percent; (2) the system needs to immediately and permanently reduce benefits by 13 percent (or a combination of the two); (3) the system needs a transfer from the general fund of $3.7 trillion between now and 2042; or (4) some combination of these actions (OASDI Trustees, 2004; Palmer & Saving, 2004).

Beyond the year 2078, the system will need much larger changes to maintain itself.

Some groups and individual legislators propose further changes to the system. A group called the Concord Coalition (2004) proposes that Social Security move toward a fully funded system (versus the current pay-as-you-go system). A fully funded system would set up a personal account for each worker. The system would invest these funds in Treasury notes or stocks and bonds. These accounts would earn interest on behalf of the individual. An increase in payments by workers could fund this system. This type of plan seems to have the support of the second Bush administration.

Opponents of this system say that it puts workers' retirement savings at risk. It also would leave poorer workers with very low savings to draw on in retirement. This would change Social Security from a broad program that spreads the risk and rewards in retirement among all workers to a program that would perpetuate mid-life income inequalities. Controversy over Social Security will heat up in the years ahead as legislators take on the challenge of reform.

CONCLUSION

Critics of the public pension system today say that public pensions cost too much. They warn that a large older population will lead to higher costs in the future. And they say that these costs will burden the younger generation with an increased national debt. But other policy analysts say that action today to reform the system can forestall a crisis in the future. Most workers, young and old, will benefit from a strong (if more costly) public pension system.

Today and in the future, older people will rely on the Social Security system for their well-being. Social Security programs provide a safety net for the poorest older people. Some of these people have no other source of income. Social Security led to the large decrease in poverty rates among older people since the 1960s. Even young people today benefit from the OASDI disability and survivor pension benefits. A strong public pension program provides a safety net for older people and their families.

Better private pensions have also improved the standard of living of older people. The combination of private pensions, income and savings, and Social Security can replace as much as 50 to 80 percent of income after retirement. People with these resources have many housing and life-style options. A national survey of attitudes toward aging, for example, shows that the general public appreciates the importance of a strong pension system. And most older people (72 percent) say they have built up their savings for retirement (Cutler, Whitelaw, & Beattie, 2002).

Still, the United States retirement income system needs reform. Many older people live in or near poverty. Cutler, Whitelaw, & Beattie (2002) found that 76 percent of older white people had saved for later life compared with only 43 percent of African Americans. And about 40 percent of older white people considered money a problem, compared with over 60 percent of older African Americans.

Women, minorities, and very old people make up a high proportion of poor older people. People with broken work records or women who worked in the home may not get enough from Social Security to keep them out of poverty. These people rarely have private pensions, and they get poorer as they age. Minority members run the greatest risk of poverty in old age.

Gerontologists and economists have proposed reforms for each part of the retirement income system. Reforms include increased payments into the Social Security system to prepare for more retired people in the future and better benefits for family caregivers, homemakers, and widows. Private pensions could offer better portability and vesting. They could also cover more workers. The government needs to help guard against the misuse of pension funds and corporate defaults on pension payments.

A strong retirement income system will benefit everyone. Older people will live free of the fear of poverty and will have more resources to enjoy old age. Younger people can feel secure that their parents will have enough resources to live on. And younger people can look forward to a good income in their own old age.

The United States will have to make changes in its public pension program. But it should support a balanced approach to pension planning that includes a strong public pension system as well as private pensions and savings. If people adopt this approach, the country can enter the future without a crisis in its retirement income system.

SUMMARY

- Controversy exists over the cost of federal retirement income programs for older people. Some writers think that the high cost of federal old-age pensions leads to less money and fewer programs for other age groups. These writers propose reduced funding for programs that serve older people. Other writers argue against reduced funding. They say that the public pension system accounts for improvements in older people's financial well-being. And poorer people, who gain the most from a strong public pension system, would suffer the most if the government cuts funding.
- In the early 1900s, both the change to an industrial society and the Great Depression created an economic crisis. This left many older people jobless and destitute. In response to these conditions, the federal government passed the Social Security Act. It established a social insurance program that protected workers from unemployment and gave people some income in retirement.
- The U.S. retirement income system consists of a combination of public and private income sources. These include Social Security benefits, personal savings and assets, and employment pensions.
- Social Security benefits ensure that all workers and their families will have at least a basic income in retirement. This program removed the threat of poverty from millions of older Americans.
- Older people's finances improved during the 1960s and 1970s. This came about because (1) new retirees had paid into Social Security for a longer time than retirees in the past; (2) Congress added cost of living increases to Social Security benefits; and (3) in 1972 the government increased benefits by 20 percent.
- Research shows that rich and poor older people differ in more than the amount of money they have. The sources of their income differ as well. The poorest older people rely heavily on public sources of support. Wealthier older people receive less than one-fifth of their income from public support. They get most of their income from private sources. A government policy that cuts public pension benefits hurts the poorest older people most.
- Age, gender, marital status, and minority status all affect retirement income in later life. African American and Hispanic elders, for example, have many times the poverty rate of whites in old age.
- The government needs to create a new set of Social Security policies that reflect changes in the life course today. Reforms would include changes in family care policies, spousal pensions, widows' benefits, and income standards. In addition, private pension rules that govern vesting, portability, and pension plan insurance all need reform.
- Future economic policies should encourage a balanced approach to retirement income. This approach includes balancing public supports with private pensions, savings, and work.

DISCUSSION QUESTIONS

1. What two major socioeconomic conditions resulted in the need to develop a federal old-age security system? Briefly describe the system that the Social Security Act established in 1935.
2. Define and describe the three-tiered retirement income system.
3. List the five basic principles of the Social Security program. What do these five principles ensure?
4. Who is eligible to collect Social Security? When are Social Security benefits taxed? What happens to the money collected as tax?

5. List the major reasons that the finances of older people improved during the 1960s and 1970s.
6. What effect would a decrease in Social Security benefits have on poorer older people? How would it affect the wealthier retiree?
7. What are the major factors that affect a person's retirement income? Describe the effect of work history, gender, and marital status on retirement income.
8. Explain why and how the Social Security policies must change to meet the needs of older people today.
9. What approach might a younger person use to best prepare financially for retirement?

SUGGESTED READING

Schulz, J. H. (2001). *The economics of aging (7th ed.).* Westport, CT: Auburn House.

This is the classic work on economics in later life. The author describes the major sources of income in later life. He discusses policies that govern public and private pension programs. And he looks at reforms that need to take place to maintain and improve the current system. This readable work also takes a close look at inequality in later life and argues for a system that supports the poor as well as wealthier seniors.

United States, Congressional Budget Office. (2004). *Outlook for Social Security. Washington, DC: Congressional Budget Office.* Full text available at *www.cbo.gov/showdoc.cfm?index=5530&sequence=0.*

This short but challenging work presents the details behind the current concerns about Social Security's resources. The study gives an overview of the current system and policies governing the system. It also projects revenue and expenses for the next one hundred years, an exercise in futurology. Still, this work gives a sense for how government experts look at the Social Security system. The text includes charts and graphs for easier comprehension of the issues.

GLOSSARY OF TERMS

absolute deprivation Refers to the minimal income needed to buy food, clothing, shelter, and health care. People who lack this minimum income are poor. The government sets a poverty level each year based on this minimum.

defined benefit plan A pension plan that states how much workers will get out of a plan when they retire. This may be phrased as a proportion of the best five or ten years of salary.

defined contribution plan A pension plan that states how much a worker pays in. The amount that a worker gets depends on the economic conditions at the time of the worker's retirement.

employment pension A pension from a person's place of work. Workers pay into this plan during their working years. The employer often pays into this plan as well.

homemaker credits This program would, if enacted, give homemakers pension credit based on the estimated income they would earn from their work at home. The plan would either pay pensions out of general revenue or homemakers might pay into the plan.

near poverty Family income between 100 and 199 percent of the poverty level.

pay-as-you-go plan A pension plan such as Social Security that funds current benefits to retirees from current workers' payments.

poverty Family income less than 100 percent of the poverty level. The poverty line depends on the size of the family and the number of children in the family.

relative deprivation Relative deprivation defines a person as poor in relation to people who have more money. This definition would say that the bottom tenth of income earners are poor.

Social Security (OASDI) Old Age, Survivors, and Disability Insurance. The federal government pension plan begun in 1935.

Supplemental Security Income (SSI) Program started in 1972 to help the poorest blind, disabled, and older people. SSI gets paid out of general revenues.

three-legged stool A description of the U.S. retirement income system. The system includes public pensions, private pensions, and savings (the legs of the stool).

underfunded pension plans A pension plan that does not have enough money in it to meet its future obligations to workers.

vesting This means that workers will get all or part of their earned benefit from a company when they leave. They will get this benefit even if they have moved to a different company.

chapter **10**

RETIREMENT AND WORK

Reverend Sam Wong felt bitter and angry when his church asked him to retire. "At age 65," he says, "you're no longer needed. You're no longer important. It doesn't matter what you were in your active years. You're nothing now. You don't have a place."

Rev. Wong's father had worked as a lay priest in the Chinese community on the West Coast and Rev. Wong took up his father's work. He had spent his life in the church and derived his sense of self-esteem from his work.

When the church asked him to stay on part-time after he retired, he refused. "Once you retire," he says, "they don't base your pay on your experience or on how much you know. I heard the person interviewing me say, 'Well, you know, there is really no standard for paying retired people.' In other words, 'we'll pay you what we decide to pay you. And you can take it or leave it.' "

Mandatory retirement forced Rev. Wong to give up his career for no reason other than his age. Professionals faced with this sudden break in their careers often find it hard to adjust to retirement. Given the choice, they would prefer to keep on working.

Wes Weston chose an early retirement. He worked in the state land titles office for seventeen years and then in the Department of Mines until age 63. "I retired early," Wes says, "because I had sufficient funds to do the things I've always wanted to do. My work with the government was far from what I wanted to do. I wanted to be able to sit down and systematically while away my time with these." He points to a bookcase filled with philosophy books.

Wes gets three pension checks a month—a small pension for work he did before the war, his Social Security check, and his civil service pension check. Wes has few money worries and spends his free time on his hobbies. His living room, for example, contains a piano and an electric organ. "I want to think, maybe write my memoirs. I also want to improve the little knowledge I have of music. I've got a number of works that I want to explore more thoroughly."

Wes has only one problem. He's still too busy. "I'm busier now than ever," he says. He serves on the board of directors of three seniors organizations, and he and his wife have designed a tabletop golf game that he hopes will sell well enough to create a legacy for his grandchildren.

Pat Larmond, a professor of classics, shows a third way to retire. She eased into retirement. She took her pension at age 65, but continued to teach one course in her specialty, Greek theater, for the next three years. At 68 she gave up this course to a younger professor. She now has the title Professor Emeritus. The university gives her an office that she shares with another retired professor. She comes in two or three times a week to do research, give guest lectures, and take lunch in the faculty club. She keeps in touch with colleagues and her field of study.

Professor Larmond adjusted to retirement without a hitch. She found that she could leave work a little at a time over a period of a few years. Flexible retirement offers an option to the shock of sudden retirement at a fixed age.

These three people show three different responses to retirement. One person experienced retirement as a shock, another as a relief, and the third as an easy transition. These older people show some of retirement's pitfalls and possibilities. They also show that retirement today offers more options than ever before. Savishinsky (2000, p. 13) says that "one size—and one theory—does not fit all." The more people know about retirement, the more they can plan for it and shape it to suit their needs. Responses to retirement differ by personal preference. They also differ by gender, social class, and race.

This chapter looks at (1) retirement policies and trends, (2) the decision to retire and options to retirement at age 65, and (3) the future of retirement in the United States.

THE SOCIAL ORIGINS OF RETIREMENT

Retirement in the U.S. today forms a normal part of the life cycle. Most people will spend some time in retirement. In 2002, for example, 32.2 percent of men and 20.8 percent of women aged 65 to 69 worked in the labor force. But for 65 to 74 year olds these figures drop by almost half to 17.5 percent of men and 11.2 percent of women still in the labor force (Rix, 2004).

Myles (1984) traces the trend toward retirement to two factors. First, industrial societies developed and applied the "retirement principle." This principle proposed that people should leave work at a fixed age regardless of physical or mental ability. Until this principle came into play, people worked as long as they could. In agricultural societies, landowners withdrew from work as they grew more frail. Then, in late old age they gave their property to their children. They would still work in the household if they had the strength.

Schulz and Myles (1990) say that a fixed retirement age began with Bismarck's national pension plan in Germany in the 1880s. Bismarck first set the age of retirement at 70, then lowered it to 65. This then became the standard age for retirement. In the United States, the retirement principle served an economy that valued faster, stronger, younger workers. It allowed companies to let older workers go without firing them (Schulz, 2001).

Employers and unions both supported a fixed retirement age. Employers supported retirement because they could retire high-priced older workers and hire cheaper younger workers. Also, younger workers could work faster. Companies wanted to speed up production and get more out of workers. Unions agreed to a faster work pace if workers could get a shorter workday. Older workers had a hard time working at this faster pace. Retirement gave them a graceful way out of work.

Unions also wanted companies to bring in a seniority system (first hired, last fired) in deciding layoffs. Seniority gave the oldest workers the most job security. This forced companies to keep the oldest, most expensive workers the longest. Retirement solved this problem. It offered seniority rights only up to the age of retirement. At retirement age, companies could let older workers go. The unions traded older workers' rights to a job for job security in middle age (Haber, 1978, cited in Atchley, 1985, p. 54). The retirement principle opened the door to retirement, but few workers walked through. The absence of private pension plans for most people kept them at work.

The second factor that made retirement almost universal, Myles (1984) says, was the "retirement wage." In the United States this took the form of the Social Security program begun in 1935. The retirement wage at first provided only small benefits. Later, increases in benefits meant that Social Security replaced a larger part of a person's preretirement income.

The retirement wage makes it possible for nearly everyone (even people with very low incomes) to retire. Myles (1984; *also* Schulz, 2001) traces current high rates of retirement at age 65 or earlier to the retirement wage. "It was the rising entitlements made available by the state," Myles (1984, p. 21) says, "that increasingly allowed [workers] to withdraw from the labor market before they wore out. . . . By 1980, the institution of retirement had been consolidated and old age had become a period in the life cycle defined and sustained by the welfare state."

RETIREMENT IN THE UNITED STATES TODAY

Men and Retirement

The retirement principle and the retirement wage have led to changes in work patterns in the United States. Coile (2003) found that both men and women show retirement spikes at ages 62 and 65. These choices of retirement age reflect the ages when Social Security and private pension plans encourage older workers to retire. These age spikes show the impact of pension policies and finances on a retiree's decision to leave work.

But men and women differ in their labor force participation. Participation for older men, for example, dropped between 1950 and 1985 (Rix, 2004). In 1950, 49.6 percent of men aged 65 and over worked in the labor force. By 1960 this figure dropped to 35.9 percent and by 1985 to 17.1 percent. This trend toward decreased labor force participation hit bottom in the mid-1980s.

Since then, studies show some increase in labor force participation for older men. Rix (2004) says that (1) an end to mandatory retirement, (2) a more liberal Social Security earnings test, and (3) an increase in the normal retirement age for Social Security all encourage older men to stay at work. Also, smaller age cohorts of young people have led some employers to keep older workers on the job. An AARP study (2002) found that 69 percent of workers aged 45 and over said they planned to work into their retirement years. Projections show a labor force participation rate of 17.3 percent for older men in 2050 (Rix, 2004).

Men typically have a long continuous work record. This means that, for a man, retirement comes as a break from a long-standing routine. Some men experience retirement as a rite of passage from one stage of life to another. Some men experience retirement as a crisis. A *Businessweek* report described the case of Bernard Salevitz (Gutner, 2004, p. 88). He retired at age 65 from a busy medical practice in New York. He and his wife moved to a new home in Scottsdale, Arizona, where one of their children lived. Salevitz says that after a period of golf and travel, "I mentally and physically collapsed. . . . There was no challenge or stimulation in my life, and that was a big mistake." He went back to work at the Mayo Clinic in Scottsdale. Three days a week he sees patients and teaches residents. He says, "It brought me back to civilization."

Szinovacz (2003) uses a life course perspective to show that retirement forms one part of a longer process. This process begins with a man's first job and ends when he enters the status of retiree. A man unprepared for the transition to retirement will face at least a temporary crisis. Most men adapt to re-

BOX 10.1
THE OLDER WORKER TODAY

Many older workers leave jobs that place too great a physical demand on them. They may transfer to a less-demanding job or retire early. Welford says that this can lead to a loss of potential. A company can lose the work of a skilled mechanic because of a single problem, such as back pain. Welford proposes better design of the workplace and more retraining designed for older workers.

Some companies have taken this approach. They have found ways to keep older, motivated, skilled employees on the job. Levin reports that auto companies have redesigned factories with the older worker in mind. Companies now include training for problem solving and teamwork, and they have equipment that eases physical strain. Machinery tilts the auto bodies so workers can work with less strain. Workers use air guns to drive screws, mitts to prevent arm and wrist injury, and floor mats to reduces stress on the back and legs.

McNaught reports that Days Inn of America uses older workers in its national reservation center. Days Inn provides older workers with special phones to control volume. The company also adjusted its training course to suit older workers and to train them in the same time as younger workers. The company finds that, compared with younger agents, older agents have about one-fifth the turnover rate. Also, though older agents take more time than younger agents on each call, they more often get a reservation. The company found that older workers cost no more than younger workers (including health insurance), and that they worked more effectively.

Many reports now document older peoples' abilities and potential. But resistance to older workers still exists. McNaught says that "managers nearly always underestimate the capabilities of seniors" and "most employers believe that older people cannot perform well, despite evidence to the contrary." Instead of seeing older workers as reliable and hard working, many employers see them as rigid and hard to train. As reported by Fein, a study by the AARP shows that employers resist hiring older workers. "It does just come down to "ageism'," says an AARP spokesperson, "and we haven't found a way to crack it."

Sources: "Work Capacity Across the Adult Years," by A. T. Welford, 1993, in R. Kastenbaum, (Ed.). *Encyclopedia of adult development,* pp. 541–553. Phoenix, AZ: Onyx; "The Graying Factory," by D. P. Levin, 1994, *New York Times,* February 20, Section B, p. 1; "Realizing the Potential: Some Examples," by W. McNaught, 1994, in M. W. Riley, R. L. Kahn, & A. Foner (Eds.). *Age and structural lag,* pp. 219–236. New York: Wiley; "Frustrating Fight for Acceptance," by E. B. Fein, 1994, *New York Times,* January 4, Section B, p. 1.

tirement within a year or so. More and more options now exist for retirees that can buffer the shock of leaving work.

New career options like a **second career**, a part-time job, or a **bridge job** also give older men more work options (AARP, 2002). Some men return to school or engage in volunteer work. A single pattern of work and retirement cannot describe the many options open to male retirees today (Rix, 2004).

Women and Retirement

Women in 2003 made up 47 percent of the total labor force (U.S. Department of Labor Women's Bureau, 2004). The proportion of women aged 55 to 64 in the labor force doubled from 1950 to 2002 (from 28.2 percent to 55.1 percent). Over this same period older women (aged 65 and over) showed a small decrease in labor force participation (10.7 to 9.9 percent). This decrease in participation may reflect better Social Security benefits that allow older women to retire.

Until the mid-1980s, the retirement literature reported almost entirely on men. But more recent work has looked at the work careers and retirement choices of women. Studies show that women have different work histories than men. Many women still spend all or part of their work career in the home. This gives women incentive to stay at work in later life. They started their careers later than men and have not built up as much pension savings. Single women, in particular, may stay at work because they need the income.

Earlier research found that married women often timed their retirement to their husbands' (Weaver, 1994). McBride (1988) reported that women with an older spouse and a high income tended to retire early or at age 62. But, Coile (2003) says, as more women spend more years in the labor force, husbands and wives have a mutual influence on their decisions to retire. Husbands' resources and opportunities still have a strong influence on retirement decisions of wives (Pienta & Hayward, 2002). But researchers find that today a husband may also time his retirement to fit his wife's plans. Husbands and wives respond to one another's resources and opportunities. Coile (2003) says that the practice of couples retiring together may increase in the future as two-earner couples decide to leave work at the same time.

Women, compared with men, follow more varied career paths. Some work, then take time off to raise a family, then return to work; others work during their childrearing years; others never enter the labor force (U.S. Department of Labor, 2004). Hill (2002) found that older women who had worked, spent only a little over one-half their adult years in the labor force. Single women may show unbroken work records similar to those of men. This makes it hard to describe one retirement pattern for women.

Beehr and Adams (2003) say that the study of women and retirement must take into account a woman's life cycle. This includes her history in the workforce and childrearing responsibilities. It also includes taking account of marital status. Divorced women, for example, plan to retire later than married women. Widows without private pensions also plan for later retirement. These findings show that finances shape single women's retirement plans.

Many women work past age 55 because they have to support themselves. More often than men, they use bridge jobs to lengthen their work careers because they need the income (Quinn & Kozy, 1996). Logue (1991), for example, found that about one in six single female new retirees lived near or below the poverty line. Married women did better because they could rely on a spouse's income. Hogan, Perrucci, and Wilmoth (2000, p. 27) say that "the path to privilege seems to be through marriage."

Family responsibilities throughout life shape women's retirement decisions. For example, women more often than men retire because they have family caregiving responsibilities (caring for an infirm parent or spouse) (Savishinsky, 2000). A lifetime of gender discrimination in the workplace also affects womens' retirement decisions. For example, poor pensions, low pay, and broken work careers due to family caregiving all lead to low income in retirement. These facts have a great impact on women's retirement decisions.

Edith Irby Jones, MD (age 65 when this photo was taken), practices internal medicine in Houston, Texas. She also serves as Clinical Assistant Professor of Medicine at Baylor College of Medicine and at the University of Texas School of Medicine, Houston. Dr. Jones served as the first president of the National Medical Association. She has focused her practice on poor people, minorities, and the elderly. Patients aged 65 and over make up 70 percent of her patient load. Professionals such as Dr. Jones often work into late old age.

Szinovacz (1983) predicted that in the future more women would have longer unbroken work records and a strong commitment to work. They may have retirement experiences similar to those of men. This seems true for many women today.

Still "we know little about women's retirement as compared to men" (Taylor & Doverspike, 2003, p. 73). Researchers need to compare men and women in retirement. This would include research on male and female differences in resources, coping methods, and outcomes. Research also needs to look at women's decisions to retire or stay at work, their work options in later life, and the effects of family life on retirement decisions. (See Figure 10.1 and Table 10.1 for more information.)

Minorities and Retirement

African Americans show a variety of retirement patterns. For one thing, African Americans make up a diverse group. The African American community contains professionals, executives, blue collar workers, and people in poverty. People in each social and economic class respond to retirement differently.

For example, the 2003 Minority Retirement Confidence Survey found that the attitudes and behavior of different income segments "often mirror the attitudes and behavior of similar segments of the overall worker population. For example, minority workers with annual household income under $35,000 respond the same way on some retirement indicators as workers overall within this income category" (EBRI, 2004b, p. 1).

This study found that poorer African Americans focus attention on issues of income adequacy and retirement choice. These African American retirees tend to have poorer pensions than whites. They tend to have broken work careers due to lower education levels, lower income levels, and racial discrimination. For example, a smaller proportion of African American workers, compared with the general population, report that their employers pay into a pension plan on their behalf (EBRI, 2004b). This keeps them from building up large private or public pension benefits. They often must work in their later years to survive.

A greater proportion of African Americans, compared with the general population, say that they do not feel confident that they will have a job that will help them prepare for retirement. And a large proportion of African Americans (42 percent compared with 33 percent of the general population) do not feel confident that they will have enough money to live comfortably in retirement (EBRI, 2004b). More than non-Hispanic white workers, African American workers say they will rely on Social Security as their main source of retirement income (AARP, 2004a).

Cook and Welch (1994) studied the coping strategies of middle-aged and older women with low incomes. They conducted focus groups with 56 low-income women in Chicago. They found that white women rarely mentioned paid work, but nearly all of the African American women did part-time and in some cases steady work "off the books." A 68-year-old woman named Lena, for example, makes floral corsages and centerpieces to bring in extra money. She also helps another woman sell Avon products. Winfred, 81, works in a variety

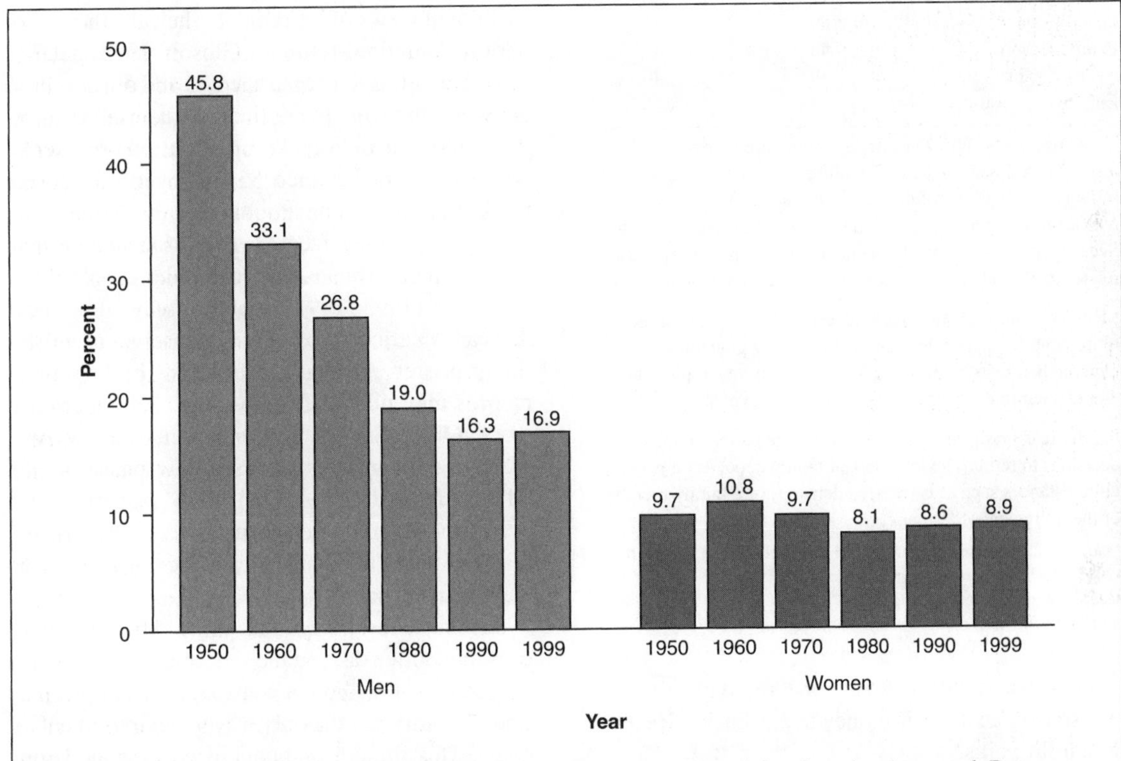

This chart shows a decrease by two-thirds in male labor force participation after age 65 from 1950 to 1999. Older women show little change in labor force participation over this period. Because of the decrease in older male workers, the proportion of older women workers in the labor force has increased. Better pensions for men encourage retirement. Women (especially widows) may find that to maintain their standard of living they have to keep working or begin working after age 65.

FIGURE 10.1
Labor Force Participation
Civilian Labor Force Participation Rates for People Age 65 and Over

Source: Adapted from P. J. Purcell. Table 2. Labor force participation rates by age and sex, 1950–2008. In Older workers: Employment and retirement trends. *Monthly Labor Review Online,* 123(10), October, 2000. *www.bls.gov/opub/mlr/w000/10/contents.htm*; *www.bls.gov/opub/mlr/2000/10/art3full.pdf.*

TABLE 10.1
Reasons for Retiring

Cutler and his colleagues (2002) on behalf of the National Council on the Aging asked the following question of retirees in a nationally representative sample: "How important was ______ in your decision to retire—very important, somewhat important or not important at all?" The following table gives the proportion of men and women who responded "very" or "somewhat important" to this question.

Reason for Retiring	*Men*	*Women*
Social Security	74	71
Money saved	77	66
Specific age	60	43
Family reasons	44	47
Health decline	39	40
Employer pressure	25	16

These responses show that employer pressure to leave work least often influenced the decision to retire (though it did influence one-quarter of the men in the sample). Financial reasons most often influenced the retirement decision—Social Security and money saved. The mention of a specific age also relates to eligibility for public or private pension benefits.

Men and women about equally report health as a reason for retirement. Some people use poor health as a graceful way to explain their exits from work. And some retirement plans take this as a legitimate reason to begin benefit payments.

Family reasons clearly play a role for some people in their decisions to retire. The influence of family depends on personal circumstances such as caregiving demands of a family member or the retirement of a spouse.

Source: Adapted from Cutler, N. E., Whitelaw, N. A., and Beattie, B. L. (2002). *American perceptions of aging in the 21st century.* The National Council on the Aging. Washington, D.C., Table 3-2, p. 23. Used with permission of The National Council on the Aging.

store and a laundromat two or three days a week. These women use this money to pay basic expenses like utility bills.

African Americans tend to work in the **secondary labor market** in retail work and service jobs. These jobs offer low pay, few benefits, and often lead to disability. Taylor and Doverspike (2003) found that, compared with whites, African American older men show high disability rates and poor health. Poor pensions and disability lead to fewer options in retirement for African Americans.

Gibson (1987) says that the concept of retirement may not apply to poorer African American workers. She reviewed the meaning of retirement in major studies in the literature. These studies assume that people retire at age 65, that a clear line exists between work and nonwork, that retired people draw income primarily from retirement sources, and that they view themselves as retired. She says that older members of minority groups such as African Americans and Hispanics often don't fit these criteria. Gerontologists need to rethink the meaning of retirement in light of minority experiences.

Gibson (1993), for example, found that some older African Americans form a category missed by traditional views of retirement. She calls these people the "unretired-retired" (Gibson, 1993, p. 277). This term refers to people aged 55 and older who do not work, but who do not think of themselves as retired. These people make up about one-quarter of African Americans aged 55 and over who do not work. Few studies have looked at this group. But, Gibson says, they face greater disadvantage than any group of African American older people.

Gibson (1993, 1991) explored why some older African Americans do not see themselves as retired. First, poorer African Americans' broken work records may blur the line between retirement and work. Older African Americans may not view a lack of work in later life as a new phase of life. African Americans who still work part-time have even less reason to see themselves as retired. For many of them, this pattern of work carries on from their middle years.

Second, Gibson says that older African Americans more often take on the sick role than the retired role. A person without a pension, for example, may find disability pay the only way to get retirement income. This finding accounts in part for the strong link found between poor health and retirement (Taylor & Doverspike, 2003). Gibson's work shows how inequality affects poorer African Americans' work patterns in middle age and their economic opportunities in later life. "Poor health and disadvantaged labor force experiences," Gibson (1993, p. 282) says, "are more influential for blacks, whereas financial readiness is more influential for whites."

Gibson also finds differences in retirement patterns *within* the African American group. A small proportion (15 percent) of older African Americans, many with very low incomes, work past the age of 70. These people may end up "dying from, rather than retiring from the work force" (Jackson, n.d., cited in Gibson, 1993). Another group (about one-half the older people in the National Survey of Black Americans) retired early, before age 64 (Gibson, 1993). This may be due to choice or the lack of jobs.

Hardy (1991) studied the labor force participation of 2,095 people aged 50 and older in Florida. She compared the backgrounds of people who reentered the workforce after retirement and those who wanted to but could not. She found that African Americans, women, and people with low socioeconomic status had trouble reentering the workforce. These findings suggest that African Americans have fewer retirement options than whites.

Compared with what we know about whites in retirement, we know little about whether older African Americans retire, why they retire, or what they do in retirement (Taylor & Doverspike, 2003). Gibson (1993) says that future research needs to recognize that many types of retirement exist. For example, current definitions exclude the unretired-retired from research studies. This leads to little knowledge about a large group of African American older people.

Also, researchers know almost nothing about African American professionals. This group has grown in recent years and will increase in the future. Gerontologists know little about their pension arrangements, career stability, or views of retirement (Richardson & Kilty, 1992). Richardson and Kilty (1992) report on one of the few studies of African American professionals. They found that professionals who felt they had to work to earn a living planned for early retirement and expected to enjoy retirement. These workers may see work as a means to an independent life when they retire. Those who felt committed to work (beyond just getting a paycheck) tended to avoid retirement planning.

The 2003 Minority Retirement Confidence Survey (EBRI, 2004b) found that middle-class African Americans tend to hold attitudes and behave in ways similar to the overall middle-class population. Richardson and Kilty (1989) also studied financial planning by these professionals. They report that African American professionals show patterns of planning similar to those of white professionals.

High proportions of both groups, for example, planned to rely on Social Security, continued professional income, and public employee pensions. African Americans, compared with whites, expected to retain more of their present income after retirement. Gibson (1993) calls for national research to further compare the retirement experiences of African Americans and whites. Longitudinal research would also allow researchers to assess the impact of civil rights legislation on African American retirees.

Minority groups other than African Americans pose unique problems to the study of retirement. Gerontologists know relatively little about retirement among minorities like Hispanic Americans. Many members of this group live as migrant workers and speak little or no English. This makes research on this population difficult.

Flippen and Tienda (2000) used large-scale survey data to study work and retirement among minority workers. They focused on the preretirement work experience of minority and female workers. They found that black, Hispanic, and female older workers, compared with white workers, faced more involuntary joblessness just before retirement. The loss of a job late in a minority worker's career often meant *retirement* or the end of the person's labor force participation.

They found that black men and Hispanic women, compared with similar white workers, showed the greatest likelihood of work loss in later life. The researchers trace the loss of work to racial and ethnic discrimination in the workplace, poorer health, less education, and fewer job skills. They say that a broken work record in youth makes it hard for these workers to stay in the labor force as they age. The loss of work late in life increases the risk of poverty in retirement. It also increases the risk of poor mental and physical health (Gallo, Bradley, Liegel, & Kasl, 2000).

Zsembik and Singer (1990) conducted one of the few studies on retirement among Mexican Americans. Zsembik and Singer (1990, p. 750) say that "given the lifetime work patterns of Mexican Americans, it is unclear how best to define retirement, identify when it occurs, and determine what retirement means." Many Mexican Americans, for example, fit Gibson's unretired-retired type. They work at part-time and seasonal jobs throughout their lives. And this leads to unclear lines between work and nonwork.

The 2003 Minority Retirement Confidence Survey (EBRI, 2004b) captures some more information about Hispanic American workers and their views on retirement. The study found that middle-class Hispanics and the overall population respond similarly to questions about retirement. But, the survey (EBRI, 2004b, p. 4) found that Hispanics, as a group, compared with the general population, felt "substantially less confidence" in their finances in retirement.

This finding reflects the large number of poorer workers in the Hispanic population. Only 20 percent of respondents felt "very confident" in their financial preparation for retirement. Only 14 percent felt "very confident" that they would have money for basic expenses. And only 13 percent of the Hispanic respondents felt that they would not outlive their retirement savings.

Hispanics say that they will rely primarily on Social Security for their retirement income. Non-native-born Hispanics, compared with native-born Hispanics, report one-half the rate of employers paying into a pension plan for them (22 percent compared with 41 percent). Poorer Hispanic workers, compared with the non-Hispanic poorer population, reported less chance of having an employer-sponsored pension plan. And less chance that an employer paid into a plan on their behalf. These findings reflect the part-time work that poorer Hispanics do and the small companies they work for.

The research to date shows that many minority members have a unique experience in the American workforce. Discrimination, low education levels, language barriers, and broken work careers all shape minority members' work experiences. These experiences lead to retirement options and decisions for many minority members that differ from the non-Hispanic white population. Gerontologists need to do more research on the forces that shape retirement for minorities and on the meaning of retirement for minority group members.

ALTERNATIVES TO RETIREMENT

People retire for many reasons: poor health, loss of a job in later life, eligibility for Social Security, a good private income, the retirement of a spouse, or

BOX 10.2

FORCES LEADING TO RETIREMENT

Individual Reasons	*Institutional Forces*
Finances	Working conditions and employer policies
Health	Retirement age policies, pension policies, and rules
Attitudes to work and retirement	Societal economic conditions
Social supports or pressures	Historical events and social values

The table presents the broad forces that lead to retirement. These forces play different roles in the retirement decisions of men, women, and minority group members. Pension policies, working conditions, and discrimination influence men, women, and minority workers differently. This leads to different views of retirement.

Source: Adapted from "Work and Retirement," by P. K. Robinson, S. Coberly, & C. E. Paul (1985), in R. H. Binstock & E. Shanas (Eds.). *Handbook of aging and the social sciences* (2nd ed.), p. 513. New York: Van Nostrand.

the desire for leisure activity. Cutler, Whitelaw, and Beattie (2002) conducted a national survey on aging for the National Council on the Aging (NCOA). Sixty-nine percent of the people in the survey said that having enough savings motivated them to retire. Forty percent said that eligibility for Social Security would motivate their retirement. Fifteen percent of retirees in this study reported that they worked full- or part-time and another 35 percent said they did volunteer work.

These findings point to a shift in the meaning of retirement for the older worker. Early research on retirement saw retirement as a life crisis and a time of disengagement (Hardy, 2002). But today, people generally retire early in good health. And they report high life satisfaction, good mental health, and for some people, an improvement in physical health in retirement (Betancourt, 1991).

Neal Cutler, the Director of the NCOA survey, says that

> We will see more and more people who describe themselves as retired but continue to work. Many of these people are working by choice, not because they have to. In the 21st century, retirement will encompass a wide range of options. We will see some 75-year-olds working two jobs and some 40-year-olds lounging poolside. Retirement used to be defined by what one was no longer doing—not parenting, not working, not actively involved. Increasingly, it will be defined by what one does do—second career, volunteer work, travel, sport activities.

James Firman, President and CEO of the NCOA, says that

> Sixty-five may be meaningful as a speed limit, but it means less and less as a retirement age. . . . The stereotypical notion of working until age 65, moving to a warm and sunny climate and rocking on the porch has gone the way of the gold retirement watch. . . . We are in the midst of a fundamental reformulation of retirement. (NCOA, 2000)

Costa (1998, p. 133, cited in Rix, 2004, p. 3) in an economic history of retirement in the United States says that retirement now looks like a "time of personal discovery and fulfillment rather than one of withdrawal, a situation made possible by rising incomes and the abundance and declining cost of leisure activities." These opportunities, of course, depend on a person having a middle class income and stable work career that provides a good pension. Still, most people retire as soon as they can afford to. And retirees now have many options in retirement. Options range from early retirement, to partial retirement, to work at second careers.

Quinn and Burkhauser (1990, p. 307) say that "if retirement from the labor force marks the passage into old age, then the old among us have grown considerably younger in recent years." U.S. workers now retire at earlier ages than ever before. Clark and Quinn (2002) found that between the mid-1960s and mid-1980s, labor force participation for men aged 55 and over declined by about 1 percent per year. From the mid-1980s to the present, this rate accelerated. By the early 2000s men had a retirement rate 20 percentage points lower than the 1980s rate would predict.

Changes in Social Security's retirement age in part explain this trend. Retirees can now draw Social Security benefits at age 62. Also, many companies offer early retirement packages to workers. Some plans give workers bonuses like health insurance and cash settlements to leave work at age 55 or 60. These options grew in the 1960s and 1970s. Companies see early retirement as a way to save on the high salaries of older workers. In 2004, by age 65 only 16 percent of men remain in the U.S. labor force (Economist, 2004).

Why do older workers retire early? First, people quit work when they can get their best deal on retirement benefits; second, they leave work because they do not enjoy working. A study based on Social Security data supports this view. This study found that people who wanted to retire said they felt tired of work and had pension income (Henretta, Chan, & O'Rand, 1992). Quinn and Burkhauser (1990) report that the age of eligibility for Social Security has a strong impact on when people retire. Studies also find that people in private pension plans retire when they think they will get the most benefits from their plans (Hayward & Liu, 1992).

Stanford and his colleagues (1991) found that the reasons for early retirement differed by ethnicity.

Early retired whites, for example, tended to come from white-collar jobs. They take early retirement because of their good pension programs. Early retired African Americans and Mexican Americans tended to come from blue-collar and service jobs. Minority group members tended to retire due to health problems or physical impairment (Taylor & Doverspike, 2003).

Policymakers have begun to worry about the trend toward early retirement. A growing older population, retired in late middle-age, may put a strain on Social Security and other pension plans. Recent changes to Social Security rules attempt to remove some of the incentive to retire. First, Social Security will raise the age for full benefits from age 65 today to age 67 by the year 2027. Second, Social Security will reduce benefits at age 62 from 80 percent to 70 percent. Third, workers will get increased Social Security benefits for putting off retirement. These changes may decrease the rate of early retirements.

Recent changes to private pension plan benefits could also lead to fewer early retirements in the future. Companies have begun to shift from **defined benefit** to **defined contribution** pension plans. Defined benefit plans pay out a defined amount at a set age according to a formula. These plans encourage retirement at a prescribed age or earlier. Defined contribution plans offer less incentive to retire at a set age. These plans work like a savings account. The employer and the employee pay in a percentage of the worker's wages. The longer people work, the more money they add to their plan and the more they will have when they retire.

Most people still belong to a defined benefit plan, but membership in defined benefit plans fell from 73 percent of private plan members in 1975 to 42 percent in 1998 (Rajnes, 2002, cited in Rix, 2004). An increasing proportion of people now belong to defined contribution plans. Rix (2004, p. 22) says that "these workers face considerable market and other risks that threaten retirement income security." These changes to pension plan rules and policies will affect workers' retirement decisions. Still, the trend toward early retirement over the past forty years shows that many workers retire as early as they can. Changes to pension rules may make early retirement harder, but these changes will not erase workers' desire to retire.

Partial Retirement

Clark and Quinn (2002; Rix, 2002) say that the trend toward early retirement has slowed. Some people delay retirement to get larger pensions when they retire. But, many retirees, often people who retire early, return to work part-time. Definitions of partial retirement differ. Some researchers say people have partially retired if they earn less than one-half their past maximum yearly income. Some researchers say people have partially retired if they earn less than 80 percent of their past maximum monthly income. Some researchers define partial retirement as work in the two years after a person begins to get Social Security benefits.

Studies find that, depending on the definition used, between 5 and 30 percent of retired wage workers work at some time during retirement. A U.S. Department of Labor report (2000) found that 25 percent of retirees said they worked part-time. And 67 percent of workers said they expected that they would work in retirement. (See Table 10.2.)

Quinn, Burkhauser, and Myers (1990, p. 26) say that part-time work "is one logical way for individuals to ease out of the labor force" and that it is "a popular route of labor force withdrawal." Rix (2004) says that 60 percent of retirees, who still worked, saw partial retirement as the ideal. Moen and colleagues (2000, cited in Rix, 2004) found that most older workers preferred less than full-time work. These preferences show up in the trend toward part-time work for men and women aged 65 and over.

From 1960 to 2001, the proportion of older men who worked part-time rose from 30.0 to 43.9 percent. The proportion of older women who worked part-time rose from 44.0 percent to 58.2 percent (Rix, 2004; U.S. Senate, 1991). Hayward (Gerontology Center, 1994) says that about one-third of retirees return to work today, usually within a year after retirement. "It is not tenable," he says, "to assume that someone who retires from the labor force will never return. . . . For a growing minority of workers there appears to be a revolving door between work and retirement."

Elder and Pavalko (1993) studied 517 men from the Stanford-Terman longitudinal study of high-IQ children. This study began in 1922 and collected twelve waves of data until 1986. Most of the men in this study had managerial or professional jobs. The researchers found three retirement patterns: abrupt, sporadic, and gradual retirement.

About one-third of the group (30 percent) made a single abrupt exit from work. These people tended to leave work at age 62. Another 16 percent showed a sporadic pattern of leaving work fully, then returning to the workforce. These people made more than five work transitions and about half of them made two or more exits from the labor force. On average, they first left the labor force at age 61. Nearly half (46 percent) of the sample showed a gradual pattern of retirement. Gradual retirees either reduced their work time or had at least two transitions out of work. They averaged three to four transitions between their career and retirement. On average, they left the labor force for the first time at age 63. About one-half these men worked between 16 and 75 percent of full-time in their first jobs after retirement. They fully retired on average at age 70, later than any other group.

TABLE 10.2
Part-time Workers by Age and Sex, 2001

Age	*Both Sexes*	*Men*	*Women*
25–54	11.1	4.2	19.1
55+	24.2	18.2	31.5
55–64	16.6	10.1	24.3
65+	50.0	43.9	58.2
65–69	44.8	37.4	54.6
70–74	56.4	51.0	63.6
75+	55.0	51.2	61.2

Rix (2004) says that many older people work part-time in retirement. This differs for men and women. Women, compared with men, show a higher rate of full-time work in the early retirement years. Note that the proportion of people who work part-time increases significantly after age 65 (an increase from 16.6 percent for workers aged 55 to 64 to 50 percent for workers aged 65 and over). More than one-half of men and women in later old age (75 and over) continue to work part-time. Also note that at every age (including age 75 and over) a higher proportion of women, compared with men, work part-time. Older women have smaller pensions and in some cases no pensions. This reflects a lifetime of low pay, part-time work (note the difference in part-time work for men and women aged 25 to 54). Older women need to work in order to pay their bills.

Source: Rix, S. E. (2004). Aging and work: A view from the United States. Washington, D.C.: AARP Public Policy Institute. Retrieved September 17, 2004, *http://research.aarp.org/econ/2004_02_work.pdf.10.* Citing U.S. Department of Labor, Bureau of Labor Statistics, January 2002, and unpublished data. Reprinted with permission.

In the national Health and Retirement Study (U.S. Department of Health, 1993; cited in Rix, 2004) about three-fourths of workers aged 51 to 61 said they would like to work part-time. They said they would like to stay at their current jobs with fewer hours per week. Workers say that more flexible work options would allow them to stay in the labor force longer. But few of them thought that their employers would agree to this. Most people find that they either have to work full-time or retire (Moen et al., 2000).

Some companies hire retired workers to help with training or to work on special projects. Some workers retire and then do the same work for another company. Quinn and Burkhauser (1990) report that about one-third of all workers in retirement move to a different type of work. More than one-half end up in a new industry. Of self-employed men who retired, three-quarters who kept working did so at something new.

These new jobs often demand lower skill levels than the job a person held before retirement. They often involve routine work. They include work in fast-food chains, bank teller jobs, and part-time factory work. Days Inn, McDonald's, and Sears all hire older employees. These companies offer flexible schedules and part-time work. But they also offer low pay. Workers who move into these jobs face a cut in wage rates of 30 percent. Some people decide to retire rather than work at these rates. Others see these jobs as ways to earn extra money and stay socially active. Rix (2002) says that the sudden transition to retirement in the past has begun to change into a more gradual process of withdrawal from work.

One study showed that about three-quarters of people stayed at transitional jobs two years after retirement (Quinn, Burkhauser, & Myers, 1990). This trend toward part-time work will increase in the years ahead. Quinn, Burkhauser, and Myers (1990, p. 189) sum up the current research. "Something is happening," they say. "Part-time and full-time work on a new job is a serious alternative to continued work on the career job and to complete labor force withdrawal. . . . a substantial number of older Americans are willing and able to continue working despite the financial disincentives that often penalize the decision to do so." Hayward and Liu (1992, p. 46) say that "for a small minority of workers, there appears to be a revolving door between part-time work and full retirement."

Second Careers

Some retirees leave work and begin a second career. Stern (1993, p. 52) says that retirement used to mean an end to productive life. "Now," she says, "it's more likely to mean 'the day on which you take your first pension and move on to something new.' " For many people, a second career means work at something they love to do or something they have always wanted to do. Paul Tournier (1972, p. 129) called a second career a "free career." This career differs from leisure or from a person's mid-life career. A second career stands outside the hierarchy of corporate life. People set their own goals, use their own approaches to solving problems, and express their own identities.

Savishinsky (2000, p. 144) gives the example of Zoe, a retired woman in her 60s who became a T'ai chi enthusiast. (T'ai chi is an ancient Chinese spiritual practice and exercise program.) She gained skill in the practice of T'ai chi after about eighteen months. She then apprenticed to her instructor and became a teacher of T'ai chi. She said she had wanted to teach for decades. So this new role fulfilled one of her dreams. "What they're paying me is nice," she said, "but the money's incidental." Zoe believed in the good that T'ai chi does for her students. And this gave her new role a deeper meaning. Zoe serves as a good example of Tournier's free career.

A questionnaire on second careers in *Modern Maturity,* the magazine of the AARP, drew 36,000 responses from people aged 50 and over. The responses ranged from a lawyer who now works as a salmon fisher to an office administrator who now grooms dogs. Caroline Bird, who wrote a book on second careers, says that many of the jobs "were dead-end, small-scale and off the organizational charts," but that "these 'bad new jobs' are ideally suited to older people who want flexibility and maybe just a little income—and they will be models for younger workers as the American work force changes" (Beck, Denworth, & Christian, 1992, p. 58).

Jack and Elaine Wyman, for example, sold their advertising agency in San Francisco and moved to Scottsdale, Arizona. They grew bored with their leisure life-style and opened a new company called Wyman Communications based in their home. Reporter Linda Stern (1993, p. 34) said at that time that, "the Wymans handle advertising for a few favored clients, have self-published a book called *Retired? Get Back in the Game!,* . . . are working on a television special for WETA in Washington, DC, and travel regularly on the lecture circuit." Other couples have opened child daycare centers, personal service businesses for homebound older people, and bed and breakfasts.

Henry M. Wallfresh, 55, worked for a firm that helped corporate retirees on retirement planning. His company laid him off during a corporate shake up. After the shock wore off, he began a second career that includes what he liked most about his former job. "He still advises corporations, writes articles and gives speeches on all aspects of retirement through his own fledgling firm, Whale Communications. Only now, he works at home in T shirts and starts most of his talks 'And then it happened to me . . .' " (Beck, Denworth, & Christian, 1992).

These jobs express the personalities, interests, and in some cases the fantasies of their creators. For many people, a second career opens a new life. As Tournier says, a second career "has a goal, a mission, and that implies organization, loyalty, and even priority over other more selfish pleasures—not in the line of duty, since professional obligations are not involved, but for the love of people. It is, therefore, not an escape, but a presence in the world" (Tournier, 1972, p. 130).

PERSONAL RESPONSES TO RETIREMENT

Atchley and Barusch (2004) describe retirement as an event, a social role, a phase of life, and a process. The event of retirement—stopping work, getting a pension, having a retirement party—signals entry into the social role of retiree. Atchley (1976; *also* Atchley and Barusch, 2004) says that this role has two characteristics: First, people must stay out of work; second, they must have the health to carry on retirement activity.

The retirement phase of life begins with taking on the retirement role, but the start of this phase has gotten blurry. Early research on retirement saw this phase as a break with the past and a crisis in a person's identity. But research finds that people show continuity between their work lives and their lives in retirement. Many people today move in and out of retirement more than once. This makes it useful to view retirement as a process.

Atchley and Barusch (2004) describe retirement as a series of stages. A condensed version of this model follows. This five-phase model takes a life-course perspective on retirement. It shows the interplay between a person's past, their current life, and external events. Some people skip phases or go back and forth between one or more phases. Researchers now speak of **revolving retirement**. This term applies to retirees who later decide to return to work (Francese, 2004). Atchley cautions that these phases "represent a device for making it easier to view retirement as a process, not as an inevitable sequence that everyone must go through" (1985, p. 196).

This model serves best as a way to discuss the decisions people make and the experiences they have in retirement. It applies best to one type of worker: the white man who retires at age 65. The model does less well at describing someone who retires early, someone who gets laid off, women, and minority group members. We know less about the patterns that these types of retirees follow. Some recent research suggests that they follow very different patterns than the one described here.

Phase 1: Preretirement

The preretirement phase has two stages—a near and remote stage. The **remote stage** takes place long before retirement. People in their 30s, for example, may start to track their contributions to a company pension plan. They read about retirement savings plans and make investments for the future. Later, in their 40s or 50s, they travel to look at possible retirement sites.

One of my colleagues in his mid-40s did some remote-stage planning. Last year he and his wife decided to sell their northern lakeside cottage. They took the money and made a down payment on a condominium apartment in Florida. I asked him why they bought a home so far from the city they live in. He said that they use the condo a few weeks a year now for vacations, but "It will be paid off in a few years. Then it will be there for us when we retire. So it's an investment in our future."

Today, people may choose to retire early, on time, or late. People after age 50 think about the options. They look at their pensions, long-term incomes, working conditions, families, spouse's retirement, and success at work (Henretta, 2003). People in good health and with enough income often decide to retire.

The **near phase** takes place just before retirement. People make plans to leave their jobs. They learn about pension payments, fill out forms, and may train someone to take their places. Ekerdt and DeViney (1993) studied 1,365 male workers' views of work during a four-year longitudinal study. Workers ranged in age from 50 to 69. The researchers found that as workers came closer to retirement age, they tended to view their jobs as a source of tension and fatigue. The researchers say that workers in a preretirement phase begin to see work as less positive. This allows them to move away from their identity as workers.

Karp (1986) found something similar in a study of academics aged 50 to 60. He describes an "exiting consciousness" that shapes these workers' priorities at the end of their careers. Vinick and Ekerdt (1992) say that some people never intend to retire. Still, they read about retirement and talk about it with friends as they near retirement age.

Most people pass through the near phase in good spirits. A person who decides to retire often sees the retirement process as fair. A person who feels forced to retire, or who retires due to ill health, will more likely feel dissatisfied with the process (Knesek, 1992).

Phase 2: The Honeymoon

The honeymoon phase takes place just after retirement. People catch up on chores and projects they postponed while they worked. They fix the storm gutters, get more involved with grandchildren, and travel. A couple may decide to take a winter cruise or a trip to New England in the fall. A person in this phase enjoys the freedom that retirement brings.

Prentis (1992, p. 77) reports the case of a 60-year-old social work administrator who retired early. Retirement gave her the chance to stay longer at her cottage, spend more time with her grandchildren, and spend more time visiting her mother in a nursing home. "For the first time in my life," she says, "I am free."

Some people cut back on their mid-life activities during this phase. They explore the limits of doing nothing. These people then increase their activities until they find the amounts that suit them best.

BOX 10.3

REFLECTIONS ON AN EARLY RETIREMENT

I retired twenty-five years ago. Well, almost—I took my first sabbatical leave. A sabbatical lasts only a year and in this way it differs from retirement. I think of a sabbatical as a long arching basketball shot. It starts on an upward swing, reaches a peak, then turns back to earth. In retirement, you go into orbit and stay there. But in many ways a sabbatical and retirement are the same. My sabbatical began as a dream, but in the end I was glad to wake up safely back at the university a year later.

In graduate school I had plenty of time to read, write, and talk about my work. Then the teacher's world of lectures, tests, grading, and worst of all, committee meetings, closed in on me. Seven years later, having earned a sabbatical, I could devote myself to creative work again, free of the chains that kept me from being the genius I knew I was inside.

For the first two months I lived my dream. Words poured out of my pen. Everything I read led to a new idea. I went to the library to browse the stacks. I met with colleagues for coffee in the afternoons. I would sip my coffee at my leisure, while they checked their watches to make sure they would get to class on time. Poor mortals. Aside from these contacts, I didn't see many people. I hadn't set up any formal ties with other researchers. I wanted to stay free to explore uncharted lands.

Like all good retirees, I had planned to travel. Just after Christmas my family and I headed to Cambridge, England, where I had a visiting position in the Medical Psychology Unit. Again, I made no commitment to work with another researcher on a project. I wanted the freedom to read, write, and soak up Cambridge culture.

Cambridge took me closer than I'd have liked to one version of life in retirement. In Cambridge, I had not only freed myself from my university, my colleagues, and my students; I had freed myself from my society. In Cambridge, I walked the streets, free from mundane concerns. I visited the library, "the Backs" or banks of the River Cam, Kings College Chapel, and other sites dozens of times. But, except for my family and a few people in my unit, no one in Cambridge knew me. No one cared if I came into the office. No one at the university cared if I lived or died. I had no obligations, but I also had no place in that world, no role. I made no difference.

I also felt the loss of income that sometimes comes with retirement. Just after we arrived in England, the dollar took a dive against the British pound. Bread cost twice what it did at home. A trip to the London Zoo for my son's birthday, including transportation, admission, and snacks, cost well over $100 (and we brought our own lunch). I began to eat more bread and

BOX 10.3
(Continued)

jam than ever before. We treated ourselves to steak and roast beef only twice in our six-month stay. To save on our heating bill, we turned the heat off during the day. I worked in an overcoat with gloves on.

I began to feel trapped, and at times depressed, by the mess I'd gotten us into. I counted the days until we could leave. What started out as a dream had turned into a nightmare. I wanted to wake up.

At last on an overcast day in June—we only had four sunny days in six months—we headed for London and our flight home. I could hardly wait to pick up my mail at the university again. I began to think about my courses in the fall. I started making notes and thinking about new lectures. We went out for dinner, to the movies, and I drove my car without worrying about the cost.

I reentered the university with excitement, and I guess a sabbatical should bring you back refreshed. But I felt as much relieved as refreshed. I'd done all I set out to do; I had written, and read, and travelled. But after all this freedom, what I wanted most was my old routine. I wanted classes and students and, well, maybe even committees. I found that I needed to be needed. If I didn't attend a meeting, I needed to know that I was missed.

Sociologists talk about the importance of social integration. The retired person, like me on my sabbatical, faces the threat of disintegration. Like me, a retiree loses income, a social role, and colleagues. But I could return to my work—this time. Someday, I'll retire for real. Then I'll have to find a new way to relate to my society, not through my position and not as a member of the university hierarchy, but in some other way. Every retired person faces this challenge. Many succeed in finding new roles and a new purpose beyond work. In the meantime, I have another sabbatical coming up in a few years. This will give me another chance to practice for retirement. I'll have a chance to do better this time. With enough practice I may get it right before I retire for real.

What do you think I should do to prepare for my next sabbatical? Based on this story, what do you think a retiree should do to ensure a good retirement?

Many people first cut back on work-related activities like board memberships. They then rebuild an active life based on their personal interests.

A retired librarian reports that after she retired, she filled her schedule as if she still worked. I "signed up for a million activities," she says. "I programmed myself really crazy" (Prentis, 1992, p. 59). Then she calmed down and worked out a more leisurely routine.

A high school principal in Prentis' (1992) study describes his honeymoon phase. First, he and his wife traveled to England. Then he started teaching at a local university in his hometown. He also got active in community work. He joined a men's club and served on the board of education and on his church council. "I have been retired now for five years," he says, "and to tell the truth, I have enjoyed every minute of it. I have no regrets" (Prentis, 1992, p. 71).

Many retirees, like this principal, report an easy adjustment to retirement. Bikson and Goodchilds (1991) studied retired and working professional men in California. They found that current workers imagined they would have many problems in retirement. A study of retirees found that they had few of these problems. Compared with workers, retirees showed the same levels of self-esteem, felt better about their use of time, and made more new friends.

Price (2003) studied women professionals. She found that they had to "reestablish order" after retirement. They adjusted best to retirement if they could use their work-related skills, stayed active, and found new roles in the community. Savishinsky (2000, p. 52) reports that after travel, for example, retirees report that "their new identity as a retiree was 'more real.' . . . the things around them were still the same; yet *they* had somehow changed."

"Harold's easing into retirement."

Phase 3: The Retirement Routine

After some time, the retiree takes up the *retirement role.* This role gives a person the right to collect a pension, but the person has the obligation not to work full-time. Atchley (1985, p. 196) says that people who adjust to this phase "know what is expected of them and they know what they have to work with—what their capabilities and limitations are. They are self-sufficient adults, going their own way, managing their own affairs."

These people have gone beyond the excitement of the honeymoon phase. Their retirement routine may include leisure, volunteer work, or a second career. People keep this routine as long as they find it satisfying, and they can change it over time. Some people take life easy. They do only what they find enjoyable and spend more time socializing with friends. Others keep a busy schedule of activity.

Ekerdt (1986) says that many retirees subscribe to what he calls the **busy ethic**. This ethic values an active life. People who subscribe to this ethic often carry electronic organizers and have telephone answering machines, so they won't miss messages. Ekerdt says that the busy ethic helps retirees ease into retirement. The busy ethic allows retirees to maintain the same values they held while working—engagement in community affairs, an active social life, and self-development. Retirees legitimate their retirement through "involvement and engagement . . . [the busy ethic] esteems leisure that is earnest, occupied, and filled with activity" (Ekerdt, 1986, pp. 239–240).

The busy ethic, Ekerdt says, domesticates or tames retirement. It supports energetic activity and healthful life-styles, two long-standing American values. The busy ethic keeps retirement and retirees in the mainstream of American life.

A person's retirement routine changes over the ten, twenty, or more years of retirement. Activities change to reflect changes in health and interests. Still, as Ekerdt shows, social ideals and expectations shape the retirement routine.

Phase 4: Disenchantment

Some people feel disenchanted with retirement. They find that relief from work loses its charm after a few months. This can occur before the retirement routine takes hold. It may come after the honeymoon and a period of rest and relaxation. Or, people may find that they can't carry out their preretirement plans. An accurate view of retirement creates a greater chance for retirement satisfaction. Unrealistic plans can lead to disenchantment.

I interviewed Phil Granger, a television cameraman, a few years ago for a study of successful aging. Phil planned to move to a piece of land he had bought in the northwest. He imagined himself living in a beautiful setting—birdwatching, hiking, camping. Unfortunately for him, his wife had other plans. She enjoyed living near her sisters and her bridge club. She refused to move. Phil broke into tears of frustration as he told me about his dream. He felt angry and disillusioned with retirement.

People who have little say in their retirement decisions can feel disenchanted. A businessman, who sold his business, said that he resented retirement and felt envious of people who worked (Prentis, 1992). "When the doors were closed on my business," he says, "I would sit in my office alone, with no one around, no one calling me. I had nobody to call. I had money, but I didn't know what to do. I

BOX 10.4
THE RETIREMENT PLANNING COUNTDOWN

Planning for retirement should begin early in a person's career. PRE should begin just after a person enters the workforce. This will allow time to make long-range plans. The schedule below suggests some of the plans a person needs to make at various points.

Time Before Retirement	*Action*
About 30 years	• Budget 10 percent of your income for savings. The magic of compounding interest makes this an attractive option. A person who puts $5,000 per year into a retirement plan each year from age 30 to retirement would save $180,000 over the thirty-six years. Assuming an interest rate of 10 percent and tax-free growth of the money, the savings would be worth $1,650,000 at retirement.
	• Start a retirement savings plan. These plans ensure that money saved will grow tax free. Plans include individual retirement accounts (IRA), 401(k) plans through an employer, and simplified employee pension (SEP) plans for self-employed people. A registered financial planner can help sort out the options and create the best plan for you.
	• Plan for large future expenses such as children's education, a home purchase, or vacation home.
	• Make out a will.
20 years	• Begin exploring retirement options such as early retirement, partial age 55 or 60, or work after age 65.
	• Consider the kind of retirement you want. Where do you want to live? How do you want to spend your time? How does your family fit into the picture (children and grandchildren, elderly parents)?
	• Develop skills, interests, and friends apart from your job.
	• Begin a diet and fitness program that you can maintain into retirement.
	• Review your will to see that it still suits your needs. Changes in your assets, in your marital status, or the arrival of grandchildren may lead you to change your will.
15 years	• You're now officially a senior—at least according to the AARP. You can begin to claim your senior discounts at the movies, at drug stores, and in restaurants.
	• Actively begin to think about and plan for retirement. Talk about these plans with your partner. And let your adult children in on your plans.
	• Review your legal papers with your partner.
	• Check on financial goals such as paying off your mortgage. Also review your asset allocation (bonds, equities, real estate) to see if your investments will meet your goals. If not, rebalance your portfolio.
10 years	• Review your housing situation. Plan for renovations if you plan to live in your home after retirement. Ensure that you save for future renovations.
	• Consider second career options. Check on legalities of running a business from your home.
	• Look into postretirement benefits such as dental plans and health care and into pensions from work.

(continued)

BOX 10.4
(Continued)

	• Look into long-term care insurance to protect yourself and your family from the costs of in-home or nursing home care.
5 years	• Review your choices for annuities and pension income.
	• Check out your Social Security benefits and decide when you want to start collecting. You can start collecting benefits as early as age 62, but at a reduced rate. Consider consulting a financial advisor, a lawyer, or an estate planner, if you haven't done so already.
	• Try a dry run of your retirement plan. For example, if you plan to move to another country or another part of the United States after retirement, live in your new setting for a while. Take some vacations there. Try to visit during various seasons of the year. Check into real estate costs and housing options. If you plan to travel in a motor home, rent one for some time to try out the life-style.
	• Get training and develop new skills you will need if you plan to keep working after retirement.
Year of retirement	• Give yourself time to adapt. Don't move in your first year. Don't make drastic changes in your plan for the year.
	• Continue to review your assets. Continue to diversify your sources of income. Plan for the long run. Make sure that large retirement payments at the start of retirement won't leave you with too small an income later on.
	• Accept that you will have to modify your retirement plan. You will make some mistakes, your interests will change, and you will learn as you go. If you have planned well, you can expect a good result after some adjustment.

had no plans. I wanted to run" (Prentis, 1992, p. 66). This man tried golf, fishing, and walking. All of these activities left him feeling empty.

These two men needed to take a step back and rethink retirement. Family and friends can help here. Phil Granger began taking classes at a local education center for older people. He says he has taken more classes than anyone he knows. He developed interests in foot massage, politics, and history. He became a leader in this group and adjusted to a new vision of retirement. The executive in Prentis' study began to look into a new business venture that he hoped would give meaning to his life.

Disenchanted people reorient themselves after some time. Some, like Phil, find new interests. Others, like the businessman, come out of full retirement and return to work part- or full-time. Betty Friedan (1993) tells the story of 66-year-old Bernie Lovitsky, who retired to a "beach lifestyle" after he sold his Michigan discount store. After a while he got bored and depressed. He joined the Peace Corps and went to Tonga for two and a half years. He returned to the United States after he helped the Tongans create a $4 million business that they now run.

Most people in good health, with a good income, a strong support network, and a flexible personality eventually adjust to retirement. They come through this stage of disenchantment and set up a retirement routine.

Phase 5: Termination

Retirement ends when people return to work or when they lose their independence. Francese (2004) refers to a return to work as a revolving retirement. He says that about 13 percent of families with a head aged 55 and over fall into this category. He sees a growth in the desire for workers to move in and out of the workforce after retiring.

Health, the availability of jobs, a person's skill level or professional background all determine a person's ability to return to work. More options to full retirement may decrease feelings of disenchantment in the future. Also, more control over the timing and content of retirement will lead to smoother transitions. Nuttman-Shwartz (2004) says that preretirement preparation for emotional issues can help smooth the retirement transition.

PRERETIREMENT EDUCATION

Preretirement education (PRE) programs began in the United States in the 1950s at midwestern universities (Deren, 1990). The programs then spread to business and industry. They focused on financial planning and often took place a few years before a person retired. Programs mostly served white, middle-class, professional men. They took place in larger companies or unions for workers with pensions plans.

Overall, few people get formal PRE. Most people find information on their own, learn from friends and relatives, or get advice from financial advisors. But studies find that PRE or counseling lead to better adjustment in retirement (Feldman, 2003). People who get good information about retirement feel more confident about their futures (Hayes & Deren, 1990).

Louis Harris (1979, cited in Rix, 1990, p. 5) says that planning "is perhaps the single most important factor in assuring a comfortable retirement life free from financial worries." What should a good preretirement program contain? A good program should help people understand their financial options. This part of the program should start early in a person's career. Financial planning comes too late if it takes place a year or two before retirement. People should understand their retirement benefits. They should know the amount of their monthly pension, and they should know what decisions they have to make (e.g., about pension benefits for a spouse).

Brady and colleagues (1994) studied PRE programs at 245 companies in New England. He found that about one-half the firms offered PRE programs. The companies that sponsored these programs felt that workers needed to understand their retirement benefits. Eighty-seven percent of the companies that offered programs provided individual counseling or planning. Programs spent most of the time on financial issues.

A good program should go beyond finances. It should include a variety of health and life-style topics, including legal issues, information on housing, work after retirement, fitness, and relationships. A program should also involve the spouse of the retiree. It should encourage discussion of each spouse's retirement plans and goals. A good program should help a couple look at their life-style, decide what changes they want to make (if any) after retirement, and plan how to make the transition (Feldman, 2003).

Women have less chance to plan for retirement than men. Women tend to hold service, wholesale, and retail jobs at low pay with poor pensions. These jobs seldom offer PRE. Women in professional positions have a better chance to get retirement advice than nonprofessionals. But Hayes and Deren (1990) report that less than 20 percent of women aged 35 and over hold professional jobs. Women who do have access to a PRE program may find that it ignores a woman's specific concerns (Deren, 1990).

Several programs in the 1990s focused on the needs of women (Deren, 1990; Keddy & Singleton, 1991). Sessions in these programs focus on finances, a major concern. But these programs found that women also needed to discuss with their spouses task sharing after retirement, sexual relations, and life-style changes (Hayes, 1990). The women in these programs reported that they valued the personal and psychological advice they received as much as the financial information (Houlihan & Caraballo, 1990). PRE programs for women may need to include topics of specific interest to them.

Deren (1990) says that PRE programs for women meet needs not met by programs designed for male workers. Women's programs have a content, design, and sensitivity to women's issues that other programs lack. Deren calls for programs that will meet the needs of Hispanic and other minority women. These programs, she says, must do more than translate English language programs. They must contain information relevant to minority women and sensitive to their cultures.

SOCIAL STRUCTURES AND RETIREMENT

Retirement studies since the 1940s and 1950s have focused on the individual experience of retirement. Studies have looked at retirement planning, activities in retirement, and retirement satisfaction. Researchers often take disengagement, activity, or continuity theory as the basis for their analyses. They assume that retirement will cause problems and that people need to cope with and respond to these problems. Most importantly, McDonald and Wanner (1990, p. 9) say, each of these theories views retirement "as a problem caused and solved by individual behavior." These theories (and others like modernization or age stratification theory) take social structures as given.

A **political economy** view of retirement looks at the effect of social structures on retirement. Social structure refers to the economy, the social stratification system, and social institutions. A person's place in the economic order, for example, shapes that person's retirement options. For example, second careers best fit the backgrounds of middle-class workers. Executives, engineers, and technicians, she says, have the privilege of retirement due to their good pension plans, good health, and education. They also have skills that they can use as consultants for pay or as volunteers to community groups.

Middle-class and upper middle-class workers with orderly work careers and good pensions report high satisfaction in retirement. People with less orderly careers, low incomes, and few skills have less opportunity.

The Dual Economy

Some social scientists divide the economy into the goods-producing and the service sectors. The goods-producing or core sector includes agriculture, mining, construction, and manufacturing. (The government sector has many of the characteristics of the core sector.) The service or periphery sector includes personal care, food services, general office work, and childcare. Dowd (1980, p. 77) says that the core sector is "highly organized and characterized by high wages and pensions systems, and the other [the periphery sector] is marked by low wages and few, if any fringe benefits."

These sectors offer unequal opportunities to retirees. Workers in the core sector (with higher wages and pensions) tend to follow traditional retirement patterns. DeViney (1995) found that core sector companies (mostly large firms) offered workers good pension plans in retirement. Hogan, Perrucci, and Wilmoth (2000) found that white men in core sector jobs had higher incomes than others in the sample, including women in the core sector.

White men also had much larger incomes in retirement. These trends reflect the tendency for workers in the core sector to work for larger firms and to have more stable work careers. Core workers' pension plans encourage and allow retirement from the labor force (Mitchell, Levine, & Pozzebon, 1988).

Those in the periphery sector (with lower pay and no pensions) show less traditional patterns of retirement. Women more often than men work in this sector. They tend to have broken work records and less chance of having a pension. This, in part, explains why single older women have some of the poorest incomes. It also explains why they often work past age 65. The type of work they do gives them few resources in retirement. Quinn, Burkhauser, and Myers (1990) found that the poorest and richest workers tended to stay in the labor force: the richest (many of them professionals) because they chose to work; the poorest, many in the service sector, because they needed the money. Low-wage men and women showed the greatest likelihood of working.

Even within a sector, the type of job a person does influences retirement options. Ruhm (1991) studied bridge jobs among retirees aged 50 to 64. Bridge jobs (jobs after a life career but before full retirement) included part-time work, second careers, and self-employment that a person held after retirement. Ruhm found that people, who held bridge jobs, most often had worked in higher status jobs in the core sector. They worked as professionals, managers, or technical workers. More than one-half of these people (57 percent) judged their bridge jobs as the most enjoyable job they had ever held. Ruhm found that few people in bridge jobs worked in production. Women, nonwhites, and people with little education left work early and had trouble finding bridge jobs. Their lack of marketable skills made it hard for them to find work after retirement.

Displaced Workers

Large shifts in the economy can also affect retirement options. Recently, many workers have been laid off due to changes in the economy. Even white male workers with seniority in union jobs find themselves out of work when an industry declines. The restructuring of the economy has led to plant closures in core industries like steel, textiles, and auto manufacturing.

This change in the economy creates long-term unemployment for large numbers of people. The U.S. Department of Labor, Bureau of Labor Statistics (2002, cited in Rix, 2004), reports that between January 1999 and December 2001 almost 10 million workers lost their jobs due to displacement. People aged 55 and older made up 1.2 million of these workers. Older workers (55 and over) made up 18 percent of long-tenured workers (in their jobs at least three years) who lost their jobs.

Moody (1988b) says that economic restructuring leads to the loss of middle-income jobs. High-tech jobs for professionals open up due to restructuring. Likewise, low-paying service jobs open up. Older workers in the middle often lack the skills to fill jobs in fields like computers and electronics. Displaced factory workers, who want to stay at work, have little choice but to move into service jobs. These jobs pay much less than many **displaced workers** made in union manufacturing jobs.

Moody (1988b) says that nearly 60 percent of older workers face a drop in job status and income. Also, some of these jobs require a move to another part of the country. Older workers with paid-off homes and roots in their communities find it hard to move. Structural changes in the economy, in part, account for individual choices in retirement today. "In a growing number of cases," Moody (1988b, p. 217) says, "'retirement' actually becomes a euphemism for discouraged or dislocated workers in the U.S. economy." (See Figure 10.2.)

A recent report by the Bureau of Labor Statistics (2002, cited in Rix, 2004) says that, compared with younger workers, older workers who lost their jobs from 1999 to 2001, had less chance of getting back to work after displacement. One-quarter of these displaced workers aged 55 to 64 had left the labor force by January 2002. This figure jumps to 55 percent of displaced workers aged 65 and over who left the labor force. "For the oldest displaced workers (65+), most of whom were eligible for Social Security benefits, labor force exit was nearly twice as common as reemployment" (Rix, 2004, p. 17).

The literature on worker displacement calls these *discouraged workers.* These workers give up looking for work. They may give up for a number of reasons. Some older workers with long work records may prefer to retire on their pensions. Other workers leave the labor force because they can't get the kind of jobs they prefer, they want to avoid facing age discrimination in the hiring process, or they gave up looking for jobs.

Controversy exists about how many workers fall into the discouraged worker category. Definitions of discouragement differ. The Bureau of Labor Statistics used a fairly strict definition and put the discouraged worker rate (nonworkers aged 55 and over) in 1994 at 8 percent (U.S. Department of Labor, Bureau of Labor Statistics, January 1995, cited in Rix, 2004).

A more recent 1999 Harris poll (Taylor, 1999, cited in Rix, 2004, p. 20) found that about 10 percent of nonworkers aged 55 or over said they "want to work and could accept a suitable job" if one were available. Rix (2004) reports that about 1 million men and women aged 55 and over say they would work if they could. She says that if statistics on unemployment included older men and women not in the labor force in 2002, the unemployment rate would have more than doubled from 3.8 to 7.8 percent.

Middle-aged workers (aged 45 and over) worry about age discrimination in the workplace. An

AARP study (2002) found that two-thirds of middle-aged workers believed that age discrimination exists in the workplace. They said they felt concerned about their ability to reenter the workforce or to get promotions as they aged. Sixty percent of these workers said they felt that employers let older workers go first when they cut staff. Almost one person in ten said they felt their firm had passed them up for a promotion. Six percent of the people in the AARP study said their firm fired them or forced them out of work due to their age. And 15 percent said they failed to get hired for a job due to their age. A number of experimental studies document age discrimination in the workplace. The studies found that "younger job applicants were favored over older applicants who were identical in all respects save age" (Rix, 2004, p. 15).

An analysis of social structural changes shows their influence on individuals' retirement options. This perspective points to social structural and economic change as the cause of some retirement trends today. Social structural change promotes

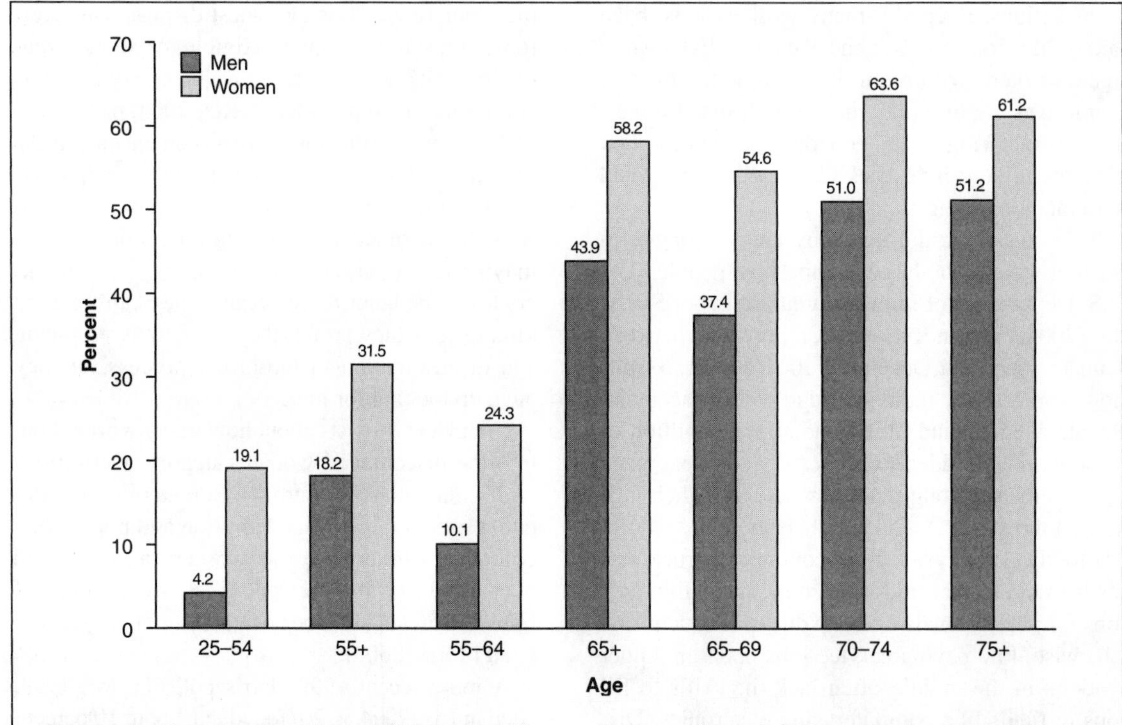

This graph shows the effect of unemployment on different age groups. Compared with the younger displaced workers, the workers (aged 55 to 64 and 65 and older) had a lower rate of reemployment over the two-year period. Also, the oldest group of workers showed a greater likelihood of leaving the labor force. Older workers tend to get discouraged looking for work. They may face (or feel they face) age discrimination in their job searches. They will opt for retirement rather than continue to look for a job. In this way, unemployment in later life effectively ends many workers' careers.

Percent employed as of January 2002 refers to all workers regardless of tenure on previous jobs.

FIGURE 10.2

Employment Status by Age of Workers Displaced from Jobs between 1999 and 2001

Source: Rix, S. E. (2004). *Aging and work: A view from the United States.* Washington, D.C.: AARP Public Policy Institute. Retrieved September 17, 2004, *http://research.aarp.org/econ/2004_02_work.pdf.10.* Citing U.S. Department of Labor, Bureau of Labor Statistics, August 2000.

part-time work, small business start-ups, work in service sector jobs, and early retirement. People accept these changes and may even feel that they have chosen these options. But the political economy perspective shows that, in part, large social forces shape these individual retirement choices.

THE FUTURE OF RETIREMENT

Gerontologists, economists, and other social scientists predict changes in retirement in the future. First, the U.S. population will have more people of retirement age than ever before. These people will form diverse groups based on age, ethnicity, race, region, work history, life experience, and income. No single pattern of retirement will describe how future retirees will end their work careers. Individual choice, the economy, marital status, and personal finances will shape workers' retirement decisions.

Second, longer life expectancy and better health for older workers will encourage many people to stay at work longer. They will need to add to their pensions (public or private) to maintain their lifestyles for more years. Bridget A. Macaskill, president and CEO of OppenheimerFunds, Inc., says that "the estimate of 70% of pre-retirement income built into many planning models may fall short, particularly given emerging healthcare concerns and the changing nature of retirement lifestyles. Even if these levels prove sufficient, they will be required for more years than most people plan for" (National Council on the Aging, 2000). Retirees in the future may decide to delay drawing their pension so that they can get higher payments into later old age.

Third, older workers will have more options in later life than ever before. Their choices will depend on their resources, skills, and experience. But they will also have more choices available to them. Options will include gradual retirement, flexible hours, bridge jobs, part-time work, second careers, or remaining at their current jobs (due to projected labor shortages) (Rix, 2002).

Rix (2004) lists a number of policy changes that would also extend workers' careers:

- Raising the earliest age that a person could get Social Security benefits;
- Raising the age that a person could get full Social Security benefits beyond the proposed future age of 67;
- Increasing the age of Medicare eligibility to encourage people to stay at work;
- Encouraging employers to use **phased retirement** programs that allow workers to leave work gradually;
- Encouraging employers to offer part-time and flexible work options to keep older workers on the job.

Fourth, future changes in the economy—such as a shortage of workers as the Baby Boom generation ages, the need for more service workers, and electronic offices that allow people to work from home—will open new work options for older people. This will encourage more workers to stay on the job or to find bridge jobs before they retire. Rix (2004, p. 22) says that "a primary reason workers are likely to postpone retirement will be the demand for labor. With slowing labor force growth, employers may have little choice but to turn to older workers."

Guillemard (1991) sees a worldwide trend in industrial nations away from a fixed retirement age. She sees this as a major change in the last stages of life. First, she sees a breakdown in the usual age-based distinctions between younger and older people. Second, she sees a breakdown in the link between old age and retirement. Retirement now occurs at younger ages than ever before. Partial retirement—flexible retirement, part-time work, job sharing, self-employment, and many other options—questions the concept of retirement itself. Retirement in the future will depend not on age but on how well people can perform a job, whether they can afford to retire, and whether they want to work.

Henretta (2003) adds a further point. More workers in the United States than ever before have employment pensions. These pensions offer more flexible retirement options. Some allow retirement at age 55. On average, people with employment pensions retire at age 61 or 62. Employee pensions free people from the lockstep of a single retirement system like Social Security.

The variety of people in old age, due to differences in social class, gender, minority group status, and occupation, leads to varied choices and opportunities in retirement. Vierck (2002) says that due to longer life expectancies, some people will work into their 80s. These people may have two or three careers. Retirement policies and the changing structure of the economy also influence retirement options. Many policymakers see longer work lives as a way to avoid a crisis in financing pensions for long-lived Baby Boomers. This suggests that retirement needs further study.

CONCLUSION

Economists trace old age in modern society to the retirement principle and the retirement wage. These two social inventions created a stage of active life beyond work. Workers earn an income from the state and can devote their time to leisure activities. Increases in public pensions have led to higher proportions of people who choose retirement. Retirement now exists as a normal part of the life cycle.

The research on retirement has focused mostly on white men. But studies of women and minorities show that they have unique patterns of work and retirement. Women, compared with men, often have broken work records and less pension income. Many women stay at work because they need the money. Minority members too have broken work records and they may have a different view of retirement. They also have fewer retirement options because they lack private pensions or savings. Researchers need to do more studies of female and minority workers' retirement.

Researchers also need to do more work on alternatives to retirement. Changes in Social Security rules and changes in the economy have led to more retirement options for older workers. These include early retirement, partial retirement, and second careers. Most of us will live through these changes. We will create the retirement of the future. The more we know about retirement, the more we can plan for a successful retirement transition.

SUMMARY

- Today, retirement is an established social institution. The trend toward retirement results from two historical events: the development of the *retirement principle* in industrialized societies, and the creation of the *retirement wage* or Social Security.
- Mandatory retirement assumes that older people work less well than younger people. However, many studies show less difference in the performance of older or younger workers when experience is taken into account. Ageism still creates resistance to keeping and hiring older workers.
- A large proportion of men choose to retire between the ages of 62 and 65 because of the retirement principle and the retirement wage. Because women follow more varied career paths than men, they do not show the same retirement pattern.
- Minorities tend to have poorer pensions, fewer benefits, and fewer options in retirement because of lower education levels, lower income levels, and racial discrimination.
- Retirees can now receive Social Security benefits at age 62. Also, many companies encourage retirement by offering early retirement packages to older workers. These incentives account for the trend toward early retirement, partial retirement, and second careers.
- The role of the retiree requires that a person (1) stay out of work and (2) have the health to carry on a retirement activity. Some theorists describe retirement as a series of phases. Briefly, a person enters the retirement role, sets up a retirement routine, and at some point leaves retirement.
- People who plan for their retirements tend to enjoy their retirements more. They report high life satisfaction and better financial resources. Guides to help with retirement planning exist. Some companies offer PRE programs, seminars for workers and spouses, and counseling.
- Researchers observe a major trend in industrialized nations away from a fixed retirement age. Retirement now occurs at younger ages than ever before. The older worker can also choose from options such as partial retirement, flexible retirement, part-time work, job sharing, and self-employment.
- In the future, ability rather than age will decide a person's retirement status. Older workers in the future may move in and out of the labor force more than once as their interests, abilities, and financial resources change.

DISCUSSION QUESTIONS

1. Define the term *retirement.* How and why did our society develop the institution of retirement?
2. Compare the working abilities of older people with those of younger people. Use research findings to back up your points. Why do employers resist hiring older workers?
3. How do retirement patterns for men and women differ? What are the major reasons for these differences?
4. Why is retirement different for African Americans than for whites? Explain the term *unretired-retired* as it applies to older African Americans.
5. List and describe some of the occupational choices older workers now have as they enter retirement.
6. List and describe the five phases of retirement.
7. How can people benefit from planning for retirement? Give an example of a good PRE program. Describe the topics covered in a good program. How does this type of information help a person plan for retirement?
8. Describe some of the trends in retirement that gerontologists predict for the future.

SUGGESTED READING

Adams, G. A., & Beehr, T. A. (Eds.). (2003). *Retirement: Reasons, processes, and results.* New York: Springer.

The authors organize this collection around three phases of the retirement process—preretirement, the retirement decision, and postretirement. The articles cover many of the topics discussed in this chapter. Articles discuss financial, social, and psychological issues that people face in retirement. The articles look at trends including bridge jobs, early retirement, and extending work life.

Bauer-Maglin, N., & Radosh, A. (Eds.). (2003). *Women confronting retirement: a nontraditional guide.* New Brunswick, NJ: Rutgers University Press.

Thirty-eight women from many professions and life conditions look at retirement. The authors discuss the need to find a new self-image beyond work, the need to balance work with recreation, and the need to shape public policies to create better opportunities in retirement. Many of these women played an activist role in the 1960s and 1970s. They continue to challenge the system as they work to overcome their negative views of retirement. This book offers a chance to learn what retirement looks like through the eyes of these articulate and socially aware women.

GLOSSARY OF TERMS

bridge job The job a person holds after a career job, but before full retirement. Bridge jobs include part-time work, second careers, and self-employment after retirement.

busy ethic The flip side of the work ethic, this ethic values the active life in retirement. It allows people to justify retirement in terms of mainstream social beliefs and values.

defined benefit A pension plan that defines how much a worker will receive after retirement.

defined contribution A pension plan that states how much a person must pay into the plan. The amount a person gets as a pension depends on economic conditions at the time of retirement.

displaced workers People who have lost their jobs due to economic slowdowns, plant closings, or an end to their positions.

near phase The phase of retirement planning that comes just before retirement. This may include filling out forms to release pension funds.

phased retirement A gradual reduction in the workweek at a person's career job.

political economy A perspective that looks at social organization and how political and economic conditions shape life experiences such as retirement.

preretirement education (PRE) Programs and information that help a person plan for retirement.

remote stage The stage in retirement planning that comes early in a person's career. It may include buying long-term investments thirty years before retirement.

revolving retirement A retirement pattern in which the retiree later decides to return to work.

second career A new career after retirement; a career shaped by a person's interests and passions.

secondary labor market Jobs that offer low pay, few benefits, and require physical labor. These jobs often lead to disability and they exist in the retail and service industries.

chapter 11

HOUSING AND TRANSPORTATION

Mrs. Carrington lived alone after her husband died. She lived in the same one-bedroom apartment that they had shared. At first, this seemed fine, but after a few years she began to have trouble climbing the six flights of stairs to her apartment. She found it hard to go out for groceries. She even had trouble getting to her ground-floor mailbox every day. The building superintendent helped her with rides to the supermarket. He got her mail for her and did small repairs around her apartment. But this depended on his schedule and personal plans.

The apartment building mostly housed people in late middle age. They worked during the day, and Mrs. Carrington had few friends in the building. Her long-time friends kept in touch on the telephone daily, but they could get around less as they aged. She spent more and more of her time watching television, alone in her apartment. Her daughter, Ruth, who lived two hours away, spoke to her at least once a day.

Ruth noticed about this time that her mother's refrigerator contained little meat, vegetables, or milk. Mrs. Carrington's inability to get out meant that she could not get fresh food. Ruth began to worry about her mother's health. She decided to look for an apartment in a seniors' housing complex closer to her home. Mrs. Carrington resisted, but she finally agreed to move.

The new setting brought her out of isolation. The apartment had a recreation room, a lobby where people gathered in the afternoon, and social events like birthday parties. The apartment complex offered a bus service to a shopping center twice a week. The bus driver brought her groceries to her door. Mrs. Carrington moved into a first-floor apartment. That meant she could get outside in the nice weather and could easily walk to the lobby to sit with her new neighbors. The staff kept an eye on the tenants for signs of illness or other problems. The move improved the quality of Mrs. Carrington's life.

Many people, like Mrs. Carrington, prefer not to move. They feel anxious about the cost of new housing and about losing touch with their friends and neighbors. They also feel comfortable with the places and things they have lived with for many years. Studies show, however, that a move to planned housing can improve morale, increase activity, and increase social interaction. Lawton (1987) emphasizes that people feel most satisfied if they move by choice and if the housing they move to suits their personal preferences.

The United States today offers older people a wide range of housing options. These options make it possible for people to live in the kind of housing they prefer. Still, problems with the housing supply exist. Some older people, those in inner cities and rural settings, for example, have few housing options. This chapter looks at: (1) the continuum of housing options and living arrangements open to older people today, (2) new developments in housing and transportation for older people, and (3) the future of housing and transportation in an aging society.

LIVING ARRANGEMENTS

Living arrangements include living with a spouse, alone, with other relatives, or with nonrelatives. Nearly all older people (85 percent) live alone or with a spouse. The rest live with another relative or with a nonrelative. Older women live in this type of arrangement at twice the rate of men. Widowhood, the tendency for women not to remarry, and low income account for the living arrangement differences between men and women.

Most older people who lived in the community (54 percent) lived with a spouse in 2003. But this, too, differs for men and women. Seventy-one percent of older men live with a spouse, compared with only 41 percent of older women. This difference between men and women increases with age. For people aged 85 and over, 56 percent of men but only 13 percent of women live with a spouse (U.S. Census Bureau, 2003a). High rates of widowhood among very old women and the tendency of men to remarry in later life account for this difference.

About one-third of all older people who live in the community lived alone in 2000 (up from 28 percent in 1989). (See Figure 11.1.) Women outnumbered men in this category by more than three to one. About 40 percent of older women lived alone compared with only 17 percent of older men. And this difference between men and women living

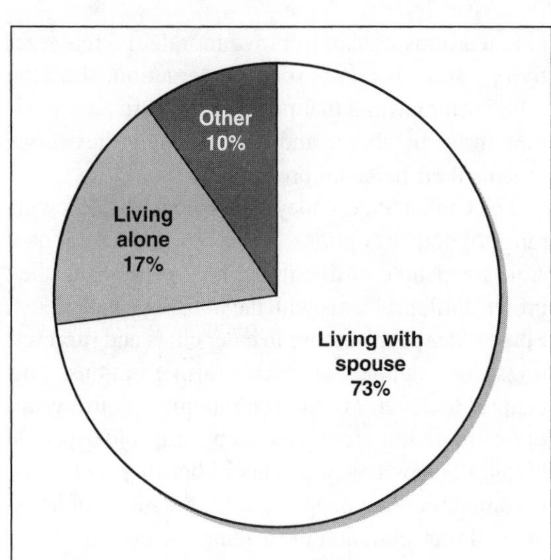

The figure shows that most noninstitutionalized older people lived with their spouses in 2000. But older men and women differ in the likelihood of living with a spouse. Nearly three-quarters of men (73 percent) but only two-fifths of women (41 percent) lived with a spouse. The proportion who lived with a spouse decreased with age. But it decreased more dramatically for women. Only 28.8 percent of women aged 75 and over lived with a spouse.

In 2000 about one-third (30 percent) of older people lived alone. Older men and women differ in the likelihood that they will live alone. Only 17 percent of men lived alone compared with 40 percent of older women. The proportion of people who live alone increases with age largely due to widowhood. Nearly one-half (49.4 percent) of women aged 75 and over live alone.

A relatively small proportion of older people (4.5 percent) lived in nursing homes in 2000. But the proportion differs by age group and increased with age. Only 1.1 percent of people aged 65 to 74 lived in a nursing home. This figure rose to 4.7 percent of people aged 75 to 84 years, and 18.2 percent of people aged 85 and over.

FIGURE 11.1

Living Arrangements of Men Aged 65 and Over, 2000

Source: Based on data from U.S. Census Bureau. See "America's Families and Living Arrangements; Population Characteristics: June 2001, Current Population Reports, P20-537" and "The 65 Years and Over Population: 2000, Census 2000 Brief, October, 2001." Retrieved October 2, 2004, *www.aoa.gov/prof/Statistics/profile/4.asp.*

alone grows with age. For women aged 75 and over, nearly one-half (49.4 percent) lived alone, compared with only 21 percent of older men (Administration on Aging, 2002d; AARP, 1993).

Engelhardt and colleagues (2002) say that increased Social Security benefits in part account for an increase in older women living alone. They found, for example, that each 1 percent increase in Social Security benefits led to a 1.3 percent increase in widows living alone. Divorced older women showed an even greater tendency to live alone as their Social Security benefits increased. Higher benefits give older women more living arrangement options.

The number of older people who live alone will likely increase in the future. Higher divorce rates in the middle and later years will add to the number of people who live alone. So will the increased number of people who choose never to marry. Also, older people today prefer what Rosenmayr and Kockeis (1963) first called "intimacy at a distance." They prefer to live near, but not with, their children.

The trend toward living alone could lead to problems in the future. People who live alone, compared with people who live with others, have more unmet needs for personal help with ADL. These people risk weight loss, falls, and burns (LaPlante, Kaye, Kang, & Harrington, 2004). Many people who live alone will need community services in order to stay out of institutions.

AN ECOLOGICAL MODEL OF HOUSING

Older people want to age in place. They want to stay in their homes as long as they can (AARP, 2003b). The AARP found similar results in a series of surveys. One survey (AARP, 1993) found that between 1986 and 1992, the proportion of older people who said they wanted to age in place increased from 78 to 85 percent. A later survey found that over 80 percent of adults aged 55 and over wanted to remain in their current homes. (See Figure 11.2.)

These people said they never wanted to move (Ethel Percy Andrus, 1995). A survey completed in January 1996 by the AARP found that 89 percent of

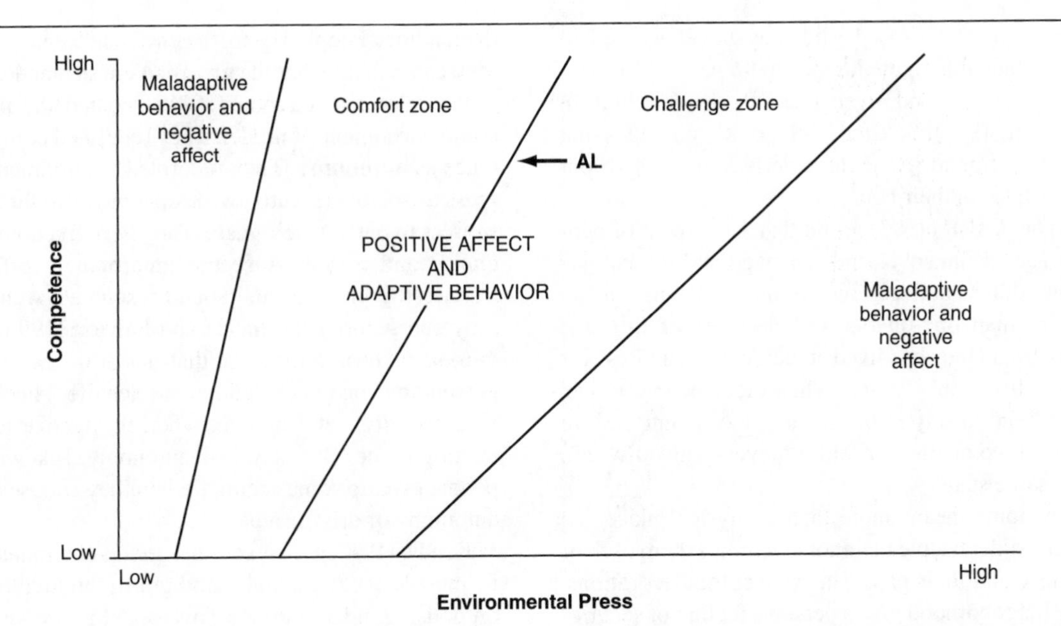

This figure describes the relationship between a person's ability and the demands of their environment. The line AL represents an average level of demand at a given level of competence. To the immediate left of the midpoint lies the comfort zone. People have enough competence here to easily get along in their environment. Here they feel most at ease. To the immediate right of the midpoint (line AL) lies the challenge zone. The environment makes the maximum demand on a person's ability.

As demand increases, adaptation takes place until environmental demand goes beyond the person's ability to adapt (right diagonal). As demand decreases below a person's adaptation level, the person will feel bored (left diagonal).

No matter how high the competence, at some level of demand a person will lose the ability to adapt. No matter how low the competence, a person will still have some adaptive ability.

The greater a person's competence, the greater the adaptive ability; the lower the competence, the lower the adaptive ability. A person with low competence can be challenged by even a small increase in demand. Lawton calls this the "environmental docility" hypothesis. Likewise, a person with low competence can benefit from even small decreases in environmental demand.

This model shows that improvement in person-environment fit can take place in three ways: (1) A person can live in a less demanding environment. This may mean a move to a more supportive setting such as a nursing home. Or it can mean adaptation of the environment to suit a person's ability. A change in housing design (e.g., an entry ramp or lower countertops) can make a problem environment comfortable. (2) A person can improve competence (e.g., through physiotherapy). (3) A person can do both.

Too often, Sheehan says, improvements take the form of decreased demand. She suggests that professionals look at both sides of this model. Increased competence can also lead to better adaptation. Sometimes a single change, such as better lighting, can increase a person's competence *and* decrease environmental demand. This model encourages people to use their full ability within safe limits.

FIGURE 11.2

The Lawton-Nahemow Ecological Model

Sources: From "Ecology and the Aging Process," by M. P. Lawton & L. Nahemow (1973), in C. Eisdorfer & M. P. Lawton (Eds.), *Psychology of Adult Development and Aging,* Washington, D.C.: American Psychological Association. Copyright © 1973 by the American Psychological Association. Adapted with permission. Also, *Successful Administration of Senior Housing,* by N. W. Sheehan (1992). Newbury Park, CA: Sage.

people aged 65 to 84 said they never wanted to move, and this figure jumped to 96 percent for people aged 85 and over (AARP, 1996, cited in Schafer, 1999). Schafer (1999, p. 8) concludes that "the vast majority of the elderly want to live out their lives in their homes. . . ."

The AARP (1993) found that 19 percent of people aged 55 and over said they had lived at their current address between twenty-one and thirty years. More than one-quarter (28 percent) of this age group said they had lived at their current address for more than thirty years. When older people move, they tend to stay in the same city or county. More than three-quarters of older movers moved within the same state.

A home means more than a physical place. To many older people their home reminds them of their family and their past. The rooms, the decorations, the neighborhood give a person a feeling of security and well-being. Fogel (1992, p. 16) says that the meaning of home goes beyond logic. People give all the good reasons why they should move, "but then conclude that the only way they would leave their home would be in a box." **Aging in place** requires that people have the resources they need to live in the setting they choose (Wagnild, 2001).

Lawton and Nahemow (1973; Lawton, 1990) created a model that describes the relationship between a person's **capability (competence)** and **environmental demand** (environmental press) (refer to Figure 11.2). Capability refers to the total of a person's physical, mental, and social abilities. Environmental demand refers to the forces that, combined with need, lead a person to make a response. This model shaped housing policy in the United States and continues to influence thinking about aging and housing today (Gitlin, 2003a; Scheidt & Norris-Baker, 2004).

This model shows that people function at their best when their capability suits the environment's demands. This allows them to fulfill their needs. If the environment demands too little or too much, the person feels out of balance and makes maladaptive responses. A healthy retiree who loves to garden and do home repairs but lives in a high-rise apartment may feel unchallenged. An older person who uses a walker may find life in a two-story house too demanding. People try to find a fit between what they can do and what the environment demands.

Parmelee and Lawton (1990) updated the person-environment fit model. They redefined competence as **autonomy**. They redefined environmental press as **security**. Autonomous people have the resources to pursue their goals. They have freedom of choice and action. A secure environment offers trustworthy physical and social resources. Autonomy and security, Parmelee and Lawton (1990, p. 466) say, "form a dialectic that lies at the heart of person-environment relations in later life." People gain security, for example, when they move to a nursing home. But they lose autonomy. Likewise, people give up some security when they choose the autonomy of driving a car.

Kendig (1990, p. 288) calls the person-environment fit model the "dominant paradigm in the literature on housing older people." This model allows us to put housing options on a continuum from least to most demanding. We can then look at the demands of each option and the adaptations needed to live in each setting.

HOUSING OPTIONS

A continuum of housing options exists today (see Box 11.2, page 289). This continuum, in theory, offers older people a chance to match their abilities to an environment that maximizes their autonomy. Each type of housing has costs and benefits. An older person may move from one type of housing to another as abilities change. (See Figure 11.3.)

Single-Family Homes

The Administration on Aging (2002a) reports that of all households headed by older people, 80 percent lived in homes that they owned (20 percent lived in rented housing). About three-quarters of older homeowners in 2001 lived mortgage free. Older people own homes on average valued less than the average for all homeowners.

Older people in nonmetropolitan settings, compared with city dwellers, more often own their own homes. (See Figure 11.4, page 290.) But nonmetropolitan homeowners tend to live in older homes that, compared with city homes, have low market value.

Margie Wilson lives in the Redwoods Retirement Community in Mill Valley, California. She has chosen a setting that will allow her to age in place.

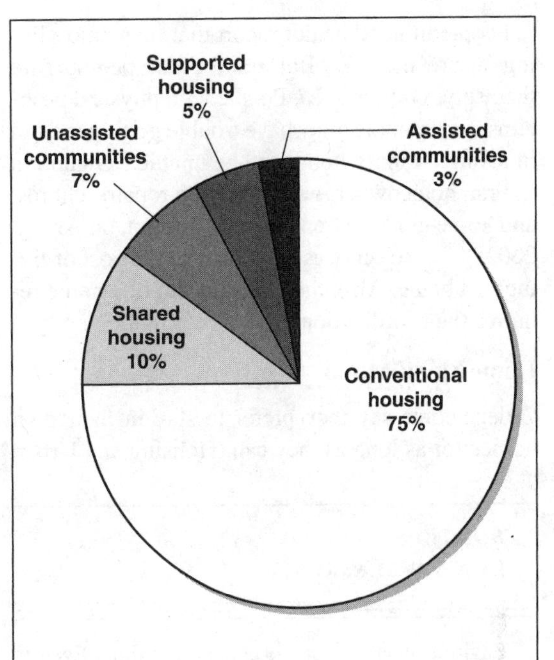

Definitions:

- Older people in conventional housing tend to own their own homes.
- In shared housing, the older person lives with a nonelderly person for support.
- In unassisted communities, healthy older people live in an age-restricted setting without special supports.
- In supported housing, the older person gets either formal or informal help from outside the home.
- In assisted communities, the older person gets help from outside the home. This often includes meals and may include personal care and nursing services.

This figure shows that the large majority of older people live on their own in the community. Most older people live in their own homes. Eighty-two percent of older people in conventional housing live in owner-occupied homes. People tend to move to more supportive settings as they age. Also, people without children tend to live in supportive setting. Supportive settings provide help with ADL and may provide health care. This figure does not include people who live in nursing homes or other facilities.

FIGURE 11.3

Choice of Housing, Age 70 and Over

Source: Schafer, R. (2000). Joint Center for Housing Studies of Harvard University. Cambridge, MA: Joint Center for Housing Studies of Harvard University. Chart 9, p. 10.

Older people lived in homes that were on average seven years older than those of all householders. And 5.4 percent of these homes had physical problems (Administration on Aging, 2002b). McGough (1993) reports that older homes have problems with maintenance, plumbing, and kitchen equipment.

Older people live in older homes in part because they tend to age in place. Older homeowners stay put for a number of reasons. First, they enjoy the comfort and familiarity of their homes. The Administration on Aging (2002b) says that a home means security and independence to older people. Second, selling a home may create a loss of tax savings and an increase in taxes because of an increase in a person's liquid assets. Third, increased liquid assets may make a person ineligible for certain health or income supports. Some people have little choice but to stay in their homes.

People in good health report that they enjoy living where they do. But some older people find themselves *overhoused.* People with physical problems, for example, may have trouble getting around in a single-family home and be unable to maintain it. Frail homeowners need help with repairs, chores, and home modifications (Administration on Aging, 2002e). These services can increase the cost of living in a home. Also, the management of a home requires the coordination of service providers.

Home Modification

Older people say they prefer to stay in their own homes for as long as they can (Housing and Urban Development, 2000b). Aging in place may entail modifying a home to suit a person's changing physical condition. Many people live in "Peter Pan Housing" (Ethel Percy Andrus, 1995, p. 4), housing designed as if people will never grow old. As many as 1 million older households need at least one modification such as a grab bar or ramp, but less than 1 percent of older people's households have these modifications. The U.S. Public Health Service says that older people could prevent as many as two-thirds of falls in part by home modification (Ethel Percy Andrus, 1995). Hare (1992, p. 36) says that if you choose to age in place, "your remodeller may be almost as important to you as your doctor."

BOX 11.1
DON'T WALK, RUN!

Environmental demand occurs all the time. Even in places where we least think about it. Traffic lights, for example, challenge us to walk to the other side of the street before the light changes. Younger people rarely feel this demand because engineers time lights to suit their bodies. Older people may feel more demand because they walk more slowly. Hare says "the timing of 'walk' phases on traffic lights seems based on the assumption that there is no one who walks slowly." Jane E. Brody reports a research study that measured the effects of traffic-light timing on older people's well-being.

Don't walk, run! This, in effect, is the message given to many elderly people who try to cross busy city streets while the traffic light signals "Walk" and then flashes "Don't Walk" to warn that the light is about to change. A study of pedestrians at a busy intersection in Los Angeles found that 27 percent of elderly people who began to cross as soon as the light flashed "Walk" were unable to reach the opposite curb before the light changed against them. At least one-fourth of those who were unable to cross in time were left stranded by at least one lane of traffic. . . .

In the study, Dr. Russell E. Hoxie and Dr. Laurance Z. Rubenstein of the University of California at Los Angeles School of Medicine watched 1,200 people trying to cross a street in an area where a lot of older people live. They found that all the younger pedestrians, who walked at an average speed of 1.27 meters a second, managed to get across the street in time. But among older pedestrians, whose walking speed averaged 0.86 meters per second, only 73 percent crossed in time.

Nearly all the elderly pedestrians observed walked more slowly than the 1.22 meters a second that city traffic engineers use in timing the interval between red lights. The researchers suggested that crossing times be increased, especially where many older people live.

The researchers believe their findings may largely explain why elderly people account for the largest share of the 7,000 pedestrian fatalities that occur annually in the United States. And, they suggested that the number of fatalities might be even higher if not for the fact that many elderly pedestrians are reluctant to cross streets they consider dangerous. Three-fourths of the elderly pedestrians interviewed by the researchers said fear kept them from crossing the street as often as they would like to.

Sources: From "Health Watch: Don't Walk, Run!" by J. E. Brody, 1994, *New York Times,* March 23, p. C12. Copyright © 1994, The New York Times Co. Reprinted with permission. Also, "Frail Elders and the Suburbs," by P. H. Hare, 1992, *Generations,* Spring, p. 37.

About one-half of older people in a series of national studies (Newman, 2003) reported at least one home modification. Twenty-three percent said they had an unmet need for a modification, and about 14 percent said they had a house-related disability. This study found that one-half the people who had made modifications still had an unmet need for modifications. An AARP (1993) study found that the most common modifications included added lighting (23 percent), living on a single floor (18 percent), using levers to replace knobs (18 percent), and adding handrails (17 percent). People with a health problem showed the greatest likelihood of modifying their homes.

Home modification allows many older people to stay in their homes into late old age. And this seems

BOX 11.2

A HOUSING CONTINUUM FOR THE ELDERLY

Many housing options exist for older people and more seem to spring up all the time. They go by many names. Sometimes the same option has more than one name. The list below sorts out and describes the most common types of housing options. The continuum ranges from the most demanding environment (single-family home) to the least demanding environment (nursing home).

1. *Single-family home (detached, attached, or mobile home, rented or owned).* This type of housing makes the most demands on the resident. It requires indoor and outdoor maintenance. It may also require good mobility if the home has stairs.
2. *Apartment, condominium, or townhouse.* This type of housing can range from a retirement hotel to an age-segregated retirement community. Tenants share common areas. Management does repairs and maintains common indoor and outdoor spaces. Services or facilities, such as a recreation room or a pool, may be provided for a fee.
3. *Continuing care retirement community or life care community.* This type of housing ranges from detached homes to congregate housing and may include a nursing home in the development. Residents move to the kind of housing that suits their abilities best. Life care communities have contracts to offer certain services for a resident's entire life. Fees for these services vary.
4. *Granny flats or ECHO housing.* Self-contained units on a child's or relative's property. Attached to the main house. The older person lives independently but gets support as needed from the family.
5. *Congregate housing (many self-contained units, rented).* This type of housing can include retirement hotels with hotel-like services. Planned and designed for older people, they provide management and support services such as communal meals, transportation, and recreation.
6. *Shared housing (house or apartment).* Two or more people live together and share expenses. Each has a private bedroom. One person usually owns and rents to tenants. Chores may be shared, or the tenant may exchange chore services for rent.
7. *Board and care and assisted living.* Board and care and foster homes offer small-scale settings with housekeeping and personal care help (bathing, dressing, eating). Assisted living is like board and care but larger and with 24-hour supervision. Intermediate care facilities offer meals in a common dining room and 24-hour help with ADL.
8. *Nursing home.* Skilled nursing care is offered 24 hours a day. This is the highest level of care available. This type of housing is for people with serious illnesses.

Huttman says that the continuum of housing offers support that fits older people's varied needs. At its best, it allows a person to choose the kind of housing that maximizes independence. The continuum shows the close link between housing and services for older people. Housing options should offer the right mix of supportive services to ensure that the elderly have control over their environments.

Sources: Chart based on "Designs for living," by J. Porcino (1993), *Modern Maturity,* April–May, pp. 24–33. Adapted with permission. Also, "Continuum of Care," by E. Huttman (1987), in G. L. Maddox (Ed.). *The Encyclopedia of aging,* pp. 145–147. New York: Springer.

like an increasingly popular way to help older people stay independent. For example, Newman (2003) found that home modification nearly doubled between 1978 and 1995. But an AARP (2003b) study of people aged 45 and over found that only about one-half of them expected to modify their homes as they aged. Only one-third of them said that they saw an older relative make home modifications. And only one in eight felt that their older relatives need to make changes to their homes.

This response may, in part, reflect the different meanings of home modification. Middle-aged adults may not think of adding lighting or changing doorknobs as "home modification." Or it may reflect a broader issue. People in good health often resist making modifications. Richard Duncan, an expert in adaptive design, says that "it's the first tangible expression of their aging, and often that's a shocking thing they have to contemplate" (cited in Sit, 1992, p. 74).

Home modification projects exist throughout the United States. Some of these programs use volunteers and donated material. Others use professionals to take on major construction projects. Some government agencies, such as the Rural Development–Rural Housing Service, provide loans to pay for repairs like fire hazards and plumbing.

This agency has also built apartment housing for older people who can no longer maintain their homes. The agency spent $32.5 million in 1999 (two-fifths of all funds lent) to build forty-nine apartment complexes for older people. This program served about 1,900 older people and people with disabilities. Older low-income women made up the majority of people served by this program (Rural Development, 2004).

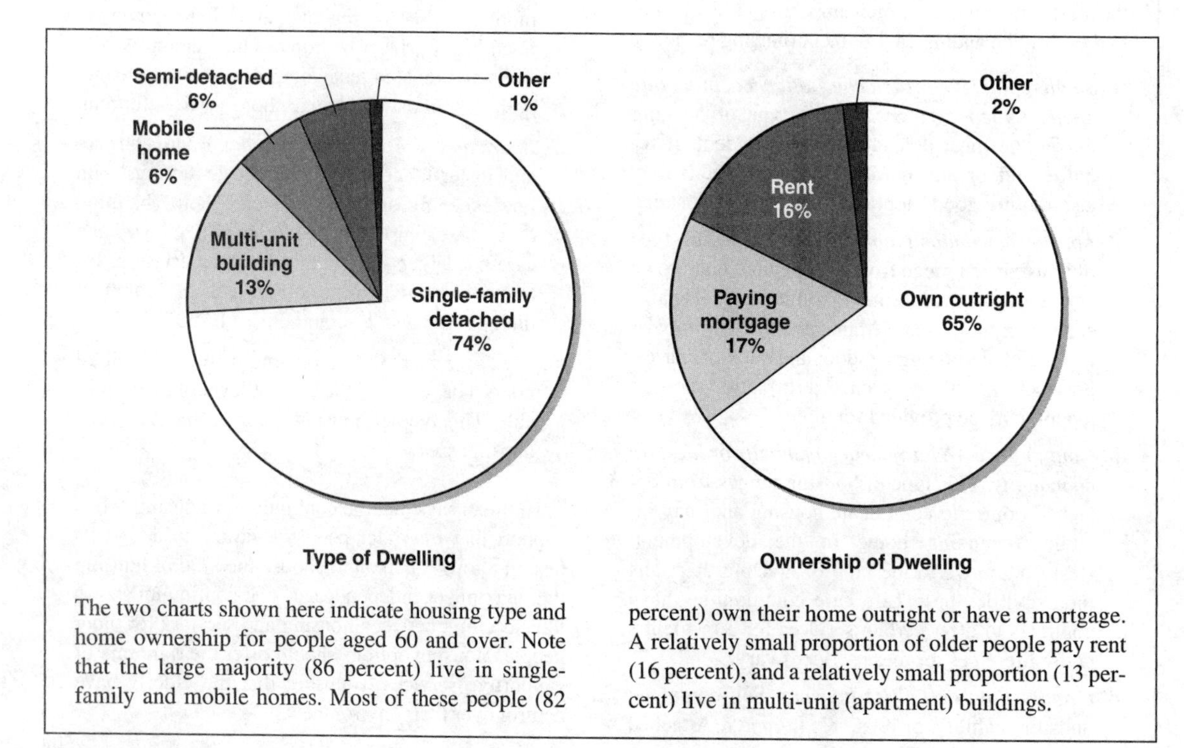

The two charts shown here indicate housing type and home ownership for people aged 60 and over. Note that the large majority (86 percent) live in single-family and mobile homes. Most of these people (82 percent) own their home outright or have a mortgage. A relatively small proportion of older people pay rent (16 percent), and a relatively small proportion (13 percent) live in multi-unit (apartment) buildings.

FIGURE 11.4
Housing Type and Ownership

Source: Understanding Senior Housing: For the 1990's, American Association of Retired Persons (AARP), 1993, Washington, DC: Author, p. 47.

The federal government announced in 2003 that it would provide $593 million to fund the construction or improvement of housing for low-income older people. This program will also subsidize rents for five years to ensure that low-income older people pay only 30 percent of their income for rent (National Resource Center, 2004).

The AARP (2002) proposes a "universal" house. This would make home modifications unnecessary. The house would include "wheelchair-accessible entryway, kitchens, and bathrooms; single-lever faucets; nonslip flooring; easy to reach temperature controls; anti-scald devices; and grab bars." A universal house (with anti-scald faucets, for example) would benefit children as well as older people. A person could move into a house like this with a young family and could stay there until late old age.

Schafer and Harvard University (2000) project an increase in major and minor modifications to housing units in the future. They report this trend for owned and rented housing. They project that people aged 85 and over will make the most home modifications.

Home Equity Conversion Loans (Reverse Mortgages)

Some people who want to stay in their homes find that they have excessive housing costs.[1] They may own a home worth $50,000 or more, but not have enough money for heat and taxes. These people live house rich, but cash poor. They may have to sell their home and move to cheaper housing. **Home**

BOX 11.3
THE HOMEBOUND SUFFER IN PRIVACY

Suburban homes built for the young families of the 1950s create problems for older people today. Suburbs demand cars to get around. Suburban split-level homes and high thresholds between rooms create barriers to movement. The wide lawns and yards of suburban homes can make maintenance a problem for older people. Reporter Esther B. Fein describes the problems faced by older women in suburban housing.

"I'm trapped," said one 73-year-old woman in Port Washington, who, like many of the elderly living alone in the suburbs, said she felt too vulnerable to have her name printed in an article. "And I don't really know anybody in the neighborhood. Who would even hear or know if something happened to me?"

Since she became ill with cancer of the thymus gland and with a nerve disorder, and can no longer climb stairs, she has lived on the bottom floor of her two-story house, sleeping in her son's childhood bedroom.

The basement was flooded months ago, but she has been unable to do anything about the mess. The various medications she takes cause severe hunger, yet she can no longer drive to the supermarket, and there are none in the area that deliver. . . .

She gets out occasionally to church, she said, but only when friends drive her. "There are a lot of people there with walkers and wheelchairs," she said. "I guess we were all young once here. We all fit in once. . . ."

Myna Lavine, an 80-year-old widow living in Bergenfield, NJ, . . . had to give up driving several years ago when glaucoma clouded her vision and arthritis slowed her movements. She leaves her small brick house only to sit on the front porch and water the lawn. Once a week, a social service worker goes to the supermarket and then unloads the groceries into Mrs. Lavine's cupboards.

"See, I love living here," Mrs. Lavine said. "I'm out on my porch almost every day watching the traffic go by. Sometimes people stop at the fence and say 'hi.' But I'm alone here."

Source: From "Elderly: Find Hardship in Haven for Young: The Homebound Suffer in Privacy," by E. B. Fein, 1994, *New York Times*, July 19, A1, B5.

BOX 11.4
REVERSE MORTGAGE OPTIONS

The federal department of HUD lists five ways to get income from a reverse mortgage. In each case the lender strikes a deal with the homeowner (borrower). The owner gets to stay in the house and collect payments from the lender. The lender owns the home and will take possession when the older person dies, moves out, or when the lender has paid the full amount owed. The payment arrangement can take one of the several forms:

- Tenure: equal monthly payments as long as at least one borrower lives and continues to occupy the property as a principal residence.
- Term: equal monthly payments for a fixed period of months selected.
- Line of credit: unscheduled payments or in installments, at times and in amounts of borrower's choosing until the line of credit is exhausted.
- Modified tenure: combination of line of credit with monthly payments for as long as the borrower remains in the home.
- Modified term: combination of line of credit with monthly payments for a fixed period of months selected by the borrower.

These options differ from one another in one important respect. The homeowner can opt to either stay in the home for life and accept payments at a certain rate (based on life expectancy, interest rates, and the value of the home). Or the homeowner can get payments at a set rate for a fixed number of months. At the end of that time, the lender owns the home and the older person may need to move. A set rate for a fixed number of months may pay more money monthly than in the first instance, in which the person can stay in the home for life. The decision to take a reverse mortgage and the specific terms of the deal require careful consideration. Most older people will want to seek the advice of a financial advisor before choosing a reverse mortgage.

Source: U.S. Department of Housing and Urban Development, Homes and Communities. Retrieved October 2, 2004, *www.hud.gov/offices/hsg/sfh/hecm/rmtopten.cfm.*

equity conversion loans (HECs) can provide homeowners with the income they need.

A number of HEC programs exist. Through one program, a person gets a monthly loan based on the person's age, current interest rates, and the house's value. The person repays the loan on a set date. Another HEC is called a deferred payment loan. Through this method, people borrow against the value of their home. Their estate repays the loan when they die, or they repay it when they move and sell the home. Many variations on these two options exist.

The older the person, the greater the house's value, and the lower the interest rate, the better the income from an HEC. Critics of reverse mortgages say that banks get too large a share of the house's value. Also, the National Resource Center on Supportive Housing and Home Modification (2004) says that reverse mortgages can include unexpected costs. These include "high set-up costs for the loans which include an origination fee, a monthly service charge of about $30 to $35, mortgage insurance premium, appraisal fee and other closing costs."

According to Bronwyn Belling, a reverse mortgage specialist with AARP, the total costs can range anywhere from $8,000 to $12,000 for homes with market values of $200,000 to $300,000.

Smith (1992, p. 77) gives an example of the high costs of this kind of loan:

> Take a 75-year-old woman with a paid-up, $100,000 home. A typical reverse mortgage would give her $362 a month for as long as she stayed put. In ten years, she would have received $43,520 but would owe $85,273

[1]The U.S. Department of Housing and Urban Development says that renters have excessive housing costs if they spend 30 percent of their before-tax income on housing, and homeowners have excessive costs if they spend 40 percent of their income on housing (U.S. Senate, 1991)

on the loan. And after seventeen years, she would have lost all the equity, even though the home would be worth $194,790 (assuming 4 percent annual appreciation). Yet during that period she would have received only $73,984.

The Federal Housing Administration (FHA), a part of the U.S. Department of **Housing and Urban Development (HUD)** has set up a program that responds to these issues. The program overcomes some of the objections to reverse mortgages. The HUD program serves people aged 62 or over who have paid off their homes or who have small mortgages. The FHA oversees and guarantees these reverse mortgages. It assesses a person's situation—based on their age and home value—and will then tell a lender how much they can lend.

So, for example, "based on a loan at today's interest rates of approximately 9 percent, a 65-year-old could borrow up to 26 percent of the home's value, a 75-year-old could borrow up to 39 percent of the home's value, and an 85-year-old could borrow up to 56 percent of the home's value" (HUD, 2004). The FHA puts limits on the cost of loans and guarantees that lenders will do what they promise (AARP, 2004b).

The AARP says that FHA-guaranteed mortgages cost less than other similar reverse mortgages, and this program lends older people the most money. This program also allows the most freedom in how a person can use the funds. A person can use the equity in their home to pay debts or live a more comfortable life. They can get a lump sum payment or monthly payments. They can borrow against the full value of their home, but they (or their heirs) will not have to pay back more than the house is worth. If the house sells for more than the loan amount due, the estate gets to keep the profit.

Some people in financial need may still choose to avoid a reverse mortgage. First, the reverse mortgage uses up a large part of their estate, second, they may not want to go into debt late in life, and third, they may not understand the risks and gains (Ronkin, 1989). The HUD offers free information on reverse mortgages on its website. Also, an older person will want to consult with family members and a financial advisor before deciding on whether a reverse mortgage works for them. Used wisely, a reverse mortgage can raise a person's standard of living and improve their sense of well-being.

The AARP (1991) says that single women in their 70s make up the largest group of people who take reverse mortgages. The Older Women's League (1993) of Washington, D.C., says that women often take out reverse mortgages because they need the cash. They care less about the high cost of the loans in the long run and more about maintaining their life-style now. As one woman told Smith (1992b, p. 78), "I felt like the loan put wings on me. It's quite a thing to say I can make it on my own."

The United Seniors Health Council (2004) says that older people could use reverse mortgages to pay for health care and long-term care. Jacobs and Weissert (1987) report that reverse mortgages could finance long-term care for the lifetime of about one-half of high-risk single people. Likewise, about one-half of the high-risk single group could use their reverse mortgage payments to buy nursing home insurance. This would protect them against catastrophic health care costs.

Home improvements and home equity conversions offer two ways for older homeowners to age in place. They expand a person's ability to maintain a home and pay the high cost of maintenance and taxes.

Apartment Living

Apartments account for the greatest proportion of older people's housing after single-family homes. The American Housing Survey of 1999 found that apartment dwellers accounted for almost 20 percent of the 21.4 million households headed by older people in 1999 (Housing and Urban Development, 2001). Renters tend to spend a high proportion of their income (more than 30 percent) on housing. They tend to be older women and many of them have a low income (Mutschler, 1992). Renters have fewer options than owners when it comes to home modification. Apartment leases often limit the kinds of changes a person can make to an apartment. For this reason, many older people choose to move into apartment buildings designed for older people.

Age Segregation versus Age Integration

Age segregation refers to a setting where older people live only with people their own age. **Age integration** refers to a setting that includes people of all ages. Eighty percent of the people in an AARP survey said they prefer to live in a neighborhood with people of all ages. But 42 percent of respondents said they preferred to live in an apartment building only with older people (AARP, 1993). One study

BOX 11.5
DESIGNS FOR SAFETY AND COMFORT

The ITT Hartford Insurance group in cooperation with the AARP has built a model home to show off new designs for older persons' housing. The model (actually part of a home) displays more than one hundred products. Some of these designs require little expense or trouble to install (such as rubber grips that fit over wooden spoon handles). Some require expert installation (such as climate control boxes). All of them improve the safety and comfort of an older person's home, for example:

- A bathroom sink has a valve that stops scalding water from reaching the faucet.
- A stove has controls at the front so that a person can get at them without reaching over the hot elements. The stove also staggers the elements so that a person can get to a back element without reaching over a front element.
- The bathroom has rubber flooring to prevent falls when wet.
- The house has a smoke-penetrating flashlight that goes off when a smoke detector sounds.
- A portable intercom allows a person to talk from anywhere in the house to visitors at the front door.
- Couch and chair colors contrast with the floor color to make seating easier.
- Window shades have small holes that let light in with less glare.
- Lamps turn on and off at a touch on the base or column.
- The thermostat, phone, oven, alarm clock, and bathroom scale all have large numbers.
- Pot handles have angles that make lifting easier.
- Large print cookbooks and large cabinet handles make cooking easier.

Companies will produce more products for older people in the future as the market grows. New technology will increase ease and comfort of living at home and alone. For example, lights can now sense when a person enters or leaves a room. They go on and off without a touch. Remote control units and computer chips can control many appliances, including the television, radio, and fans. Home computers will give homebound older people access to the world. They will offer information, friendship, and entertainment.

Research engineers at Stanford, Carnegie Mellon, the University of Pittsburg, and the University of Michigan have applied computer technology to the needs of older people. They developed a walker with sonar detectors and mapping software to help frail older people get around. They also developed a first-generation robot named Pearl that will (in future generations of development) react to an older person's needs. The robot and other computerized devices will add to the support given by family members and professional caregivers (Rotstein, 2004).

Technology-enhanced designs make life easier for people of all ages. Door levers that help older people with arthritis, for example, also make it easier for children to enter and leave rooms. Technology and invention will make houses safer and more enjoyable for everyone. Designs for older people can lead the way.

Are there other products that you know about or have seen that would help an older person live more comfortably? Can you suggest some home modification or invention that would make life easier for older people?

Source: Adapted from "The Hartford House: Home Modifications in Action," by G. B. Hynes, 1992, *Generations, 16*(2), pp. 33–34. Adapted with permission of American Society on Aging, *www.asaging.org*.

found that older tenants in age-integrated housing resented the "disruption of others' peaceful enjoyment." The study found that older tenants felt that younger tenants caused most of the disruptions (Sheehan & Stelle, 1998).

Golant (1985) says that age-segregated housing helps people develop good relationships, allows for greater security, and offers more access to support services. Older people in age-segregated communities can create their own subcultures. People in these communities value one another, see the world in roughly the same way, and focus on activities they enjoy together.

An Australian study (Davidson, Brooke, & Kendig, 2001, p. 123) compared older people in age-segregated housing with a similar group in mixed housing in the community. The researchers found that "the age-segregated sample had relatively more interaction with friends and had less risk of isolation from friends." This finding applied especially to people aged 75 and over. The researchers conclude that age-segregated housing helps older people who have physical problems and can't easily visit others. People who lived in age-segregated housing, compared with those who lived in the community, received more visits from friends. For this reason, some older people benefit from age-segregated communities.

Lawton (1987) said that older people do well in either age-segregated or age-integrated housing. The choice depends on what an individual prefers and on the individual's needs. It also depends on good design. Lawton says that the right design can make age-integration and age-segregation enjoyable.

Normal Design versus Special Design

Older people say they want to live near amenities like a grocery, drugstore, and doctor's office. About one-quarter of older people say they want to live near a senior center (AARP, 1993). Publicly sponsored apartment developments for older people in the past gave little thought to the issues raised by aging in place. They contained few supports for people as they aged. They assumed that as people needed more care, they would move to a nursing home. This rarely happens. Instead, people stay in their apartments but need more supports.

Sheehan (1992) estimates that between one-quarter and one-third of people in older persons' housing are age 80 or over. As one housing manager said to me, "We didn't expect it, but we've built high-rise nursing homes." These buildings now need to add supports for their tenants. Congregate housing meets this need.

Congregate Housing and Assisted Living

Housing can mean simply a roof and four walls, or it can mean a setting that enhances a person's well-being. Housing for some older people demands an integration of housing and services. The U.S. Department of Housing and Urban Development (2000b) says that about 10 percent of people aged 70 to 74 live in some kind of special care environments (either with another person or with some living assistance). This increases to approximately 60 percent at age 90. **Congregate (or enriched) housing** provides one type of supportive environment.

A congregate housing complex offers meal service and may also offer health care support, and recreation programs. The Assisted Living Federation of America (2000) estimates that between 611,300 and 777,800 people live in assisted living settings. Congregate housing reduces older residents' isolation and gives them a sense of safety and emotional security. Fifty-one percent of older people in an AARP survey (1993) said they had an interest in enriched housing. Altus and Mathews (2002) surveyed people who live in congregate apartments. Tenants reported high satisfaction with their housing.

Golant (2003) found that many people who live in subsidized high-rise housing lack health and personal care supports. These people risk institutionalization. The oldest people (aged 85 and over), many of them women, face the greatest risk. A high proportion of these people have ADL and IADL deficiencies. They need help in maintaining themselves in the community. Golant (2003) reports that 12 percent of people in rent-assisted apartments have mental deficiencies that interfere with their everyday lives. These tenants need help with housekeeping and personal care. But relatively few subsidized buildings offer supports.

Assisted living apartments serve people with these health care and personal care needs. Assisted living apartments add personal services and some health care to congregate housing amenities. Only about 3 percent of older people outside nursing homes use this option (Housing and Urban Development, 2000b). These settings provide some help with ADL (dressing, grooming, bathing). They do not provide skilled nursing services. Regnier (2003) reports that assisted living projects average 52.2 units. Most of the units (61 percent) are studio apartments. Residents average 83 years old and have an average of three ADL restrictions. About 45 percent have cognitive impairments. A majority (65 percent) need help bathing and more than one-quarter (29 percent) need help toileting.

This problem reflects federal HUD policies on older persons' housing. First, cost cutting led to an absence of recreation, activity, and service space (like a dining room) in these buildings (Scott-Webber & Koebel, 2001). Second, HUD housing until recently assumed that older tenants had good health and could perform ADL. Third, HUD policies assumed that supports led to dependency, so HUD-supported buildings provide little space and almost no services for older tenants.

Koff and Park (1993, p. 238) sum up the effects of public policy on older people's housing. "Too few federal housing policies for the elderly," they say, "have considered the quality of life in the housing but instead have mainly focused on providing 'maintenance' environments that are only just adequate as shelter." Housing must offer older people services that enhance their autonomy, allow them to age in place, and provide them the chance for personal growth.

Subsidized Housing

The federal government provides rent subsidies to older people who live in nongovernment housing. The government does this through Section 8 of the federal Housing and Community Development Act. This program helps low-income families pay the difference between a fair market rent and their ability to pay. The family pays a percentage of their income for rent; the program pays the rest.

BOX 11.6

SPECIAL HOUSING DESIGN FOR HOMELESS OLDER MEN

The Aging Health Policy Center (1985, cited in Elias and Inui) says that between 15 and 28 percent of homeless people are aged 50 or over. Most of these people are men aged 50 to 65. These men have many health problems. They often have an alcohol addiction and have adapted to poverty, violence, and life on the street.

Elias and Inui describe a single-room occupancy (SRO) program that serves older men in Seattle. It offers private SRO rooms and complete meal services in a safe setting. The program charges the men 60 percent of their income for room and board. It has television rooms, a pool table, and a library. A residents' council makes policy.

The men in this setting felt they had a stable address. They invited friends and family to their building. They also improved their self-care. On the street, one man said, you feel like a "nonentity." But in this building "You feel like you're entitled to courtesy and respect and things like that."

Elias and Inui say that the building may have a limited effect on the residents' alcoholism, but the men "pointed to improvement in hygiene, service utilization, and reconciliation with family members as indicators of progress."

This building fulfills many of the residents' needs for a home. It offers them physical safety, comfort, and a stable center for their lives.

Source: From "When a House Is Not a Home: Exploring the Meaning of Shelter Among Chronically Homeless Older Men," by C. I. Elias & T. S. Inui, 1993, *The Gerontologist, 33*(3), pp. 396–402.

Folts and Yeatts (1994) predict an increased demand for low-cost or subsidized seniors housing in the future. In 2004, for example, HUD funded a program to help meet this demand. HUD awarded $740 million to develop or improve apartment housing for very low-income older people and people with disabilities. Of this total, $593 million went toward housing improvements for the very low-income elderly. HUD grants will also subsidize rents for low-income older people for five years. This will keep very poor older tenants' rents at only 30 percent of their income (homesmod.org, 2003).

Golant (2002) studied subsidized housing in Florida. He found that the state provided subsidized housing for older people. But it concentrated subsidized housing in certain counties. This meant that most low-income older people, who lived in other parts of the state, had no access to this type of housing. Golant refers to this as "geographic inequality." As the current stock of housing ages, it will get harder to maintain. This may lead to a decline in the quality of subsidized housing in the future (Blank, 1993). It may also lead to a severe shortage of supported housing for older people in the future. The United States needs more programs like the recent HUD grants to ensure adequate housing for low-income seniors.

Single Room Occupancy

HUD defines a single room occupancy (SRO) as "a residential property that includes multiple single room dwelling units. Each unit is for occupancy by a single eligible individual. The unit need not, but may, contain food preparation or sanitary facilities, or both" (Housing and Urban Development, 2000a).

SRO conjures up images of older people who live in rundown inner-city hotels. These hotels typically house men, over age 75, widowed or never married, and poor. Many of these men have lived in this kind of housing throughout their lives. They choose to live in an SRO because they value their privacy and independence. SROs that house older men often lack services like medical care and meals (Keigher & Berman, 1991). In the past few years, many central cities have torn down the old hotels that served as SRO housing. This has decreased the number of men who live like this (Mutschler, 1992).

Kovar (1987) takes a broader view of SROs. She defines a single room occupant as anyone who lives in a single room and is unrelated to anyone else in the same housing unit. She includes houses, hotels, and apartments. She says that nearly two-thirds of these people live in one-room apartments. One-quarter live in other people's homes. Kovar estimates that about 1.5 million people aged 62 and older live in single rooms.

By Kovar's definition, people who live in single rooms look similar to any group of older people. She reports, for example, that white women aged 65 to 74 make up the majority of SROs. Most have good health and remain active. Many have low incomes. Women tend to live in single rooms in other people's houses. Men tend to live in one-room apartments.

Supportive Housing

Some housing options provide older people with assisted living: personal and health care supports. These options include board and care homes and nursing homes.

Board and Care Homes

Board and care homes go by the names adult care homes, halfway houses, shelter care homes, domiciliary care, personal care homes, community residence facilities, rest homes, and foster care homes. These many names for the same type of housing can lead to confusion. Also, two places that use the same name can offer different services.

Most board and care homes "provide a room, meals, and help with daily activities. Some states will allow some nursing services to be provided" (Administration on Aging, 2004a). Board and care homes generally care for a small number of residents (two to ten typically). These homes do not serve as medical facilities, but they do offer personal care services like help with eating, bathing, and dressing. Residents in a board and care home eat together. The manager of the home takes responsibility for the residents' well-being.

Mollica (2002) found that, in 2002, the United States had 36,399 board and care and assisted living facilities. These facilities served almost 1 million people—an increase of 14.5 percent over 2000. Homes can range in size from one to more than one hundred residents, although most homes have thirty or fewer residents. Residents range in age from 60 to 75 years old on average. More women than men live in these facilities.

Residents choose to live in a board and care home because they have too little income to pay for the services they need in their own homes. They need an affordable way to get personal care and supervision. The board and care home gives them service in a homelike setting. Most owners run board and care homes for profit. Homes vary widely in the services they provide and in their costs. All homes provide meals. Other services can range from help with eating to letter writing. Sometimes monthly fees include all services, sometimes not. All states license board and care homes.

Owners in some states must pass a test to get licensed. Most states have approval to cover service costs through Medicaid (Mollica, 2002). A board and care home can also solve a financial and housing problem for the manager/owner. Nell Stone, a 66-year-old retired home health aid, runs a board and care home in Teaneck, New Jersey. She gives care to two women, aged 95 and 76. The women live in her home, and she provides them with meals, some personal care, and rides to services. Stone says the income from her boarders allows her to maintain her home. "Without the ladies," she says, "I would have to move to a one-room apartment" (Gilman, 1994, p. 9C).

Many board and care homes now house people with cognitive impairments. This places new demands on home managers and on residents. Mollica (2002) says that thirty-six states have set out requirements for homes that house people with cognitive impairments or dementia. But some researchers raise questions about the ability of board and care homes to meet the needs of these residents (Hawes, 1999).

A person who decides to live in a board and care home needs to know the details of life in the home. What services does the home provide? When and how often do meals get served? Does the home offer activities outside the building? Most people who live in board and care homes say they like where they live. They say their home offers a safe and private setting with the services they need. Kane and Wilson (1993) studied assisted living programs (including board and care homes) in twenty-one states. They found that this type of program can offer care at moderate cost. It especially meets the needs of low-income and disabled older people.

Nursing Homes

People who need medical care in addition to personal care may enter a nursing home. Nursing homes provide skilled nursing care. A relatively small number of older people (1.56 million) lived in nursing homes in 2000. This came to about 4.5 percent of the total older population. But the percentage of older people who live in a nursing home increases dramatically with age. For example, only 1.1 percent of people aged 65 to 74 lived in a nursing home. But this figure jumps to 18.2 percent of people aged 85 and over (Administration on Aging, 2002b).

The quality of nursing homes has improved in the past few years. This improvement came about in part through stronger regulations and more government enforcement. The Omnibus Budget Reconciliation Act of 1987, called OBRA-87 nursing facility reform regulations, set out precise standards for nursing home care. This included the following requirements:

1. All nursing homes must assess patients at least once a year. Assessments cover ADL as well as health care needs. The nursing home must create a detailed care plan based on this assessment.
2. All nursing homes must inform residents orally and in writing about their legal rights. This includes the right to choose a doctor, the right to freedom from restraints, and the right to privacy and confidentiality.
3. Staff must include a registered nurse for at least eight hours each day and at least one li-

Patients playing cards in a nursing home. Note that one woman uses a rack to hold her cards in front of her. She may have arthritis in her hands. This makes it hard for her to hold the cards. A nursing home environment can match environmental demands to patients' abilities.

censed nurse at all times every day. Large facilities with 120 beds must have a full-time social worker. Nurse's aides must pass a training course of seventy-five hours. States must test the competency of aides.

4. States must ensure that nursing homes comply with these new regulations.

Kane and Kane (2001, p. 417) call nursing homes "the most heavily regulated health industry." Due to past scandals over poor care and misuse of funds, "the nursing home industry has been viewed as one that must be closely overseen." Government regulations require that facilities meet "the highest practicable physical, medical and psychological well-being" of every resident (American Medical Directors Association, 2003).

Congress refined the original act in 1990 and debate goes on over new technical points. The legislation allows the government to take over the management of a facility that does not comply with the new policies. Or it can remove the nursing home from the Medicare or Medicaid program (U.S. Senate, 1990, cited in Koff & Park, 1993).

Kane and her colleagues (1990, cited in Fogel, 1992) found that older people in nursing homes value autonomy and privacy. Fogel (1992) says that institutions should allow people to control some private space. Some nursing homes do this. They manage to create a homelike atmosphere. Older people in these settings build strong relationships with staff and other residents. They decorate their rooms with mementos. They create a comfortable place for themselves. People with long-term illnesses may find more comfort in good nursing homes than in their former homes.

Good nursing home design can also increase patient autonomy. Kitchens near living areas help cognitively impaired patients expect meal time by the smell of cooking food. L-shaped rooms add to feelings of privacy in semiprivate rooms. An award-winning facility called Woodside Place, in Pittsburgh, Pennsylvania, uses design to enhance the autonomy of patients with Alzheimer's disease (Presbyterian, 2004). The facility houses thirty-six people in three twelve-person *houses* (Deely & Werlinich, 1992, p. 35). Each house has a different visual theme—star, tree, and house. The houses contain wallpaper borders, quilt designs, and old photos of Pittsburgh that use these themes. The themes give variety to the decor and help residents remember where they live (Deely & Werlinich, 1992). The small units give residents a feeling of place and a sense of home.

People with Alzheimer's tend to wander. They will walk out of a facility and get lost. Woodside solves this problem through design. The designers built an internal street that allows the residents to wander from space to space in the building freely and safely. The facility also has a fully fenced yard so that residents can go out without getting lost. Finally, each resident wears a name tag that contains a computer chip. This chip locks the entrance doors if a patient comes near.

Woodside Place shows that good design can support older people with special needs. This same attention to patient comfort and well-being can create a good environment in any nursing home.

Elder Cottages and Accessory Apartments

Elder cottages began under the name *granny flats* in the district of Victoria, Australia. They also go by the name elder cottage housing opportunities (ECHO). An elder cottage is a small moveable cottage that sits in the yard of an adult child's house. The cottage attaches to the house's electrical and water systems. It contains a bathroom, kitchen, bedroom, and sitting area. The small size of the cottage allows the older person to save on maintenance. Some elder cottages fit into an attached garage next to a child's house. Elder cottages give older people the freedom to live on their own with the support of their family next door. The cottage gets moved when the older person dies or moves to a nursing home.

Accessory apartments exist within or are added onto a single-family home. An adult child may set up an accessory apartment for a parent. Or an older person may set up one and rent the space to another older person. The tenant gives the older owner companionship, and they may share services. The U.S. Census Bureau says that 2.5 million accessory apartments exist. Sometimes an accessory apartment produces income that allows an older person to keep his or her home (Chapman & Howe, 2001). For renters, accessory apartments provide affordable housing and companionship. Accessory apartments lead to a more stable neighborhood because older people can stay in their homes longer.

Elder cottages and accessory apartments face zoning restrictions (Chapman & Howe, 2001). The cottages decrease lot size, and apartments create multiple-family dwellings in residential neighborhoods. Neighbors fear these options will lower housing values. Zoning laws that restrict accessory apartments have driven some people to develop them illegally. Zoning laws may explain why few people have chosen accessory apartments and elder cottages.

The cost of high-quality ECHO housing also sets up a barrier. A person has to pay for the building as well as for delivery and installation. Lazarowich (1991) studied ECHO housing around the world. He found that in most places where ECHO housing has succeeded, families rent the units from the government. The government delivers the unit and arranges to move it when the older person dies or moves. This system controls the number of cottages in a community, their size, quality, and removal. Direct government support and grants to the private sector have led to the success of ECHO housing in a number of countries (Pollak & Gorman, 1989).

Home Sharing

Home sharing in the United States dates back to the eighteenth and nineteenth centuries (Jaffe, 1989). Home sharing most often takes place when an older homeowner rents out one or more rooms. The tenant pays rent and may help around the house as part of the payment. The homeowner and tenant have separate bedrooms but share the kitchen, dining room, and living room.

Home sharers lose some of their privacy, but they gain companionship, help with housekeeping, and some income. "The money isn't essential," one home sharer said, "though it helps. I did it mainly for the company. I really don't like living alone. I like being with people" (Mantell & Gildea, 1989,

BOX 11.7
A BOARDWALK BACK TO NATURE

"I'm going out," announced Clarence, early last winter, wearing his jacket and fedora. He was wheeling himself toward the door at the end of the "C" wing to go onto the boardwalk. "I try to get out some every day the weather lets me," he said to me that day, smiling broadly. Clarence was an avid hunter and outdoorsman all his life. Even though multiple sclerosis had totally debilitated his legs, Clarence continued his love affair with the outdoors. Propelling his wheelchair along the tree-lined boardwalk to the overlook at Knapps Creek, he savored the sights, sounds and smells of creation. . . .

For two years, my office window faced the boardwalk. Often I would look up from interminable paperwork at the nursing home to watch the action outside. Even now, memories of those days come back—of different faces and voices and qualities of light. Vernon, convinced that exercise would fend off aging, methodically walking twenty or more roundtrips a day, laying twigs on the handrail to count his progress. Charlie, struggling to maintain his own ambulatory ability, helping fellow resident Oleta to make it "all the way up and back." Volunteers pushing wheelchair residents along the slightly rough boards to explore once again the sensory mystery of sun and shade, gentle breeze, and the smell of the earth. . . .

It is a wintry day as I write this, but before long a day will arrive warm enough to ask Mrs. Harper for a "date."

Lulu Harper is past her mid-nineties now, with a narrow temperature comfort zone. But she is still the quintessential nature girl and possesses a sharp inquisitive mind.

On that special day, we'll roll out onto the boardwalk in her carriage. Like a prince, I will pluck for her fresh-born leaves, budding twigs, and dainty spring flowers. I may even bring back a handful of dank wood dirt from beneath the pines to present to this silver-haired queen of nature. And she will gently run her fingers over these jewels, while sunbeams dance on her cheeks.

The boardwalk, as you can tell, has affected us all—put us back in touch with our natures.

Source: "A Boardwalk Back to Nature," by A. Johnson, 1994, *Aging Magazine, 366,* pp. 54–55. Reprinted with permission.

p. 18). Stich (2000) reports that home sharers feel safer, less lonely and healthier. They report eating and sleeping better now than when they lived alone.

Today, services exist to match homeowners with a person who wants to share living costs. These services often work as small nonprofit organizations, sometimes as part of a larger agency (Rahder, Farge, & Todres, 1992). They interview sharers and owners, check references, and help make the match work. Stich (2000) sees home sharing as a growing option for single older people. She gives an example of this growth. An agency called Housemates Match began in the mid-1980s by matching about fifty people per year. The program now matches 650 people per year.

Pynoos, Hamburger, and Arlyne (1990) studied a program in San Jose, California, titled Project MATCH. The program served providers and seekers aged 24 to 96. The study found that women made up 82 percent of clients. Forty-four percent of the clients said they wanted to home-share to save money. One-fifth of the people said they wanted companionship. Sharers helped one another with household maintenance, meals, and housework. Most of the people in the study (55 percent) said they had no problems with their partners. About one-quarter of the people had a moderate or serious problem, and another 20 percent had two or more problems. Eighty percent of the people questioned said they felt moderately or highly satisfied.

Project Match in 2004 managed thirty-seven units of shared rental housing for low-income seniors (San Jose Community Connections, 2004). Home sharing appeals to only a small proportion of older people. A study conducted by the AARP asked people whether they had tried home sharing or would consider it. Only 7 percent of the sample had shared someone else's home and only 9 percent would consider. Still, it meets the needs of the older person who wants companionship and a relatively low-cost housing option.

Retirement Communities

Retirement communities can take at least two forms: (1) **naturally occurring retirement communities (NORCs)**; and (2) **planned retirement communities**.

About one-quarter of older people live in a building or neighborhood where at least one-half the people are aged 60 or over. Gerontologists call these naturally NORCs. The populations in most of these neighborhoods and apartment buildings grew older as people aged in place. People in these communities say they like living with older people. They say this keeps the neighborhood peaceful and quiet, they share common interests with neighbors, and they find their neighbors friendly and helpful.

Minority older people may find themselves in a NORC because of racial segregation. This applies to African American older people more than to any other group. Skinner (1992) says that lifelong housing segregation has restricted where older African Americans could live. This has left many of them in inner cities or rural settings. Older African Americans tend to stay in place as they age, in part because they have little choice. Skinner (1992, p. 50) says that "economic disadvantage from low incomes, racial segregation, and ageism join to create formidable barriers to housing and the free choice or movement to other housing options."

Inner-city neighborhoods or rural settings do not always turn into ideal NORCs. Many of these neighborhoods lack easy shopping, transportation, and safety. They can leave older people afraid and isolated in their homes. "With few options available to them, they are not only aging in place, they are stuck in place, prisoners in their own homes, without the ability to move to more appropriate housing" (Skinner, 1992, p. 51). Krause (2004), for example, reports that people in inner-city neighborhoods may not have the resources available to help the older person. A rundown neighborhood can also create stress and health problems for the older person.

But this isn't true of all urban settings. And Krause (2004) notes that the lack of support may apply to only the worst neighborhoods. Some urban communities offer amenities that keep older people in place and attract others. For example, older people in inner-city neighborhoods live near the churches, shops, and neighbors they've known for years. This makes the local community an important resource for older minority group members. Krause (2004) found that the amount of support available to an older person depended on their needs, the quality of the urban environment, and the amount of resources available in their neighborhood network.

Other groups of older people have also begun to value the diversity and culture of city life. Smith (2004a; 2004b) says that "whether they are new arrivals, savoring their liberation from lawn mowing and automobiles, or veteran urbanites, deeply rooted in communities they helped to build and surrounded by neighbors they have known all their lives, many older Americans find that the services they need and the amenities they enjoy are more plentiful and more accessible in the city."

Marshall and Hunt (1999; *also* Hunt, Marshall, & Merrill, 2002) describe another type of NORC. These communities occur in rural areas. They found that rural communities could become one of three types of NORC—amenity, convenience, and bifocal.

An amenity community attracted people who wanted the charm of a rural life-style and country environment. Amenity communities had younger, affluent, well-educated residents.

A convenience community attracted people who wanted the benefits of living in a community that could meet their health care and service needs. These communities, compared with those of amenity migrants, had older, less well-educated, and less wealthy residents.

A bifocal community attracted people who wanted amenities but also nearness to family and friends. Members of these communities shared characteristics of the other two groups.

BOX 11.8
RETIREMENT COMMUNITIES WITH SPECIAL APPEAL

Deciding where to retire used to be like deciding on a summer camp—there were day camps and sleep-away camps, but the activities were pretty much the same. But just as summer camps now cater to interests ranging from archery to zoology, retirement communities are springing up that let you grow old in the company of people with similar backgrounds or mutual passions that go far deeper than a shared interest in golf.

They range from communities for gay men and lesbians to centers shaped for members of specific ethnic groups. Retired military officers have formed communities around the country. Sunset Hall in Los Angeles bills itself as a "home for free-thinking elders." Other examples include a residence for artists in the works in Manhattan; the ElderSpirit Center, a cohousing retirement community based on spiritual principles that is opening this summer at Abingdon, VA; and an assisted-living center in Gresham, OR, for retirees who are deaf or blind, where the employees know sign language and there are rooms with door lights instead of bells.

Experts say that one force behind the trend is the lengthened lifespan of those retiring. Choosing where to live after work is no longer mostly a matter of deciding the best place to be when you fall apart.

Decades ago, the most common kind of partnership for a retirement community was with health care companies, said Bill Silbert, the marketing director for the Kendal Corporation, which runs retirement centers operating "in the Quaker tradition" near Cornell, Dartmouth and Oberlin. Now the partnerships are often with universities. "Health care is an important part of the concept," Mr. Silbert said, "but it's not the reason to come."

Ron Manheimer, executive director of the North Carolina Center for Creative Retirement in Asheville, NC, said he expects to see more retirement communities in which older people can live among peers who share their specific interests and values. "These are pretty much the people you're going to end up living with for the rest of your life," he said. "People want to be with people they will be comfortable with and where there will be a high level of mutual trust."

"The whole idea that there's this homogenous group of elders is simply not true," he said. "There are cultures of aging, and there are more and more of them."

Robert G. Kramer, executive director of the National Investment Center for the Seniors Housing and Care Industries in Annapolis, MD, said the diversification is being driven in part by baby boomers seeking more options for their parents. This generation, he said, is used "to forcing the market to deliver what they want; they've done it all their life."

"What we see today," Mr. Kramer said, "will be absolutely nothing compared to what we'll see in 10 or 15 years."

Drew Leder, a professor at Loyola College in Maryland who has studied the spirituality of aging, agreed. "When the baby boomers were growing up there were three flavors of ice cream; now there are 1,000," he said. "Similarly, there are going to be 1,000 different flavors of retirement."

Here is a sampling of those flavors:

Jeanne Dolan, who bought land with her partner at Carefree Cove, a Gated community for gay men and lesbians in Zionville, NC, said, "I think most people would like to retire with at least somewhat like-minded people, especially now that we're living a lot longer and going to be retired a lot longer."

But living in a community aimed at a specific group has its pros and cons. Pei Yang Chang, 88, lives with his wife, Rose, at Aegis Gardens, an assisted-living center in Fremont, CA, where everything from the food to the building design is Chinese. "The good thing," he said, "is there are so many old friends. The bad thing is we are out of touch with general public. We don't want to be too excluded."

Lorraine Carvalho dreamed of retiring in a community with other gay women. At 57, she learned about Carefree Cove, a gated community for gay men and lesbians in North Carolina's Blue Ridge Mountains. "I was like, 'Oh my God—there's my dream right there,' " Ms. Carvalho said.

(continued)

BOX 11.8
(Continued)

Gay retirement living is a concept on the edge of a boom. The Palms of Manasota in Palmetto, FL, the first gay and lesbian retirement community, opened in 1998, and several others are being planned or close to breaking ground. Carefree Cove began selling lots in 2001.

David Aronstein, president of Stonewall Communities, a nonprofit corporation developing a co-operative in Boston for gay men and lesbians, said, "Especially for gay men and women who have spent their lives as a minority, the security of living with people with like-minded values is very valuable."

Aegis Gardens, a development for Chinese older people, shows how a housing development can adapt to the culture of its residents. The first street address assigned to the Aegis Gardens assisted-living center contained the number four. Chinese tradition associates the number with death, so Aegis Assisted Living petitioned for a change. Blue also connotes death, so the company's navy blue uniforms were changed to dark red, which means happiness. Brochures were printed in green, "a much more prosperous color," the president and chief executive, Dwayne J. Clark, said.

At Aegis Gardens, one of a small number of retirement centers catering to ethnic groups, the employees speak Mandarin or Cantonese. Activities include a daily tai chi exercise class, Chinese calligraphy and Chinese opera singing, as well as table tennis, mah jong and bingo.

To build Aegis Gardens, Mr. Clark said the company sought help from an advisory group of Chinese-Americans on details down to the size of the guardian lions at the entrance.

Mr. Clark, whose company runs a dozen retirement centers in the northwest, said a community aimed at Chinese retirees would not have been possible 10 or 15 years ago; tradition required adult children to care for their parents.

"As people become more Americanized, that's changing," he said. "The wives of Asian-Americans are working just like Americans that are born here."

Source: Adapted from Appelman, H. (2004). All Your Neighbors Are Just Like You. *The New York Times,* April 13, 2004 p. G1. Retrieved June 23, 2004.

People in all three types of communities tended to stay in a community that met their unique needs. Most newer planned retirement communities come about when a developer builds and sells houses to healthy active retirees. These communities supply health services, shopping centers, and recreation facilities. Communities range in size from towns like Sun City, Arizona, with around 40,000 people, to small communities of 9,000 people like Leisure World near Silver Spring, Maryland.

Kastenbaum (1993b) says that people who settle in these communities value the new homes, clean streets, easy access to shopping, and middle-class neighbors. The weather and relaxed life-style appeal to most migrants. They also look for safety and freedom from fear of crime. Many have left northern communities where crime has increased. One woman told Kastenbaum (1993b, p. 163), "Our [old] neighborhood was just not the pleasant place it had always been."

The new communities often have gates and guards, and residents in *posses* watch out for strangers (Dychtwald & Flower, 1990). They also have age restrictions that only allow people aged 55 or older to move in. Critics of these communities say they create barriers between older people and the rest of society. Kastenbaum (1993b, pp. 170–171) says that these communities can develop a "fortress mentality" and set up "barricades against physical or symbolic invasion." Only a small proportion of Americans choose to live in this kind of enclave, but those who do express satisfaction with their choices (Streib, 1987).

A new type of housing for older people has emerged—housing communities based on or near a university campus. As many as fifty to one hundred housing centers for older people exist or are being built on U.S. university campuses. These include communities associated with the University of Indiana, Notre Dame, and Arizona State University.

Projects that develop in partnership with a university work the best. They integrate the residents with university life. These developments attract people interested in campus cultural life, in personal growth, or in getting a degree. Retired faculty and staff often choose this type of community so they can maintain contact with the campus. Campuses benefit from having older students in the classroom, from older residents' volunteer activities, and from donations from older residents.

Regnier (2003) reports that members of a community near Iowa State University donated $3 million to the university over a five- to six-year period. Regnier (2003, p. 109) says that "although this is a very small segment of the U.S. elder population, it nonetheless represents a growing and influential sector."

Continuing Care Retirement Communities

Nursing home costs can wipe out a person's savings and put the person's family in debt. To protect against these costs, some older people have moved to **continuing care retirement communities (CCRCs)**. "Continuing Care Retirement Communities (CCRCs) or communities offering Life Care are designed to offer active seniors an independent life-style and a private home from which to enjoy it, regardless of future medical needs" (Senior*resource*.com, 2004).

Some communities ask for a payment up front and then monthly payment for services and medical expenses. These communities offer residents multiple care options (Seniorresource.com, 2004). An AARP study (Ejaz et al., 2003) found that most people moved to a CCRC because of their own or their spouse's health care needs.

Residents sign a contract with the facility that guarantees them access to housing and defined types of care for the rest of their lives. Gonyea, Hudson, and Seltzer (1990) found that older people in a Boston suburb ranked this as their preferred option if they had to move. Regnier (2003) reports that between 1,900 and 2,000 CCRCs exist in the United States. The American Seniors Housing Association (Schless & Preede, 2000) estimates that between 1997 and 2000 the United States added to its housing stock about 200,000 assisted living, congregate housing, senior apartments, and CCRCs.

People in CCRCs live in private apartments that have kitchens, so residents can make their own meals. Some communities have common dining rooms where residents can eat if they choose. Most CCRCs provide transportation, fitness centers, and social activities. They also offer round-the-clock nursing care in a nursing home wing attached to the main building or in a separate building.

About 75 percent of CCRCs also offer long-term care in units without kitchens. These units have twenty-four-hour nursing care and help with activities of daily living. Most CCRCs that offer this kind of help require that a person move from independent housing to a special unit. Fees for long-term care services vary, depending on the CCRC's entrance fee and monthly charges.

Most CCRCs charge high entrance fees. All communities charge a monthly fee for rent and some services. CCRCs accept people who can live on their own, have good health, and have the ability to pay higher monthly fees in the future. Entrance fees in most communities range from $40,000 to $90,000 for a one- or two-bedroom apartment. But they can run as high as $400,000. Monthly fees average between $200 and $2,500 (AARP, 2004c). Couples pay more than single people. Monthly fees can increase as the cost of services increases. Some communities will return a part of the entrance fee to a person's family or estate when the older person dies or leaves.

CCRCs attract older old people. The typical resident is a single woman around 80 years old (Netting, 1991). They want the security of future nursing home care. Moen and Erickson (2001) found that, compared with men, women showed the most overall satisfaction with life in a CCRC. One 80-year-old woman described her reasons for moving to a CCRC this way:

> I have always done for myself. I have some very good friends and a dear house-mate, but I don't have any family nearby. Of course, my friends and house-mate are all in their eighties too. So, I realized that if I was going to continue doing for myself, I needed to make some changes. Here I have reliable backup. (Lavizzo-Mourey & Eisenberg, 1992, p. xvii)

CCRCs offer benefits but also create some risks for older people. First, monthly payments can go up. Second, a person does not own the property. Third, the company that owns the community may go out of business. Older people can lose their investment and their housing if this happens. Some states regulate CCRCs, and the industry has set up an accreditation system. But even state regulation will not protect against future community failure. And the accreditation system does not ensure that a CCRC will fulfill its promises.

Somers and Spears (1992) see a growing interest in CCRCs. In the future, more people will fit the profile of current CCRC residents (single women aged 80 and older). They will want protection from crippling long-term care costs. But the high cost may limit the number of people who can move to this type of housing. New types of CCRCs will emerge to meet the needs of a growing market. They will appear in more flexible forms with varied services. Potential residents will attempt to match a community with their assets, their needs, and their expectations about community life.

THE FUTURE OF HOUSING

The current generation of older people will need more supportive housing. This will include housing designed so people can age in place, and it will include more long-term care facilities. The future will see a blending of housing and services to help older people live as independently as possible.

Integration of Housing and Services

Improved housing in the future for all older people will depend on a better integration of housing and services. The key to aging in place often has little to do with the size and shape of a building. It has to do with the social and health care supports that allow people to stay in their homes. Newcomer and Weeden (1986, p. 6) say that "unfortunately, if integration or coordination occurs among [housing, health care, and social service] programs within any community, it is more likely by accident than design."

Newcomer and Weeden (1986) say that the lack of coordinated housing and services leaves many older people without the supports they need. They estimate that between 10 and 20 percent of nursing home residents could live outside institutions if they had supportive housing.

Regnier (1993, p. 46; 2003) studied supportive housing for older people in northern Europe. A number of countries (Sweden, Denmark, Norway) have developed something called the "mixed-use service house." This design provides services to older people in a housing complex and to people in the nearby community. Services include meals, recreation, and health treatment. One service house in Sweden shares space in a community center for middle-school students. The students and older people share a crafts room and gymnasium. A restaurant serves residents, students, and the local community.

Another type of housing puts older people's apartments over shops such as a pharmacy, cafe, and grocery store. These housing units often have balconies and courtyards linked to children's playgrounds. Service houses create links between older people and the community. Europeans in their design of housing for older people "integrate, connect, protect, overlook, enliven and facilitate" (Regnier, 1993, p. 51). This type of housing could serve as a model for supportive housing in the United States (Regnier, 2003). It would suit people, especially city dwellers, who want to stay in their communities but need help to do so.

Low-Income, Rural, and Minority Housing

A review of housing options shows that a wide range of options exists. But "a significant fraction of the elderly either cannot afford adequate housing or

BOX 11.9
IT'S BACK TO THE OLD ALMA MATER

People join continuing care retirement communities for many reasons. Most people join for the health care and social service benefits. But communities also offer life-style options that appeal to specific groups of people. Pamela Sherrid reports on the growing interest in communities linked to university campuses. These communities provide not only services and health care supports, but also intellectual stimulation and access to the arts.

Imagine life on a college campus with no required courses and no homework. Students can forget it, but for a growing number of senior citizens, it's no idle daydream. Retirement communities are suddenly opening in university towns across the country; residents get the lifestyle students wish *they* had. Classes, no grades. Parties in the common room with no all-nighters afterward. Residents of Meadowood, near Indiana University, get more than 100 free concerts each year by students and faculty of the top-notch School of Music. As the University of Virginia women's basketball team climbed to the '93 Eastern regional finals, James Harper, a resident of nearby Colonnades community, rooted at every game.

The appeal to retirees of a vital intellectual climate combined with the sophisticated medical care often available at university centers is so obvious it's a wonder the notion hasn't caught fire before. A few pioneering communities, like Meadowood and those at Iowa State in Ames and the University of Connecticut in Storrs, got settled in the early or mid-80s. The current crop, including the Colonnades and communities near Dartmouth, Duke University and the University of Washington in Seattle, have opened in the past three years. . . . In some cases, the college is the developer; in others, a complex is built by a developer but maintains close informal ties with the college. Residents of privately owned Kendal at Hanover (NH) for instance, can take free classes sponsored by Dartmouth on everything from Milton to international politics.

Retired faculty and alumni of a school may be the first to receive a community's promotional literature, but all retirees are welcome. Anyone who responds is likely to find the drill similar to that at any "continuing care" retirement community: Residents typically enter in their mid-to-late 70s, then live independently in apartments or cottages, usually taking at least one meal a day in the community dining room. A person who becomes too frail to bathe, dress or eat without help can move to an apartment or room in the assisted living areas, where a home-health aide is on call. Nursing-home care is available, too—in many communities, it's covered by the price of admission. One reason Isabelle and Cabell Bailey live at the Colonnades, says Isabelle, is that if one should enter the nursing home, "the other would be right next door."

Residents who are completely happy with their choice warn that the transition to community life can be rocky; many recall with pain the process of emptying and selling the family home. But the link to a vibrant intellectual community—plus the lively group of older people that these retirement villages attract—is uniquely inspiring to many. Take Peter Bien, a professor of English at Dartmouth who helped found Kendal and whose 88-year-old mother is a resident. "Living there is a creative experience," he says. Bien, 63, will retire in about four years. He and his wife are already signed up.

Would you want to live near your university campus in retirement? What do you see as the advantages and disadvantages of this kind of retirement community? Would you prefer another type of community? Would you prefer one that focuses on a marina or a sports stadium and attracts people with these interests? What type of retirement community would you like to live in, if you could invent one for yourself?

Source: From "It's Back to the Old Alma Mater," by P. Sherrid, 1993, *U.S. News & World Report,* June 14, pp. 101–103.

live in a residence that is inappropriate for their present need" (Ehrlich, 1986, p. 189). Many poor older people live in rundown housing and cannot afford to move out. Ruth Sachs, who directs a housing program called Sarah's Circle in Washington, DC, says that "there is no continuum of care for low-income people" (Keyser, 1994, p. 93).

A person in a rural setting often has fewer housing options than a person in a city. Rural older people tend to live in single, detached houses that they own (Shafer & Harvard University, 2000). Krout (1986, cited in Hubbard, Blieszner, & London, 1992) reports that rural older people risk living in substandard housing—without either hot water, a private toilet, or a private bathtub. Also, compared with urban residents, older rural residents have "a smaller and less diverse array of community-based supportive services" (Golant, 2004, p. 299). "Despite mental images of decaying urban neighborhoods and run-down boarding houses," Coward (1988, p. 170) says, "it is the *rural* elderly, as a whole, that seem to be disadvantaged." The housing continuum needs more options for low-income, minority, and rural older people.

Minority older people also need more access to the choices on the housing continuum. For example, minority members have made little use of alternative unsubsidized housing (like home sharing or CCRCs). Few of these options suit poor older people. "If innovative housing alternatives remain untried among minority elderly," Lacayo (1991, p. 45) says, "then the disparity between their living arrangements and those of the dominant older population can only become more pronounced. This would mean increasing isolation and persistent poverty for minority elders."

Lacayo (1991) suggests a number of changes that would improve housing for minority older people:

- More funding for Section 202 loans to create housing for older people; also, more funding for home repair programs.
- More subsidized housing in minority neighborhoods near services; government incentives to builders to create and maintain minority housing.
- More innovative housing designed for minority older people. This should include creative financing options for minority elders.

Many older people cannot move along the housing continuum to find housing that meets their needs. Barriers to living in a supportive environment include the availability and affordability of options. Future housing policies need to ensure that options exist and that older people can choose the options that best suit their needs.

TRANSPORTATION

Transportation gives older people a sense of independence and control over their lives. It allows them to visit friends, attend cultural events, go shopping, and get health care. A lack of transportation can lead to isolation, poor health, and decreased well-being. Rural, suburban, and urban older people have different transportation options and needs.

Public Transportation

Public transportation and other forms of mobility (like walking) account for only 8 percent of trips older people make outside their homes (Stutts, 2003). Still, people who live in cities report the need to live near public transport. Low-income people who live alone and have health problems also express a need to live near public transport (AARP, 1993). Even older people who drive need public transportation at times. For example, they may need to make a trip at night, but hesitate to drive after dark. Stutts (2003) says that American public transit options lag behind those in most European countries. And Bailey (2004) reports that more than one-half of older nondrivers (3.6 million people), on any given day, have to stay at home at least partly because they have no transportation options.

People in rural areas have fewer transportation options than people in cities. Bailey (2004) reports that people in rural areas tend to make less use of public transportation (usually due to lack of available services). And, compared with people who live in cities, they tend to stay home more because they lack transportation. Fewer people in rural areas, compared with people in urban areas, have access to cars. And most towns under 10,000 people have no intercity bus line. Poor quality rural roads and bridges make travel hard. And rural people pay more for public transportation due to large distances and the small numbers of users. All of these things increase the chance of isolation for rural seniors (Coward, 1988).

Bailey (2004) recommends increases in federal funding to expand public transportation, especially in rural areas. She also recommends increased funding for special transportation services (like paratransit buses) to help older people with disabilities.

Private Transportation

Hare (1992) proposes that gerontologists include driving as an ADL in their assessments of a person's abilities. Older people who live in rural areas and suburbs must drive to survive. These areas often have no public transportation systems (Burkhardt, 2000). People need cars to get to friends, shops, and almost anywhere else. Suburban and rural buses and taxi services help older people get around. They cannot overcome the isolation of living outside a city without a car. "If they were affordable," Hare (1992, p. 36) says, "chauffeurs would rank next in importance to doctors and remodellers."

Even in cities relatively few older people take public transportation if they have a car. Burkhardt (2000, p. 109) says that "even in areas where a variety of transportation options are available, the number one mode of transportation for older people remains the car, preferably with them as the driver." Stutts (2003) reports that two-thirds of the time older people drive themselves when they take an automobile trip. And even people aged 85 and over more often travel by car as a driver than as a passenger. Travel by car accounts for 92 percent of trips made outside the home. And, compared with nondrivers, those who drive make twice as many trips outside the home each day. Between 1983 and 1995 the proportion of older people with driver's licenses increased, older people took more trips with their cars, and they drove more miles per day. Stutts (2003) says that the trend toward more older drivers and more use of cars by older drivers will continue in the future.

Studies disagree on the effects of age on driving ability. For example, studies that measure millions of miles driven find that people aged 75 to 84 have a crash rate slightly higher than middle-aged people. This rate increases with age. But, people aged 85 and over still have a crash rate only as great as that of people aged 20 to 24. They have a better safety record than 16 to 19 year olds (the age group with the highest crash rate).

Bruce (1994) argues that the measure of accidents per million miles driven works against older people. They tend to take shorter trips and drive on city streets. This boosts the risk of accidents. He prefers the use of accidents per 1,000 drivers. By this measure, older people make the safest drivers. Studies that use crashes per thousand drivers show that older people (even those aged 75 and older) have the best safety records (Bryer, 2000). Compared with the crash rate of all other drivers, they have about one-half the rate of accidents (Stutts, 2003).

Stutts (2003, p. 193) says that "there is no question" that physical changes in later life impair a person's ability to drive. Decreased vision, cognitive impairment, decreased strength and mobility, and slower reaction time all decrease a person's ability to drive safely. But older people compensate for some of these declines (Rudinger & Jansen, 2003; Burkhardt, 2000). They may ride more often as passengers, they may limit their driving to the daytime, and they may limit their driving to familiar places in their neighborhoods.

Physical ability varies among older drivers. Vision and reaction time tend to decline with age. But age alone cannot predict a person's driving ability. The right to drive should depend on a person's ability, not age. Stutts (2003) also reports that injury rates per 1,000 people decrease with the age of the driver. Drivers aged 75 and over, for example, show the lowest injury rate for any age group. But fatality rates on a variety of measures increase with age and

BOX 11.10
TAKE AWAY MY LICENSE

For many of us, getting a driver's license in our teen years symbolized entry into adulthood. Giving up a driver's license symbolically signals a loss of freedom and autonomy. Few people would willingly give up the right to drive. But Max Israelite, a 75-year-old Pennsylvanian, plans to do just that. He gives his reasons below.

I celebrated my 75th birthday recently. Sometime soon, I plan to put my car up for sale, tear up my driver's license and never get behind the wheel of a car again. It will not be easy to give up the automobile, and I take this step reluctantly. I enjoy driving. It permits a mobility impossible with any other mode of transportation. The sense of omnipotence one experiences when wheeling down the highway at 70 miles per hour is irreplaceable. Having been a motorist for so long, I'll find it difficult to become a pedestrian again.

Beyond being an ingrained habit, the automobile is a necessity, especially for those of us who live in suburbia. There is little or no public transportation, the corner grocery has become extinct and people must get to a shopping center or mall—usually several miles away—to replenish the family larder.

I recognize that I am not a first-rate driver. I was not a great driver when I was a young man, and the aging process has not enhanced my driving skills. While it is true that in more than half a century of driving, I have had only two accidents for which I was to blame—both fender benders that caused minimal damage and no injuries—I attribute this to good luck rather than good driving. In a case of rare unanimity my children concur with this opinion, adding the observation, "It's not only good luck; it's that everyone else is a good driver."

I took the only driver's test I would ever take when I was 21 years old, when my eyes were sharp enough to count the fleas on the hind leg of a shaggy dog at 100 paces. Twenty years later, I had begun to wear glasses. Today, I wear bifocals. Simply stated, I do not see as well in 1994 as I did in 1940. . . .

Since they cannot conduct the normal business of living without their cars, the majority of my contemporaries continue to drive, although most of us have made concessions to maturity. We no longer take long trips, nor do we drive after dark. We rarely venture out during rush hours, and we shun areas of high-density traffic whenever possible.

That's most of us. Some refuse to bow to the inevitable, and continue to drive as they always drove. . . .

All too frequently, I see an item on the 6 o'clock news about an elderly gentleman who, having driven accident-free since 1928, has run into and through a crowd of people waiting at a bus stop. He cannot understand how it happened. He is certain the accident was caused by mechanical failure. "I was pushing down on the foot brake as hard as I could," he asserts. Sure he was. Or maybe it was the gas pedal. And an eightysomething lady drives through the window of a restaurant at lunchtime, and is at a loss to explain the aberration. These are adventures I would like to forgo.

And in an effort to forgo them, I will be moving in with my son and his family later on this year, when the house he is building is completed. This will make it possible for me to manage without a car.

Undeniably, I will suffer a loss of mobility when I give up driving. I will give up a measure of my cherished independence when there is no longer a car parked in my driveway, available for instant use. But I would rather stop driving five years too soon than one millisecond too late.

Do you agree with this author's decision? Do you agree with his view of older drivers? What can society do to ensure that people can drive as long as they have the ability, but not so long that they endanger themselves and others?

Source: From *Newsweek,* May 9, p. 11, © 1994, Newsweek, Inc., "Take Away My License," by M. Israelite.

increase dramatically from age 75 and older. The fatality rate for the oldest drivers equals or surpasses that of the youngest drivers (aged 16 to 19). Other data show that, compared with younger drivers, older drivers more often bear the fault for an accident. And this tendency to be at fault increases with age.

The concern over seniors' driving ability has led some states to test older drivers before reissuing licenses. Some states require vision tests for older drivers. Studies show that these states have lower fatal accident rates for drivers aged 70 and over (Levy, Vernick, & Howard, 1995). A majority of states issue limited licenses for older people with a history of accidents. The license limits driving to daytime, low speeds, and near the person's home. The District of Columbia and the state of New Hampshire require that older people take a knowledge test after age 75 (Bruce, 1994). California requires that doctors report people with dementia who may have a problem driving (Stutts, 2003, citing Staplin, Lococo, Stewart, & Decina, 1998).

The AARP prefers education rather than age-based testing. It offers a course for older drivers called "55 Alive/Mature Driving." Several million people aged 50 and over have taken the course, which includes discussions of how to adapt to physical changes. A German study (Rudinger & Jansen, 2003) supports the value of education and self-regulation over a general driving test based on a person's age.

The Federal Highway Administration has published a report with over 100 recommendations for improvements to highways that will help the older driver. These include improvements in lighting on roads, larger and brighter signs, better signage at intersections, and clearer lines on roadways (Stutts, 2003; Jovanis, 2003). These changes will give older drivers more confidence, better guidance, and allow them to drive more safely at later ages.

Auto engineers have also created designs that benefit the older driver. These include side airbags, speedometer information projected on the windshield, and global positioning systems that use voice commands to give directions. These changes can reduce accidents and lower the fatality rate for older drivers in a crash. Future designs could include collision warning devices and software to adjust speed in the presence of potential dangers (like too short a distance between vehicles) (Jovanis, 2003; Färber, 2003).

Kastenbaum (1993a) says that older people in the United States link driving to freedom, competence, and youthfulness. A Florida woman expressed her frustration at life without a car. "I live alone and don't like to depend on friends. . . . I walk to the grocery, get rides from the Red Cross to the doctor's office. The logistics are driving me up a wall. If I had to do it over again, I wouldn't give up my car . . ." (Burkhardt, 2000, p. 111). Education programs, changes in driving patterns, and new highway designs can all extend the number of years an older person drives safely.

CONCLUSION

Dychtwald and Flower (1990) envision new forms of retirement communities in the future. These will include an *Olympic village* with nonstop athletic activities, a *Tron center* with high-tech computers, videos, and entertainment, and a time-share village where people can move from place to place every few years. These options may emerge to serve people with good incomes, good health, and a focus on leisure.

The large majority of older people, however, prefer to age in place. Many older people vacation in the Sun Belt. There they enjoy a relaxed life style and leisure activities. But they prefer to live most of the year near life-long neighbors, friends, and family. New housing options, including home modification, elder cottages, and accessory apartments, can help older people achieve this goal. New housing will have to meet the needs of a diverse older population. Their needs will range from more long-term care beds, to new types of housing developments with integrated services, to modified homes to allow people to stay in their homes longer, to new communities for active Baby Boomers. The continuum of housing for older people will expand in the future and will include more options than ever before.

SUMMARY

- Living arrangements include living with a spouse, alone, with other relatives, or with nonrelatives. Eighty-five percent of older people live alone or with a spouse. The rest live with another relative or with a nonrelative.
- The number of older people who live alone will increase in the future. Higher Social Security benefits, widowhood, and divorce all contribute to this trend.
- People who live alone report a high rate of chronic illness and activity limitation. As people age, their competence or ability may decline and environmental press or demand may increase. When this happens, people need supports to stay in their homes.
- Older people prefer to age in place. They want to stay in their homes as long as they can. Aging in place requires that people have the resources they need to live in the setting they choose.
- Many housing options exist for older people today. The most common types of housing, ranging from the most demanding to the least demanding environments, include (a) single-family homes, (b) apartments and condominiums, (c) life-care communities, (d) granny flats, (e) congregate housing, (f) shared housing, (g) assisted living, and (h) nursing homes. This housing continuum offers options that fit older people's varied needs.
- The large majority of people aged 60 and over live in single-family homes. Most people own their homes, with the majority living mortgage free. Suburban homes, built for the families of the 1950s, create problems for older people. These homes may not suit the physical abilities of people who have aged in place. They may also leave a person isolated, with few transportation options. Home modifications and new transportation services can help older people in suburban homes.
- Many people aged 60 and over live in apartments. Renters tend to be older women with low incomes. They have fewer options when it comes to home modification. For this reason, older renters often choose to move into apartments designed for older people.
- Some older people require less demanding environments than single-family homes or apartments. They can choose from other options that offer more support and services. These options include congregate housing, subsidized housing, single rooms, or board and care homes.
- Interest in new types of housing options will grow in the future. Designers have developed many new housing alternatives to meet the needs of people as they age. Some of these alternatives include elder cottages, home sharing, retirement communities, and continuing care retirement communities.
- Most older people today prefer to age in place. This depends on the integration of supportive housing, social services, transportation, and health care. Living arrangements will have to meet the needs of a diverse older population. These needs will range from long-term care in institutions to new communities for active Baby Boomers.
- As people age, they feel more need to live near public transportation. Physical changes can affect driving, but older drivers vary in their driving abilities. Education programs and new highway designs can help extend the number of years that older people can drive a car. This will allow seniors to live independently for a longer time.

DISCUSSION QUESTIONS

1. What types of living arrangements are available to older people? Arrange them on a continuum from least to most supportive housing.
2. What has led a greater proportion of older people than ever before to live alone? Why do gerontologists think this trend will continue?
3. Discuss some of the problems that an older person who lives alone can face. What are some methods for overcoming these problems?
4. Describe the relationship between a person's capability (competence) and environmental demand (press). How do these two things affect a person's ability to live alone?
5. What kinds of problems do older people face if they live in a single-family home? What kinds of home modifications can help a person live in safety and comfort?
6. Describe several housing options, besides single-

family homes or apartments, that are available to older people today. How do these options differ from single-family homes and apartments?

7. List and describe several alternatives to traditional housing that are now available to older people. What benefits do they offer older residents? What risks do these alternatives present?

dep

9. How people? W that will imp portation?

SELECTED READING

Wahl, H-W., Scheidt, R. J., & Windley, P. G. (Eds.). (2004). *Focus on aging in context: socio-physical environments.* New York: Springer.

The editors have organized this collection around the ecological framework first proposed by Lawton and Nahemow and discussed in this chapter. The essays look at the fit between the person and the environment from various points of view. Topics include the effect of the environment on everyday life, competence, and problem solving; design of interior space; and the supportive neighborhood. The essays show the importance of looking at how a supportive environment can create the conditions for successful aging.

Gubrium, J. F. (1993). *Speaking of life: Horizo nursing home residents.* Hawthorne, NY: Aldi

Gubrium uses ethnographic analysis to study the life in nursing homes. He presents older residents' f and perceptions of nursing home life. Few other studies h asked older people to talk about the meaning of life in a nursing home. Few other researchers have listened carefully and reported what residents have to say. Chapter titles like "Worried to Death," "It's Come to This," and "Lovin' the Lord" give a flavor of residents' concerns and the stories they tell.

GLOSSARY OF TERMS

age integration Housing for many age groups; for example, an apartment building that houses people of all ages from children to retirees.

age segregation Housing for only one age group; for example, an apartment complex for older people.

aging in place Living in the same location, usually a home or apartment, until late old age or death.

assisted living Provides personal care such as meals and bathing, and 24-hour supervision.

autonomy Similar to capability; the ability of a person to independently carry out daily activities.

capability (competence) A measure of a person's ability to live comfortably in an environment.

congregate (or enriched) housing Housing that provides amenities such as meals on site for residents.

continuing care retirement communities (CCRCs) Offer health and social services to members for a fee.

Department of Housing and Urban Development (HUD) A primary source of subsidized housing for older people in the United States.

environmental demand (press) A measure of the demand that an environment places on an older person.

home equity conversion loans (HECs) Methods for freeing up the equity (or value) of a home.

naturally occurring retirement community (NORC) A building or neighborhood with at least one-half the people aged 60 or over. This occurs without conscious planning as people in a community age in place.

planned retirement community A community planned, usually by a developer, to house and serve older people.

security The feeling that a person can manage independently in an environment.

8. Explain the future trend in housing for older people.
What kinds of things will help older people live in-
[illegible]endently in the future?
[illegible]oes the lack of transportation affect older
[illegible]hat kinds of services can society provide
[illegible]rove older people's access to trans-

[illegible]s of meaning for
[illegible]e de Gruyter.
[illegible]quality of
[illegible]elings
[illegible]ve

chapter 12

AND EDUCATION

I first met Sarah Bowles at a suburban YMCA. Sarah ran a fitness program for older adults called the Retired People's Participaction Club. The program enrolled 215 members. It involved gym exercises, followed by a swim in the pool, with lots of time to kibbitz and schmooze. "You want a political discussion," she once told me, "you'll find it in the sauna."

I first talked with Sarah as part of my research for my book *Successful Aging*. I considered Sarah a model of active living. She was 72 years old at the time. I decided to call Sarah again to see what she was doing ten years later. How had this active, successfully aging woman fared over the years? I had no idea where to find her, so I tried the Y where I first visited with her. "Yes," a receptionist said, "Sarah still works here. But she's gone for the day."

I left my number and Sarah called me back the next day. She told me that she still leads the club in the gym and swim program five days a week in the winter and three days a week in the summer. The program has now grown to over 300 registrants, with about five new people enrolling each month. She has trained eight of the club members to work as instructors.

"The program must be benefiting people," she says, "because they just keep coming. As for me, I'm on nitro now. I keep working in the program because otherwise I would be at home stagnating."

"If I don't lead the program one day, my body doesn't work. I have a bad case of arthritis in both my wrists. So I wear a cast when I lead the gym session. I can barely get down on the mat because I broke both my knees some years ago and that bothers me. Plus, I'm afraid I might break my wrists. Last month I fell and cracked some ribs, so that bothered me for a while. But I still get down there. I do what I can. Sometimes I tell the people, 'Do as I say, not as I do.' I try the exercises out on me first. I hear some of them say, 'If she can do it, I can do it.' "

In addition to running her program, Sarah lectures to groups on health and fitness. She travels to small towns and teaches older people to lead fitness programs in their own communities. She also helps train university students in how to run fitness programs for older people. She does all this as a volunteer and says that dedication to her program keeps her fit and alert. "The program is the most important thing in my life," she says. "I feel guilty if I miss a day."

Many studies now support the value of active life-styles like Sarah's. And the YMCA now offers "active older adult" programs in Ys throughout the United States Research reports now show that an active leisure life-style directly benefits health and helps buffer the influence of life events and illness.

This chapter looks at (1) the activity patterns of older people in the United States today, (2) some of the barriers that keep older people from active living, and (3) some model programs for overcoming barriers to active living.

LEISURE

The dictionary defines *leisure* as "freedom from time-consuming duties, responsibilities, or activities." And Robinson (1991) reports that retirement frees up an average of 25 hours per week for men and 18 hours per week for women (Robinson, 1991). But what do older people do with this freedom? Do they take up new activities, maintain old activities, or become disengaged in later life?

Most studies find that older people maintain the leisure activities of their middle years (Strain, Grabusic, Searle, & Dunn, 2002). People with enough income and good health show more continuity than change in leisure activities. Kelly (1993, p. 120) says, "They are, after all, still the same persons."

In general, studies find that older people spend most of their leisure time alone and on sedentary **core leisure activities**. Horna (1994) defines core activities as those that need few resources, have a low cost, and easy access. Core activities include reading, watching television, and visiting with family. Strain and her colleagues (2002) studied 380 people aged 60 to 85 in Manitoba, Canada. They found that people most often engaged in watching television, reading, and shopping. Eight years later in a follow-up study they found that these people listed watching television and reading as their most frequent activities. U.S. studies find similar results.

Lee and King (2003) asked samples of community-dwelling men and women (aged 49 and over) about their activities. Ninety-five percent of the people in the study reported talking on the phone and reading as frequent activities. Over 80 percent said they talked with friends, listened to the radio, or watched television. Compared with men, women spent more time on social activities and household maintenance.

This pattern of sedentary leisure activity seems resistant to change. Lee and Kind (2003) set up an intervention program to increase physical activity and change eating habits. They found that the intervention led to increased physical activity directly related to the program. But it did not change the other, more sedentary, patterns of leisure activity. Wu (2000) found similar results in a survey of 136 older people in South Dakota. The people in the study said that they most often engaged in visiting family or friends and watching movies or television. They said that they participated least in physical activities like tennis and skiing.

Horna (1994) defines **peripheral leisure activities** as those that require more resources, take place outside the home, and need more effort to engage in. Peripheral activities include exercise, sports, outdoor recreation, and travel. Teague and MacNeil (1992; *also* Wu, 2000) say that people aged 65 and over show the lowest rates of participation in outdoor activities. Older people tend to avoid strenuous activities like swimming, tennis, and waterskiing. Studies report that participation in leisure activities differs by age, gender, and race.

Age and Leisure

Researchers find that the rate of leisure activity declines with age (see Figure 12.1). This decline begins in midlife and gets more extreme as a person ages (Wilcox, 2002). Decline affects certain activities more than others. Horna (1994) says that core activities such as "reading, culture, conversation, entertaining, and home improvements" all show a gradual decrease with age. But core leisure activity stays high for all age groups into late old age. Certain home-based activities, such as hobbies, increase with age (Jackson, 1993, cited in Horna, 1994). A person's environment can influence the person's activities.

Pruchno and Rose (2002) compared activities for three groups of frail older people. One group lived in a nursing home, a second group lived in an assisted living facility, and a third group got home health care. The researchers found that the assisted living group spent more time than either group on housework. The frail older people in a nursing home tended to read less than the people in the other groups. But they engaged in more recreation activity than people who lived in their own homes. The nursing home provides opportunities for recreation and encourages this activity. People in assisted living or on their own had to spend more time on maintenance activities like housework and shopping.

Younger old people with higher incomes engage in more peripheral activities like sports and travel. But peripheral activities compared with core activities show an even greater decline with age. Leisure that demands exertion drops off dramatically. The oldest age groups show the least peripheral leisure activity. Frailty and decreased physical ability account for much of this decline.

Gender and Leisure

Leisure participation differs by gender as well as age. Studies show that women have less leisure time in later life than men. They do more of the household tasks than men and often take on the role of caregiver to a spouse or relative. The University of Michigan studied housework throughout the life course. The study found that the amount of housework a person does stays stable throughout life. Women aged 25 to 75 averaged 23 hours of housework a week. Men in this age group averaged only 8 hours a week (cited in "Age Brings No Drop," 1991).

The American Time Use Survey conducted by the Bureau of Labor Statistics (2004, cited in Douthat & Poe, 2004) found that working women spent just under two hours on housework each day. Working men spent one hour and ten minutes. These women spent forty-five minutes on care for

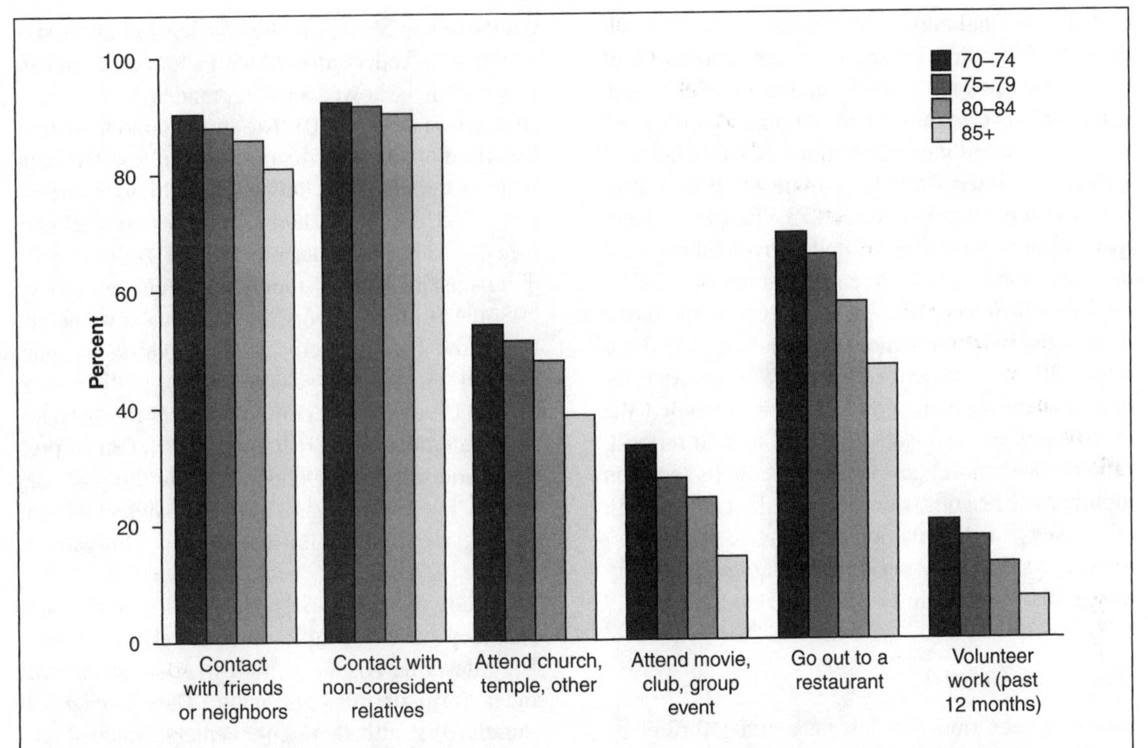

This figure reports social activity in the two weeks prior to the survey. It shows that the older the group, the less they engaged in social activity. But even in later old age (aged 85 and over) people maintained contact with family, neighbors, and friends. Nearly one-half of the oldest group went out to a restaurant and about 40 percent attended religious services.

Declines in health and mobility lead to decreases in activity with age. The more strenuous the activity, the greater the decline (e.g., attending movies or a club). But these figures show that older people stay in touch with their social network into late old age. The majority of men and women, about two-thirds, felt satisfied with the amount of social activity in their lives.

FIGURE 12.1

Percentage of Persons Aged 70 and over Who Reported Engaging in Social Activities, by Age Group, 1995

Source: Federal Interagency Forum on Aging-Related Statistics. (2004). Older Americans 2000: Key indicators of well-being. Health Risks and Behaviors. Indicator 19—Social Activity. Retrieved January 11, 2005, *www.agingstats.gov/chartbook2000/healthrisks.html.*

family members. Men spent 24 minutes on family care. Working men said they spent forty minutes on leisure activity each day. Women spend this time running errands, engaging in civic activities, and personal care.

Robinson (1991) says that gender roles affect the kind of housework people do. Men, for example, show increases in time spent on yardwork, repairs, and gardening. Men spend much less time than women on laundry and child care. Men and women also prefer different activities in retirement (as they did in their middle years). Men, for example, prefer sports activities and competition. Women tend to avoid sports and male-dominated activities. They prefer dance and aerobics (Horna, 1994). Horna (1994, p. 111) concludes that leisure in later life "represents an extension of the earlier life and leisure patterns and preferences." Garber and Blissmer (2002, p. 39) say that "the socialization patterns established earlier in life appear to be salient into old age."

Satariano and colleagues (2000) studied "avoidance of leisure time physical activity" in a sample of over 2,000 people aged 55 and over in Sonoma, California. They found that, compared with men, women reported more limitations and avoidance of physical activity. But a large majority of both genders (81 percent of women and 73.5 percent of men) gave reasons why they limited or avoided physical activity. Some people gave medical reasons for decreasing their activity. And this reason increased with age. But nonmedical reasons accounted for about 20 to 30 percent of people who reported reduced activity. Nonmedical reasons included the absence of an exercise companion and no interest. The researchers suggest that interventions focus on nonmedical reasons (like the lack of a companion). They suggest the creation of exercise teams or a buddy system to increase participation in activity programs. (See Table 12.1.)

Race and Leisure

Some studies find that leisure activity differs by race and ethnicity. For example, compared with whites, older minority group members report less participation in physical activity (Garber & Blissmer, 2002; Fitzgerald et al., 1994). Kamimoto and colleagues (1999, cited in Wilcox, 2002) found that 36 percent of white women aged 65 to 74 reported no leisure physical activity in the month before their study. Fifty-three percent of African American women in this age group reported no activity.

These figures for inactivity rose to 47 percent for white women and 61 percent for African American women aged 75 and over. Older African American women showed a lower rate of participation, compared with whites, when the researchers controlled for age, income, and education (Brown & Tedrick, 1993; *also* Wilcox, 2002). These women said that they lacked information about programs, family kept them from these activities, and they had transportation problems.

A study of 2,912 women aged 40 and over looked at leisure activity by ethnic and racial group. The study found that, compared with white and Hispanic women, African American and American Indian/Alaskan Native showed the least likelihood of exercising. And, compared with white women, Hispanic women showed a greater tendency to exercise (Brownson et al., 2000). The study found that about one-third of white, African American, and Hispanic women reported no leisure activities (exercise, recreation, or physical activity) in the two weeks before the survey. About one-half of American Indian/Alaskan Natives reported no leisure activity.

Some studies support the idea that low income limits the outdoor activity participation of older African Americans (Conn, 1997). Allison and Smith (1990) say that cultural barriers can keep minority members from recreation. Also, fear of prejudice and the lack of opportunity in the past may inhibit the current generation of older African Americans in their leisure choices (Freysinger, 1993).

A study of older African American women found that they have a unique view of leisure activity. They describe leisure as both freedom from work and a form of self-expression. They engaged in church work, attended senior centers, watched television, and did crafts. These women also engaged in self-care and care for others in their social network (Allen & Chin-Sang, 1990). They thought of caregiving as part of their leisure activities. They say that caregiving gives meaning to their lives and creates a way for them to relate to others.

Studies of minority group leisure activities often compare minority and majority older people. They use majority behavior as the norm. This often makes minority members look deficient. But it ignores minority members' unique social context and values (Freysinger, 1993). Allen and Chin-Sang (1990; *see also* Chin-Sang & Allen, 1991) say that leisure may have a different meaning for people from different backgrounds. For example, Wilcox (2002, p. 21) says, "little is known about rates of [physical activity] in older Asian American women." Freysinger (1993, p. 223), in a review of the literature on minority groups and recreation, says, "Not one study was found exploring the activities of [older Asian/Pacific Americans and Native Americans]. . . . They are indeed neglected minority groups."

TABLE 12.1

Gender and Age Differences in Time Use

Time Spent on Activities in Hours Per Day, 2003

	Men		*Women*	
	15+	*65+*	*15+*	*65+*
Personal care	9.13	9.51	9.54	9.76
Eating and drinking	1.24	1.65	1.18	1.43
Household activities	1.33	1.89	2.30	3.06
Purchasing goods and services	0.68	0.90	0.94	0.89
Caring for and helping household members	0.34	0.15	0.75	0.12
Caring for and helping nonhousehold members	0.26	0.31	0.31	0.31
Working and related activities	4.57	1.20	2.87	0.43
Organizational, civic, and religious activities	0.29	0.41	0.35	0.46
Leisure and sports	5.41	7.52	4.83	6.88
Telephone calls, mail, and email	0.13	0.16	0.24	0.36
Other activities	0.18	0.29	0.20	0.28

Not surprisingly, compared with younger age groups, men and women aged 65 and over spend less time working and more time on leisure activities. Older people also spend more time on personal care and personal activities like shopping, eating and drinking, and household activities. This reflects the greater amount of leisure time available for nonworking adults. Older people also spend more time on social activities such as talking on the phone and engaging in civic and religious activities.

Gender roles explain many of the differences in time use between older men and older women. Older women spent more time than men on household activities and less time on leisure and sports. Also, older men, compared with older women, spent nearly three times as much time working. This difference reflects the lifelong tendency of men to focus on work and in some cases to stay at work past age 65. Life course theory says that roles and patterns of behavior in earlier life shape life in old age. These figures on time use support this theory.

Source: U.S. Department of Labor. Bureau of Labor Statistics. Time Use Survey. Table 3. Average hours per day spent in primary activities (1) for the total population, by age, sex, race, Hispanic or Latino ethnicity, and educational attainment, 2003 annual averages. Retrieved January 11, 2005, *www.bls.gov/news.release/atus.t03.htm.*

Plonczynski (2003, p. 215) includes volunteer work and religious activities in her definition of physical activity. "These activities," she says, "are particularly important with older adults and minority older adults, respectively. This inclusion reflects the broad range of lifestyle physical activities within community life." Other studies of leisure need to take minority differences into account when studying the physical activity of older people and when assessing the minority person's leisure choices.

Leisure Education

Studies of older people's leisure attitudes show that they often picked up their views of leisure in their childhoods. Many older men and women today were taught that play in adulthood meant wasted time. They learned that only young people should play sports or exercise. These attitudes work against an active leisure life-style. Older people today need to learn the value of leisure activity, and they need to learn new ways to use their free time. Lehr (1992) says that leisure education should include an appreciation of leisure as fun and enjoyment.

Mobily (1992) says that a wide leisure repertoire gives people more options in later life. Searle and Mahon (1991) found that older people can expand their range of activities through leisure education. They conducted a controlled study of leisure education in a day hospital. The program attempted to increase leisure awareness, social interaction, and leisure skills. They found that through education, people expanded their knowledge of leisure choices. People also improved their skill at leisure activities.

MacNeil (2001) predicts greater leisure activity among older people in the future. He reports an 18 percent increase between 1988 and 1995 in sport, fitness, and outdoor leisure activities for the Baby Boom generation. He reports a 21 percent increase in fitness activities during this same time. He says that this reflects life-style differences between Baby Boomers and the current generation of older people. He says that these people will bring their interest in fitness and activity with them into old age. And they will demand more recreation opportunities in later life.

McGuire, Dottavio, and O'Leary (1987) studied data from a nationwide recreation survey. They identified two groups of older people, each with different leisure patterns. They called one group **contractors**. These people had stopped at least one outdoor activity in the past year and had not learned any new activity since age 65. At best, contractors continued the same activities they had learned in childhood. The researchers called the second group **expanders**. This group kept up their former activities but also added at least one new outdoor activity since age 65. Expanders added new activities throughout life.

The researchers say that leisure service providers need to create many options for older people. Leisure education programs can help both groups. Contractors can learn how to add new activities. Expanders can develop skills in the new activities they have begun.

NEW ACTIVITIES IN OLD AGE

Older people today show a strong interest in fitness and health promotion programs. They also take part in more active recreation. Better incomes, better health, and new attitudes toward aging account for this increase in interest. Older people have also begun to explore new leisure activities. These people serve as role models for people in their middle years. Their discoveries will create new opportunities for aging in the future.

Outdoor Recreation

The federal government encourages older people to use outdoor recreation sites. It offers "Golden Age Passports" to people aged 62 and over. The passports cost ten dollars and allow free entry for the older person and companions to all U.S. national parks, historic sites, wildlife refuges, and recreation areas (National Park Service, 2004). Many older people combine outdoor activity with travel. A number of airlines, bus lines, and hotels offer discounts for older people.

MacNeil (2001) predicts a future interest in extreme sports by Baby Boom elders. These will include biking, skiing, water sports, and mountain climbing. Travel tour companies now offer challenging outdoor adventure tours. One adventure travel company said that people aged 55 and over made up 30 percent of its clients (Dychtwald & Flower, 1990). These companies sponsor tours to Tibet, the Amazon, the Galapagos Islands, and Antarctica. Some of the tours include hiking, climbing, rafting, and other demanding activities. Others include more support, such as a Jeep journey through the mountain passes of Tibet. This kind of outdoor activity will attract more older people in the future, especially people with good incomes and good health.

Fitness, Health, and Well-Being

Some years ago Kraus and Raab (1961) labeled disuse of the body in old age **hypokinetic disease**. This syndrome leads to much of the decline in the body in later life. Other gerontologists say simply, "Use it or lose it." Disuse leads to slow decline in the body. A national study in the United States of over 6,000 people aged 60 and over, for example, found that 39 percent of the sample were overweight and 23.3 percent were obese (Anderson et al., 2001).

The study reports that the proportion of overweight and obese older people grew during the 1990s. The study found that overweight and obese people reported low levels of participation in leisure time physical activity. The lack of activity puts older people at risk for heart disease, osteoporosis, depression, and disability.

A large literature reports on the good effects of exercise in later life. For many years, for example, researchers thought that cardiovascular ability declined steadily by about 10 percent per year. Recent research shows that regular exercise can reduce the rate of decline. Some studies show no decline over a decade or more in cardiovascular performance among highly trained older people. Plonczynski (2003, p. 214) reports that regular physical activity can reduce the incidence of diabetes and osteoporosis. Active people tend to live longer and in better health. They show a decreased risk of falling and better functional ability than nonactive older people.

The American College of Sports Medicine (2000, cited in Plonczynski, 2003) says that physical activity also leads to more fitness, greater endurance, increased strength, and improved flexibility. Exercise increases aerobic capacity, increases cardiac output, and leads to better use of muscles Even an increase in normal physical activity—housework, shopping, volunteer work can improve health.

Dunn and colleagues (1999, cited in Plonczynski, 2003) report improvements in blood pressure readings for nonactive older adults after the start of a physical activity program. Adults with mild hypertension show benefits from increased exercise (Blumentahl et al., 2000, cited in Plonczynski, 2003). These benefits in turn lead to better functioning in daily life for older people. Coleman and Iso-Ahola (1993) report that leisure produces self-determination and social supports that buffer stress.

Cousins and Burgess (1992, p. 461) say that "regular, sweat-inducing physical activity appears to be 'the one percent solution,' that is, a way to reverse the overall average 1 percent annual decline in many human functions." Iso-Ahola (1993) says that millions of people each year would avoid illness and extend their lives by adopting healthier life-styles. This in turn might reduce medical costs. He considers prevention of sedentary life-styles an important social issue.

Challenges to Fitness in Later Life

For all of the benefits that older people can gain from exercise, older people show low participation rates in physical activity. And they generally show declines in physical activity with age (Plonczynski, 2003). The Center for Disease Control (cited in

BOX 12.1
TRAVELS WITH GRANDPA

New kinds of outdoor leisure activities fit the life-styles of today's new retiree. Journalists Beck, Gordon, and Dallen describe outdoor adventures that bring grandparents and grandchildren closer together.

A pair of rubber rafts floated onto the swift Snake River last week with unusual passengers on board: eight grandparents and 10 grandchildren, ranging in age from 6 to 69. Blue herons soared overhead in Wyoming's Grand Teton National Park. Snowcapped peaks towered in the distance. "Did you know that interest rates went down one-quarter percent this weekend?" asked Joe Rault, 64, reading *The Wall Street Journal.* His grandsons Miles Clements, 6, and Eddie Clements, 8, ignored him, too engrossed in the white water that sometimes threatened to upend the raft. Halfway through the 10-mile trip, Grandpa Rault put his paper aside for a pretend nap. Miles and Eddie tried to pry his eyelids open, whereupon Rault wrestled them to the bottom of the raft. As his wife, Bonnie, looked on, Rault said with a gleam in his eye, "They started it!"

Humorist Robert Benchley said there are two kinds of travel—"first class, or with children." But that distinction is fast disappearing. With more money, more energy and more leisure time than ever, growing numbers of grandparents are travelling with their grandchildren, says Tom Frenkel of the National Tour Association, and many join escorted trips. The idea is "definitely catching on—for several good reasons," says Dorothy Jordon, publisher of the newsletter *Family Travel Times.* "Many children get 12 to 18 weeks of vacation a year. Their parents generally don't get that much." What's more, grandparents often live in distant cities and rarely get time with their grandchildren. . . .

Grandchildren can make ideal escorts for single older women who want to see the world. "When I was first widowed, I thought that was the end of travelling," said Flora Carlberg, 61, accompanying her 13-year-old grandson on a Grandtravel Western Parks tour last week. Now she hopes to take each of her nine grandchildren on a trip, one at a time. . . .

"Our children keep reminding us that we never did this for them," laughs Bonnie Rault, 58. "But they're pretty tickled that we can do this for *their* children."

Source: From "Travels with Grandpa," by M. Beck, J. Gordan, & R. Wallen, *Newsweek,* July 30, p. 48.

Center for Healthy Aging, 2004) reports that 28 to 34 percent of adults aged 65 to 74 engage in no leisure activity. This increases to 35 to 44 percent of people aged 75 and over. Only 25 to 35 percent of older people engage in the recommended amounts of leisure activity. A National Health Interview Survey of 27,000 people aged 65 and over found that only 7.5 percent of them engaged in vigorous exercise (Rooney, 1993). "It is clear," Kelly (1993, p. 123) says, "that no type of activity is as likely to be abandoned or avoided by the old as regular physical exercise."

Three gerontological theories give at least partial explanations for these findings: disengagement theory, continuity theory, and age stratification theory. Briefly, **disengagement theory** (Cumming & Henry, 1961) sees disengagement from activity as a natural process. It allows the older person to withdraw from social roles and activities prior to death. **Continuity theory** (Atchley, 1999a) proposes that older people follow the same pattern of activity or inactivity in old age that they followed in middle age. Most people lead a sedentary life in middle age. They carry this pattern into later life. **Age stratification theory** (Riley, 1971) says that society expects certain behaviors from people in later life. Society also offers older people a narrow range of social roles to play. An older person who wants to live an active life-style may find few supports.

Two women enjoy active leisure time at the beach.

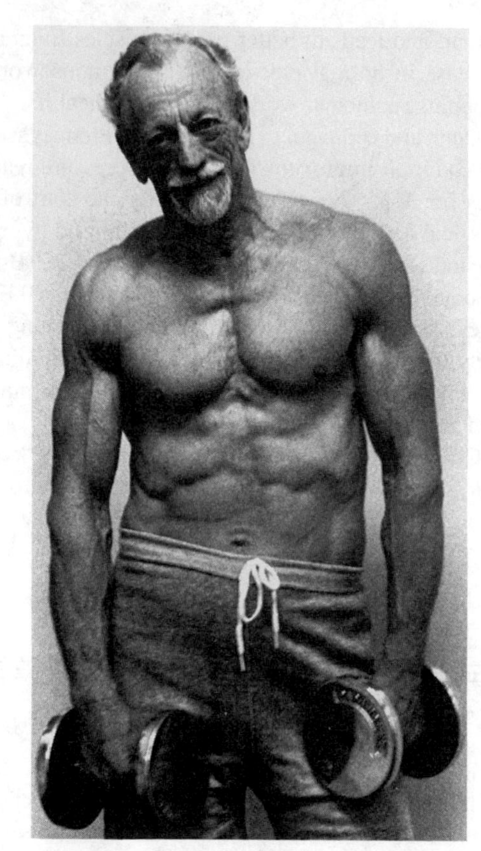

Dr. John Turner, age 67 in this photo, is a weightlifter and bodybuilder. (Etta Clark)

These theories point to social forces that can either encourage or inhibit an active life-style. **Activity theory**, a fourth major theory of aging, serves as a counterpoint to the three theories mentioned previously. Activity theory promotes the value of ac-

tive living. It says that people experience high life satisfaction if they stay active. Activity theory leads to a search for ways to overcome barriers to active living in older people's lives. (See Chapters 2 and 6 for more details on these theories; *also* Figure 12.2.)

Programs That Overcome Barriers to Active Living

Sport, leisure, and recreation programs can break the inertia of disengagement, continuity, and age stratification. To do this they need to attract sedentary older and middle-aged people. Shephard (1990, p. 67) says that "the social norm that old age is a time to slow down and take a well-earned rest must be corrected."

First, older people need access to leisure and recreation programs. Disengagement theory views withdrawal as a normal social-psychological adaptation to aging. But disengagement may be as much a function of physical disability as of psychosocial withdrawal. A decline in health, for example, can challenge a person's ability to stay active (Conn, 1997). Poor health or activity limitation in part explains disengagement from a more active life-style with age. Interventions that help people overcome physical barriers show that, given the chance, people can and do stay physically active into late old age.

One woman had always wanted to tap dance, but she now had arthritis in her legs and could barely stand. A recreation program that served homebound older people solved her problem. The program arranged for another senior, a dance instructor, to visit this woman. The instructor had the woman sit on a kitchen stool so she could dance without putting weight on her legs. This program helped fulfill this woman's lifelong wish. The program also runs special T'ai chi classes for people with visual impairments or other major health challenges (Penning & Wasyliw, 1992).

Continuity theory says that people will follow patterns of activity in later life that they followed in their middle years. They do this in part to maintain a stable sense of self throughout life. Continuity reduces the threat to loss of self-esteem and self-worth. People avoid leisure and recreation activities that might threaten their self-images or well-being. Continuity can keep a person within boundaries that limit personal growth and development. Women in the past, for example, had little exposure to sports. Their lower levels of participation (compared with men) suggest that they will continue to avoid these activities. Past prejudices and current fears keep them from activities that they might enjoy (Paxton, Browning, & O'Connell, 1997).

Continuity theory suggests that activity programs will need to meet the needs of minority elders. These people will tend to take part in programs that fit their understanding of leisure, recreation, and activity. Program designers need to understand how people from different cultures define leisure, recreation, and activity. They also need to provide programs in languages other than English so that minority older people can take part in them.

Cousins and Burgess (1992) say that leisure and recreation programs must minimize physical and psychological risk to participants. Shephard (1990) presents a good discussion of the physical risk that exercise poses for people in their 70s and older. This includes injury, extreme fatigue, and in some cases, sudden death. Methods exist to avoid these dangers. Psychological risk includes fear of embarrassment, ridicule, and failure. People may fail to meet their own or others' expectations. This can even be true of former athletes who set unrealistic goals for themselves.

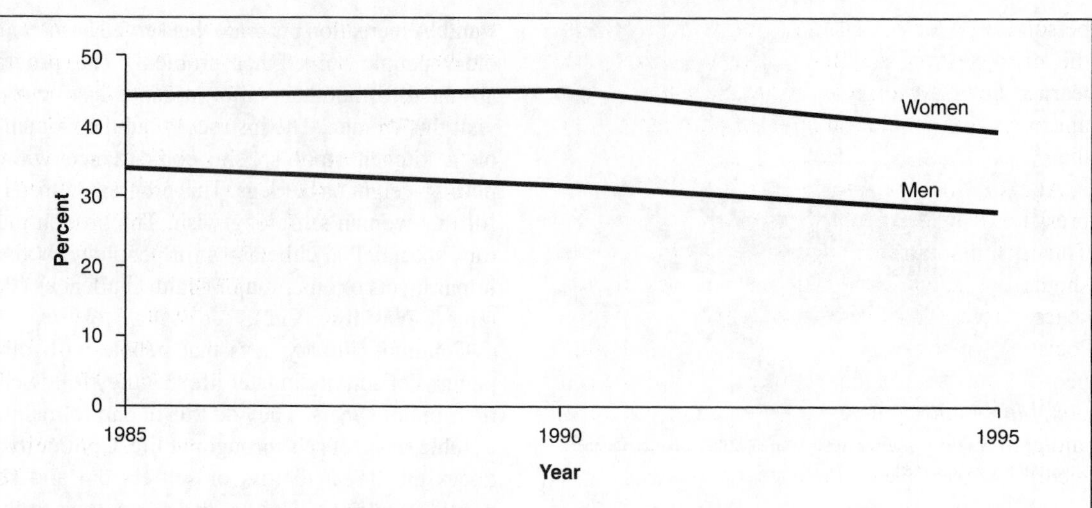

This figure shows a decline in the proportion of older people who reported a sedentary life-style (engaging in no leisure-time physical activity). The proportion of sedentary older people dropped from 34 to 28 percent for men and from 44 to 39 percent for women. Most people who engaged in exercise did light-to-moderate activities including walking, gardening, and stretching.

Note that women showed a greater tendency to live a sedentary life-style. This may have to do with higher rates of chronic illness among older women (especially in late old age). It also reflects the life-style differences of men and women in the past. Society encouraged male physical activity during the school years in sports and in more strenuous jobs at work. Society tended to type active girls as *tomboys* and to discourage an active life-style in the middle years.

This stereotype has decreased. The lower rates of sedentary activity in 1995 for both men and women suggest that older people engage in more activity today. Health promotion programs and an awareness of fitness encourage activity. Also, more people now come into old age with a desire to stay active and fit. This will lead to a more active older generation in the future. And this will translate into less risk of chronic disease and more independent living.

FIGURE 12.2

Percentage of Persons Aged 65 and over Who Reported Having a Sedentary Life-style, by Sex, 1985, 1990, and 1995

Source: Federal Interagency Forum on Aging-Related Statistics. (2004). Older Americans 2000: Key indicators of well-being. Health Risks and Behaviors. Indicator 20—Sedentary Lifestyle. Retrieved January 11, 2005, *www.agingstats.gov/chartbook2000/healthrisks.html.*

A program should allow people to take risks without fear of ridicule or failure. McAuley (1993; *also* Paxton, Browning, & O'Connell, 1997) says that programs should create a sense of **self-efficacy**. Self-efficacy refers to what people believe they can do. People with a strong sense of efficacy take on more challenging tasks and put out more effort. **Mastery accomplishments**, successful achievements, and knowledge of achievements all enhance efficacy (McAuley, Lox, & Duncan, 1993).

Sarah Bowles, described at the start of this chapter, traces the success of her program to the development of efficacy and self-confidence (although she wouldn't use these terms). Sarah studies her people carefully. She listens to them, watches how they perform, and builds the program to suit their needs. Sarah's program reduces threats to members' self-worth. She has no music, no competition between class members, and no failures. People attend with walkers and canes if they need to. "Each person keeps their own time," she says. "I try out the exercises on me first. Over the years I've learned how fast to go and what's dangerous. It's amazing what people can do if the pace is right for their age."

Age stratification theory points to the societal pressures that keep people from an active life-style. This includes narrow notions of what older people should and shouldn't do. It also includes the absence of roles for active older people to play. We associate lawn bowling, walking, and golf with older people. Only recently have older people begun to break this mold by taking up swimming, aerobics, and gymnastics. Some senior athletes have set new records for their age group in track and field events.

Still, older athletes may seem like exceptions to the rule. Many people have imbibed the image of the older person as ill, at risk, and sedentary. Cousins and Burgess (1992) say that stereotypes of seniors' abilities exist among recreation specialists as well as the public, and due to stereotyping, professionals may underestimate seniors' abilities. The habit of typing people by age poses one of the greatest challenges to older people who want to live an active life-style. This can lead to programs that fail to challenge participants. This, in turn, reinforces stereotypes about seniors' lack of ability.

For example, forty years ago, few people would have thought that T'ai chi would become one of the most popular activities among seniors. Older people who have taken up this ancient Chinese form of exercise often go on to develop great skill. Some have become amateur masters of this art and have become teachers. Activity programs should make the most of the abilities that older people have. Appropriate programs can help people develop a positive self-image and discover new potential as they age. Good program design can overcome other barriers that keep older people from living active lives.

Professionals who work with older people need to listen to program members. Good communication between a program leader and participants creates a successful program. Professionals can then set individual goals for clients, with realistic expectations. Older people need varied types of programs to suit their varied needs. Gentler activities like walking or swimming may serve older people better than jogging or running. A brisk walking program may best meet certain older people's needs.

The growth of mall walking programs in the past few years shows the appeal of walking as a form of exercise. I recently arrived at a shopping mall at 7:30 AM on a frigid December morning. I had a meeting in one of the offices attached to the mall. To my surprise, I found a group of senior mall walkers already suited up and into their routine. Programs that fit the needs of their members and allow people to participate at their own pace will encourage attendance.

Above all, program leaders must make programs enjoyable and rewarding. Cousins and Burgess (1992) say that instructors often speak too quickly, use slang or jargon, or start when the audience has not understood instructions. These researchers suggest that instructors break movements down into small units. Then the instructor should allow self-paced practice of the new skill.

Leaders should include participants in planning, assessing, and developing activity programs. This builds commitment to the program and leads to ongoing participation. Leaders also need to understand the life circumstances of the program members. Wilcox and King (2004) conducted a controlled study of an exercise program that enrolled ninety-seven older people. The researchers found that negative life events during the course of the program led to lower program attendance. The more life events, the greater the effect on attendance.

Many studies have found that seniors join and stay with a program if the program offers social interaction. Older people often take part in physical activities in order to be with others (Garber & Blissmer, 2002). Leaders need to ask seniors about their goals and design programs to meet these goals. Older people's goals often differ from those of younger people in exercise, fitness, or sports programs.

Again, Sarah Bowles' program contains a principle that other professionals could apply. She puts people first. She gives people permission to enjoy themselves during their workout. "During the program, people just talk, and talk, and talk. Sometimes the noise is terrific," she says. "That has got a lot to do with the program's success." Younger old people, compared with the very old, have a more positive attitude toward exercise, fitness, and active living. This, in part, reflects a difference in the health of young-old and old-old people. Younger cohorts have better health and can still take part in many of the activities of their middle years.

A more positive attitude toward active living also probably reflects the effects of health promotion in recent years. Younger old people almost daily hear reports on the value of exercise for good health. Future cohorts of older people will come into old age with even more knowledge about the value of exercise and active living. They will bring a more positive attitude toward activity in later life.

BOX 12.2

BALL-PLAYING SENIORS STEP UP TO PLATE

Long before the sun hits high noon at Nottoway Park in Vienna, a dedicated band of aging athletes will have smacked dozens of softballs into the outfield—some to soar high in the trees, others to hug the ground.

A mid-May sun warms the playing field, where players stretch and loosen their joints in preparation for a slow-pitch softball tournament. Dozens of teams are competing for the chance to go to the Senior Softball World Series in September in Palm Springs, Calif. This is a fight not just for first place, but for the pleasure of defeating stereotypes about what the body is capable of achieving after age 50.

"At our age, we're lucky to be playing," says a cheerful Tom Rios, who has driven from Pittsburgh to compete in the 12th annual Senior Softball Capital Classic, in a bid for a chance to win the Super Bowl–sized ring awarded to winners of the Senior Softball World Series.

His team loses, but there are no real losers in senior softball. Anyone who can play in these games must be fighting fit. Players are lean, muscular and limber. Some move with a grace and dexterity rivaling the performance of men 20 and 30 years younger. Even a few pushing 85 still can hit, run and field at an astonishing level of performance.

Men Can Be Boys Again

For all its competitive drive, senior softball also is a social focal point for players, many of whom have formed deep friendships after years of playing together. Winning teams travel all over the country to take part in national competitions.

"They have a boys' room here?" jokes a player as he scans the field for his teammates.

"Hey, skinny," shouts another man to a player he recognizes.

"How are you feeling today—stiff?" another asks.

A group of men doing leg stretches speaks reverently of a 70-year-old man who slammed the ball sky-high the previous day in a breathtaking moment of athletic power. "Man, that guy has prostate cancer, but he sure can hit."

The game attracts its share of fans from loyal wives who cheer on their husbands' teams—and bring ice for bruises.

The players share a common enemy: old age. They are keenly aware of one another's limitations and gloat when they can overcome the aches and pains to hit a home run. Softball requires not just a powerful swing and fast legwork, but also the ability to exert the body in sudden spurts of energy to catch a ball or tag another player out.

"These people are going to live longer because they are in better shape now than when they were younger," says Dave Scheele, publicity chairman for the Northern Virginia Senior Softball Association.

Source: Veigle, A. (1998). Ball-playing seniors step up to plate. *The Washington Times,* July 21, p. 10. Full Text COPYRIGHT 1998 News World Communications, Inc. Reprinted with permission of the *Washington Times.*

Masters Athletes and the Senior Olympics

Sports leagues for older athletes have grown up throughout the United States. These athletes, who range in age from 30 to their 70s, refer to themselves as **masters**. Streisand (1992, p. 68) reports that the National Men's Senior Baseball League, for example, has 3,200 teams nationwide with 45,000 members. The league holds a World Series every fall and its national tournaments host 490 teams. The league claims to hold the largest amateur baseball tournaments in the world (Men's Senior Baseball, 2004). Masters cyclists now number more than 15,000, and over 133,000 men and women compete in masters tennis. These leagues hold local and national competitions.

Streisand (1992, p. 69) says, "There is a masters or senior division for nearly every sport, from rodeo to drag racing." The National Senior Games Association is "dedicated to motivating active adults to lead a healthy lifestyle through the senior games movement" (National Senior Games, 2004). It sanctions and coordinates sports and games activities for people aged 50 and over throughout the country. Warren Blaney organized the first Senior Olympics in California in 1969 (Pepe & Gandee, 1992). The program lasted four days and drew 175 participants to three events (marathon, swimming, and track and field) (Leitner & Leitner, 1985).

By 1980, over 4,000 people took part in fifty events. "In that year," Pepe and Gandee (1992, p. 192) say, "a seventy-two-year-old woman won the First Annual Equestrian Competitive Trail Ride, a fifteen-mile rider-and-horse event." By 1985, thirty-five states had Senior Olympic programs. By 1987, 50,000 people took part in regional Senior Olympic events in fifty cities in the United States. (Dychtwald & Flower, 1990). In that same year, the first National Senior Olympic games took place (Kamm, 1992). By 2003, the Summer Games in Hampton Roads, Virginia, attracted 10,700 athletes. Competition took place in eighteen sports included bicycling, badminton, triathlon, track and field, and basketball.

The Senior Olympics encourages older people to stay active and make new friends. A study of senior Olympians found that they engaged in fitness programs to maintain their health and for the competition (Fontane & Hurd, 1992). O'Brien and Conger (1991) say that older elite athletes use sports to find meaning and to gain a sense of achievement in later life. One-half the people in an Ohio study said they took part to keep fit, one-third said they took part because they enjoyed the activity, and one-third took part to meet others socially (Pepe & Gandee, 1992). Many people participated with a friend, spouse, or family member (Schreck, 1992).

SENIOR CENTERS

Barriers to active living exist. These include negative attitudes toward exercise and poorly designed activity programs. But, other more stubborn barriers to participation also exist. These include lack of transportation to programs, lack of money to take part in programs, fear of neighborhood crime, and bad weather. These barriers most often affect poorer old people. They may live in inner-city neighborhoods or in rural areas that lack easy access to programs and facilities. Local senior centers help meet the needs of these older people. Senior centers in communities throughout the country include an exercise, yoga, T'ai chi, or other fitness programs. These centers also offer transportation, meal programs, and social activities that attract older people who face barriers to active living.

Senior centers form the nearest thing to a nationwide recreation and service delivery program for older people. The National Institute of Senior Centers defines a senior center as a place where "older adults come together for services and activities that reflect their experience and skills, respond to their diverse needs and interests, enhance their dignity, support their independence, and encourage their involvement in and with the center and the community" (National Council on the Aging, 2004). The first club for older people began in Boston in 1870. New York City opened its first senior center more than seventy years later in 1943 (Leitner & Leitner, 1985).

The National Council on the Aging (2004, citing the U.S. Administration on Aging) reports that by 1961 about 218 centers existed across the United

States. Since the mid-1960s the Older Americans Act provided some funding through service contracts to support more than 6,000 centers. By the year 2000, 15,000 centers existed in the United States. They served almost 10 million older people each year. Many centers today get funding from local governments and nonprofit agencies (such as the United Way). Senior centers provide services and activities that support independence and social contact. Most senior centers have a full-time administrator, an activity director, and volunteers.

The National Council on the Aging (2004) reports on a survey of more than 400 senior centers (Krout, 1990). The survey found that 10 percent of the participants were over age 85. The survey also found that almost 60 percent of centers reported an increase in the number of frail participants. The centers reported high use by white women. Rural centers tend to serve frail older people with in-home services (National Council on the Aging, 2004). Centers must meet the needs of both frail and active older people in their communities. Most centers offer education programs in arts and the humanities, health services (such as foot care clinics and fitness activities), legal and income counseling, and meals.

Standards exist for senior centers in the United States through the National Institute of Senior Centers. A National Senior Center Accreditation Board accredits centers nationwide. About one hundred centers have met the Board's standards, and sixty more have started the application process.

The National Council on the Aging (2004; *also* Beisgen & Kraitchman, 2003) lists a dozen of the programs most often offered at senior centers. These include health and wellness programs, arts and humanities programs, intergenerational programs, and employment assistance programs. Centers also offer meal and nutrition programs. These serve a number of functions. They provide members with a hot meal once a day or several times a week, they bring people together to socialize, and they allow more able members to volunteer in meal preparation. Meal programs build camaraderie and an informal support network among members. Centers also link older people to other services in the community.

Krout, Cutler, and Coward (1990) reviewed national data on senior center participation. They found that, among people aged 60 and over, 13.7 percent used a center during the past year. They found that centers attracted women, people with lower incomes, and older seniors (*see also* Cutler & Danigelis, 1993). Participants tended to live alone and had fewer problems with ADL than nonparticipants. People attend centers mostly for companionship and activities, and they stop attending because of poor health.

Wagner (1995) studied senior centers and found two models of center membership: the **social agency model** and the **voluntary organization model**. The social agency model serves people with few resources, like single older people in poor health. These people use the center as a social service agency. They attend lunch or dinner programs and get health checkups. The voluntary organization model serves people with strong community contacts, like married older people in better health. They use the center as a social club.

Sabin (1993) used national data and found support for both models of center use. Senior centers of each type serve a specific clientele. But some groups rarely attend either type of center. Rural older people tend to make less use of centers. They may find centers inaccessible or even unavailable. Only 25 percent of all senior centers are in rural areas (Teague & MacNeil, 1992). Where they do exist, centers serve an important function. In small towns, senior centers may offer the only chance for social contacts outside a person's family.

Researchers need to look at racial differences in senior center use. Ralston (1993) reviewed the literature on senior centers and found little useful information on African Americans and almost no research on Hispanics, Asian Americans, or American Indians. Freysinger (1993) found that minority participation in senior centers depends on whether people feel a fit between their cultural identity and the staff, programs, and members at a center. Ego and Shiramizu (1992) trace the absence of older people with an Asian/Pacific background to a lack of knowledge of programs, cultural and language differences between clients and services, and fear of government by these older people.

Pardasani (2004) studied 220 senior centers in New York state. The study found that most centers had white administrators (86.2 percent) and attracted white participants (80 percent). But multi-purpose centers (that offered meals, recreation, education, and other programs) had the largest proportion of minority participants (27.3 percent). Also, urban centers had the highest proportion of minority older people (41 percent). Programs that attracted minority older people tended to have minority staff and to offer linguistically and culturally diverse programming. This study points to the need for more diverse staffing and for culturally sensitive programming. Minority elders feel most comfortable in a setting that recognizes and respects their languages and cultures.

Ego and Shiramizu (1992) report that San Jose, California, has developed a successful senior center program for Asian/Pacific Americans. The city draws on the support of the Asian/Pacific community to help fund the program. The city now offers programs tailored to specific groups including Korean, Chinese, Indochinese, and East Indian older people. The centers help older immigrants with translation needs, health care, and legal help.

Senior centers not only exist in the community, but they create a community for their members. Life in a thriving senior center reflects the backgrounds and needs of the people who belong to it and use it. A study of three rural senior centers in Minnesota found that people dropped by to socialize, relax, and drink coffee. They had a strong sense of ownership and control of their center (Havir, 1991). Many members volunteered their time to help make their center work.

EDUCATION

In 2002, less than one person in ten (9 percent) aged 75 and over had a Bachelor's degree. But nearly one-quarter (23.2 percent) of people aged 25 to 34 had a Bachelor's degree. The younger the age group, the greater likelihood that someone will have a university education. This trend will lead to higher levels of education among future cohorts of older people. And studies show that the more education a person has, the greater the chance that they will enroll in an education program in later life (Danner, Danner, & Kuder, 1993). This could lead to a boom in education programs for older people.

So far, traditional education programs have had a limited attraction for older people. Although the numbers of older people who take courses has increased in recent years, only a small number of seniors enroll in schools today.

An older person who wants to take a course at a university, for example, faces many barriers. First, the older student may face a long walk from a car park or bus stop to classes. The cost of parking and bad weather in some regions add to the problem of getting to class. Second, most classes take place in one- or two-hour time blocks. A person who wants to take one course may have to visit the university three times a week. Even a short commute can add three or more hours of travel to a three-hour-per-week course.

Third, the tell-'em-and-test-'em lecture style of most postsecondary classes misses the point of why most older people want education. They do not want a credential and have no interest in tests or credits. They want knowledge, understanding, and insight.

A few authors have explored the content and purpose of learning in old age. Psychologist Carl Jung (1976), for example, saw the need for a unique educational experience in later life. Jung uses the image of the day to describe two phases of life: the morning and evening. Each phase, he says, has its specific purpose and content, and at each phase a person has specific educational needs. Jung says that in the morning of life (up to middle age), education prepares a person for a career and for participation in society.

Jung describes later life as a time of individuation. He proposes that education in the evening of life serves self-discovery. He asks, "Are there perhaps colleges for forty-year-olds which prepare them for the coming life and its demands as the ordinary colleges introduce our young people to knowledge of the world and of life?" He answers that no such colleges exist. These colleges would deal with what Jung calls "culture." They would explore spiritual issues and death and dying, and would encourage self-discovery through the study of literature, art, and music.

Schools will have to adapt if they want to attract older students. First, they will have to offer courses in easy-to-reach places. Some schools already offer courses in shopping centers where students can park and get to class easily. Second, they will have to offer courses at more convenient times. Single three-hour blocks, weekends, or even week-long courses better suit older learners' needs. Third, instructors will have to learn adult education methods. Older students have little patience with long lectures. They want to interact with their teachers and fellow students. They want to share their knowledge. Universities in the future will need to remove many of these barriers if they want to serve adult students. Some schools have begun to do this.

Elderhostel

Except for the small number of older people enrolled in higher education credential programs, only 19 percent of older people said they engaged in any educational activity in the past year (U.S. Census Bureau, 2003b). This may change as more people enter old age with more education. Some programs have gained popularity because they fit the older person's interests and life-style.

Elderhostel is one of the fastest growing education programs in the world. It combines university education with European hosteling. David Bianco

BOX 12.3

TEACHING METHODS FOR OLDER STUDENTS

Some teaching methods can help older people learn better in the classroom. They include taking breaks, giving immediate feedback on tests, and presenting material in a number of ways to meet the needs of different learners. These techniques target some of the barriers that keep older people from enjoying classroom life.

1. Remove time pressure and other sources of anxiety in the classroom. Let people set their own pace for discussion of topics or in the case of assignments. Let people get used to new ideas.
2. Decrease competition and encourage cooperation between students. Encourage participation in classroom discussion. Avoid talking-head lectures. Give people a chance to comment and respond.
3. Give people breaks often or cut down the length of each session. Avoid fatigue.
4. Start with simple tasks and problems and build up to harder ones. Break the work into segments. Give people a chance to practice what they know and to use it in different ways.
5. Give people feedback on their work as soon as possible.
6. Give people visual and aural cues to help them with their work. Use clear diagrams, speak clearly, repeat questions from the class so everyone can hear. For example, don't speak while facing the blackboard.
7. Group the information. Use memory aids such as pictures, mental images, and verbal cues.
8. Build on what students already know. Older students are the best learning aids in the classroom. Use them wisely by allowing them to take part in class activities.

Some people say that teachers should use these methods with students at any age. How do these suggestions fit some of the special needs of older learners? Are there other teaching or learning methods that you think would improve education for older people?

Source: Adapted from D. F. Hultsch & F. Deutsch (1981). *Adult development and aging: A life-span perspective.* New York: McGraw-Hill, p. 152.

BOX 12.4
PATTERNS OF EDUCATION FOR OLDER PEOPLE

Gerontologist Harry Moody explored the "philosophical presuppositions of education in later life." He describes four modal patterns of education. Each of these patterns has spawned education programs that exist today. For example, people learn as a form of leisure, they learn to prepare for new active roles, and they learn as a means of self-actualization. Moody proposes that education for older people move toward patterns 3 and 4: participation and self-actualization.

1. *Rejection.* This pattern assumes the obsolescence of the older person. It views older people as worn out and unproductive. Education for older people wastes resources. This pattern sees education as a means to an end: production and economic success. It supports the functionalist view of education as a way to prepare young people for work. Older people have no place in this educational system.
2. *Social services.* This pattern sees older people as a needy group. They need services such as education to fill in their time and live a happy life. Professionals can best provide this service. This pattern supports access to education for older people. Free tuition programs at universities fit this pattern. Whether older people use these programs makes little difference to society. Older people learn for their own private enjoyment. Education for older people has a low social priority.
3. *Participation.* This pattern sees education as a way to prepare older people for active community life. Older people learn how to care for themselves and one another. Education can take the form of self-help groups, study groups that look at social issues, or lobby groups that work for social change. Education in this pattern builds bridges between generations. It brings older people into the mainstream of community life.
4. *Self-actualization.* Psychologist Abraham Maslow saw self-actualization as the peak of human functioning. He felt that older people had the best chance of living this way. This pattern sees education as a way to discover new possibilities in life. Education should lead to ego integrity, wisdom, and fulfillment in later life. Older people who express these values will serve as a resource to society and as role models for the young.

Few education programs follow the last two patterns, but they present the highest ideals for education in later life. Some new programs such as Elderhostel and ILRs express these ideals.

Sources: Copyright 1988 From *Abundance of life,* by H. R. Moody, New York: Columbia University Press; "What philosophical justification is there for educating older adults?" by H. R. Moody, 1976, *Educational Gerontology, 1,* pp. 1–16. Reproduced by permission of Taylor & Francis, Inc., http://www.taylorandfrancis.com.

and Martin Knowlton, a social activist and educator, started the program in New Hampshire in 1975. They designed a series of challenging intellectual courses for older people. Then they arranged for the students to live on a university campus.

Elderhostel began with 220 people aged 55 and over enrolled in five schools. The program in 2003 enrolled almost 200,000 students at over 10,000 programs in more than ninety countries (Elderhostel, 2004a). Elderhostel offers courses in England, Scotland, Wales, Mexico, Bermuda, the Scandinavian countries, Germany, the Netherlands, France, and Italy, as well as in North America.

The original programs lasted one to two weeks—from Sunday night to Saturday morning. But today "traditional programs" (similar to the first programs offered by Elderhostel) can last from three to twelve days. Traditional programs typically include three academic courses that meet for ninety minutes each day. Students take all three courses. Programs include field trips and evening activities. Elderhostel tries to keep the class size small: Most courses enroll from thirty-five to forty-five people at a time. The total fee for a number of the one-week programs in 2005—including food, rooms, course fees, and costs for extracurricular tours and activities—came to under $600 (Elderhostel, 2005).

Elderhostel has expanded beyond its traditional format to include active outdoor programs, service programs, shipboard, and intergenerational programs (for grandparents and grandchildren). International programs usually last two to three weeks. A thirteen-day program in England, for example, studies art and life in London. The program includes visits to major art galleries, museums, and Kensington Palace. Experts give lectures during the program and students enjoy evenings at the theater and London pubs. The cost is about $2,730, not including air fare (Elderhostel, 2004b). More adventurous hostellers can sign up for a two-week safari in Kenya (cost, $3,171, not including air fare). The program includes visits to major game preserves with lectures on the ecology and wildlife of the region.

In the United States, programs often play up local resources and points of interest. A four-night program in California focuses on the desert ecology in and around Palm Springs. Students hike through the desert and nearby oases. This program offers accommodations with a pool, Jacuzzi, and golf courses nearby. A program in Colorado explores the culture and life-style of three Native American tribes—the Ute, Anasazi, and Navajo. Students learn about the history of the tribes and their current struggle to maintain their cultures.

Elderhostelers share the joys and frustrations of student life. At some sites students share rooms; often they have to share bathrooms and eat in a university dining hall. A "Circumpolar Studies" program in Alaska and Siberia a few years ago came with the following warning set in bold type: "The sidewalks in Yakutsk and at the health resort are not well-maintained; cracked pavements and potholes are common. Walking over rough, unpaved roads is required for some field trips. Transportation during field trips will be via local school buses" (Elderhostel, 1995a, p. 6).

Elderhostel attracts older people for a number of reasons. Students say they take the programs to gain new knowledge, to try something new, and to visit a new place (Roberto & McGraw, 1990). Ruth Neleski (1995) reports that she took her first course, a canoe-study course in Maine, because she had a frequent flyer ticket that she wanted to use up. As a bonus, on the way to the course she met her husband-to-be in a Maine restaurant. They married six months later. Inez Ross (1995), an Elderhosteler from Los Alamos, New Mexico, says that since taking an Elderhostel course she has become one of the OPALS—Older Person with an Active Life-Style.

At a time when education programs face cutbacks across North America, Elderhostel has grown stronger and more independent. Elderhostel takes no money from the government, nor does it ask for any. It supports its programs through tuition and donations from alumni and other supporters. Moody (1988a, p. 205) traces Elderhostel's success to its founders' insight that older people had "a potential for growth and continued learning."

Lifelong Learning Institutes

Elderhostel spawned a program called Institutes for Learning in Retirement (ILRs), now called Lifelong Learning Institutes (LLIs). LLIs attract students such as those who attend Elderhostel programs, but students in LLIs study in their own communities. The programs come in varied formats—lectures, seminars, and travel courses. In most cases, older people decide together on the topics they will study. Each institute has a distinct organizational structure, but "central to the ILR philosophy are 'peer-teaching' and 'self-governance' " (Meyers, 1987, cited in Swedburg, 1992).

These programs have grown rapidly throughout North America. The New School for Social Research in New York started the first LLI in 1962 (Beck, Glick, Gordon, & Picker, 1991). The first ILRs had several things in common: first, they all had affiliations with universities to ensure academic integrity and to link the programs to campus life. Second, the programs encouraged learners to take ownership of their institutes, become members, and pay dues. Third, institutes encouraged members to manage the institute and in some cases teach classes. By 1991, 161 LLIs existed in the United States.

Elderhostel set up an Elderhostel Institute Network throughout North America. Network affiliates grew from thirty-two in 1988 to more than 300 by 2004. Elderhostel Institute Network affiliate programs offer over 4,000 courses each term. Members of LLIs generally take two or three courses per term. And most programs offer two or three terms per year. About 200 to 300 people belong to a typical LLI. Elderhostel estimates that more fifty LLIs start each year. And over 60,000 people belong to a network-affiliated LLI (Elderhostel, 2004b).

LLI courses have no grades or tests. They often take the form of study groups. Sometimes students in the LLIs, some of them retired professors or other professionals, lead the classes. But they may teach subjects far from their specialties. A retired chemical engineer, for example, "leads a class on mythologies of the Middle East." A dentist leads a study group on opera. A group of five people, with no experience in flying, built an ultralight aircraft.

LLI students come for education, but students in university-affiliated programs often give back to the university as much as they get. Some programs attract politicians, physicians, and business leaders. These LLI students mentor undergraduates and may give lectures in some required university courses. Members of other programs donate time to help the libraries at their institutions, or they may host dinners for foreign students. Students at California State, Fullerton, built a 15,000 square-foot gerontology center for the university. The center includes space for research, teaching, and public outreach.

Some people say that programs such as Elderhostel or LLIs segregate older people. Van der Veen (1990), for example, calls for "inter-age universities" that serve mixed age groups. These universities would take into account the special needs of older adults, but would mix older people with younger people in classes. Some older people might prefer this kind of education. In either case (age-mixed or age-segregated programs), older people will develop new educational alternatives to meet their needs. New generations of older people will challenge traditional models of education. People in LLIs will challenge educators and bring fresh interest and ideas to the classroom. In age-mixed settings they will create role models for younger students. Universities benefit if they include older people in their vision of the future (Scholz, 1993).

The Future of Education for Older People

The use of media, such as interactive television and computers, will make education more accessible to older people. Even a bedbound person can take courses and interact with classmates via the computer. More of these options will exist in the future. More people will make use of these options as new cohorts of well-educated, computer-literate people enter old age.

New education programs hold out promise, but also raise important issues. People with higher education will know how to use computers; they will lead and join education programs. But Moody (1988a) sees a growing gap in educational opportunity in later life between older people who have many years of education and those who have few.

Moody notes that new programs, including Elderhostel and LLIs, often serve an elite group of older people. Many of these people have some higher education. Some have worked as educators. Older people, as a group, in the future will have better education than older people today, but the older population in the future will also show more diversity in education, income, racial and ethnic background, and health.

How will future education programs serve people with little education and low income? How will they serve people who failed in school or who dislike formal education? How will future programs meet the needs of minority elders who may speak little English? Will these groups miss out on new opportunities for personal growth through education as they age?

Moody (1988a) says that public policy needs to address these issues. He suggests public funding for programs to help poorer and less educated older people get education in later life.

COMMUNITY SERVICE AND VOLUNTEER WORK

A survey conducted by the AARP found that 43 percent of people aged 65 and over work as volunteers. They did this mostly for personal satisfaction and to help others (Cutler, Whitelaw, & Beattie,

2002; Silberman, Cantave Burton, & AARP, 2004). Another study found that volunteers averaged one day a week, and one-quarter of them said they would have volunteered more time if asked (Eldercare Volunteer, 1992).

A U.S. Department of Labor study (cited in U.S. Senate, 1991) defined volunteer work as unpaid work for an organization like a church or school. The study reports that, overall, older people in the community volunteer at a slightly lower rate than younger people (17 percent for people aged 65 and over compared with 20 percent for people aged 16 to 64). But older people, compared with people aged 16 to 64, volunteer at a higher rate in hospitals and health organizations, social or welfare organizations, and church or religious groups. Older people compared with younger people on average also spent slightly more hours per week as volunteers (4.7 hours compared with 4.4 hours). And they volunteer for more weeks per year (34.9 weeks compared with 21.9 weeks).

Among older people, those aged 65 to 74 had the greatest percentage of volunteers (Eldercare Volunteer, 1992; *also* Silberman, Cantave Burton, & AARP, 2004). But, McNaught (1994) says, even among people aged 75 and over, one in four gives some time to a charity. This equals the rate of volunteering among 50 year olds. Older volunteers, compared with nonvolunteers, tend to be younger, female, better educated and have higher family incomes and better subjective health (Cutler & Danigelis, 1993). People with these characteristics tend to put in more time volunteering.

Silberman and her colleagues (2004) studied older volunteers in North Dakota. They found that religious organizations serve as the most popular context for volunteering in later life. Sixty-one percent of older volunteers worked for churches or religious organizations. About one-quarter (27 percent) of older volunteers worked for civic organizations, and 22 percent worked for schools or educational organizations. These people serve as resources in their communities and improve the quality of life for all age groups.

Chamber (1993) says that a better educated older population will take on more volunteer work in the future. A few writers have suggested ways to harness this energy. Historian Thomas Cole (1991, p. 36) proposes a National Elder Corps that "would encourage a highly visible form of service and social integration for older people." Local, state, and federal governments would fund the Elder Corps. Community groups would match local needs with this pool of elder talent. Schools, hospitals, and nursing homes, for example, could apply for an Elder Corps volunteer to enhance the lives of their clients.

The National Retiree Volunteer Center comes close to this model of an Elder Corps. The National Retiree Volunteer Center grew out of a 1977 volunteer project in Minneapolis. The program uses corporate retirees to work on local problems throughout the country. By 1988, the program had twenty-two corporate-based programs in Minnesota and eleven others across the country. The National Retiree Volunteer Center trains the retiree, and a company gives office space to support the project. Part of the volunteer training takes place through the Humphrey Institute of Public Affairs at the University of Minnesota.

Companies support this project. The Honeywell Corporation in Minneapolis, for example, encourages its engineers to design and create equipment for handicapped people through a local agency called the Courage Center. 3M supports mentoring programs in public schools. Unisys supports a program at the William Mitchell School of Law, where volunteers serve as mock jurors in student trials. Other programs, such as the Service Corps of Retired Executives, find volunteer slots for retired executives.

Fischer and Schaffer (1993) say that volunteer programs depend on active and successful recruitment. Personal contact remains one of the best recruitment methods. Henley-Smith (1992) says that volunteer job fairs and second career days can increase the number of older volunteers. Volunteer programs can help volunteers cope with grief, frustration, and the time demands that volunteering places on people (Fischer & Schaffer, 1993). Greenfield and Marks (2004) found that volunteering helped people cope with the loss of major role identity.

CONCLUSION

Leisure, recreation, and physical activity can enhance life satisfaction in old age. Activities such as education, volunteering, or exercise give people personal satisfaction. Ekerdt (1986), in a classic article on the "busy ethic," says that keeping busy, in itself, helps people adjust to retirement in our action-oriented society. Activities, such as exercise, fit our national belief in the value of good health (Becker, 1993). The active older person can feel a part of the wider society through active living.

Becker (1993) cautions that too much focus on health promotion or on frenetic activity leads to a meaningless (if healthy) life. He suggests a balanced life based on reasonable goals of health and wellness. He also suggests that in later life "for the sake of our society and of humanity in general, we must begin to turn our concerns outward" (Becker, 1993, p. 5). Many older people have begun to do this through volunteer work and community service programs.

In later life people need varied activities to fulfill the ideals of physical, social, and spiritual well-being. Mobily (1992) says that a wide range of leisure options creates the best condition for successful aging, and that "a vital leisure self is more probable if the personal pool of recreational activities contains many alternatives. Those who have more leisure choices can avoid, circumvent, or overcome the constraints and barriers to leisure that arise in old age" (Mobily, 1992, p. 193).

Today, a **structural lag** can exist between the changing lives of older people and the opportunity to live a good old age. Riley and Riley (1994, p. 16) say that "there is a mismatch or imbalance between the transformation of the aging process . . . and the role opportunities, or places in the social structure, that could foster and reward people" in later life. Many of the programs and activities reported previously come as responses to this mismatch or imbalance. Master athlete programs, national volunteer centers, and lifelong learning institutes all respond to the growing leisure, recreation, and education needs of older people today. Longer lives, better health, better education, and more affluence will call for more creative responses in the future.

SUMMARY

- Gerontologists define leisure as free or unobligated time. Most studies of leisure support the continuity theory of aging. This theory suggests that older people tend to maintain the leisure activities of their middle years. Retired people usually have more time for these activities. With enough time, income, and good health, retirees tend to show more continuity than change in their leisure activities.
- Older people spend most of their leisure time on core leisure activities like socializing and reading. These activities need few resources, have a low cost, and have easy access. Peripheral activities such as sports and exercise usually take place outside the home. They require more resources, effort, money, and time. Seniors today tend to avoid strenuous outdoor activities like tennis, skiing, and swimming.
- Leisure participation differs by gender as well as by age and race. Studies show that men and women prefer different activities in retirement (as they did in their middle years). African American older people compared with white older people report less participation in outdoor activities. Gerontologists need to do more research on minority group members and leisure.
- Young people enjoy more leisure today than younger people in the past. They also have a greater interest in health, fitness, and activity. Because they will carry these characteristics into their old age, interest in leisure activity among older people will increase.
- Three social theories—disengagement, continuity, and age stratification—all point to social forces that inhibit an active leisure life-style. Sport, leisure, and recreation programs for older people can overcome these barriers. Activity theory promotes an active life-style in old age.
- Senior centers provide recreation programs for older people. These centers offer varied programs and activities, including crafts, exercise, socializing, education, and meals.
- Studies show that people with more education have a greater tendency to enroll in education programs in later life. But an older person who wants to take a college course faces many barriers. A long commute to

campus, long distances between buildings, and the lecture-style class do not appeal to most older people.
- Elderhostel combines university education with European hosteling. The program typically consists of three academic courses that meet for one or two weeks. Elderhostel offers programs worldwide. This allows older people to combine travel with education. ILRs or LLIs offer older people a chance to learn in groups in their own communities.
- A high proportion of people aged 60 and over do volunteer work. They do this mostly for personal satisfaction. Gerontologists predict that a more educated and affluent older population in the future will take on even more volunteer work.
- In later life, people enjoy varied activities such as recreation, exercise, education, and volunteer work. These activities lead to physical, social, and spiritual well-being.

DISCUSSION QUESTIONS

1. Define the term *leisure* and explain the continuity theory of aging as it applies to leisure activities.
2. In general, how do older people spend their leisure time?
3. What effect does age have on participation in core and peripheral leisure activities? What accounts for this pattern?
4. What major factors influence an older person's choice of leisure activities?
5. Why do researchers predict a greater interest in leisure activities among older people in the future?
6. What benefits can people gain from exercise and physical activity?
7. List and describe the three sociological theories that explain why older people prefer to live sedentary lives. How can older people learn to enjoy a more active life-style?
8. What services do senior centers provide for older people in the community?
9. Why do schools have a limited attraction for older people? Suggest some methods that can help older people learn better in a classroom situation.
10. Describe the Elderhostel and ILR programs. Give several reasons why Elderhostel attracts older people. Why do some gerontologists criticize programs like Elderhostel?
11. Suggest several ways to encourage older people to do more volunteer work.

SUGGESTED READING

Alfred, M. V. (2002). *Learning and sociocultural contexts: Implications for adults, community, and workplace education.* San Francisco, CA: Jossey-Bass.

The author collects nine essays on adult learning. The essays focus how culture and context influence adult learning. This text sensitizes the reader to the issues that minority group learners face. Topics include cross-cultural mentoring, immigrant students' learning in adult education programs, and online learning. A stimulating look at the many contexts where adult learning takes place, including the workplace, online, and in professional practice. It expands our thinking about education.

Beisgen, B. A., & Kraitchman, M. C. (2003). *Senior centers: Opportunities for successful aging.* New York: Springer.

The authors base this book on twenty years' experience managing a senior center in Pittsburgh, Pennsylvania. They discuss how to create a successful center, how to design programs, and how to create a satisfying environment for older people. The book is filled with insights into the needs and interests of older center clients. Topics include activities, education programs, and the future of senior centers. A practical guide written by people experienced in the field and a broad view of successful aging.

GLOSSARY OF TERMS

age stratification theory Society provides older people with specific roles to play and with expectations about activity in later life.

activity theory People tend to enjoy old age most if they stay active.

continuity theory People tend to enjoy old age most if they perform the same activities in later life as in middle age.

contractors People who do not take up new activities in later life to replace activities of their younger years.

core leisure activities Activities such as reading and socializing, often home-based and inexpensive.

disengagement theory People tend to enjoy old age most if they withdraw from activity as they age.

expanders People who begin new activities later in life to replace activities from their younger years.

hypokinetic disease Poor health related to lack of movement.

masters High-performance senior athletes.

mastery accomplishments Achievements that demonstrate skill and ability. This leads to feelings of self-efficacy.

peripheral leisure activities Activities such as sports and travel; they often take place outside the home and at some expense.

self-efficacy People's belief that they can meet environmental demands.

social agency model The use of a senior center as an agency that provides social and health care services.

structural lag Change in social structures (such as educational institutions) lags behind individual change; for example, few educational organizations today respond to the educational preferences of older people.

voluntary organization model The use of a senior center as social club.

chapter 13

FAMILY LIFE AND SOCIAL SUPPORT

Glenda and Al care for Al's father, Mr. Simkin. Mr. Simkin has lived with them for the past three years since his wife died. Recently, Mr. Simkin's ability to care for himself has declined. He now relies on Glenda and Al for personal care like bathing and toileting. For the past six months, they have felt the strain.

For example, they can no longer leave Mr. Simkin alone. Al says they feel tied down, "like a mother to a baby." Glenda says they have begun to argue over Mr. Simkin's care and "we share a feeling of frustration because we can't escape from caregiving." Some nights Glenda sleeps on a mat on the floor in Mr. Simkin's room. She does this so she can get him water or help him to the bathroom in the middle of the night. Lately, she's begun to lose patience with Mr. Simkin. Once she screamed, "I want a divorce from you, Pop."

Caregiving can put a strain on the caregiver and on family life. But Glenda will tell you that she loves Mr. Simkin, and she wants to care for him at home until he dies. Today, family members, like Glenda and Al, provide most of the support that older people get. Families provide income support, emotional support, social integration, and health care. The family also provides a network of social contacts that enhance the older person's self-image and sense of well-being.

Family support often flows two ways. Older people give to their networks as much as they receive, sometimes more. Through help with child rearing, financial support, and good advice, older people enrich family life.

Part one of this chapter looks at three topics related to family life: (1) marital status (including marriage, widowhood, divorce, and lifelong singlehood), (2) sexuality and aging, and (3) gay and lesbian older adults.

Part two of this chapter examines three topics related to social support: (1) informal support given to older people from family members and friends including the task of caregiving; (2) older people as a source of support, including their role as grandparents; and (3) elder abuse. The chapter concludes with a look at changing family structures and their impact on older people.

PART I: FAMILY LIFE, MARRIAGE, AND WIDOWHOOD

Age-graded normative life events take place at expected times in a person's life. These events (e.g., high school graduation, religious confirmation, and retirement) mark entry into a new **status** or position in society.

Marriage and widowhood are both age-graded normative life events. Marriage leads to the status of being a married person in our society. It also leads to expectations about behavior such as monogamy, expressions of love, and sharing financial resources. Most people today marry for the first time in their 20s or early 30s. Kahana and her colleagues (1994) say that by age 34, 80 percent of Americans have married; by age 45, 95 percent.

Marriage Demographics

Marital Status

Nearly all adults (96 percent) in the United States marry at least once. But the proportion of people married at a given age decreases from middle age onward. Divorce accounts for only a small proportion of this decrease. On average, less than two older people per 1,000 divorce each year. Widowhood explains most of the decrease in marriage rates. So, by age 65, men, compared with women, show a greater likelihood of being married.

In 2001, for example, 73 percent of older men were married compared with only 41 percent of older women. Almost one-half of all older women in 2001 were widows (46 percent). There were over four times as many widows (8.9 million) as widowers (2.0 million). Divorced and separated (including married/spouse absent) older persons represented only 10 percent of all older persons in 2001. But this percentage has increased since 1990, when about 7 percent of the older population were divorced or separated/spouse absent (Administration on Aging, 2002b). (Look ahead to Figure 13.1.)

The Advantages and Disadvantages of Marriage. Marriage offers a number of advantages to people as they age. First, married couples have more financial resources than single people. Married couples on average are younger than single older people, and one member of the couple may still work. Also, a number of lifelong trends account for why married people have more resources. Married couples tend to have a higher combined lifetime income than a single person, and they may have two pensions in old age. They also tend to spend less per person on food, rent, and other expenses because two people share the costs.

Second, married couples report greater life satisfaction than do single people (Cotten, 1999; Stack & Eshleman, 1998). Most older couples, especially those in good health, say they are happy. And couples report greater satisfaction in later life than earlier in their marriages. A study of older African Americans (mean age, 67), for example, found that marriage enhances subjective well-being (Tran, Wright, & Chatters, 1991). Other studies find increases in love, intimacy, and bonding between married partners in the later years of marriage. Goodman (1999) reports that affection and companionship grow in importance in marriage in later life. People who have remarried express satisfaction with their new spouses and their new relationships.

Couples in long-term marriages enjoy a new freedom in later life. They can focus on one another and their own enjoyment. They live adult-centered lives. They travel, visit friends, and do things together. Couples also have more chances than single people to engage in sexual relations. Research shows that the "empty nest: leads to increased marital satisfaction. Heidemann, Suhomlinova, and O'Rand (1998, p. 221) call the empty nest "a period of euphoria in marriages that have survived the demands of childraising."

Third, marriage leads to better adjustment to aging and to better health. A good marriage provides intimacy, greater life satisfaction, and more social support (Cotten, 1999). Marriage also provides emotional stability and a sense of security (Fitzpatrick & Wampler, 2000). Married older people, compared with single older people, live longer (especially men) and in better health (Schone & Weinick, 1998; Rowe & Kahn, 1998).

Couples have lower rates of hospitalization and nursing home placement. Spouses offer one another a live-in support system in times of need (Connidis, 2001). Couples in long-term marriages have a lifetime of shared experiences to draw on. This can help the couple cope with physical and psychological changes in old age. Peters and Liefbroer (1997) say that researchers need to look at the quality of a marriage to understand marriage's impact on well-being.

The previously mentioned findings apply to good marriages. A poor relationship will not necessarily improve over time. A relationship that includes bickering, fighting, and abuse may only get worse over time. A single person with a strong network of friends and family will feel more life satisfaction than someone in a bad marriage.

Even a good relationship faces a number of strains in later life. First, interests may diverge in later life. Activity limitations in later old age account for some of this change. Second, a relationship may suffer from changes in roles. Retirement, for example, can lead to confusion about household roles and responsibilities. Disagreements over everyday roles can lead to feelings of unfairness and anger. Third, ill health later in life can lead to strains in marital satisfaction. Caregiving can strain a couple's romantic relationship. Caregiving can also strain the caregiver spouse's mental and physical health. (Caregiving forms a separate topic later in this chapter.)

Married couples will live longer together than ever before, and long-term marriages face challenges in later life. Some couples will feel a decrease in marital satisfaction. These couples may benefit from professional counseling and other formal supports. Other marriages will have the resources to meet new challenges and thrive. Today, a good marriage provides an older person with a built-in support system, a companion, a friend, and a sexual partner.

Common-Law Unions. Some older people choose to live together and not marry. Research shows that the rate of cohabitation among older people has increased over the past few decades. In the United States, the rate went from nearly zero in 1960 for

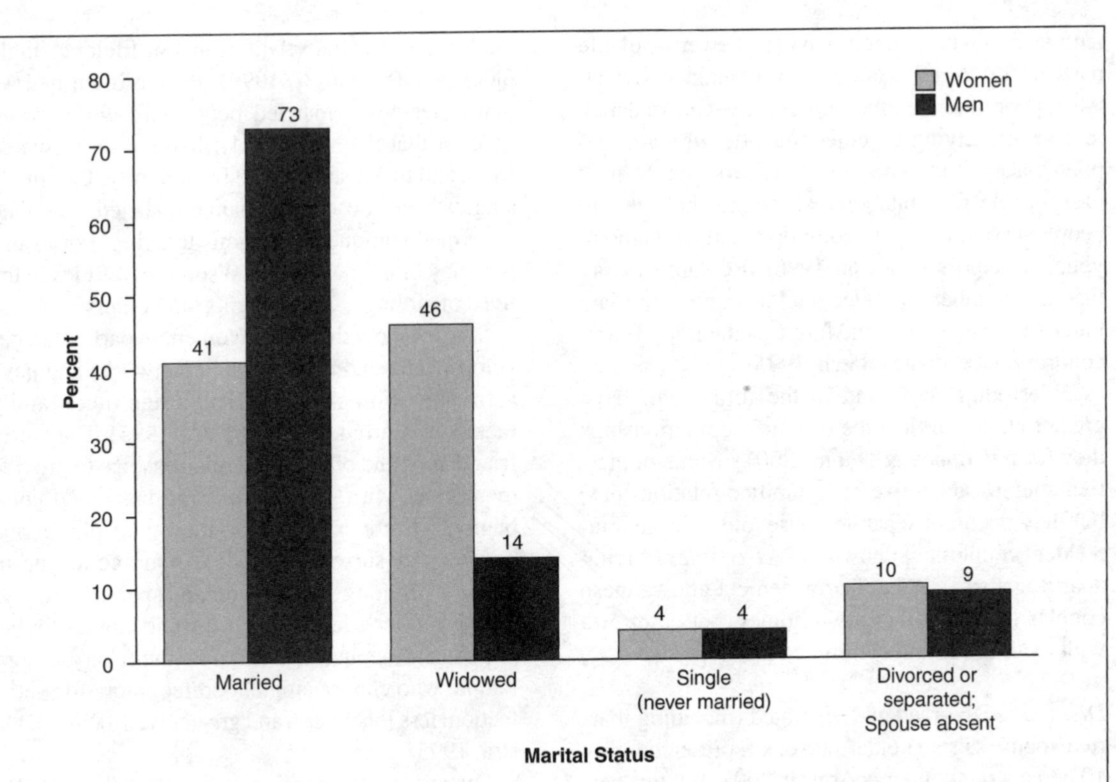

The figure shows 2001 data for the marital status of people aged 65 and over. Only a small proportion of older men or women remained single throughout life. Also, only a small proportion of older people are divorced at any one time. (Some formerly divorced people now appear in the married column.)

Note that a greater proportion of men than women are married. A greater proportion of women are widowed. (Even at age 85 and over most men have a spouse compared with only small proportion of women.) This means that most men will live with a spouse throughout their lives. Most women will live many years alone as widows.

These differences in marital status in later life lead to differences in the experience of old age. Older women, for example, often face the stresses of spousal caregiving in later life. They may play this role more than once if they remarry in old age.

Some of the differences between men and women shown here will change in the future. Men will have longer life expectancies in the years ahead. This will lead to more married couples in later life and to a lower rate of widowhood for women.

FIGURE 13.1
Marital Status of Older People

Source: Administration on Aging. (2002a). Profile of older Americans. Retrieved November 24, 2004, www.aoa.gov/prof/Statistics/profile/3.asp.

people aged 60 and older to 2.4 percent of this group in 1990 (Chevan, 1996). Older people tend to enter common-law relationships after the end of a first marriage. This may come before a remarriage or the couple may want an intimate relationship without the formal bonds of marriage (Leigh, 2000).

Chevan (1996) says that, compared with older women, more older men cohabit. These older men tend to live with younger women. Fewer available partners for older women may explain this fact. Also, poor older people show the greatest tendency to cohabit. Living together (outside of marriage) may make good economic sense for the poorest older people. Cohabitation is also more likely among people who have separated or divorced, and among younger seniors (Chevan, 1996). Researchers say that the number of older adults in common-law unions will increase in the future as the Baby Boom cohorts enter old age (Hatch, 1995).

Older adults now and in the future will have greater choice in the type of intimate relationships they form (Cooney & Dunne, 2001). Some unmarried couples today live in committed relationships, but they maintain separate households. These nonresident couples are known as *LAT couples* ("living apart together"). A LAT arrangement allows these couples to live in their own homes, but enjoy life with an intimate and committed partner.

Divorce. Divorced and separated (including married/spouse absent) older persons represented only 10 percent of all older persons in 2001. But this percentage represents a significant increase since 1990. In that year only about 7 percent of the older population were divorced or separated/spouse absent (Administration on Aging, 2002a). New cohorts entering old age with more liberal attitudes toward divorce may account for this increase. Divorce rates differ for men and women. Divorced men made up 8 percent of the male population aged 65 to 74.

But divorced women made up almost 11 percent of the female population aged 65 to 74 (U.S. Census Bureau, 2002b). Cohen (1999) says that people who divorce in middle or later life rarely remarry. But compared with women, men show a greater tendency to remarry after divorce. Divorce in later life often means economic insecurity, particularly for women (Miller, Hemesath, & Nelson, 1997). For men, it often means loss of social contact with children and relatives (Barrett & Lynch, 1999).

Lifelong Singlehood. A small proportion (about 4 percent) of older people have never married (U.S. Census Bureau, 2002b). Little research exists on the lives and social relationships of lifelong single older people (Barrett, 1999). People often believe that older never married people are *unmarriageable,* or that they feel lonely, live socially isolated lives, and feel disconnected from family. But, many singles have chosen to remain unmarried. And they have made unique adaptations to aging. For example, they often play vital and supportive roles in the lives of siblings, older parents, and others.

Studies show that older women, in particular, develop strong and diverse social networks and have active ties with siblings, friends, and other family members (Barrett, 1999; Dykstra, 1995). They form friendships and other social relationships to provide themselves with supporters, confidants, and companions. For example, they may treat nieces and nephews as surrogate children. One colleague of mine, a lifelong single woman, spends holidays with her sister's family, buys toy and clothes for her nieces and nephews, and takes them on outings. People who choose singlehood feel more life satisfaction, less loneliness, and greater well-being (Dykstra, 1995).

Overall, never married older people report that they lead active lives and feel happy. They have good health and feel satisfied with their standard of living. Singles feel they have freedom and control over their lives. In general, single women feel more satisfied with their lives than single men (Barrett, 1999). Davies (1995) found that older single women reported greater psychological well-being than younger single women or older single men. Older single people do report more loneliness than married seniors. But, single people, particularly single women, tend to feel less lonely than divorced and widowed older people (Dykstra, 1995).

Overall, the literature on singlehood suggests that never married people have good support networks (Connidis & McMullin, 1999). Still, compared with married couples, they lack spousal and child support in later life. This leads singles to use more formal supports and to develop more supportive friendships than married older people (Barrett & Lynch, 1999; Liebler & Sandefur, 2002). Older single people who need care are more likely to require institutional care because they lack a spouse or children.

Researchers project an increase in the proportion of old single people as Baby Boomers enter later life. These singles, as they age happily and in good health, may change societal attitudes about permanent singlehood. Researchers say that future studies should look at the coping strategies that never-married people use to maintain their high quality of life (O'Brien, 1991).

Widowhood

There were over four times as many widows (8.9 million) as widowers (2.0 million) in the United States in 2001. Almost one-half of all older women were widows (46 percent) compared with only 14 percent of older men (Administration on Aging, 2002a). Older women, particularly those aged 75 and older, are more likely than older men to live their final years in widowhood, most often living alone. At least three things account for the higher rate of widowhood for women: (1) women tend to marry older men; (2) women have a longer life expectancy than men; and (3) men tend to remarry after loss of a spouse. Gerontologists describe widowhood as an expectable or age-graded normative life event (especially for women), one that creates a great deal of stress (Lopata, 1996).

Bereavement. Widows and widowers face some common problems. These include not enough time to grieve, a lack of emotional support after the official mourning period, and lack of support from adult children during grieving. O'Bryant (1991a) found that forewarning about a spouse's death allowed a person to work out some grief. Surviving spouses could plan for the future and this eased adjustment to widowhood. Still, strong emotions may come and go for many months after a spouse's death. Lund (1993b, p. 539) describes this as an emotional "roller coaster ride." Feelings of grief can include disbelief, shock, numbness, sadness, or guilt. A person can also feel abandoned, angry, and depressed.

Many widows report that widowhood stripped them of their identities. Van den Hoonaard (1997) calls this "identity foreclosure." Widowhood signals the end of a woman's former identity (as a wife) and begins the need to build a new identity. MacDougall (1998, pp. 1–2), a widow, says that "part of the pain has to do with our sense of self; without our life-long partner, it becomes necessary to redefine our place in the world. When one has been part of a couple for a very long time, the adjustment can seem impossible."

Bereavement can go on months and even years after the formal mourning period. Many women hold onto their wife roles for years after their husbands' deaths. Zisook and Schuchter (1991a, 1991b) found that 70 percent of widows and widowers yearned for their spouses after seven months. Twenty-three percent showed symptoms of depression after seven months, and 16 percent showed these symptoms after thirteen months. A comparison group of married older people had depression rates of only 4 percent.

Rosenbloom and Whittington (1993) studied the effects of widowhood on nutrition. They found that widowhood led to changes in eating habits and a decline in nutrient quality. A large majority (84 percent) of widows said they lost weight (an average of almost eight pounds) after widowhood. The researchers say that a continuation of this pattern could lead to illness.

Most people eventually bounce back from the shock of widowhood. Van den Hoonaard (1999) says that the opportunity for widowed women to talk about the last days of their husband's lives can give them comfort. These stories can also act as *bridges* on their journeys from being a wife to being a widow.

Lund (1989, cited in Lund, 1993b) found that only 15 to 25 percent of widows and widowers have long-term problems with bereavement. A five-year longitudinal study of women in Massachusetts looked at the effects of widowhood on health and psychological well-being (Avis, Brambilla, Vass, & McKinlay, 1991). The study found no difference in health between widows and married women over this time. Widows showed more psychological distress than married women throughout the study, but distress decreased over time.

Compared with men, few women remarry after their spouses die. This, in part, reflects the smaller number of eligible men compared with eligible women in later life. Also, men tend to remarry younger women. Women who do remarry say they want a companion and the feeling that they add to another person's happiness. Talbott (1998) found that many older widows reported an interest in men. But they also reported negative attitudes toward remarriage and an increased enjoyment in their independence.

Some women experience widowhood as a release. Widowhood allows them to rediscover parts of their identities they had lost in marriage. One woman I interviewed said she would not marry again (for the fourth time). "I'm tired of taking care of sick old men," she said. "I want to enjoy myself for a while." Widows sometimes set new goals, take up new activities, and take on new challenges.

Widows and Widowers: Coping with Loss. Most studies of widowhood contain too few men to compare with women. But a few studies show how the loss of a spouse affects each gender. First, studies of family supports, friendship, and confidants (someone to confide in) show that widowed women have more social supports than widowed men (Campbell, Connidis, & Davies, 1999). Gallagher and Gerstel (1993), for example, studied the social networks of 106 women aged 60 and over. They found that over 90 percent of women, married or widowed, provided help to someone. Married women tended to care for husbands and a small group of family members. Widows tended to provide practical help to a large network of friends. Both groups of women had active social networks. These networks help widows maintain a satisfying social life.

Men typically name their spouses as their confidants. But women, compared with men, more often have confidants other than their spouses (Gurung, Taylor, & Seeman, 2003). Widows, for example, often chose a sister or friend as a confidant. Campbell and her colleagues (1999) found that siblings, particularly sisters, provide emotional support to their widowed sisters. Sisters also serve as confidants and companions, especially if they live nearby. Siblings can connect a person to their past, while giving support in the present.

Confidants can contribute to good morale. They can lessen anxiety, tension, and depression. A number of studies suggest that men experience more social isolation and have fewer sources of support than widows (Barer, 1994; van den Hoonaard, 1994). Most older men spent their lives focused on their careers, while older women spent their lives focused on people (Patterson, 1996).

So, women have more close relationships than men in old age. Because men have fewer supports than women, they more often experience loneliness after their spouses die (Moore & Stratton, 2002). They also may experience a decline in their social functioning and mental health status. Chipperfield and Havens (2001) say that while life satisfaction declines for both men and women following the death of a spouse, men show a greater decline.

Second, wives link men to wider social networks. More often than men, women say they have close relationships with family and friends besides their husband. They often name these friends, relatives, and children as their confidants, and they keep up these relationships when their husbands die (Campbell, Connidis, & Davies, 1999; McCandless & Conner, 1997). A widowed woman with children will usually continue in the role of mother and grandmother.

A widower loses a wife, a companion, and his link to other family and social ties. This may explain why many men rush into another marriage after they lose a spouse. Wu (1995) found that widowed men remarry sooner than widowed women. After five years, less than 6 percent of widowed women had remarried. But over 22 percent of widowed men had remarried. Within ten years 35 percent of men had remarried (compared with only 11 percent of women).

Third, widowed men, compared with women, find it harder to make new friends or to join self-help groups. Men have a higher risk of dying within the six months following the death of their spouses (Lee, Willetts, & Seccombe, 1998). Compared with women, widowers also run a higher risk of suicide.

Moore and Stratton (2002) found that, in spite of these challenges, some older widowed men bounce back from widowhood. The men in their study reestablished meaningful lives after the loss of their spouses. Many of them found companionship and got involved in social activities.

Studies in general have judged men as less involved than women in relationships. But self-reports by men show that they often see themselves as having strong bonds of affection and closeness to family members. Sometimes they rate higher than women on self-reports of closeness. Boxer and his colleagues (1986, p. 102) say that:

> by unquestioningly imposing a "female model" of interpersonal relationships on men's experiences, investigators may be missing relevant information. . . . Male bonds may require more subtle measurement techniques and may manifest themselves in ways or in settings that are different from women's bonds.

The research suggests that men and women may have different social network needs and different types of relationships in later life. This may reflect differences in how men and women develop relationships earlier in life. More research needs to look at the social lives of widows and widowers to understand how their needs differ.

Fourth, the loss of a spouse can have a devastating effect on a woman's finances in later life. The longer life expectancy of older women, their broken employment records, low wages for working women, fewer women with pension plans, and the tendency of women to remain widowed all lead to many of the financial problems that older women face. Inflation, for example, will eat away at a survivor's pension, if the widow has one.

Both widows and widowers run a greater risk of institutionalization than a married person because they lack spousal supports if they get sick. Widowhood, in spite of good social supports, puts men and women at risk as they age. Supportive relationships with family and friends help widowed men and women deal with the challenges they face.

Dating and Remarriage. Men tend to remarry after widowhood and women tend to stay single, but studies report little about how widows and widowers form new intimate relationships. Bulcroft and Bulcroft (1991, cited in McElhaney, 1992) looked at dating patterns of single people aged 55 and over. The study found that about one-third (30 percent) of the men and 6.7 percent of the women reported having one or more dates in the past month. The study also focused on those people who said they had dates. The researchers found that one-half of the men and nearly one-third of the women daters said they went out with more than one person in the past year. Almost one-half of the men and women said they had a steady dating relationship with one partner.

Montenegro (2003) reports on a study of 3,501 single men and women aged 40 to 69. She found that about one-third of the people in the study had an exclusive dating arrangement. Another third had a nonexclusive dating arrangement. Nine percent expressed no interest in dating. Moore and Stratton (2002, p. 145) say that men in their study found dating stressful. One widow described dating as "akin to an hour on the rack" and "my worst nightmare." Another said he would only ask a woman out for one date in order not to get too involved.

Those people in Montenegro's study who dated regularly said they enjoyed the freedom of singlehood, but dating helped them cope with loneliness. Men and women said they looked for a dating partner with a good personality and a sense of humor. Many men in the study looked for physical attractiveness and sexual satisfaction in a dating partner. Most people in the study found dating prospects through friends, family, or work. Some used an online dating service.

Older people say they date for two main reasons: They want to find a marital partner, and they like to stay socially active. Older women say it increases their prestige. They say that other women envy them for dating. Men say they date in order to talk about their personal concerns (McElhaney, 1992). Dating also acts as an outlet for romance, sex, and love. More than one-third of the daters in Montenegro's (2003) study reported that they had sexual intercourse at least once per month.

Pieper and Petkovsek (1991) studied remarriage in a sample of fifty remarried older couples. They found that less than 10 percent of the people in the couples had felt a strong desire to remarry. About one-third of the sample said they had not thought much about remarriage. About one-half the men

BOX 13.1
THE SHOCK OF WIDOWHOOD

I am sitting on a sofa, sipping tea with Joanna in her living room high above the city, in one of the wealthiest sections of town. Joanna has lived alone since her husband died twelve years ago. She describes the stress she felt as a caregiver at that time.

We had a comfortable middle-class life—two cars, a cottage, a house, children, and friends. We were involved in everything. Then he became ill with cancer of the brain.

Well, it was a matter of carrying on. I was going to stop working in real estate and be with my husband when he was sick, but I didn't. My supervisor thought it wasn't a good thing to dwell on it, to be at home a lot. He was right. So I carried on with my job. Of course, I had to do it well. It's part of the picture. You have to do it well. It has to be perfect.

I seemed to have this idea that I was going to carry it all on, that I could do it. I did for two years, and I ran myself into the ground, running up to the hospital at noon and helping him with his lunch, going up again after work. And then at night just sacking out so I could go on with another day. It was very hard.

I think all this running up to the hospital constantly wasn't really genuine. I did it. I cared for his suffering. But I was human. I wished someone else could be doing it. So I was not being true to myself. I think that led to a lot of things later.

Even after my husband died, I was determined to carry on as though nothing had happened. I was so determined that nothing like my husband's death was going to throw me, and I didn't allow myself a grievance time.

After his death, I travelled. At Christmas I went to Spain, Hawaii, or wherever. At Easter I went somewhere. I went to Europe. There was never a day—I didn't allow myself any time at all. Do you get the picture? No time to breathe.

It was unbelievable. No wonder I needed something. I didn't want to lean on people. I think I got hooked on a sleeping pill every night when my husband was sick, plus I drank a bit. Well, for a year after he died I was hospitalized off and on. I was using different kinds of pills. The doctor would change prescriptions, but I wouldn't discard the old one. I took more alcohol than I'd like to admit along with the pills. I was a very, very confused person. That was my way of coping, my way of standing the pain. I needed some kind of anesthetic. You finally have to get floored to realize you can't do it alone.

Well, I finally got floored. The last time I drove my car I drove right into a restaurant—right through the window.

I had the car washed that day. And I was parked in front of this pizza parlor having a cup of coffee. I thought the sidewalk was quite a distance from the front of the car. I didn't want it sticking out so I put it in low and just eased it up. I drove right through the window.

I just stepped out of the car—over these shards of plate glass, big pieces of plate glass on the road—and I said, "I'd like a cup of coffee." "Lady," the owner said, "you get back in that car." He was quite certain I was out of my tree. But I didn't get back. I just sat in the booth until the police came.

That's the last time I drove. That was getting near the end. I guess for me the change had to come in the form of a crisis. That's the only way I would accept it. I resist change, especially change imposed on me. Now, if I had to let it all go, I know I could do it. I have something here [pointing to herself] that I can be comfortable with.

Joanna took a year's leave of absence from her job, sold her house, cottage, and car, and joined Alcoholics Anonymous. It took her two years to start a new life based on A.A., social commitments to groups she wants to help, and her family. Today Joanna has retired from work. She tutors young people after school, spends time cross-country skiing, and time alone at her cottage. She also has a strong relationship with her granddaughter.

Summing up her life today, Joanna says: "What really gives my life meaning now is inside. It's not external anymore. I have my inner resources—I always had them, but I didn't use them. For me widowhood was very painful at first because I resisted change. Now I'm changed and it's okay. I would say I have a new freedom."

and one-third of the women in these marriages had dated between their marriages.

Most of these men and women reported little support from their adult children for dating or remarriage. After remarriage, adult children showed a tendency not to accept the new spouse. Pieper and Petkovsek (1991) say that adult children may feel protective toward their parents and worry about the wisdom of the remarriage. Children may also feel some jealousy and a rivalry with the new spouse.

Remarried people reported satisfaction with their new spouse. They said they had more in common with their present spouse than with their former spouse. They also gave a more positive rating to their present spouse's personality. They considered their current spouse more friendly, interesting, considerate, and affectionate.

Couples most often said they remarried for companionship. This item rated first or second on nearly every person's list of reasons. Couples also expressed a strong need to love and be loved. Overall, the couples in this study expressed high satisfaction with their new marriages.

Sexuality

Sexual activity serves two functions: reproduction and pleasure. The western tradition, from the Old Testament onward, emphasized reproduction. In the Judeo-Christian tradition, sex for pleasure is sinful and immoral. This view leaves little room for sex in later life and may have led to the notion that older people live (or should live) asexual lives.

Today, attitudes toward sexuality in later life have begun to change. Leitner and Leitner (1985, p. 325) refer to sex as "a uniquely beneficial leisure activity for elders." Older people in good health can enjoy an active sex life into late old age, and the more active the sex life, the better their sexual response. Cutler reports that sex at least once a week increases and regulates hormone flow for men and women (cited in "Sex by Schedule," 1992). Greeley (1992, cited in Mayo Clinic, 1993) found that "the happiest men and women in America are married people who continue to have sex frequently after they are 60. They are also most likely to report that they are living exciting lives."

Alex Comfort (1972), author of *The Joy of Sex,* says that most people give up sex for the same reason they give up riding a bicycle: (1) they think it looks silly (attitude); (2) they have arthritis and can't get on (health); and (3) they don't have a bicycle (widowhood). People report an interest in sex into late old age. Given good health and a partner, older people can (and do) have sexual relations into late old age (Schlesinger, 1996).

Greeley (1992, cited in Mayo Clinic, 1993) reviewed studies that asked 5,738 people over age 60 about their sex lives. Thirty-seven percent of married people in these studies said they had sex at least once a week. Sixteen percent had sex several times a week. The Duke University Longitudinal Study on Aging found that the best predictor of a good sex life in old age is a good sex life in the younger years. Palmore (1981, p. 89) concludes from the data that "most older married persons are not asexual; on the contrary, substantial proportions remain sexually active until at least their 80s. They also show that impotence and sexual problems in old age are reversible, and that substantial proportions at all ages report increasing sexual activity."

The Duke study found that sexual activity leads to high life satisfaction and good health for older people. Many older couples say that sex is more satisfying now than when they were younger. Sexual expression often evolves with age to include forms of intimacy other than sexual intercourse, including touching, hugging, and holding hands (Cooley, 2002).

Research shows that good health and marriage hold the key to a woman's continued sexual activity (Metz & Miner, 1998). Jacoby (1999, p. 41) refers to a "partner gap." She says that, compared with older women, older men tend to have sexual partners. And this difference between women and men increases with age. Widowhood or a husband's decision to stop having sex often puts an end to a woman's sexual activity (Loehr, Verma, & Seguin, 1997). "The saddest truth . . . ," Jacoby (1999, p. 43) says, "is that for most (though not all) older widows, the loss of a husband translates into the end of sex."

Older people can have a satisfying marriage without an active sex life. But continued sexual activity leads to well-being and happiness for older couples (Matthias, Lubben, Atchison, & Schweitzer, 1997). Cooley (2002, p. 2) says that "while expressing our sexuality isn't as essential for survival as food or water, it fulfills a need for affection and belonging." This in turn has a positive impact on our self-esteem and quality of life. People in institutional settings face unique challenges to the expression of their sexuality.

Fairchild, Carrino, and Ramirez (1996) studied twenty-nine U.S. nursing homes. They report that twenty-eight had no formal program to train staff about residents' sex-related issues. And almost one-half of the facilities did not address sexuality at all within their staff training programs. Furthermore, social workers described staff attitudes toward residents' sexuality as "mixed" or "largely negative." They used terms such as "intolerant," "humorous," or "condemning." They also reported that nursing home staff members had "intolerant" or "condemning" attitudes toward homosexuality and lesbianism.

Research supports the need for more formal staff training programs that teach workers about the sexual needs and feelings of older residents (Fairchild, Carrino, & Ramirez, 1996; Walker & Ephross, 1999). Staff members should consider residents' need for privacy. Also, staff need to assess a confused resident's ability to consent to sexual relations. Staff members may need to protect dementia patients from sexual exploitation or abuse (Lichtenberg, 1997).

Physical Changes and Sexual Adaptations

Physical changes due to aging require adaptations in sexual performance. For example, with age a man's sexual response slows from first excitement through orgasm. Cross (1993) says that a man can adapt to this change by learning to enjoy more varied forms of sexual relations. This can include intercourse without ejaculation or touching to stimulate his partner.

Sometimes illness can interfere with sexual function. Damage to blood vessels in the penis, for example, accounts for about one-half of all impotence in men past age 50. Also, hardening of the arteries can limit the flow of blood to the genitals. It can stop a man from having an erection and can lead to swelling of tissues in the vagina for women.

A heart attack, prostate surgery, or hysterectomy do not necessarily decrease sexual activity or enjoyment. Illness may require an adjustment in sexual patterns or in life-style. Cooley (2002) says that good eating habits, weight control, limits on the use of alcohol, and an active sex life can all enhance and prolong sexual activity. The *Mayo Clinic Health Letter* (1993) also says that rest before sex, exercise to loosen joints, and touching can overcome problems caused by illness.

Women can use vaginal jelly to decrease dryness during intercourse (*see also* Karlen, 1992). Older people without a partner can masturbate for sexual pleasure (Zeiss & Kasl-Godley, 2001). Weg (1983b) says that masturbation can lead to a release of tension and increased well-being. Counseling may help for nonmedical problems.

Goldman and Carroll (1990) offered a sex education program to couples experiencing problems with the man's getting an erection. The researchers found that education about physical and psychological changes in old age improved the couples' sex lives. Couples in the program reported a greater ability to express their sexuality. Many books and videos exist that can help couples explore ways to adapt to these changes.

Drugs like Viagra and Levitra now exist to restore or enhance sexual performance in older men. The AARP conducted a study of sexual behaviour and found that 10 percent of men used a new drug treatment or other therapy to overcome impotence (Jacoby, 1999). About one-half of the men in the study who took some form of medication took Viagra. Most Viagra users and their partners in this study said it increased their sexual enjoyment. The success of Viagra in the marketplace will lead to new forms of drug therapy for impotence. The use of drug therapies and a greater interest in sexual activity among younger seniors will lead to more active sex lives among older adults in the future.

All of this talk about physical change and adaptation misses a key part of the sexual equation: the relationship of the people involved. People can adapt to many changes in their bodies and still enjoy a good sex life. But this requires knowledge about sex in later life and good communication between the partners. The National Institute on Aging (1994) reminds us that sexuality includes emotional as well as physical response. The National Institute on Aging says that a man's fear of impotence, for example, can create enough stress to cause it. A woman's feeling of lost beauty can interfere with enjoyment of sex.

Sex therapist David Schnarch separates genital prime from sexual prime. He says that "sexual intensity is more a function of emotional maturation than of physiological responsiveness" (cited in "Getting Older, Getting Better," 1992, p. 17). Good sex, he says, depends on intimacy.

Butler and Lewis (2002) say that older couples can develop a unique intimacy as they age. They refer to a "second language of sex—a growing capacity . . . to develop intimacy and communication in a love relationship . . ." (Butler, Lewis, & Sunderland, 1991, p. 225). Weg (1983a, p. 8) says that researchers too often ignore "the walking hand-in-hand or arm-in-arm; the caring for one another; the touching and holding, with or without intercourse."

This makes later life a good time to explore sexual potential. Touch, foreplay, a good setting, and mood can all enhance sex. Slower response time can lead to more intimacy and a deeper relationship. The *Mayo Clinic Health Letter* (Mayo Clinic, 1993) gives some sound advice here: "Whether you seek intimacy through non-sexual touching and companionship or through sexual activity, you and your partner can overcome obstacles. The keys are caring, adapting, and communicating."

Gay and Lesbian Older People

Cantor, Brennan, and Shippy (2004) say that few national surveys ask about sexual orientation or identity. And they say that surveys likely miss people who will not reveal their sexual preferences. So, only a rough estimate exists of the number of lesbian, gay, or bisexual (LGB) older people in the United States. Cantor and her colleagues conclude, from the few studies that do exist, that from 3 to 8 percent of the U.S. population has a LGB orientation. This would mean that the United States has from 1 to 2.8 million LGB seniors. They estimate that this figure could grow to between 2 and 6 million LGB seniors by 2030.

A myth exists that LGB and transgender (LGBT) seniors live lonely, pathetic lives. The myth pictures them as ugly and rejected by young lovers. Friend (1980, p. 245) refers to "the popular view of the older gay male as lonely, maladjusted, and living marginally to the institutions of society."

Research findings on aging LGBTs fail to support this myth. Studies show that LGBT seniors play active roles in the gay and straight communities. Older LGBTs may play a parent or grandparent role to a younger person. LGBT older people may also play the role of caregiver to parents in their family (Cantor, Brennan, & Shippy, 2004). Their single status, mobility, or willingness to live with a parent may select them for this role.

Quam and Whitford (1992) found high life satisfaction in a study of eighty midwestern lesbians and gays. A study of seventy-eight lesbians (Deevey, 1990) found that they had excellent mental health and a positive view of aging. Cruz (2003) studied 125 gay and bisexual men aged 55 to 84. These men reported little depression and good health. Lipman (1986) found that older lesbians and gays have more friends than do older heterosexuals.

Kimmel (1992) found that older gay white men created their own support systems. These friends serve as surrogate families. Friendship leads to good health and psychological well-being (de Vries & Blando, 2004). Research shows that older gay men and lesbians are concerned about the same things as heterosexual older people—health, finances, and loneliness. For example, having a committed partner increases life satisfaction and decreases loneliness for older gay men and lesbians (Brown, Sarosy, Cook, & Quarto, 1997).

Gays and lesbians do face certain unique problems as they age. First, the LGB community, like the heterosexual community, values youth. Bergling (2004) reports that gay men have learned and believe many of the stereotypes of aging. Some writers (Hammond, 1987) say that lesbians feel less of this prejudice against age. But both gay and lesbian seniors lack role models of good aging.

Second, the law and social institutions often do not recognize gay or lesbian relationships. This can lead to problems with legal custody of disabled partners, discrimination in housing, and barriers to the use of social services designed for heterosexual partnerships (Cahill & South, 2002). Hospitals, for example, sometimes limit access to intensive care units to family members. They may not recognize a gay or lesbian partner as family.

Third, living in a homophobic and hostile environment causes some of the greatest stress for gays or lesbians of any age. The controversy over gay marriage shows that many people oppose giving gay couples the same rights and recognition as heterosexual married couples. Older gays and lesbians have suffered under this attitude for a lifetime. Self-help groups, more research on gay and lesbian aging, and more societal acceptance of gay and lesbian life styles will all lead to a better age for gays and lesbians in the future.

The double social stigma of being gay and being old increases the challenges that older gays and lesbians face in later life (Grossman, 1997). For example, societal homophobia led many gay and lesbian older people to hide their same sex relationships. They feared that exposure might cost them their jobs. Gay working class men, for example, have a difficult time disclosing their sexual orientation (Chapple, Kippax, & Smith, 1998).

Friend (1996) says that adaptation to living in a hostile society may improve the gay and lesbian person's ability to cope with aging. First, he says that gays and lesbians have experience in constructing a positive image of themselves in spite of social definitions. This can help them construct a positive image of themselves as they age (*see also* Jones & Nystrom, 2002).

Second, gays and lesbians have experience in creating supportive relationships. This can help them create the support networks they need as they age. Third, many gays and lesbians have experience with political advocacy and will be better able to defend their rights as they age. This activist experience can help aging gays and lesbians get the social supports they need in later life (Brotman, Ryan, & Cormier, 2002).

Like older heterosexual adults, older gays and lesbians need a broad range of social supports and services. Gays and lesbians can best meet these needs by planning and implementing programs for their community (Beeler, Rawls, Herdt, & Cohler, 1999; Jacobs, Rasmussen, & Hohman, 1999). Informal supports also play a significant role. Long-term relationships with a committed partner provide both gay men and lesbians with companionship, acceptance, and support (Berger, 1996). Ties to other family members and friends also provide support (Fullmer, 1995).

Research on gays and lesbians in later life has only begun. A number of research topics still need study (Grossman, 1997). These include the longitudinal study of aging gay and lesbian couples (O'Brien & Goldberg, 2000), ethnic and cultural issues faced by gays and lesbians, gay widowhood (Shernoff, 1997), and aged gays and lesbians in their community. Researchers also need to study the relationships between gay older parents and their adult children and grandchildren (Connidis, 2001). Studies of gay and lesbian aging show that societal influences and past experiences shape a person's life in old age. They also show that sexuality plays an important part in gay and lesbian as well as heterosexual aging.

Weg (1983b, p. 76) summarized the research on sexuality in later life: "There is no one way to love or to be loved; there is no one liaison that is superior to another. No one life-style in singlehood or marriage, heterosexual or homosexual, will suit all persons. Self-pleasuring, homosexuality, bisexuality, celibacy, and heterosexuality are all in the same human sexual repertoire. . . . In a social climate that is more open and accepting, the reality of numbers is helping to return the 'old' to the mainstream of living and sexuality to the elderly."

PART II: SOCIAL SUPPORT

Social support refers to help and assistance we give to and receive from others. Older people benefit from the support they get from family members and friends in the form of emotional support, companionship, help with household chores, and a range of other help. Merrill (1997) estimates that over 80 percent of informal support received by older adults comes from family.

But older family members also give help to others through financial support and help with childcare. They may provide a home for unmarried, divorced, or unemployed adult children. Part two of this chapter looks at (1) informal supports for older people and caregiving; (2) older people as a source of support, including their role as grandparents; and (3) elder abuse.

Family Life and Family Supports

Over the past 150 years, the family has changed in size and structure in the United States. In the past, one child, a "parent keeper," often stayed at home to look after aging parents (Hareven, 1992, p. 10). Hareven says that family members spent more time together and helped one another more. Even in the early years of industrialization, families often lived in multigenerational households.

Today, the family has gotten smaller as parents have fewer children, and children often move long distances from their parents in order to find or keep jobs. Even when parents and children live near one another, they rarely live in the same household. These and other changes in the family have led some writers to assume that families no longer support their older members. Frequent moves and the fast pace of modern life make it seem as if the family has abandoned its older members.

But studies in the United States find that families still provide most of the support for older people. Families help older members in times of illness, they exchange services with older members, and they often visit older relatives. Many adult children live within a short drive of their parents. Troll and Bengtson (1992) reported on a study of people aged 85 and over in the San Francisco area. They found that three-fourths of the women and one-half of the men saw their children at least weekly. Older people also keep in contact with family members through letters and by telephone (Sotomayor & Applewhite, 1988). And now families keep in touch through email and instant messaging.

Health care professionals and social services take on many jobs the family did in the past, but children often help their parents get access to these services (Neuharth & Stern, 2000). Children also monitor their parents' well-being and need for more help. Grandchildren may help a grandparent with household chores. Brody (1983, p. 597; 1995, p. 20) sums up the research on family support based on a study of three generations. "Values about family care of elderly adults," she says, "have not eroded despite demographic and socioeconomic changes. The old values were holding very firm indeed." Shanas (1979) called the idea of family breakdown a "hydra-headed myth." The myth persists in spite of the evidence.

Informal Supports for Older People

Formal support refers to paid help from professional caregivers such as doctors, nurses, and social workers. Informal support refers to unpaid help given by friends, neighbors, and family. Informal support takes many forms, including advice, affection, companionship, helping older family members with transportation, and nursing care.

Relatives make up more than 80 percent of the caregivers of older people with disabilities (Brody, 1995). Stone (1995) says that even when formal care exists, informal care forms the basis of care for older people.

Studies find that few older people who need help with daily chores or health care use only formal care. More often people use both the formal and informal support systems (Spillman & Pezzin, 2000). Keating and her colleagues (1997, p. 24) call this a "caring partnership." They say that social policies now favor this mix of informal and formal care. Studies show that people usually turn to the formal system only after the informal system no longer meets their needs. Penning (2002) finds that even those who make extensive use of formal care services still rely on their informal care network.

Four Models of Informal Support

Four models describe the roles of informal supporters. The **task specificity model** says that different groups (spouse, child, neighbor) have different abilities and different resources to offer the older person

"It's your grandparents, claiming their visitation rights."

(Litwak, 1985). Each group has a specific role to play in the older person's support system.

The **hierarchical compensatory model** says that supporters come first from the older person's inner family circle (Cantor, 1979). Older people then move outward to get support from less intimate people as they need more help (Cantor & Little, 1985). This model says that married older people turn to a spouse first, then to a child. Older people turn to friends, neighbors, and formal supports (in that order) if they still have unmet needs (Walker, 1991).

The **functional specificity of relationships model** (Simons, 1983–84) recognizes that "one tie may provide one type of support or a broad range of support, dependent on how that particular relationship has been negotiated" over the life course (Campbell, Connidis, & Davies, 1999, p. 118). For example, the gender, marital status, parenthood, and proximity of helpers all influence the amount and type of support a person will get.

The **convoy model of support** (Kahn & Antonucci, 1980) sees people as having a dynamic network of close ties with family and friends. This model uses concentric circles to describe relationships around the older individual, with the strongest relationships in the closest circle. Outer circles show weaker relationships (Haines & Henderson, 2002). These relationships form a *convoy* that travels with individuals throughout life, exchanging social support and assistance. The relationships of people in this convoy grow and change with changing life circumstances.

Powers and Kivett (1992) found some support for the hierarchical compensatory model in a study of rural older adults. They found that older people expected more help from closer relatives and less help from more distant relations. They found less support for the task specificity model. Older people in this study expected all family members to visit and help during an illness.

Penning (1990) studied informal supports of people aged 60 and over. She found that different groups of supporters did different tasks (supporting the task specificity model). But she found little support for the hierarchical compensatory model. People in this study used a variety of formal and informal supports at the same time.

Luckey (1994) studied African American elders' support networks. She found little support for the hierarchical compensatory model. Instead she reports that African American elders drew on a broad range of kin for support. Their support systems included second and third generations of nieces, nephews, and grandchildren. These relatives provided a broad range of supports that complemented formal supports.

Few studies have found strong support for the hierarchical compensatory model. This model may present too rigid a picture of the give and take of family life. It also fails to account for aging under different socioeconomic conditions. Low-income African American elders, for example, may lack the full hierarchy of available supports. They use substitute kin (like nieces and nephews) to fill in for a missing spouse or children. This pattern differs from support system use among whites.

Campbell, Connidis, and Davies (1999) found support for the functional specificity of relationships model. They found that siblings provide a range of social support for certain groups, including single women, the childless, single men, and widowed women. But siblings provide little support for divorced and married men. In general, siblings give support when they live nearby. Siblings also tend to serve as companions and confidants, and they more often provide practical support to sisters than to brothers. These findings show that particular groups of older adults develop supportive ties with siblings, "not as substitution or compensation for lost ties but based on a lifetime of negotiating unique ties with siblings" (p. 144).

Haines and Henderson (2002) assessed the convoy model of social support. They found that while the model helps to identify supportive relationships, not all strong ties provide support. They found that weak ties, typically ignored in the convoy model of support, provide instrumental support, emotional support, and companionship.

Older people use formal supports along with informal supports for at least two reasons. First, an older person may have an incomplete informal network and need specific kinds of help (like someone to do the shopping). Second, some older people who have intact networks have high health care needs. For example, caregivers who care for older family members with dementia use more in-home services than other caregivers (Hawranik, 2002). The informal and formal systems work together in these cases to share the overall load.

Ward-Griffin (2002) found that both formal and informal care providers perform physical and emotional care work. Formal care providers, specifically nurses in this study, have professional knowledge and skills that differentiate them from family care providers. However, as Ward-Griffin says, the boundary between professional and family caregivers blurs when family members develop caregiving skills and knowledge.

Other research findings add another dimension to this complexity. Living arrangements influence the type of supports older people use. For example, an older person who lives with someone will likely get support for the ADL from that person (Boaz, Hu, & Ye, 1999). Shared living arrangements (between siblings or friends) can help widowed or childless older people live in the community. Strain and Blandford (2003) find that caregivers who live with an older parent provide daily help with meal preparation and household chores.

Penning (1990, p. 227) concludes that "the issue of who provides assistance to whom, of what type, and under what conditions is complex." Researchers need more sophisticated models to describe the reality of informal supports. More research on rural, minority, and low-income older people will also lead to more accurate models of social support.

Spousal Support

Studies show that a spouse, if available, will take on the caregiving role. In two national studies, spouses made up between one-quarter and almost two-fifths of caregivers (Cantor, 1992). They most often served as **primary caregivers**. Wives more often than husbands play this role. Wives tend to outlive their husbands and care for their husbands during the husbands' terminal illnesses. This makes caregiving in later life another expectable life event for a married woman.

Only 10 percent of men serve as caregivers to their spouses, compared with 37 percent of women (Manton & Liu, 1984, cited in U.S. Senate, 1991). Spousal support decreases with age, but formal support increases. This affects women more than men. Even in late old age (age 85 and over), 20 percent of men who need care have a spouse as their caregiver, but only 2 percent of women in this age group have a spouse as a caregiver.

Mackenzie and MacLean (1992) say that even after a spouse enters an institution, the spouse in the community feels stress. Spouses report loneliness, a desire to get on with their lives, and feelings of guilt. They feel loyalty to the institutionalized spouse and yet feel the loneliness of widowhood. Novak and Guest (1989, 1992) studied caregivers of cognitively impaired older people. They found five dimensions of caregiver burden: time dependence, developmental burden, physical burden, social burden, and emotional burden. They found that even after a spouse enters an institution, the community-dwelling spouse feels some burden.

Loos and Bowd (1997) found that caregiver spouses felt guilty after institutionalization. Spouses of institutionalized older people, compared with adult children, feel more physical and developmental burden. Physical burden referred to the strain of long visits and travel to the institution. Hallman and Joseph (1999) found that women, compared with men, spend more time travelling to give care. Developmental burden referred to spouses' feelings of being unable to get on with life. One wife told Gladstone (1995, p. 56) that "when you're apart after never being apart it has an effect on you. You seem to be in a turmoil. We'd known each other since we were 14 years old so we were together a long, long time."

Rosenthal and Dawson (1991) studied sixty-nine wives of institutionalized men. They found that women went through a transition to "quasi-widowhood." During the first days following institutionalization, these women said they felt relief from the stress of caregiving at home. But they also displayed poor health, low morale, and depression. These women reported feeling guilty, sad, and lonely.

Most women over time adapt to living with a spouse in an institution (Loos & Bowd, 1997). Some women accept the loss of their spouses as a friend and companion and restructure their lives outside the institution. Other spouses keep close ties to the institution. Ross, Rosenthal, and Dawson (1997a; 1997b) found that more than 80 percent of the wives in their study visited their husbands at least several times a week. About 20 percent visited every day. But the researchers found that active visitors felt more depressed at the end of nine months and felt dissatisfied with the care their husbands got.

This study suggests that wives who begin to give up the caregiver role do better after their husbands are institutionalized. The researchers found that about two-thirds of spouses gave up some of their caregiving responsibility. These wives had cognitively impaired spouses. They visited less and allowed staff to take on the job of caring. This group felt less depressed and said they felt "sort of like a widow" (Ross, Rosenthal, & Dawson 1994, p. 29). Healing began to take place as wives gained distance from the caregiver role.

Children and Other Relatives

Spousal care declines with a person's age, but care from a child and other relatives increases with age. About 2.7 million adult children provide personal care to disabled older people (Cantor, 1992). Even among younger cohorts (aged 65 to 74) who need care, children and other relatives (often siblings and nieces) make up as much as two-fifths of caregivers for men. Most adult children give secondary care; they serve as a backup and give respite to spousal caregivers. Children also serve as financial managers and provide links to formal services.

Dupuis and Smale (2004) report that even older people who reside in long-term care institutions get informal help from their children. Children who help care for a parent in an institution say they feel strong attachment to a parent and they recognize past help and support (Keefe & Fancey, 2000). Other studies report that daughters, compared with sons, provide more care to parents. Daughters (compared with sons) also report greater feelings of stress (Penning, 1998). Daughters-in-law often provide care to their husband's parents. They may feel responsible to give care even if they don't feel affection for the parent (Guberman, 1999). Walker (1996) traces this fact to cultural pressures on women to give care. One woman put this simply: "Who else is going to do it?" (Walker, 1996).

Keefe and Fancey (2002) found another reason daughters give care to their mothers: They felt obliged to return their mothers' earlier care. The researchers found that daughters recalled the past when their mothers provided help and support to them. This motivated them to give care in the present.

Studies of older care receivers finds that they tend to downplay the amount of care they get from their children. They often report that they receive less support from their children than they give. Bengtson and Kuypers (1971) explained this odd finding some years ago by reference to what they call "developmental stake." This theory says that, compared with their children, older people feel a greater stake in having good parent–child relations. This leads older parents to emphasize family harmony and solidarity. They may deemphasize the support their children give them in order not to see themselves as a burden.

This difference in perception can create family tensions. Adult children can feel that their parents do not appreciate what they do for them, even though the children do as much as they can.

Relatives other than children also offer routine support and support in emergencies. Consider the following case. Bea Whitlea, a 75-year-old widow, stood next to her shopping cart waiting for the bus to take her back to her housing complex. She leaned forward to rest on the cart for support, but the cart scooted out from under her. Bea fell and caught herself on her outstretched hand. The weight of the fall caused her wrist to snap and caused a bruise on her knee. She fell forward onto her face and damaged her teeth.

An ambulance rushed her to the hospital, where they put a cast on her wrist and gave her first aid for cuts on her face. She would have to see her dentist about her teeth. Bea could have returned to her apartment later that day, but the shock of the injuries, the pain, and the cast on her wrist made it hard for her to stay by herself. Bea called her brother, who came over immediately. They arranged for her to move in with her younger sister in a nearby town for two weeks until she felt better. Bea's daughter arranged for doctors' appointments and helped set her up in her apartment again.

Bea relies on a network of kin that includes her children and her siblings. Because her children live several hours away and have their own demanding schedules, she often relies on her brother and sister when she needs help. Her brother takes her shopping for special items like clothes or furniture. Her sister has her over for holidays and family dinners.

Older people who have at least one remaining brother or sister report frequent interaction with their siblings. Siblings more often socialize with each other than provide health care support. Their closeness rests, in part, on their shared experience of aging. Older sisters, for example, may both have experienced widowhood. They often form close friendship bonds and provide emotional support to one another. Avioli (1989) says that 74 percent of older adults think of at least one of their siblings as a close friend.

Supports for Childless Older People

Some older people have never married. Others, who married, had no children. These people adapt to aging without the support of adult children. They create a network of supportive family and friends. Those who have chosen to remain childless report high life satisfaction and happiness (Connidis & McMullin, 1999). They have about the same satisfaction with life as married older people who have close relations with their children and higher satisfaction than parents with distant ties to children. McMullin and Marshall (1996, p. 356) report that "compared to parents, childless individuals experience less life stress and similar levels of well-being." Connidis and McMullin (1999) also find that childless older adults report financial benefits, greater freedom, and career flexibility.

Still, the social networks of older childless people offer less support when the older person becomes sick (Rubinstein, 1996). Childless older people who report disadvantages point to a lack of companionship, missed experiences and incompleteness. They also report a lack of care in old age (Connidis & McMullin, 1999). This group tends to be disadvantaged in other ways as well. They tend to be unmarried, older, female, less financially secure, in poorer health, and living alone. Widows in particular feel less advantage if childless. Because childless older people may lack informal support, they may need more formal supports than do older parents. They also face a greater risk of institutionalization than do people with children (Giranda, Luk, & Atchison, 1999).

Friends and Neighbors

Older people without families often rely on friends and neighbors for support. Lilly, Richards, and Buckwalter (2003) found that friends provided emotional support and social integration. Barker and Mitteness (1990) found that women more often than men took on the role of nonkin caregiver. They found that neighbors made up the largest category of nonkin caregivers. Caro and Blank (1988) found

These friends attend an inner-city nutrition site in San Francisco for lunch each day. At the site they meet people, enjoy sociability, and share an understanding based on their life experience.

that nearly three-quarters (72 percent) of nonkin caregivers live with the older person or in the same building.

O'Bryant (1991b) says that dependence on friends and neighbors prevents isolation and loneliness. Studies report that friends or neighbors make up from 5 to 24 percent of caregivers. This fits the estimate of most national studies. By this estimate, about 140,000 frail older people have nonkin caregivers.

Studies show that friends' social and emotional support improves the well-being of older people (O'Connor, 1995). This especially applies to older people who have no spouse or whose children live far away. Friends do more than provide services to older people. Researchers say that friendships can help older people overcome problems caused by lost work roles and the lost spouse role in old age (Field, 1999). Older people use friends for social and emotional support (Lilly, Richards, & Buckwalter, 2003).

This suggests that different people in the older person's social network play different support roles. A spouse or child will help with household chores. But friends serve as social partners. They help each other cope with life difficulties and stressful events. Friends who are the same age often share the same physical limits, the same interests, and the same historical background. Lifelong friends also share experiences and memories. Research shows the importance of close and supportive friendships in the lives of older adults (Adams & Blieszner, 1995). A variety of relationships, including friendships, create a full and satisfying support network.

Siblings as a Source of Informal Support

Most older people have at least one living brother or sister. Siblings can serve as an important source of social support for older people. The support provided by a sibling will vary by individual need. For example, a married older person with many children nearby may make little use of sibling support. Single people and women make the most use of sibling supports (Barrett & Lynch, 1999). Childless older people, compared with people with children, set up more supportive ties with their siblings They tend to get more support from siblings when they get ill. Childless siblings also tend to give support to their brothers and sisters (Barrett & Lynch, 1999). Rubinstein (1996) reports that childless women often build relationships with siblings' children or the children of nonrelatives.

In general, older women tend to have more active sibling ties than older men, with ties between sisters stronger than ties between brothers or a brother and sister (Connidis, 2001). Geographic proximity influences some types of support but not others. For example, while companionship requires in-person contact, people can confide in one another and give emotional support even over a distance. Siblings more often provide emotional support than practical support, even for those who live close by (Miner & Uhlenberg, 1997).

Minority Differences in Social Support

Some research suggests that minority groups offer strong support to their older members. Dilworth-Anderson (1992) describes the African American family as a mutual aid system that expresses many of the traditional values of the African American community. For example, African American families absorb needy members and give them help to survive in harsh economic times.

The National Long Term Care Demonstration Project found that African American families give their older members medical care supports (White-Means, 1993). Older African Americans also rely on the church for support. Church membership gives older African Americans a group of friends and confidants in addition to their families. Krause (2002) reports that older African Americans who actively take part in church activities report more spiritual and emotional support from their fellow parishioners.

Gibson and Jackson (1992) say that the oldest old (aged 85 and over) made the most use of *both* family and church supports. Walls (1992) reports that African American elders rely on the family for emotional support and the church for instrumental support. People with strong family and church networks felt a sense of well-being.

Kivett (1993) found that African American grandmothers, compared with white grandmothers, give and receive more support from their grandchildren. African American grandmothers sometimes play the role of surrogate parents for grandchildren. Older African Americans also provide needy adult children with shelter, food, and money.

Hispanic families show a strong interdependence of older and younger members. Sotomayor and Randolph (1988) report that Hispanic families (in most Hispanic subgroups) value mutual support between the generations. They report that the family still plays an important role in supporting older people.

Sotomayor and Randolph (1988) studied family support for Puerto Rican and Mexican American elders. They found that Hispanic families engage in mutual support "when ill, making important decisions, and handling financial problems" (Sotomayor & Randolph, 1988, p. 155). They say that older members, when ill, get more help from their families than the family expects the older person to give. Older Hispanics rely on their children for help with shopping, transportation, and home maintenance.

Most older Hispanics in this study (about 70 percent) say that their children both love and respect them. They say they know this because their children visit them and check on their needs. On the other hand, older people say they give more advice than they get. They also take unemployed children into their homes, babysit for grandchildren, and give religious instruction to young family members (Sotomayor & Randolph, 1988). Sotomayor and Randolph (1988, p. 143) say that for these elders "the extended family is a vital social support system that includes a special role for the elderly family members."

Cultural values, love, and respect in part explain the supports that younger Hispanic family members give to their elders. But Sotomayor and Randolph (1988) say that poverty and a lack of suitable social services sometimes force Hispanic elders to rely on their families. Bastida (1988) studied Puerto Rican elders and found that none of them considered formal services as a major source of support.

Past work has idealized the informal supports available to minority older people. Lockery (1991) says that under current conditions these beliefs create a simplistic view of minority aging. Some families do give support. But other families lack the resources to give support, and this may even create more stress for older family members. Lockery (1991) says that diversity within minority groups leads to different amounts and types of support to older members. Also, changing social and economic conditions create new challenges for minority families.

Longer life expectancies, poverty, and declining health in later life will place a greater burden on African American and Hispanic families in the years ahead. This feeling of strain within minority families may already have begun. Eggebeen (1992), for instance, reports that Mexican Americans showed no greater exchange between the generations than whites. And African Americans showed lower levels of intergenerational help than either Mexican Americans or whites.

Eggebeen (1992) says that demands on minority families have increased at the same time that resources have shrunk. "Perhaps," he says, "these data point to how much has changed among black families in the past decade more than they correct erroneous characterizations drawn from past ethnographic work" (Eggebeen, 1992, p. 49).

Lockery (1991, p. 61) says that future studies of minority supports need to focus on the needs of each minority group. Future policies must take care "not to perpetuate the myth that racial and ethnic minorities take care of their own. Not only may their elderly need more caregiving services, they may also lack the primary support systems that many assume are there."

Caregiving

Male and Female Caregivers

Harris (2002) reports that sons make up 10 to 12 percent of primary caregivers to elderly parents. They make up as much as 52 percent of secondary caregivers. Husbands make up about 13 percent of all caregivers. But we know less about these male caregivers than about women who give care. Research on husbands shows that men look at caregiving differently than do women. Socialization teaches women to form empathic relations and to respond to the needs of others (Hooyman, 1990). Women then have more trouble setting limits on others' and their own expectations.

Barker and Mitteness (1990) found that male caregivers set limits on their caregiving activities. They tend to avoid tasks that involve intimacy (like skin care or changing a person's diapers). They more often tend to offer help with transportation, money, or the management of services (Barker & Mitteness, 1990).

Many studies report that, compared with wives who give care, husband caregivers feel less distress and depression. But qualitative research and a quantitative study by Kramer and Lambert (1999) describe a more complex picture of husbands as caregivers. They find that they feel a sense of pride and accomplishment as caregivers. But husbands also report "a decline in happiness, an increase in depression, and a decline in emotional support and marital satisfaction" (Harris, 2002, p. 214). These findings present a more realistic picture of the ups and downs that come with caregiving.

Caregiver sons report the least distress (Biegel, Sales, & Schulz, 1991). Studies found that sons get involved in care primarily in the absence of a female caregiver. Sons, compared with daughters, get less involved in their parents' emotional needs and less often get involved in routine household work. They seem better at setting limits on how much help they give. They also feel less guilty about setting these limits. Male caregivers rely more on formal help for their care receivers. Studies of caregiving husbands and sons show that gender roles influence caregiving activities. Men favor a more administrative, managerial role. Women more often give emotional support and personal care.

Caregiver Burden

Many studies report that giving care to a physically disabled or cognitively impaired older person leads to **caregiver burden**. This refers to problems and stress due to caregiving. Longer life expectancy now and in the future will lead to more older people needing support for more years. This will place an increased demand on more family caregivers. It may lead to more cases where caregivers feel burdened.

Schulz and Martire (2004) found that older people with many chronic conditions can stretch the limits of caregivers' energy, health, and emotions. Caregivers often feel emotional and mental strain. This can lead to depression, anxiety, and emotional exhaustion. Caregiving often restricts the caregiver's social contacts outside the home. It can lead caregivers to feel trapped and at a dead end in life. The greater the impairment of the caregiver, the greater the feeling of depression (Biegel, Sales, & Schulz, 1991).

Family caregivers report that they feel a loss of control and autonomy. One caregiver says, "I feel like, like now, I'm all on tenterhooks. I feel like I'm on a treadmill, all the time, all the time, and I can't get off this thing" (cited in O'Connor, 1999, p. 226). Family caregivers also report stress due to tasks like cleaning, doing laundry, and shopping. Still, O'Connor reports that many spouse caregivers refuse to use outside help. They feel an obligation to their spouses and they feel that they can give the best care.

Caring for someone with Alzheimer's disease (and other cognitive impairments) can put the greatest strain on an informal caregiver. Caregivers feel the physical strain of caregiving, but also the emotional strain of seeing someone they love deteriorate. Writers have described caregiving for an Alzheimer's patient as a "36-hour day" (Mace & Rabins, 1981). A person with Alzheimer's disease may wander the house all night or wander outside. One caregiver reports that one night her husband filled the toilet with oranges. She had to call a plumber to unclog the bowl. Another time he got out of the house at night with the car keys. He drove for one hundred miles before the car ran out of gas and someone found him wandering near a farmhouse.

This woman, like many caregivers of cognitively impaired spouses, lives in constant anxiety. She suffers from a lack of sleep and physical exhaustion. This has led to a decline in her health. Her doctor has advised her that she may need medical help unless she gets some respite from her caregiving chores.

Caregiving also leads to conflicting demands on the caregiver. Abel (1990) found, for example, that some caregiving daughters had to quit their jobs, give up promotions, or take time off from work to give care. Daughters also gave up vacations and leisure activities.

A daughter in one caregiver study said, "I wouldn't want to put my kids through what I am going through" (Lund, 1993a, p. 60). Another caregiver said that a person who had "to work a full day, raise a family, and take care of an impaired relative would be susceptible to suicide, parent-abuse and possibly murder." A daughter-in-law in this study said, "I hope I die before I have her kind of problems" (Lund, 1993a, p. 60).

Men and women differ in their responses to the demands of caregiving. Like women, men who take on the caregiving role feel stress and burden. Husbands may need care themselves. And sons may juggle multiple responsibilities (husband and worker as well as caregiver) in order to provide care. But sons typically take on tasks related to the male role. They will help with yard work, financial management, and home maintenance. They tend to avoid domestic work and personal care that female caregivers often take on.

Campbell and Martin-Matthews (2003) say that men with higher incomes pay for personal care services and hire people to do domestic chores. Men say they feel good about caregiving and that caregiving gives them "a chance to pay their parents back for their care, a sense of purpose and personal growth, and the importance of being a role model for their children" (Harris, 1998, p. 347).

Research shows that wives, daughters, and other female relatives give most of the informal support to older family members. Women do the domestic chores and provide the personal care that a parent or spouse may need. Myles (1991) called the trend toward more women working outside the home and having less time available to provide care to older parents a "caregiving crunch." Working women feel the "crunch" because society expects women to serve as caregivers. These women experience more stress and greater absenteeism from work (Martin-Matthews & Campbell, 1995). Researchers say that caregivers need to work out family strategies to cope with stress. They also need job flexibility and community supports to help them stay at work.

The Rewards of Caregiving

Caregiver research has focused on burden and the costs of caregiving, but some caregivers report feelings of satisfaction and achievement. Some people who feel committed to the caregiver role report a sense of well-being (Pierce, Lydon, & Yang, 2001). Cohen, Colantonio, and Vernich (2002) found that 73 percent of caregivers could identify at least one positive thing about caregiving. An additional 7 percent identified more than one positive thing. Caregivers enjoyed helping their care receiver feel better. They also felt duty and love toward their care receiver (Ross, Rosenthal, & Dawson, 1997a). These caregivers respond to the demands of caregiving "with a sense of challenge and . . . in fact, seem to thrive in the situation" (Chiriboga, Weiler, & Nielsen, 1990, p. 135).

Some people say that caregiving made them more caring and compassionate toward others. They say they learned patience and learned to value life more (Lund, 1993a). Sometimes these people carry heavy loads of caregiver demand, but they view caregiving as a calling, a responsibility, and an expression of their love for their care receiver. Heru, Ryan, and Iqbal (2004) found that caregivers of moderately impaired family members showed the least burden if they had a supportive family.

Research shows that caregivers who have positive feelings about caregiving have lower depression, less burden, and better self-reported health (Cohen, Colantonio, & Vernich, 2002). Lund (1993a) says that successful caregivers (1) provide good care, (2) want to give care, (3) protect their own well-being, and (4) develop new skills and abilities. The research on successful family caregiving shows that informal caregivers in general do better when they use formal care services (Chiriboga, Weiler, & Nielsen, 1990). A flexible system of services can support the work of informal caregivers and provide the care that the older person needs.

Care for the Caregiver

A number of researchers have proposed ways to ease caregiver burden. *Family counseling* can help ease the burden of caregiving. Counseling works best when it takes into account the entire family system—the caregiver's spouse, children, and siblings, as well as the older person. Counseling can help caregivers deal with moral conflicts about how much protection to give a care receiver. Counseling or psychotherapy can help a caregiver deal with stress and depression. Gendron and her colleagues (1996) report the value of skill training. They found that assertiveness training and cognitive restructuring (taking a more positive view of caregiving) led to decreased feelings of burden.

Support groups give caregivers information about how to cope with caregiving demands. They also give caregivers emotional support. The Alzheimer's Society, hospitals, and churches offer support groups. Some groups offer support based on a specific disease (e.g., dementia or cancer). Some of these groups have a professional leader; others work as self-help groups. People in support groups often report feelings of relief and greater ability to manage as caregivers (Gallagher & Hagen 1996; Hagen, Gallagher, & Simpson 1997).

Respite services in the community give caregivers a break from the demands of caregiving (Chappell, 1997). These services range from friendly visitors who stay with the care receiver for a few hours to full-day adult daycare, to longer institutional respite. Institutional respite programs can last from several days to several weeks, allowing caregivers to take vacations, deal with personal needs such as medical treatment, or simply rest.

Eldercare programs at work can help family caregivers cope. These programs include counseling services, information on community services and supports, and flexible work schedules.

Good programs and other interventions cannot completely do away with all feelings of burden, nor should we expect them to. Spouses and children feel loss, anger, and frustration as they see a person close to them suffer through an illness. These feelings reflect a legitimate response to a parent's or spouse's suffering. But interventions can help caregivers understand caregiving; they can help caregivers cope with the everyday demands of care; and they can give caregivers social and emotional support.

The Future of Informal Support

Brody (1995a, p. 17) says that "the needs of the old for care have far exceeded the capacity of the family to fulfill." Cantor (1992) describes changes in family structure that will make this even more true in the future. First, families now have more generations alive than ever before. "By the year 2020," Cantor (1992, p. 67) says, "the typical family will consist of at least four generations." Families have a vertical or **bean-pole family structure** (Bengtson, Rosenthal, & Burton, 1990). Each generation will have fewer members and fewer potential supporters from within their own generation. Family members will have to support one another across generational lines.

Second, kin networks are becoming top-heavy. An average married couple today and in the future

BOX 13.2
KEEPING MOTHER GOING

Researcher Elaine Brody (1981) coined the term *woman in the middle* to describe the strains felt by middle-aged women who care for children, a spouse, and an elderly parent. Mary Anne Montgomery describes the pressures she faced caring for three generations.

For Mother the fracture was catastrophic. I was appalled that a "minimal fracture" behind the knee could have such a devastating effect on the entire mind and body. Mother seemed like a balloon that had been pricked and lost all its air. She lay, sometimes pale and listless, other times in pain, with periods of confusion, disorientation, and memory loss. I often found myself visiting an eighty-year-old, helpless, sad, whiney child who barely resembled the mother I knew. The brief episodes when she looked at me strangely and didn't recognize me were eerie and frightening. . . .

For me those weeks were full of new experiences, responsibilities, uncertainties, decisions to be made, and always, pressures. The trip to the hospital twice a day left little time or energy for household matters. As one who owned four different books on organizing and using one's time wisely, I couldn't find time to read them; I was swamped with work to be done. The house was a mess. Our beloved twelve-year-old basset hound suddenly developed incontinence problems, creating additional chores. I longed for just one full day at home alone to work and gather my thoughts in peace. Yet I seemed always to be driving—to see Mother, or to do errands for her or for my family of five. The children frequently needed to be chauffeured here and there or to be watched in this school program or that game. With the Christmas shopping season upon us, there were family gifts to be purchased. Mother began to have shopping requests for me, too. The physical demands on my time plus the emotional strains of dealing with an unpredictable and different mother reduced me almost to a state of shock. I was mentally and physically numbed.

Numbness was no help in trying to figure out the complexities of Medicare, doctor, and hospital bills or in making plans for Mother's extended care when I didn't know where to turn for guidance. Her own files and health insurance records were a jumble. The policies seemed to be lost. Household and medical bills arrived at her apartment daily, and I found her checkbook stubs a mystery of incompleteness. Having so many tasks and responsibilities dumped on me all at once was terribly difficult. Not even my husband, Mike, truly understood the enormity of the pressures I felt. (He was busy trying to cope with the children, the meals, and the household work I had neglected.) From way back in my childhood came to mind the cry for rescue: "Mother! Please help me!" But of course it was *my* turn to help Mother.

Source: From "Keeping Mother Going," by M. A. Montgomery, 1988, in J. Norris (Ed.). *Daughters of the elderly: Building partnerships in caregiving,* pp. 51–64. Bloomington: Indiana University Press. Reprinted with permission.

will have more parents than children. Middle-aged women will spend more years with parents over 65 than with children under age 18.

Third, some members of the oldest generation in a family will be age 85 and over. These people will need a lot of support. Many of them will be widowed, and some of their children will need care themselves. Cantor (1992) predicts that caregiving will move to later ages as more older people stay well until late old age. Add to these changes the increased number of middle-aged women, traditional family caregivers, who work in the labor force. Many of these women will in the future stay in the labor force past age 65. They will not have the time or energy to serve as caregivers to older relatives.

Brody (1995) says that caregiving demands today peak in later middle age. More than one-quarter (28 percent) of women in one study reported quitting work to care for an older relative. Another quarter thought about quitting (Brody, 1995). More women in the future may decide to stay at work and hire help rather than care for a parent.

All of these changes will increase the need for supports to older people. They will also reduce the amount of informal support available. In the future, informal supporters will rely on formal supports to help them care for older family members. These formal programs need to offer flexible services—like adult daycare, night care, respite care, and support groups—to meet the needs of individual families.

Policymakers often speak of partnerships between state programs and informal supports. But a number of researchers ask whether this new focus on the family will provide better care or simply shift the burden of care to families (Keating et al., 1999). Harlton and her colleagues (1998) found that older people and policymakers differed in their view of care to older people. Policymakers thought that family and neighborhood (informal) supports gave older people more control over their lives. But older people felt that family support made them more dependent and a burden on their families. They did not feel that family members should provide housing, financial support, or personal care (Kemp & Denton, 2003). They preferred state-funded supports, believing that these supports gave them the most control over the services they received.

A decade ago, Rosenthal (1994, p. 421) said that formal support should play the central part in social support. Families (middle-aged women) could then decide how much or how little of this support they need. "We should not overestimate the availability or quality of family care," Rosenthal said. "Some older people do not have family members who are able to provide care." Others may have family members who do not have the time or energy to give more than emotional support. Still others may prefer professional help to family care. Policymakers need to learn more about the views of older clients and their families to create programs that meet older people's needs. Kunemund and Rein (1999) find that generous state-funded social and health care supports strengthen rather than weaken family solidarity.

Eldercare and the Workplace

More women work outside the home today than ever before. Many of them care for a dependent parent or spouse. Some also care for young children. Wagner (1991, p. 378) defines eldercare as "a process of caring for an older person in order that he or she may remain as independent as possible for as long as possible." Eldercare can range from calling a parent once a week to providing personal care like bathing or feeding. Eldercare can create stress for a middle-aged person who also has a family and a job.

The AARP (Dinger, 2003b) surveyed 639 companies in Ohio to learn about eldercare issues faced by workers. The companies reported that 55 percent of their employees provided care to an older person. And 55 percent of the companies said that caregiving had an effect on worker performance. Almost 40 percent of workers had asked for time off to give eldercare.

In an earlier national study, Stone and colleagues (1987) found that 21 percent of caregivers with jobs worked fewer hours in order to devote time to caregiving. Nineteen percent took time off without pay, and 29 percent rearranged their work schedules to give time to caregiving. Nine percent of caregivers (almost 200,000 people) said they quit their jobs to take on the caregiver role. Eldercare can lead to absences, lateness, and decreased productivity (Helfrich & Dodson, 1992).

Studies estimates that between 10 and 31 percent of caregiver workers leave their jobs because of caregiving demands. Some people retire early. Others quit their jobs (Wagner, 2003, citing National Alliance for Caregiving & AARP, 1997; Statewide Resources Consultant, 2002).

Gottlieb and Kelloway (1995, p. 339) also found that people who give eldercare cut back on "leisure,

BOX 13.3

ELDERCARE AND WORK: A BALANCING ACT

A Case Study

Ron, a 35-year-old editor for a large publishing firm, provides care for his mother who has Alzheimer's disease. During the day, Ron's mother, Alice, attends an adult day program 3 days a week and has a paid caregiver who comes to the apartment two days a week. Ron and his mother live in Manhattan in a small rent-controlled apartment that has been their home since Ron was a child. Once the disease was diagnosed and it became clear that living alone was a dangerous proposition for Alice, Ron moved back into his childhood home to manage the everyday needs of his mother.

For the past three years, Ron has come home from work in time to pick up his mother at the day program or relieve the paid caregiver, and he spends his evenings on domestic chores and caregiving tasks. Lately Ron has taken to sleeping in the same room as his mother because of her sleep problems and fear that she might injure herself when she gets up in the night. Ron's cousin, who helps on the weekend, has encouraged Ron to begin to look for care facilities for his mother. While he realizes that moving Alice to a facility is inevitable, Ron has delayed making a decision based upon frequent conversations he had with his mother over the years about her fear of moving to a care facility in old age. Like many other caregivers of persons with cognitive impairment, Ron is distressed by the changes he observes in his mother and feels guilty and conflicted about providing care for his mother and managing the beginning of his career as an editor.

Ron has curtailed all of his work-related travel and often has to leave work early or come in late in order to take his mother to doctor's appointments. Lately, on the days after his mother has had a difficult night he has also noticed that he is making small mistakes at work because of his fatigue. He hasn't spoken to his supervisor or co-workers about his mother or his caregiving situation. After hearing them speak about a woman on their team who is also caring for her mother, he was concerned that he might be viewed as lacking the proper attitude and commitment for work if he brought his family life into the office. He did, however, use the 800 number available to employees for advice on eldercare because it was confidential and he didn't have to give his name. The phone call resulted in a list of adult day programs and phone numbers that eventually led to the services his mother is now using. Ron feels increasingly isolated in his work and in his caregiving tasks—and all too aware of the fact that relief will only come when it becomes necessary for him to break a promise he made to his mother many years ago.

Many workers face the challenge of balancing work and care for an older relative. Wagner, the author of the case study above, published by Family Caregiver Alliance, estimates that as many as 15 percent of workers care for chronically ill relatives. The number of people who face this challenge will increase in the years ahead as more women in the workforce, the U.S. has more older people in the population, and families have fewer adult children to care for aging parents. What are some of the ways that businesses can help workers cope with the dual demands of eldercare and work?

Source: From Wagner, D. L. (2003). Workplace Programs for Family Caregivers: Good Business and Good Practice. Retrieved November 25, 2004, *www.caregiver.org/caregiver/jsp/content/pdfs/op_2003_workplace_programs.pdf.* Reprinted with permission. Family Caregiver Alliance/National Center on Caregiving.

continuing education, and volunteer activities." The researchers found that caregivers who gave personal care, such as nursing care, and dual caregivers (who care for children and an older person) showed the greatest tendency to cut back on personal activities. Gottlieb and Kelloway (1995, p. 339) say that "paradoxically, it appears that, in their efforts to balance family demands and job responsibilities, employees are cutting back on those activities that afford relaxation, rejuvenation, and personal or career development."

The AARP (Dinger, 2003b) study in Ohio found that 57 percent of the companies offered funeral and bereavement leave, about one-third offered flexible work schedules, and one-third offered job security. Peterson (1993) says that as many as 10 percent of Fortune 500 companies offer help to caregivers. Still, nearly one-third of the Ohio companies (29 percent) offered no support to workers who provided eldercare. (A similar study in Delaware [Dinger, 2003a] found that 22 percent of companies offered no support to employee–caregivers).

Companies that offer eldercare services say that the programs improve morale and productivity (Gottlieb & Kelloway, 1995). Services include counseling referrals, support groups, and adult daycare (Helfrich & Dodson, 1992). The Travelers insurance company holds on-site support groups for workers who give eldercare (Wagner, 1991). Other companies offer Employee Assistance Programs where a worker can get help from a professional counselor outside the company.

Gottlieb and Kelloway (1995) say that even simple, low-cost options such as flex time, seminars on eldercare, and more information about services help. They lower stress and lead to more job satisfaction. Wagner (2003) says that the most progressive companies offer a "decision-support model." This model offers employees access to a care manager. The manager helps employees with care planning and with insurance and legal issues. The employer may hire a care manager or retain a company to supply this service.

More companies might offer these programs if they knew of the benefits to their workers. But Wilson and her colleagues (1993) say that, due to cost-cutting, companies show little interest in developing new eldercare programs. The researchers propose that caregivers locate and make the best use they can of existing programs and community services.

Older People as Family Supporters

Most of the writing on older people in families focuses on their needs and on what other people do for them. But older people also give help to their families (Keefe & Fancey, 2002). Very early work by Shanas (1967) found that "far from being the passive recipients of their adult children's bounty, reciprocal help is given in the form of home services, monetary assistance, assistance in time of illness and other crisis situations and, in addition, older parents often provide childcare services."

Researchers find that over a lifetime, parents give more support than they receive. Further, older people provide support to their children throughout their later years. McNaught (1994) reports that one older household in five provides a large proportion of income to their children's or grandchildren's household. Stone and his colleagues (1998, p. 24) say, "If we had included the monetary value of services provided informally by one generation to another we would increase markedly the relative size of the figure for flows that benefit the young."

Support from older parents to their children includes more than money. They often help their children with health care and daily chores. This can include help with housework or yard work. Also, older people help with personal care. Some older parents provide daily and lifelong care to children with disabilities (Joffres, 2002). Many older parents also share their homes with adult children. These are children who delay leaving home or who return home in adulthood. Adult children who live with older parents often do so because they have no spouse, attend school, or have no job.

McNaught (1994) says that younger families also benefit from the care that grandparents give to grandchildren. He reports that 44 percent of people aged 55 and over say they still care for children. Many older people look after grandchildren while their middle-aged children work. Some grandparents care for grandchildren in what gerontologists call "skipped generation" households (without the child's parents present) (Thomson, Minkler, & Driver, 2000).

Grandparents take on other productive roles in their families. They link family members, buffer the stress of divorce, and even act as surrogate parents. Research shows that adult children rely on their parents as role models throughout their lives. Many adult children turn to their parents for emotional support and help during and after a divorce (Hamon, 1995). Parents can also act as role models for their adult children as they experience important later life transitions such as grandparenthood, widowhood, and retirement. Older family members derive great satisfaction from the help they give to their children and to other younger family members.

Older people in families often play the role of *kinkeeper*. Kinkeepers keep in touch with family members and form a hub of family communication. In our family, my mother played the role of kinkeeper. She kept in touch with her brothers and sisters weekly. She heard from my aunts and uncles on my father's side of the family a few times a year. She attended weddings and birthdays. Cousins, who live throughout the United States, called once or twice a year to keep my mother up to date on their lives. When I called, my mother would relay the latest news of family members' relationships, careers, and health. When I came to visit, my mother would arrange a dinner and invite our extended family. These people rarely saw one another except on these occasions.

A woman usually takes on the role of kinkeeper. Often a kinkeeper's daughter will take her place when the kinkeeper dies. Troll and Bengtson (1992) say that a younger woman may serve as an assistant kinkeeper when the kinkeeper gets feeble. Sometimes more than one person takes on this role and they become co-kinkeepers.

Troll and Bengtson (1992, p. 43) say that even the oldest old have a role to play in their families. Very old family members may withdraw from active roles like kinkeeping. They then serve to strengthen family solidarity. They give to their families "the memory of what they did for them and the model of how the next generation can carry on the pattern. . . . Their contribution to the young is perhaps also more symbolic than instrumental."

Family roles can give meaning and purpose to an older person's life. Research finds that older people have the highest emotional well-being when they give as well as receive support. Reciprocity makes older people feel useful, independent, and worthwhile. Research shows that giving support to others—family, friends, and neighbors—even leads to longer life (Brown, Nesse, Vinokur, & Smith, 2003).

These findings overall show that most older people live interdependently with family, neighbors, and friends. They give and receive help with practical activities, finances, and advice throughout their lives. Older people's supportive roles can strengthen intergenerational ties and create more fulfilling relationships between parents and their children, as well as their grandchildren.

Grandparenting

Crispell (1993) reports that one person in ten between ages 30 and 44 has a grandchild. This figure jumps to 50 percent of people aged 45 to 59, and 83 percent of people aged 60 and over. The number of grandparents will increase by 15 percent by the year 2000. Nearly one-half of these grandparents will come from the Baby Boom generation.

Grandparents now play complex roles in the lives of their grandchildren (Kemp, 2003). Some grandparents feel that they do enough by simply being present; but others play a more active role as family arbitrators, watchdogs, or family historians. Grandparents often look out for the well-being of younger relatives, help them when they can, and create links between family members. The grandparent role offers older people one of the most satisfying and enjoyable ways to give to other family members.

Some grandparents involve themselves in the daily lives and care of their grandchildren. Cherlin and Furstenberg (1985), in a study of 510 grandparents in the United States, found five styles of grandparenting: detached, passive, supportive, authoritative, and influential. Older grandparents tend to use the detached or passive styles. They tend to see their grandchildren less than other types of grandparents, and they tend to live far away from their grandchildren. Influential grandparents live closer and see their grandchildren more than other types.

One grandfather said that if his grandson has a problem, "he'll come over to see me. . . . And if I need some help, like getting some screens down . . . for the summer, I'll get him to help me" (Cherlin & Furstenberg, 1985, p. 108). These findings suggest that grandparents' influence on and involvement with grandchildren decrease with age. Some grandparents use *selective investment* to focus on their closer and more compatible grandchildren.

A grandmother and granddaughter from Maine share a quiet moment in the garden. Grandparents give grandchildren extra attention that enriches both their lives. They also link grandchildren to traditions and family values.

Sanders and Trygstad (1993) studied the attitudes of college students toward their grandparents. They found that only about one-quarter of the students saw their grandparents monthly or more. But the students considered their relationships with their grandparents important. They saw this relationship as a sign of family strength.

In another study, college students said they saw their grandparents (or significant elders) as parent surrogates, buddies, storytellers, and confidants (Franks, Hughes, Phelps, & Williams, 1993).

A young man says about his grandmother that "it is great to be able to go round and complain about home or about dad being ridiculous or whatever. She will always be lovely and agree how stupid he is" Jerrome (1996, p. 91). Many of them said that a grandparent babysat for them or cared for them in their youth. Most of these students said their grandparents had a strong influence on their values, goals, and choices in life. The students also felt that their grandparents created a link between the generations in their families. This gave students a sense of their history and roots.

Studies show that children's feelings about their grandparents also depend on the relationship between the grandparents and the parents. Holladay and colleagues (1997), for example, found that parental attitudes influenced teenaged granddaughters' feelings of closeness to their grandmothers. An absence of criticism of the grandmother by the parent, and parents' comments on the importance of the grandmother led to greater feelings of closeness. Older grandchildren have closer ties with their grandparents if they see the relationship between their parents and grandparents as close (King & Elder, 1995).

Hagestad (1985) reported that grandmothers more often than grandfathers changed their own views on social issues, dress, and education due to their grandchildren's opinions on them. Hagestad (1985, p. 41) called this "reversed socialization." Hagestad's early work, and other research that has followed, shows that grandchildren and grandparents have an influence on one another's lives (Kemp, 2004).

In general, research shows that while the bond between adult grandchildren and their grandparents remains high across the life course, the relationship involves continuity and change over time. Mills (1999) finds that as grandchildren age, they grow closer to grandmothers but less close to grandfathers.

Other research suggests that a gradual decline takes place in the relationship over time, with some increased closeness in the grandparents' later years (Silverstein & Long, 1998). Hodgson (1995) finds that grandchildren feel a continued closeness to grandparents over time, with some grandchildren reporting an increased appreciation for their grandparents as they themselves age. The literature shows that the grandparent role allows room for personal expression and that older people can use it as a source of emotional satisfaction.

Gender can also influence the quality of the grandparent–grandchild relationships. For example, grandchildren tend to be closer to their maternal grandparents (Chan & Elder, 2000). Grandparents are closer to granddaughters than to grandsons. And grandmothers have closer and more active ties with both granddaughters and grandsons than do grandfathers (Silverstein & Long, 1998). What a grandparent makes of the grandparent role also depends on the older person's gender, age, marital status, and relationship with his or her adult children.

Research by Kemp (2004) looks at the expectations grandparents and grandchildren have of themselves and each other within what she terms these 'grand' roles. Kemp finds that while the roles and relationships are diverse, grandparents and grandchildren do have expectations related to behaviors and responsibilities within the relationship. For example, both grandparents and grandchildren feel that grandparents should provide love, support, encouragement, and assistance to grandchildren, but should not interfere in their lives unless asked for help or advice.

As one grandmother says, "I think being a grandparent is to listen and not to criticize" (Kemp, 2004, p. 11). A granddaughter says "grandparents are just supposed to be there when you need them and they always are . . . they don't give advice unless you ask for it" (Kemp, 2004, p. 15). Grandparents were also seen as role models, teachers, and sources of family history and lived experience.

Grandchildren felt they should be respectful to grandparents and to give them their time and attention. They felt an obligation to give back to grandparents for all the love and support grandparents had given to the family. This came in the form of spending time with grandparents and doing things to make grandparents proud of their accomplishments. Grandparents also hoped that their grandchildren would spend time with them and be an important part of their lives. However, for both grandchildren and grandparents, independence was important. Grandchildren sought to establish their own independence. And grandparents wanted to maintain their independence (Kemp, 2004).

Grandparenting and New Family Structures

High divorce rates among children lead to new relationships for older people. Johnson (1988, cited in Johnson, 1992) studied suburban families in northern California in which divorce had occurred. She studied the relationship between grandparents, their divorced children, and their grandchildren. The grandparents had a median age of 65. All of the grandparents lived near their grandchildren.

Johnson found that after a child's divorce, the older generation may stay in touch with their child's spouse and their grandchildren. If the child remarries, the older person gains new in-laws. Almost one-half (48 percent) of the people in Johnson's research on grandmothers report **expanded kinship networks** after a child's divorce (Johnson & Barer, 1987, cited in Johnson, 1992). "These relatives occupy positions along divorce and remarriage chains that are three generations deep, and new linkages, disconnections, and relinkages are continually being made" (Johnson, 1992, p. 19).

A grandmother, for example, may stay in touch with her former daughter-in-law after her son's divorce in order to keep in contact with her grandchildren. She may even develop a close personal friendship with her former daughter-in-law. If her former daughter-in-law remarries, she may meet and get to know a new family of grandparents and children from this new marriage. This will expand her kinship and social network.

Johnson (1992) says that older people often benefit from increases in family size due to divorce and remarriage of children and in-laws. Grandparents may include step-grandchildren in their list of grandchildren. Johnson (1992, p. 19) says that "some older people have busy lives managing a complex kinship system created by frequent marital changes of more than one child." These complexities increase as many children marry and divorce, sometimes more than once.

Grandparent remarriage due to divorce or widowhood only adds to the complexity of modern family life. These remarriages add more step and in-law relations to the family network. The modern flexible and elastic family system leads to enriched relationships for many older people. The modern family shows new complexities that researchers have only begun to study.

Grandparent Visitation Rights

Grandparents can have strong or weak relationships with their grandchildren. Grandparents set up relationships that fit their life-styles, interests, and compatibility with their grandchildren. Eggebeen and Hogan (1990, cited in Eggebeen, 1992) say that, in general, older people tend to give support to their grandchildren. Help ranges from childcare to household help. But parents mediate this relationship (Gladstone, 1989). Grandparents negotiate their relations with grandchildren through the child's parents, and parents may put boundaries on this relationship.

Gladstone (1987) studied 110 grandparents of families in which the parents had divorced or separated. He found that adult children can arrange or obstruct grandparents' visits. If the former son- or daughter-in-law had custody, contact with grandchildren depended on the grandparent's relationship to the former son- or daughter-in-law (Johnson, 1992). The issue of a grandparent's right to visit a grandchild has grown in importance with increases in the divorce rate.

More recent work by Hilton and Macari (1997) found that maternal grandparents stay more involved in the grandparent role than paternal grandparents when their daughter gains custody of her children. The reverse takes place when a son gains custody of his children. Kruk (1995) found that denial of access by a son- or daughter-in-law (often in the case of divorce) accounted for most cases of contact loss.

In the past, all fifty states (not including the District of Columbia) had some grandparent visitation statute. Advocacy groups helped set these in place. But the courts in many states have struck down these statutes (AARP, 2005b). In states where permissive visitation statues exist, a grandparent can petition the courts for visitation rights. The statutes state under what conditions a grandparent can petition and how the courts should decide on granting rights. But these statutes do not ensure that the court will grant this right. The court attempts to assess the child's best interest in deciding on visitation rights. Jackson (1994) says that clear legal guidelines do not exist on how to determine the child's best interests. States often allow petitions only in cases of divorce or death of a parent or if the child has lived with the grandparent for some time (Purnell & Bagby, 1993).

One case of a state court's action to strike down a visitation statute found its way to the U.S. Supreme Court. In 2000, the Supreme Court reviewed a grandparent visitation case in Washington State. A court in that state struck down a permissive grandparent visitation statute. The state court held that the statute was unconstitutional because it weakened parents' decision-making power with respect to their children. The Supreme Court overturned the lower court and upheld the statute. The Supreme Court did not think a permissive visitation statute was unconstitutional. Nor did it agree that the statute compromised parents' ability to make decisions for their children.

Fernandez (1988) says that state statutes make vague statements that do not help judges make decisions. She proposes a model statute that assumes the autonomy of the nuclear family. It allows access only when access maintains a relationship that benefits the child. Fernandez proposes that a "substantial" relationship must exist between the child and grandparent as the basis for visitation. Grandparent visitation risks constitutional infringement on the rights of parents to control access to a child. Burns (1991) says that future legal action will focus on visitation rights of grandparents whose grandchildren live in intact homes.

Grandparents who go to court risk increasing the tension with the son- or daughter-in-law. Kruk (1995) says that legislative support for grandparent rights would decrease the need for legal action. Today, grandparents have to show the courts why they should have access to their grandchildren. They also have to show that denying access would be harmful to grandchildren (Goldberg, 2003). Given the constitutional right of parents to control access to their children, it seems unlikely that grandparents will get any guaranteed visitation rights.

Advisors on this subject say that grandparents should maintain good relations with their son- or daughter-in-law in the case of a divorce. This provides the simplest means of access to grandchildren. The son- or daughter-in-law may fear that the grandparent will try to turn the child against the parent. A trusting relationship between the grandparent and the adult child can remove this fear. The AARP (2005b) says that a grandparent can use a trained mediator to improve a relationship between the grandparent and the grandchild's parent. This can sometimes resolve the issue without involving lawyers and the courts.

Grandparents as Surrogate Parents

The AARP (2005b) reports that almost 2.5 million grandparents aged 65 and over had the primary responsibility for their grandchildren who lived with them. Some inner-city schools report that between 30 and 70 percent of children live with their grandparents or other relatives (Gross, 1992, cited in Minkler & Roe, 1993). Thomson and her colleagues (2000) found that, compared with all grandparents, African American grandparents had twice the odds of caring for a grandchild.

Grandparents often wind up caring for their grandchildren because their own children cannot provide the care. This can occur because of divorce or separation, mental health difficulties, substance abuse, or the death of an adult child (Waldrop & Weber, 2001). Caring full-time for a grandchild can create a close emotional bond, particularly for grandmothers (Bowers & Myers, 1999). Caregiving grandparents most often reported the rewards of caregiving if they felt a strong family bond and obligation to give care (Giarrusso, Silverstein, & Feng, 2000).

Grandparents feel rewarded when they raise their grandchildren, but they also face challenges. These can include worries about their own health, problems with social isolation, and financial difficulties (Roe & Minkler, 1998; Sands & Goldberg-Glen, 2000). At a time when older people expect more freedom in their retirement years, these grandparents take on unanticipated childcare responsibilities. And often they do this with high-risk grandchildren (Minkler, 1999a).

Minkler & Roe (1993, p. 83) studied African American grandmothers of crack cocaine–addicted children in Oakland, California. The researchers found that these grandmothers faced financial strain. Eighty-seven percent of the grandparents reported "significant financial difficulty since assuming full-time caregiving." One woman said, "We were doing so well before—now it's a disaster!"

Johnson (1992) says that in the case of divorce, a child (often a daughter) may return to her parents' home with her own children. Almost 40 percent of divorced children showed a pattern of return to parents' support. Grandparents in these cases will find themselves actively supporting two generations. Johnson (1992) found that about 75 percent of parents of divorced children provided them with financial aid. Almost 60 percent of the children depended on their parents for their well-being. In these cases, the parents got involved in the day-to-day lives of their divorced children and grandchildren. Grandparents accepted the role, but often felt angry about this new responsibility.

Dilworth-Anderson (1992) asks whether families headed by single grandparents can survive increased stress in the future. Giarrusso and her colleagues (2000) found that social support buffered the stressful effects of caring for grandchildren. Minkler and Roe (1993) propose a number of supports that would help buffer stress. These include support groups, a *warm line* to give grandparents advice and emotional support, peer counseling, and respite services.

Giarrusso and her colleagues (2000, p. 88) end their report on grandparent caregiving by calling for a balanced view of the stresses and rewards of this role. "Attention to only the stressful and obligatory nature of grandparent caregiving," they say, "may mask the full social and psychological range of the experience and deny the underlying value and meaning that grandparents often attribute to this important societal role."

Elder Abuse

Until the late 1980s, few studies existed on elder abuse. Studies often used small convenience samples. Estimates on the amount of abuse ranged from 4 percent (Block & Sinott, 1979, cited in Pillemer & Finkelhor, 1988) to as low as 1.5 percent (Gioglio & Blakemore, 1983, cited in Pillemer & Finkelhor, 1988). Pillemer and Finkelhor (1988) conducted the first large random sample survey of elder abuse in the United States. The study took place in the Boston metropolitan area and included interviews with over 2,000 older people in the community. The study focused on physical abuse, psychological abuse, and neglect. The study found an elder abuse rate for all types of abuse of 32 per 1,000, a physical violence rate of 20 per 1,000, a verbal aggression rate of 11 per 1,000, and a neglect rate of 4 per 1,000.

In the late 1990s, Congress requested a study of elder abuse in the United States (National Center for Health Statistics, 2003). The government released the study in the fall of 1998, titled the "National Elder Abuse Incidence Study." The study estimated that in 1996 450,000 people aged 60 and over in domestic settings experienced abuse or neglect (a rate of about 10 per 1,000). This figure fits with data collected in a 1999 study of all types of elder abuse in seventeen states. That study found a rate of 8.6 per 1,000 older adults (Jogerst et al., 2003). The national study found that about one-fifth of all cases got reported to an official agency. In other words, reported cases represent only a small portion (about 20 percent) of the almost half million elder abuse cases in the United States.

The study also found that women experienced a higher rate of abuse than men. Women made up 58 percent of the older population, but they made up 76 percent of emotional/psychological abuse cases, 71 percent of physical abuse cases, 63 percent of financial exploitation cases, and 60 percent of neglect cases. And very old people (aged 80 and over) were abused or neglected at two to three times their proportion of the older population.

Black older people were abused at roughly twice their proportion of the older population. Ninety percent of the time the abuser was a family member. And of these family members, two-thirds were adult children or spouses. Neglect most often occurred with people who were depressed, confused, or frail (National Center, 1998).

The study found that men accounted for 83.4 percent of abandonment incidents and 62.6 percent of physical abuse cases. Most perpetrators were between the ages of 36 and 59. Nearly one-third of abusers were aged 60 and over (National Center on Elder Abuse, 1998; *also* Carp, 2000). These findings and others have led to a number of theories of elder abuse. Some of these theories focus on family violence.

Theories of Abuse

Researchers have developed a number of theories to explain the causes of elder abuse (Carp, 2000). Theories of abuse focus on the causes of abuse. Quinn and Tomita (1997) describe five of the most common explanations in the literature: (1) the dependency of the older person; (2) caregiver stress; (3) learned violence in the family; (4) impairment of the abuser (by alcohol, drugs, mental retardation, etc.); and (5) societal attitudes toward older people, the disabled, and women.

Aronson, Thornewell, and Williams (1995; *also* Hightower, 2004) take a feminist view of elder abuse. They say that elder abuse reflects women's lack of power throughout life. Quinn and Tomita (1997) find that some studies support the theory that elder abuse is a continuation of spousal abuse into later life.

Quinn and Tomita (1997) say that theories of abuse are not mutually exclusive. Abuse can arise from more than one cause. A stressed caregiver may also come from a violent family and may be an alcoholic. A caregiver may hold both ageist and sexist views and the stress of caregiving may trigger

BOX 13.4

WHAT ARE YOUR ATTITUDES AND BELIEFS ABOUT ELDER ABUSE?

Researcher Michael J. Stones created a research tool, the Elder Abuse Aptitude Test (EAAT), to study attitudes and beliefs about elder abuse. Fill out the EAAT below and total your score to assess your attitudes and beliefs. The EAAT will also sensitize you to the many types of abuse that older people can face.

The following statements refer to how people sometimes act toward older adults. They only refer to behavior by someone an older adult has reason to trust. That person could be a relative or someone who takes care of the older person. That person could also be someone paid to help or look after the older person's affairs, such as a doctor, nurse, homemaker, or lawyer. The questions do not refer to how strangers treat older people. Do you understand the kinds of people the questions refer to?

Please indicate whether the actions below are (1) not abusive, (2) possibly abusive, (3) abusive, (4) severely abusive, or (5) very severely abusive toward an older person if done by someone that person has reason to trust. Remember that the questions don't apply to an act by a stranger. Circle a number next to each statement, given that:

1 means Not Abusive
2 means Possibly Abusive
3 means Abusive
4 means Severely Abusive
5 means Very Severely Abusive

A person a senior has reason to trust who

1. Steals something a senior values	[1]	[2]	[3]	[4]	[5]
2. Makes a senior pay too much for things like house repairs or medical aids	[1]	[2]	[3]	[4]	[5]
3. Pushes or shoves a senior	[1]	[2]	[3]	[4]	[5]
4. Lies to a senior in a harmful way	[1]	[2]	[3]	[4]	[5]
5. Opens a senior's mail without permission	[1]	[2]	[3]	[4]	[5]
6. Pressures a senior to do paid work when that senior doesn't want to	[1]	[2]	[3]	[4]	[5]
7. Doesn't take a senior places that senior has to go (like a doctor's appointment)	[1]	[2]	[3]	[4]	[5]
8. Withholds information that may be important to a senior	[1]	[2]	[3]	[4]	[5]
9. Unreasonably orders a senior around	[1]	[2]	[3]	[4]	[5]
10. Doesn't provide a senior with proper clothing when needed	[1]	[2]	[3]	[4]	[5]
11. Tells a senior that he or she is "too much trouble"	[1]	[2]	[3]	[4]	[5]
12. Fails to provide proper nutrition for a senior	[1]	[2]	[3]	[4]	[5]
13. Disbelieves a senior who claims to be abused without checking that claim	[1]	[2]	[3]	[4]	[5]

Add the numbers you circled and divide the total by 13. How did you score? How did your classmates score? Stones reported average scores of 4.07 for 22 to 40 year olds, 3.83 for 41 to 64 year olds, and 3.50 for 65 to 93 year olds.

Sources: M. J. Stones (1994). *Rules and tools: The meaning and measurement of elder abuse: A manual for milestones.* Newfoundland; M. J. Stones and D. Pittman (1995). "Individual differences in attitudes about elder abuse: The Elder Abuse Attitude Test (EAAT)," *Canadian Journal on Aging* 14 (Suppl. 2): 61–71. Reprinted with permission from the Canadian Association of Gerontology, *www.utpjournals.com.* M. J. Stones and M. Bédard (2002). "Higher thresholds for elder abuse with age and rural residence," *Canadian Journal on Aging 21*(4): 577–86.

violence. Research shows that a number of conditions—the relationship of the caregiver to the older person, a history of family violence, lack of support for the caregiver, the gender of the caregiver, and caregiver competence—all play a role in determining whether abuse occurs.

Responses to Abuse

Researchers and practitioners disagree over the definition of elder abuse (Carp, 2000). They apply the term to many types of unhappy family relationships. This has led to confusion over what counts as elder abuse and disagreement about the prevalence of abuse. Lachs and Pillemer (1995) say that arguments over the definition of abuse overlooks the needs of the victims. They say that physical frailty, devalued social status, and elder abuse do exist, and that practitioners don't need to get hung up in this debate. They should focus on the needs of abuse victims.

Pillemer and Finkelhor (1988) suggest three responses to elder abuse: (1) professionals who work with older people need to know more about the prevalence of abuse and potential abusers (*see also* Cook-Daniels, 2004); (2) older people need to know more about abuse and what they can do about it; and (3) responses to abuse need to focus on parental and spousal abuse.

Responses could include safe apartments in congregate housing or self-help groups for older abused spouses. Florida, for example, funds a statewide system of shelters for abused family members. More use could be made of these centers. Vinton (1992) found that older women made up less than 2 percent of people in these shelters (although they made up an average of 27 percent of the population in that area).

Studies show that the type of abuse depends on the physical and mental conditions of the abuser and the abused. It depends on the past and present relationship of the abuser and the abused. It also depends on social supports in the environment the abuser and abused live in. Interventions can improve these conditions and decrease the rate of abuse.

Elder Abuse Policies

Policy refers to regulations and guidelines on how to deal with elder abuse. Policies can include criminal court action, mandatory reporting, guardianship and power of attorney, and mediation to resolve disputes. But these methods use public means (by a social worker or police) to improve a family relationship. This course of action often fails. The law assumes that two people in a dispute have only a limited relation to each other. But an abused spouse or parent often has a long-term relationship with his or her abuser, and he or she may want to maintain this relationship (sometimes at personal risk).

For example, a study of the effectiveness of adult protective legislation (Bond, Penner, & Yellen, 1995) found an unwillingness by both the alleged abuser and the victim to cooperate during investigations. They also found a general reluctance to report cases of abuse. The researchers found that few cases get to court.

Legal action may do little to improve the abused person's life. A legal outcome, such as removing the abused person from a setting, may cause more stress to the abused person. Likewise, the abused person may reject legal remedies such as jailing an abusing child or spouse because they depend on that person for help. Pittaway and Gallagher (1995) found that nearly one-fifth (18 percent) of abused older people in their study said they feared reprisal.

Researchers support the need for intervention strategies for both the abused older person and the abuser. Nahmiash and Reis (2000) examined the effectiveness of intervention strategies in cases of abuse. The most successful strategies involved concrete help from nurses and other medical professions as well as homemaking services. Other successful interventions helped to empower older people. These included support groups, volunteers who acted as advocates, and information about a person's rights and available resources (also World Health Organization/International Network for the Prevention of Elder Abuse, 2002).

Barriers exist to implementing these changes. For example, Wolf (2001) finds that many victims of family violence refuse to join a support group. She suggests that support groups have an older group leader or co-leader, someone familiar with issues these older people face. Other research (Lithwick, Beaulieu, Gravel, & Straka, 1999) finds that many abused older people refuse services that might reduce stress. These included medical services, home care assistance, daycare centers, and respite programs. Roberto, Teaster, and Duke (2004) found that, compared with white women, African American older women tended to refuse intervention even though they ran a higher risk of repeated abuse.

Future Issues in Elder Abuse

Elder abuse and neglect have existed throughout history. What then accounts for the sudden interest in abuse and neglect? Four social changes account for this interest: (1) the growth of the older population, (2) the increased political power of older people, (3) the women's movement and a critical analysis of the family, and (4) the state's willingness to intervene in family life.

Some authors (Callahan, 1986; Crystal, 1986) argue that formal service agencies have adopted the cause of elder abuse to expand their influence and get more funding. This view links the sudden interest in abuse to the expansion of the welfare state. Other authors say that special programs aimed at reducing abuse reinforce negative stereotypes of older people as feeble and helpless (Harbison, 1999).

Wolf and Pillemer (1989) take a different view. They see health and social service professionals' intervention in child abuse and in elder abuse as parallel. In both cases, professionals, on behalf of the state, set out to protect a vulnerable minority (Otto, 2000). Through this process, elder abuse has become a legitimate social problem. They see this attention as a first step in creating social policies to protect abused older people.

The research on elder abuse supports the idea that older people suffer from varied forms of mistreatment. Some subgroups may have a higher-than-average risk of abuse and may need special attention. This includes older women, those who are physically or cognitively frail, and those who depend on their abuser for financial security or caregiving (Brandl, 2000). Mason (2003) describes a twelve-week program called S.E.A.M.—Stop Elder Abuse and Mistreatment. This program helps abusers change their behavior. It discusses their past unacceptable behavior and helps them develop acceptable alternatives.

Researchers have explored the causes, theories, and responses to elder abuse. More research is needed on the role of race, ethnicity, and culture in the abuse and neglect of older people. More research is also needed on elder abuse in residential settings. Glendenning (1999), for example, reviewed the literature on abuse and neglect in long-term care settings. This review found that the facility environment, the characteristics of the resident, and the characteristics of the staff (including the problem of staff burnout) all influenced the existence of abuse. Researchers say that professionals need more education about abuse and the tools to assess and detect abuse (Cook-Daniels, 2004; Ramsey-Klawsnik, 2004).

Research shows that the large majority of older people do not experience abuse. Still the number of abuse cases will grow in the future as the older population expands. This makes elder abuse an ongoing concern. Future studies should propose policies and practices to help ensure the safety of a growing and diverse older population.

CONCLUSION

Studies in the past looked at families with a husband, wife, and children from one marriage. Studies of widowhood, for example, generally refer to loss of a lifelong mate. But changes in the family today will change family life for older people in the years ahead.

Married couples, for example, tend to make little use of formal supports. Even in late old age, when people have severe functional problems, compared with unmarried older people, married people have a much lower rate of institutionalization. Caregiving spouses may feel that the use of a nursing home, respite care, or other services means that they have failed. A couple may ignore the buildup of stress in their relationship until abuse or some other form of breakdown occurs. Studies can look more closely at couples and how they manage as they age.

More studies of aging in alternative relationships will give a more varied picture of aging. Researchers need to do more studies of gay, lesbian, and bisexual older people, of never married older people, of unmarried men, and of divorced older people.

People who enter old age today will bring with them more open attitudes toward sex. And these attitudes will shape their behavior in later life. Johnson (1997) already finds evidence of this trend in a study of seniors' attitudes toward sex. This research found a more positive and accepting attitude toward sexuality among older people, particularly the young-old. Researchers need to look at changes in attitudes toward sexuality and the sexual behavior of new cohorts of older people

Few studies have compared family and social relations in different ethnic and racial groups. Researchers need to study cultural and social class differences that lead to unique social relationships. Researchers need to look more closely at minority family relations in later life. Some of this work has begun, for example, in the study of surrogate parenting in African American families. But researchers need to tease out the roles that cultural values and necessity play in these adaptations.

Studies of fictive kin and play siblings, for example, give insights into alternative cultural adaptations. The terms *fictive kin* and *play relatives* (a term used by older people themselves) refer to nonrelatives who the older person thinks of as family. A study of 122 African Americans aged 85 and over in Oakland, California, for example, found that 45 percent of the sample had fictive kin. And 80 percent of these people said they enjoyed these relationships (Johnson, 1999).

More studies need to look at male relationships in later life. Few studies exist on male friendships, male approaches to coping with widowhood, or grandfathers. Research on elder abuse points to high rates of spouse abuse. More research needs to look at the stresses married people face in later life.

New patterns of family life have begun to emerge: gay relationships, serial monogamy (multiple marriages in a lifetime), widowhood, and remarriage. These all lead to more complex family structures in later life. Grandparents will have grandchildren from several marriages of their children. They will have multiple in-laws from these marriages. Their grandchildren may in turn have several marriages. Older people themselves may have children, grandchildren, and great-grandchildren from their own multiple marriages.

What will future studies make of a child with two mothers, one woman who donates the egg and the other woman who bears the child? What relation do these people have to one another? Gerontologists Matilda White Riley and John Riley (1994, p. 31) say that English does not even have names "for such confusing relationships." Will family (blood) bonds hold families together in the future? Or will people choose as relatives the people they like best? Will people invent new family structures to suit their needs? Who will feel obligated to support whom in this complex network? What will motivate older and younger people to care for one another? The changing family will create new questions for gerontologists. It will also pose new challenges for all of us as we age and sort out our family relations.

SUMMARY

- Age-graded normative life events take place at expected times in a person's life. These events define a person's position in society. Expectable (normative) events, such as marriage or widowhood, often lead to a passage from one social role to another.
- The proportion of people married at a given age decreased from middle age onward. Divorce accounts for only a small proportion of this decrease. Widowhood explains most of this decrease. Women, compared with men, have a greater chance of living as widows. Most men will live with a spouse throughout their lives. Most women will live many years as a widow.
- The advantages to marriage in later life include (1) a greater combined income and the benefits of sharing the cost of expenses; (2) greater life satisfaction; and (3) better adjustment to aging. The disadvantages of marriage in later life include (1) interests may diverge; (2) a relationship may suffer during a role change like retirement; and (3) ill health may strain a relationship.
- People report an interest in sex into late old age. Substantial proportions of people remain sexually active until at least their 80s. Any decline in interest takes place gradually over many years. Studies show that the

best predictor of a good sex life in old age is a good sex life in a person's younger years.

- Most illnesses do not decrease sexual activity or enjoyment. Research shows that good eating habits, weight control, limiting alcohol, and an active sex life all enhance and prolong sexual activity.
- Women more than men risk widowhood as they age. Three major factors account for this: (1) women tend to marry older men; (2) women have a longer life expectancy than men; and (3) men tend to remarry after the loss of a spouse. Researchers call widowhood an expectable life event for older women.
- Men tend to remarry after widowhood, but women tend to stay single. Remarried people expressed satisfaction with their new spouses. Couples most often reported that they remarried for companionship and a strong need to love and be loved.
- In the past, at least one child often stayed home to look after aging parents. Today, children move long distances from their families to find and keep jobs. In addition, families have gotten smaller as parents have fewer children. These changes in the family have led people to assume that families no longer support their older members. But studies show that families still provide most of the support for older people.
- Relatives provide most of the care for older people even when formal (paid or professional) care exists. Studies show that a spouse, if available, will take on the caregiving role.
- Sociologists describe the African American family as a mutual aid system. Older African Americans receive support from family members and help these members in turn. Older African Americans turn to the family for emotional and financial support. They turn to the church for instrumental support. People with strong family and church ties feel a sense of well-being.
- Women often take on the work of informal support for older family members. Male caregivers tend to feel less distress and depression than female caregivers. Men, compared with women, seem better at setting limits on their caregiving.
- Caregivers of older family members with chronic conditions or with cognitive impairments often feel caregiver burden. Many caregivers find the role rewarding, but few find it easy. Successful informal caregiving entails: (1) providing good care, (2) wanting to give care, (3) protecting one's own well-being, (4) developing new skills and abilities, and (5) using formal care systems when necessary. Older people and their caregivers need flexible services that they can tailor to their specific needs.
- Families in the future will need to rely on formal supports to supplement informal caregiving. Pressures on the family in the future will include (1) more generations alive at one time, (2) top-heavy kin networks, (3) older members living to a very old age, and (4) more middle-aged women (traditional caregivers) in the labor force.
- Researchers have discovered many types of elder abuse. Studies show that the type of abuse depends on the physical, mental, and environmental conditions of the abuser and the abused. It also depends on the past relationships of these people and the social supports available to them. Education programs and shelters for abused family members can help decrease the rates of abuse.
- A study of grandparents in the United States found five styles of grandparenting: (1) detached, (2) passive, (3) supportive, (4) authoritative, and (5) influential. Grandparents' influence on and involvement with grandchildren decrease with age. Some grandparents use selective investment to focus on their closer and more compatible grandchildren.
- New patterns of family life have begun to emerge. Gay and lesbian relationships, divorce, and remarriage can lead to more complex family structures in later life. The older generation may have children, grandchildren, and great-grandchildren from their own and their children's multiple marriages. Changes in family life today will change family life for older people in the years ahead.

DISCUSSION QUESTIONS

1. Define the term *age-graded normative life event* and give several examples of this type of event.
2. Why does the proportion of married people decrease after middle age? How does the proportion of married people differ for men and women?
3. State the advantages and disadvantages to marriage in later life.
4. List the three major factors that account for the high rate of widowhood among women.
5. In general, why do older people remarry? What do they report about their experience of remarriage?
6. What have researchers found out about older people's interest in sex?
7. What can older people do to improve their sex lives?

8. What does research show about the existence of family support for older people?
9. Who provides most of the routine support for older people in their families? What other family members will older people typically depend on?
10. What type of system best describes how African American families provide support for their older members? What other informal supports, besides the family, do African American people use?
11. What types of strains do many female caregivers face today? Why do male caregivers, compared with female caregivers, feel less distress and depression?
12. List the characteristics of a good caregiver.
13. Describe some of the major changes in family structure that have occurred in this century. How has the system of informal supports changed due to this change in structure?
14. State at least three beliefs about elder abuse that the first large studies of elder abuse called into question. How can society help reduce the rate of elder abuse?
15. What styles of grandparenting have researchers found? How do grandparenting styles change with age?
16. What effect will changing patterns in family life today have on older people in the future?

SUGGESTED READING

Kramer, B. J, & Thompson, E. H. (2002). *Men as caregivers: Theory, research, and service implications.* New York: Springer.

The authors say that caregiving research has generally looked at female caregivers. They say that, compared with women, male caregivers see caregiving differently. They respond to the needs of their care receivers differently. And the need different supports to fulfill the caregiving role. This book suggests new approaches to research on male caregiving.

Garner, J. D., & Mercer, S. O. (Eds.). (2001). *Women as they age.* New York: Haworth Press.

This collection looks at the challenges women face as they age in a male-dominated society. It includes discussions of psychological, social, and health care issues related to older women. It also looks at the challenges that many older women face. These include surrogate parenting, membership in an ethnic minority, and intimacy. The book can also serve as a resource guide for women in later life. It encourages empowerment and the development of self-determination.

Starkman, E. M. (1993). *Learning to sit in the silence: A journal of caretaking.* Watsonville, CA: Papier-Mache.

A book based on a ten-year journal kept by a daughter-in-law caregiver. She describes the everyday feelings of satisfaction and frustration in her role. A unique and valuable look at the inner world of caregiving. Starkman concludes that families need to talk more about caregiving decisions.

GLOSSARY OF TERMS

age-graded normative life events Life events linked to a specific age or stage of development. Society often structures these events (a graduation, a wedding) to mark a status passage.

bean-pole family structure A family that has many generations alive at the same time, but with few people in each generation.

caregiver burden The feeling of physical and emotional exhaustion that caregivers sometimes feel.

convoy model of support This model of support uses an image of concentric circles to describe relationships with the older person. The strongest relationships exist in the closest circle. Outer circles show weaker relationships. These rings of relationships follow a person (like a ship convoy) throughout life. The relationships of people in this convoy grow and change with changing life circumstances.

expanded kinship network The complex network of relations that can exist after a divorce.

functional specificity of relationships model This model of support to older people recognizes a person may provide one type of support or a broad range of support. This will depend on how the relationship between the supporter and the older person has developed over time. Gender, marital status, parenthood, and geographical closeness or distance all play a role in deciding the kind of support a person can give.

hierarchical compensatory model The idea that caregivers come from the care receiver's closest relations first (spouse and children). Then caregiving responsibilities move outward in a hierarchy from closer to more distant relatives and friends.

primary caregiver The person who takes on most of the responsibility for caring for an older person.

status A position in society, for example, student, retiree, widow. Sociologists say a person occupies a status.

task specificity model The idea that people take on caregiving roles according to their ability to perform a task.

chapter **14**

DEATH AND DYING

Draw a line across a piece of paper. Put the word *birth* at the left end of the line. Put the word *death* at the right end of the line. Now put a dot for today's date. Put the date of your birth under the birth dot. Now put the date you project for your death under the dot that says death.

How did you feel about fixing a date for your death? How did you come up with a date? Do people of different ages think the same way about death? Do you look forward to your next birthday? Or do you think about how few years you have left to do the things you want to do? How do older people think and feel about death?

Have you discussed death within your family? Do people in your family or among your friends talk about a good death, about their preferences for burial or cremation, or about their feelings about death and dying? This chapter looks at death in old age. It

BOX 14.1

DEATH AND DYING AMONG THE HUTTERITES

In an article on aging and death, Joseph W. Eaton reprinted the following letter from a Hutterite farmer to his sister. The letter describes the death of their younger brother.

> Dear sister, our dear brother came home on September 8, on a Wednesday morning about 5 o'clock. He said that he had a fairly nice trip. He cried a great deal because of pains. He stated that distress teaches one to pray. I went immediately the following day to visit with him. I could hardly look at him, it was so painful to me; he looked so terrible that it made my heart almost break. However, I remained with him until he died, and until the funeral was over.
>
> Two evenings before his death, his home was full of people, approximately 25 were there. He expressed a heavenly pleasure when he saw them all and said he could not express his pleasure in seeing them. It struck me almost as a miracle when I saw this starved and weak body lying there, telling us such a strong story. We listened to him, warned him not to talk so much because it may do him harm. However, he stated, "while I am still alive, I can speak. When I will be dead, then, of course, I won't be able to tell you what I have to say." . . .
>
> He stated that dying does not cause him any difficulty; he said that he had a clear conscience and is in peace with God and all people. He asked many people in my presence whether they had something against him. However, everybody replied in the negative. They said to him that they themselves were in peace with him. . . .
>
> [Just before his death] his children stood around him with a sad heart, and all realized that his departure will be soon. He called his oldest son, gave him his hand and pressed a kiss on his forehead, and advised him how he should behave in the future. Among other words he told him he should obey his preacher, the boss and the field boss, and if the community entrusted a position to him, he should execute same as well as he could, and not only superficially. . . .
>
> [He then calls to his side his daughter, the colony business manager, his wife and his brother.] He said, "I am at peace with God and with all people. I have a clear and good conscience. I am ready to depart, but now everything goes so slow. I have only one desire and that is to go to my Lord." He said quite frequently how good it is to have a clear and peaceful conscience. He advised us also that we should prepare ourselves, because the pleasure was inexpressible.
>
> So I have described to you the events and experiences which I have seen with my own eyes, and it is my request and my wish that we all should prepare ourselves. Blessed by God.

Source: Joseph W. Eaton (1964), "The art of aging and dying," *Gerontologist* 4:94–112. Reproduced with permission of the Gerontological Society of America, 2000.

focuses on (1) attitudes toward death and on where death takes place, (2) ethical questions about death and dying, and (3) mourning and grief.

DEATH AND SOCIETY

Aiken (2001) says that attitudes toward death fall on a continuum. Some societies see death as an enemy, something we fight with all our power. Other societies welcome death and even see it as a transition to a better, even blissful, world. Still others, in the middle, see death as a mystery.

Kastenbaum (1999, p. xv) says he misses the old days—"the really old days." In the ancient past, he says, people saw death as a mysterious transition. They created myths and stories to explain death to themselves. The Greek Hades, the Christian Heaven or Hell, or the Muslim Paradise all show humans grappling with the meaning of death. For some societies, death meant an eternity of darkness and shadow. For others, as Dante describes in his *Inferno,* it could mean punishment for an evil life. And for Muslims, death means a life of ease and pleasure for believers. As Kastenbaum says, "death was clearly something BIG." The power of the stories, their central role in religion and culture, tell us that people have always wondered about death.

But times have changed and we have a new view of death and dying (one that coexists with some of our traditional views). Science and technology extend life and push death and dying to late old age. Death in the United States today most often takes place in a hospital or nursing home. We rarely have a direct experience of death. Foley and his colleagues (1995), for example, studied 1,227 deaths of older people (average age, 80) in Connecticut. They found that most of these people died in an institution—45 percent died in a hospital and 25 percent died in a nursing home. Only 30 percent died at home. The National Hospice and Palliative Care Organization (2004) reports similar figures.

We see graphic scenes of death in the movies or on television. But these images distance us from death (Aiken, 2001). They have little impact on our daily lives. We can turn off the television or leave the theatre if the images scare or depress us.

Today, death challenges our moral and ethical codes. Our legal system grapples with the issue of physician-assisted suicide, our health care system deals with the long trajectory toward death that we call long-term care, and families cope with institutions such as hospitals and nursing homes where death most often occurs.

Death may still fill us with fear. But more often it confronts us with practical choices: To die in an institution or at home? To prolong care or end treatment? To opt for burial, cremation, or freezing of the body until science finds a cure? We still hear the old stories through our religious traditions and literature. But they lack mystery and sound more like fantasy. Discussions of death and dying today often focus on death and dying in old age.

DEATH IN OLD AGE

In the past, high infant mortality, childhood diseases, and high female death rates during childbearing years made death among all age groups a common event. Today, most infants will live to old age. Life expectancy at birth in the United States for the years 2000 to 2005 stood at 80.4 years for females and 74.6 years for males. Even at age 65 a woman can expect to live to age 85 and a man could expect to live to age 81 (United Nations, 2002). Longer life expectancy today means that death often takes place in old age. And today most people die of the diseases of old age—cancer, heart disease, stroke, and lung disease. These diseases result from a lifetime of accumulated stress on the body.

The trajectory of death from these diseases differs from dying in the past. People died earlier in the past and they often died quickly of an acute illness (e.g., influenza, pneumonia) or accident. Today people die in old age from more than one chronic illness (e.g., cancer, heart disease, diabetes) (Bern-Klug, Gossert, & Forbes, 2001). People often experience a slow decline along with intense crises that lead to death. Dying can include pain, delirium, swallowing problems, loss of mental function, and other forms of discomfort (Ross et al., 2002). Dying in old age makes special demands on health care providers, family members, and older people themselves.

Only a small number of studies have looked at how older people feel about death (Cicirelli, 2002). But gerontological theories suggest some of the ways that older people feel about death. According to activity theory, for example, people want to stay active throughout their lives. They substitute new roles and activities for ones that they lose as they age. When people retire, activity theory says that they will have the highest life satisfaction if they find new things to do. This theory says nothing about death.

Disengagement theory says that people want to disengage from social roles as they age. This theory also says that retirement and withdrawal from social responsibilities lead to high life satisfaction. According to this theory, an awareness of impending death starts the process of disengagement. People know that they will die soon, so they ease their way out of social life. Disengagement produces a smooth transition of power from one generation to the next. Death has a less disruptive effect on society if older people disengage from social roles as they age. This theory focuses on the social effects of dying, but it says little about death as a personal experience or about how older people feel about death.

Erikson's (1963) theory of ego development says that the last stage of life leads to a life review. A person looks over his or her life, ties up loose ends, and prepares for death. Erikson describes this as **ego integrity**. "It is the acceptance of one's one and only life cycle as something that had to be and that, by necessity, permitted of no substitutions" (1963, p. 268). The integrated person accepts his or her biography and culture, and with this acceptance "death loses its sting" (p. 268). Peck (1955, 1968) says that in the last part of this last stage a person can achieve **ego transcendence**. People in this stage feel a deep concern for others and for the culture they will leave when they die.

These theories say that older people respond to death in more than one way: Some people deny it, some accept it, and some embrace it. The few studies that have tested these theories have found complex combinations of acceptance and rejection of death (Cicirelli, 2002).

Koster and Prather (1999) report that people at the end of life had five concerns: avoiding a drawn-out death, getting pain relief, having control of treatment options, staying in touch with loved ones, and becoming a burden. People feared that they would burden family with physical care, that family members would have to witness their deaths, and that family members would have to make decisions about life-sustaining treatment.

Studies that compare older and younger people find that older people think about death more, but feel less afraid of death than the young. Cicerilli (1999), for example, studied 388 adults with an average age of 73. He found that younger people in this group reported more fear of death. A survey conducted for AARP in 2000 asked 1,815 people aged 45 and older about their attitudes toward death (cited in Vierck, 2002). The study found that the older the person, the less they felt afraid of dying and of pain at the end of life. Both Cicerilli and the AARP study found that women, compared with men, expressed more fear of dying. Women also expressed more fear of pain and of having artificial means used to keep them alive.

A study of the oldest old (people aged 85 and over) found that people in this age group understood that life had come near its end. They considered death a part of living, and they felt that they needed to make decisions as they prepared for death. The loss of friends and the many changes in the world around them made it easier for them to accept death (Johnson & Barer, 1997).

Cicirelli (2002) studied the meaning of death for 109 older people between the ages of 70 and 97. The sample included people with both high and low socioeconomic status and African Americans as well as whites. Cicirelli found that death held four meanings for this group. It meant (1) eventual meeting with God or nonexistence; (2) continued involvement in earthly life; (3) preparation to leave a legacy, something people would remember them for; and (4) a limited time left to do the things they wanted or needed to do. Some people felt more strongly about some of these items than others. And people often expressed all or more than one of these meanings at the same time. Cicirelli (2002, p. 79) says, "In short, personal meanings of death influenced both how older adults lived now and how they expected to exist beyond death."

Cicirelli (2002) found a relatively low fear of death among the people in his study. Women scored higher than men on the four fear of death scales used in his study. Cicirelli also found that fear of the process of dying and fear of the unknown peaked in the late 70s and early 80s. He suggests at this age people have not yet accepted the inevitability of death and have not come to a personal understanding of death.

Studies of the fear of death find that people with mild or uncertain religious belief fear death most, while those with strong religious beliefs or no belief at all deal with death best (Cicerilli, 1999, 2002). Clements (1998) found that people who made religious belief a central part of their lives reported the least fear of death and felt less fear about dying. People with a mild belief may accept enough of religion to believe in an afterlife, but not enough to feel they will have a good one.

INSTITUTIONAL DEATH

Religious belief and a sense of purpose can help buffer the fear of death, but how and where a person expects to die also affects how he or she feels about death. In the past, most people died at home, surrounded by family, friends, and neighbors. Some cultures still ensure this kind of death. But, in the United States, a large majority of deaths (for people of all ages) takes place in hospitals or nursing homes (Weitzen, Teno, Fennell, & Mor, 2003).

Hospitals will take in more and more dying patients as the population ages. But studies show that many doctors and nurses in hospitals feel uncomfortable with dying patients. Ross and her colleagues (2002) say that acute care hospitals often marginalize older dying patients. Staff see them as practical problems or *bed blockers.* The medical model, based on technology and cure, often fails to meet the needs of the dying older person.

A study of medical textbooks, for example, found that more than one-half the textbooks contained no information about pain management, psychological issues at the end of life, fear of death, or spirituality (Bronner, 2003). The Robert Wood Johnson Foundation has provided large grants to improve teaching about end-of-life treatment to physicians. The Foundation has also supported changes in medical textbooks so that they contain more content on end-of-life care. The Foundation reports that more needs to be done. Nurses, pharmacists, and other health care professionals also need more training in palliative care. A study of pharmacy programs in the United States, for example, found that only 62 percent of pharmacy programs provide classroom instruction in end-of-life care (Herndon et al., 2003).

Medical staff members sometimes feel guilty or angry about dying patients. And they may misunderstand patients' preferences for end-of-life care. Wenger and his colleagues (2000) report that in 54 percent of cases physicians misunderstood patients' preference to forgo cardiopulmonary resuscitation. These patients had a lower chance of getting a do not resuscitate order on their charts and therefore had a lower chance of getting the treatment they preferred.

Because they have spent all of their professional lives learning to keep people alive, they think of death as a failure. They may avoid dying patients or respond less quickly to their needs. Health care professionals need knowledge about pain management and about the unique needs of minority older people (Ross et al., 2002).

CHANGES IN THE TREATMENT OF THE DYING

The health care system has begun to change its approach to dying patients of all ages. Two doctors more than any others—Elisabeth Kübler-Ross in the United States and Dame Cicely Saunders in England—started this reform.

Stages of Death and Dying

Kübler-Ross (1969) described five stages that her patients went through before they died. First, she says, people deny that they are dying. They say, "Not me." They may believe that the doctor has the wrong x-rays or someone else's tests. They may go from specialist to specialist looking for a new diagnosis. They may not even hear the doctor tell them they have a fatal illness.

Second, she says, people feel angry. They begin to believe that they will die. "Why me?" they ask. At this point, people blame the doctors or their spouses or God for their illnesses.

Third, they begin to bargain. They say, "Yes, me, but . . ." and try to make deals with the hospital staff. They may promise to be a good patient and to follow doctor's orders, if only they will get better. They may bargain with God, promising to go to worship or to live a more pious life. They may bargain with God for one more summer at the cottage, or for enough time to see a child married, a grandchild born, or their next birthday.

Fourth, they feel depressed. Their illness gets worse, and they know they will die. They say, "Yes, me," and they feel a great sadness. Kübler-Ross says that depression has two stages. In the first stage, people mourn present losses—the loss of family, career, and the things they love, such as a home, car, or cottage. In the second stage, they mourn future losses—the loss of good times to come, the chance to see children or grandchildren grow up, and other future events. People begin to say goodbye in this stage.

Fifth, people accept death. They say, "My time is close now . . . it's okay." They say goodbye to family and friends and die in peace.

Kübler-Ross says that at every stage a person holds on to hope. At first, a person may hope the doctor has made a mistake; later there may be hope for a remission if the person has cancer, and later still there may be hope for a painless death.

Some writers question the number of Kübler-Ross's stages or their order. Shneidman (1984, p. 199) rejects Kübler-Ross's stage theory—"the notion that human beings, as they die, are somehow marched in lock step through a series of stages of the dying process"—on clinical grounds. He reports a wide range of emotions, needs, and coping methods that dying people use. "A few of these in some people, dozens in others—experienced in an impressive variety of ways." Kübler-Ross (1969) herself says that patients can skip stages; stages can overlap; and people can go back over the same stage many times. Some responses, such as anger, come up again and again.

Also, different illnesses create different trajectories of death or different patterns of response. Kübler-Ross based her model on cancer patients in a hospital, but cancer patients who have remissions may go through these stages more than once. People with other illnesses show other trajectories. Sometimes, a person can have long plateaus between times of decline. However, someone who dies shortly after an auto accident may not go through any of these stages.

Northcott and Wilson (2001) say that the dying process depends on many things—a person's age, the illness, the individual's will to live, and on the treatments used to fight or manage the disease. Lawton (2001, citing Institute of Medicine 1997; *also* Kaufman, 2002), for example, says that "sudden death, steady decline, and episodic decline" all have described unique death trajectories.

All sides of this debate share one thing: They have brought discussion and thinking about death into public life. People who have to cope with death and dying—patients, their families, and medical staff—now have a number of ways to think and talk about death. This has helped free many people from the silence that surrounded death and dying only a few years ago.

Hospice Care

The idea of a **hospice** dates back to at least the Middle Ages in Europe. Hospices at that time took in travelers who needed food, shelter, and care. Hospices today meet the special needs of dying patients. Dame Cicely Saunders opened the first modern hospice, St. Christopher's, in London, England, in 1967.

St. Christopher's has fifty-two beds, inpatient and outpatient services, a home visiting program, a daycare center for the children of staff, and private rooms for older people. The hospice welcomes visitors, including children, and allows families to cook for their dying relatives if they want to. Rooms are available for relatives who want to stay overnight. St. Christopher's does not attempt to extend life; it tries to relieve symptoms and to help patients enjoy their last days.

Hospice Program Goals

Saunders says that a "hospice is a program, not a place" (Canadian Medical Association, 1987, p. 34). First, a hospice controls pain. People fear death for many reasons, but often they fear the pain that may accompany death more than death itself. Pain relief ensures that the person will die in comfort, thus relieving much of the fear and anxiety. St. Christopher's pioneered the pain relief techniques now used by hospices around the world.

St. Christopher's created the Brompton mix—a mixture of heroin or morphine, cocaine, Stemetil syrup, and chloroform water—to relieve chronic pain. Medical staff base pain control on two techniques: First, they adjust drug dosage until it relieves a patient's pain. "The aim," Saunders (1984, p. 268) says, "is to titrate the level of analgesia against the patient's pain, gradually increasing the dose until the patient is pain free." Then, the nurses give the next dose before the previous one has worn off. Hospitals often wait until a person shows signs of pain before they give the next dose of pain reliever. By giving the analgesic "before the patient may think it necessary [usually every four hours] . . . it is possible to erase the memory and fear of pain" (p. 268).

Patients cared for by this method need lower dosages to maintain a pain-free state because the drug does not have to overcome the pain that has begun. Lower dosages mean that patients stay more alert. A study conducted by the AARP (cited in Vierck, 2002) found that the public supports pain control at the end of life. Three-fourths of people aged 45 and over in this study said that doctors should be able to use controlled substances to control pain at the end of life. The state of Oregon enacted legislation to support this view. The state passed the Intractable Pain Act in 1995. This act allows doctors to use controlled substances (like morphine) to manage patients' pain at the end of life. The act relieves doctors of the fear of censure for prescribing pain-relieving drugs.

Dr. Susan Tolle, director of the Center for Ethics in Health Care at Oregon Health and Science University (cited in Ostrom, 2000), says the Intractable Pain Act has improved the treatment of dying people. She says that Oregon, compared with the nation as a whole, has the lowest in-hospital death rate, better attention to advance planning, more referrals to hospices, fewer barriers to prescribing narcotics, and a smaller percentage of dying patients in pain (34 versus 50 percent nationally).

Second, a hospice allows a person to die a simple death. The hospice does not use respirators or resuscitators to keep someone alive. Staff members make dying a part of life in the hospice. They leave the curtains open around a dying person's bed so that patients can see that their roommates have died. Patients also know they have a say in their treatment; they can ask for medication when they feel they need it, and they can ask to die at home. Saunders (1984) reports that people who die at home often feel more pain than people who die in the hospice, and caregivers often feel burdened by the demands of care. St. Christopher's (and other hospices) agree to re-admit patients whenever the patient or the family needs more support.

Third, a hospice gives people love and care. Staff members focus on the comfort of the patient, taking the time to touch patients and hold them. The hospice will serve special foods that patients like or give them soothing scented baths. The hospice also helps patients do as much for themselves as they can; this increases patients' well-being by giving them a sense of control over their treatment. The family members of dying patients also receive care. The Family Service Project at St. Christopher's offers help to families who find it hard to cope with their grief (*see also* Levy, 1987). Saunders (1984, p. 269) says that "staff and volunteers visit to assess the need and to offer support, and if more specialized help is indicated, this can be arranged."

Hospices spread to North America during the 1970s and early 1980s. More than 1,000 hospices opened in the United States between 1974 and 1984. The National Hospice and Palliative Care Organization (2004) says that in 1977 the United States had fewer than one hundred hospices. By 2004, the number had grown to an estimated 3,200 hospice programs serving 950,000 patients (National Hospice and Palliative Care Organization,

2004). Medicare began coverage of hospice programs in 1984. This, in part, explains their rapid growth (Rybarski, 2004).

Today, at least five types of hospices exist in the United States: (1) at-home care provided by professionals and volunteers, (2) home care provided by nurses and health care agencies, (3) freestanding hospice facilities, (4) hospice within a hospital emphasizing relief of pain, and (5) in a nursing home (one of the fastest growing sites for hospice care) (Gold, 1995). The National Hospice Organization in the United States studied family satisfaction with several hundred hospice programs of all types. The study found high levels of satisfaction with services (Connor, 1998).

Palliative Care

Palliative care is "a program of active compassionate care primarily directed towards improving the quality of life for the dying" (Subcommittee on Institutional Program Guidelines 1989, p. 1). A complete program of palliative care includes symptom control and spiritual support as well as bereavement support and education. Palliative care units do the same work as hospices, but they most often exist within a large acute care hospital. Workers in palliative care programs include nurses, physiotherapists, psychologists, and volunteers.

Palliative Care for the Elderly

Palliative care units take in patients of all ages. Studies show that palliative care can help older people as well as younger people, but some older patients have unique needs.

Shedletsky, Fisher, and Nadon (1982) conducted one of the few studies of death and dying among older hospitalized patients. They studied the records of forty older patients (average age, 80.6 years) who had died in the extended care wing of a hospital. Extended care hospital settings take in many older people with long-term illnesses who need constant medical care. These units often have a palliative care treatment philosophy.

The researchers found that older extended care patients differed from younger palliative care patients. First, older patients averaged more diagnoses than the younger patients. Second, the younger patients typically had cancer, whereas the older patients typically suffered from circulatory and respiratory diseases. Third, relatively few younger patients died from respiratory failure, while respiratory failure caused about 50 percent of all deaths in the older group.

Shedletsky, Fisher, and Nadon (1982) found that drug treatment helped about 80 percent of the people with pain and skin problems. The staff reported that just before death, 75 percent of the patients felt no pain or distress and 75 percent were conscious or semiconscious. The staff found, however, that patients with respiratory problems got the least benefit from drug treatment, and this group made up the largest portion of people with discomfort before death. The researchers concluded that some groups of older extended care patients may have special palliative care needs.

Mori (1991) points out that palliative care turns some assumptions of the health care system upside down. First, palliative care acknowledges the limits of curative medicine. It accepts death as part of life. Second, palliative care takes time. It follows the natural course of an individual's death. Palliative health services adjust to suit each person's needs. It puts the individual's need for comfort first. Third, palliative care treats the whole person, which is deemed to include the person's caregivers and social support system. Palliative care calls for a different kind of health care practice, one that broadens the health care options for dying patients.

Mori (1991) describes a number of challenges that face palliative care programs. First, funding of the health care system limits some palliative care services. For example, hospitals cannot claim reimbursement for services to caregivers. So only two-thirds of palliative programs cover bereavement counselling. Also, physicians get low pay for home visits, a condition that limits their interest in palliative home care.

Second, health care workers and the public need more knowledge about palliative care. The public needs to know what this option offers. Professionals need to know how to work effectively on a palliative care team. They need better primary training and more frequent continuing education.

Third, palliative care challenges some core beliefs that people hold today. People believe in the curative power of modern medicine. And they may feel that palliative care gives up on the patient. They may feel guilty about choosing palliative care for a dying parent or spouse. Northcott and Wilson refer to the "California daughter syndrome" (2001, p. 68). A child, who may not have seen a parent for many years, refuses to accept the imminent death of the parent. The child then demands maximum medical treatment. Northcott and Wilson call for the gradual use of palliative care measures as a person approaches death. This, they say, may avoid the appearance that treatment has ended when palliative care has begun.

Fourth, nurses in one study said that the health care system often made it hard for them to deliver palliative care at home (Ross & McDonald, 1994). They blamed bureaucracy, fragmented services, and too much focus on efficiency. These forces interfered with the quality of care they wanted to provide. It kept them from giving patients the emotional support they wanted to give. This study points to the tension between the values of palliative care and the curative model that dominates the health care system.

Fifth, many older people will have no one at home to provide palliative care outside the institution. Community-based palliative care programs favor people with a primary caregiver. Older women, many of them widowed, often lack a primary caregiver. This makes them ineligible for home-based palliative care. Also multiple pathologies in an older patient may make pain control more complex.

Frail older people on palliative home care may need the use of respite beds and a day hospital. Palliative care at home places more demands on family caregivers. And some caregivers of older patients in palliative care programs report feeling stressed and exhausted (Ross et al., 2002). Families need health care and social support to carry out home-based palliative care.

Home care workers can help with cleaning and shopping. Respite care can help family caregivers get the rest they need. Quality community-based end-of-life care depends on a partnership between formal and informal caregivers. It also depends on the support of institutional care when needed. In Great Britain today, for example, most care at the end of life takes place at home (Eastaugh 1996, cited in Northcott & Wilson, 2001). But people

BOX 14.2

PRINCIPLES OF QUALITY PALLIATIVE CARE

A study titled "Last Acts," originally funded by the Robert Wood Johnson Foundation, looked at the experience of death and dying in America. The program involved more than 400 organizations in producing the following guidelines for quality palliative care.

The following Five Principles of Palliative Care describe what care can and should be like for everyone facing the end of life. Some of these ideas may seem simple or just common sense. But all together they give a new and more complete way to look at end-of-life care.

1. Palliative care respects the goals, likes, and choices of the dying person.
2. Palliative care looks after the medical, emotional, social, and spiritual needs of the dying person.
3. Palliative care supports the needs of the family members.
4. Palliative care helps gain access to needed health care providers and appropriate care settings.
5. Palliative care builds ways to provide excellent care at the end of life.

Source: A Vision for Better Care at the End of Life. Retrieved December 13, 2004, *www.partnershipforcaring.org/Resources/prineng.html.*

often go to a hospital for a short (one- to three-day) stay before they die.

The Last Acts organization (2002, 2003), originally funded by a grant from the Robert Wood Johnson Foundation, studied palliative programs in all fifty states and the District of Columbia. The study found that more programs exist today than in the past and people throughout the country show more awareness of end-of-life issues. But the study also saw room for improvements. The research found that only about 25 percent of dying patients die at home. Most people still die in hospitals and nursing homes. But many of these people would benefit from home-based palliative care. The study also found that the country needs more professionals trained in pain management.

Other studies support the need for more professional training in palliative care. One study, for example, found that primary care physicians created the most barriers to fulfilling palliative care goals (such as pain control) (Ryan, Carter, Lucas, & Berger, 2002). In another study 66 percent of physicians trained as geriatric fellows felt that they could use more training in hospice and palliative care (Medina-Walpole, Barker, & Katz, 2004).

ETHICAL ISSUES

Palliative care and other approaches to the treatment of dying patients raise a variety of ethical questions. Is it ethical to stop actively treating a person's illness? Does the decision not to put someone on a respirator or not to use a heroic life-saving measure contribute to the person's death? Philosophers, physicians, and legal experts have looked at these and other issues related to dying today.

Two ethical questions come up again and again in the writing on death and dying. First, how much information should health care providers give a dying person about their conditions? Second, when should a doctor allow a person to die?

Advance Directives

Some years ago, experts debated whether to tell dying patients about their condition or keep this knowledge from them. Today, most experts support an open awareness context. They agree that patients have a right to know about the choice of treatment the physician has made and about alternative treatments, including the choice of no treatment

Likewise, patients need to communicate their preferences for end-of-life treatment to their health care providers. At present, a person who lacks the mental competence to refuse treatment must rely on someone else to act for the person. Family members, a friend, or a medical doctor often must make this decision. Even if a person has told someone what the person wishes or has written a statement of the wish to end treatment at a certain point, these instructions have no binding effect on the decision.

Most states in the United States recognize living wills. Kelly et al. (1989) studied physicians in nine countries and found that doctors would value having specific directions on the type of care a patient wants. Using the results of the study, the researchers produced a booklet called *Let Me Decide* that offers a model of a living will and a **health care directive**. The directive gives specific information to family members and doctors about the amount of treatment the person prefers under different conditions. The person also writes out a personal statement about preferences for care as part of the directive.

Directives most often take the form of the **durable power of attorney** or a **living will**. The power of attorney gives someone (often a lawyer, but also possibly a child, spouse, or other family member) the right to make financial decisions on behalf of the older person if the person loses his or her mental capacity. The living will refers to health care wishes at the end of life. It directs the person to make decisions on the older person's behalf, if that person can't make the decision. **Advance directives** allow the older person to maintain autonomy. Directives state what medical actions a person wants under what conditions. Directives also state who has the right to make the decisions (Cramer, Tuokko, & Evans, 2001). They also help family members make health care decisions and avoid court intervention in decision-making.

The federal government and state laws govern advance directives. Each state has its own statutes governing advance directives. These statutes sometimes conflict with one another. And even within a state, advance directive statutes may conflict with other laws. In 1993 the National Conference of Commissioners on Uniform State Laws (2004) passed a draft of a Uniform Health-Care Decisions Act. The Commissioners proposed that states pass this act to bring uniformity to statutes across the country. At this writing, only a few states have passed this act. (See Figure 14.1.)

A more powerful effect on the use of advance directives comes from the federal government. The federal government passed the Patient Self-Determination Act in 1990. This act encourages people to choose the type of medical care and the extent of medical care they want at the end of life. The Patient Self-Determination Act says that hospitals, nursing homes, and other health agencies that get Medicare or Medicaid payments must recognize the living will and health care powers of attorney. The Patient Self-Determination Act affirms people's rights to make decisions for themselves. Health care agencies must ask people whether they have advance directives. They must also give people educational materials about their rights under state law (American Cancer Society, 2004).

Lawton (2001) reports that family members and physicians sometimes differ in their judgment of the person's will to live and of the person's end-of-life preferences. This potential for conflict supports the need for an advance directive. Lawton goes on to say that an advance directive allows a person to think about his or her preferences while in a sound state of mind. It allows people to control their own destinies. The courts will honor advance directives. But a person's relatives or friends need to make health care professionals aware of the directive and what it says.

Cramer, Tuokko, and Evans (2001) report that most people have heard of advance directives, but relatively few people have them. In their study, they found that only 28 percent of their sample had made out a power of attorney for finances. Only 19 percent said they had a living will for health services. People with more education tended to have these documents in place. The researchers say that advance directives work best when the older person has discussed preferences with the person's surrogate.

Some research shows that people put off making out an advance directive. They may not know about them, may not know their value, or they don't want to think about poor health or death (Hamer et al., 2002). Galambos (1998), for example, reports that relatively few people—15 to 20 percent of the population—make advance directives. She reports that only 35 percent of people aged 75 and over have an advance directive. Upper class whites show the greatest likelihood of having an advance directive. Minorities show the least likelihood.

Hopp and Duffy (2000) studied the end-of-life decisions of 540 people aged 70 and over. The study included 86 African Americans and 454 whites. The researchers found that, compared with African Americans, whites tended to discuss their preferences for treatment before their deaths. Whites also tended to have a living will and to identify a durable power of attorney. Whites also tended to make decisions about limiting care and withholding treatment at the end of life. African Americans tended to desire all possible treatments to extend life.

McAuley and Travis (2003) studied the use of advance directives in long-term care settings, specifically, living wills and orders that limited treatment. They found that, compared with the rest of the sample, African Americans were least likely to have either type of advance directive. Education about advance directives may increase their use.

Austin and Fleisher (2003) say that minority group members' choices at the end of life reflect their earlier experiences with the health care system. They say that minority group members feel distrust in the health care system. Minority group members also face cultural barriers. These include language barriers and attitude differences between minority patients and white health care providers (Krakauer, Crenner, & Fox, 2002).

These conditions account for the high proportion of African American elders who die in a hospital (Berger at al., 2002). Minority members who feel that the system has excluded them in the past tend to want all available treatment at the end of their lives (Owen, Goode, & Haley, 2001). Austin and Fleisher

INSTRUCTIONS	**FLORIDA LIVING WILL – PAGE 1 OF 2**
PRINT THE DATE	Declaration made this ________ (day) day of ____________ (month), ______ (year)
PRINT YOUR NAME	I, ______________________________, willfully and voluntarily make known my desire that my dying not be artificially prolonged under the circumstances set forth below, and I do hereby declare that:
PLEASE INITIAL EACH THAT APPLIES	If at any time I am incapacitated and ______ I have a terminal condition, or ______ I have an end-stage condition, or ______ I am in a persistent vegetative state
	and if my attending or treating physician and another consulting physician have determined that there is no reasonable medical probability of my recovery from such condition, I direct that life-prolonging procedures be withheld or withdrawn when the application of such procedures would serve only to prolong artificially the process of dying, and that I be permitted to die naturally with only the administration of medication or the performance of any medical procedure deemed necessary to provide me with comfort care or to alleviate pain.
	It is my intention that this declaration be honored by my family and physician as the final expression of my legal right to refuse medical or surgical treatment and to accept the consequences for such refusal. In the event that I have been determined to be unable to provide express and informed consent regarding the withholding, withdrawal, or continuation of life-prolonging procedures, I wish to designate, as my surrogate to carry out the provisions of this declaration:
PRINT THE NAME, HOME ADDRESS AND TELEPHONE NUMBER OF YOUR SURROGATE	Name: ______________________________ Address: ______________________________ ______________________________ Zip Code: __________ Phone: ______________________________
© 2005 National Hospice and Palliative Care Organization	

A person in the state of Florida could use this model of a living will to state their end-of-life preferences. The Partnership for Caring, Inc., website offers model living wills for each state. The example here serves as a guide to what information most living wills contain.

Will you fill out a living will in your old age? Why or why not? Do your parents or grandparents have a living will? Why or why not? Do you think that having a living will is a good idea? Why or why not?

FIGURE 14.1

Florida Living Will

Source: Retrieved December 16, 2004, *www.partnershipforcaring.org/Advance/fldoc.html.* Reprinted with permission.

FLORIDA LIVING WILL - PAGE 2 OF 2

PRINT NAME, HOME ADDRESS AND TELEPHONE NUMBER OF YOUR ALTERNATE SURROGATE

I wish to designate the following person as my alternate surrogate, to carry out the provisions of this declaration should my surrogate be unwilling or unable to act on my behalf:

Name: ______________________________

Address: ______________________________

______________________________ Zip Code: ______________

Phone: ______________________________

ADD PERSONAL INSTRUCTIONS (IF ANY)

Additional instructions (optional):

SIGN THE DOCUMENT

I understand the full import of this declaration, and I am emotionally and mentally competent to make this declaration.

Signed: ______________________________

WITNESSING PROCEDURE

TWO WITNESSES MUST SIGN AND PRINT THEIR ADDRESSES

Witness 1:

Signed: ______________________________

Address: ______________________________

Witness 2:

Signed: ______________________________

Address: ______________________________

Courtesy of Caring Connections
1700 Diagonal Road, Suite 625, Alexandria, VA 22314
www.caringinfo.org, 800/658-8898

FIGURE 14.1
(Continued)

(2003) say that community leaders can help their constituents see the benefits of palliative home-care and hospice care. Advance directives can ensure that older people get the care they want and need.

In spite of their value, advance directives pose problems that need public discussion. First, in some cases people change their minds about treatment as they near death. But they may not get a chance to change their advance directive. Lawton (2001) reviewed studies of end-of-life preferences. He found support for this concern. The research showed that about 30 percent of people change their preferences over time. Some want more intervention (10 percent) and others less (20 percent). He concludes that people need the chance to review and, if necessary, revise their advance directive as they approach death.

Second, subtle forms of coercion may influence an older person's instructions in an advance directive. Older people may propose an end to treatment because they feel that they will burden others with their care. Also, a health care provider, due to conscience or institutional policy, may refuse to abide by the older person's wishes.

These issues point to the need for better methods of communication between dying people and their

BOX 14.3

A FAMILY'S RESPONSE TO DEATH AND DYING

The academic discussions of the right to decide on prolonging life often focus on medical and legal issues. But every day, people, along with their physicians and nursing staff, make decisions about their older family members. These decisions, at their best, take place within a context of openness and trust between families and health care professionals. The following case shows how one family decided against aggressive treatment.

Mrs. Walker, 78, moved into an apartment in the Beth Sharon Senior Complex in early December. The complex offered her a supportive environment. It had a security system, access for a wheelchair, and a chance to socialize with other residents.

Mrs. Walker had played an active part in her community for many years as a hospital volunteer and businessperson. So, when she moved into her apartment complex, she joined the Beth Sharon Seniors Group and regularly attended their afternoon teas in a nearby center. On January 10, as she left for the tea, she lost her balance, fell down a flight of stairs, and severely injured her head. When an ambulance arrived, she was found to be unconscious and was taken to a nearby hospital for emergency treatment.

Mrs. Walker's daughter, Phyllis, a nurse, rushed to the hospital when she was called. The neurosurgeon on staff had already completed a CAT scan and showed it to Phyllis. "I don't like the look of this," he said. "There appears to be severe bleeding at the base of the brain stem. She's not likely to be well again, or indeed function on her own."

Phyllis left the ward to talk with her sister and other family members. They agreed that they would not press for an operation to remove the blood clot. Surgery would almost certainly lead to the necessity of a respirator and other artificial means of life support. Over the next few days, as the family waited for some change in their mother's condition, Phyllis would suggest various actions or ask for another test. Each time the surgeon in charge would ask a simple question, "Would your mother like us to do that?" And each time Phyllis agreed that her mother would not want aggressive treatment to prolong her life. The decision to wait became harder to sustain as Mrs. Walker's breathing faltered. But the family stayed with its decision, based on Mrs. Walker's many discussions with them. Family members and close friends supported the family's decision to follow their mother's wishes.

Sixteen days after entering the hospital, and without regaining consciousness, Mrs. Walker died. She was cremated, in accordance with her request, and her family held a memorial service to celebrate her life.

caregivers (Lawton, 2001). Bern-Klug and her colleagues (2001) say that older people, families, and health providers need to have more than a written advance directive. They need to have in-depth discussions about an older person's preferences for end-of-life care.

Euthanasia and Physician-Assisted Suicide

Doctors sometimes face ethical conflicts when they treat dying patients. Medical ethics say that a doctor should heal and cure patients, but the Hippocratic oath also says that a doctor should first "do no harm." What should a doctor do when machines, surgery, or drugs that extend a person's life also prolong their suffering? What should a doctor do when a patient asks to die? And what does the law say about **euthanasia** (actively helping someone achieve a painless death)?

First, when is a person dead? When he or she stops breathing? When the heart stops beating? Or when the brain waves stop? Harvard Medical School (1968) gives four criteria for death: The person (1) no longer makes a response, (2) no longer breathes or moves, (3) has no reflexes, and (4) has no sign of brain activity on two electroencephalograms taken twenty-four hours apart. But what if a machine keeps someone breathing, or a heart pump keeps someone's heart beating or medication keeps someone alive? Are these people alive or dead? When does a family or a doctor have the right to end treatment?

Walton and Fleming (1980, p. 58) say that a doctor who sets out to kill a patient—for example, by giving the patient a drug overdose—"has committed himself more firmly. He is therefore more directly accountable for the outcome." A doctor who allows death to happen—for example, by not putting a person on a respirator or by taking someone off a respirator—may or may not cause a person's death. This is **passive euthanasia**. The person may live even without the treatment. Walton and Fleming say that ethical treatment should offer the most options for the patient. "A passive course of action provides a sensible alternative to aggressive treatment and, at the same time, allows for unexplainable and unforeseen events which may be of great benefit to the patient" (Walton & Fleming, 1980, p. 60).

The current law leaves many questions open. Once treatment has begun, for instance, the law inhibits a doctor from discontinuing treatment. The doctor may know, through an advance directive, that after some time the patient would want treatment discontinued. But, by discontinuing the treatment, the doctor risks legal action. Both the law and medical ethics reject **active euthanasia** or **physician-assisted suicide (PAS)**—actively helping someone end his or her life either because the person asks for death or to relieve suffering.

The public shows ambivalence about PAS. A Harris poll taken in 1999 found that 61 percent of the U.S. public supported legalization of PAS (Yankelovich & Vance, 2001). But not all of these people would choose PAS for themselves. Fifty-one percent of older Americans supported legalizing PAS and 62 percent of Americans aged 18 to 29 supported legalizing PAS. Forty-one percent of whites opposed legalizing PAS. But a large majority of African Americans (77 percent) opposed legalizing PAS. Cultural differences, religious beliefs, closeness to death, and personal values all influence attitudes toward PAS.

St. John and Man-Son-Hing (2002) found that a request for active euthanasia most often comes from someone in pain or with depression. Symptom control can make dying less painful and can reduce the request for active euthanasia. Still, some studies show that women, minorities, older people, and people with specific diseases may not get the pain relief they need (Lee 1999; Meier, Myers, & Muskin, 1999). Doctors themselves disagree on how much a physician should assist a person who wishes to die.

Recent cases in the United States have (at least for now) settled the issue of the legality of PAS. In PAS, a doctor gives a person the means to commit suicide or advice on how to commit suicide. The patients take the action themselves. Controversy exists over this practice.

Michigan courts acquitted Dr. Jack Kevorkian of murder three times in cases where he helped patients commit suicide. But in 1999, a jury convicted Kevorkian of murder. Supporters and critics of PAS

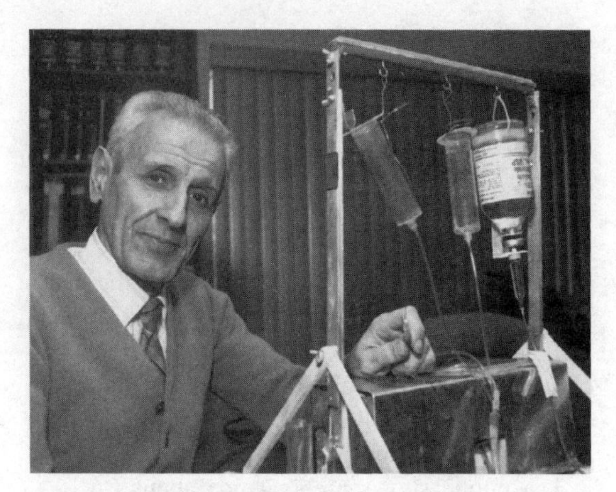

Dr. Jack Kevorkian and his suicide machine.

often argue about the issue of consent. Supporters of assisted suicide say that the patient's right to accept or refuse treatment will protect people from misuse of PAS. Critics of PAS fear that this will lead to mercy killing without patient's consent.

Krauthammer (1996) reports that this type of mercy killing occurred in the Netherlands, where legalized PAS exists. Also, some doctors may consent to patient requests too quickly. Few guidelines exist today for doctors to follow, and medical associations have begun to review their standards in light of recent court actions and social changes.

Public debate on this issue will grow. Physicians now have the ability to prolong life through technology. This could mean more years of pain and suffering for some patients. Also, the cost of keeping people alive on machines and with expensive medications will increase. Some people will support active euthanasia on economic grounds. Many people see the choice of active euthanasia as a right in modern society (Yankelovich & Vance, 2001).

A few countries today allow voluntary euthanasia or PAS. And they give some idea of the issues that legalized PAS raises. Humphry (2000) reports that Swiss law has allowed assisted suicide since 1937 as long as it relieves suffering and has a humanitarian purpose. But social sanctions keep most doctors from assisting with suicide. The Constitutional Court of Colombia on May 20, 1997, approved legalized euthanasia. The court ruled that "no person can be held criminally responsible for taking the life of a terminally ill patient who has given clear authorization to do so." The ruling still has to go before the country's Congress for adoption (Humphry, 2000, p. 49).

Humphry (2000) says that in only two places does assisted suicide have societal support—the Netherlands and the state of Oregon. Oregon passed the Death with Dignity Act in 1994 by popular vote. This act bans voluntary euthanasia (mercy killing), but it supports PAS in cases of advanced terminal illness. It allows physicians to prescribe drugs that help a person end his or her life. The law lays out a detailed process for patients and physicians to follow. The federal government challenged this law. But as of this writing, the law remains in effect.

A report in 2003 on the Oregon policy found that fifty-eight people got legal prescriptions for medication and thirty-eight used the medicine. But studies in Oregon also show the need for education about end-of-life options. Silveira and colleagues (2000), for example, studied 728 outpatients in four Oregon clinics. They found that only 23 percent understood assisted suicide and only 32 percent understood active euthanasia. Sixty-two percent of the people in the study did not know the difference between the two. The researchers say that people need education about their options before they can make intelligent decisions about end-of-life care.

The Netherlands began allowing PAS in 1973. In 1984, the Dutch Supreme Court allowed both voluntary euthanasia and PAS. These types of deaths account for about 3 percent of all deaths in the Netherlands each year. Regulations exist to guide physicians' practices. In particular, doctors have to report cases in which they have assisted with a suicide. However, technically, euthanasia remains illegal in the Netherlands. The courts allow the process, but no law exists that makes it legal (Humphry, 2000).

This debate over PAS and euthanasia will continue as Americans sort out the implications of these practices. But other approaches to end-of-life illness, such as hospice care and palliative care, will grow in importance. Likewise people need to learn more about advance directives so that they can get the end-of-life care that they want.

MOURNING AND GRIEF

When an older person dies, he or she often leaves behind children, sometimes a spouse, and other family members (such as grandchildren or siblings). The AARP reports that one person in five aged 50 and over in the United States engaged in arranging or planning a funeral in 1998 to 1999 (cited in Vierck, 2002). These survivors need to adjust to the loss, and society can help with this adjustment. Funeral practices and rituals structure the grieving process. They prescribe what mourners should say, what they should wear, and in some cultures even how they should sit.

Mourners in Christian cultures wear black; mourners in some Asian cultures wear white. North American society values silent, unemotional grieving; some Chinese families hire professional mourners to make loud wailing noises at the funeral. Jewish tradition requires that the family sit shivah for seven days after a funeral. According to this custom, mourners tear their clothes, sit on low chairs to deny themselves physical comfort, cover the mirrors in their home, and light a candle that burns for one week. The mourning family accepts visitors throughout the week, and ten men gather at the house each day for prayer. Mourning continues in less intense stages for a year until the unveiling of a commemorative stone on the grave of the deceased. Orthodox Judaism forbids mourning after the year has passed (Aiken, 2001).

Each culture has its own funeral rituals and mourning practices, but all of them have a common purpose: to help the bereaved family cope with grief and reestablish community bonds after the loss of a community member. Regardless of the culture a person belongs to or the type of funeral he or she attends, each bereaved person has to work through personal feelings of grief. Bereavement refers to the feeling of loss at death of a loved one. Kastenbaum (2001, p. 316) calls bereavement "an objective fact."

The fact of bereavement often leads to grief. Some research in North America shows that mourners go through stages of grief. Early work by Lindemann (1944) describes three such stages: an initial response phase, an intermediate phase, and a recovery phase. First, the bereaved person feels shock and disbelief. They may report feeling cold and numb, and some people say they feel dazed, empty, and confused. These feelings protect a person from feelings of sorrow. People in this phase often fear that they will break down in public. This phase can last for several weeks.

Second, the person begins to review what has happened. This takes three forms: (1) The bereaved person obsessively reviews one or two scenes related to the death, or may be very self-critical about something that should have been said or done. (2) The bereaved person searches for a meaning for the death. Religious people may find solace in knowing that God willed this death. (3) The bereaved person searches for the deceased. This may mean that a widow goes to places where she expects to see her spouse. She may also feel his presence while watching television, eating dinner, or lying in bed. Some people even call out to their spouses and expect an answer. This phase lasts about a year.

Third, the bereaved person begins to recover. Survivors look for social contacts. They may join a club or go on a cruise. They feel that they have come through an ordeal and say they feel stronger and more competent than before. This stage begins around the second year after the death.

Kastenbaum (2001) says that grief affects a person's physical as well as psychological well-being. Some research shows that grief throws the body's neuroendocrine system out of balance. Acute grief can lead to illness and may even lead to death. Grief affects a person's entire life including their social relations.

Gorer (1965) says that successful **grief work** includes three stages: (1) breaking bonds to the deceased, (2) readjusting to the environment without the deceased, and (3) forming new relationships. Not everyone makes a smooth trip through this process. Sometimes a person can show a delayed emotional response to a parent's or a spouse's death. The person seems to cope well, displaying lots of zest and energy, but may have internalized the grief. This delay can lead to emotional upset and physical illness later.

Only a small percentage of bereaved people go through morbid grieving. But research does show that people who have problems with grieving may turn to alcohol and drugs (Connor, 1998). They may also feel sorrow, anger, bitterness, rage, and despair (Northcott & Wilson, 2001, citing Clark, 1993).

Researchers note that stage models can include up to seven stages of grief and mourning (Aiken, 2001). But many people deviate from these patterns of bereavement Stages may overlap, a person may go through some stages more than once, stages can come in a different order than predicted, or a person may only go through some of the stages (Wortman & Silver, 1990). Northcott and Wilson (2001) say that the pattern of grieving by survivors depends on how the person died, whether the death took place suddenly or over time, and how old the person was. A sudden death in a fatal accident can produce a severe grief reaction. An expected death may produce a less extreme immediate reaction (Almberg, Grafstrom, & Windblad, 2000).

Older widows, for example, compared with younger widows, tend to show a less intense immediate grief response. But they may show intense grief months after the death (Aiken, 2001). Sanders (1980–1981) compared the scores on a "grief experience inventory" of forty-five bereaved spouses in two age groups (people over age 65 and those under age 63). She found that older spouses showed less grief than younger spouses at the time of a first interview (shortly after their spouse's death). At the second interview, older spouses showed higher scores than younger spouses on scales of denial and physical symptoms, and increases in ten other scales compared with younger spouses.

Wortman and Silver (1990) say many things can keep a person from coming to terms with loss—sudden death, poor health of the survivor, or the lack of social support. Under these conditions, grief can last for years. Martin and Elder (1993) also see grieving as a long-term process. They say that grief may come and go in cycles over long periods of time. Northcott and Wilson (2001, p. 156) say that, "grief is never truly over." These results show that an older person may need support long after his or her spouse's death.

Baker (1991) reports that spouses who have died continue to influence the living in many ways. People sometimes talk to a dead spouse, ask them for advice, or try to imagine what they would do in a situation the surviving spouse is facing. One woman said she felt her husband lie down next to her in bed some months after his funeral. Widows or widowers sometimes decide against remarriage because of the close ties that still exist with their dead spouses. Moss and Moss (1984–1985, p. 204) consider this a normal response to widowhood in old age and "a nourishing link to the past." More research on bereavement in old age will show how this experience differs from bereavement in younger people (Wortman & Silver, 1990).

CONCLUSION

This chapter has touched on some of the complex issues related to death and dying. Each religion has its own views on issues such as euthanasia, funeral practices, and mourning. Each culture shapes its members' beliefs about the meaning of death, about life after death, and about care for the sick and dying. People will respond in unique ways to their own death and to the deaths of people they know and love. Today, changes in technology, the management of terminal illness, and the meaning of death raise new questions about death and dying. The study of death and dying can help people to understand these issues and make better choices for themselves. An incident from my life made this clear to me.

> After my father's funeral, my mother, my sister, my father's brothers, and I got into a rented limousine and drove to the cemetery. The funeral director stopped the cars in the funeral procession at the cemetery gate. We saw the hearse pull ahead and stop a hundred yards away. I turned around to talk to one of my uncles in our car. A few minutes later, the director waved all the cars on. We stopped behind the hearse and got out. It was empty. The director led us to the graveside. We stood close to the grave, but we could not see the coffin or any earth. A blanket of fake grass covered the earth that had come from the grave. Another blanket covered the coffin. Relatives and friends gathered to the side

and behind us. The director said some prayers and a few kind words. My mother, my sister, and I stood and stared at the fake grass. I think we were supposed to leave. But I motioned to the director to pull the grass back. He looked surprised. I told him to pull the grass back. He did. We saw the corner of the coffin and the corner of the grave, and we started to cry.

I tell this story because my knowledge of death and dying gave me the confidence to act. I felt I should do something to make my father's death real and begin the grieving process. And I knew what I had to do.

Those of us in the field of aging use our knowledge of aging each day. We use it to better understand our families and friends. And we use it to understand the changes we go through as we age. Knowledge about death and dying allows us to plan for our future with less fear and denial. The study of aging can make old age a better time of life for each of us and for the people we love.

SUMMARY

- Attitudes to death vary by age, religion, and culture. Older people generally accept death more than younger people. Like younger people, older people say they want to continue living, if they feel their life has meaning.
- People with either no religious belief or a very strong belief seem to cope with death best.
- Death occurs more often in old age today than in the past, and it also occurs more often in an institution. These trends will increase as the population ages.
- Elisabeth Kübler-Ross reports five stages of dying. Not everyone goes through all of these stages in the order Kübler-Ross describes, but her writings encouraged a more open discussion of death and dying when they first appeared.
- Cicely Saunders opened the first modern hospice in England in 1967. St. Christopher's Hospice offers an alternative to hospital care for the dying. Hospices offer pain control and a home-like setting for death.
- Palliative care units in hospitals offer the same comfort and care as a hospice. Some of these units will help patients die in their own homes. They also ensure patients that they can return to the hospital at any time.
- Most experts and patients prefer an open awareness context for dying. They agree that patients have a right to know about the choice of treatment the physician has made and about alternative treatments, including the choice of no treatment. Doctors today need to understand their own feelings about death and dying, so they can give their patients the kind of care that their patients prefer.
- Doctors say that proper pain control would end the fear that leads people to ask for euthanasia. The law today does not require doctors to take heroic measures to keep a terminally ill patient alive. Clearer guidelines would help doctors decide about stopping treatment for people in certain situations. The law prohibits active euthanasia.
- Health care directives relieve doctors of criminal liability. They give family members and doctors specific information about the amount of treatment a person prefers. They also state who has the right to make decisions on behalf of the patient.
- Death leads to grief and mourning for survivors. Culture and religion help people cope with feelings of grief. Funerals, for example, bring the community together and give mourners support. Still, each person has to work through feelings of grief in his or her own way. Researchers say that mourners go through stages of grief and that if all goes well they will emerge from grieving to carry on their lives.

DISCUSSION QUESTIONS

1. Researchers have proposed three theories that describe how older people respond to death. List and explain each of these theories.
2. Describe the means that older people use to buffer their fear of death.
3. How has population aging changed the context of dying?
4. Describe how Elisabeth Kübler-Ross and Cicely Saunders each influenced thinking about death and dying.

5. Explain the main function of a hospice. What methods do hospices use to help people enjoy their last days?
6. Compare and contrast palliative care units and hospices. Why do researchers think that, compared with a normal hospital, palliative care units cost less money to care for dying patients?
7. Discuss the differences between active and passive euthanasia? Discuss the pros and cons of physician-assisted suicide.
8. Describe Lindemann's three stages of grief. Describe successful grief work. How do older and younger people differ in their grieving patterns?

SELECTED READINGS

Brian de Vries (Ed.). (1999). *End of life issues: Interdisciplinary and multidimensional perspectives.* New York: Springer.

This book contains articles on current issues in aging and death. Topics include preferences for place of death, bereavement, communicating life-prolonging treatment wishes, and physician-assisted suicide. An excellent collection of current thinking in this field.

Kastenbaum, R. J. (2001). *Death, society, and human experience* (7th ed.). Boston: Allyn & Bacon.

A classic text in the field, the text offers up-to-date information on hospice care, end-of-life decisions, euthanasia, and bereavement. The book also covers unusual topics like survival after death. The book is well written, with good summaries of the research on death and dying.

GLOSSARY OF TERMS

active euthanasia Intervening actively to end a person's life.

advance directive A precise statement of the desired treatment and care, including what medical actions to be taken under what conditions and a declaration of who has the right to decide.

durable power of attorney The power that gives someone, usually a lawyer, child, friend, or other family member, the right to make decisions on behalf of the ill person.

ego integrity The acceptance of the notion that one's life cycle is something complete and unique.

ego transcendence A late stage of psychosocial development, in which people feel a deep concern for others and for the culture they will leave when they die.

euthanasia Ending the life of someone suffering a terminal illness or incurable condition.

grief work The process of grieving, which includes breaking bonds to the deceased, readjusting to the environment without the deceased, and forming new relationships.

health care directive Instructions with specific information for family members and doctors about the amount of treatment the person prefers under different conditions.

hospice Hospices are health care services that meet the special needs of dying patients.

living will A legal document that specifies the limits of health care treatment desired in case of a terminal illness.

palliative care Care directed toward improving the quality of life for the dying, including symptom control and spiritual support as well as bereavement support and education.

passive euthanasia Withholding or ceasing treatment of someone who is ill or injured and not expected to recover.

physician-assisted suicide (PAS) Actively helping someone end his or her life either because the person asks for death or to relieve suffering.

chapter 15

POLITICS AND POLICIES

Maggie Kuhn started her career as a senior activist in 1972 at the age of 67. Gerontologists called her a "professional little old lady." She helped create and promote the causes of the **Gray Panthers**, a vocal and activist group. Through protests, speeches, and appearances on national television, she showed that older people have intelligence, energy, and political savvy. They also have experience that society needs and can use.

Maggie Kuhn said that the Gray Panthers use "the experience and survival knowledge of old people and the idealism and energy of young people to change attitudes and social policy. Our long range goals," she said, " are directed toward social change and in the direction of a more humane and just society" (Kuhn, 1976, p. 88; Kuhn, 1975, p. 360). Maggie lived these ideals until the end of her life on April 22, 1995. In its May/June 1995 issue, *Aging Today* wrote: "Young and old will remember her spirit as galvanizing the intergenerational movement she helped to foster."

Maggie Kuhn chose the activist's role. But older people stay politically involved in other ways too. Gerontologists study older people, politics, and policies from at least three points of view. First, they study voting patterns, political attitudes, and the age of people in public office. Second, they study **advocacy, activism**, and group conflict. This includes the study of **lobby groups** and the issue of **generational equity**. Third, they look at the policies and structures of government that serve older people.

This chapter looks at (1) political action including voting, attitudes, and office holding, (2) advocacy and activism, and (3) government policies and structures. The chapter concludes with a look at the future of aging, politics, and policy in America.

Maggie Kuhn, founder of the Gray Panthers, at the microphone. She inspired others with her desire to improve social life for the young and old.

VOTING

Older people take part in politics in many ways. They listen to public affairs shows on radio and television, they give money to political parties, and they work on political campaigns. They also vote, run for office, and engage in political advocacy and activism. Some of these activities demand more involvement than others. Voting, for example, takes the least effort but allows for the involvement of the most older people. Studies in the 1960s reported that the proportion of people voting peaked in middle age and dropped off in older age groups (Milbrath, 1965). These studies supported the idea that older people disengage from social and political life.

More recent studies report that older people stay engaged and consider voting an important obligation. Love (2004) conducted a survey for the AARP (see Table 15.1). He found that 89 percent of people aged 40 to 69 considered voting "a very important obligation." Ninety-three percent of people aged 70 and over held this view. This survey asked people whether they considered themselves politically active." Seven percent of people aged 40 to 57 considered themselves "very active." Six percent of people aged 58 to 69 gave this response. Nine percent of people aged 70 and over considered themselves "very active" politically.

The U.S. Census Bureau (2000d) reports that in the November 1998 election a large majority of older people registered and voted. For example, 77.1 percent of people aged 65 to 74 registered to vote and 63.3 percent voted. In that same year 73.2 percent of people aged 75 and over registered to vote and 54.8 percent voted. These figures show that older people stay active and engaged in political life into late old age. Only in late old age (age 75 and over) do declines in voting occur, mostly due to poor health. (See Table 15.2.)

Cox (1993, p. 379) says that older people are "interested and better informed about political developments and are more likely to participate actively in the process themselves." Older people have more time than younger people to stay informed about political issues and to take part in the political process (Vierck, 2000).

Participation Trends among Older Voters

Among older voters, compared with women, men have a higher proportion of registrants and a higher proportion of voters. Also, compared with women, older men show less decline in registration and voting with increased age. For example, men show no decline in registration even after age 75 (U.S. Census Bureau, 2000d).

Studies of voting show that voting participation increases with education (Burr, Caro, & Moorhead, 2002). Among those aged 65 to 74, only 38.5 percent of people with less than a grade 9 education voted in the November 1998 election. But in this same age group, 80.2 percent of men and women with five years or more of college voted (U.S. Census Bureau, 2000d). Among the oldest age group (75 and over), those with five years or more of college voted at twice the rate of people with less than a grade 9 education (72.6 percent compared with 36.7 percent). Also, the higher a person's level of education, the greater the likelihood the person will work for a campaign and for a political party (Jirovec & Erich, 1992).

TABLE 15.1
Political Activity in Later Life

In this table you will find results from a 2004 AARP survey of political activity among middle-aged and older Americans.

24. How politically active would you say you are, are you very active, somewhat active, not very active, or not active at all?

	40–57	*58–69*	*70+*
Very active	7%	6%	9%
Somewhat active	43	45	41
Not very active	31	31	27

30. These days, many people are so busy they can't find time to register to vote, or move around so often that they don't get a chance to re-register. Are you now registered to vote in your precinct or election district or haven't you been able to register so far?

	40–57	*58–69*	*70+*
Registered to vote	84%	92%	91%
Haven't registered	16	8	9

33. Do you, yourself, plan to vote in the election this November (2004)?

	40–57	*58–69*	*70+*
Yes	90%	93%	92%
No (skip to 35)	7	5	5
Don't know (skip to 35)	3	2	2

34. How certain are you that you will vote (in the election this November 2004)? Are you absolutely certain, fairly certain, or not certain?

	40–57	*58–69*	*70+*
Absolutely certain	83%	87%	85%
Fairly certain	13	9	11
Not certain	5	4	3
Don't know	—	1	1

The findings show, overall, that political activity and interest either show little difference between older and younger age groups or increase in older age groups. Older people show roughly the same commitment to voting as do younger age groups. Seventeen percent of the people in the 70 plus group said they would like to be more politically active. But they had "difficulty getting around." These findings show that people stay politically active into late old age. And only health limitations keep them from being more active.

Source: Love, J. (2004). *Political behavior and values across the generations.* AARP Strategic Issues Research. Retrieved December 5, 2004, *research.aarp.org/general/politics_values.pdf.*

People with higher incomes also show greater tendencies to vote. Only 32.2 percent of people aged 65 to 74 who reported a family income under $5,000 voted in November 1998. But 78.8 percent of people in this age group who earned $75,000 or more voted. Even among the oldest age group, the wealthiest group voted at twice the rate of the poorest group (U.S. Census Bureau, 2000d).

Educated, affluent people tend to understand the political system. They also see a strong link between voting and social policies such as taxation (Cox, 1993). This gives them a reason to vote and to believe that their vote will make a difference. It also gives them more influence over the electoral system and public policy.

Minority group elders have lower rates of voting than the general population. Among older people, a higher proportion of non-Hispanic whites compared with non-Hispanic African Americans and Hispanics report registering and voting (U.S. Census Bureau, 2000d). The gap between the proportion of white and minority voters grows with age. The oldest Hispanic women (aged 75 and over), for example, had the lowest turnout. Only 31.6 percent of this group voted in the November 1998 election (compared with 51.7 percent of non-Hispanic white women in this age group).

Culture, language, and literacy barriers may keep some minority older people from voting. Also, minority elders may feel less hopeful than whites that their vote will improve their lives.

Still, minority groups show greater voter participation among older than younger age groups. African Americans aged 65 to 74, for example, had the highest proportion of voters among African Americans in the November 1998 election. Fifty-eight percent of African Americans aged 65 to 74 voted (compared with 40 percent for all African Americans aged 18 and over). Likewise, Hispanic elders aged 65 to 74 voted at almost double the rate of Hispanics as a group in that election. Forty-five percent of Hispanics aged 65 to 74 voted (compared with 20 percent for all Hispanics aged 18 and over (U.S. Census Bureau, 2000d).

Love (2004) found that voter participation reflects the values of older people today. For example, Love reports that 91 percent of this group registered to vote and 90 percent voted in the 2000 election. Also 76 percent of people aged 70 and over consider voting "an act of patriotism." They don't necessarily believe that voting gives them a say in how the government runs things. Only 37 percent of those aged 70 and over strongly agreed with this. But they do feel that a person should vote "regardless of how they feel about the candidates."

The oldest age group believes in the democratic electoral process. Compared with younger age groups, older people also report more commitment to the two major political parties (Vierck, 2002). Historical events have shaped these views. People aged 70 and over today grew up in a more patriotic age. Many of them served in World War II. Compared with younger people today, older people feel more respect for the government. They may also identify their own sense of self-worth with the social order they helped create and maintain. Does this

TABLE 15.2

Reported Voting and Registration, by Sex and Age: November 1998

Age Group	*Percent Registered*	*Percent Voting*
18 and over	62.1	41.9
18–24	39.2	16.6
25–34	52.4	28.0
35–44	62.3	40.7
45–54	69.3	50.7
55–64	74.0	57.9
65–74	77.1	63.3
75 and over	73.2	54.8

This table shows the proportion of people in various age groups who registered to vote and then voted in the November 1998 election. The figures show that both registration and percent voting increase with age until age 75. After age 75 registration to vote remains relatively high, but the percentage of people who vote drops off. This table shows that older people maintain their interest in political life into late old age. A decline in the physical ability accounts for the decline in voting later in life.

Source: Adapted from U.S. Census Bureau. (2000). Voting and registration in the election of November 1998. Detailed tables for current population report, P20-523. Washington, D.C. Retrieved December 6, 2004, *www.census.gov/population/socdemo/voting/cps1998/tab01.txt.*

mean that older people take a conservative stance on political issues?

The AARP study shows some evidence of this. Love (2004) found that members of the oldest age group are "largely conservative on economic (59%) and social (49%) issues, and about one-third of them say they have become more conservative on economic, social, foreign policy, moral, and legal issues as they have aged."

On the other hand, the oldest group (70 plus), like the middle-aged groups, showed support for more welfare programs to help the poor and support for more environmental protection. The AARP study shows that older people's views differ by issue. Compared with middle-aged people, they tend to favor prayer in schools and increased military defence. But they support strong government-run Social Security and Medicare systems. A recent Gallup poll (Barry & Duka, 2002) found that older people, more than other age groups considered Social Security and a Medicare drug benefit as top national priorities.

Love says that issues such as environmental protection and Medicare may not reflect conservative or liberal views. They may reflect self-interest and an interest in the good of the larger community.

What will future voting patterns look like as the Baby Boom generation enters old age? Baby Boomers as a group report a slightly more liberal tendency than older cohorts on economic and social issues. For example, on economic issues 16 percent of Baby Boomers rate themselves as "moderately liberal." This compares with 12 percent of the group aged 58 to 69 and 11 percent of the 70 plus group who rate themselves this way. This same trend holds for social issues. Nineteen percent of Baby Boomers rated themselves as "moderately liberal" compared with 16 percent of the 58 to 69 year olds and 11 percent of the 70 plus group.

The Baby Boomers, more than the two other age groups, felt that they had become more conservative as they've gotten older. This may reflect their starting point. As children of the 1960s social revolution, they may feel a strong contrast between their more moderate views today and the radical views they held in the past. On the other hand, this group may continue to grow more conservative over time and may come to share the views of many seniors today.

Most studies of voting today use cross-sectional methods. They compare the voting patterns of younger and older age groups at one point in time, so they cannot tell us whether voting patterns change as people age. Probably voting behavior reflects some increase in commitment to the social order with age. It probably also reflects attitudes toward government and authority that people develop in their early years. New cohorts of older people may feel less commitment to the system and to party politics.

The AARP study reported that, compared with older cohorts, the Baby Boomers feel they owe the least obligation to the country (Love, 2004). They feel the least obligation to pay attention to the political process. They also report the strongest feelings of self-interest. The Baby Boom cohorts that came of age in the 1960s, compared with the World War II generation, will probably take a more liberal view of social policies. But they also show a skepticism toward the political process. They may take part in other kinds of political action as well, like protests and lobbying.

Will Older People Form a Voting Bloc?

Binstock (2000) reports that older people have a greater impact on election results today than in the past. He found that the proportion of total votes that older people cast rose from 15.4 percent in 1966 to 20.3 percent in 1996. This, in part, reflects the growing size of the older population. It also reflects a decline in the voter participation rate for younger people.

Vierck (2002, p. 56) calls older people "an important voting bloc." And she predicts that more older people will cast their votes in the future. First, the population of older people will increase, so older people will make up a larger proportion of voters. Second, people coming into old age today have better incomes and more education than older people in the past. This may lead to more interest in politics and greater voter turnout in the future. She says that "Older Americans are projected to become an even more powerful voting group as the aging population swells" (Vierck, 2000, p. 56).

Some writers predict that this high voter turnout and the growing number of older people will create a power bloc. They fear that older people will gain control of local and national politics (and of government budgets). Rosenbaum and Button (1989, p. 301) call this the "gray peril hypothesis."

Gerontologist Robert Binstock (2000) questions this assumption. True, when all of the Baby Boom generation reaches age 65 they will make up one-quarter of the voting age population. And they may cast between one-third and two-fifths of all votes in a presidential election. Binstock says that the large and growing number of older voters hold more symbolic than real power. They could sway an election by voting as a bloc on a specific issue (e.g., Social Security or Medicare). But he doubts that this will happen.

Binstock (2000) says that people aged 65 and over hold varied political beliefs. Older people's views differ by social class, race, and gender. People of different groups within the older population have different concerns. A study of voting patterns related to Social Security, for example, showed that, compared with wealthier voters, lower income voters showed a stronger concern for and commitment to the Social Security system. This reflects the lower income person's dependence on Social Security income. Campbell (2002) says that this shows the power of self-interest in shaping voting preferences.

"Diversity among older persons," Binstock says, "may be at least as great with respect to political attitudes and behavior as it is in relation to economic, social, and other characteristics" (Binstock, 1991a, p. 331, citing Hudson & Strate, 1985). Binstock says that older voters choose a candidate for many reasons—race, ethnicity, environmental policies. They rarely vote for someone based on one issue, such as age, or out of self-interest.

Even on age-related issues, older people differ in their views and vote for different candidates. Social class, for example, plays a bigger role in voting behavior than age. A wealthy man may decide to vote against a program to help poor older women if the program increases his taxes. Differences in ethnicity, lifelong attachment to a political party, and urban and rural differences all fragment the older vote. Older people often look at an issue with an eye to how their vote will affect their children and grandchildren.

Robert Blendon of the Harvard University School of Public Health agrees. He says that older Americans could certainly "drive a change in Congress if they just focused on seniors' issues. But with everything else going on, they may vote on other things" (cited in Barry & Duka, 2002). Barry and Duka (2002) support this conclusion. They say that "the economy, stock market, corporate scandals" terrorism, and patriotism all shape older peoples' choices on election day. Even large organizations such as the AARP, with over 35 million members, cannot deliver blocks of votes. Binstock (1991a) says that in the 1980 presidential election, for example, leaders of age-based organizations supported President Jimmy Carter, but the majority of older people in that election voted for Ronald Reagan. Binstock (1978) says,

> There is little reason to believe that a phenomenon termed "senior power" will significantly increase the proportion of the budget devoted to the aging, or redirect that portion of the budget toward solving the problems of the severely disadvantaged. Whatever senior power exists is held by organizations that cannot swing decisive voting blocs.

Still, older people as a group have influenced legislation in the recent past, although not generally through voting. Lobbying efforts, for example, helped pass the Medicare legislation of 1965. Protests to Congress helped repeal the Medicare Catastrophic Coverage Act in 1989. The growing number of older people means that politicians cannot afford to ignore their concerns. Torres-Gil (1992, p. 75) says that "senior citizens might not always have been the principal player [in policy decisions], but they have been an important one."

HOLDING POLITICAL OFFICE

Williamson and his colleagues (1982) say that in the United States older people make up a high proportion of political officeholders, and the highest political posts often have the oldest people in them. This happens, in part, because a person tends to move to higher positions over time.

Schlesinger (1966, cited in Williamson, Evans, Powell, & Hesse-Biber, 1982) found that the younger a person's age, the less important was the office held. For example, election to the House of Representatives will tend to come at an earlier age than election as governor. And this tends to come earlier than election as a senator. Presidents often get elected late in their careers. Many presidents have passed age 65 in office, although the United States has elected only two presidents over age 65—William Henry Harrison and Ronald Reagan.

Exceptions to older officeholders do occur. John F. Kennedy, Bill Clinton, George W. Bush, and other middle-aged people have reached high office in the United States. The last two presidential elections, in particular, show a trend toward younger presidents. This could reflect the Baby Boom generation's desire to elect presidents from their own cohort.

As this group ages, the trend toward older presidents could return. Still, the system favors the older officeholder. Older members of the Senate and House of Representatives, for example, have more power than younger members. They serve on and chair the most powerful committees due to Congress's seniority system. These powerful leaders can shape legislation to serve their states and districts. This gives voters an incentive to reelect older politicians, and it keeps some members of Congress in their jobs into their 80s. Supreme Court justices also tend to stay in office past age 65. Justices usually get appointed in their late 50s. Some stay on the court past age 90.

This gives a select group of older people direct access to power and influence. Does this mean that older politicians promote older people's concerns? Not necessarily. Spivack (1992) assessed Washington lobbyists' views of politicians. Lobbyists ranked some of Congress's oldest senators as opponents of programs for older people.

ADVOCACY

Senior advocacy groups have played an important role in national politics in the past half century. The earliest advocacy groups, in the 1930s, set the stage for the Social Security system. More recently, in the mid-1960s, advocacy groups promoted Medicare and Medicaid legislation. They succeeded in getting this legislation passed, over the protests of powerful groups like the American Medical Association. Today, advocacy groups lobby government officials to maintain and expand current programs for older people.

Gerontologists disagree over how best to describe senior advocacy. One perspective views older people's political actions as a form of social movement. A social movement forms when a group (1) comes together around a set of issues, (2) creates a media image of itself as concerned and important, (3) places pressure on government and policy decision makers, and (4) has expertise and can raise money or votes to support its issues (Hendricks & Hendricks, 1986). Gerontologists disagree on whether age can form the basis of a social movement. Binstock (1972), for example, says that seniors' groups lack enough financial stability, organizational rigor, and supporters to form a social movement.

Pratt (1983) disagrees. He sees a growing group consciousness among older people in the United States today. He predicts this will form the basis of a future social movement. Today, some groups show the characteristics of a social movement. They define issues, promote themselves as concerned, and put pressure on government to shape policies. But they have not succeeded in creating a social movement, and the diversity of the older population makes it unlikely that they will.

A second perspective sees older people's political influence as an example of "interest group pluralism" (Williamson, Evans, Powell, & Hesse-Biber, 1982, p. 12). This perspective views public policy as the "outcome of competition among a variety of groups." Each group expresses the interests of its members, advocates for its position, and competes with other groups for scarce public resources. Most experts agree that older people's organizations have played this role for at least sixty years.

Binstock (1991a) describes three forms of political power available to senior advocacy groups. First, these groups have access to elected officials in Congress, to government policymakers, and sometimes to the White House. They can present their views on legislation and policy issues.

The National Institute of Senior Centers and the National Council on the Aging (1993), for example, developed an advocacy manual for board members, coordinators of programs, and senior services volunteers. The manual instructs readers on how to influence local, state, and national political decisions. The manual contains instructions on how to meet with a legislator, how to influence state or national legislative bills, and how to lobby within legal limits. The manual targets increased support for senior services under the Older Americans Act.

Other groups such as the Coalition of Women in Long Term Care lobby for improvements in the long-term system. This group claims over 200 members including nursing home owners, nurses, and representatives of the home health industry (Flippen, 1998).

Second, advocacy groups have access to the media. Large and influential groups such as the AARP can speak out at congressional hearings and conferences and can play a role in national policy forums like the White House Conferences on Aging.

Third, they can use what Binstock calls "the electoral bluff." He says that politicians treat older people seriously because they do not want to offend a large group of potential supporters. Senior lobby groups use all of these methods to influence national and local policies.

Senior advocacy groups first gained national attention in the United States in the 1930s. Writer Upton Sinclair proposed a plan in California to give people aged 60 and over a $50 per month pension. Another California group, called Ham and Eggs, proposed a weekly pension for unemployed people aged 50 and over. This group held marches and rallies and sponsored radio shows. It claimed 300,000 members. Both Sinclair's program and Ham and Eggs folded before achieving their goals.

A third advocacy group, the Townsend movement, began at the same time in California. This group committed itself to legislative reform. The Townsend plan (named after the founder of the movement, Dr. Francis Townsend) proposed that the government pay older people in the United States $200 a month. Older people who got the money would agree to stay out of the labor force and would spend the money within thirty days. Townsend designed this plan to give older people an income and to stimulate the economy during the Depression. As many as 2 million people joined this movement by the mid-1930s (Burg, 1999).

The Townsend movement flexed its political muscles only once, in 1934. It successfully defeated an incumbent congressman, who showed little concern for aging issues. The movement put its own candidate, John McGroarty, 72 years old, into office. McGroarty had no success in getting the Townsend plan adopted in Washington, and the Townsend movement never reached its goal of a monthly wage for older people.

The movement's success at the polls, however, led to national recognition of its goals. The movement also pressured politicians to pass the Social Security Act. Wallace and his colleagues say that from this point on "the elderly promised to be a significant force in American politics" (Wallace, Williamson, Lung, & Powell, 1991, p. 98; *also* Burg, 1999).

Today, senior advocacy groups have greater access to politicians and to Congress than ever before. Achenbaum (2000a) notes the recent growth in size and influence of lobby groups that serve older people. These include over one hundred organizations that advocate for older adults or represent professionals who work with older people.

Gray lobby groups such as the **AARP**, for example, set out legislative agendas, open offices in state capitals, and gain pledges from lawmakers to support senior issues. They can even threaten to oppose lawmakers who renege on their pledges or fail to support senior issues (Serafini, 2002). "Whatever AARP chooses to do (or not do)," Binstock says, "tends to define the overall position of the old-age lobby" (1997, p. 65).

Wallace and his colleagues (1991, p. 103) say that senior lobby groups, such as the AARP, get their power from "organizational cohesiveness" and the claim that they represent millions of older people. Achenbaum (2000b) says that in the future, gray lobby groups will create links to women's groups and groups that represent people with disabilities. These groups share concerns that overlap with those of the older population.

A recent response to nonprofit lobby groups suggests the influence of older people on Congress. Lieberman (2000) reports on the work of a conservative think tank, the Capital Research Center. This group attempted to discredit the AARP to weaken its ability to influence Social Security and Medicare legislation. The think tank criticized the AARP's size, its support of liberal causes, and the size of its office in Washington.

This attack led to Senate hearings on the organization's finances and practices. The attack weakened the AARP's lobbying efforts for a time and led the organization to soften its support for Social Security and Medicare. Future debates over health care costs will keep senior lobby groups at the center of political action. A closer look at these groups will describe their goals, the people they serve, and how they influence lawmakers.

The American Association of Retired Persons

The AARP "is dedicated to enhancing quality of life for all as we age. We lead positive social change and deliver value to members through information, advocacy and service." The association envisions "a society in which everyone ages with dignity and purpose, and in which AARP helps people fulfill their goals and dreams" (AARP, 2003a). In 2004, the association had over 3,200 local chapters, over 35 million members, and offices in all fifty states, including the District of Columbia, Puerto Rico, and the U.S. Virgin Islands.

The AARP grew out of the National Retired Teachers Association (NRTA) that began in 1947. In 1955, the NRTA began to offer group life insurance to its members. This program grew so popular that in 1958 the NRTA formed the AARP so that people other than retired teachers could get this insurance. By 1982, the NRTA had become a division of the larger AARP.

The AARP attracts its large membership for at least two reasons. First, it has a low membership fee. Membership for one year (in 2004) cost $12.50 for a person aged 50 and over (the person's spouse gets membership for free). This includes a subscription to *AARP The Magazine* and the *AARP Bulletin* (the AARP also prints *AARP Segunda Juventud,* a quarterly newspaper in Spanish). Second, the AARP offers services to its members including life and health insurance, a discount pharmacy service, special credit card rates, travel, education programs, and other services.

In its annual report, the AARP states that it earned $770 million in revenue in 2003 from membership fees, insurance funds, and services. The association also earned $78 million from advertisers in its publications. Earnings from fees, insurance, and services allow the AARP to maintain a lobbying and public affairs staff. Research also makes up part of the AARP agenda. For example, the association joined with the National Council on the Aging to produce a study titled, *American Perceptions of Aging in the 21st Century* (Cutler, Whitelaw, & Beattie, 2002). This study surveyed American attitudes toward aging. The AARP also sponsors research on housing, social policies, and retirement in the United States. It also supports and manages the *Ageline* computerized database that contains reports on thousands of studies in the field of aging.

The AARP takes a neutral stance toward both major political parties. This broadens the association's membership base, keeps the association's tax-free status, and keeps both parties anxious to please. The organization also supports lobby groups in every state and promotes political organization in all of the U.S. congressional districts. The organization keeps members up to date on aging issues through reports and bulletins. It also attempts to shape members' opinions on current issues.

An article in the January 2005 issue of the *AARP Bulletin,* for example, contained an analysis of President Bush's plan to reform Social Security (Goozner, 2005). The article reviews the Administration's plan to allow workers to set up private savings accounts with their Social Security payroll taxes. The plan would allow workers to invest their money in the stock market and take advantage of potential gains in market value.

BOX 15.1
SILVER-HAIRED LEGISLATURES

Many lobbyists have expense accounts, $1,000 suits, and expensive watches. Behind them stand large corporations such as oil and gas companies or telecommunications giants. But a more modest breed of lobbyist also exists. These people work the state legislatures on behalf of older people. Some of them are older people themselves. Legislators respect them for their commitment to their cause and their knowledge of the issues.

Twenty-seven states in the United States have created channels for this activity. Most states call these groups Silver-Haired Legislatures. The first of these began in 1970 in Missouri. People aged 55 and over can serve in these legislatures. But, Vierck (2000) says, members average age 80. Members include teachers, doctors, and business people. These representatives meet with state legislators to express their constituents' concerns. They also keep their constituents up to date on legislation. Silver-Haired Legislatures in most cases meet for a few days each year. They then prepare and present a list of priority proposals to their legislators. Silver-Haired Legislators in Florida claim that over 100 of the issues they supported have gone on to become state law. This group worked with actual legislators to create the State Department of Elder Affairs (Vierck, 2000).

Below, journalist Linda Wagar profiles two active and successful senior lobbyists.

When most men his age were tinkering with their fly-casting equipment, John Holtermann was starting a new career.

At 74, Holtermann was elected to the Silver-Haired Legislature, a group of senior citizens who helps apprise the Texas Legislature of senior concerns. For most members that means attending the group's biannual meeting and helping draft a legislative agenda.

But for Holtermann, that's only where the job begins. Now 81, he has turned a part-time volunteer assignment into a steady unpaid labor. As one of the group's lobbyists, he makes the 45-minute drive from his home in San Marcos to Austin whenever the Texas Legislature is in session.

He's such a fixture in committee rooms and legislative offices that most lawmakers—and even the governor—greet him by name.

He speaks proudly of a 70 percent track record in passing legislation on causes as varied as more stringent licensing of nursing homes to continued funding for child abuse centers.

"If we supported just the issues that affect 65-year-olds, we wouldn't be thinking about the future," said Holtermann.

Grace Matthew Maratta cried as she watched the bill she had spent months coddling through the legislative process die on the floor of the Ohio House.

She tells the story nearly 10 years later, laughing at her own innocence.

"I was new at the time and I thought I had gotten the bill through the system," said Maratta, a volunteer lobbyist for the Police and Fire Retirees Association. "I didn't realize that at the drop of a hat things could change."

When the bill failed, she awakened to the not-so-sweet reality of the legislative process. But she kept on fighting and three years later the increase was approved.

It has become one of a number of successes for Maratta in the Ohio Legislature. She, however, shares the credit with her best friend Catherine Phillips, who lobbies alongside her.

Their latest cause is a 3 percent cost-of-living increase for the widows of firefighters and police officers.

Now 70, Maratta is impatient about getting that bill through. She enjoys lobbying, but walking the marble floors is hard on her artificial hip and she is uncertain how much longer she'll have the strength to continue.

Not that quitting would be easy. She tried to retire three years ago, but the retirees association couldn't find anyone willing to take her place. At least not for free.

Source: From "Savvy Senior Lobbyists," by L. Wagar, 1993, *State Government News,* June 16–18, pp. 16–17. Reprinted with permission.

The AARP warns that this approach puts workers' retirement savings at risk. If the market performs poorly, many older Americans could find themselves with little or no pension savings. The analysis presents the facts about the proposed policy. But it also attempts to sway the opinion of AARP's large membership against the proposal.

The article ends with a picture of army troops in a line getting ready to lob grenades at an enemy outside the picture's frame. An invitation under the photo reads: "Call to Action! Call AARP's hotline . . . and tell your members of Congress to oppose private accounts that take money out of Social Security . . ." (AARP, 2005a, p. 15).

The AARP will face a challenge as its membership increases in size. More members will increase the association's potential influence, but it will also increase differences in members' views on issues. For example, some members of the AARP will agree with the organization's opposition to privatized Social Security accounts. But some wealthier and investment-savvy members may favor the President's plan. The diversity of the AARP's membership will make focused advocacy more difficult in the future (Binstock, 1997). An organization with a diverse membership such as the AARP has a hard time speaking for its members' many interests (let alone the interests of all older people).

Many other advocacy groups for older people exist. They include the National Council on the Aging, the National Association of Retired Federal Employees, and minority group organizations such as the National Hispanic Council on Aging and the National Caucus and Center on Black Aged. Smaller groups, such as the Older Women's League, lobby on behalf of specific constituencies. All of these groups educate, give out information, and make government agencies aware of their members' needs. Some groups sponsor model social programs and support research on aging. All of them claim to speak on behalf of some group of older people.

The Limits of Advocacy

Senior advocacy groups can influence policy, but they have limited political power. Even in the past, critics say, senior organizations played only a supporting role in creating social policy (Jacobs, 1990). Non–age-based groups (like the labor unions) played a bigger role than senior advocacy groups in shaping legislation and policy.

Pratt (1983) says that at least three things stifle the impact of senior advocacy groups. First, many members join these groups for personal reasons—to get insurance benefits or discount drugs. They do not support the group's political aims. An AARP poll, for example, found that 40 percent of members join for cheap insurance and other benefits. Only 14 percent join to support lobby efforts. Only about 400,000 members (out of 33 million members) play an active part in policy debates (Novack, 1991). As a result, a group like the AARP cannot deliver the votes of its members.

Second, senior groups show surges and declines in support from members. Surges often occur when federal benefits (like Social Security or Medicare) get threatened. Otherwise, most members show relatively little interest in policy issues.

Third, senior groups have to spread their lobbying efforts in Washington. They do this because many congressional committees and government agencies deal with senior-related issues (housing, health, pensions). This means that senior groups cannot focus their efforts on one or two key players involved in aging policy.

Advocacy on behalf of older people has more impact on public policy than does voting. But, in the case of both lobbying and voting, the diversity of the older population dampens seniors' clout. Advocacy groups show their greatest strength, Pratt (1983, p. 165) says, "when it comes to defending the sanctity of existing public programs. . . ; it tends to be easier to veto change than to initiate it successfully." The case of the Medicare Catastrophic Coverage Act (MCCA) makes this clear.

The Medicare Catastrophic Coverage Act: A Case Study in Senior Advocacy

The story of the MCCA, Torres-Gil (1992, p. 80) says, reveals "much about the future of the politics of aging." It shows the government's concern for older people, the limits of government support for older people's programs, and the potential for class conflict within the older population.

Holstein and Minkler (1991, p. 189) call the MCCA of 1988 "the greatest expansion of Medicare since the program's establishment in 1965." This act (1) put a cap on hospital and physician expenses; (2) granted more coverage for prescription drugs, and some new Medicaid payments by the states; (3) included a small expansion of long-term care coverage; (4) protected some spousal assets from the *spend down* required for Medicaid-sponsored nursing home care; and (5) created a commission to study long-term care and health care for uninsured people.

The MCCA funded these benefits by asking older people to pay more for Medicare (up to $800 per year). The act also required an added Medicare payment from older people with incomes over $25,000 a year. Congress passed this legislation by a large majority. Members of both parties supported the MCCA. So did major senior lobby groups like the AARP. To Congress' surprise, the act raised a storm of protest from groups of (mostly well-off) older people.

Older people rejected this legislation for several reasons. First, the legislation improved benefits for cases of acute illness but did not include relief from the costs of long-term care. For instance, the act did not cover nursing home costs, an average cost of $29,000 a year. This left middle-class and wealthier older people without protection for one of their greatest present and future health care expenses. It failed to relieve the fear that a long-term illness could wipe out a lifetime of savings (Torres-Gil, 1990).

Second, many middle-class people had their own insurance coverage for acute care, or they had coverage through their retirement plans. These people saw little advantage to the new legislation. Third, wealthier older people rejected the idea of an extra tax on their payments.

Groups in Florida, California, and the southwest began to protest this legislation. The National Committee to Preserve Social Security and Medicare led a national drive to repeal the MCCA. This organization grew to 5 million people during the campaign. Older people from across the country wrote to Congress. Six thousand members of the AARP resigned from that organization to protest its support of the MCCA. The AARP (in a reversal of its earlier position) turned against the MCCA. By mid-1989, Congress felt enough pressure to repeal the MCCA. The repeal passed Congress by Thanksgiving of 1989.

This case study teaches at least three lessons about politics and policies for older people today. First, Congress sent a message to older people by passing the MCCA. This legislation symbolically said that Congress will support improvements in programs such as Medicare, but only if older people pay for these improvements themselves. The MCCA symbolized an end to the growth of government-supported programs for older people.

Second, the repeal of the MCCA shows the strong social class divisions that exist within the older population. Hudson (1994) says that the MCCA stirred up social class differences among older people. It charged wealthier older people more for benefits. Poorer older people paid less. Wealthier older people then acted on the basis of their class interests. They rejected the legislation. And they succeeded in having it repealed. This case shows that older people can, and will, act to protect their interests. But in this case, common economic interests, rather than age identity, led to political action.

Middle-class older people defeated a plan that would have helped poorer older people. Congressman Pete Stark, an author of the repeal, said "We are being stampeded by a small group to deny benefits to everyone else" (Binstock, 1992, p. 404). "By all accounts," Binstock says, "a relatively small, unrepresentative proportion of comparatively well-off older persons who were upset by having to pay a new progressively scaled surtax were able to cow their congressional representatives into repealing it [the MCCA]" (1992, p. 404).

Third, this case makes it clear that large lobby groups such as the AARP do not speak for all older people. The AARP supported the MCCA because its leadership supports more benefits for older people. But the AARP membership, mostly middle-class people, rejected the plan. When the AARP called for a repeal of the MCCA, it lost its chance to speak for poorer older people. Poorer people stood to gain the most from this act. But the AARP decided in the end to support its middle-class members.

The MCCA case shows the complexity of policymaking for older people today. **Compassionate ageism** in the past assumed that all older people suffered from low income, poor health, and lack of services (Binstock, 1992). This led to legislation that improved Social Security, created Medicare, and put in place the Older Americans Act. But older people as a group have diverse needs, and sometimes these needs clash. The needs of middle-class, working-class, and poor older people may differ. Middle-class people, for example, want lower taxes. Poorer people want more government services. Minority group needs may differ from those of the majority, and differences in need may exist between minority groups (Rivas & Torres-Gil, 1991). Policy in the future must take these diverse interests into account.

ACTIVISM

Some years ago Alex Comfort (1976, p. 29) gave the following advice to people entering old age:

> You are about to join an underprivileged minority. There is no way of avoiding this at present. The remedies available to you will be those available to other minorities—organization, protest and militancy. Don't get trapped into aging alone if you can help it. The time to organize and get into a posture to resist is before the floor falls out.

Activism complements the work of advocacy groups. Advocacy largely works within the system to reform or support existing programs. Rarely do advocacy groups speak out on broad social issues like inequality in later life. Activists, by contrast, work for fundamental social change. Often this change goes beyond narrow issues related to pensions and health care.

The Gray Panthers embody Comfort's call to action. The Gray Panthers call themselves "a national organization of intergenerational activists dedicated

Toles © 1989 *The Buffalo News.* Reprinted with permission of Universal Press Syndicate.

to social change. We are age and youth in action" (Gray Panthers, 2004). At the organization's high point in the 1970s and 1980s, it raised senior activism to a fine art. "Their approach to nursing-home reform, for example, was to stage a street play at the AMA Convention in Atlantic City in which a doctor sold patients to the Kill 'Em Quick Nursing Home; doctors' wives were reported to have glared in disapproval at what the old folks were doing" (Hapgood, 1978, p. 353).

Maggie Kuhn, first leader of the Gray Panthers, founded the organization in 1972 with six other retirees when her employer (a church in Philadelphia) forced her to retire. This group made a commitment to use their retirement years for public service. Maggie Kuhn's appearances on television and at rallies throughout the United States led to rapid growth in Gray Panther membership. At that time, the group claimed 50,000 members in one hundred *networks* throughout the country.

Maggie Kuhn's charisma and energy accounted for much of the Panthers' success. But this strength also points to the group's weaknesses. First, new leadership did not develop after Maggie Kuhn's death in 1995. This created a crisis that threatened the group's future. Second, the Panthers lack formal organization. The group claims fifty active local chapters but it lacks a strong central office. It also lacks long-term professional staff. Third, most Panther members want more power for older people, but they no longer get the press coverage for their views.

In 1997, the organization appointed a new board of directors and a new chair. Today, the Gray Panthers take a critical view of social policies, but they

BOX 15.2
INTEREST GROUP COALITIONS

Wallace and his colleagues call senior power "no more dangerous than a lamb in wolf's clothing." They say that older people as a group do not have the power to bring about social reform. Instead, older people most often succeed in creating change when they link their interests to those of other lobby groups.

Williamson and his colleagues support this view. They studied the start of Medicare and found that interest group coalitions formed over the ideological issue of growing state programs to redistribute services to the needy. The coalition in favor of Medicare supported more services to people in need. The coalition against Medicare opposed any transfer of funds from tax revenues. The following lists present the most influential members of the two groups.

For Medicare
AFL-CIO
American Nurses Association
Council of Jewish Federations and Welfare Funds
American Association of Retired Workers
National Association of Social Workers
National Farmers Union Federation
The Socialist Party
American Geriatrics Society

Against Medicare
American Medical Association
American Hospital Association
Life Insurance Association of America
National Association of Manufacturers
National Association of Blue Shield Plans
American Farm Bureau
The Chamber of Commerce
The American Legion

These coalitions support different social class interests. The unions and working class groups supported Medicare. Business and organized medicine opposed Medicare. Powerful pressure groups such as organized labor won the day. The overlap of labor's interests and those of older people led to success. Ironically, medical doctors and hospitals (opponents of Medicare) got some of the largest financial benefits from the program.

Sources: From J. B. Williamson, L. Evans, L. A. Powell, & S. Hesse-Biber, *The Politics of Aging: Power and Policy* (1982). Courtesy of Charles C. Thomas Publisher, Ltd., Springfield, Illinois. Also "A Lamb in Wolf's Clothing?" by S. P. Wallace, J. B. Williamson, R. G. Lung, & L. A. Powell (1991). In M. Minkler & C. L. Estes (Eds.), *Critical Perspectives on Aging,* Amityville, NY: Baywood.

BOX 15.3
THE WHITE HOUSE CONFERENCE ON AGING

Once a decade since 1961 the White House has held a Conference on Aging. As of this writing, the most recent conference took place May 2–5, 1995, with 2,217 delegates from across the country. (The next conference will take place on October 23-26, 2005).

Representatives of Congress and state governors appointed most of the delegates, who met and discussed sixty resolutions. The resolutions came from over 800 preconference meetings held around the country two years before the White House Conference on Aging. The delegates passed forty of these resolutions. They also passed ten resolutions developed in Washington by the conference delegates. Some of these resolutions may find their way into policy through executive order of the President. Others will work their way onto the legislative agenda.

The following list presents the top ten resolutions (out of forty) that passed from the list sent to the conference, and the ten resolutions that the conference delegates put forward and passed in 1995.

Resolutions

This list is ranked with the item receiving the highest number of votes at the top. The first resolution passed with 1,595 votes out of 2,002 ballots cast.

1. Keeping Social Security sound, now and for the future
2. Preserving the integrity of the Older Americans Act
3. Preserving the nature of Medicaid
4. Ensuring the future of the Medicare program
5. Preserving advocacy functions under the Older Americans Act
6. Ensuring the availability of a broad spectrum of services
7. Financing and providing long-term care and services
8. Acknowledging the contribution of older volunteers
9. Assuming personal responsibility for the state of one's health
10. Strengthening the federal role in building and sustaining a well-trained work force grounded in geriatric and gerontological education

Delegate-Generated Resolutions

This list is also ranked with the item receiving the most votes at the top.

1. Reauthorization of the Older Americans Act
2. Alzheimer's research
3. Meeting mental health needs
4. Long-term care financing
5. Social Security/entitlements
6. Protecting Medicare and Medicaid
7. Comprehensive health care
8. Need to preserve and expand elderly housing
9. Legal assistance
10. Income security

Note the similarities and differences in these two lists. Many of the items in both lists focus on basic needs like health, income, and social services.

The agenda for the 2005 conference contains the following topics: Planning Along the Lifespan, The Workplace of the Future, Community Supports, Health and Long-Term Living, Social Engagement, and The Marketplace. You can find out more about the resolutions passed and the topics discussed by going to the White House Conference on Aging website at *http://www.whcoa.gov/*.

Source: Reprinted with permission from "For the Record: 50 WHCOA Resolutions," *16*(4), pp. 6–7, 1995. Copyright © 1995 American Society on Aging, San Francisco, California. *www.asaging.org*.

look more like an advocacy group than an activist group. The group holds conventions, sells bumper stickers, buttons, and T-shirts. It raises awareness of senior issues on its website, criticizes the proposed privatization of Social Security, and supports improvements in Medicare (Gray Panthers, 2004).

A relatively small number of older people took part in senior activism in the past and even fewer do so today. But more people may choose this approach in the future. Baby Boom cohorts that protested in the 1960s and 1970s may feel more comfortable using an activist approach to social change. They may also use these methods to protest poverty, pollution, and other social problems.

GOVERNMENT AND AGING POLICY

Federal, state, and local governments now have a web of agencies, policies, and programs to serve older people. Some programs serve all older people; others target specific groups (Supplemental Security Income, for example, serves low-income older people). Some programs offer benefits for people to use as they wish (e.g., Social Security); others offer direct services, such as senior centers. These programs grew without a plan into what Gelfand (1993) calls the **aging network**.

This network creates a safety net that guarantees a minimum income and minimum health care for all older people. These programs and policies exist nationwide in rural and urban settings. They have enhanced the lives of older people for over thirty years. Many of the programs and much of the legislation related to this network comes out of the Older Americans Act.

BOX 15.4
FEDERAL GOVERNMENT INITIATIVES ON AGING

Since the 1950s the federal government has put into place a number of agencies, committees, and programs that develop and provide services for older people. The list below gives some of the most important developments in the aging network.

1959	U.S. Senate Special Committee on Aging established
1961	First White House Conference on Aging
1965	Older Americans Act passed; Medicare and Medicaid
1965	Administration on Aging established as an operating agency of the Department of Health, Education, and Welfare
1967	Age Discrimination in Employment Act signed into law
1971	Second White House Conference on Aging
1973	Older Americans Comprehensive Services Amendments (the Older Americans Act) passed; Area Agencies on Aging developed to plan services for older people statewide
1974	National Institute on Aging created
1978	Legislation raised mandatory retirement age from 65 to 70
1981	Third White House Conference on Aging
1986	Mandatory retirement eliminated
1987	Omnibus Budget Reconciliation Act set new standards for nursing home care
1988	Medicare Catastrophic Coverage Act passed
1989	Medicare Catastrophic Coverage Act repealed
1995	Fourth White House Conference on Aging
2004	Medicare prescription drug reimbursement implemented
2005	Fifth White House Conference on Aging

The greatest legislative activity on behalf of older people took place during the 1970s. The public supported these programs because they saw older people as poor and needy. By the 1980s, public opinion shifted and older people came to be seen as relatively well off. Recent attempts to create policies to help older people have met resistance due to this view. McKenzie suggests that supports for older people have peaked. He sees a trend toward higher taxes of Social Security benefits, higher costs for medical care, and a decline in older people's income.

Sources: From "Senior Status: Has the Power of the Elderly Peaked?" by R. B. McKenzie, 1993, *American Enterprise, 4*(3), pp. 74–80. www.TAEmag.com. See also, "The WHCOA and Lower Expectations," by R. Rosenblatt (1995). *Aging Today, 16*(2), p. 2.

Congressmen and seniors meet at a Capital Hill press conference to discuss prescription drug benefits to seniors under the Medicare program.

The Older Americans Act

The Older Americans Act (OAA) has served as the basis of federal government aging policy for over forty years. Congress introduced the OAA in 1965 with the goal of "assuring the well-being of the elderly." No other federal program has this single broad purpose. Funding for the act grew from $6.5 million in 1965 to just over $1.6 billion in 2002. This increase in funding reflects the OAA's increased responsibility for setting up a national service network for older people. The OAA also set up the Administration on Aging (AOA) within the federal Department of Health and Human Services.

The OAA charged the AOA "with the responsibility to serve as the advocate for older people at the national level, and to oversee the development of a comprehensive and coordinated system of care that will enable older individuals to remain at home and participate fully in the community life" (AOA, 2004c). The AOA has the responsibility to provide home and community services set out in the OAA. It is the official federal agency charged with looking after federal aging policy. It coordinates programs and services, sets policy, and conducts research on aging.

The AOA works with federal, state, local, and tribal agencies in the National Network on Aging (AOA, 2004d). The National Network on Aging serves about 7 million older people and caregivers. The Network has "56 State Units on Aging; 655 Area Agencies on Aging; 233 Tribal and Native organizations; two organizations that serve Native Hawaiians; 29,000 service providers; and thousands of volunteers" (AOA, 2004d).

The Network provides services to all older people. But most programs target poorer older people, people who live in isolation, and people with severe health problems. OAA programs (managed by the AOA) fall into six categories: supportive services, nutrition services, preventive health services, the National Family Caregiver Support Program, services that protect older people from abuse, and services to Native Americans. These services get state and local support as well as federal funding.

The federal government reauthorized the Older Americans Act in 2000. The reauthorization will extend the program through 2005. The reauthorization supports ongoing programs and provides for a new program—the National Family Caregiver Support Program. This program focuses support on family caregivers for ill or disabled older people. It recognizes the important role that family caregivers play in community long-term care. The program provided $125 million to state agencies on aging for the year 2001. The funding will provide information, counseling, support groups, respite care, and other supports to family caregivers (AOA, 2004b).

Some critics blame the AOA for not coordinating government aging policies and programs. But Torres-Gil (1992) says the position of the AOA within the federal government makes this impossible. In the United States many age-related policies and programs (like housing) come under other government departments. And each department has its own policies and programs. Representative Claude Pepper (1979, cited in Oriol, 1987), an advocate for older people's concerns, knew firsthand about the complex bureaucracy that serves older people. He called

BOX 15.5
OLDER AMERICANS ACT OF 1965, AS AMENDED 2000

TITLE 42—THE PUBLIC HEALTH AND WELFARE
CHAPTER 35—PROGRAMS FOR OLDER AMERICANS
SUBCHAPTER I—DECLARATION OF OBJECTIVES AND DEFINITIONS
SEC. 3001. CONGRESSIONAL DECLARATION OF OBJECTIVES

The Congress hereby finds and declares that, in keeping with the traditional American concept of the inherent dignity of the individual in our democratic society, the older people of our Nation are entitled to, and it is the joint and several duty and responsibility of the governments of the United States, of the several States and their political subdivisions, and of Indian tribes to assist our older people to secure equal opportunity to the full and free enjoyment of the following objectives:

1. An adequate income in retirement in accordance with the American standard of living.
2. The best possible physical and mental health which science can make available and without regard to economic status.
3. Obtaining and maintaining suitable housing, independently selected, designed and located with reference to special needs and available at costs which older citizens can afford.
4. Full restorative services for those who require institutional care, and a comprehensive array of community-based, long-term care services adequate to appropriately sustain older people in their communities and in their homes, including support to family members and other persons providing voluntary care to older individuals needing long-term care services.
5. Opportunity for employment with no discriminatory personnel practices because of age.
6. Retirement in health, honor, dignity—after years of contribution to the economy.
7. Participating in and contributing to meaningful activity within the widest range of civic, cultural, education and training and recreational opportunities.
8. Efficient community services, including access to low-cost transportation, which provide a choice in supported living arrangements and social assistance in a coordinated manner and which are readily available when needed, with emphasis on maintaining a continuum of care for vulnerable older individuals.
9. Immediate benefit from proven research knowledge which can sustain and improve health and happiness.
10. Freedom, independence, and the free exercise of individual initiative in planning and managing their own lives, full participation in the planning and operation of community-based services and programs provided for their benefit, and protection against abuse, neglect, and exploitation.

Source: U.S. Code Online via GPO Access, *wais.access.gpo.gov.* Laws in effect as of January 7, 2003. Document not affected by Public Laws enacted between January 7, 2003 and February 12, 2003. CITE: 42USC3001. Retrieved January 11, 2005, *http://frwebgate.access.gpo.gov/cgi-bin/getdoc.cgi?dbname=browse_usc&docid=Cite:+42USC3001.*

this tangle of agencies and services "fragmented, inefficient, unmanageable, and incomprehensible."

Some people suggest that the Area Agencies on Aging should coordinate all community programs, but all aging programs will probably never come under one authority. Instead, all parts of the government in the future will take the aging population into account. They will adjust programs to meet older people's needs.

State and local governments have begun to do this. They have developed innovative programs in case management and home care (Liebig, 1992). They also advocate on behalf of older people and their families for better federal funding of long-term

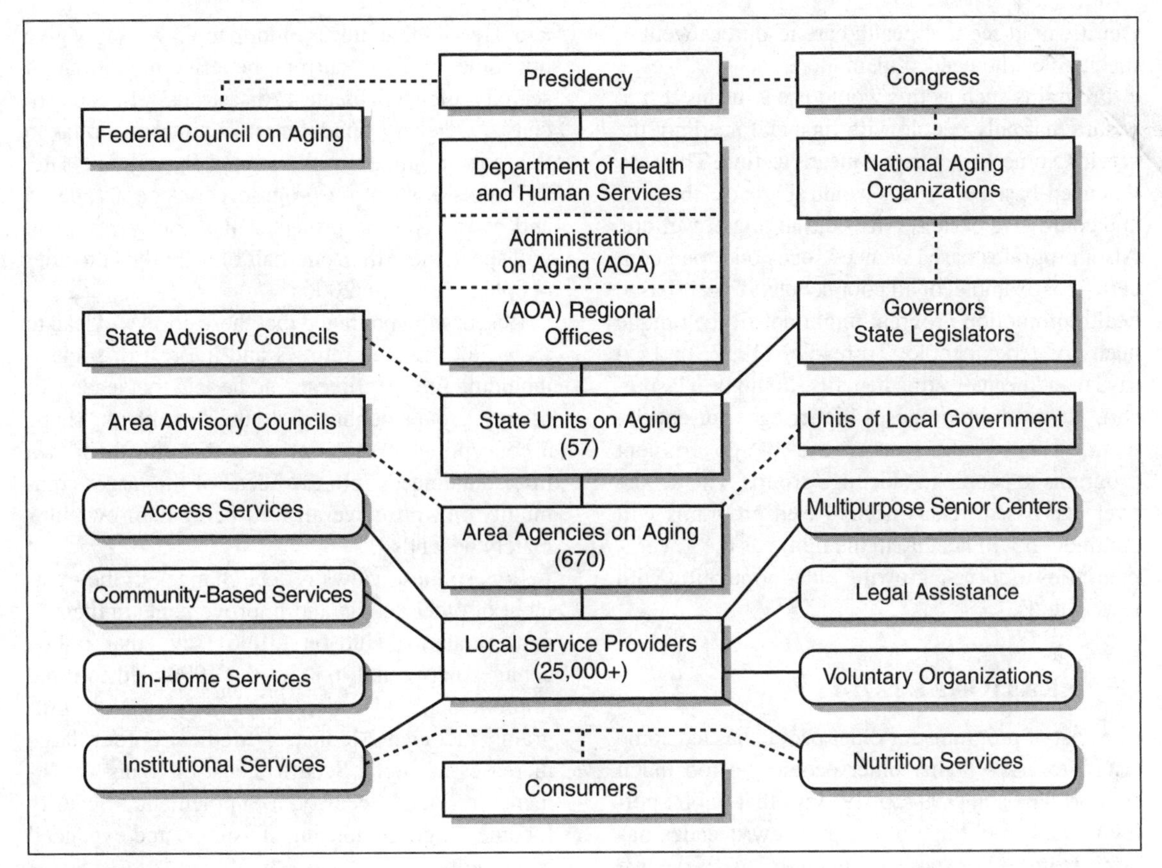

FIGURE 15.1
The Aging Network
Sources: Based on National Association of State Unity on Aging (1985); and The National Academy on Aging (1995). "Facts on the Older Americans Act," *Gerontology News,* November, 6.

care. Quirk (1991, p. 26) says that the state and local aging network in the years ahead will "play a key role in advancing the social, economic, and political agendas of the older population it was designed to serve." (See Figure 15.1.)

Still, Torres-Gil (1992) says, the existing web of services and programs needs improvement. The lack of coordination of programs and their lack of focus, for example, increases costs. Broad-based programs, such as community health clinics, sometimes fail to serve the older people who need them most (the poor, the very old, and minority elders). A community clinic designed to serve all older people, for example, may lack the funds to focus on very old homebound people. Likewise, the program may lack the staff to develop an outreach program for minority elders.

Critics of current policy say that government programs should serve people based on their needs, not their age (Hudson, 1997). A health care agency, for example, might set up a community health clinic in an Hispanic neighborhood. This program would serve all poorer people in the neighborhood. The program might serve fewer older people than a clinic for the aged (since some older people might have incomes too high to qualify for the service).

But it would see that health care resources went to the people who needed them most.

Programs such as this would use a means test to ensure that only people with financial need got the service Some writers reject means testing. They say that need-based programs would single out the poor and could give basic services the stigma of welfare. Also, programs based on need focus on broad concerns, for example, of all poor people. A need-based health promotion program might not fit the unique needs of older people. Torres-Gil (1992, p. 145) says that "means-testing benefits should be a last resort." Instead, he proposes higher ages for entitlement. This would restrict use of government programs to people in older age groups. The debate over age-based versus needs-based programs will continue. It will heat up in the future as the government tries to serve a growing older population with fewer funds.

GENERATIONAL EQUITY

The cost of programs for older people has led some critics to ask whether older people get too much support. Hudson (1997, p. 39) says that public policy related to old age in the past few decades has gone from " 'We can't do enough' to 'Have we done too much?' " Discussions of support for older people, given the costs of age-based programs, often come down to the issue of the fair distribution of resources to the older and younger generations (Jacobs, 1990).

A *New York Times* article, for example, reported that "on Capitol Hill there are increasing complaints that the elderly are casting too large a shadow over the Congress, and receiving more than their fair share of Federal benefits at the expense of the middle-aged and young" (Aid to Elderly, 1988, cited in Quadagno, 1991). This article suggests that older people, formerly portrayed as needy and helpless, now get too much support. Terms like *greedy geezers* portray older people as well off and anxious to grab more benefits if they can (Fairlie, 1988).

Rosenzweig (1991), for example, dealt with this topic in an address given at the annual meeting of the Gerontological Society of America some years ago. He said that unless older people willingly give up some of their current benefits in a time of scarcity, they will create a "disastrous" effect on society. "Of every nondefense, noninterest dollar in the federal budget [in the United States]," he said, "47 cents is spent on programs for people age 65 and over." And he projected that the government will spend more than one-half of its budget on older people in the early 2000s.

Rosenzweig predicted that these costs will lead to a conflict between retirees and the rest of society, including future retirees. And he said that leaders of interest groups ought to help their members "shape a conception of their interests that fits their own immediate needs into the needs of the larger community on whose overall well-being their own ultimately depends."

In part, these views reflect changes in the treatment of older people and improvements in their financial status. Hudson (1996) says that policy changes between 1965 and the 1990s led to rapid improvements in older people's lives New programs included Medicare, Medicaid, four large increases in Social Security, cost of living adjustments to Social Security, a Supplemental Security Income program, housing subsidies, and expanded community care.

This led to a rapid decrease in poverty rates among older people, one of the great social achievements of this century. Between 1959 and the mid-1990s, for example, the poverty rate for older people dropped by two-thirds, from 39 percent to around 13 percent (Hudson, 1996). "Social Security," Hudson (1997, p. 5) says, "has done more to alleviate poverty and inequality among old people than either the tax system or other social programs, including welfare."

Three assumptions underlie the generational equity debate: (1) older people get an unfair share of the nation's resources; (2) a larger older population will place an intolerable burden on younger people; and (3) younger people pay high taxes for Social Security today, but will get little benefit from the system when they retire. Each of these points focuses on the distribution of resources to younger and older people.

BOX 15.6

AGING IN CALIFORNIA

Conflict in the Making?

The generational equity debate predicts potential future conflict between older and younger people. David Hayes-Bautista says that the demographics of California add an ethnic dimension to this potential conflict. Census data show that California's Anglo population decreased from 79 to 54 percent of the population between 1970 and 1990. It will drop to below 50 percent by the later part of the 1990s.

At the same time, the Latino population grew from 10.9 to 25.7 percent of the population. Hayes-Bautista says that Latinos could make up 35 percent of the state population in the future. These figures point to a potential clash over the state's resources. Hayes-Bautista explains the issue and ends with a poignant question.

As the baby boomers turn 65 and swell the ranks of the elderly, the younger, working age population will increasingly be composed of Latinos. . . . The economy of the state is quickly and increasingly being driven by Latinos and others of the emergent (non-Anglo) majority population. Their economic success, or failure, will influence the future economic and social well-being of the largely Anglo elderly population in California.

The shrinking Anglo population lives a world apart from the growing, youthful Latino community. Some overall indicators for 1990 present a portrait of a society perilously close to apartheid-like conditions.

Education: Anglos had an average of 13.4 years of educational attainment; Latinos had barely 9.1 years.

Income and Poverty: The Anglo population has a median family income of $43,400; Latino families earned just $26,900. Overall, Anglos had a low rate of poverty—7.1 percent.

Even the Anglo elderly, who do experience a drop in income, nonetheless rarely experience poverty; 5.0 percent of those aged 65 and over lived in poverty. In contrast, children of all ethnic groups were over four times as likely to live in poverty; 21.5 percent did so. And Latinos of all ages were the most likely of any group to live in poverty—22.0 percent.

Putting these percentages in absolute numbers will tell a story. Five times as many Latino children live in poverty (566,117) as do Anglo elderly (112,788).

On the surface, it would appear that the conditions for a very bitter interethnic and intergenerational conflict exist: a well-educated elderly Anglo population that has rarely experienced poverty expecting to be supported in its retirement by a poorly educated, younger Latino population for which poverty is a common occurrence.

Can a conflict be avoided?

Hayes-Bautista holds out hope for a win-win outcome. Support for Anglos in old age, he says, depends on the economic success of young Latinos. Older Anglos and Latinos will both win through support of good education and a strong economy. "The key step," he says, "will be to forge alliances across ethnic groups and across generations."

Source: Reprinted with permission from "Young Latinos, older Anglos, and public policy: Lessons from California," by D. E. Hayes-Bautista, *Generations,* Fall/Winter, pp. 37–39, 1991. Copyright © 1991 American Society on Aging, San Francisco, California. *www.asaging.org*.

At the same time that poverty has decreased for older people, poverty among children has increased. Some writers make a connection between these two facts. Smith (1992a, p. 68), for example, says that "in order to pay for the oldsters' Big Rest, other worthy causes, most critically investment in children, increasingly get pushed aside." He suggests that money for old-age programs go to expand Head

Start, vaccination, and school lunch programs for children. Lacayo (1990, p. 40) agrees. He says that the government should "trim spending on affluent older people to free up funds for nutrition, schooling and health care for impoverished kids." Lacayo suggests that the government means test Social Security and Medicare or tax Social Security benefits.

The issue of **generational equity** has sparked debate and controversy. It led to the creation of a group called Americans for Generational Equity. This group grew from fewer than a hundred members in 1985 to more than a thousand members in 1990 (Wisensale, 1993). Americans for Generational Equality believes that young and middle-aged people cannot pay the high costs for services to older and younger people. Americans for Generational Equality proposes cuts to programs for older people to free up money for the young. For example, it proposes to replace Social Security in the United States with a system of welfare for the poorest older people (Quadagno, 1991).

Other U.S. groups such as the **Concord Coalition** propose a means test for Social Security and Medicare. The coalition says that only people who earn under $40,000 per year should get Social Security and Medicare. Cruikshank (2003, p. 27) reports that in 1999 the Concord Coalition "took out a full-page ad in the *New York Times* to attack a proposal to use part of the budget surplus to strengthen Social Security and Medicare." These groups gather support by pitting the interests of older people against those of the young. They argue that programs for older people take money from programs for poor children. Townson (1994, p. 14) says the media have taken up the cause of "kids versus canes." Hudson (1993, p. 79) says that "the aged find themselves transformed into an overindulged and singularly greedy population.

Minkler (1991, p. 36) calls the idea that young people suffer because of older people "flawed and dangerous." Generational equity supporters assume that most older people no longer need Social Security and other government programs. This view ignores the diversity of the older population (Hudson, 1996). Large proportions of the very old, minority older people, and older women still live near or below the poverty line.

Robert Butler (1993), first Director of the National Institute on Aging, says that support for older people has nothing to do with poverty rates for children. Poverty exists among children because social policies and policymakers allow it to exist. Critics of childhood poverty, Butler says, should emphasize society's failure to deal with this issue. Poor children, for example, live in poor families. Often women with low incomes head these families. Reduced support for older people will not solve the problem of poverty in youth. It will only lead to a return to high rates of poverty at the later end of life.

The argument that a larger older population will place an intolerable burden on younger people assumes that older people will demand more resources and that younger people will have to pay for them. It further assumes that younger people will find these increased costs burdensome. This view assumes that nothing will change either in the economy or in public policy in the future. But a stronger economy would make programs for older people more affordable, and containment of health care costs (the cause of much of the increase in program costs for older people) would make programs for older people less expensive. Public policies related to health care and Social Security need to change now to prepare for future demands. Changes will include the adjustment of benefit levels, an increase in the retirement age, and an increase in payments into the system.

Some of these changes have begun to take place. For example, the 1986 amendments to the federal Age Discrimination in Employment Act abolished mandatory retirement. This protects workers in the public and private sector from forced retirement (Koff & Park, 1993). It allows workers to choose to stay at work longer. Federal policy has increased Social Security taxes. It will also raise the age for full Social Security eligibility from age 65 to age 67 by the year 2027. This policy will keep people at work longer. It will allow the Social Security trust fund to grow and meet the needs of a large older population.

Further increases in payroll taxes could cover Social Security costs over the next seventy-five years without an intolerable burden on the young. "According to the Social Security trustees," Goozner writes (2005, p. 12) "if the tax on wages today were raised by less than 1 percent each for employee and employer (from the current rate of 6.2 percent each), Social Security would be solvent through 2077."

The facts about Social Security do not support the argument that young people pay high taxes for Social Security today but will get little benefit from the system when they retire. First, many of the people who get income from the Social Security system are younger men, women and children, dependents, survivors, and disabled people. In 2000, for example, children, young people, and adults under age 64 made up 30 percent of all people who received Social Security benefits. This came to almost 10 million people. Nearly 3 million children under age 18 got benefits in that year. Of these, almost 1.9 million children under age 18 got survivor benefits. Six million disabled workers in 2000 also got benefits from the Social Security system (Generations United, 2004).

Claude Pepper served as a congressman from Florida into his late 80s. He fought for many years to improve services and programs for older people. In 1990, the Pepper Commission proposed improved home care and long-term care insurance to protect older people from poverty.

Social Security policies may change in the future. Some authors have suggested a means test for Social Security. This would limit Social Security benefits to poor older people. But policy analysts (Hudson, 1997) say such a move would erode support for Social Security among more affluent older people. And this would weaken the system and lower benefits for the poor. A strong Social Security program will benefit middle-class workers by providing them with income security in later life. Wealthier older people may see some reduction in benefits, but they will still benefit from the system Poorer people, in particular, will benefit from a strong Social Security system. A weakened Social Security system would reverse the achievements of "America's most effective poverty-reduction program" (Marmor, Mashaw, & Harvey, 1990).

Studies of generational conflict disagree on the potential for conflict in the future. A study by the AARP (1995) found that out of fourteen possible points that show attitudes of generational conflict, most Americans score only two or three points. Most people felt that older people could get *more* respect, and "there was virtually no evidence of attitudes that older people were getting more than their fair share of local government resources" (AARP, 1995, p. vi).

In a more recent study, Cutler and his colleagues (2002) found that only 6 percent of the people 18 and over in their national survey considered older people *greedy geezers*. Curiously, older people agreed with this statement at more than twice the rate of other age groups. These authors concluded "there is more evidence of a generation consensus than a generation gap" (Cutler, Whitelaw, & Beattie, 2002, p. 64).

Torres-Gil (1992) proposes some reforms of public policies that would dampen real and potential age group conflict. First, government policies should move away from entitlements to all older people. For example, policies such as cost of living increases go to all older people, regardless of need. New policies could restrict cost of living increases to poor older people. Other programs should focus support on subgroups of older people in need, like women, minorities, and the disabled.

Second, the government should move away from policies that give support based only on age. The government should instead move to needs-based programs that would serve people of all ages. For example, family caregivers at every age could benefit from a change in Social Security rules. These rules count years out of work for caregiving as years of zero income. This lowers Social Security payments in the future. A rule could allow caregivers to drop out up to five years of low or no income due to caregiving (Torres-Gil, 1992).

Third, older people can show active support for non–age-related programs, such as programs to overcome drugs abuse, homelessness, and poor education. The AARP (1995) study of attitudes toward aging found that people felt intergenerational tensions if they believed that older people opposed services for others and only supported programs for themselves. "The real challenge to this aging, politically powerful generation," Torres-Gil (1992, p. 137) says, "will be to avoid becoming selfish."

Butler (1993) calls for more groups that advocate for both children and older people. A coalition group called Generations United takes this approach. Generations United began with the National Council on the Aging and the Child Welfare League of America as co-chairs. The group represents more than one hundred national, state, and local organizations including the United Way and Volunteers of America (Generations United, 2004). It claims to speak for over 70 million Americans. Generations United supports an expansion of funding for the National Senior Service Corps and policy changes that would allow more older people to serve as Foster Grandparents. Generations United also supports training programs that would teach Housing and Urban Development workers about the needs of grandparents who raise children in public housing.

Generations United also maintains a website that informs people about intergenerational issues. It sponsors meetings and conferences that bring the generations together. Organizations such as this help buffer potential conflict between the generations.

The debate over the cost of an older population will go on in the years ahead. And the growing size of the older population will draw attention to the costs of public pensions, health care, and other services. Blaming older people for this shift in resource allocation will not lead to a better life for older or younger people. The public needs good information about the costs and the benefits of social policies. We all have parents and grandparents. We will all be old someday. And we want a society that cares for people at every age.

THE FUTURE OF AGING, POLITICS, AND POLICY

Older people will probably not control political decision making either through voting, advocacy, or activism in the future. But they will influence public policy. Pampel and Williamson (1989, cited in Wallace, Williamson, Lung, & Powell, 1991) studied the effects of an aging population on welfare spending in eighteen societies, including the United States. They found that an increased older population leads to more money spent on pensions and medical care. This held true in spite of social class and governmental differences in these countries.

Hudson (1988) studied developed nations, including Sweden, Canada, France, Great Britain, West Germany, and the United States. He found increases in expenditures on social security in all of these countries between the mid 1950s and the late 1970s. All of these societies will see an increase in the number of older people who get a public pension. This will increase the amount of money devoted to programs for older people. And this in turn will lead to more lobbying and debate around seniors' issues. Wallace and his colleagues (1991, p. 108) say that "numbers alone will give the elderly considerable power in the basic operation of the society."

Two images of older people in the future emerge from the literature. One is an image of selfish, mean-spirited bullies willing and able to sway social programs and policies to serve their needs. The other is an image of wise, intelligent people able to look at broad societal needs and to the future. Minkler (1991) proposes the ideal of generational interdependence (rather than generational equity) as a way to view relations between different age groups. The younger and older generations need one another.

The old need the young to provide social resources for them in old age. The young need the old to plan for the well-being of future generations. Some programs need the support of all generations. A program such as national health insurance, for example, would benefit people of all ages and backgrounds.

Hudson (1994) sees the diversity of the older population as a source of generational interdependence. He says that on certain issues, such as antipoverty programs, some older people have more in common with younger people than with people in their age group. Other writers think that age may no longer serve as a useful way to think about the needs of the population. Torres-Gil (1992, pp. 90–91; *also* Achenbaum, 2000b) proposes "vertical alliances" across age groups based on common needs. "The poor, the disabled, minorities, women, and other disadvantaged groups of all ages will find more in common with each other than with those who simply share their age."

The ideal of generational interdependence changes the discussion of aging, politics, and policy. Voting and the interest group perspective look at politics as a competition between age groups. In a time of scarce resources, this leads to conflict and makes everyone poorer. Interest group politics have also created a deadlock on social policy reform.

Rosenblatt (1995a), for example, reports that Medicare costs grow each year, but no politician wants to tamper with the program. The concept of generational interdependence calls for rethinking our image of older people as a homogeneous group in need. This concept looks for ways to serve people in need from every age group.

Maggie Kuhn (Kerschner, 1976, cited in Hessel, 1977, p. 93) offered some wisdom on this point. She said that she and the Gray Panthers, "have worked through and gone beyond the so-called "Senior Power" view of ourselves. . . . We do not wear *Senior Power* buttons or think of ourselves as special pleaders for the cause of old people and old people's campaigns." She said that older people should do more than argue for cheap travel fares and lower taxes for themselves. Instead, they should become advocates and activists for a better society. They can serve both young and old in this role.

CONCLUSION

Older people take an active part in political life even in late old age. They vote, hold public office, work as advocates for social causes, take an activist stance on social issues. Older people advise the government on policy (through Silver-Haired Legislatures and participation in White House Conferences on Aging). They also form coalitions with other groups (like unions) to pass legislative reform.

Older people have succeeded in improving their condition through political action. Government programs such as Social Security, Medicare, and the Older Americans Act have all improved the quality of life in old age. Political action and its outcomes have transformed the image of older people. The public once saw older people as weak and needy. It now sees them as powerful and sometimes greedy. This change in image could lead to a backlash against programs for older people. This would hurt the poorest older people most.

Gerontologists propose a more balanced view of older people and their role in political life. They propose a generational interdependence perspective. This view shows that older and younger people can work together to create a better society.

SUMMARY

- Gerontologists study aging and politics from three points of view: (1) voting patterns, (2) activism, and (3) the policies of government that serve older people. Older people take part in politics in many ways. They give money to political parties, work in political campaigns, vote, run for office, and engage in advocacy and activism.
- Studies show that the proportion of people who vote increases with age and declines only in late old age. The increasing number of older people and their tendency to vote adds to their influence on government policy. This influence has its limits because older people do not vote as a single bloc.
- Minority older people have lower rates of voting than the general population. Culture, language, and literacy barriers prevent some of these older people from voting. Also, they may feel less hopeful that their votes will have an effect.
- The elderly differ by social class, race, gender, and age. They also differ in their views, and they vote for different candidates as well. Research shows that social class, for example, plays a bigger role in voting behavior than age.
- In the United States, older people make up a high proportion of officeholders. This occurs because a person tends to move to higher positions over time.
- Gerontologists disagree about whether older people can and will form a social movement. Older people do form interest groups that compete with other groups for public resources.
- Senior advocacy groups have access to three forms of political power. First, these groups have access to elected officials. Second, they have access to national media. Third, they can use the *electoral bluff,* the idea that they can sway votes against a politician. Senior lobby groups use all of these methods to influence national and local policies.
- The AARP takes a neutral position toward both major political parties. It supports lobby groups in every state and promotes political organization in all the U.S. congressional districts.
- The AARP has a diverse membership, which makes it difficult to express a single unified view on issues. As the AARP membership grows larger, its diversity will increase.
- Senior advocacy groups such as the AARP attract many members for personal reasons (like discounts on travel). Most members have little interest in political advocacy. Interest in advocacy surges when the government threatens programs like Social Security.
- Older people most often succeed in creating social change when they link their interests to other lobby groups. Coalitions form around interests that serve social class interest.
- Activism complements the work of advocacy groups. Advocacy works within the system to reform or support existing programs. Activists work for fundamental social change. They use methods such as protest and scrutiny of corporate practices to bring about change.
- Federal funding for the elderly has more than doubled since the 1960s. This reflects the increased number of older people and the increase in services and programs for older people. These programs and services form a social safety net that ensures a minimum standard of health care and income for all older people.
- The Older Americans Act has served as the basis of federal government aging policy since 1965. The Older Americans Act attempts to ensure the well-being of older people. It does this through a national network of services. The Administration on Aging has the job of carrying out the Older Americans Act. It coordinates programs and services, sets policies, and conducts research on aging.
- Federal government policy has led to improvements in the well-being and financial status of older people. Some groups such as Americans for Generational Equity and the Concord Coalition say that too much of the national budget goes to older people. They call for more funding for children's programs and cutbacks to programs for the elderly.
- Three assumptions underlie the generational equity debate: Older people get an unfair share of the nation's resources; a large older population places an intolerable burden on younger people; young people pay taxes for Social Security but will get few benefits when they retire. Gerontologists find little evidence to support these assumptions.
- Gerontologists suggest at least two ways to avoid generational conflict. First, the government should offer programs based on need, not age. Second, older people can show support for non–age-based programs and for programs that benefit other age groups.

DISCUSSION QUESTIONS

1. Gerontologists study at least three types of senior political activity. List them and give several examples of these activities.
2. Describe the voting patterns of older people. How does this influence their political decisions?
3. Explain why older minority group members have a lower voting rate than the general population.
4. Why don't older people vote as a bloc? What plays the biggest role in determining how people vote?
5. Why do some gerontologists think that older people can and will form a social movement? Why do other gerontologists disagree?
6. What methods do older people use to influence national and local policies?
7. What does the AARP do? What strengths does this organization have? What weaknesses? How does the AARP differ from the National Council of Senior Citizens?
8. What type of advocacy has the most impact on public policy?
9. Explain the term *interest group coalition.* How do these coalitions help older people?
10. How do activist groups differ from advocacy groups? What issues do advocacy groups deal with? How do groups like the Gray Panthers achieve their goals?
11. Why has federal funding for the elderly increased over the years? Explain the benefits to older people of federal programs.
12. List and explain the objectives of the Older Americans Act. What government agency carries out these objectives?
13. Define *generational equity.* Will the United States see conflict between the older and younger generations in the future? Give reasons to support your answer.
14. What assumptions underlie the generational equity debate? How might conflict be avoided?

SUGGESTED READING

Wallace, S. P., & Williamson, J. B. (1992). *Senior movement: Reference and resources.* New York: G. K. Hall and Maxwell Macmillan.

An annotated bibliography of over 800 works on the senior movement in the United States. The bibliography has four sections: (1) general works; (2) the movement's leaders, organizations, strategies; (3) issues such as Social Security; and (4) research and advocacy resources. The authors include an introductory essay on the senior movement in the United States.

Butler, R. N., & Kiikuni, K. (Eds.). (1992). *Who is responsible for my old age?* New York: Springer.

A look at the relationship between self-reliance and community support in an aging society. The contributors use this theme to look at the role of government in the future, women and old-age policy, and intergenerational relations. The authors propose that self-reliance for older people (for all of us?) depends on strong formal and informal social supports.

GLOSSARY OF TERMS

AARP (American Association of Retired Persons) The largest senior advocacy group in the United States. The AARP lobbies government, supports research on older people, and informs members about political issues.

activism Working outside the system through protest, monitoring elected officials' behaviors, and street theater.

advocacy Working within the system through lobbying and presentations to government to achieve political change.

aging network The collection of programs and services that provide supports to older people.

compassionate ageism The belief that older people are needy and deserve special policies to help them.

generational equity Refers to the concern that middle-aged people will be burdened with the costs of caring for a large older population (e.g., high Social Security, Medicare, and other service costs). Some groups propose cuts to programs for older people to free up money for the young.

Gray Panthers Founded in 1972 as a multiage activist group. The Panthers used protests and street theater to achieve their goals.

lobby groups Groups that attempt to influence politicians' behavior on certain issues.

chapter 16

GERONTOLOGY CAREERS AND YOU

A *New Yorker* cartoon shows two kids looking at a family photo album. One says to the other, "And this one is my grandmother and her current lover." This cartoon plays on our sense that older people don't have *lovers*. It also tells us that they do now. And it shows that the younger generation takes this for granted.

The cartoon makes us laugh at the sophistication of children today. But it also says something about the life-styles of older people. The past few years have seen a change in the reality of aging and in the public view of old age. And aging will change more in the future. This makes gerontology an exciting field of study and practice. Students who want to enter this field will find many ways to work with and for older people.

This chapter discusses (1) some of the major issues that aging raises for us today, (2) educational opportunities in gerontology, and (3) careers in the field of aging.

CHALLENGES FOR AMERICAN SOCIETY

The previous chapters reviewed many topics in the field of aging. Each of these topics raises issues that challenge Americans and American society today. Some issues span more than one topic. Consider three issues that have changed our thinking about aging: (1) age irrelevance, (2) diversity, and (3) generational interdependence.

AGE IRRELEVANCE

Some years ago Bernice Neugarten (1980) coined the term "age irrelevant society." She said that in an older society we would judge people by their ability rather than their age. For example, we have associated old age with age 65 for over a century. The first pension plans used this as the age of retirement. This may have made sense in the past, when few people would live to age 65, but increased life expectancy, better health, later onset of disability, and more flexible pension options make age 65 a poor predictor of a person's activity, life-style, or needs.

Today many people still retire at age 65. Pension plans encourage this. But more and more people retire before age 65, and others retire and then start second careers in a new field. Age 65 also serves as a poor predictor of a person's health and well-being. Most people today report good health into their 70s. Some people even see improvements in health after retirement. Older people exercise, travel, and take part in education. Some live more active and varied lives than younger people.

The division of life activities by age—schooling for the young, work for the middle aged, and leisure for the old—no longer fits. Masters athletes and senior Olympians, for example, give new meaning to the concept of leisure. These people have turned athletic achievement into a second career. Older people have returned to school in record numbers. Not for degrees, but for personal development. Organizations such as Elderhostel and Lifelong Learning Institutes meet this need, and other programs such as travel study tours will grow in the future.

Consider this case: A 47-year-old friend of mine, Art, has just returned to school to get his MBA degree. He and his wife Phyllis took up ballroom dancing ten years ago. They now compete and give exhibitions. Art works as an executive for a communications company; Phyllis works as a nurse. Their youngest child, a teenage daughter, still lives with them. Their older daughter got married a year ago. They became grandparents this fall. At 47, Art is a father, husband, student, worker, and grandfather as well as an amateur show dancer. Does Art's age tell you much about who he is and what he is able to do? Does his life-style fit the traditional model of midlife as a stable (and boring) plateau?

Historian Peter Laslett (1989) says that recent changes in demography, health, and life-styles call for "a fresh map of life." He says that the **third age**, a French term for the age of physical decline, no longer fits the early years of retirement. Laslett says that the third age now refers to an active time of life after middle age. He adds a **fourth age**, to describe what most people think of as old age—a time of physical decline. But even here, a person's ability rather than age best defines this stage in life.

Diversity

Gerontologists in fields as varied as housing, minority relations, physiology, cognitive psychology, and social policy point to the diversity of the older population. Older people differ as much among themselves as they differ from other age groups. For example, older people differ in physical ability, gender, ethnicity, race, geographic region, and age.

Studies of minority groups and aging report differences even within one minority group. Puerto Rican, Cuban, and Mexican American elders have different histories and cultures. And they have different experiences in the United States. Differences between these groups lead to differences in family relations, language ability, and socioeconomic status. Likewise, men and women live different lives in old age. Women, compared with men, run a higher risk of widowhood, chronic illness, and poverty in later life. These differences reflect differences between the sexes throughout life.

Gerontologists caution against treating older people as a homogeneous group. A policy or service that suits one group of older people will not necessarily suit another. Minority elders, for example, tend to underuse community health care services. Some gerontologists say that these settings put up language and cultural barriers that discourage use. Professionals from the majority culture who set up these services may not see these barriers. An exercise program that works for one group, for example, may not work for another.

The diversity of the older population adds an extra challenge to working with older people, and the need for sensitivity to diversity applies to researchers as well as practitioners. I recall one survey where we interviewed nursing assistants about stress on the job. One question asked these women if they ever felt they were "at the end of their rope." A Pakistani woman looked horrified and shook her head. She thought the question asked whether she had ever attempted suicide.

The older population in the future will be even more diverse. It will have a higher proportion of minority elders. It will include people from many generations. It will include more people with diverse backgrounds, who will have unique personal histories. The diversity of the older population puts gerontology researchers' and practitioners' knowledge to the test. It demands a greater sensitivity to and awareness of the uniqueness of older people.

Generational Interdependence

Minkler (1991) calls for generational interdependence. Interest group politics led to new programs and better funded programs for older people. Social Security and Medicare, for example, account for much of the improvement in well-being among older people in the past thirty years. But gerontologists see little likelihood that funding for older people's programs will increase. At best, these programs can hope to survive cutbacks in government spending.

Older people in the future will serve their own interests best when they can lobby for change along with other age groups. Some programs, such as a national medical care system, would serve the old and the young. So would a strong Social Security system or better services for people with disabilities. Young people today could count on this system in planning their retirement or in coping with disability, and they would know that their parents will have a basic pension.

Some writers propose to shift government spending from older to younger people. But generational interdependence calls for more creative solutions to people's needs. It asks young and old people to recognize their mutual needs, and it calls for a balanced use of resources to serve all age groups.

Gerontological research allows us to understand these and other issues in aging today. This research has asked and answered scientific and practical questions. It has also helped guide social policy. Gerontology will play an even more important role in guiding public policy as the United States ages into the twenty-first century. People in every profession and occupation will benefit from this research and practice. Educational programs now offer a variety of ways for students and professionals to learn about aging.

GERONTOLOGY EDUCATION

The University of Michigan in 1955 conducted a survey of 312 colleges and universities in the United States. The survey asked about gerontology programs at these schools. Only fifty schools at that time offered courses related to aging and only seventy-two schools reported some gerontology research. During the next forty years, programs and courses sprang up on most large and many smaller campuses across the country. American higher education had discovered aging.

Wilbur (2004) reports that of the 3,000 colleges and universities in the United States, 500 currently offer one or more courses in gerontology. Williams (2003) reports that the *National Directory of Educational Programs in Gerontology and Geriatrics* lists more than 1,000 gerontology programs. While some programs have been discontinued over the years, Wilbur (2004) says that four times as many have thrived. At least 200 schools offer degrees or majors in gerontology, 235 offer credit certificates, and nearly 100 offer a Masters degree in gerontology (AGHE, 1996; Williams, 2003).

The University of Michigan, Duke University, the University of Chicago, and the University of Southern California have some of the most established programs in the country. They began in the 1950s and 1960s. Other schools more recently began to offer specialized training for health care professionals. Williams (2003) says that the federal Bureau of Health Professions has designated some higher education centers as Geriatric Education Centers.

In 2000, thirty-four of these centers got $7.4 million to develop and offer their programs. Geriatric Education Centers offer a range of interdisciplinary programs that bring together expertise from schools of medicine and other health fields (e.g., dentistry, public health, nursing, etc.) Programs include staff training, continuing education, and clinical geriatrics training.

Types of Gerontology Programs

Some years ago the Carnegie Commission on Higher Education (1973) found that three philosophies guided higher education: scientific, professional, and liberal arts. These philosophies apply to gerontological study. The scientific approach relies on research and data collection to study aging. The professional approach teaches how to provide services to older people and solve social problems. The liberal arts approach teaches about the process of aging and human development. Undergraduate and master's degree programs often take a liberal arts or professional approach to aging studies. Bachelor's programs, for example, may include a course in research methods and in the sociology of aging.

Most gerontology programs include a course in the psychology of aging and in social gerontology. A large proportion of programs also include courses in the biology and physiology of aging. The scientific approach most often shows up in graduate programs. Some education programs combine these approaches. Professional undergraduate programs (e.g., in nursing or social work) often combine a liberal arts and professional approach. Graduate programs (in administration, for example) sometimes combine professional and scientific approaches.

The Gerontological Society of America and the Association for Gerontology in Higher Education cosponsored a project entitled Foundations for Establishing Education Program Standards in Gerontology. The report asked 111 experts what knowledge students of aging needed most. Over 90 percent of the experts said that all students, regardless of their field, needed to know about (1) the normal psychological changes that come with age; (2) health and aging; and (3) normal biological changes that come with age. Almost 90 percent of the experts also included sensory changes, demography of aging, and the sociology of aging. Almost 90 percent of the experts agreed on a single basic skill for anyone who would practice in the field: "understanding aging as a normal experience" (Johnson et al., 1980, p. 26).

University and College Programs

University education in gerontology now takes at least four forms: (1) doctoral degrees for teachers and researchers, (2) master's degrees for practitioners, (3) undergraduate degrees and courses, and (4) certificate programs.

Some schools have graduate programs that lead to a master's or doctoral degree in gerontology. Other schools locate specializations in aging within traditional disciplines. In this case, a student would get a sociology master's degree, but would focus course papers and the thesis on aging-related topics. Some graduate programs offer special training in topics like public policy and health sciences research.

Peterson, Wendt, and Douglass (1994) found that campuses that offered doctorate and other graduate degrees had the highest proportion of gerontology, geriatrics, and aging (GGA) courses and programs. Eighty-eight percent of schools with doctoral programs and 77 percent of schools with other graduate programs offered GGA education.

Undergraduate courses exist on aging in almost every college and university today. The tendency to offer programs differs by school size. About 60 percent of small schools (2,500 or fewer students) had GGA programs, compared with over 90 percent of large schools (more than 20,000 students) (Peterson, Wendt, & Douglass, 1994). Beland and Kapes (2003) studied university programs for future parks and recreation employees. They found that about one-half of the 112 schools they studied offered aging-related courses to undergraduates in these programs. Thirteen of the sixty-six schools (about 20 percent) with graduate programs offered a graduate course related to aging.

Some departments offer majors in gerontology. Other schools offer interdisciplinary certificates or diplomas to students who complete a cluster of degree credit courses. Schools offer these programs for undergraduates and graduates. MacNeil and his colleagues (2003), for example, studied leisure and recreation programs in the United States. They found that 61 percent of the sixty-six schools they surveyed offered a major, certificate, or concentration in gerontology. Most schools offered these programs for undergraduates.

Peterson and his colleagues (1994) found that two-year colleges (offering an associate degree) had the lowest proportion of GGA courses and programs (52 percent). These schools also had a lower proportion of GGA programs and courses than four-year and graduate institutions. Most of the two-year colleges (255 out of 299) offered GGA courses, but no programs. This study found that two-year colleges between 1985 and 1992 had a greater tendency (compared with other institutions) to reduce the number of GGA courses and size of their programs.

The researchers call for a reversal of this trend. They say that "colleges serving general education undergraduates should offer all students a sensitization to aging" of at least one course (Peterson & Wendt, 1990, cited in Peterson, Wendt, & Douglass, 1994, p. 37). This would open a new field of study to many college students. It might also point them to new career options. Colleges will have to consciously keep or add gerontology courses to achieve this goal.

Some schools have built up interest in gerontology by offering service learning courses (Dorfman et al., 2004; Weinreich, 2004). These courses combine course work with community service. Service learning gerontology courses generally focus on intergenerational service learning. These courses ask students to work with older people in the community as part of their course work. Some courses encourage students to serve as advocates for older adults and to work for social change (Lagana, 2003). Service learning offices on campuses can help gerontology instructors find placements for their students.

Cummings and her colleagues (2003) studied undergraduate and graduate students in the field of social work. They found that undergraduate social work majors, who had a good field experience working with older people, tended to work with older people after graduation. These students also felt confidence in their gerontology skills and knowledge. Service learning courses provide one way for students in health and social service disciplines to have positive relations with older people.

This may lead more of these students to work with older people when they graduate.

Many undergraduate and Master's degree gerontology programs require a field placement or **internship**. Internships can take place in a variety of settings, including nursing homes, senior centers, and recreation programs. Nearly 80 percent of the experts in the Foundations project (Johnson et al., 1980) said they favored required field projects in gerontology programs. Field placements allow students to apply their knowledge and develop practical skills. They also help students form social networks that can lead to jobs. Students say that internships linked them to the workforce and in some cases led to jobs. (The best field placements have good supervision and evaluation. They require good communication between the school and the placement setting.

Sizemore and Coover (1993) developed a program to increase undergraduate students' sensitivity to cultural differences among older people. They placed non–Spanish-speaking undergraduate students in a social service agency that serves Hispanic elders. Students did routine agency work and observed how agency staff served clients. The researchers say that this type of placement can enhance classroom teaching on minority aging. It can also increase future professionals' awareness of minority members' needs. This will remove one of the barriers that keeps minority elders from getting the services they need.

The Foundation project proposed three career clusters for students with an interest in aging: biomedicine, psychosocial studies, and socioeconomic environmental studies. Clusters included core items and special courses for each cluster. The biomedical cluster, for example, included the study of diseases in old age. The socioeconomic cluster included the study of public policy. Gerontology programs could offer a single core curriculum or career clusters. In both cases, programs need cooperation between disciplines and support from faculty members from different departments. Gerontology programs break down departmental barriers. They offer faculty members and students a chance to integrate knowledge around the theme of aging.

Peterson and Wendt (1990, cited in Peterson et al., 1994) propose six general goals for gerontology education on U.S. campuses.

Two students interview an older patient at the Village Nursing Home in New York City. They learn about aging directly from an older person. They also get to visit a setting where professionals work with the elderly.

1. All undergraduates should take at least one course to sensitize them to aging.
2. Practicing professionals should take at least one course in aging to improve their understanding of the uniqueness of old age.
3. Science students should learn about age, period, and cohort issues through research.
4. Teachers in the field should have academic training and field experience in gerontology and geriatrics.
5. Degree and certificate students need a full range of instruction laid out in the Association for Gerontology in Higher Education (AGHE) *Standards and Guidelines.*
6. Professionals need to learn how to adapt their skills to serve the unique needs of older people.

At least two of the goals described by Peterson and Wendt focus on education and training for practicing professionals. But few professionals return to campus to take undergraduate or graduate courses in gerontology. The pressures of work and family, parking problems on most campuses, and the schedule of most university classes make enrollment in conventional programs difficult. Many universities recognize this. They offer nondegree certificate programs in gerontology through their continuing education or extension divisions.

Most of these programs include courses on the core topics mentioned previously. They also offer courses on topics like housing, social policy, death and dying, and gender issues. Certificate programs often take place in the evenings or on weekends. And classes generally consist of fellow professionals. These programs often offer shorter courses that give professionals an update on a topic in six or eight sessions. A cluster of courses leads to a nondegree certificate. These programs meet the needs of busy professionals who want knowledge that they can apply in their work.

In-Service Programs

Gerontology education today also takes place outside universities and colleges. Health care and social service professionals can choose from a range of educational options. Programs include on the job training, attendance at in-service training sessions, and conferences. Some professions require that members get a certain number of **continuing education units (CEUs)** each year. Professionals can get CEUs by attending conferences, taking courses, reading books, or listening to audio taped talks. These programs keep professionals up to date on research findings and methods for serving their clients.

Some legislation has proposed grants for student traineeships and advanced training for work with older people (Torres-Gil, 1992). The AGHE Standards Committee (1990) calls for more courses, minors, majors, and specializations in gerontology at the undergraduate and graduate levels. Programs also need to focus on professional training in long-term care administration, public policy, and research. Programs should include training that improves the competencies of professionals in the field. Yeo (1991; *see also* Damron-Rodriguez, Dorfman, Lubben, & Beck, 1992) says that professionals need more training for work with minority elders.

In California, 40 percent of older people will come from non-Anglo backgrounds by the year 2020. Professionals in health care fields will need training in **ethnogeriatrics**, the study of how ethnicity affects aging and health. Ethnogeriatrics includes information on diseases such as diabetes and dementia in different minority groups. Students also study the health beliefs of minority group members and their use of the health care system. Students learn the value systems of other cultures and these cultures' views of illness.

No formal accreditation of gerontology programs exists, but the AGHE produces guidelines and standards for undergraduate and graduate programs as well as certificate programs (AGHE Standards Committee, 1990). Hickey (1995) says that gerontology programs need to have a clear purpose. Some programs focus on keeping professionals in touch with their field. Others focus on job training for undergraduates. Practice-related programs need a **competency-based curriculum**. They should provide students with marketable skills. To do this, they need a close tie to the field and constant updating in light of employers' needs (Peterson, Wendt, & Douglass, 1991).

The large number of programs available and their different goals make finding the right program a challenge. The AGHE has a *Program Database on Gerontology in Higher Education* that contains a listing of programs throughout the United States (www.aghe.org/site/aghewebsite/section.php?id=8219). Students can specify a region of the country, the credential they seek, and their discipline (e.g., medicine, education) or any combination of these items. The AGHE will conduct the search and provide a list of suitable programs for a small fee ($10 for students in 2004).

Students may wonder whether it pays to get further education and training in aging. Most programs imply that they lead to jobs in the field. But does gerontology education really lead to jobs? Studies show that many people who graduate from gerontology and geriatrics programs find work with older people (Lobenstine, 1994). Peterson (1985) found that 59 percent of master's degree graduates in gerontology held full-time jobs in the field of aging. Graduates reported satisfaction with their degrees and their progress in their careers. Work experience with older people also helps students find jobs.

In general, the more education a person has, the higher the position held in the **aging network**. A study of workers in State Units on Aging and Area Agencies on Aging found that people with graduate degrees held more administrative or specialist positions. They earned more money than people with bachelor's degrees. Oddly, though, over 60 percent of Agencies on Aging jobs and about 75 percent of State Units on Aging jobs did not require any gerontology education (Peterson, Wendt, & Douglass, 1991).

In jobs that required gerontology education, only 11 percent of Area Agencies on Aging and 8.6 percent of State Units on Aging professionals had a credential in gerontology. A large majority of these professionals (85 percent) said that future professionals should have specialized training in gerontology. Wendt and Peterson (1992) project a transition to a better trained workforce in aging. They say that the aging network will probably update job qualifications to require more training in aging.

These findings suggest that a general undergraduate or graduate degree (even with no gerontology training) offers the most opportunity for work in the aging network. Some training (not necessarily a credential) in gerontology will open the door to more jobs in this network. Jobs at the highest levels in the aging network (administrators) favor people with a master's degree. People in these positions often had master's degrees in administration (Peterson, Wendt, & Douglass, 1991).

WORK AND CAREERS IN GERONTOLOGY

> Do you find enjoyment in being with older persons? Do you empathize with the needs of the elderly and feel a desire to be an advocate for them? Are you intrigued with wanting to understand the process of why we age? Do you have a basic concern for people and their special needs?
>
> Consider preparing for a career in the field of aging! (Lobenstine, 1994, p. 1)

A larger older population will create new jobs for young people. This will include jobs for health care professionals like doctors, occupational therapists, physiotherapists, and nurses. The National Institute on Aging (1984, cited in Peterson, 1987) estimates that the need for nurses in nursing homes, for example, will increase by two and a half times between 1985 and the early years of this century. Many nurses will also work in community settings. The National Institute on Aging says that community health nurses will quadruple in number between 1985 and the early 2000s.

Cohen (2004) says that the medical profession recognizes the need for more trained geriatricians. It has responded by creating new geriatrics and gerontology curricula. Warshaw and Bragg (2003) report that the number of fellowship programs in geriatric medicine almost doubled between 1988 and 2001 to 2002.

In 2001 to 2002 120 geriatric medicine fellowship programs were training 338 fellows. The

A health care worker with an older patient. Students in fields such as medicine, nursing, and occupational therapy often get jobs working directly with older people.

researchers note that over 10,000 physicians earned Certificates of Added Qualifications in Geriatrics between 1988 and 2001. This brings the number of physicians trained in geriatrics to 5.5 per 10,000 people aged 75 or over in the United States. Still, the researchers say, even this rapid growth in the number of trained physicians will not meet the needs of a growing older population.

An older society will need more architects, engineers, clergy, family counselors, senior center directors, and professors who know about aging (Williams, 2003). Engineers, for example, will work on problems in biomechanics and the development of artificial limbs and joints. They will also create new assistive devices for older people with disabilities.

Professionals in fields such as banking, travel, and sales will need to orient their marketing and services to an older clientele. People in retail sales will benefit from a positive attitude toward older customers. Even factory managers will benefit from knowing more about aging. This will give them more knowledge of the people they supervise.

Workers in nearly every field will see more older people as clients and customers in the future. But some people will want to focus their careers entirely on work with older people. How can a student develop a career in the field of aging?

Finding Work in the Field of Aging

Students often enjoy the study of aging. They then want to know how they can enter a career in gerontology. Some students will find work with older people relatively easily. Students in fields such as nursing, social work, physiotherapy, and occupational therapy have the greatest chance of working with older people. A study of social workers, for example, estimated that 26 percent of social workers in the National Association of Social Workers work with the elderly (Peterson, 1990). The 2000 to 2001 *Occupational Outlook Handbook* ranks geriatric social work as the field needing the most social workers (Williams, 2003).

Students in programs such as recreation studies, business, or law may decide to focus their interests on serving older clients. These students will need to take elective courses in aging. Many schools now offer these courses asynchronously online over the Internet (Shenk, Moore, & Davis, 2004). St. Hill and Edwards (2004) offer an undergraduate aging course online. They say that the online format has increased the enrollment of undeclared majors in their course.

Students in a general arts and science program may have to build their own gerontology program (if their school does not offer a formal program). Undergraduates need to choose electives on aging from varied disciplines (courses like the sociology of aging or the psychology of aging). They can also choose term paper topics related to aging.

These students will have a broad knowledge of aging when they graduate. This will rarely prepare them to give direct service to older people. Programs such as nursing and social work do this best. But an undergraduate degree can lead to work, for example, as a program specialist, someone who sets up and monitors programs in the aging network. Kansas State University has a website entitled Academic Careers and Internet Resources (*www.ksu.edu/acic/career/options/Gerontology.html*). The site provides links to career opportunities in the field of gerontology. The AGHE also provides information on its website entitled Careers in Gerontology (*www.careersinaging.com/careersinaging/*). This site includes video testimonials by professionals in the field. It also includes the text of a booklet entitled *Careers in Aging: Consider the Possibilities.*

Any student who wants to work with older people can benefit from some simple job search strategies. For example, many jobs come from personal contacts. Students should get to know people who work in the field of aging. This will provide one of the best ways to find out about and get a job working with older people. Bolles (1995) calls this the **hidden job market**. Many jobs in the field of aging never appear in the paper or in a professional journal. Some of them get filled before they even open up.

People who work in the field of aging tend to know one another. They know about job openings and they ask one another to suggest candidates. Someone linked to this informal group will learn about these jobs or sometimes get offered one of these jobs without asking. But this leads to a classic bind. If you don't work in the field, you don't know anyone in the field, so you can't find work in the field. How can you break into this hidden job market? Career development professionals suggest several things you can do now to improve your job chances in the future.

Join Your Local or State Gerontology Association

Larger towns and cities will have an association. Otherwise, a state association probably exists. See if the association has a student group within the main organization. Woody Allen said that "50 percent of success is just showing up." Increase that percentage by doing something: get active, attend meetings, join committees. You will learn about local, state, and national aging issues. You will get to know researchers, scholars, and practitioners who can tell you about opportunities in the field. You will also enjoy the company of other people interested in the topic of aging.

Contact your university or college center on aging (if your school has one). This center conducts research, sponsors lectures, and may have a student discussion group. Ask your center about volunteer or paid research work. You may not think of yourself as a researcher, but the center may need interviewers for a survey study or someone to code data in the office. The center may need the computer or library research skills you have. If you belong to a minority group, you may have special skills to offer. Research studies need interpreters and interviewers with varied backgrounds.

Seek an Internship

Internships place students in a community work setting related to their field. They receive academic credit for this work. Students also gain knowledge about professional practice, learn about the issues that professionals face every day, and make valuable personal contacts. Some academic programs require an internship. Others may leave this as an option. You can choose an internship that allows you to work with older people. This could turn into a job when you graduate. If not, you will at least gain valuable experience that you can refer to when you apply for other positions.

Do Volunteer Work

Find the kind of setting you might like to work in and volunteer. This will give you experience, references, and future job contacts. It will also tell you whether you really like this kind of work. Ideally, choose a volunteer job that fits with your college or university program.

Wayne Jensen, a former physical education student, volunteered to work at a new housing complex. The complex soon opened a gym and recreation center. He helped design the center and eventually got hired as the assistant director. He became the director of the center when his boss retired. Fifteen years later, he runs the recreation center's activity program and has a staff of three assistants. He now offers field placements in the center to university and college students.

Meg Wolsley, a student in a gerontology certificate program, volunteered at an educational program for older people. She helped around the office and co-taught some large fitness classes. The staff got to know her and noted that the students liked her teaching style. They hired her a year later to run a grant-funded community outreach program.

Jobs like Meg's don't always turn into lifelong careers. Meg, for example, worked on contract for two years. She then worked on another contract for the same education program for another year. So far, she has stayed employed since she graduated, although she would like a more stable position. Her work has given her valuable experience and contacts with people in the field of aging. This will serve her well as she searches for a permanent job.

Informational Interviewing

Bolles (2004) describes this method of job hunting in his best-selling book, *What Color Is Your Parachute? 2004 A Practical Guide for Job-Hunters and Career Changers.* Every student (in any field) who wants to find a satisfying career ought to read and work through this book. Bolles now has a website entitled JobHuntersBible.com (www.jobhuntersbible.com/index.php). The site lists dozens of ideas and contacts to help kickstart a job search, including the U.S. government's *Occupational Outlook Handbook, 2004-05* (www.bls.gov/oco/). Bolles considers the Internet a great new tool in the job hunter's toolbox.

Gerontology students will benefit from Bolles' (2004, p. 182) advice on *informational interviewing.* This type of interviewing has two goals: (1) you want to find out whether a career in aging will allow you to use your skills and talents, and (2) you want to know what it's like to work with older people.

First, choose someone to interview. If you think you would like to work in an exercise program, you talk with two or three people who work in these kinds of programs. If you think you would like to work as a hospital administrator, you interview two or three hospital administrators. In other words, you interview people who have the information you need about the career you think you would like. Bolles (2004, p. 197) says that you should ask all of your interviewees the same four questions:

- How did you get into this work?
- What do you like the most about it?
- What do you like the least about it?
- Where else could I find people who do this kind of work so I can talk with them?

Bolles (1995, p. 283) says that by interviewing for information you are "trying on jobs to see if they fit you."

I began my career in gerontology this way. I received a grant one summer in the early 1970s to make a documentary video on aging. The video included interviews with leaders in the field of aging in my city. I spent hours learning about aging firsthand from these people. I not only learned about the issues in the field. I learned about their careers, their concerns, and their passion for gerontology. These people became some of my closest supporters and friends over the years.

Informational interviewing will put you in contact with people who know their field from the inside. They can tell you what it takes to get into the field, and they can tell you about the future prospects of their profession. Bolles cautions that you should not use this method as a way to ask for a job. This ploy will poison an employer against you and get you tagged as an untrustworthy person. You only want information at this point. You will get to know and enjoy good relations with the people you meet if you simply try to learn from them. Also, send a thank you note to anyone you see.

Keep Learning

Subscribe to newsletters and journals in your field. Or, at least, go to the library and browse through the latest issues of journals that interest you. Read the latest books on aging, the life cycle, and human development. Many popular books appear on these subjects every year. Search the Internet for sites related to your interests. Most national associations and government agencies that work with the elderly maintain websites. Check these sites regularly. Keep up on the latest issues.

Do you enjoy books on widowhood, women's issues, housing, health care, relationships, or policy? Your choice of reading reveals what interests you most about aging. Explore your interests further. Take courses, attend seminars, and attend lectures by visiting scholars. Go with a friend, if you feel shy about going alone. Try to meet some new people at each event, even if it's the person sitting next to you in the lecture hall. This will expand your network further. You will probably see people more than once if you attend events regularly. Eventually people will come over to talk to you.

BOX 16.1

NATIONAL ASSOCIATIONS THAT SERVE OLDER PEOPLE

National associations provide information about their services and programs. Go to their websites to learn about opportunities for work with older people. Many of these agencies have local offices throughout the country. You can call the local offices to interview for information and learn about the field of gerontology firsthand. The websites and information below may change over time. They represent the information at the time of this writing.

American Association of Retired Persons (AARP)
601 E St., NW
Washington, DC 20049
202/434–2277
www.aarp.org

American Society on Aging (ASA)
833 Market St., Suite 511
San Francisco, CA 94103
415/974–9600
www.asaging.org

Association for Gerontology in Higher Education (AGHE)
1030 15th St., NW, Suite 240
Washington, DC 20005
202/289–9806
www.aghe.org/site/aghewebsite/

Gerontological Society of America (GSA)
1030 15 St., NW, Suite 250
Washington, DC 20005
202/842–1275
www.geron.org

National Association of Area Agencies on Aging (NAAAA)
1112 16th St., NW, Suite 100
Washington, DC 20036
202/296–8130
www.n4a.org/

National Association of State Units on Aging (NASUA)
1225 I St., NW, Suite 725
Washington, DC 20005
202/898–2578
www.nasua.org/

National Council on the Aging (NCOA)
409 Third St., SW, Second Floor
Washington, DC 20024
202/479–1200
www.ncoa.org/index.cfm

National Institute on Aging (NIA)
Public Information Office
9000 Rockville Pike
Bethesda, MD 20892
301/496–1752
www.nih.gov/nia

U.S. Administration on Aging (AoA)
330 Independence Ave., SW
Washington, DC 20201
202/619–0441
www.aoa.dhhs.gov

U.S. Census Bureau
Age and Sex Statistics Branch
Population Division
Washington, DC 20233
301/457–2378
www.census.gov

Start a Student Gerontology Club

Talk to your instructor about this. Schools often have funds for student clubs. You and one or two friends can apply for these funds. You will probably need a faculty advisor. Then, hold an afternoon get together with refreshments. Arrange for a guest speaker and invite students from across campus to attend. You will meet fellow students (future professional colleagues) this way. Faculty will also get to know you in a new way, as a club leader.

Know Yourself

Write out a personal mission statement. Write out your vision of an ideal career. Write out specific career goals. Again, *What Color Is Your Parachute?* (a new edition comes out each year) can help here. It contains exercises that can help you figure out what you ought to do and how you can get to do it. Also, ask your teachers and the professionals you meet how you can create the kind of career you want in the field of aging. Get more than one person's advice. Then find out how to develop this career and take steps to make this happen. Students who do a little more, who put a little more focus on their career, and who show enthusiasm for the field will have an edge in the job market. Make a career in aging a priority.

One of my undergraduate assistants developed a career in aging through persistence. Rita dropped by my office one July day to ask whether I had any work for her to do. She explained that she wanted to learn about academic work in the field of aging and would work for free. I had never met her before and I was busy with research work at the time. I told her to come back in September. I never expected to see her again, but she came back in early September with the same request. I still didn't have any plans to take on a student assistant, even for free, so I told her to try again in a month or so.

To my surprise, she came back again in early October. I had just gotten some money to hire a student assistant, and since I had no one else in mind, I hired Rita to grade introductory sociology papers for me that term. Rita stayed on as my research assistant for the next two years. She worked winters grading papers. She worked summers on research projects. She met a number of my colleagues through this work. She graduated and got strong references from me and several other professors. Rita got accepted to a top graduate school, in part because of her references and her academic work experience.

All of this may sound exhausting. You can't (and won't) do all of this, and you certainly won't do this all in one day. Pick the suggestions that seem easiest to do and that appeal to you most. Some of these things you can do informally. For example, if interviewing for information seems scary, don't make a big thing of it. Begin talking to relatives, family friends, or neighbors who may work with older people. You may find opportunities to interview for information at a church picnic. A friend's mother, for example, may work in an agency where she counsels many older clients. You can subtly ask her your four questions when the time seems right. Above all, keep looking for opportunities to expand your knowledge and experience.

GERONTOLOGY AND YOU

My mother died suddenly on October 29, 1992. She lived in her own apartment to the end. For about a year before her death, she had a number of physical problems, including a bad fall that resulted in a broken wrist. The fall and recovery left her weak and at risk of further illness. But she managed to stay in her apartment with support from my sister, her own brother and sister, a visiting nurse, and a homemaker.

One afternoon she came back to her apartment after a visit to her doctor. My uncle helped her to the couch to rest after the walk from the car. She sat down, slumped over on her side, and closed her eyes. My uncle shook her, called her name. But she was gone. She died of a burst aneurysm near the heart.

I arrived a day and a half later to make funeral arrangements. The funeral director asked if I wanted to view the body. I hesitated. I had never seen a dead body before. But I said that I would. The day of the funeral, the director led me to a room. He showed me the coffin and opened the lid.

There I saw my mother for the first time in over a year. She looked tiny, smaller than I remembered. Her body was wrapped in a cotton shroud. I could see only her face. It looked like wax. I stood for a moment, said a last goodbye, turned, and walked away.

My sister asked me later why I wanted to see our mother's body. I explained that I needed to make her death real for me. I needed to satisfy myself that she was gone, to convince myself that the beautiful polished coffin we saw in the chapel really contained her body. Viewing the body disturbed me, but it also brought me a peace that stays with me today.

The study of aging has done more than teach me facts and theories of aging. It has given me useful knowledge about my own aging, life, and relationships. This knowledge gave me the courage to say "Yes" to the funeral director and to see my mother a last time. The study of aging has shaped my personal and professional life. It has also increased my understanding of current events and the people I know. I hope it will do the same for you.

SUMMARY

- Three issues have changed our thinking about aging today: (1) age irrelevance, (2) diversity, and (3) generational interdependence. Increased life expectancy, better health, and more flexible pension plans have led to new life-styles and opportunities in old age. Older people differ in physical ability, ethnicity, race, geographic region, and gender. This makes age a poor predictor of ability, performance, life-style, and interests. The older age group in the future will include people from several generations. They will need to take a broad intergenerational interest in society and social policies.
- University programs can take a professional, scientific, or liberal arts approach to the study of aging. All students of aging should have knowledge of (1) normal psychological changes that come with age, (2) health and aging, (3) normal biological changes, and (4) demography and the sociology of aging. Anyone studying aging should understand aging as a normal process.
- The Association for Gerontology in Higher Education predicts that a larger older population will need more health care professionals. These people will need to know more about aging and the unique needs of older people.
- Students can take an active approach to finding work with older people. They can join a gerontology association, volunteer at a university center on aging, work as an intern in a setting that allows them to work with older people, and volunteer to do community work. Students can also interview professionals in the field of aging for information about the profession.

DISCUSSION QUESTIONS

1. List and explain three issues that have changed our views on aging today.
2. List the three approaches to the study of aging in universities. What basic information about aging should all gerontology students know?
3. What kinds of jobs will an aging population create for younger people?
4. How can students improve their chances of finding a job in the field of aging?
5. What is informational interviewing? How is it done? What are its goals?

SUGGESTED READING

Williams, E. (2003). *Opportunities in gerontology and aging services careers.* Chicago, IL: VGM Career Books.

This book provides a guide to careers in gerontology and aging services. Individual chapters focus on exploring careers in gerontology, career choices in the field (including careers in advocacy, business, communications, criminal justice/law, education, health services, ministry, recreation, rehabilitation, and social services), challenging ageist stereotypes, training for careers in gerontology, trends impacting aging services, and the future of the field.

Peterson, D. A. (1987). *Career paths in the field of aging: Professional gerontology.* Lexington, MA: Lexington Books.

The author reviews educational programs in aging and job opportunities in the field. He presents information on degree programs and proposals for continuing professional education.

Association for Gerontology in Higher Education. (1994). *National directory of educational programs in gerontology and geriatrics* (6th Ed.). Washington, DC: AGHE.

This guide lists over 1,000 programs in gerontology and geriatrics throughout the United States. It describes the focus of each program, the address, and the type of certification the program offers. A valuable resource if you plan to go on in your study of aging. Your school library or center on aging may have a copy. You may also be able to get a copy through interlibrary loan. (The volume costs $85 from AGHE, 1001 Connecticut Avenue, NW, Suite 410, Washington, DC 20036.)

GLOSSARY OF TERMS

aging network The federal network of agencies that grow out of the Older Americans Act. They include State Units on Aging and Area Agencies on Aging.

competency-based curriculum A curriculum that specifies what a graduate should be able to do. Only students who show minimum competence graduate.

continuing education units (CEUs) Credits given to professionals for education activities such as attendance at conferences or seminars. Some professional associations require that members get a minimum number of CEUs each year or two to stay licensed.

ethnogeriatrics The study of how ethnicity affects aging and health. This field studies diseases such as diabetes and dementia in different minority groups. It also looks at the value systems of other cultures as they influence aging and health.

fourth age A stage of life that historian Peter Laslett adds to the French third age. He adds this because of life expectancy and the differences between younger and older old people.

hidden job market The jobs that never reach the newspapers or employment agency files; jobs known only to those who work in a field and have access to the latest information about job openings.

internship A program that finds a work placement for a student in a community setting. The student gets university credit for the work.

third age A French term for old age. Laslett suggests that this may best apply today to the younger years of old age.

WORKS CONSULTED

AARP (American Association of Retired Persons). (1984). *Prescription drugs: A survey of consumer use, attitudes and behavior.* Washington, DC: Author.

AARP (American Association of Retired Persons). (1990). *Report on the survey of older consumer behavior.* Washington, DC: Author.

AARP (American Association of Retired Persons). (1991). *Home equity conversion in the United States: Programs and data.* Washington, DC: Public Policy Institute.

AARP (American Association of Retired Persons). (1992). *Making wise decisions for long-term care.* [Pamphlet]. Washington, DC: Author.

AARP (American Association of Retired Persons). (1993). *Understanding senior housing: For the 1990's.* Washington, DC: Author.

AARP (American Association of Retired Persons). (1995). *Images of aging in America: Final report.* Chapel Hill, NC: FGI Integrated Marketing.

AARP (American Association of Retired Persons). (1996). *Understanding senior housing.* Washington, DC: Author.

AARP (American Association of Retired Persons). (1999). *Consumer behavior, experiences, and attitudes: A comparison by age groups.* Princeton, NJ: Princeton Survey Research Associates. Retrieved: December 20, 2004, http://research.aarp.org/consume/d16907_behavior.pdf.

AARP (American Association of Retired Persons). (2001). *Income, poverty, and health insurance in the United States in 2001.* Retrieved: September 5, 2004, http://research.aarp.org/econ/fs93_income.html.

AARP (American Association of Retired Persons). (2002). Get a grip. *Modern Maturity, 45*(5), 106.

AARP (American Association of Retired Persons). (2003a). *Annual report 2002.* Retrieved: December 6, 2004, http://assets.aarp.org/www.aarp.org_/articles/aboutaarp/annualreport2002_f.pdf.

AARP (American Association of Retired Persons). (2003b). *These four walls . . . : Americans 45+ talk about home and community.* Retrieved: October 2, 2004, http://research.aarp.org/il/four_walls.pdf.

AARP (American Association of Retired Persons). (2003c). *2002 AARP Montana consumer fraud survey.* Retrieved: March 6, 2004, www.research.aarp.org/consume/mt_fraud.html.

AARP (American Association of Retired Persons). (2004a). *Baby boomers envision retirement II: A survey of baby boomers' expectations for retirement.* Washington, DC: Author. Knowledge Management. Retrieved: December 30, 2004, http://research.aarp.org/econ/boomers_envision.pdf.

AARP (American Association of Retired Persons). (2004b). *Federally insured loans. Eligibility and repayment.* Retrieved: October 3, 2004, www.aarp.org/Articles/a2003-03-21-elig.html.

AARP (American Association of Retired Persons). (2004c). *Housing choices. Continuing care retirement communities.* Retrieved: November 7, 2004, www.aarp.org/life/housingchoices/Articles/a2004-02-26-retirementcommunity.html.

AARP (American Association of Retired Persons). (2004d). *Staying ahead of the curve: The AARP work and career study.* Washington, DC: Author. Retrieved: September 17, 2004, www.research.aarp.org/econ/multiwork.html.

AARP (American Association of Retired Persons). (2005a). Call to action! *AARP Bulletin, 46*(1).

AARP (American Association of Retired Persons). (2005b). *Caring for your grandchild.* Retrieved: January 7, 2005, www.aarp.org/life/grandparents/grandchild/Articles/a2004-09-01-grandparents-visitation.html.

AARP and the University of Southern California. (2004). *Images of aging in America 2004: A summary of selected findings.* Retrieved: December 20, 2004, http://research.aarp.org/general/images_aging.pdf.

Abel, E. K. (1990). Daughters caring for elderly parents. In J. F. Gubrium & A. Sankar (Eds.), *The home care experience: Ethnography and policy* (pp. 189–206). Newbury Park, CA: Sage.

Abrams, S. (2001). Inebriated elders: The problem of substance abuse among the elderly. *Elder Law Journal, 9*(2), 229–255.

Achenbaum, W. A. (1983). *Shades of gray: Old age, American values, and federal policies since 1920.* Boston: Little, Brown.

Achenbaum, W. A. (1985). Societal perceptions of aging and the aged. In R. H. Binstock & E. Shanas (Eds.), *Handbook of aging and the social sciences* (2d ed.), (pp. 129–148). New York: Van Nostrand.

Achenbaum, W. A. (1987). Can gerontology be a science? *Journal of Aging Studies, 1,* 3–18.

Achenbaum, W. A. (1993). One way to bridge the two cultures: Advancing qualitative gerontology through professional autobiographies. *Canadian Journal on Aging, 12*(2), 143–156.

Achenbaum, W. A. (2000a). Afterword. In T. R. Cole, R. Kastenbaum, & R. E. Ray (Eds.), *Handbook of the humanities and aging* (2d ed.), (pp. 419–431). New York: Springer.

Achenbaum, W. A. (2000b). The elderly's future stake in voluntary associations. *Journal of Aging and Social Policy, 11*(2–3), 41–47.

Achenbaum, W.A., & Stearns, P. N. (1978). Old age and modernization. *The Gerontologist, 18,* 307–312.

Adams, C., Smith, M. C., Pasupathi, M., & Vitolo, L. (2002). Social context effects on story recall in older and younger women: Does the listener make a difference? *The Journals of Gerontology Series B: Psychological Sciences and Social Sciences, 57,* 28–40.

Adams, R., & Blieszner, R. (1995). Aging well with family and friends. *American Behavioral Scientist, 39*(2), 209–224.

Aday, R. H., & Austin, B. S. (2000). Images of aging in the lyrics of American country music. *Educational Gerontology, 26*(2), 135–154.

Administration on Aging. (2002a). *A profile of older Americans.* Retrieved: November 24, 2004, www.aoa.gov/prof/Statistics/profile/3.asp.

Administration on Aging. (2002b). *A profile of older Americans: 2002.* Retrieved: November 24, 2004, www.aoa.gov/prof/Statistics/profile/2002profile.pdf.

Administration on Aging. (2002c). *A profile of older Americans: 2002. American housing survey for the United States in 2001, current housing reports.* H150/01. Retrieved: September 26, 2004, www.aoa.gov/prof/Statistics/profile/9.asp.

Adminstration on Aging. (2002d). *A profile of older Americans: 2002. Living arrangements.* Retrieved: October 2, 2004, www.aoa.gov/prof/Statistics/profile/4.asp.

Adminstration on Aging. (2002e). *Housing.* Retrieved: September 26, 2004, www.aoa.gov/eldfam/housing/Housing_pf.asp.

Administration on Aging. (2003). *A profile of older Americans: 2003.* Washington, DC: U.S. Department of Health and Human Services. Retrieved: September 6, 2004, www.aoa.gov/prof/Statistics/profile/2003/2003profile.pdf.

Administration on Aging. (2004a). *Board and care.* Retrieved: October 31, 2004, www.aoa.gov/eldfam/housing/housing_services/board_care.asp.

Administration on Aging. (2004b). *Fact sheets—Challenges of global aging.* U.S. Department of Health and Human Services. Retrieved: March 15, 2004, www.aoa.gov/press/fact/alpha/fact_global_aging.asp.

Administration on Aging and U.S. Department of Health and Human Services. (2004). *Alzheimer's resource room.* Retrieved: June 26, 2004, www.aoa.gov/alz/public/alzprof/research/research.asp.

Administration on Aging. (2005). *Legislation and budget.* Retrieved: May 27, 2005, www.aoa.gov/about/legbudg/current_budg/legbudg_current_budg.asp.

Age brings no drop in hours of housework. (1991). *Aging, 362,* 48.

AGHE (Association for Gerontology in Higher Education). (1996). *Careers in aging: Opportunities and options.* Washington, DC: Author.

AGHE Standards Committee, (1990). *Standards and guidelines for gerontology programs* (2d ed.), T. A. Rich, J. R. Connelly, & E. B. Douglass (Eds.). Washington, DC: Author.

Aging Health Policy Center. (1985). The homeless mentally ill elderly. Working paper. San Francisco: University of California.

Aiken, L. R. (2001). *Dying, death, and bereavement* (4th ed.). Mahwah, NJ: Lawrence Erlbaum.

Aldwin, C. M., & Gilmer, D. F. (2004). *Health, illness, and optimal aging: Biological and psychosocial perspectives.* Thousand Oaks, CA: Sage.

Allen, K. R., & Chin-Sang, V. (1990). A lifetime of work: The context and meanings of leisure for aging African American women. *The Gerontologist, 30*(6), 734–740.

Allison, M. T., & Smith, S. (1990). Leisure and the quality of life: Issues facing racial and ethnic minority elderly. *Therapeutic Recreation Journal, 24*(3), 50–63.

Almberg, B. E., Grafstrom, M., & Winblad, B. (2000). Caregivers of relatives with dementia: Experiences encompassing social support and bereavement. *Aging and Mental Health, 4*(1), 82–89.

Altus, D. E., & Mathews, R. M. (2002). Comparing the satisfaction of rural seniors with housing co-ops and congregate apartments: Is home ownership important? *Journal of Housing for the Elderly, 16*(1–2), 39–50.

Ambrosius, G. R. (1994, July/August). Virtual marketing and the deyouthing of America. *Aging Today,* 11.

American Cancer Society. (2004). *The patient self-determination act.* Retrieved: December 16, 2004, www.cancer.org/docroot/MIT/content/MIT_3_2X_The_Patient_Self-Determination_Act.asp?sitearea=MIT.

American College of Sports Medicine. (2000). *ACSM's guidelines for exercise testing and prescription* (6th ed.). Baltimore: Lippincott Williams & Wilkins.

American Medical Directors Association. (2003). *Synopsis of federal regulations in the nursing facility: Implications for attending physicians and medical directors.* Retrieved: November 6, 2004, www.amda.com/federal affairs/regulations_synopsis.htm.

Amoss, P. (1999). Coyote looks at grandmother: Puget Sound Salish grandmothers in myth and message. In M. M. Schweitzer (Ed.), *American Indian grandmothers: Traditions and transitions* (pp. 79–101). Albuquerque: University of New Mexico Press.

Amoss, P. T., & Harrell, S. (1981). Foreword. In P. T. Amoss & S. Harrell (Eds.), *Other ways of growing old: Anthropological perspectives* (pp. 1–24). Stanford, CA: Stanford University Press.

Anderson, R. E., Franckowiak, S., Christmas, C., Walston, J., & Crespo, C. (2001). Obesity and reports of no leisure time activity among older Americans: Results from the third national health and nutrition examination survey. *Educational Gerontology, 27,* 297–306.

Anderson, R. M., Minino, A. M., Fingerhut, L. A., Warner, M., & Heinen, M. A. (2004). *Deaths: Injuries, 2001.* National vital statistics reports, 52(21). Hyattsville, MD: National Center for Health Statistics.

Andrews, G. J., Gavin, N., Begley, S., & Brodie, D. (2003). Assisting friendships, combating loneliness: Unsers' view on a 'befriending' scheme. *Ageing and Society, 23*(3), 349–362.

Andrews, J. (1989). *Poverty and poor health among elderly Hispanic Americans.* Baltimore, MD: Commonwealth Fund Commission on Elderly People Living Alone.

Andrews, M. (2000). Ageful and proud. *Ageing and Society, 20*(6), 791–795.

Annon, T. A. K., & Lee, D. W. (1994). Reading speed and prose memory in older and younger adults. *Psychology and Aging, 9*(2), 216–223.

Antonovsky, A., & Sagy, S. (1990). Confronting developmental tasks in the retirement transition. *The Gerontologist, 30,* 362–368.

Antonucci, T. C., & Akiyama, H. (1993). Stress and coping in the elderly. *Applied and Preventive Psychology, 2,* 201–208.

Anzick, M. A., & Weaver, D. A. (2001). Reducing poverty among elderly women. ORES Working Paper Series Number 87. Division of Economic Research. Washington, DC: Social Security Administration. Retrieved: September 11, 2004, www.ssa.gov/policy/docs/workingpapers/wp87.pdf.

AOA (Administration on Aging). (2004a). *GAO, IG & U.S. Senate hearings.* Retrieved: December 10, 2004, www.aoa.gov/prof/research/research.asp.

AOA. (Administration on Aging). (2004b). *Older Americans Act.* Retrieved: December 10, 2004, www.aoa.gov/about/legbudg/oaa/legbudg_oaa.asp.

AOA (Administration on Aging). (2004c). *Welcome.* Retrieved: December 10, 2004, www.aoa.gov/about/legbudg/oaa/legbudg_oaa.asp.

AOA (Administration on Aging). (2004d). *Welcome. Mission.* Retrieved: June 29, 2005, www.aoa.gov/about/over/over_mission.asp.

Apt, N. (1998). Keynote address. *Bulletin on Aging, 1&2,* 13–15.

Ardelt, M. (2000). Antecedents and effects of wisdom in old age. *Research on Aging 22*(4), 360–394.

Arias E. (2004). *United States life tables, 2001.* National vital statistics reports, 52(14). Hyattsville, MD: National Center for Health Statistics. Retrieved: March 21, 2004, www.cdc.gov/nchs/data/nvsr/nvsr52/nvsr52_14.pdf.

Arias E., & Smith B. L. (2003). *Deaths: Preliminary data for 2001.* National vital statistics reports; Vol. 51, no. 5. Hyattsville, MD: National Center for Health Statistics.

Aristotle. (1941). *The basic works of Aristotle.* R. McKeon (Ed.). New York: Random House.

Arking, R. (1991). *Biology of aging: Observations and principles.* Englewood Cliffs, NJ: Prentice Hall.

Aronson, J., Thornewell, C., & Williams, K. (1995). Wife assault in old age: Coming out of obscurity. *Canadian Journal on Aging, 14*(Suppl.), 72–88.

Assisted Living Federation of America. (2000). *ALFA's overview of the assisted living industry.* Fairfax, VA: ALFA.

Atchley, R. C. (1976). *The sociology of retirement.* New York: Schenkman.

Atchley, R. C. (1980). *The social forces in later life.* Belmont, CA: Wadsworth.

Atchley, R. C. (1985). *Social forces and aging* (4th ed.). Belmont, CA: Wadsworth.

Atchley, R. C. (1989). A continuity theory of normal aging. *The Gerontologist, 29,* 183–190.

Atchley, R. C. (1994). *The social forces in later life* (7th ed.). Belmont, CA: Wadsworth.

Atchley, R. C. (1999a). *Continuity and adaptation in aging: Creating positive experiences.* Baltimore: Johns Hopkins University Press.

Atchley, R. C. (1999b). Continuity theory, self, and social structure. In V. W. Marshall & C. D. Ryff (Eds.), *The self and society in aging processes* (pp. 94–121). New York: Springer.

Atchley, R. C., & Barusch, A. S. (2004). *Social forces and aging* (10th ed.). Belmont, CA: Wadsworth/ Thomson Learning.

Atkinson, R. (1994). Late onset problem drinking in older adults. *International Journal of Geriatric Psychiatry, 9,* 321–326.

Ausman, L. M., & Russell, R. M. (1990). Nutrition and aging. In E. L. Schneider & J. W. Rowe (Eds.), *Handbook of the biology of aging* (3d ed.), (pp. 384–406). San Diego: Academic Press.

Austad, S. N. (2001). Concepts and theories of aging. In E. J. Masoro & S. N. Austad (Eds.), *Handbook of the biology of aging* (5th ed.), (pp. 3–22). San Diego: Academic Press.

Austin, B. J., & Fleisher, L. K. (2003). *Financing end-of-life care: Challenges for an aging population.* Academy of Health. Retrieved: December 13, 2004, www.hcfo.net/pdf/eolcare.pdf.

Austin, E. (2000). Geriatrics in medical education: Curricular examples. *Gerontology and Geriatrics Education, 20*(3), 87–92.

Avioli, R. (1989). The social support functions of siblings in later life. *American Behavioral Scientist, 33*(1), 45–57.

Avis, N. E., Brambilla, D. J., Vass, K., & McKinlay, J. B. (1991). Effect of widowhood on health: A prospective analysis from the Massachusetts Women's Health Study. *Social Science and Medicine, 33*(9), 1063–1070.

Bäckman, L., Small, B. J., Wahlin, A., & Larsson, M. (2000). Cognitive functioning in very old age. In F. I. M. Craik & T. A. Salthouse (Eds.), *The handbook of aging and cognition* (2d ed.), (pp. 499–558). Mahwah, NJ: Lawrence Erlbaum.

Backman, L., Small, B. J., & Wahlin, A. (2001). Aging and memory: Cognitive and biological perspectives. In J. E. Birren & K. W. Schaie, (Eds.), *Handbook of the psychology of aging* (5th ed.). San Diego: Academic Press.

Bailey, L. (2004). *Aging Americans: Stranded without options.* Washington, DC: Surface Transportation Policy Project. Retrieved: October 31, 2004, www.transact.org/library/reports_html/seniors/aging.pdf.

Baker, P. M. (1991). Socialization after death: The might of the living dead. In B. Hess & E. Markson (Eds.), *Growing old in America* (4th ed.). New York: Transaction Books.

Baldridge, D. (2002). Indian elders. In D. L. Infeld (Ed.), *Disciplinary approaches to aging: Vol. 4, Anthropology of aging* (pp. 255–267). New York: Routledge.

Ball, M. M., Perkins, M. M., Whittington, F. J., Connell, B. R., Hollingsworth, C., King, S. V., Elrod, C. L., & Combs, B. L. (2004). Independence in assisted living. *Journals of Gerontology: Series B: Psychological Sciences and Social Sciences, 59B*(4), S202–S212.

Ball, R. M. (2001). Don't drain the Social Security fund. *Washington Post* (August 30), C7.

Baltes, P. (1987). Developmental psychology. In G. L. Maddox (Ed.), *The encyclopedia of aging* (pp. 170–175). New York: Springer.

Baltes, P. B. (1992, February). Wise, and otherwise. *Natural History, 26,* 50–51.

Baltes, P. B. (1993). Aging mind: Potential and limits. *The Gerontologist, 33*(5), 580–594.

Baltes, P. B. (1997). On the incomplete architecture of human ontogeny: Selection, optimization, and compensation as foundations of developmental theory. *American Psychologist, 52,* 366–380.

Baltes, P. B., & Baltes, M. M. (1990). Psychological perspectives on successful aging: The model of selective optimization with compensation. In P. B. Baltes & M. M. Baltes (Eds.), *Successful aging: Perspectives from the behavioral sciences* (pp. 1–34). Cambridge, England: Cambridge University Press.

Baltes, P. B., & Schaie, K. W. (1982). The myth of the twilight years. In S. H. Zarit (Ed.), *Readings in aging and death: Contemporary perspectives* (2d ed.). New York: Harper & Row.

Baltes, P. B., & Willis, S. L. (1982). Plasticity and enhancement of intellectual functioning in old age: Penn State's Adult Development and Enrichment Project (ADEPT). In F. I. M. Craik & S. E. Trehub (Eds.), *Aging and cognitive processes* (pp. 353–389). New York: Plenum.

Bane, S. D. (1991). Rural minority populations. *Generations, 15*(4), 63–65.

Banks, M. R., & Banks, W. A. (2002). Effects of animal-assisted therapy on loneliness in an elderly population in long-term care facilities. *Journals of Gerontology:*

Series A: Biological Sciences and Medical Sciences, 57A(7), M428–M432.

Banks, W. A., & Banks, M. R. (2003). Putting more heart in the nursing home: What we learned from the dogs. *Geriatrics and Aging, 6*(2), 66.

Barer, B. M. (1994). Men and women aging differently. *International Journal of Aging and Human Development, 38*(1), 29–40.

Barer, M. L., Hertzman, C., Miller, R., & Pascali, M. V. (1992). On being old and sick: The burden of health care for the elderly in Canada and the United States. *Journal of Health Politics, Policy and Law, 17*(4), 763–782.

Barker, J. C., & Mitteness, L. S. (1990). Invisible caregivers in the spotlight: Non-kin caregivers of frail older adults. In J. F. Gubrium & A. Sankar (Eds.), *The home care experience: Ethnography and policy* (pp. 101–127). Newbury Park, CA: Sage.

Barnea, Z., & Teichman, M. (1994). Substance misuse and abuse among the elderly: Implications for social work intervention. *Journal of Gerontological Social Work, 21,* 113–148.

Barnes, D. E., Tager, I. B., Satariano, W. A., & Yaffe, K. (2004). The relationship between literacy and cognition in well-educated elders. *The Journals of Gerontology Series B: Psychological Sciences and Social Sciences, 59,* M390–M395.

Barresi, C. M. (1990). Ethnogerontology: Social aging in national, racial, and cultural groups. In K. F. Ferraro (Ed.), *Gerontology: Perspectives and issues* (pp. 247–265). New York: Springer.

Barrett, A. E. (1999). Social support and life satisfaction among the never married. *Research on Aging, 21*(1), 46–72.

Barrett, A. E., & Lynch, S. M. (1999). Caregiving networks of elderly persons: Variations by marital status. *The Gerontologist, 39*(6), 695–704.

Barrett, J., & Wright, M. (1981). Age-related facilitation in recall following semantic processing. *Journal of Gerontology, 2,* 194–199.

Barry, P., & Duka, W. (2002). Older vote carries clout. Experts say it could sway elections, set future course for critical issues. *AARP Bulletin Online, 43*(9), 3–6. Retrieved: December 6, 2004, www.aarp.org/bulletin/news/Articles/a2003-08-26-clout.html.

Bartels, S. J., & Smyer, M. A. (2002, Spring). Mental disorders of aging: An emerging public health crisis? *Generations,* 14–20.

Bartke, A., & Lane, M. (2001). Endocrine and neuroendocrine regulatory functions. In E. J. Masoro & S. N. Austad (Eds.), *Handbook of the biology of aging* (5th ed.), (pp. 297–323). San Diego: Academic Press.

Bartoshuk, L. M., & Weiffenbach, J. M. (1990). Chemical senses and aging. In E. L. Schneider & J. W. Rowe (Eds.), *Handbook of the biology of aging* (3d ed.), (pp. 429–443). San Diego: Academic Press.

Barzilai, N., & Gabriely, I. (2001). The role of fat depletion in the biological benefits of caloric restriction. *Journal of Nutrition, 131,* 903S–906S.

Bass, S. A., & Caro, F. G. (1996). The economic value of grandparent assistance. *Generations, 20*(1), 29–38.

Bastida, E. (1988). Reexamining assumptions about extended families: Older Puerto Ricans in a comparative perspective. In M. Sotomayor & H. Curiel (Eds.), *Hispanic elderly: A cultural signature* (pp. 163–183). Edinburg, TX: Pan American University Press.

Bastida, E., & Juarez, R. (1991). Older Hispanic women: A decade in review. In M. Sotomayor (Ed.), *Empowering Hispanic families: A critical issue for the '90s* (pp. 155–172). Milwaukee, WI: Family Service America.

Bates, C. J., Benton, D., Biesalski, H. K., Stachelin, H. B., van Staveren, W., Stehle, P., Suter, P. M., & Wolfram, G. (2002). Nutrition and aging: A consensus statement. *Journal of Nutrition, Health and Aging, 6*(2), 103–116.

Bazargan, M. (1994). Effects of health, environmental, and socio-psychological variables on fear of crime and its consequences among urban black elderly individuals. *International Journal of Aging and Human Development, 8,* 99–115.

Beard, B. B. (1991). *Centenarians: The new generation.* New York: Greenwood.

Beard, R. L. (2004). In their voices: Identity preservation and experiences of Alzheimer's disease. *Journal of Aging Studies, 18*(4), 415–428.

Becerra, R. M. (1983). The Mexican American: Aging in a changing culture. In R. L. McNeely & J. L. Colen (Eds.), *Aging in minority groups* (pp. 108–118). Beverly Hills, CA: Sage.

Beck, M. (1990). Going for the gold. *Newsweek,* April 23, 74–75.

Beck, M., Denworth, L., & Christian, N. (1992). Finding work after 50. *Newsweek,* March 16, 58–60.

Beck, M., Glick, D., Gordon, J., & Picker, L. (1991). School days for seniors. *Newsweek,* November 11, 60–63.

Beck, M., Quade, V., Roberts, E., Gordon, J., & Annin, P. (1990). A home away from home. *Newsweek,* July 2, 56–58.

Beck, S., & Page, J. W. (1988). Involvement in activities and the psychological well-being of retired men. *Activities, Adaptation and Aging, 11*(1), 31–47.

Becker, M. H. (1993, March). A medical sociologist looks at health promotion. *Journal of Health and Social Behavior, 34,* 1–6.

Beckman, K. B., & Ames, B. N. (1998). The free radical theory of aging matures. *Physiological Review, 78*(2), 547–581.

Beehr, T. A., & Adms, G. A. (2003). Concluding observations and future endeavors. In G. A. Adams & T. A. Beehr (Eds.), *Retirement: Reasons, processes, and results* (pp. 293–298). New York: Springer.

Beeler, J. A., Rawls, T. W., Herdt, G., & Cohler, B. J. (1999). The needs of older lesbians and gay men in Chicago. *Journal of Gay and Lesbian Social Services, 9*(1), 31–49.

Beisgen, B. A., & Kraitchman, M. C. (2003). *Senior centers: Opportunities for successful aging.* New York: Springer.

Bekey, M. (1991, April/May). Dial s-w-i-n-d-l-e. *Modern Maturity,* 31ff.

Beland, R., & Kapes, C. (2003). Gerontology education for recreation service majors: Meeting the demands of the 21st century. *Educational Gerontology, 29*(7), 617–626.

Belden, Russonello, & Stewart Research/Strategy/Management. (2001). *In the middle: A report on multicultural boomers coping with family and aging issues: A national survey conducted for AARP.* Washington, DC: AARP. Retrieved: July 14, 2004, http://research.aarp.org/il/in_the_middle.pdf.

Belgrave, L. L, & Bradsher, J. E. (1994). Health as a factor in institutionalization: Disparities between African Americans and whites. *Research on Aging, 16*(2), 115–141.

Bell, D., Kassachau, P., & Zellman, G. (1976). *Delivering services to elderly members of minority groups: A critical review of the literature.* Santa Monica, CA: RAND.

Bengtson, V., Rosenthal, C., & Burton, L. (1990). Families and aging: Diversity and heterogeneity. In R. H. Binstock & L. K. George (Eds.), *Handbook of aging and the social sciences* (pp. 263–287). San Diego: Academic Press.

Bengtson, V. L. (1993). Is the "contract across generations" changing? Effects of population aging on obligations and expectations across age groups. In V. L. Bengtson & W. A. Achenbaum (Eds.), *Changing contract across generations* (pp. 3–23). New York: A. de Gruyter.

Bengtson, V. L., Burgess, E. O., & Parrott, T. M. (1997). Theory, explanation, and a third generation of theoretical development in social gerontology. *Journals of Gerontology Series B, 52*(2), S72–88.

Bengtson, V. L., & Kuypers, J. A. (1971). Generational differences and the developmental stake. *International Journal of Aging and Human Development, 2,* 249–260.

Bengtson, V. L., Rice, C. J., & Johnson, M. L. (1999). Are theories of aging important? Models and explanations in gerontology at the turn of the century. In V. L. Bengtson & K. W. Schaie (Eds), *Handbook of theories of aging* (pp. 3–20). New York: Springer.

Bennett, A. T., & Collins, K. A. (2001). Elderly suicide: A 10-year retrospective study. *American Journal of Forensic Medicine and Pathology, 22*(2), 169–172.

Berg, B. L. (1998). *Qualitative research methods for the social sciences* (3d ed.). Boston: Allyn & Bacon.

Berg, C. A., & Sternberg, R. J. (2002). Multiple perspectives on the development of adult intelligence. In J. Demick & C. Andreoletti (Eds.), *Handbook of adult development* (pp. 121–130). New York: Kluwer Academic/Plenum.

Berg, C. A., & Sternberg, R. J. (2003). Multiple perspectives on the development of adult intelligence. In J. Demick & C. Andreoletti (Eds.), *Handbook of adult development* (pp. 103–119). New York: Kluwer Academic.

Berger, A., Pereira, D., Baker, K., O'Mara, A., & Bolle, J. (2002). Commentary: Social and cultural determinants of end-of-life care for elderly persons. *The Gerontologist, 42* (Special Issue 3), 49–53.

Berger, P., & Luckmann, T. (1967). *The social construction of reality.* Garden City, NY: Anchor.

Berger, R. (Ed.). (1996). *Gay and grey: The older homosexual man* (2d ed.). New York: Harrington Park.

Bergling, T. (2004). *Reeling in the years: Gay men's perspectives on age and ageism.* New York: Harrington Park.

Bergman, G. (1991, April). Aging confab focuses on older women of color. *Sun Reporter,* 17.

Berman, L., & Sobkowska-Ashcroft, I. (1986). The old in language and literature. *Language and Communication, 6,* 139–145.

Berman, L., & Sobkowska-Ashcroft, I. (1987). *Images and impressions of old age in the great works of Western literature (700 B.C.–1900 A.D.).* Lewiston, NY: Edwin Mellen.

Bern-Klug, M., Gessert, C., & Forbes, S. (2001). Need to revise assumptions about the end of life: Implications for social work practice. *Health and Social Work, 26*(1), 38–48.

Bernstein, A. B., Hing, E., Moss, A. J., Allen, K. F., Siller, A. B., & Tiggle, R. B. (2003). *Health care in America: Trends in utilization.* Hyattsville, MD: National Center for Health Statistics.

Betancourt, R. L. (1991). *Retirement and men's physical and mental health.* New York: Garland.

Beyene, Y., Becker, G., & Mayen, N. (2002). Perception of aging and sense of well-being among Latino elderly. *Journal of Cross-Cultural Gerontology, 17*(2), 155–172.

Bharucha, A. J. (2003). Late-life suicide. In J. M. Ellison & V. Sumer (Eds.), *Depression in later life: A multidisciplinary psychiatric approach* (pp. 297–305). New York: Marcel Dekker.

Biafora, F. A., & Longino, C. F. (1990). Elderly Hispanic migration in the United States. *Journal of Gerontology: Social Sciences, 45*(5), S212–S219.

Biegel, D. E., Sales, E., & Schulz, R. (1991). *Family caregiving in chronic illness.* Newbury Park, CA: Sage.

Bigler, R. (2002). *Lack of pension coverage a reality for more than half of U.S. workers* (Jan. 29, 2002). LRA Online—Labor Research Association. Retrieved: September 5, 2004, www.laborresearch.org/story.php?id=95.

Bikson, T. K., & Goodchilds, J. D. (1991). *Experiencing the retirement transition: Managerial and professional men before and after* (Rand Note, N-3430-MF). Santa Monica, CA: Rand.

Binstock, R. H. (1972). Interest-group liberalism and the politics of aging. *The Gerontologist, 12*(3, pt. 1), 265–280.

Binstock, R. H. (1978, November 11). Federal policy toward the aging—its inadequacies and its politics. *National Journal,* 1838–1845.

Binstock, R. H. (1983). The aged as scapegoats. *The Gerontologist, 23*(2), 136–143.

Binstock, R. H. (1991a). Aging, politics, and public policy. In B. B. Hess & E. W. Markson (Eds.), *Growing old in America* (4th ed.), (pp. 325–340). New Brunswick, NJ: Transaction.

Binstock, R. H. (1991b, Summer/Fall). From the great society to the aging society—25 years of the Older Americans Act. *Generations,* 11–18.

Binstock, R. H. (1992). The oldest old and "intergenerational equity." In R. M. Suzman, D. P. Willis, & K. G. Manton (Eds.), *The oldest old* (pp. 394–417). New York: Oxford University Press.

Binstock, R. H. (1993). Healthcare costs around the world: Is aging a fiscal "black hole"? *Generations, 17*(4), 37–42.

Binstock, R. H. (1997). The old-age lobby in a new political era. In R. B. Hudson (Ed.), *The future of age-based public policy* (pp. 56–74). Baltimore, MD: The Johns Hopkins University Press.

Binstock, R. H. (1999). Public policies and minority elders. In M. L. Wykle & A. B. Ford (Eds.), *Serving minority elders in the 21st century* (pp. 5–24). New York: Springer.

Binstock, R. H. (2000). Older people and voting participation: Past and future. *The Gerontologist, 40*(1), 18–31.

Binstock, R. H., & George, L. K. (Eds.). (1990). *Handbook of aging and the social sciences* (3d ed.). San Diego: Academic Press.

Binstock, R. H., & Kahana, J. (1988). An essay on setting limits: Medical goals in an aging society. *The Gerontologist, 28*(3), 424–426.

Birren, J. E., & Schroots, J. F. (1996). History, concepts, and theory in the psychology of aging. In J. E. Birren & K. W. Schaie (Eds.), *Handbook of the psychology of aging* (4th ed.), (pp. 3–23). San Diego: Academic Press.

Blanchard-Fields, F., & Abeles, R. P. (1996). Social cognition and aging. In J. E. Birren & K. W. Schaie (Eds.), *Handbook of the psychology of aging* (4th ed.), (pp. 159–161). San Diego: Academic Press.

Blank, T. O. (1993). Housing as a factor in adult life. In R. Kastenbaum (Ed.), *Encyclopedia of adult development* (pp. 215–222). Phoenix, AZ: Oryx.

Blau, P. M. (1964). *Exchange and power in social life.* New York: Wiley.

Blazer, D. G. (2003). Depression in late life: Review and commentary. *The Journals of Gerontology Series A: Biological Sciences and Medical Sciences, 58,* M249–M265.

Blondell, R. D. (1999). Alcohol abuse and self-neglect in the elderly. *Journal of Elder Abuse and Neglect, 11*(2), 55–75.

Blow, F. C., Oslin, D. W., & Barry, K. L. (2002, Spring). Misuse and abuse of alcohol, illicit drugs, and psychoactive medication among older people. *Generations,* 50–55.

Bluck, M. G., & Reno, V. (Eds). (2001). *Reflections on implementing Medicare.* Washington, DC: National Academy of Social Insurance.

Blumenthal, J. A., Sherwood, A.I., Gullette, E. C., Babyak, M., Waugh, R., Georgiades, A., et al. (2000). Exercise and weight loss reduce blood pressure in men and women with mild hypertension. Effects on cardiovascular, metabolic and hemodynamic functioning. *Archives of Internal Medicine, 160*(13), 1947–1958.

Boaz, R. F., Hu, J., & Ye, Y. (1999). The transfer of resources from middle-aged children to functionally limited elderly parents: Providing time, giving money, sharing space. *The Gerontologist, 39*(6), 648–657.

Boegeman, M. (1989). Teaching creative writing to older women. *Women's Studies Quarterly, 17*(1–2), 48–55.

Boeri, M. M., & Baunach, D. M. (2002). Effects of education on retirement: A continuity perspective. *Southwest Journal on Aging, 17*(1–2), 15–21.

Bolles, R. N. (1995). *What color is your parachute? 1995. A practical guide for job-hunters and career changers.* Berkeley, CA: Ten Speed Press.

Bolles, R. N. (2004). *What color is your parachute? 2004. A practical guide for job-hunters and career changers.* Berkeley, CA: Ten Speed Press.

Bonanno, A., & Calasanti, T. M. (1988). Laissez-faire strategies and the crisis of the welfare state: A comparative analysis of the status of the elderly in Italy and in the United States. *Sociological Focus, 21,* 245–263.

Bond, G. E., Rice, M. M., McCurry, S. M., Graves, A. B., Teri, L., Bowen, J. D., McCormick, W. C., & Larson, E. B. (2003). Alcohol, aging, and cognitive performance: A cross-cultural comparison. *Journal of Aging and Health, 15*(2), 371–390.

Bond, J. B., Jr., Penner, R. L., & Yellen, P. (1995). Perceived effectiveness of legislation concerning abuse of the elderly: A survey of professionals in Canada and the United States. *Canadian Journal on Aging, 14* (Suppl. 2), 118–135.

Bortz, W. M., & Bortz, W. M., II. (1992). Aging and the disuse syndrome—Effect of lifetime exercise. In S. Harris, R. Harris, & W. S. Harris (Eds.), *Physical activity, aging and sports: Practice, program and policy. Vol. II* (pp. 44–50). Albany, NY: Center for the Study of Aging.

Botwinick, J. (1984). *Aging and behavior* (3d ed.). New York: Springer.

Bowd, A. D. (2003). Stereotypes of elderly persons in narrative jokes. *Research on Aging, 25*(1), 22–35.

Bowers, B. F., & Myers, B. J. (1999). Grandmothers providing care for grandchildren: Consequences of various levels of caregiving. *Family Relations, 48*(3), 303–311.

Boxer, A. M., Cook, J. A., & Cohler, B. J. (1986). Grandfathers, fathers, and sons: Intergenerational relations among men. In K. A. Pillemer & R. S. Wolf (Eds.), *Elder abuse: Conflict in the family* (pp. 93–121). Dover, MA: Auburn House.

Brach, J. S., Simonsick, E. M., Kritchevsky, S., Yaffe, K., & Newman, A. B. (2004). Association between physical function and lifestyle activity and exercise in the Health, Aging and Body Composition Study. *Journal of the American Geriatrics Society, 52*(4), 502–509.

Bradley, D. E., & Longino, C. F. (2001). How older people think about images of aging in advertising and the media. *Generations, 25*(3), 17–21.

Brady, E. M., Andrus Foundation, Edmund S. Muskie Institute of Public Affairs, AARP. (1994). Pre-retirement education: Views from the organization: Final report. Portland, ME: Edmund S. Muskie Institute of Public Affairs.

Brandl, B. (2000). Power and control: Understanding domestic abuse in later life. *Generations, 24,* 39–45.

Braun, P., & Sweet, R. (1983–84). Passages: Fact or fiction? *International Journal of Aging and Human Development, 18,* 161–176.

Breytspraak, L. M. (1995). The development of self in later life. In M. Novak (Ed.), *Aging and society: A Canadian reader* (pp. 92–103). Toronto: Nelson Canada.

Bringle, R. G., & Kremer, J. F. (1993). Evaluation of an intergenerational service learning project for undergraduates. *Educational Gerontology, 19*(5), 407–416.

Brody, E. (1981). "Women in the middle" and family help to older people. *The Gerontologist, 21*(5), 471–480.

Brody, E. (1983). Women's changing roles and help to elderly parents: Attitudes of three generations of women. *Journal of Gerontology, 38,* 597–607.

Brody, E. (1995a). Prospects for family caregiving: Response to change, continuity, and diversity. In R. A. Kane & J. D. Penrod (Eds.), *Family caregiving in an aging society* (pp. 15–28). Thousand Oaks, CA: Sage.

Brody, J. (1995b, April 19). Study links vigorous exercise, longevity: Sweating it out beats moderation. *The Globe and Mail,* 1.

Brody, S. J., & Morrison, M. H. (1992, Winter). Aging and rehabilitation: Beyond the medical model. *Generations,* 23–25.

Brogden, M. (2001). *Gerontocide: Killing the elderly.* London: Jessica Kingsley.

Bronner, E. (2003). *The foundation's end-of-life programs: Changing the American way of death.* Retrieved: December 13, 2004, www.rwjf.org/publications/publicationsPdfs/anthology2003/chapter_04.html.

Bronnum-Hansen, H., & Juel, K. (2001). Abstention from smoking extends life and compresses morbidity: A population based study of health expectancy among smokers and never smokers in Denmark. *Tobacco Control, 10*(3), 273–278.

Bronson, R. T., & Lipman, R. D. (1991). Reduction in rate of occurrence of age-related lesions in dietary restricted laboratory mice. *Growth, Development and Aging, 55,* 169–184.

Brotman, S., Ryan, B., & Cormier, R. (2002). Mental health issues of particular groups: Gay and lesbian seniors. In *Writings in gerontology: Mental health and aging,* 56–67. Cat. No. H71-s2/1-18-2002E. Ottawa: Minister of Public Works and Government Services Canada.

Brown, A. (1989). A survey on elder abuse at one Native American tribe. *Journal of Elder Abuse and Neglect, 1*(2).

Brown, L. B., Sarosy, S. G., Cook, T. C., & Quarto, J. G. (1997). *Gay men and aging.* New York: Garland.

Brown, M. B., & Tedrick, T. (1993). Outdoor leisure involvements of black older Americans: An exploration of ethnicity and marginality. *Activities, Adaptation and Aging, 17*(3), 55–65.

Brown, S. C., & Park, D. C. (2003). Theoretical models of cognitive aging and implications for translational research in medicine. *The Gerontologist, 43,* 57–67.

Brown, S. L., Nesse, R. M., Vinokur, A. D., & Smith, D. M. (2003). Providing social support may be more beneficial than receiving it: Results from a prospective study of mortality. *Psychological Science, 14*(4), 320–327.

Brownson, R. C., Eyler, A. A., King, A. C., Brown, D. R., Shyu, Y. L., & Sallis, J. F. (2000). Patterns and correlates of physical activity among US women 40 years and older. *American Journal of Public Health, 90,* 264–270.

Bruce, J. (1994). To drive or not to drive. *Aging, 366,* 49–51.

Bryant, D. P., & Bryant, B. R. (2003). *Assistive technology for people with disabilities.* Boston: Pearson.

Bryer, T. (2000). Characteristics of motor vehicle crashes related to aging. In K. W. Schaie, & M. Pietrucha (Eds.), *Mobility and transportation in the elderly* (pp. 157–206). New York: Springer.

Buckingham, R. W. III, Lack, S. A., Mount, G. M., MacLean, L. D., & Collins, J. T. (1976). Living with the dying. *Canadian Medical Association Journal, 115,* 1211–1215.

Bulcroft, R., & Bulcroft, K. (1991). The nature and functions of dating in later life. *Research on Aging, 13*(2), 244–260.

Bull, C. N., & Bane, S. D. (1993). Growing old in rural America: New approach needed in rural health care. *Aging Magazine, 365,* 18–25.

Bureau of Labor Statistics and the U.S. Bureau of the Census. (2003). *Annual demographic survey: March supplement.* Retrieved: September 6, 2004, http://ferret.bls.census.gov/macro/032004/hhinc/new02_001.htm.

Burg, S. B. (1999). Gray crusade: Townsend Movement, old age politics, and the development of Social Security. Ann Arbor, MI: UMI Dissertation Services.

Burggraf, V. (2000). Older woman: Ethnicity and health. *Geriatric Nursing, 21*(4), 183–187.

Burkhardt, J. E. (2000). Limitations of mass transportation and individual vehicle systems for older persons. In K. W. Schaie & M. Pietrucha (Eds.), *Mobility and transportation in the elderly* (pp. 97–123). New York: Springer.

Burns, E. M. (1991). Grandparent visitation rights: Is it time for the pendulum to fall? *Family Law Quarterly, 25*(1), 59–81.

Burr, J., Caro, F. G., & Moorhead, J. (2002). Productive aging and civic participation. *Journal of Aging Studies, 16*(1), 87–105.

Burr, J. A., & Mutchler, J. E. (2003). English language skills, ethnic concentration, and Household composition: Older Mexican immigrants. *The Journals of Gerontology Series B: Psychological Sciences and Social Sciences, 58,* S83–S92.

Burrows, N., Geiss, L., Engelgau, M., & Acton, K. (2000). *Prevalence of diabetes among Native Americans and Alaskan Natives, 1990–1997.* Diabetes Care (n.d.). Retrieved: April 15, 2002, www.findarticles.com/cf_0/mOCUH/12_23/68322723/p1/articlejhtml.

Burt, V. L., Whelton, P., Roccella, E. J., Brown, C., Cutler, J. A., Higgins, M., Horan, M. J., & Labarthe, D. (1995). Prevalence of hypertension in the U.S. adult population: Results from the Third National Health and Nutrition Examination Survey, 1988–1991. *Hypertension,* 25.

Burton, L., & DeVries, C. (1992, Summer). Challenges and rewards: African American grandparents as surrogate parents. *Generations,* 51–54.

Butler, R. (2001–2002). Is there an "anti-aging'"medicine? *Generations, 25*(4), 63–65.

Butler, R. N. (1969). Age-ism: Another form of bigotry. *The Gerontologist, 9,* 243–246.

Butler, R. N. (1975). *Why survive? Being old in America.* New York: Harper & Row.

Butler, R. N. (1987). Ageism. In G. Maddox (Ed.), *The encyclopedia of aging.* New York: Springer.

Butler, R. N. (1993). Dispelling ageism: The cross-cutting intervention. *Generations, 17*(2), 75–78.

Butler, R. N., & Lewis, M. I. (1988). *Love and sex after sixty.* New York: Harper & Row.

Butler, R. N., & Lewis, M. I. (2002). *New love and sex after 60* (3d rev. ed.). New York: Ballantine Books.

Butler, R. N., Lewis, M. I., & Sunderland, T. (1991). *Aging and mental health* (4th ed.). New York: Macmillan.

Cahill, S., & South, K. (2002). Policy issues affecting lesbian, gay, bisexual, and transgender people in retirement. *Generations, 26*(2), 49–54.

Calasanti, T. (2002). Work and retirement in the 21st century: Integrating issues of diversity and globalization. *Ageing International, 27*(3), 3–20.

Calasanti, T. M. (1996). Incorporating diversity: Meaning, levels of research, and implications for theory. *The Gerontologist, 36,* 147–156.

Calasanti, T. M., & Slevin, K. F. (2001). *Gender, social inequalities, and aging.* Walnut Creek, CA: AltaMira Press.

Calkins, M. P. (2003). Lighting for older eyes. *Nursing Homes Long Term Care Management, 52*(11), 68+.

Callahan, D. (1987). *Setting limits: Medical goals in an aging society.* New York: Simon & Schuster.

Callahan, J. J. (1986). Guest editor's perspective. *Pride Institute Journal of Long-Term Home Health Care, 5,* 2–3.

Campbell, A. L. (2002). Self-interest, Social Security, and the distinctive participation patterns of senior citizens. *American Political Science Review, 96*(3), 565–574.

Campbell, L. D., & Martin-Matthews, A. (2003). The gendered nature of men's filial care. *Journals of Gerontology Series B, 58*(6), S350–S358.

Campbell, L. D., Connidis, I. A., & Davies, L. (1999). Sibling ties in later life: A social network analysis. *Journal of Family Issues, 20*(1), 114–148.

Canadian Medical Association. (1987). *Health care for the elderly: Today's challenges, tomorrow's options.* Ottawa: Canadian Medical Association.

Cantor, M. H. (1979). Neighbors and friends: An overlooked resource in the informal support system. *Research on Aging, 1,* 434–463.

Cantor, M. H. (1992, Summer). Families and caregiving in an aging society. *Generations,* 67–70.

Cantor, M. H., & Brennan, M. (2000). *Social care of the elderly: The effects of ethnicity, class and culture.* New York: Springer.

Cantor, M. H., & Little, V. (1985). Aging and social care. In R. H. Binstock & E. Shanas (Eds.), *Handbook of aging and social sciences* (pp. 745–781). New York: Van Nostrand Reinhold.

Cantor, M. H., Brennan, M., & Shippy, R. A. (2004). *Caregiving among older lesbian, gay, bisexual, and transgender New Yorkers.* New York: National Gay and Lesbian Task Force Policy Institute.

Carcagno, G. J., & Kemper, P. (1988). Evaluation of the National Long Term Care Demonstration: Overview of the channeling demonstration and its evaluation. *Health Services Research, 23*(1), 1–22.

Carnegie Commission on Higher Education. (1973). *The purposes and the performance of higher education in the United States.* New York: McGraw-Hill.

Caro, F. G., & Blank, A. E. (Eds.). (1988). Quality impact of home care of the elderly. [Special issue] *Home Health Care Services Quarterly, 9*(2-3).

Carp, F. M. (2000). *Elder abuse in the family: An interdisciplinary model for research.* New York: Springer.

Carstensen, L. L. (1991). Selectivity theory: social activity in life-span context. In K. W. Schaie & M. P. Lawton (Eds.), *Annual review of gerontology and geriatrics, Vol. 11* (pp. 195–217). New York: Springer.

Casperson, C. J., Powell, K., & Christenson, G. M. (1985). Physical activity, exercise, and physical fitness: Definitions and distinctions for health related research. *Public Health Reports, 100,* 126–130.

Cataldo, J. K. (2003). Smoking and aging: clinical implications. Part 1: Health and consequence. *Journal of Gerontological Nursing, 29*(9), 15–20.

Cattell, M. G. (1994). "Nowadays it isn't easy to advise the young": Grandmothers and granddaughters among Abaluyia of Kenya. *Journal of Cross-Cultural Gerontology, 9,* 157–178.

Cattell, R. B. (1963). Theory of fluid and crystallized intelligence: An initial experiment. *Journal of Educational Psychology, 54,* 105–111.

Cavanaugh, J. C. (1983). Comprehension and retention of television programs by 20- and 60-year-olds. *Journal of Gerontology, 38,* 190–196.

Center for Healthy Aging. (2004). *Best practices in physical activity.* Retrieved: November 23, 2004, http://healthyagingprograms.org/content.asp?sectionid=31&ElementID=144.

Center for Medicare and Medicaid Services. (2004a). *Medicaid beneficiary demographics. Selected fiscal years.* Retrieved: December 28, 2004, www.cms.hhs.gov/researchers/pubs/datacompendium/2003/03pg35.pdf and www.cms.hhs.gov/researchers/pubs/datacompendium/2003/03pg34.pdf.

Center for Medicare and Medicaid Services. (2004b). *Medicaid payments by basis of eligibility. Selected fiscal years.* Retrieved: December 28, 2004, www.cms.hhs.gov/researchers/pubs/datacompendium/2003/03pg10a.pdf.

Center for Medicare and Medicaid Services. (2004c). *Program information on Medicare, Medicaid, SCHIP, and other programs of the Centers for Medicare and*

Medicaid Services, PowerPoint presentation. June 2002 edition.

Cerella, J. (1990). Aging and information-processing rate. In J. E. Birren & K. W. Schaie (Eds.), *Handbook of the psychology of aging* (3d ed.), (pp. 201–221). San Diego: Academic Press.

Chamber, S. M. (1993). Volunteerism by elders: Past trends and future prospects. *The Gerontologist, 33*(2), 221–228.

Chan, C. G., & Elder, Jr, G. H. (2000). Matrilineal advantage in grandchild-grandparent relations. *The Gerontologist, 40*(2), 179–190.

Chan, L. (2003). Is spirituality healthful? *Wellness Options, 4*(12), 26–27.

Chapman, N. J., & Howe, D. A. (2001). Accessory apartments: Are they a realistic alternative to ageing in place? *Housing Studies, 16*(5), 637–650.

Chappell, N. L. (1995). Gerontological Research in the '90s: Strengths, weaknesses, and contributions to policy. *Canadian Journal on Aging, 14* (Suppl. 1), 23–36.

Chappell, N. L. (1997). *National respite project: Evaluation report.* Victoria: Centre on Aging, University of Victoria.

Chappell, N. L., & Blandford, A. (1991). Informal and formal care: Exploring the complementarity. *Ageing and Society, 11*(Pt. 3), 299–317.

Chappell, N. L., Strain, L. A., & Blandford, A. A. (1986). *Aging and health care: A social perspective.* Toronto, Ontario: Holt, Rinehart & Winston of Canada.

Chapple, M. J., Kippax, S., & Smith, G. (1998). 'Semi-straight sort of sex': Class and gay community attachment explored within a framework of older homosexually active men. *Journal of Homosexuality, 35*(2), 65–83.

Charness, N. (2003). Access, motivation, ability, design, and training: Necessary conditions for older adult success with technology. In N. Charness & K. W. Schaie (Eds.), *Impact of technology on successful aging* (pp. 15–27). New York: Springer.

Chatterji, P., Burstein, N. R., Kidder, D., & White, A. J. (1998). *Evaluation of the Program of All-Inclusive Care for the Elderly (PACE).* Cambridge, MA: Abt Associates.

Chatters, L., Taylor, R., & Jayakody, R. (1994). Fictive kinship relationships in Black extended families. *Journal of Comparative Family Studies, 25,* 297–312.

Chatters, L. M., & Taylor, R. J. (1993). Intergenerational support: The provision of assistance to parents by adult children. In J. S. Jackson, L. M. Chatters, & R. J. Taylor (Eds.), *Aging in African American America* (pp. 69–83). Newbury Park, CA: Sage.

Chen, Y. (1994). Improving the economic security of minority persons as they enter old age. In *Minority elders: Five goals toward building a public policy base* (2d ed.), (pp. 32–39). Washington, DC: Gerontological Society of America.

Chen, Y-P. (2001). Social Security benefits for the family: An issue in social protection. In F. L. Ahearn (Ed.), *Issues in global aging* (pp. 17–23). New York: Haworth.

Cheong, J. M. K., Johnson, M. A., Lewis, R. D., Fischer, J. G., & Johnson, J. T. (2003). Reduction in modifiable osteoporosis-related risk factors among adults in the Older Americans Nutrition Program. *Family Economics and Nutrition Review, 15*(1), 83–91.

Cherlin, A., & Furstenberg, F. F. (1985). Styles and strategies of grandparenting. In V. L. Bengtson & J. F. Robertson (Eds.), *Grandparenthood* (pp. 97–116). Beverly Hills: Sage.

Chernoff, R. (2002). Health promotion for older women: Benefits of nutrition and exercise programs. *Topics in Geriatric Rehabilitation, 18*(1), 59–67.

Cherry, R., & Magnuson-Martinson, S. (1981). Modernization and the status of the aged in China: Decline or equalization? *The Sociological Quarterly, 22,* 253–261.

Chevan, A. (1996). As cheaply as one: Cohabitation in the older population. *Journal of Marriage and the Family, 58*(3), 656–667.

Chin-Sang, V., & Allen, K. R. (1991). Leisure and the older black woman. *Journal of Gerontological Nursing, 17*(1), 30–34.

Chipperfield, J. G., & Havens, B. (2001). Gender differences in the relationship between marital status transitions and life satisfaction in later life. *Journal of Gerontology: Psychological Sciences, 56B*(3), P176–P186.

Chiriboga, D. A., Weiler, P. G., & Nielsen, K. (1990). The stress of caregivers. In D. E. Biegel & A. Blum (Eds.), *Aging and caregiving: Theory, research, and policy* (pp. 121–138). Newbury Park, CA: Sage.

Cicirelli, V. G. (1999). Personality and demographic factors in older adults' fear of death. *The Gerontologist, 39*(5), 569–579.

Cicirelli, V. G. (2002). *Older adults' views on death.* New York: Springer.

Clark, P. G. (1993). Moral discourse and public policy in aging: Framing problems, seeking solutions, and 'public ethics.' *Canadian Journal on Aging, 12*(4), 485–508.

Clark, R. L. (1993). Population aging and retirement policy: An international perspective. In A. M. Rappaport & S. J. Schieber (Eds.), *Demography and retirement:*

The twenty-first century (pp. 255–284). Westport, CT: Praeger.

Clark, R. L., & Quinn, J. F. (2002). Patterns of work and retirement for a new century. *Generations, 26*(2), 17–24.

Clarke, L. C. H. (2002). Beauty in later life: Older women's perceptions of physical attractiveness. *Canadian Journal on Aging, 21*(3), 429–442.

Clements, R. (1998). Intrinsic religious motivation and attitudes toward death among the elderly. *Current Psychology: Developmental, Learning, Personality, Social, 17*(2-3), 237–248.

Clifford, J. C. (1989). What DRGs mean to the patient and the provider. *Journal of Geriatric Psychiatry, 22*(2), 201–210.

Cohen, C. A., Colantonio, A., & Vernich, L. (2002). Positive aspects of caregiving: Rounding out the caregiver experience. *International Journal of Geriatric Psychiatry, 17*(2), 184–188.

Cohen, E. S. (2001). Complex nature of ageism: What is it? Who does it? Who perceives it? *The Gerontologist, 41*(5), 576–577.

Cohen, G. D. (1994). Journalistic elder abuse: It's time to get rid of fictions, get down to facts. *The Gerontologist, 34*(3), 399–401.

Cohen, G. D. (1999). Marriage and divorce in later life: Editorial. *American Journal of Geriatric Psychiatry, 7,* 185–187.

Cohen, J. J. (2004). Health care for seniors: Are our nation's physicians ready? *Caring, 23*(6), 30–32.

Cohn, R. (1982). Economic development and status change of the aged. *American Journal of Sociology, 87,* 1150–1161.

Coile, C. (2003). *Retirement incentives and couples' retirement decisions.* Chestnut Hill, MA: Center for Retirement Research at Boston College. Retrieved: September 17, 2004, www.bc.edu/centers/crr/papers/wp_2003-04.pdf.

Cole, T. (1991). The specter of old age: History, politics, and culture in an aging America. In B. B. Hess & E. W. Markson (Eds.), *Growing old in America* (4th ed.), (pp. 23–37). New Brunswick, NJ: Transaction.

Cole, T. R., & Ray, R. E. (2000). Introduction. In T. R. Cole, R. Kastenbaum, & R. E. Ray (Eds), *Handbook of the humanities and aging* (2d ed.), (pp. xi–xxii). New York: Springer.

Coleman, D., & Iso-Ahola, S. E. (1993). Leisure and health: The role of social support and self-determination. *Journal of Leisure Research, 25,* 111–128.

Collings, P. (2000). Aging and life course development in an Inuit community. *Arctic Anthropology, 37*(2), 111–125.

Collings, P. (2001). "If you got everything, it's good enough": Perspectives on successful aging in a Canadian Inuit community. *Journal of Cross-Cultural Gerontology, 16*(2), 127–155.

Comfort, A. (1972). *The joy of sex.* New York: Crown.

Comfort, A. (1976). *A good age.* New York: Simon & Schuster.

Concord Coalition. (1993). *The zero deficit plan: A plan for eliminating the federal budget deficit by the year 2000.* Washington, DC: Author.

Concord Coalition. (2004). *Facing facts: Social Security reform—facing up to the real trade-offs.* Retrieved: September 12, 2004, www.concordcoalition.org/facing_facts/alert_v10_n1.html.

Conn, V. S. (1997). Older women: Social cognitive theory correlates of health behavior. *Women & Health, 26*(3), 71–85.

Connell, B. R. (1998). A picture is worth 1000 Words: Using video-based technology to understand behavior problems in long term care settings. In G. M. Gutman (Ed.), *Technology innovation for an aging society: Blending research, public and private sectors* (pp. 69–82). Vancouver: Gerontology Research Centre, Simon Fraser University.

Connidis, I. A. (2001). *Family ties and aging.* Thousand Oaks, CA: Sage.

Connidis, I. A., & McMullin, J. A. (1999). Permanent childlessness: Perceived advantages and disadvantages among older persons. *Canadian Journal on Aging, 18*(4), 447–465.

Connor, S. R. (1998). *Hospice: Practice, pitfalls, and promise.* Washington, DC: Taylor and Francis.

Conway-Turner, K. (1999). Older women of color: A feminist exploration of the intersections of personal, familial and community life. *Journal of Women and Aging, 11*(2-3), 115–130.

Conwell, Y. (2001). Suicide in later life: A review and recommendations for prevention. *Suicide and Life-Threatening Behavior, 31*(1, Suppl. S), 32–47.

Conwell, Y., Duberstein, P. R., Connor, K., Eberly, S., Cox, C., & Caine, E. D. (2002). Access to firearms and risk for suicide in middle-aged and older adults. *American Journal of Geriatric Psychiatry, 10*(4), 407–416.

Cook, F. L., & Welch, A. S. (1994). Economic hardship and the coping strategies of middle-aged and elderly low income women. Paper presented at the annual meeting of the Gerontological Society of America, November 18–20, Atlanta, GA.

Cook-Daniels, L. (2004). Training of adult protective services workers: A survey report. *Victimization of the Elderly and Disabled, 7*(3), 37+.

Cool, L., & McCabe, J. (2002). The 'scheming hag' and the 'dear old thing': The anthropology of aging women. In D. L. Infeld (Ed.), *Disciplinary approaches to aging, Vol. 4, Anthropology of aging* (pp. 133–147). New York: Routledge.

Cooley, M. E. (2002). Sex over sixty. *Expression: Bulletin of the National Advisory Council on Aging, 15*(2).

Cooney, T., & Dunne, K. (2001). Intimate relationships in later life, current realities, future prospects. *Journal of Family Issues, 22*(7), 838–858.

Corbin, J. M. (2002). Participant observations of a participant observer. In G. D. Rowles & N. E. Schoenberg (Eds.), *Qualitative gerontology* (2d ed.), (pp. 93–108). New York: Springer.

Corr, C. A., Nabe, C. M., & Corr, D. M. (1994). *Death and dying, life and living.* Pacific Grove, CA: Brooks/Cole.

Corti, M-C., Guralnik, J. M., Ferrucci, L., Izmirlian, G., Leveille, S. G., Pahor, M., Cohen, H. J., Pieper, C., & Havlik, R. J. (1999). Evidence for a Black-White crossover in all-cause and coronary heart disease mortality in an older population: The North Carolina EPESE. *American Journal of Public Health, 89*(3), 308–314.

Costa, D. L. (1998). *The evolution of retirement.* Chicago: University of Chicago Press.

Cott, C. A., & Gignac, M. A. M. (1999). Independence and dependence for older adults with osteoarthritis or osteoporosis. *Canadian Journal on Aging, 18*(1), 1–25.

Cotten, S. (1999). Marital status and mental health revisited: Examining the importance of risk factors and resources. *Family Relations, 48*(3), 225–233.

Coughlin, T. A., McBride, T. D., & Liu, K. (1990). Determinants of transitory and permanent nursing home admissions. *Medical Care, 28*(7), 616–631.

Couper, D. P. (1994). What's wrong with this picture? Aging and education in America. *Aging Today,* September/October, 3.

Cousins, S. O., & Burgess, A. (1992). Perspectives on older adults in physical activity and sports. *Educational Gerontology, 18,* 461–481.

Coward, R. T. (1988). Aging in the rural United States. In E. Rathbone-McCuan & B. Havens (Eds.), *North American elders: United States and Canadian perspectives* (pp. 161–178). New York: Greenwood.

Coward, R. T., & Rathbone-McCuan, E. (1985). Delivering health and human services to the elderly in rural society. In R. T. Coward & G. R. Lee (Eds.), *The elderly in rural society: Every fourth elder.* New York: Springer.

Cowart, M. E., Sutherland, M., & Harris, G. J. (1995). Health promotion for older rural African Americans: Implications for social and public policy. *Journal of Applied Gerontology, 14*(1), 33–46.

Cowgill, D. O. (1972). A theory of aging in cross-cultural perspective. In D. Cowgill & L. Holmes (Eds.), *Aging and modernization.* New York: Appleton-Century-Crofts.

Cowgill, D. O. (1974). Aging and modernization: A revision of the theory. In J. F. Gubrium (Ed.), *Late life.* Springfield, IL: Charles C. Thomas.

Cowgill, D. O., & Holmes, L. D. (Eds.). (1972). *Aging and modernization.* New York: Appleton-Century-Crofts.

Cowley, M. (1980). *The view from 80.* New York: Viking Press.

Cox, H. (1993). Political beliefs and activities. In R. Kastenbaum (Ed.), *Encyclopedia of adult development* (pp. 377–381). Phoenix, AZ: Oryx.

Coyle, J. M. (1990). Understanding female retirement: Future research needs. In C. L. Hayes & J. M. Deren (Eds.), *Pre-retirement planning for women: Program design and research* (pp. 151–162). New York: Springer.

Craik, F. I. M. (2000). Age-related changes in human memory. In D. C. Park & N. Schwarz (Eds.), *Cognitive aging: A primer* (pp. 75–92). Philadelphia: Taylor and Francis.

Craik, F. I. M., & T. A. Salthouse (Eds.). (2000). *The handbook of aging and cognition* (2d ed.). Mahwah, NJ: Lawrence Erlbaum.

Cramer, K., Tuokko, H., & Evans, D. (2001). Extending autonomy for health care preferences in late life. *Aging Neuropsychology and Cognition, 8*(3), 213–224.

Crews, D. E. (1993). Biological aging: Book review essay. *Journal of Cross-Cultural Gerontology, 8,* 281–290.

Crimmins, I. M., & Saito, Y. (2001). Trends in healthy life expectancy in the United States, 1970–1990: Gender, racial, and educational differences. *Social Science and Medicine, 52*(11), 1629–1641.

Crimmins, I. M., Saito, Y., & Ingegneri, D. (1989). Changes in life expectancy and disability-free life expectancy in the United States. *Population and Development Review, 15,* 235–267.

Crimmins, I. M., Saito, Y., & Ingegneri, D. (1997). Trends in disability-free life expectancy in the United

States, 1970–1990. *Population Development and Review, 23,* 555–571.

Crispell, D. (1993). Grandparents galore. *American Demographics, 15*(10), 63.

Crispell, D., & Frey, W. H. (1994). American maturity. In H. Cox (Ed.), *Aging* (9th ed.), (pp. 119–125). Guildford, CT: Dushkin.

Cross, R. J. (1993). What doctors and others need to know: Six facts on human sexuality and aging. *SIECUS Report, 21*(5), 7–9.

Cruikshank, M. (2003). *Learning to be old: Gender, culture, and aging.* Lanham: Rowman & Littlefield.

Cruz, J. M. (2003). *Sociological analysis of aging: The gay male perspective.* New York: Harrington Park.

Crystal, S. (1986). Social policy and elder abuse. In K. A. Pillemer & R. S. Wolf (Eds.), *Elder abuse: Conflict in the family* (pp. 331–340). Dover, MA: Auburn House.

Cubillos, H., & Prieto, M. (1987). *The Hispanic elderly: A demographic profile.* Washington, DC: National Council of La Raza.

Culture and caregiving. (1992). *Aging, 363–364,* 29–30.

Cumming, E., & Henry, W. E. (1961). *Growing old: The process of disengagement.* New York: Basic Books.

Cummings, S. M., Galambos, C., & DeCoster, V. A. (2003). Predictors of MSW employment in gerontological practice. *Educational Gerontological, 29*(4), 295–312.

Curley, L. (1987). Native American aged. In G. L. Maddox (Ed.), *The encyclopedia of aging* (pp. 469–470). New York: Springer.

Curtin, S. (1972). *Nobody ever died of old age.* Boston: Little, Brown.

Cutler, N. E., Whitelaw, N. A., & Beattie, B. L. (2002). *American perceptions of aging in the 21st century. A myths and realities of aging chartbook.* Washington, DC: National Council on the Aging and the AARP Foundation.

Cutler, S. J., & Danigelis, N. L. (1993). Organized contexts of activity. In J. R. Kelly (Ed.), *Activity and aging* (pp. 146–163). Newbury Park, CA: Sage.

D'Mello, D. A. (2003). Epidemiology of late-life depression. In J. M. Ellison & V. Sumer (Eds.), *Depression in later life: A multidisciplinary psychiatric approach* (pp. 1–26). New York: Marcel Dekker.

Dalaker, J. (2001). *Poverty in the United States: 2000. U.S. Census Bureau, Current Population Reports, Series P60-214.* Washington, DC: U.S. Government Printing Office. Retrieved: September 5, 2004, www.census.gov/prod/2001pubs/p60-214.pdf.

Dalaker, J., & Proctor, B. D. (2000). *Poverty in the United States, 1999. U.S. Census Bureau, Current Population Reports, Series P60-210.* Washington, DC: U.S. Government Printing Office. Retrieved: July 14, 2004, www.census.gov/prod/2000pubs/p60-210.pdf.

Damron-Rodriguez, J., Dorfman, R., Lubben, J. E., & Beck, J. C. (1992). A geriatric education center faculty development program dedicated to social work. *Journal of Gerontological Social Work, 18*(3-4), 187–201.

Damron-Rodriguez, J-A. (1998). Respecting ethnic elders: A perspective for care providers. *Journal of Gerontological Social Work, 29*(2-3), 53–72.

Dancy, J. Jr., & Ralston, P. A. (2002). Health promotion and Black elders: Subgroups of greatest need. *Research on Aging, 24*(2), 218–242.

Danner, D. D., Danner, F. W., & Kuder, L. C. (1993). Late life learners at the university: Donovan Scholars program at age twenty-five. *Educational Gerontology, 19*(3), 217–239.

Darling, L. (1994, January 23). Age, beauty and truth. *New York Times,* 1, 5.

Davidson, S., Brooke, E., & Kendig, H. (2001). Age-segregated housing and friendship interaction for older people. In L. A. Pastalan & B. Schwarz (Eds.), *Housing choices and well-being of older adult: Proper fit* (pp. 123–135). New York: Haworth.

Davies, L. (1995). A closer look at gender and distress among the never married. *Women and Health, 23*(2), 13–30.

Davies, M. (1993). Theories of ageing and their implications for pre-retirement education. *Journal of Educational Gerontology, 8*(2), 67–74.

Davis, T. J. (1993). Investment scam line. *Secure Retirement, 2*(6), 34–36.

Day, J. C. (1996). *Population projections of the United States by age, sex, race, and Hispanic origin: 1995–2050.* U.S. Bureau of the Census, Current Population Reports, P25-1130. Washington, DC: U.S. Government Printing Office.

De Leo, D., Carollo, G., & Buono, M. D. (1995). Lower suicide rates associated with a tele-help/tele-check service for the elderly at home. *American Journal of Psychiatry, 152,* 632–634.

De Leo, D., Rozzini, R., & Bernardini, M., et al. (1992). Assesment of quality of life in the elderly assisted at home through a tele-check service. *Quality of Life Research, 1,* 367–374.

de Luce, J. (2001). Silence at the newsstands. *Generations, 25*(3), 39–43.

De Vries, B., & Blando, J. A. (2004). The study of gay and lesbian aging: Lessons for social gerontology. In G. Herdt & B. de Vries (Eds.), *Gay and lesbian aging:*

Research and future directions (pp. 3–28). New York: Springer.

Deder, J., Komisar, H. L., & Niefeld, M. (2001). The financing and organization of health care. In R. H. Binstock & L. K. George (Eds.), *Handbook of aging and the social sciences* (5th ed.), (pp. 387–405). San Diego: Academic.

Deely, B., & Werlinich, K. (1992). Woodside Place: A personal care home for people with Alzheimer's disease. *Aging, 363–364,* 35–36.

Deevey, S. (1990). Older lesbian women: An invisible minority. *Journal of Gerontological Nursing, 16*(5), 35–37+.

DeGenova, M. K. (1992). If you had your life to live over again: What would you do differently? *International Journal of Aging and Human Development, 34,* 135–143.

DeNavas-Walt, C., Proctor, B. D., & Mills, R. J. (2004). *Income, poverty, and health insurance coverage in the United States: 2003.* U.S. Census Bureau, Current Population Reports, P60-226. Washington, DC: U.S. Government Printing Office. Retrieved: September 5, 2004, www.census.gov/prod/2004pubs/p60-226.pdf.

Deren, J. M. (1990). Challenges and constraints: Creating nationally available programs for midlife women. In C. L. Hayes & J. M. Deren (Eds.), *Pre-retirement planning for women: Program design and research* (pp. 77–88). New York: Springer.

Der-McLeod, D., & Hansen, J. C. (1992). On Lok: The family continuum. *Generations, 17*(3), 71–72.

DeViney, S. (1995). Life course, private pension, and financial well-being. *American Behavioral Scientist, 39*(2), 172–185.

Diamond, T. (1992). *Making gray gold.* Chicago: University of Chicago Press.

Digiovanna, A. G. (2000). *Human aging: biological perspectives* (2d ed.). Boston: McGraw-Hill.

Dilworth-Anderson, P. (1992, Summer). Extended kin networks in black families. *Generations,* 29–32.

Dilworth-Anderson, P., Williams, I. C., & Williams, S. W. (2001). Urban elderly African Americans. In L. K. Olson (Ed.), *Age through ethnic lenses: Caring for the elderly in a multicultural society* (pp. 95–102). London: Rowman & Littlefield.

Dinger, E., & AARP. Knowledge Management. (2003a). *AARP Delaware caregiving in the workplace survey.* Washington, DC.

Dinger, E., & AARP. Knowledge Management. (2003b). *AARP Ohio caregiving in the workplace survey.* Washington, DC.

Dixon, R. A., Backman, L., & Nilsson, L-G (Eds.) (2004). *New frontiers in cognitive aging.* Oxford, England: Oxford University Press.

Dixon, R. A., & Cohen, A-L. (2001). The psychology of aging: Canadian research in an international context. *Canadian Journal on Aging, 20* (Suppl.1), 125–148.

Dorfman, L. T., Murty, S. A., Ingram, J. G., Evans, R. J., & Power, J. R. (2004). Interngenerational service-learning in five cohorts of students: Is attitude change robust? *Educational Gerontology, 30*(1), 39–55.

Douthat, R., & Poe, M. (2004, December). A woman's work is never done. *The Atlantic Monthly,* 70.

Dowd, J. J. (1975). Aging as exchange: A preface to theory. *Journal of Gerontology, 30,* 584–594.

Dowd, J. J. (1980). *Stratification among the aged.* Monterey, CA: Brooks/Cole.

Downs, B. (2003) *Fertility of American women: June 2002.* Current population reports, P20-548. Washington, DC: U.S. Census Bureau. Retrieved: March 27, 2004, www.census.gov/prod/2003pubs/p20-548.pdf.

Doyle, D. P. (1990). Aging and crime. In K. F. Ferraro (Ed.), *Gerontology: Perspectives and issues* (pp. 294–315). New York: Springer.

Du Bois, B. C., Yavno, C. H., & Stanford, E. P. (2001). Care options for older Mexican Americans: Issues affecting health and long-term care service needs. In L. K. Olson, (Ed.), *Age through ethnic lenses: Caring for the elderly in a multicultural society* (pp. 71–85). London: Rowman & Littlefield.

Duberstein, P. R., Conwell, Y., Seidlitz, L., Denning, D. G., Cox, C., & Caine, E. D. (2000). Personality traits and suicidal behavior and ideation in depressed inpatients 50 years of age and older. *The Journals of Gerontology Series B: Psychological Sciences and Social Sciences, 55*(1), P18–P26.

Dugan, E., & Kivett, V. R. (1994). Importance of emotional and social isolation to loneliness among very old rural adults. *The Gerontologist, 34*(3), 340–346.

Duke University. (1991). *Duke Institute for Learning in Retirement.* Durham, NC: Duke University Continuing Education.

Dunkle, R., Roberts, B., & Haug, M. (2001). *The oldest old in everyday life: Self perception, coping with change, and stress.* New York: Springer.

Dunlop, J., Manghelli, D., & Tolson, R. (1990). Older problem drinkers: A community treatment continuum. *Aging, 361,* 33–37.

Dunn, A. L., Marcus, B. H., Kampert, J. B., Garcia, M. E. Kohl, H. W., III, & Blair, S. N. (1999). Comparison of lifestyle and structured interventions to increase physical activity and cardiorespiratory fitness. *Journal of the American Medical Association, 28*(4), 327–334.

Dupuis, S. L., & Smale, B. J. A. (2004). *In their own voices: Dementia caregivers identify the issues.* Final report prepared for the Ministry of Health and Long-Term Care and the Ontario Senior's Secretariat as part of Initiative No. 6 of Ontario's Alzheimer Strategy. Waterloo, ON: Murray Alzheimer Research and Education Program.

Durkheim, E. (1951). *Suicide: A study in sociology.* New York: Free Press.

Durkheim, E. (1956). *The division of labor in society.* New York: Free Press.

Dychtwald, K. (1999). *Age power: How the 21st century will be ruled by the new old.* New York: Tarcher/Putnam.

Dychtwald, K., & Flower, J. (1990). *Age wave: The challenges and opportunities of an aging America.* New York: Bantam Books.

Dykstra, P. A. (1995). Loneliness among the never and formerly married: The importance of supportive friendships and a desire for independence. *Journal of Gerontology: Social Sciences 50B,* S321–329.

Easom, L. R. (2003). Concepts in health promotion: Perceived self-efficacy and barriers in older adults. *Journal of Gerontological Nursing, 29*(5), 11–19.

Eastaugh, A. M. (1996). Approaches to palliative care by primary health care teams: A survey. *Journal of Palliative Care, 12*(4), 47–50.

Easterlin, R. A. (1987). *Birth and fortune* (2d ed.). Chicago: University of Chicago Press.

Easterlin, R. A. (1991). The economic impact of prospective population changes in advanced industrial countries: An historical perspective. *Journal of Gerontology, 46,* S299–S309.

EBRI (Employee Benefit Research Institute). (2004a). *FAQs about benefits—Retirement issues.* Retrieved: February 11, 2005, www.ebri.org/benfaq.

EBRI (Employee Benefit Research Institute). (2004b). *The 2003 minority retirement confidence survey.* Retrieved: September 18, 2004, www.ebri.org/rcs/2003/03mrcssf.pdf.

Economist. (2004). Survey: Retirement. Forever young. The Economist.com, March 25. Retrieved: September 25, 2004, www.economist.com/surveys/showsurvey.cfm?issue=20040327.

Edmonds, M. M. (1993). Physical health. In J. S. Jackson, L. M. Chatters, & R. J. Taylor (Eds.), *Aging in African American America* (pp. 151–166). Newbury Park, CA: Sage.

Educating hard-to-reach minority groups about Alzheimer's disease. (1992). *Aging, 363–364,* 42–45.

Effros, R. B. (2001). Immune system activity. In E. J. Masoro & S. N. Austad (Eds.), *Handbook of the biology of aging* (5th ed.), (pp. 324–350). San Diego: Academic Press.

Eggebeen, D. J. (1992, Summer). From generation unto generation: Parent-child support in aging American families. *Generations,* 45–49.

Ego, M. M., & Shiramizu, B. (1992). Older Asian/Pacific Americans: Provision of responsive leisure programming and research paradigms. In R. Rothschadl (Ed.), *Proceedings of the Sandra A. Modisett symposium on aging and leisure in the 1990s* (pp. 77–83). Indianapolis, IN.

Ehrlich, P. (1986). Hotels, rooming houses, shared housing, and other housing options for the marginal elderly. In R. Newcomer, M. P. Lawton, & T. Byert (Eds.), *Housing an aging society* (pp. 189–199). New York: Van Nostrand Reinhold.

Eisdorfer, K. (1981). Foreword. In P. T. Amoss & S. Harrell (Eds.), *Other ways of growing old: Anthropological perspectives* (pp. xiii–xxi). Stanford, CA: Stanford University Press.

Ejaz, F. K., Schur, D., Fox, K., Blenkner, M., & AARP Andrus Foundation. (2003). *Consumer satisfaction in continuing care retirement communities.* Cleveland, OH: Margaret Blenkner Research Institute.

Ekerdt, D. J. (1986). The busy ethic: Moral continuity between work and retirement. *The Gerontologist, 26*(3), 239–244.

Ekerdt, D. J. (Ed.). (2002). *Encyclopedia of aging* (4 vols.). New York: Macmillan Reference USA. Retrieved January 22, 2005, from Gale Virtual Reference Library via Thomson Gale: http://find.galegroup.com/gvrl/infomark.do?&type=retrieve&tabID=T002&prodId=GVRL&docId=CX3402299999&source=gale&userGroupName=csusj&version=1.0.

Ekerdt, D. J., & DeViney, S. (1993). Evidence for a preretirement process among older male workers. *Journals of Gerontology, 48*(2), S35–S43.

Elder, G. H., Jr. (2000). The life course. In E. F. Borgatta & R. J. V. Montgomery (Eds.), *The encyclopedia of sociology. Vol. 3* (2d ed.), (pp. 939–991). New York: Wiley.

Elder, G. H., & Johnson, M. K. (2003). The life course and aging: Challenges, lessons, and new directions. In R. A. Settersten (Ed.), *Invitation to the life course: Toward new understandings of later life* (pp. 49–81). Amityville, NY: Baywood.

Elder, G. H., & Pavalko, E. K. (1993). Work careers in men's later years: Transitions, trajectories, and historical change. *Journal of Gerontology, 48*(4), S180–S191.

Eldercare Volunteer Corps begins recruitment drive. (1992). *Aging, 363–364,* 54–60.

Elderhostel. (1995a). *Elderhostel: International catalogue, July(1).* Boston: Elderhostel.

Elderhostel. (1995b). *Elderhostel: United States and Canada catalogue, May.* Boston: Elderhostel.

Elderhostel. (2004a). *The learning in retirement movement.* Retrieved: November 23, 2004, www.elderhostel.org/ein/learning_na.asp.

Elderhostel. (2004b). *What is Elderhostel?* Retrieved: November 24, 2004, www.elderhostel.org/about/what_is.asp.

Elderhostel. (2005). *Programs under $600.* Retrieved: July 4, 2005, www.elderhostel.org/programs/bargains.asp.

Elias, C. J., & Inui, T. S. (1993). When a house is not a home: Exploring the meaning of shelter among chronically homeless older men. *The Gerontologist, 33*(3), 396–402.

Elo, I. T., & Preston, S. H. (1997). Racial and ethnic differences in mortality at older ages. In L. Martin & B. J. Soldo (Eds.), *Racial and ethnic differences in the health of older Americans.* Washington, DC: National Academy Press.

Eng, C., Pedulla, J., Eleazer, G. P., McCann, R., & Fox, N. (1997). Program of All-inclusive Care for the Elderly (PACE), an innovative model of integrated geriatric care and financing. *Journal of the American Geriatric Society, 45,* 223–232.

Engelhardt, G. V., Gruber, J., Perry, C. D., & National Bureau of Economic Research. (2002). *Social Security and elderly living arrangements.* Cambridge, MA: National Bureau of Economic Research.

Erikson, E. H. (1959). Identity and the life cycle: Selected issues. *Psychological Issues, 1,* 50–100, Appendix.

Erikson, E. H. (1963). *Childhood and society* (2d ed.). New York: W. W. Norton.

Erikson, E. H. (1982). *The life cycle completed.* New York: W. W. Norton.

Estes, C. L. (1979). *The aging enterprise.* San Francisco: Jossey-Bass.

Estes, C. L. (1999). The aging enterprise revisited. In M. Minkler & C. L. Estes (Eds.), *Critical gerontology: Perspectives from political and moral economy* (pp. 135–146). Amityville, NY: Baywood.

Estes, C. L. (2000). The uncertain future of home care. In R. H. Binstock & L. E. Cluff (Eds.), *Home care advances* (pp. 239–256). New York: Springer.

Ethel Percy Andrus Gerontology Center. (1995, Winter). Research update: Home safe home. *Vitality,* 4–5.

Eyetsemitan, F. E., & Gire, J. T. (2003). *Aging and adult development in the developing world: Applying Western theories and concepts.* Westport, CT: Praeger.

Fairchild, S. K., Carrino, G. E., & Ramirez, M. (1996). Social workers' perceptions of staff attitudes toward resident sexuality in a random sample of New York State nursing homes: A pilot study. *Journal of Gerontological Social Work, 26*(1–2), 153–169.

Fairlie, H. (1988). Talkin' 'bout my generation. *New Republic, 198*(13), 19–22.

Färber, B. (2003). Microinterventions: Assistive devices, telematics, and person-environment interactions. In K. W. Schaie, H-W. Wahl, H. Mollenkopf, & F. Oswald (Eds.), *Aging independently: Living arrangements and mobility* (pp. 248–262). New York: Springer.

Featherman, D. L., Smith, J., & Peterson, J. G. (1990). Successful aging in a post-retired society. In P. B. Baltes & M. M. Baltes (Eds.), *Successful aging: Perspectives from the behavioral sciences* (pp. 50–93). Cambridge, England: Cambridge University Press.

Feder, J., Komisar, H. L., & Niefeld, M. (2001). The financing and organization of health care. In R. H. Binstock & L. K. George (Eds.), *Handbook of aging and the social sciences* (5th ed.), (pp. 387–405). San Diego: Academic Press.

Federal Interagency Forum on Aging-Related Statistics. (2000). *Older Americans 2000: Key indicators of well-being.* Appendix A: Detailed Tables. Retrieved: March 6, 2004, www.agingstats.gov/tables%202001/tables-healthrisks.html#Indicator%2024; www.agingstats.gov/chartbook2000/tables-economics.html#Indicator%208; www.agingstats.gov/tables%202001/Tables-population.html#Indicator%201.

Fees, B. S., Martin, P., & Poon, L. W. (1999). A model of loneliness in older adults. *The Journals of Gerontology Series B: Psychological Sciences and Social Sciences, 54*(4), P231–P239.

Feldman, D. C. (2003). Endgame: The design and implementation of early retirement incentive programs. In G. A. Adams & T. A. Beehr (Eds.), *Retirement: Reasons, processes, and results* (pp. 83–114). New York: Springer.

Ferber, M. A. (1993). Women's employment and the Social Security system. *Social Security Bulletin, 56*(3), 33–55.

Fernandez, P. S. (1988). Grandparent access: A model statute. *Yale Law and Policy Review, 6*(88), 109–136.

Ferraro, K. F. (1989). Reexamining the double jeopardy to health thesis. *Journal of Gerontology: Psychological Sciences, 44*(1), S14–S16.

Ferraro, K. F. (1990). The gerontological imagination. In K. F. Ferraro (Ed.), *Gerontology: Perspectives and issues* (pp. 3–18). New York: Springer.

Ferraro, K. F. (1992). Cohort change in images of older adults, 1974–1981. *The Gerontologist, 32*(3), 296–304.

Ferraro, K. F., & Farmer, M. M. (1993). Double jeopardy to health for black older Americans?: A longitudinal analysis. Report. West Lafayette, IN: Purdue University.

Ferraro, K. F., LaGrange, R. L., & McCready, W. C. (1990). *Are older people afraid of crime? Examining risk, fear, and constrained behavior.* DeKalb, IL: Northern Illinois University.

Ferris, M. (2000). Racial disparities in health care for the elderly. *Geriatric Times, 1*(4). Retrieved March 7, 2002, www.medinfosource.com/gt/2000/209html.

Ferrucci, L., Izmirlian, G., Léveillé, S. G., Phillips, C. L., Corti, M. C., Brock, D. B., & Guralnik. J. M. (1999). Smoking, physical activity, and active life expectancy. *American Journal of Epidemiology, 149*(7), 645–653.

Field, D. (1999). Continuity and change in friendships in advanced old age: Findings from the Berkeley older generation study. *International Journal of Aging and Human Development, 48*(4), 325–346.

Fierst, E. U., & Campbell, N. D. (Eds.). (1988). *Earnings sharing in Social Security: A model for reform.* Washington, DC: Center for Women Policy Studies.

Fillit, H. (1994). Challenges for acute care geriatric inpatient units under the present Medicare prospective payment system. *Journal of the American Geriatrics Society, 42*(5), 553–558.

Fischer, D. H. (1978). *Growing old in America.* Oxford, England: Oxford University Press.

Fischer, L. R., & Schaffer, K. B. (1993). *Older volunteers: A guide to research and practice.* Newbury Park, CA: Sage.

Fiske, A., & Arbore, P. (2000–2001). Future directions in late life suicide prevention. *Omega: Journal of Death and Dying, 42*(1), 37–53.

Fitzgerald, J. T., Singleton, S. P., Neale, A. V. Prasad, A. S., & Hess, J. W. (1994). Activity levels, fitness status, exercise knowledge, and exercise beliefs among health, older African-American and White women. *Journal of Aging and Health, 6*(3), 296–313.

Fitzpatrick, J. A., & Wampler, K. S. (2000). Marital relationships: A life course perspective. In S. J. Price, P. C. McKenry, & M. J. Murphy (Eds.), *Families across time: A life course perspective* (pp. 92–104). Los Angeles: Roxbury.

Flanigan, K. M., Lauria, G., Griffin, J. W., & Kuncl, R. W. (1998). Age-related biology and diseases of muscle and nerve. *The Neurology of Aging, 16*(3), 659–669.

Flippen, C., & Tienda, M. (2000). Pathways to retirement: Patterns of labor force participation and labor market exit among the pre-retirement population by race, Hispanic origin, and sex. *Journals of Gerontology Series B: Psychological Sciences and Social Sciences, 55*(1), S14–S27.

Flippen, S. (1998). Why there's a coalition for women in long-term care. *Nursing Homes Long Term Care Management, 47*(1), 54–56.

Fogel, B. S. (1992, Spring). Psychological aspects of staying at home. *Generations,* 15–19.

Foley, D. J., Mile, T. P., Brock, D. B., & Phillips, C. (1995). Recounts of elderly deaths: Endorsements for Patient Self-Determination Act. *The Gerontologist, 35*(1), 119–121.

Folts, W. E., & Yeatts, D. E. (1994). *Housing and the aging population: Options for the new century.* New York: Garland.

Foner, N. (1993). When the contract fails: Care for the elderly in nonindustrial cultures. In V. L. Bengtson & W. A. Achenbaum (Eds.), *The changing contract across generations* (pp. 101–117). New York: Aldine De Gruyter.

Fontane, P. E., & Hurd, P. D. (1992). Self-perceptions of national senior olympians. *Behavior, Health, and Aging, 2*(2), 101–111.

Foot, D. K., & Stoffman, D. (1998). *Boom, bust, and echo 2000: Profiting from the demographic shift in the new millennium.* Toronto: Macfarlane Walter & Ross.

Foundations Project. (1980). Foundations for gerontological education. *The Gerontologist, 20,* Pt. II.

Fowler, L. (1990). Colonial context and age group relations among Plains Indians. *Journal of Cross-Cultural Gerontology, 5,* 149–168.

Fowles, D. G. (1992). The numbers game: Projections of long-term care needs. *Aging, 363–364,* 76–77.

Francese, P. (2004). Labor of love. *American Demographics, 26*(2), 40–41.

Frank, A. G. (1969). *Latin America: Underdevelopment or revolution.* New York: Monthly Review.

Frankl, V. (1990). Facing the transitoriness of human existence. *Generations, 15*(4), 7–10.

Franks, L. J., Hughes, J. P., Phelps, L. H., & Williams, D. G. (1993). Intergenerational influences on Midwest college students by their grandparents and significant elders. *Education Gerontology, 19*(3), 265–271.

Freeman, J. T. (1979). *Aging: Its history and literature.* New York: Human Sciences.

Freedman, V. A., Aykan, H., Wolf, D. A., & Marcotte, J. E. (2004). Disability and home care dynamics among older unmarried Americans. *Journal of Gerontology: Series B: Psychological Sciences and Social Sciences, 59B*(1), S25–S33.

Freid, V. M., Prager, K., MacKay, A. P., & Xia, H. (2003). *Chartbook on trends in the health of Americans. Health, United States, 2003.* Hyattsville, MD: National Center for Health Statistics.

Freidenberg, J. N. (2000). *Growing old in El Barrio.* New York: New York University Press.

Frere-Jones, S. (2005, January 17). When I'm sixty-four. *The New Yorker,* pp. 94ff.

Frey, W. H. (1999). *Beyond social security: The local aspects of an aging America.* Washington, DC: Center on Urban and Metropolitan Policy, The Brookings Institution.

Freysinger, V. J. (1993). The community, programs, and opportunities. In J. R. Kelly (Ed.), *Activity and aging* (pp. 211–229). Newbury Park, CA: Sage.

Friedan, B. (1993). *The fountain of age.* New York: Simon & Schuster.

Friedland, R. B., & Summer, L. (1999). *Demography is not destiny.* Washington, DC: National Academy on an Aging Society.

Friedman, M. (1992). Confidence swindles of older consumers. *Journal of Consumer Affairs, 26*(1), 20–46.

Friend, R. A. (1980). Gaying: Adjustment and the older gay male. *Alternative Lifestyles, 3,* 231–248.

Friend, R. A. (1996). Older lesbian and gay people: A theory of successful aging. In R. Berger (Ed.), *Gay and grey: The older homosexual man* (2d ed.), (pp. 277–298). New York: Harrington Park.

Fries, J. F. (1980). Aging, natural death, and the compression of morbidity. *New England Journal of Medicine, 303,* 130–136.

Fries, J. F. (1983). Compression of morbidity. *Milbank Memorial Fund Quarterly, 61*(3), 397–419.

Fries, J. F. (1984). Compression of morbidity: Miscellaneous comments about a theme. *The Gerontologist, 24*(4), 354–359.

Fries, J. F. (1987a). Disease postponement and the compression of morbidity. In G. L. Maddox (Ed.), *The encyclopedia of aging* (pp. 183–186). New York: Springer.

Fries, J. F. (1987b). Life-span. In G. L. Maddox (Ed.), *The encyclopedia of aging* (pp. 401–402). New York: Springer.

Fries, J. F. (1990). Medical perspectives upon successful aging. In P. B. Baltes & M. M. Baltes (Eds.), *Successful aging: Perspectives for the behavioral sciences* (pp. 35–49). Cambridge, England: Cambridge University Press.

Fry, C. L. (1990). Cross-cultural comparisons of aging. In K. F. Ferraro (Ed.), *Gerontology: Perspectives and issues* (pp. 129–146). New York: Springer.

Fry, C. L. (2003). The life course as a cultural construct. In R. A. Settersten Jr. (Ed.), *Invitation to the life course: Toward new understandings of later life* (pp. 269–294). Amityville, NY: Baywood.

Fullmer, E. M. (1995). Challenging biases against families of older gays and lesbians. In G. C. Smith, S. S. Tobin, E. A. Robertson-Tchabo, & P. W. Power (Eds.), *Strengthening aging families: Diversity in practice and policy* (pp. 99–119). Thousand Oaks, CA: Sage.

Fullmer, E. M., Shenk, D., & Eastland, L. J. (1999). Negating identity: A feminist analysis of the social invisibility of older lesbians. *Journal of Women and Aging, 11*(2-3), 131–148.

Gafni, A. (2001). Protein structure and turnover. In E. J. Masoro & S. N. Austad, (Eds.), *Handbook of the biology of aging* (5th ed.), (pp. 59–83). San Diego: Academic Press.

Galambos, C. M. (1998). Preserving end-of-life autonomy: The Patient Self-Determination Act and the Uniform Health Care Decisions Act. *Health and Social Work, 23*(4), 275–281.

Gallagher, E. M., & Hagen, B. (1996). Outcome evaluation of a group education and support program for family caregivers. *Gerontology and Geriatrics Education, 17*(1), 33–50.

Gallagher, S. K., & Gerstel, N. (1993). Kinkeeping and friend keeping among older women: The effect of marriage. *The Gerontologist, 33*(5), 675–681.

Gallegos, J. S. (1991). Culturally relevant services for Hispanic elderly. In M. Sotomayor (Ed.), *Empowering Hispanic families: A critical issue for the '90s* (pp. 173–190). Milwaukee, WI: Family Service America.

Gallo, W. T., Bradley, E. H., Liegel, M., & Kasl, S. V. (2000). Health effects of involuntary job loss among older workers: Findings from the Health and Retirement Survey. *The Journals of Gerontology Series B: Psychological Sciences and Social Sciences, 55,* S131–S140.

GAO studies find employers expanding eldercare slowly. (1994, July/August). *Aging Today,* 11–12.

Garber, C. E., & Blissmer, B. J. (2002). The challenge of exercise in older adults. In P. M. Burbank & D. Riebe

(Eds.), *Promoting exercise and behavior change in older adults* (pp. 29–56). New York: Springer.

Garcia, C. (1993). What do we mean by extended family? A closer look at Hispanic multigenerational families. *Journal of Cross-Cultural Gerontology, 8,* 137–146.

Garfield, B. (2004). Why TV can only get better. *AARP Bulletin, 45*(4), 10.

Garfinkel, H. (1967). *Studies in ethnomethodology.* Englewood Cliffs, NJ: Prentice-Hall.

Gaugler, J. E., & Zarit, S. H. (2001). The effectiveness of adult day services for disabled older people. *Journal of Aging & Social Policy, 12*(2), 2347.

Gavrilov, L. A., & Gavrilova, N. S. (1991). *The biology of life span: A quantitative approach.* New York: Harwood Academic. (Revised and updated English edition, V. P. Skulachev, Ed. Translated from the Russian by John Payne & Linda Payne.)

Gavrilov, L. A., & Gavrilova, N. S. (2001). Reliability theory of aging and longevity. *Journal of Theoretical Biology, 213*(4), 527–545.

Gee, E. (1982). Discussion of John F. Myles' "Social Implications of a Changing Age Structure." In G. M. Gutman (Ed.), *Canada's changing age structure: Implications for the future* (pp. 59–66). Burnaby, Canada: Simon Fraser University Publications.

Gelfand, D., & Yee, B. W. K. (1991, Fall/Winter). Trends and forces: Influence of immigration, migration, and acculturation on the fabric of aging in America. *Generations,* 7–10.

Gelfand, D. E. (1993). *The aging network: Programs and services* (4th ed.). New York: Springer.

Gelfand, D. E. (Ed.). (2003). Aging *and ethnicity: Knowledge and services* (2d ed.). New York: Springer.

Geller, P. Z. (1994). Taking the next steps in adult day care. *Perspective on Aging, 23*(1), 13–17.

Gendron, C., Poitras, L., Dastoor, D. P., & Perodeau, G. (1996). Cognitive-behavioral group intervention for spousal caregivers: Findings and clinical considerations. *Clinical Gerontologist, 17*(1), 3–19.

Generations United. (2004). *Fact sheet: Social Security: A program that benefits all ages.* Retrieved: December 10, 2004, www.gu.org/Files/Social%20Security%202001.pdf.

George, L. K. (1996). Missing links: The case for a social psychology of the life course. *The Gerontologist, 36*(2), 248–255.

Gerber, J., Wolff, J., Klores, W., & Brown, G. (1989). *Lifetrends: The future of baby boomers and other aging Americans.* New York: Macmillan.

Gerhard, G. S., & Cristofalo, V. J. (1992, Fall/Winter). The limits of biogerontology. *Generations,* 55–59.

Gerontology Center Newsletter. (1994). Work after retirement: Demographer reveals a trend. *Gerontology Center Newsletter, 9*(2), 1–2.

Gesser, G., Wong, P. T. P., & Reker, G. T. (1986). Death attitudes across the life-span: The development and validation of the death attitude profile (DAP). Personal communication.

Getting older, getting better. (1992, March/April). *Psychology Today,* 16–17.

Giarrusso, R., Silverstein, S., & Feng, D. (2000). Psychological costs and benefits of raising grandchildren: Evidence from a national survey of grandparents. In C. B. Cox (Ed.), *To grandmother's house we go and stay* (pp. 71–90). New York: Springer.

Gibson, D. (1996). Broken down by age and gender—'The problem of old women' redefined. *Gender and Society, 10*(4), 433–448.

Gibson, R. C. (1986). Outlook for the black family. In A. Pifer & L. Bronte (Eds.), *Our changing society* (pp. 181–197). New York: W.W. Norton.

Gibson, R. C. (1987). Reconceptualizing retirement for black Americans. *The Gerontologist, 27,* 691–698.

Gibson, R. C. (1989). Minority aging research: Opportunity and challenge. *Journal of Gerontology: Social Sciences, 44*(1), S2–S3.

Gibson, R. C. (1991). Subjective retirement of black Americans. *Journals of Gerontology, 46*(4), S204–S209.

Gibson, R. C. (1993). The black American retirement experience. In J. S. Jackson, L. M. Chatters, & R. J. Taylor (Eds.), *Aging in Black America* (pp. 277–297). Newbury Park, CA: Sage.

Gibson, R. C., & Jackson, J. S. (1992). The black oldest old: Health, functioning, and informal support. In R. M. Suzman, D. P. Willis, & K. G. Manton (Eds.), *The oldest old* (pp. 321–340). New York: Oxford University Press.

Gilleard, C. J., & Gurkan, A. A. (1987). Socioeconomic development and the status of elderly men in Turkey: A test of modernization theory. *Journal of Gerontology, 42,* 353–357.

Gillin, C. T. (1986, June). Aging in the developing world. Paper presented at the Canadian Sociology and Anthropology Association meetings, Winnipeg, Manitoba.

Gilman, E. (1994, February 20). Matching the elderly with foster families. *New York Times,* Section NJ, p. 9C.

Giranda, M., Luk, J. E., & Atchison, K. A. (1999). Social networks of elders without children. *Journal of Gerontological Social Work, 31*(1-2), 63–83.

Gist, Y. J. (1994). Aging trends—Southern Africa. *Journal of Cross-Cultural Gerontology, 9,* 255–276.

Gitlin, L. N. (2003a). M. Powell Lawton's vision of the role of the environment in aging processes and outcomes: A glance backward to move us forward. In K. W. Schaie, H-W. Wahl, H. Mollenkopf, & F. Oswald (Eds.), *Aging independently: Living arrangements and mobility* (pp. 62–76). New York: Springer.

Gitlin, L. N. (2003b). Next steps in home modification and assistive technology research. In N. Charness & K. W. Schaie (Eds.), *Impact of technology on successful aging* (pp. 188–202). New York: Springer.

Gladstone, J. W. (1987). Factors associated with changes in visiting between grandmothers and grandchildren following an adult child's marriage breakdown. *Canadian Journal on Aging, 6,* 117–127.

Gladstone, J. W. (1989). Grandmother-grandchild contact: The mediating influence of the middle generation following marriage breakdown and remarriage. *Canadian Journal on Aging, 8,* 355–365.

Gladstone, J. W. (1995). The marital perceptions of elderly persons living or having a spouse living in a long-term care institution in Canada. *The Gerontologist, 35*(1), 52–60.

Glascock, A. P., & Feinman, S. L. (1981). Social asset or social burden: Treatment of the aged in non-industrial societies. In C. L. Fry (Ed.), *Dimensions: Aging, culture, and health.* New York: Praeger.

Glass, J. C. Jr., & Huneycutt, T. L. (2002). Grandparents parenting grandchildren: Extent of situation, issues involved, and educational implications. *Educational Gerontology, 28*(2), 139–161.

Glendenning, F. (1999). Elder abuse and neglect in residential settings: The need for inclusiveness in elder abuse research. *Journal of Elder Abuse and Neglect, 10*(1-2), 1–11.

Gluck, M. E. (Ed.), Reno, V. P. (Ed.), & National Academy of Social Insurance (U.S.). (2001). *Reflections on implementing Medicare* (2d ed.). Washington, DC: National Academy of Social Insurance.

Golant, S. (2002). Geographic inequalities in the availability of government-subsidized rental housing for low-income older persons in Florida. *The Gerontologist, 42,* 100–109.

Golant, S. (2004). The urban-rural distinction in gerontology: An update of research. In H-W. Wahl, R. J. Scheidt, & P. G. Windley (Eds.), *Annual Review of Gerontology and Geriatrics, Vol. 23, 2003, Focus on aging in context: Socio-physical environments* (pp. 280–312). New York: Springer.

Golant, S. M. (1985). In defense of age-segregated housing. *Aging, 348,* 22–26.

Golant, S. M. (2003). Political and organizational barriers to satisfying low-income U.S. seniors' need for affordable rental housing with supportive services. *Journal of Aging & Social Policy, 15*(4), 21–48.

Golant, S. M., & La Greca, A. J. (1995). The relative deprivation of U.S. elderly households as judged by their housing problems. *Journal of Gerontology: Social Sciences, 50B*(1), S13–S23.

Gold, D. P., Andres, D., Etezadi, J., Arbuckle, T., & Schwartzman, A. (1995). Structural equation model of intellectual change and continuity and predictors of intelligence in older men. *Psychology and Aging, 10*(2), 294–303.

Gold, M. F. (1995). Hospice care allows death with dignity. *Provider, 21*(9), 84–86.

Goldberg, D. L. (2003). Grandparent-grandchild access: A legal analysis. Paper presented to Family, Children, and Youth Section, Department of Justice Canada. Minister of Justice and Attorney General of Canada.

Golden, F. (2004, January 19). Still sexy after sixty. *Time.*

Goldman, A., & Carroll, J. L. (1990). Educational intervention as an adjunct to treatment of erectile dysfunction in older couples. *Journal of Sex and Marital Therapy, 16*(3), 127–141.

Gonyea, J. G., Hudson, R. B., & Seltzer, G. B. (1990). Housing preferences of vulnerable elders in suburbia. *Journal of Housing for the Elderly, 7*(1), 79–95.

Goodman, C. (1999). Intimacy and autonomy in long term marriage. *Journal of Gerontological Social Work, 32,* 83–97.

Goodman, C., & Silverstein, M. (2002). Grandmothers raising grandchildren. *The Gerontologist, 42,* 676–689.

Goozner, M. (2005). Don't mess with success. *AARP Bulletin, 46*(1), 12–15.

Gordon, P., Ronsen, B., & Brown, E. R. (1974). Antiherpesvirus action of isoprinosine. *Antimicrobial Agents and Chemotherapy, 5,* 153–160.

Gorer, G. (1965). *Death, grief, and mourning in contemporary Britain.* London: Cresset.

Gottlieb, B. H., & Kelloway, E. K. (1995). Eldercare and employment. In M. Novak (Ed.), *Aging and society: A Canadian reader* (pp. 336–341). Scarborough, Ontario: Nelson Canada.

Gratton, B., & Haber, C. (1993). Rethinking industrialization: Old age and the family economy. In T. R. Cole, W. A. Achenbaum, P. L. Jakobi, & R. Kastenbaum (Eds.), *Voices and visions of aging* (pp. 134–159). New York: Springer.

Gray Panthers. (2004). *Gray panthers information.* Retrieved: December 10, 2004, www.graypanthers.org/graypanthers/info.htm.

Gray, D., & Calsyn, R. J. (1989). Relationship of stress and social support to life satisfaction: Age effects. *Journal of Community Psychology, 17,* 214–219.

Green R., & Galambos, C. (2002). Social work's pursuit of a common professional framework: Have we reached a milestone? *Journal of Gerontological Social Work, 39*(1-2), 7–23.

Greenfield, E. A., & Marks, N. F. (2004). Formal volunteering as a predictive factor for adults' psychological well-being. *Journals of Gerontology: Series B: Psychological Sciences and Social Sciences, 59B*(5), S258–S264.

Greer, G. (1991). *The change: Women, aging and the menopause.* Toronto: Alfred A. Knopf.

Gregory, R. F. (2001). *Age discrimination in the American workplace: Old at a young age.* New Brunswick, NJ: Rutgers University Press.

Gribble, J. N., & Preston, S. H. (Eds.). (1993). *The epidemiological transition.* Washington, DC: The National Academy Press.

Grobman, M. (1991). Managed care meets the long-term care challenge. *HMO Magazine, 32*(5), 32–36.

Grossman, A. H. (1997). The virtual and actual identities of older lesbians and gay men. In M. Duberman (Ed.), *A queer world: The center for lesbian and gay studies reader* (pp. 615–626). New York: New York University Press.

Grune, T., & Davies, K. J. A. (2001). Oxidatie processes in aging. In E. J. Masoro & S. N. Austad (Eds.), *Handbook of the biology of aging* (5th ed.), (pp. 25–58). San Diego: Academic Press.

GSA Task Force on Minority Issues in Gerontology. (1994). *Minority elders: Five goals toward building a public policy base* (2d ed.). Washington, DC: Gerontological Society of America.

Guberman, N. (1999). Daughters-in-law as caregivers: How and why do they come to care? *Journal of Women and Aging, 11*(1), 85–102.

Gubrium, J. F. (1993). Voice and context in a new gerontology. In T. R. Cole, W. A. Achenbaum, P. L. Jakobi, & R. Kastenbaum (Eds.), *Voices and visions of aging* (pp. 46–63). New York: Springer.

Gubrium, J. F., & Holstein, J. A. (1997). *The new language of qualitative methods.* New York: Oxford University Press.

Gubrium, J. F., & Holstein, J. A. (1999). Constructionist perspectives on aging. In V. L. Bengtson & K. W. Schaie (Eds.), *Handbook of theories of aging* (pp. 287–305). New York: Springer.

Guillemard, A. M. (Ed.). (1983). *Old age in the welfare state.* Beverly Hills, CA: Sage.

Guillemard, A. M. (1991). International perspectives on early withdrawal from the labor force. In J. Myles & J. S. Quadagno (Eds.), *States, labor markets, and the future of old age policy* (pp. 209–226). Philadelphia: Temple University Press.

Guinness Book of World Records. (1988). *Guinness book of world records* (27th ed.). New York: Sterling.

Gurung, R. A. R., Taylor S. E., & Seeman, T. E. (2003). Accounting for changes in social support among married older adults: Insights from the MacArthur Studies of Successful Aging. *Psychology and Aging, 18*(3), 487–496.

Gutmann, M. P. (1995). Older lives on the frontier: The residential patterns of the older population of Texas, 1850–1910. In D. I. Kertzer & P. Laslett (Eds.), *Aging in the past: Demography, society, and old age* (pp. 175–202). Berkeley: University of California Press.

Gutner, T. (2004, July 25). Getting psyched to retire. *BusinessWeek,* 88–90.

Haber, C. (1983). *Beyond sixty-five: The dilemma of old age in America's past.* Cambridge, England: Cambridge University Press.

Haber, C. (1993, Spring/Summer). "And the fear of the poorhouse": Perceptions of old age impoverishment in early twentieth-century America. *Generations,* 46–50.

Haber, C. (2000). Historians' approach to aging in America. In T. R. Cole, R. Kastenbaum, & R. E. Ray (Eds.), *Handbook of the humanities and aging* (2d ed.), (pp. 25–40). New York: Springer.

Haber, C., & Gratton, B. (1992). Aging in America: The perspective of history. In T. R. Cole, D. D. Van Tassel, & R. Kastenbaum (Eds.), *Handbook of the humanities and aging* (pp. 352–370). New York: Springer.

Haber, D. (2003). *Health promotion and aging: Practical applications for health professionals* (3d ed.). New York: Springer.

Hagen, B., Gallagher, G. M., & Simpson, S. (1997). Family caregiver education and support programs: Using humanistic approaches to evaluate program effects. *Educational Gerontology, 23*(2), 129–142.

Hagestad, G. O. (1985). Continuity and connectedness. In V. L. Bengtson & J. F. Robertson (Eds.), *Grandparenthood.* Beverly Hills: Sage.

Hahn, R., & Eberhardt, S. (1995). Life expectancy in four U.S. racial/ethnic populations: 1990. *Epidemiology, 6,* 352–356.

Haines, V. A., & Henderson, L. J. (2002). Targeting social support: A network assessment of the convoy model of social support. *Canadian Journal on Aging, 21*(2), 243–256.

Hall, M., & Havens, B. (2002). Social isolation and social loneliness. In *Writing in gerontology: Mental health and aging, No. 18,* (pp. 33–44). Ottawa: National Advisory Council on Aging,

Hallman, B. C., & Joseph, A. E. (1999). Getting there: Mapping the gendered geography of caregiving to elderly relatives. *Canadian Journal on Aging, 18*(4), 397–414.

Hamel, M. B., Lynn, J., Teno, J. M., Covinsky, K. E., Wu, A. W., Galanos, A., Desbiens, N. A., & Phillips, R. S. (2000). Age-related differences in care preferences, treatment decisions, and clinical outcomes of seriously ill hospitalized adults: Lessons from SUPPORT. *Journal of the American Geriatrics Society, 48*(5, Suppl.), S176–S182.

Hamer, C. F., Guse, L. W., Hawranik, P. G., & Bond, J. B., Jr. (2002). Advance directives and community dwelling older adults. *Western Journal of Nursing Research, 24*(2), 143–158.

Hammond, D. B. (1987). *My parents never had sex.* Buffalo, NY: Prometheus Books.

Hamon, R. R. (1995). Parents as resources when adult children divorce. *Journal of Divorce and Remarriage, 23*(1-2), 171–183.

Hancock, J. A. (1987a). Appendix A. In J. A. Hancock (Ed.), *Housing the elderly* (pp. 267–272). New Brunswick, NJ: Center for Urban Policy Research.

Hancock, J. A. (1987b). Introduction. In J. A. Hancock (Ed.), *Housing the elderly* (pp. xiii–xiv). New Brunswick, NJ: Center for Urban Policy Research.

Hapgood, D. (1978). The aging are doing better. In R. Gross, B. Gross, & S. Seidman (Eds.), *The new old* (pp. 345–363). Garden City, NY: Anchor.

Harbison, J. (1999). Models of intervention for "elder abuse and neglect": A Canadian perspective on ageism, participation, and empowerment. *Journal of Elder Abuse and Neglect, 10*(3–4), 1–17.

Hardy, M. A. (1991). Employment after retirement: Who gets back in? *Research on Aging, 13*(3), 267–288.

Hardy, M. A. (2002). The transformation of retirement in twentieth-century America: From discontent to satisfaction. *Generations, 26*(2), 9–16.

Hare, P. H. (1992, Spring). Frail elders and the suburbs. *Generations,* 35–39.

Hareven, T. K. (1992, Summer). Family and generational relations in the later years: A historical perspective. *Generations,* 7–12.

Harlton, S. V., Keating, N., & Fast, J. (1998). Defining eldercare for policy and practice: Perspectives matter. *Family Relations, 47*(3), 281–288.

Harman, S. M., Metter, E. J., Metter, J., Tobin, J. D., Pearson, J., & Blackman, M. R. (2000). Longitudinal effects of aging on serum total and free testosterone levels in healthy men. *Journal of Clinical Endocrinology & Metabolism, 86*(2), 724–731.

Harootyan, R. A. (1993). Aging, functional abilities, and life-span design. In American Association of Retired Persons & Miami Jewish Home and Hospital for the Aged (Eds.), *Life-span design of residential environments for an aging population: Proceedings of an invitational conference* (pp. 111–118). Washington, DC: AARP.

Harris, D. K., Changas, P. S., & Palmore, E. B. (1996). Palmore's first Facts on Aging Quiz in a multiple-choice format. *Educational Gerontology, 22*(6), 575–589.

Harris, L. (1991). 1.9 million seniors ready and able to go back to work. *Aging, 362,* 51.

Harris, P. B. (1998). Listening to caregiving sons: Misunderstood realities. *The Gerontologist, 38*(3), 342–352.

Harris, P. B. (2002). The voices of husbands and sons caring for a family member with dementia. In B. J. Kramer & E. H. Thompson, Jr. (Eds.), *Men as caregivers: Theory, research, and service implications* (pp. 213–233). New York: Springer.

Hart, J. (1992). *Beyond the tunnel: The arts and aging in America.* Washington, DC: Museum One Publications.

Hartocollis, A. (1988, March 18). I don't know why I be living this long. *Newsday.*

Harvard Medical School. (1968). A definition of irreversible coma: Report of the ad hoc committee of the Harvard Medical School to examine the definition of brain death. *Journal of the American Medical Association, 205*(5), 677–679.

Hatch, R. G. (1995). *Aging and cohabitation.* New York: Garland.

Havens, B., & Hall, M. (2001). Social isolation, loneliness, and the health of older adults in Manitoba, Canada. *Indian Journal of Gerontology, 15*(1-2), 1126–1144.

Havir, L. (1991). Senior centers in rural communities: Potentials for serving. *Journal of Aging Studies, 5*(4), 359–374.

Hawes, C. (1999). Key piece of the integration puzzle: Managing the chronic care needs of the frail elderly in residential care settings. *Generations, 23*(2), 51–55.

Hawranik, P. (2002). Inhome service use by caregivers and their elders: Does cognitive status make a difference? *Canadian Journal on Aging, 21*(2), 257–272.

Hayes, C. L. (1990). Social and emotional issues facing midlife women: The important role of pre-retirement planning. In C. L. Hayes & J. M. Deren (Eds.), *Pre-retirement planning for women: Program design and research* (pp. 27–40). New York: Springer.

Hayes, C. L., & Deren, J. M. (1990). Preface. In C. L. Hayes & J. M. Deren (Eds.), *Pre-retirement planning for women: Program design and research* (pp. xiii–xvi). New York: Springer.

Hayes-Bautista, D. E., Hsu, P., Perez, A., & Gambon, C. (2002). The 'browning' of the graying of America: Diversity in the elderly population and policy implications. *Generations, 26*(3), 15–22.

Hayflick, L. (1981). Prospects for human life extension by genetic manipulation. In D. Danon, N. W. Shock, & M. Marois (Eds.), *Aging: A challenge to science and society* (pp. 162–179). Oxford, England: Oxford University Press.

Hayflick, L. (1996). *How and why we age.* New York: Ballantine.

Hayflick, L., & Moorehead, P. S. (1961). The serial cultivation of human diploid cell strains. *Experimental Cell Research, 25,* 585–621.

Hayslip, B. Jr., Shore, R. J., & Henderson, C. E. (2000). Perceptions of grandparents' influence in the lives of their grandhchildren. In B. Hayslip & R. Goldberg-Glen (Eds.), *Grandparent raising grandchildren: Theoretical, empirical, and clinical perspectives* (pp. 35–46). New York: Springer.

Hayward, M. D., & Liu, M. (1992). Men and women in their retirement years. In M. Szinovacz, D. J. Ekerdt, & B. H. Vinick (Eds.), *Families in retirement* (pp. 23–50). Newbury Park, CA: Sage.

Hazelrigg, L. E., & Hardy, M. A. (1995). Older adult migration to the sunbelt: Assessing income and related characteristics of recent migrants. *Research on Aging, 17,* 209–234.

Healey, S. (1994). Diversity with a difference: On being old and lesbian. *Journal of Gay and Lesbian Social Services, 1*(1), 109–117.

Healey, T., & Ross, K. (2002). Growing old invisibly: Older viewers talk television. *Media, Culture and Society, 24*(1), 105–120.

Health and Human Services. (2001). *Indicators of welfare dependence, 2001. Appendix A: Supplemental Security Income.* Retrieved: September 5, 2004, www.aspe.hhs.gov/hsp/indicators01/apa-SSI.htm.

Health and Retirement Study. (2004). NIA U01 AG09740. *An overview of Health and Retirement Study components.* Accessed: December 18, 2004, http://hrsonline.isr.umich.edu/docs/irb/HRS_IRB_Information.pdf and http://hrsonline.isr.umich.edu/intro/sho_uinfo.php?hfyle=overview&xtyp=2.

Hedlund, A. L. (1999). Give-and-take: Navajo grandmothers and the role of craftswomen. In M. M. Schweitzer (Ed.), *American Indian grandmothers: Traditions and transitions* (pp. 53–77). Albuquerque: University of New Mexico Press.

Hedrick, S. C., Rothman, M. L., Chapko, M., Ehreth, J., & Kiehr, P. (1993). Summary and discussion of methods and results of the adult day health care evaluation study. *Medical Care, 31*(9, Suppl.), SS94–SS103.

Heidemann, B., Suhomlinova, O., & O'Rand, A. M. (1998). Economic independence, economic status, and empty nest in midlife marital disruption. *Journal of Marriage and the Family, 60,* 219–231.

Helfrich, T. E., & Dodson, J. L. (1992). Eldercare: An issue for corporate America. *Journal of Case Management, 1*(1), 26–29.

Hendricks, J. (1982). The elderly in society: Beyond modernization. *Social Science History, 6,* 321–345.

Hendricks, J. (1997). Bridging contested terrain: Chaos or prelude to a theory. *Canadian Journal on Aging, 16*(2), 197–217.

Hendricks, J. (1999). Creativity over the life course—A call for a relational perspective. *International Journal of Aging and Human Development, 48*(2), 85–111.

Hendricks, J., & Hendricks, C. D. (1986). *Aging in mass society: Myths and realities* (3d ed.). Boston: Little, Brown.

Hendrix, L. R. (2003). Intercultural collaboration: An approach to long term care for urban American Indians. *Care Management Journals, 4*(1), 46–52.

Henley-Smith, L. (1992). Untapped wealth of senior volunteers. *Spectrum, 6*(2), 40–43.

Henretta, J. C. (2003). The life-course perspective on work and retirement. In R. A. Settersten, Jr. (Ed.), *Invitation to the life course: Toward new understandings of later life* (pp. 85–105). Amityville, NY: Baywood.

Henretta, J. C., Chan, C. G., & O'Rand, A. M. (1992). Retirement reason versus retirement process: Examining the reasons for retirement typology. *Journals of Gerontology, 47*(1), S1–S7.

Hermann, N. (1991). Confusion and dementia in the elderly. In *National Advisory Council on Aging, Mental Health and Aging* (pp. 31–48). Ottawa: NACA.

Herndon, C. M., Jackson, K. II, Fike, D. S., & Woods, T. (2003). End-of-life care education in United States pharmacy schools. *American Journal of Hospice and Palliative Care, 20*(5), 340–344.

Heru, A. M., Ryan, C. E., & Iqbal, A. (2004). Family functioning in the caregivers of patients with dementia. *International Journal of Geriatric Psychiatry, 19*(6), 533–537.

Hess, B. B. (1987). Poverty. In G. L. Maddox (Ed.), *The encyclopedia of aging* (pp. 530–532). New York: Springer.

Hess, B. B., & Soldo, B. J. (1985). Husband and wife networks. In W. J. Sauer & R. T. Cowards (Eds.), *Social support networks and the care of the elderly* (pp. 67–92). New York: Springer.

Hess, T. M., Rosenberg, D. C., & Waters, S. J. (2001). Motivation and representational processes in adulthood: The effects of social accountability and information relevance. *Psychology and Aging, 16*(4), 629–642.

Hessel, D. (Ed.). (1977). *Maggie Kuhn on aging: A dialogue.* Philadelphia: Westminster Press.

Hetzel, L., & Smith, A. (2001). *The 65 Years and Over Population: 2000—Census 2000 Brief. U.S. Census Bureau.* Retrieved: March 21, 2004, www.census.gov/prod/2001pubs/c2kbr01-10.pdf or www.census.gov/population/www/cen2000/briefs.html.

Heumann, J. E. (2004). *Consumer-directed personal care services for older people in the U.S.* Retrieved: December 28, 2004, http://research.aarp.org/health/ib64_cd.pdf.

Hey, R. P. (1995). Cuts loom for Medicare enrollees. *AARP Bulletin, 36*(6), 1ff.

Hickey, T. (1995). Gerontology program development. Seminar presentation sponsored by the Centre on Aging, University of Manitoba, Winnipeg, Manitoba, February 23.

Hightower, J. (2004). Age, gender and violence: Abuse against older women. *Geriatrics and Aging, 7*(3), 60–63.

Hill, E. T. (2002). Labor force participation of older women: Retired? Working? Both? *Monthly Labor Review, 125*(9), 39–48.

Hilton, J. M., & Macari, D. P. (1997). Grandparent involvement following divorce: A comparison in single-mother and single-father families. *Journal of Divorce and Remarriage, 28*(1-2), 203–224.

Hinrichsen, J. J. (1990). Heart of treatment for alcoholism: Alcoholics Anonymous. *Aging, 361,* 12–17.

Hobbs, F. B., & Damon, B. L. (1996). *65+ in the United States. P23-190 Current population reports: Special series.* Retrieved April 26, 2004, www.census.gov/prod/1/pop/p23-190/p23190-i.pdf.

Hobbs, F., & Stoops, N. (2002). *Demographic trends in the 20th century.* U.S. Census Bureau, Census 2000 Special Reports, Series CENSR-4. Washington, DC: U.S. Government Printing Office. Retrieved: January 19, 2004, www.census.gov/prod/2002pubs/censr-4.pdf.

Hodgson, L. G. (1995). Adult grandchildren and their grandparents: The enduring bond. In J. Hendricks (Ed.), *The ties of later life* (pp. 155–170). Amityville, NY: Baywood.

Hoenig, H., Taylor, D. H., & Sloar, F. A. (2003). Does assistive technology substitute for personal assistance among the disabled elderly? *American Journal of Public Health, 93*(2), 330–337.

Hogan, R., Perrucci, C. C., & Wilmoth, J. M. (Eds.). (2000). Gender inequality in employment and retirement income: Effects of marriage, industrial sector, and self-employment. In *Advances in gender research, vol. 4* (pp. 27–54). Stamford, CT: JAI.

Holladay, S., Denton, D., Harding, D., Lee, L., Lackovich, R., & Coleman, M. (1997). Granddaughters' accounts of the influence of parental mediation on relational closeness with maternal grandmothers. *International Journal of Aging and Human Development, 45*(1), 23–38.

Holmberg, A. R. (1969). *Nomads of the long bow.* Garden City, NY: Natural History Press.

Holmen, K., Ericsson, K., Andersson, L., & Winblad, B. (1992). Loneliness among elderly people living in Stockholm: A population study. *Journal of Advanced Nursing, 17*(1), 43–51.

Holmes, E. R., & L. D. Holmes. (1995). *Other cultures, elder years* (2d ed.). Thousand Oaks, CA: Sage.

Holstein, M. H. (2001–2002). Feminist perspective on anti-aging medicine. *Generations, 25*(4), 38–43.

Holstein, M., & Minkler, M. (1991). The short life and painful death of the Medicare Catastrophic Coverage Act. In M. Minkler & C. L. Estes (Eds.), *Critical perspectives on aging: The political and moral economy of growing old* (pp. 189–206). Amityville, NY: Baywood.

Homans, G. C. (1961). *Social behavior: Its elementary forms.* New York: Harcourt Brace Jovanovich.

Homesmod.org. (2003). "$740 million to be made available . . ." Retrieved: December 31, 2002, www.homemods.org.

Honig, M. (1999). *Minorities face retirement: Work-life disparities repeated?* New York: International Longevity Center. Retrieved: September 6, 2004, www.ilcusa.org/_lib/pdf/publicationsminoritiesface.pdf.

Hooyman, N. R. (1990). Women as caregivers of the elderly. In D. E. Biegel & A. Blum (Eds.), *Aging and caregiving: Theory, research, and policy* (pp. 221–241). Newbury Park, CA: Sage.

Hooyman, N. R., Browne, C. V., Ray, R., & Richardson, V. (2002). Feminist gerontology and the life course: Policy, research, and teaching issues. *Gerontology and Geriatrics Education, 22*(4), 3–26.

Hooyman, N. R., & Kiyak, H. A. (1993). *Social gerontology: A multidisciplinary perspective* (3d ed.). Boston: Allyn & Bacon.

Hopp, F. P., & Duffy, S. A. (2000). Racial variations in end-of-life care. *Journal of the American Geriatrics Society, 48*(6), 658–663.

Horn, J. L. (1982). The aging of human abilities. In B. B. Wolman (Ed.), *Handbook of developmental psychology* (pp. 847–870). Englewood Cliffs, NJ: Prentice-Hall.

Horn, J. L., & Cattell, R. B. (1966). Age differences in primary mental ability factors. *Journal of Gerontology, 21,* 210–220.

Horn, J. L., & Cattell, R. B. (1967). Age differences in fluid and crystallized intelligence. *Acta Psychologia, 26,* 107–129.

Horna, J. (1994). *The study of leisure: An introduction.* Toronto, Ontario: Oxford University Press.

Houlihan, P., & Caraballo, E. (1990). Women and retirement planning: The development of Future Connections, Inc. In C. L. Hayes & J. M. Deren (Eds.), *Pre-retirement planning for women: Program design and research* (pp. 63–76). New York: Springer.

Housing and Urban Development. (2000a). *Homes and Communities. Community planning and development. SRO terms.* Retrieved: October 30, 2004, www.hud.gov/offices/cpd/homeless/library/sro/understandingsro/terms.cfm.

Housing and Urban Development. (2000b). Trends in elderly housing. *Urban Research Monitor, 5*(2), 1. Retrieved: October 29, 2004, www.huduser.org/periodicals/urm/urm_07_2000/urm1.html and www.huduser.org/periodicals/urm/urm_07_2000/urm2.html.

Housing and Urban Development. (2001). *Housing assistance for low income elderly.* Retrieved: October 30, 2004, www.hud.gov/local/mo/library/archives/stl109.cfm.

Housing and Urban Development (HUD). (2004). *Homes and communities. Home buying. How HUD's reverse mortgage program works.* Retrieved: October 3, 2004, www.hud.gov/buying/reverse.cfm.

Hoyert, D. L., Arias, E., Mith, B. L., Murphy, S. L., & Kochaneck, K. D. (1999). Deaths: Final data for 1999. *National Vital Statistics Report, 49*(8). DHHS Publication No. (PHS) 2001-1120. Hyattsville, MD: National Center for Health Statistics.

Hubbard, W. S., Blieszner, R., & London, J. W. (1992, Spring). Moving from outdoor to indoor plumbing: Decreasing the risk of institutionalization among Appalachian elders. *Generations,* 67–68.

Hubert, H. B., Block, D. A., Oehlert, J. W., & Fries, J. F. (2002). Lifestyle habits and compression of morbidity. *Journals of Gerontology: Series A: Biological Sciences and Medical Sciences, 57A*(6), M347–M351.

Hudson, R. B. (1988). Social policy in the United States. In E. Rathbone-McCuan & B. Havens (Eds.), *North American elders: United States and Canadian perspectives* (pp. 55–68). New York: Greenwood.

Hudson, R. B. (1993). 'Graying' of the federal budget revisited. *Generations, 17*(2), 79–82.

Hudson, R. B. (1994). The "graying" of the federal budget revisited. In D. Shenk & W. A. Achenbaum (Eds.), *Changing perceptions of aging and the aged* (pp. 145–153). New York: Springer.

Hudson, R. B. (1996). Changing face of aging politics. *The Gerontologist, 36*(1), 33–35.

Hudson, R. B. (1997). The history and place of age-based public policy. In R. B. Hudson (Ed.), *The future of age-based public policy* (pp. 1–12). Baltimore, MD: The Johns Hopkins University Press.

Hudson, R. B. (1999). The evolution of the welfare state: Shifting rights and responsibilities for the old. In M. Minkler & C. L. Estes (Eds.), *Critical gerontology: Perspectives from political and moral economy* (pp. 329–343). Amityville, NY: Baywood.

Hudson, R. B., & Strate, J. (1985). Aging and political systems. In R. Binstock & E. Shanas (Eds.), *Handbook of aging and the social sciences* (2d ed.), (pp. 554–585). New York: Van Nostrand Reinhold.

Humphry, D. (2000). *Supplement to final exit.* Junction City, OR: Norris Lane Press.

Hunt, M. E., Marshall, L. J., & Merrill, J. L. (2002). Rural areas that affect older migrants. *Journal of Architectural and Planning Research, 19*(1), 44–56.

Hutlock, T. (2003). 'Smart technology' future is now. *Nursing Homes Long Term Care Management, 52*(1), 84+.

Huttman, E. (1987). Continuum of care. In G. L. Maddox (Ed.), *The encyclopedia of aging* (pp. 145–147). New York: Springer.

IHS (Indian Health Service). (1990). *Trends in Indian health—1990.* Washington, DC: U.S. Government Printing Office.

Institute of Medicine. (1997). *Approaching death.* Washington, DC: National Academy Press.

International Longevity Center and AARP. (2003). *Unjust desserts: Financial realities of older women. New York: ILC and AARP.* Retrieved: September 6, 2004, www.ilcusa.org/_lib/pdf/unjustdesserts.pdf.

Iso-Ahola, S. E. (1993). Leisure lifestyle and health. In D. Compton & S. Iso-Ahola (Eds.), *Leisure and mental health.* Park City, UT: Family Development Resources.

Jackson, A. M. (1994). Coming of age of grandparent visitation rights. *American University Law Review, 43,* 563–601.

Jackson, J. J. (1972). African American women in a racist society. In C. Willie, B. Kramer & B. Brown (Eds.), *Racism and mental health* (pp. 185–268). Pittsburgh, PA: University of Pittsburgh Press.

Jackson, J. J. (1985). Aged black Americans: Double jeopardy re-examined. *Journal of Minority Aging, 10*(1), 25–61.

Jackson, J. J. (1987). African American aged. In G. L. Maddox (Ed.), *The encyclopedia of aging* (pp. 71–73). New York: Springer.

Jackson, J. J., & Ensley, D. E. (1991). Ethnogerontology's status and complementary and conflicting social and cultural concerns for American minority elders. *Journal of Minority Aging, 12*(2), 41–78.

Jackson, J. J., & Jackson, J. S. (1992). *Ethnogerontology and American blacks: Brief bibliography: A selective annotated bibliography for gerontology instruction.* Washington, DC: Association for Gerontology in Higher Education.

Jackson, J. S. (1989). Race, ethnicity, and psychological theory and research. *Journal of Gerontology: Psychological Sciences, 44*(1), P1–2.

Jackson, J. S., Chatters, L. M., & Taylor, R. J. (1993). Status and functioning of future cohorts of African-American elderly: Conclusions and speculations. In J. S. Jackson, L. M. Chatters, & R. J. Taylor (Eds.), *Aging in African American America* (pp. 301–318). Newbury Park, CA: Sage.

Jackson, R., Howe, N., Center for Strategic International Studies (Washington, DC), & Watson Wyatt Worldwide. (2003). *Aging vulnerability Index: An assessment of the capacity of twelve developed countries to meet the aging challenge.* Washington, DC: Center for Strategic International Studies (Washington, DC); & Watson Wyatt Worldwide.

Jackson, J. S., Taylor, R. J., & Chatters, L. M. (1993). Roles and resources of the African American elderly. In J. S. Jackson, L. M. Chatters, & R. J. Taylor (Eds.), *Aging in African American America* (pp. 1–20). Newbury Park, CA: Sage.

Jacobs, B. (1990). Aging and politics. In R. H. Binstock & L. K. George (Eds.), *Handbook of aging and the social sciences* (pp. 349–361). San Diego: Academic Press.

Jacobs, B., & Weissert, W. (1987). Home equity financing of long-term care for the elderly. In J. A. Hancock (Ed.), *Housing the elderly* (pp. 151–176). New Brunswick, NJ: Center for Urban Policy Research.

Jacobs, R. J., Rasmussen, L. A., & Hohman, M. M. (1999). The social support needs of older lesbians, gay men, and bisexuals. *Journal of Gay and Lesbian Social Services, 9*(1), 1–30.

Jacobs, S-E. (1999). Being a grandmother in the Tewa world. In M. M. Schweitzer (Ed.). *American Indian grandmothers: Traditions and transition* (pp. 125–144). Albuquerque: University of New Mexico Press.

Jacoby, S. (1999). Great sex: What's age got to do with it? *Modern Maturity* (October), 41ff.

Jaffe, D. J. (1989). An introduction to elderly shared housing research in the United States. In D. J. Jaffe (Ed.), *Shared housing for the elderly* (pp. 3–12). New York: Greenwood.

Janelli, L. M., & Sorge, L. (2001). Portrayal of grandparents in children's storybooks: A recent review. *Gerontology and Geriatrics Education, 22*(2), 69–88.

Jennison, K. M. (1992). Impact of stressful life events and social support on drinking among older adults: A general population survey. *International Journal of Aging and Human Development, 35,* 99–123.

Jerrome, D. (1996) Continuity and change in the study of family relationships. *Ageing and Society, 16*(1), 93–104.

Jirovec, R. L., & Erich, J. A. (1992). Dynamics of political participation among the urban elderly. *Journal of Applied Gerontology, 11*(2), 216–227.

Joffres, C. (2002). Barriers to residential planning: Perspectives from selected older parents caring for adult offspring with lifelong disabilities. *Canadian Journal on Aging, 21*(2), 303–311.

Jogerst, G. J., Daly, J. M., Brinig, M. F., Dawson, J. D., Schmuch, G. A., & Ingram, J. G. (2003). Domestic elder abuse and the law. *American Journal of Public Health, 93*(12), 2131–2136.

John, R. (1994). The state of research on American Indian elders' health, income security, and social supports. In J. S. Jackson (Ed.), *Minority elders: Five goals toward building a public policy base* (2d ed.), (pp. 46–58). Washington, DC: Gerontological Society of America.

John, R., & Baldridge, D. (1996). *The National Indian Council on Aging report: Health and long-term care for Indian elders.* Washington, DC: National Indian Policy Center.

John, R., Hennessy, C. H., & Denny, C. H. (1999). Preventing chronic illness and disability among Native American elders. In M. L. Wykle & A. B. Ford (Eds.), *Serving minority elders in the 21st century* (pp. 51–71). New York: Springer.

Johnson, B. (1997). Older adults' suggestions for health care providers regarding discussions of sex. *Geriatric Nursing, 18,* 65–66.

Johnson, C. (1999). Fictive kin among oldest old African Americans in the San Francisco Bay area. *Journals of Gerontology: Series B: Psychological Sciences and Social Sciences, 54B*(6), S368–S375.

Johnson, C. L. (1992, Summer). Divorced and reconstituted families: Effects on the older generation. *Generations,* 17–20.

Johnson, C. L., & Barer, B. M. (1990). Families and networks among older inner-city African Americans. *The Gerontologist, 30*(6), 726–733.

Johnson, C. L., & Barer, B. M. (1992). Patterns of engagement and disengagement among the oldest old. *Journal of Aging Studies, 6,* 351–364.

Johnson, C. L., & Barer, B. M. (1997). *Life beyond 85 years: The aura of survivorship.* New York: Springer.

Johnson, H. R., Britton, J. H., Lang, C. A., Seltzer, M. M., Stanford, E. P., Yancik, R., Maklan, C. W., & Middleswarth, A. B. (1980). Foundations for gerontological education. *The Gerontologist, 20*(3), 1–61.

Johnson, J. C., & Smith, N. H. (2002). Health and social issues associated with racial, ethnic, and cultural disparities. *Generations, 26*(3), 25–32.

Jones, T. C., & Nystrom, N. M. (2002). Looking back . . . looking forward: Addressing the lives of lesbians 55 and older. *Journal of Women and Aging, 14*(3-4), 59–76.

Jovanis, P. P. (2003). Marcointerventions: roads, transportation systems, traffic calming, and vehicle design. In K. W. Schaie, H-W. Wahl, H. Mollenkopf, & F. Oswald (Eds.). *Aging independently: Living arrangements and mobility* (pp. 234–247). New York: Springer.

Jung, C. G. (1976). The stages of life. In J. Campbell (Ed.), *The portable Jung.* Harmondsworth, England: Penguin.

Kahana, E., & Kahana, B. (2003). Contextualizing successful aging: New directions in an age-old search. In R. A. Settersten (Ed.), *Invitation to the life course: Toward new understandings of later life* (pp. 225–255). Amityville, NY: Baywood.

Kahana, E., Kahana, B., Johnson, J. R., Hammond, R. J., & Kercher, K. (1994). Developmental challenges and family caregiving: Bridging concepts and research. In E. Kahana, D. E. Biegel, & M. L. Wykle (Eds.), *Family caregiving across the lifespan* (pp. 3–41). Thousand Oaks, CA: Sage.

Kahana, E., Kahana, B., & Kercher, K. (2003). Emerging lifestyles and proactive options for successful aging. *Ageing International, 28*(2), 155–180.

Kahn, K. L., Draper, D., Keeler, E. B., Rogers, W. H., & Rubenstein, L. V. (1992). Effects of the DRG-based prospective payment system on quality of care for hospitalized Medicare patients: Final report. Report prepared by RAND, Santa Monica, CA, for the Health Care Financing Administration.

Kahn, R. L., & Antonucci, T. C. (1980). Convoys over the life course: Attachments, roles, and social support. *Life-Span Development and Behavior, 3,* 253–86.

Kaiser Commission. (2004). *Uninsured workers in America.* The Kaiser Commission on Medicaid and Uninsured Workers. Retrieved: August 14, 2004, www.kff.org/uninsured/7117.cfm.

Kaiser Family Foundation. (2003). The Kaiser Family Foundation D.C. health care access survey, 2003. Retrieved: December, 29, 2004, www.kff.org/minorityhealth/loader.cfm?url=/commonspot/security/getfile.cfm&PageID=23624.

Kalish, R. A. (1979). The new ageism and the failure models: A polemic. *The Gerontologist, 19,* 398–402.

Kamimoto, L. A., Easton, A. N., Maurice, E., Husten, C. G., & Macera, C. A. (1999). Surveillance for five health risks among older adults—United States, 1993–1997. *MMWR, 48,* 89–156.

Kamm, A. (1992). Illinois senior olympics. In S. Harris, R. Harris, & W. S. Harris (Eds.), *Physical activity, aging and sports: Practice, program and policy. Vol. II* (pp. 199–202). Albany, NY: Center for the Study of Aging.

Kane, R. A. (1995, July/August). The quality conundrum in homecare. *Aging Today,* 7.

Kane, R. A., & Kane, R. L. (1987). *Long-term care: Principles, programs and policies.* New York: Springer.

Kane, R. A., & Wilson, K. B. (1993). Assisted living in the United States: A new paradigm for residential care for frail older persons? Report published by AARP, Public Policy Institute.

Kane, R. L. (1991). SHMO outlook: Is the cup half full or half empty? Comments in response to "Adding long-term care to Medicare: The Social HMO experience." *Journal of Aging and Social Policy, 3*(4), 89–92.

Kane, R. L. (1999). Setting the PACE in chronic care. *Contemporary Gerontology: A Journal of Reviews and Critical Discourse, 6*(2), 47–50.

Kane, R. L., Illston, L. H., & Miller, N. A. (1992). Qualitative analysis of the program of all-inclusive care for the elderly (PACE). *The Gerontologist, 32*(6), 771–780.

Kane, R. L., & Kane, R. A. (2001). Emerging issues in chronic care. In R. H. Binstock & L. K. George (Eds.), *Handbook of aging and the social sciences* (5th ed.), (pp. 406–425). San Diego: Academic Press.

Kang, T. S., & Kang, G. E. (1983). Adjustment patterns of the Korean-American elderly: Case studies of ideal types. *Journal of Minority Aging, 8*(1–2), 47–55.

Kaplan, D. (1997). Access to technology: Unique challenges for people with disabilities. *Generations, 21*(3), 24–27.

Kaplan, F. S. (1987). Osteoporosis: Pathophysiology and prevention. *Clinical Symposia, No. 4* (Canada). Mississauga, Ontario: CIBA-GEIGY.

Karlawish, J. (2004). Ethics of research in dementia. In S. Gauthier, P. Scheltens, & J. L. Cummings (Eds.), *Alzheimer's disease and related disorders annual 2004* (pp. 123–136). London: Martin Dunitz.

Karlen, A. (1992). Appreciating the sexual you. *Modern Maturity, 35*(2), 52–54+.

Karp, D. A. (1986). Academics beyond mid-life: Some observations on changing consciousness in the fifty to sixty year decade. *International Journal of Aging and Human Development, 33,* 81–103.

Kart, C. S. (1990). Diversity among aged African American males. In Z. Harel, E. A. McKinney, & M. Williams (Eds.), *African American aged: Understanding diversity and service needs* (pp. 100–113). Newbury Park, CA: Sage.

Kasper, J. D. (1988). *Aging alone: Profiles and projections.* A Report of the Commonwealth Fund Commission on Elderly People Living Alone, Baltimore, MD.

Kastenbaum, R. (1993a). Driving: A lifespan challenge. In R. Kastenbaum (Ed.), *Encyclopedia of adult development* (pp. 134–139). Phoenix, AZ: Oryx.

Kastenbaum, R. (1993b). Encrusted elders: Arizona and the political spirit of postmodern aging. In T. R. Cole, W. A. Achenbaum, P. L. Jakobi, & R. Kastenbaum, (Eds.), *Voices and visions of aging: Toward a critical gerontology* (pp. 160–183). New York: Springer.

Kastenbaum, R. J. (1999). Foreword. In B. de Vries, (Ed.), *End of life issues* (pp. xv–xvii). New York: Springer.

Kastenbaum, R. J. (2001). *Death, society, and human experience.* Boston: Allyn & Bacon.

Kastenbaum, R. J., & Candy, S. (1973). The four percent fallacy: A methodological and empirical critique of extended care facility program statistics. *Aging and Human Development, 4,* 15–21.

Katz, S. (2001–2002). Growing older without aging? Positive aging, anti-ageism, and anti-aging. *Generations, 25*(4), 27–32.

Katz, S., & B. Marshall. (2003). New sex for old: Lifestyle consumerism, and the ethics of aging well. *Journal of Aging Studies, 17*(1), 3–16.

Kaufert, P. A., & Lock, M. (1997). Medicalization of women's third age. *Journal of Psychosomatic Obstetrics and Gynaecology, 18,* 81–86.

Kaufman, S. R. (1993, Spring/Summer). Reflections on "the ageless self." *Generations,* 13–16.

Kaufman, S. R. (2002). Commentary: Hospital experience and meaning at the end of life. *The Gerontologist, 42*(Special Issue 3), 34–39.

Kayser-Jones, J., & Koenig, B. A. (1994). Ethical Issues. In J. F. Gubrium & A. Sankar, (Eds.), *Qualitative methods in aging research* (pp. 15–32). Thousand Oaks, CA: Sage.

Keating, N. C., Fast, J. E., Connidis, A., Penning, M., & Keefe, J. (1997). Bridging policy and research in eldercare. *Canadian Journal on Aging/Canadian Public Policy, 16*(Suppl.), 22–41.

Keating, N. C., Fast, J. E., Frederick, J., Cranswick, K., & Perrier, C. (1999). *Eldercare in Canada: Context, content, and consequences.* Cat. No. 89-570-XPE. Ottawa: Minister of Industry.

Keddy, B. A., & Singleton, J. F. (1991). Women's perceptions of life after retirement. *Activities, Adaptation and Aging, 16*(2), 57–65.

Keefe, J. M., & Fancey, P. (2000). Care continues: Responsibility for elderly relatives before and after admission to a long-term care facility. *Family Relations, 49*(3), 235–244.

Keefe, J. M., & Fancey, P. J. (2002). Work and eldercare: Reciprocity between older mothers and their employed daughters. *Canadian Journal on Aging, 21*(2), 229–41.

Keigher, S. M., & Berman, R. H. (1991). How SRO hotels meet the needs of older Chicagoans. *Journal of Housing for the Elderly, 8*(1), 111–126.

Keith, J. (1990). Age in social and cultural context: Anthropological perspectives. In R. H. Binstock & L. K. George (Eds.), *Handbook of aging and the social sciences* (3d ed.), (pp. 91–111). San Diego: Academic Press.

Kellerman, V. (1994, April 24). Other end of spectrum: AIDS strikes elderly. *New York Times,* LI, 12.

Kelley-Moore, J. A., & Farraro, K. F. (2004). Black/white disability gap: Persistent inequality in later life? *Jour-*

nals of Gerontology: Series B: Psychological Sciences and Social Sciences, 59B(1), S34–S43.

Kelly, J. L., Elphick, G., Mepham, V., & Molloy, D. W. (1989). *Let me decide.* Hamilton: McMaster University Press.

Kelly, J. R. (1993). Varieties of activity. In J. R. Kelly (Ed.), *Activity and aging* (pp. 119–124). Newbury Park, CA: Sage.

Kemp, C. (2003). The social and demographic contours of contemporary grandparenthood: Mapping patterns in Canada and the United States. *Journal of Comparative Family Studies 34*(2), 187–212.

Kemp, C. (2004). "Grand" expectations: The experiences of grandparents and adult grandchildren. *Canadian Journal of Sociology, 29*(4), 499–525.

Kemp, C. L., & Denton, M. (2003). The allocation of responsibility for later life: Canadian reflections on the roles of individuals, government, employers, and families. *Ageing and Society 23*(6), 737–760.

Kemper, P. (1990). Case management agency systems of administering long-term care: Evidence from the channeling demonstration. *The Gerontologist, 30*(6), 817–824.

Kemper, P., & Murtaugh, C. (1991). Lifetime use of nursing home care. *New England Journal of Medicine, 324*(9), 595–600.

Kemper, P., Spillman, B., & Murtaugh, C. (1991). A lifetime perspective on proposals for financing nursing home care. *Inquiry, 28*(4), 333–344.

Kendig, H. L. (1990). Comparative perspectives on housing, aging, and social structure. In R. H. Binstock & L. K. George (Eds.), *Handbook of aging and the social sciences* (3d ed.), (pp. 288–306). San Diego: Academic Press.

Kendis, R. J. (1989). *An attitude of gratitude: The adaptation to aging of the elderly Japanese in America.* New York: AMS Press.

Keyser, C. M. (1994). Housing program makes investment in community. *Managing Senior Care, 3*(10), 93–94.

Kim, P. K. H., & Kim, J. S. (1989). Curriculum development for social work with Asian-American elderly. *Gerontology and Geriatrics Education, 10,* 89–98.

Kimmel, D. C. (1992, Summer). The families of older gay men and lesbians. *Generations,* 37–38.

King, V., & Elder, Jr., G. H. (1997). The legacy of grandparenting: Childhood experiences with grandparents and current involvement with grandchildren. *Journal of Marriage and the Family, 59*(4), 848–859.

Kinsella, K., & Velkoff, V. A. (2001). *An aging world: 2001.* U.S. Census Bureau, Series P95/01-1. Washington, DC: U.S. Government Printing Office. Retrieved: February 10, 2005, www.census.gov/prod/2001pubs/p95-01-1.pdf.

Kirchoff, S., & Adams, M. (2004). Pension insurer goes deeper in red. *USA Today,* November 16, 1.

Kirk, A. B., Waldrop, D. P., & Rittner, B. A. (2001). More than a meal: The relationship between social support and quality of life in daytime meal program participants. *Journal of Gerontological Social Work, 35*(1), 3–20.

Kirwin, P. M. (1991). *Adult day care: The relationship of formal and informal systems of care.* New York: Garland.

Kivett, V. R. (1993). Grandparenting: Racial comparisons of the grandmother role: Implications for strengthening the family support system of older black women. *Family Relations, 42*(2), 165–172.

Kleyman, P. (2002). Journalism's age-beat continues steady heartbeat despite ageist media economics. *Contemporary Gerontology: A Journal of Reviews and Critical Discourse, 8*(4), 115–118.

Knesek, G. E. (1992). Early versus regular retirement: Differences in measures of life satisfaction. *Journal of Gerontological Social Work, 19*(1), 3–34.

Knight, J., & Traphagan, J. W. (2003). The study of the family in Japan: Integrating anthropological and demographic approaches. In J. W. Traphagan & J. Knight (Eds.), *Demographic change and the family in Japan's aging society* (pp. 3–24). Albany: State University of New York Press.

Koch, T. (2000). *Age speaks for itself: Silent voices of the elderly.* Westport, CT: Praeger.

Koff, T. H., & Park, R. W. (1993). *Aging and public policy: Bonding the generations.* Amityville, NY: Baywood.

Koitz, D., Bobb, M. D., Page, B., & United States Congressional Budget Office. (2002). *Looming budgetary impact of society's aging.* Washington, DC: Congressional Budget Office.

Kolb, P. J. (2000). Continuing to care: Black and latina daughters' assistance to their mothers in nursing homes. *Affilia, 15*(4), 502–525.

Koncelik, J. A. (2003). The human factors of aging and the micro-environment: Personal surroundings, technology and product development. *Journal of Housing for the Elderly, 17*(2), 117–134.

Korczyk, S. M., & Public Policy Institute, AARP. (2002). Back to which future: The U.S. aging crisis revisited. Washington, DC: Public Policy Institute, AARP.

Koster, J., & Prather, J. (1999). Around the world: Canada. AARP Global Aging e-Report, April. E-mail communication.

Kotlikoff, L. (1993). Economic impact of the demographic transition: Problems and prospects. In American Association of Retired Persons (Ed.), *Aging of the U.S. population: Economic and environmental implications: Proceedings of an invitational workshop* (pp. 31–46). Washington, DC: AARP.

Kovar, M. G. (1987). Single room occupancy. In G. L. Maddox (Ed.), *The encyclopedia of aging* (pp. 610–611). New York: Springer.

Koyano, W., Hashimoto, M., Fukawa, T., Shibata, H., & Gunji, A. (1994). The social support system of the Japanese elderly. *Journal of Cross-Cultural Gerontology, 9,* 323–333.

Kozak, K. J., Owings, M. F., & Hall, M. J. (2004). *National hospital discharge survey: 2001.* Vital Health Statistics, 13(156). Hyattsville, MD: National Center for Health Statistics.

Krakauer, E. L., Crenner, C., & Fox, K. (2002). Barriers to optimum end-of-life care for minority patients. *Journal of the American Geriatrics Society, 50*(1), 182–190.

Kramer, B. J., & Lambert, J. D. (1999). Caregiving as a life course transition among older husbands: A prospective study. *The Gerontologist, 39*(6), 658–667.

Kramer, D. A. (2003). The ontogeny of wisdom in its variations. In J. Demick & C. Andreoletti (Eds.), *Handbook of adult development* (pp. 131–151). New York: Kluwer Academic.

Kramer, J. B. (1992). Serving American Indian elderly in cities: An invisible minority. *Aging, 363–364,* 48–51.

Kraus, H., & Raab, W. (1961). *Hypokinetic disease.* Springfield, IL: Charles C. Thomas.

Krause, N. (2002). Church-based social support and health in old age: exploring variations by race. *Journals of Gerontology: Series B: Psychological Sciences and Social Sciences, 57B*(6), S332–S347.

Krause, N. (2004). Neighborhoods, health, and well-being in late life. In H-W. Wahl, R. J. Scheidt, & P. G. Windley (Eds.), *Annual review of gerontology and geriatrics, Vol. 23, 2003, Focus on aging in context: Socio-physical environments* (pp. 223–249). New York: Springer.

Krauthammer, C. (1996). First and last, do no harm. *Time,* April 15, 61.

Krishnan, P. (1990). Aging in developed and developing countries. *University of Alberta Centre for Gerontology Newsletter,* Fall.

Krout, J. A. (1990). *Organization, operation, and programming of senior centers: A seven year follow up.* Freedonia, NY: State College of New York at Freedonia.

Krout, J. A. (1991). Rural advocates must raise their voices. *Perspective on Aging, 20*(1), 4–9+.

Krout, J. A., Cutler, S. J., & Coward, R. T. (1990). Correlates of senior center participation: A national analysis. *The Gerontologist, 30*(1), 72–79.

Krueger, B. (2001). How aging is covered in the print media. *Generations, 25*(3), 10–12.

Kruk, E. (1995). Grandparent-grandchild contact loss: Findings from a study of 'grandparent rights' members. *Canadian Journal on Aging, 14*(4), 737–754.

Kübler-Ross, E. (1969). *On death and dying.* New York: Macmillan.

Kuhn, M. (1975). Learning by living. *International Journal of Aging and Human Development, 8*(4), 359–365.

Kuhn, M. (1976). What old people want for themselves and others in society. In P. Kerschner (Ed.), *Advocacy and age.* Los Angeles: University of California Press.

Kunemund, H., & Rein, M. (1999). There is more to receiving than needing: Theoretical arguments and empirical explorations of crowding in and crowding out. *Ageing and Society 19*(1), 93–121.

Kuypers, J. A., & Bengtson, V. L. (1973). Social breakdown and competence: A model of normal aging. *Human Development, 16,* 181–201.

Kyomen, H. H., & Gottlieb, G. L. (2003). Barriers to the safe and effective treatment of late-life depression. In J. M. Ellison & V. Sumer (Eds.), *Depression in later life: A multidisciplinary psychiatric approach* (pp. 27–53). New York: Marcel Dekker.

Lacayo, C. G. (1991, Fall/Winter). Living arrangements and social environment among ethnic minority elderly. *Generations,* 43–46.

Lacayo, R. (1990). The generation gap. *Time,* October 29, p. 40.

Lachs, M. S., & Pillemer, K. (1995). Abuse and neglect of elderly persons. *The New England Journal of Medicine, 332,* 437–443.

Laditka, J. M. M., & Laditka, S. B. (2000). Morbidity compression debate: Risks, opportunities, and policy options for women. *Journal of Women & Aging, 12*(1–2), 23–38.

Lagana, L. (2003). Using service-learning research to enhance the elderly's quality of life. *Educational Gerontology, 29*(8), 685–701.

LaGrange, R. L., & Ferraro, K. F. (1987). Elderly's fear of crime: A critical examination of the research. *Research on Aging, 9,* 372–391.

Lamme, S., & Baars, J. (1993). Including social factors in the analysis of reminiscence in elderly individuals. *International Journal of Aging and Human Development, 37,* 297–311.

Lantz, M. S., & Giambanco, V. (2001). Key to treating older smokers? Don't quit helping. *Geriatrics, 56*(5), 58–59.

LaPlante, M. P., Kaye, S. H., Kang, T., & Harrington, C. (2004). Unmet need for personal assistance services: Estimating the shortfall in hours of help and adverse consequences. *Journals of Gerontology: Series B: Psychological Sciences and Social Sciences, 59B*(2), S98–S108.

LaRock, S. (1992). Both private and public sector employers use early retirement sweeteners. *Employee Benefit Plan Review, 47*(2), 14–16+.

Laslett, P. (1976). Societal development and aging. In R. H. Binstock & E. Shanas (Eds.), *Handbook of aging and the social sciences.* New York: Van Nostrand.

Laslett, P. (1985). Societal development and aging. In R. H. Binstock & E. Shanas (Eds.), *Handbook of aging and the social sciences* (2d ed.), (pp. 199–230). New York: Van Nostrand.

Laslett, P. (1989). *A fresh map of life: The emergence of the third age.* London: Weidenfeld & Nicolson.

Last Acts Campaign. (2003). State-by-state report card on care for the dying finds mediocre care nationwide. *Journal of Pain and Palliative Care Pharmacotherapy, 17*(2), 111–115.

Last Acts. (2002). *Means to a better end: A report on dying in America today.* Washington, DC: Last Acts National Program Office.

Lavizzo-Mourey, R., & Eisenberg, J. M. (1992). Foreword. In A. R. Somers & N. L. Spears (Eds.), *The continuing care retirement community: A significant option for long-term care?* (pp. xvii–xx). New York: Springer.

Lawton, M. P. (1970). Ecology and aging. In L. A. Pastalan & D. H. Carson (Eds.), *Spatial behavior of older people.* Ann Arbor, MI: University of Michigan.

Lawton, M. P. (1980). *Environment and aging.* Monterey, CA: Brooks/Cole.

Lawton, M. P. (1987). Housing. In G. L. Maddox (Ed.), *The encyclopedia of aging* (pp. 333–336). New York: Springer.

Lawton, M. P. (1990). Residential environment and self-directedness among older people. *American Psychologist, 45*(5), 638–640.

Lawton, M. P. (2001). Quality of life and the end of life. In J. E. Birren & K.W. Schaie (Eds.), *Handbook of the psychology of aging* (5th ed.). San Diego: Academic Press.

Lawton, M. P., & Nahemow, L. (1973). Ecology and the aging process. In C. Eisdorfer & M. P. Lawton (Eds.), *Psychology of adult development and aging* (pp. 619–674). Washington, DC: American Psychological Association.

Lazarowich, N. M. (Ed.). (1991). *Granny flats as housing for the elderly: International perspectives.* New York: Haworth.

Lazenby, H. C., & Letsch, S. W. (1990, Winter). National health expenditures 1989. *Health Care Financing Review, 12,* 1–26.

Leavitt, T. D., & Schulz, J. H. (1988). The role of the asset test in program eligibility and participation: The case of the SSI. Working Paper. Waltham, MA: Policy Center on Aging, Heller School, Brandeis University.

Lee, B. C. (1999). Should it be legal for physicians to expedite death. Yes: What experience teaches about legalization of assisted dying. *Generations 23*(1), 59–60.

Lee, G. R., Willetts, M. C., & Seccombe, K. (1998). Widowhood and depression: Gender differences. *Research on Aging, 20,* 611–630.

Lee, J. A. (1987). What can homosexual aging studies contribute to theories of aging? *Journal of Homosexuality, 13*(4), 43–70.

Lee, J. J. (1992). *Development, delivery, and utilization of services under the Older Americans Act: A perspective of Asian American elderly.* New York: Garland.

Lee, J., Yeo, G., & Gallagher-Thompson, D. (1993). Cardiovascular disease risk factors and attitudes towards prevention among Korean-American elders. *Journal of Cross-Cultural Gerontology, 8,* 17–33.

Lee, J. S. (2002). Aging curriculum and research capacity in schools of social work: A national survey. *Educational Gerontology, 28*(9), 805–815.

Lee, R. E., & King, A. C. (2003). Discretionary time among older adults: How do physical activity promotion interventions affect sedentary and active behaviors? *Annals of Behavioral Medicine, 25*(2), 112–119.

Lehr, U. M. (1992). Physical activities in old age: Motivation and barriers. In S. Harris, R. Harris, & W. S. Harris (Eds.), *Physical activity, aging and sports: Practice, program and policy. Vol. II* (pp. 51–62). Albany, NY: Center for the Study of Aging.

Leigh, G. K. (2000). Cohabiting and never-married families across the life course. In S. J. Price, P. C. McKenry, & M. J. Murphy (Eds.), *Families across time: A life course perspective* (pp. 77–89). Los Angeles: Roxbury.

Leinweber, F. (2001). Older adult market: New research highlights 'key values.' *Generations, 25*(3), 22–23.

Leitner, M. J., & Leitner, S. F. (1985). *Leisure in later life.* New York: Haworth.

Lenski, G., & Lenski, J. (1974). *Human societies: An introduction to macrosociology* (2d ed.). New York: McGraw-Hill.

Leon, J., & Lair, T. (1990). Functional status of the noninstitutionalized elderly: Estimates of ADL and IADL difficulties. DHHS Pub. No. (PHS)90-3462. National medical expenditure survey research findings, 4. Agency for Health Care Policy and Research. Rockville, MD: Public Health Service.

Leonard, F. (1993). Home alone: If your parents need help and you're miles away, call a care manager. *Modern Maturity,* December–January, 46–51, 77.

Leutz, W., Abrahams, R., & Capitman, J. (1993). Administration of eligibility for community long-term care. *The Gerontologist, 33*(1), 92–104.

Leutz, W., Greenlick, M., Ervin, S., Feldman, E., & Malone, J. (1991). Adding long-term care to Medicare: The Social HMO experience. *Journal of Aging and Social Policy, 3*(4), 69–87.

Levin, D. P. (1994). The graying factory. *New York Times,* February 20, Section 3, p. 1.

Levine, R. L., & Stadtman, E. R. (1992, Fall/Winter). Oxidation of proteins during aging. *Generations,* 39–42.

Levy, D. T., Vernick, J. S., & Howard, K. A. (1995). Relationship between driver's license renewal policies and fatal crashes involving drivers 70 years or older. *Journal of the American Medical Association, 274*(13), 1026–1030.

Levy, J. A. (1987). A life course perspective on hospice and the family. *Marriage and Family Review, 11,* 39–64.

Lichtenberg, P. A. (1997). Clinical perspectives on sexual issues in nursing homes. *Topics in Geriatric Rehabilitation, 12*(4), 1–10.

Lichtenstein, M. J., Pruski, L. A., Marshall, C. E., Blalock, C. L., Murphy, D. L., Plaetke, R., & Lee, S. (2001). Positively Aging teaching materials improve middle school students' images of older people. *The Gerontologist, 41*(3), 322–332.

Lieberman, T. (2000). *Slanting the story: The forces that shape the news.* New York: New Press.

Liebig, P. S. (1992). Federalism and aging policy in the 1980s: Implications for changing interest group roles in the 1990s. *Journal of Aging and Social Policy, 4*(1–2), 17–33.

Liebler, C. A., & Sandefur, G. D. (2002). Gender differences in the exchange of social support with friends, neighbors, and co-workers at midlife. *Social Science Research, 13*(3), 364–391.

Lilly, M. L., Richards, B. S., & Buckwalter, K. C. (2003). Friends and social support in dementia caregiving: Assessment and intervention. *Journal of Gerontological Nursing, 29*(1), 29–36.

Lincoln, Y., & Guba, E. (2000). Paradigmatic controversies, contradictions, and emerging confluences. In N. Denzin & Y. Lincoln (Eds.), *Handbook of qualitative research* (2d ed.), (pp. 163–187). Thousand Oaks, CA: Sage.

Lindemann, E. (1944). Symptomatology and management of acute grief. *American Journal of Psychiatry, 101,* 141–148.

Lindenberger, U., & Baltes, P. D. (1997). Intellectual functioning in old and very old age: Cross-sectional results from the Berlin Aging Study. *Psychology and Aging, 12,* 410–432.

Lipman, A. (1986). Homosexual relationships. *Generations, 10*(4), 51–54.

Lippert, B., & Scott, Z. (2003). What's wrong with this picture? *My Generation, 12,* 48+.

Lithwick, M., Beaulieu, M., Gravel, S., & Straka, S. M. (1999). Mistreatment of older adults: Perpetrator–victim relationships and interventions. *Journal of Elder Abuse and Neglect, 11*(4), 95–112.

Litwak, E. (1985). *Helping the elderly: The complementary roles of informal networks and formal systems.* New York: Guilford.

Liu, L. L., & Park, D. C. (2003). Technology and the promise of independent living for adults: A cognitive perspective. In N. Charness & K. W. Schaie (Eds.), *Impact of technology on successful aging* (pp. 262–289). New York: Springer.

Lobenstine, J. C. (1994). *Consider a career in the field of aging.* A brochure for the Association for Gerontology in Higher Education.

Lockery, S. A. (1991, Fall/Winter). Family and social supports: Caregiving among racial and ethnic minority elders. *Generations,* 58–62.

Loehr, J., Verma, S., & Seguin, R. (1997). Issues of sexuality in older women. *Journal of Women's Health, 6*(4), 451–457.

Logue, B. J. (1991). Women at risk: Predictors of financial stress for retired women workers. *The Gerontologist, 31,* 657–665.

Long, M. V., & Martin, P. (2000). Personality, relationship closeness, and loneliness of oldest old adults and their children. *The Journals of Gerontology Series B: Psychological Sciences and Social Sciences, 55,* P311–P319.

Longino, C. F. (1990). Geographical distribution and migration. In R. H. Binstock & L. K. George (Eds.), *Handbook of aging and the social sciences* (3d ed.), (pp. 45–63). San Diego: Academic Press.

Longino, C. F. (1992). The forest and the trees: Micro-level considerations in the study of geographic mobility in old age. In A. Rogers (Ed.), *Elderly migration and population redistribution: A comparative study* (pp. 23–34). London: Belhaven Press.

Longino, C. F. (2001). Geographical distribution and migration. In R. H. Binstock & L. K. George (Eds.), *Handbook of aging and the social sciences* (5th ed.), (pp. 103–124). San Diego: Academic Press.

Longino, C. F., Jr. (2004). Socio-physical environments at the macro level: The impact of population migration. In H-W. Wahl, R. J. Scheidt, & P. G. Windley (Eds.), *Annual review of Gerontology and Geriatrics, Vol. 23, 2003, focus on aging in context: Socio-physical environments* (pp. 110–129). New York: Springer.

Loos, C., & Bowd, A. (1997). Caregivers of persons with Alzheimer's disease: Some neglected implications of the experience of personal loss and grief. *Death Studies, 21*(5), 501–514.

Lopata, H. Z. (1996). *Current widowhood: Myths and realities.* Thousand Oaks, CA: Sage.

Louis Harris and Associates. (1989). *Older Americans: Ready and able to work.* New York: Author.

Love, J. (2004). Political behavior and values across the generations. AARP Strategic Issues Research. Retrieved: December 5, 2004, http://research.aarp.org/general/politics_values.pdf

Lucchino, R., Lane, W., & Ferguson, K. D. Aging content in elementary and secondary school curriculum. *Gerontology and Geriatrics Education, 18*(2), 37–49.

Luckey, I. (1994). African American elders: The support network of generational kin. *Families in society. Journal of Contemporary Human Services, 75*(2), 82–89.

Lugaila, T. (1998). *Marital status and living arrangements: March 1997.* Current Population Reports, P20-154. Washington, DC: U.S. Census Bureau.

Lum, Y-S., Chang, H. J., & Ozawa, M. N. (1999). Effects of race and ethnicity on use of health services by older Americans. *Journal of Social Service Research, 25*(4), 15–42.

Lund, D. A. (1993a). Caregiving. In R. Kastenbaum (Ed.), *Encyclopedia of adult development* (pp. 57–63). Phoenix, AZ: Oryx.

Lund, D. A. (1993b). Widowhood: The coping response. In R. Kastenbaum (Ed.), *Encyclopedia of adult development* (pp. 537–541). Phoenix, AZ: Oryx.

Luttropp, N. (1995). Minnie Mouse matures. *Aging Today, 16*(4), 5.

MacDougall, B. (1998). A time to grieve. *Expression, 12*(1), 1–2.

Mace, N., & Rabins, P. (1981). *The 36-hour day.* Baltimore, MD: Johns Hopkins University Press.

Mackenzie, P., & MacLean, M. (1992). Altered roles: The meaning of placement for the spouse who remains in the community. *Journal of Gerontological Social Work, 19*(2), 107–120.

MacKnight, C., & Powell, C. (2001). Effect of a home visit on first year medical students' attitude towards older adults. *Geriatrics Today, 4*(4), 182–185.

MacNeil, R. D. (2001). Bob Dylan and the Baby Boom generation: The times they are a changin'—again. *Activities, Adaptation and Aging, 25*(3-4), 45–58.

MacNeil, R. D., Winkelhake, K., & Yoshioka, N. (2003). Gerontology instruction in recreation and leisure studies curricula: A two-decade status report. *Educational Gerontology, 29*(4), 279–294.

Madden, D. J. (2001). Speed and timing of behavioral processes. In J. E. Birren & K.W. Schaie (Eds.), *Handbook of the psychology of aging* (5th ed.) San Diego: Academic Press.

Maddox, G. L. (Ed.). (1987). *The encyclopedia of aging.* New York: Springer.

Maddox, G. L. (1988). Aging, drinking, and alcohol abuse. *Generations, 12,* 14–16.

Maddox, G. L., & Campbell, R. T. (1985). Scope, concepts, and methods in the study of aging. In R. H. Binstock & E. Shanas (Eds.), *Handbook of aging and the social sciences* (2d ed.), (pp. 3–31). New York: Van Nostrand.

Maguire, K., Pastore, A. L., & Flanagan, T. J. (1993). *Bureau of Justice statistics sourcebook of criminal justice statistics—1992.* NCJ-143496. Washington, DC: U.S. Department of Justice.

Malveaux, J. (1987). Comparable worth and its impact on black women. In M. C. Simms & J. Malveaux (Eds.), *Slipping through the cracks: The status of black women* (pp. 47–62). New Brunswick, NJ: Transaction Books.

Malveaux, J. (1993). Race, poverty, and women's aging. In J. Allen & A. Pifer (Eds.), *Women on the front lines: Meeting the challenge of an aging America* (pp. 167–190). Washington, DC: Urban Institute Press.

Mantell, J., & Gildea, M. (1989). Elderly shared housing in the United States. In D. J. Jaffe (Ed.), *Shared housing for the elderly* (pp. 13–23). New York: Greenwood.

Manton, K. G., & Gu, X-L. (2001). Dramatic decline in disability continues for older Americans. *Proceedings of the National Academy of Sciences (PNAS).* May 8. Cited in National Institutes of Health. Retrieved: May 4, 2004, www.nia.nih.gov/news/pr/2001/0507.htm.

Manton, K. G., & Soldo, B. J. (1992). Disability and mortality among the oldest old: Implications for current and future health and long-term-care service needs. In R. M. Suzman, D. P. Willis, & K. G. Manton (Eds.), *The oldest old* (pp. 199–250). New York: Oxford University Press.

Markides, K. (1987a). Hispanic Americans. In G. L. Maddox (Ed.), *The encyclopedia of aging* (pp. 322–323). New York: Springer.

Markides, K. (1987b). Minorities and aging. In G. L. Maddox (Ed.), *The encyclopedia of aging* (pp. 449–451). New York: Springer.

Markides, K. S. (1983). Minority aging. In M. W. Riley, B. B. Hess, & K. Bond (Eds.), *Aging in society: Selected reviews of recent research* (pp. 115–137). Hillsdale, NJ: Erlbaum.

Markides, K. S., & Coreil, J. (1988). The health status of Hispanic elderly in the Southwest. In S. R. Applewhite (Ed.), *Hispanic elderly in transition: Theory, research, policy and practice* (pp. 35–59). New York: Greenwood Press.

Markides, K. S., Hoppe, S. K., Martin, H. W., & Timbers, D. M. (1983). Sample representativeness in a three generation study of Mexican Americans. *Journal of Marriage and the Family, 45,* 911–916.

Markides, K. S., & Mindel, C. H. (1987). *Aging and ethnicity.* Newbury Park, CA: Sage.

Markides, K. S., Timbers, D. M., & Osberg, J. S. (1984). Aging and health: A longitudinal study. *Archives of Gerontology and Geriatrics, 3,* 33–49.

Markson, E. (1987). Menopause: Psychosocial aspects. In G. L. Maddox (Ed.), *The encyclopedia of aging* (pp. 437–438). New York: Springer.

Marmor, T. R. (2001). How not to think about Medicare reform. *Journal of Health Politics, Policy and Law, 26*(1), 107–117.

Marmor, T. R., Mashaw, J. L., & Harvey, P. L. (1990). Attack on Social Security. In T. R. Marmor, J. L. Mashaw, & P. L. Harvey (Eds.), *America's misunderstood welfare state: Persistent myths, enduring realities* (pp. 128–174). New York: Basic Books.

Marshall, L. J., & Hunt, M. E. (1999). Rural naturally occurring retirement communities: A community assessment procedure. *Journal of Housing for the Elderly, 13*(1-2), 19–34.

Martin, K., & S. Elder. (1993). Pathways through grief: A model of the process. In J. D. Morgan (Ed.), *Personal care in an impersonal world: A multidimensional look at bereavement* (pp. 73–86). Amityville, NY: Baywood.

Martin, L. G., & Kinsella, K. (1994). Research on the demography of aging in developing countries. In L. G. Martin & S. H. Preston (Eds.), *Demography of aging* (pp. 356–397). Washington, DC: National Academy Press.

Martinez, I. L. (2002). Elder in the Cuban American family: Making sense of the real and ideal. *Journal of Comparative Family Studies, 33*(3), 359–375.

Marx, K. (1967, orig. 1867–1895). *Das Kapital.* New York: International Publishers.

Mason, A. (2003). S.E.A.M., Stop Elder Abuse and Mistreatment: A psycho-educational program for abusers of the elderly. *Victimization of the Elderly and Disabled, 5*(5),67.

Masoro, E. J. (2001). Dietary restriction: An experimental approach to the study of the biology of aging. In E. J. Masoro & S. N. Austad, (Eds.), *Handbook of the biology of aging* (5th ed.), (pp. 396–420). San Diego: Academic Press.

Matsuoka, J. K., & Ryujin, D. H. (1989–1990). Vietnamese refugees: An analysis of contemporary adjustment issues. *The Journal of Applied Social Sciences, 14*(1), 23–45.

Matthews, A. (1991). *Widowhood in later life.* Toronto, Ontario: Butterworths.

Matthews, A. M., & Campbell, L. D. (1995). Gender roles, employment and informal care. In S. Arber & J. Ginn (Eds.), *Connecting gender and aging: A sociological approach* (pp. 129–43). Buckingham, UK: Open University Press.

Matthias, R. E., Lubben, J. E., Atchison, K. A., & Schweitzer, S. O. (1997). Sexual activity and satisfaction among very old adults: Results from a community-dwelling Medicare population survey. *The Gerontologist, 37*(1), 6–14.

Mayer, M. (1993). Pensions: The naked truth. *Modern Maturity,* February/March, 40–44.

Mayo Clinic. (1993, February). Sexuality and aging. Mayo Clinic Health Letter.

McAdams, D. P. (1996). Narrating the self in adulthood. In J. E. Birren et al., (Eds), *Aging and biography: Exploration in adult development* (pp. 31–148). New York: Springer.

McAuley, E. (1993). Self-efficacy, physical activity, and aging. In J. R. Kelly (Ed.), *Activity and aging* (pp. 187–205). Newbury Park, CA: Sage.

McAuley, E., Lox, C., & Duncan, T. E. (1993). Long-term maintenance of exercise, self-efficacy, and physiological change in older adults. *Journals of Gerontology, 48*(4), P218–P224.

McAuley, W. J., & Travis, S. S. (2003). Advance care planning among residents in long-term care. *American Journal of Hospice and Palliative Care, 20*(5), 353–359.

McBride, T. D. (1988). *Retirement behavior of women: Findings from the 1982 new beneficiary survey* (Working paper No. 3063-01). Washington, DC: Urban Institute.

McCabe, K., & Gregory, S. S. (1998). Elderly victimization: An examination beyond the FBI's index crimes. *Research on Aging, 20*(3), 363–372.

McCall, N., Petersons, A., Moore, S., & Korb, J. (2003). Utilization of home health sevices before and after the Balanced Budget Act of 1997: What were the initial effects? *Health Services Research, 38*(1, Part 1), 85–106.

McCandless, N. J., & Conner, F. P. (1997). Older women and grief: A new direction for research. *Journal of Women and Aging, 9,* 85–91.

McCrae, R. R., & Costa, P. T., Jr. (1990). *Personality in adulthood.* New York: Guilford.

McDaniel, S. A. (1986). *Canada's aging population.* Toronto: Butterworth.

McDonald, P. L., & Wanner, R. A. (1990). *Retirement in Canada.* Toronto, Ontario: Butterworth.

McElhaney, L. J. (1992, Summer). Dating and courtship in the later years: A neglected topic of research. *Generations,* 21–23.

McFadden, S. H. (1996). Religion, spirituality, and aging. In J. E. Birren & K. W. Schaie (Eds.), *Handbook of the psychology of aging* (4th ed.), (pp. 162–177). San Diego: Academic Press.

McGarry, K., & Schoeni, R. F. (1995). *Transfer behavior within the family: results from the asset and health dynamics survey.* Working Paper No. 5099. Cambridge, MA: National Bureau of Economic Research.

McGough, D. (1993). Housing. In J. F. Van Nostrand (Ed.), *Common beliefs about the rural elderly: What do national data tell us?* Hyattsville, MD: National Center for Health Statistics.

McGuire, F. A., Dottavio, F. D., & O'Leary, J. T. (1987). The relationship of early life experiences to later life leisure involvement. *Leisure Sciences, 9,* 251–257.

McGuire, F. A., O'Leary, J. T., Alexander, P. B., & Dottavio, F. D. (1987). Comparison of outdoor recreation preferences and constraints of black and white elderly. *Activities, Adaptation and Aging, 9*(4), 95–104.

McHugh, K. E. (2000). "Ageless self"? Emplacement of identities in Sun Belt retirement communities. *Journal of Aging Studies, 14*(1), 103–115.

McKee, P., & Barber, C. (1999). On defining wisdom. *International Journal of Aging and Human Development, 49*(2), 149–164.

McKenzie, R. B. (1993). Senior status: Has the power of the elderly peaked? *American Enterprise, 4*(3), 74–80.

McKinlay, J. B. (1985). A case for refocusing upstream: The political economy of illness. In P. Conrad & R. Kern (Eds.), *The sociology of health and illness: Critical perspectives* (pp. 484–498). New York: St. Martin's Press.

McLeod, D. (1995). Fake bank examiners bilk the unsuspecting. *AARP Bulletin, 36*(5), 1, 14.

McLeroy, K. R., & Crump, C. E. (1994, Spring). Health promotion and disease prevention: A historical perspective. *Generations,* 9–17.

McMellon, C. A., & Schiffman, L. G. (2002). Cybersenior empowerment: How some older individuals are taking control of their lives. *Journal of Applied Gerontology, 21*(2), 157–175.

McMullin, J. A., & Marshall, V. W. (1996). Family, friends, stress, and well-being: Does childlessness make a difference? *Canadian Journal on Aging, 15*(3), 355–73.

McNaught, W. (1994). Realizing the potential: Some examples. In M. W. Riley, R. L. Kahn, & A. Foner (Eds.), *Age and structural lag* (pp. 219–236). New York: John Wiley.

McPherson, B. D., & Kozlik, C. A. (1987). Age patterns in leisure participation: The Canadian case. In V. W. Marshall (Ed.), *Aging in Canada: Social perspectives* (2d ed.), (pp. 211–227). Toronto, Ontario: Fitzhenry & Whiteside.

Mead, G. H. (1934). In C. W. Morris (Ed.), *Mind, self, and society: From the standpoint of a social behaviorist.* Chicago: University of Chicago Press.

Medicare. (2004a). *Medicare plan choices.* Retrieved: July 25, 2004, www.medicare.gov/Choices/Overview.asp.

Medicare. (2004b). *Alternatives to nursing home care: About PACE.* Retrieved: February 28, 2004, www.medicare.gov/Nursing/Alternatives/Pace.asp?PrinterFriendly=True.

Medina-Walpole, A., Barker, W. H., & Katz, P. R. (2004). Strengthening the fellowship training experience: findings from a national survey of fellowship trained geriatricians 1990–1998. *Journal of the American Geriatrics Society, 52*(4), 607–610.

MedlinePlus. (2004a). *Medical encyclopedia.* Retrieved: May 7, 2004, www.nlm.nih.gov/medlineplus/ency/article/004013.htm#Information.

MedlinePlus. (2004b). Menopause. *Medical encyclopedia.* Retrieved: May 7, 2004, www.nlm.nih.gov/medlineplus/ency/article/000894.htm#Symptoms.

Meier, E. E., Myers, H., & Muskin, P. R. (1999). When a patient requests help committing suicide. *Generations, 23*(1), 61–68.

Melzer, D., McWilliams, B., Brayne, C., Johnson, T., & Bond, J. (2000). Socioeconomic state and the expectation of disability in old age: Estimates for England. *Journal of Epidemiology and Community Health, 54*(2), 28–92.

Men's Senior Baseball League. (2004). *Home page.* Retrieved: November 24, 2004, www.msblnational.com/.

Mendoza, L. (1981). *The servidor system: Policy implications for the elder Hispano.* San Diego: University Center on Aging, San Diego State University.

Mermelstein, R., Miller, B., Prohaska, T., Benson, V., & Van Nostrand, J. F. (1993). In J. F. Van Nostrand, S. E. Furner, & R. Suzman (Eds.), *Health data on older Americans: United States, 1992* (pp. 9–21). Hyattsville, MD: National Center for Health Statistics.

Merrill, D. M. (1997). *Caring for elderly parents: Juggling work, family, and caregiving in middle and working class families.* Westport, CT: Auburn House.

Metz, M. E., & Miner, M. H. (1998). Psychosexual and psychosocial aspects of male aging and sexual health. *Canadian Journal of Human Sexuality, 7*(3), 245–259.

Meyer, J., & Speare, A. Jr. (1985). Distinctively elderly mobility: Types and determinants. *Economic Geography, 61*(1), 79–88.

Miedema, B., & Tatemichi, S. (2003). Gender, marital status, social networks and health: Their impact on loneliness in the very old. *Geriatrics Today, 6*(2), 95–99.

Milbrath, L. W. (1965). *Political participation: How and why do people get involved in politics?* Chicago: Rand McNally.

Miller, A. M., & Iris, M. (2002). Health promotion attitudes and strategies in older adults. *Health Education and Behavior, 29*(2), 249–267.

Miller, B., Prhoaska, T., Mermelstein, R., & Van Nostrand, J. F. (1993). In J. F. Van Nostrand, S. E. Furner, & R. Suzman (Eds.), *Health data on older Americans: United States, 1992* (pp. 41–75). Hyattsville, MD: National Center for Health Services.

Miller, B. G. (1999). Discontinuities in the statuses of Puget Sound grandmothers. In M. M. Schweitzer (Ed.), *American Indian grandmothers: Traditions and transitions* (pp. 103–124). Albuquerque: University of New Mexico Press.

Miller, J. A. (1991). On Lok Senior Health Services consolidated model of long-term care, San Francisco, California. In J. A. Miller, (Ed.) *Community-based long-term care: Innovative models* (pp. 202–215). Newbury Park, CA: Sage.

Miller, R. B., Hemesath, K., & Nelson, B. (1997). Marriage in middle and later life. In T. D. Hargrave & S. M. Hanna (Eds.), *The aging family: New visions in theory, practice, and reality.* New York: Brunner/Mazel.

Mills, T. L. (1999). When grandchildren grow up: Role transition and family solidarity among baby boomer grandchildren and their grandparents. *Journal of Aging Studies, 13* (2), 219–239.

Miner, S., & Uhlenberg, P. (1997). Intergenerational proximity and the social role of sibling neighbors after midlife. *Family Relations, 46*(2), 145–153.

Minkler, M. (1985). Building supportive ties and sense of community among the inner-city elderly: The Tenderloin Senior Outreach Project. *Health Education Quarterly, 12*(4), 303–314.

Minkler, M. (1991). Generational equity or interdependence? *Generations, 15*(4), 36+.

Minkler, M. (1992). Community organizing among the elderly poor in the United States: A case study. *International Journal of Health Services, 22*(2), 303–316.

Minkler, M. (1999a). Intergenerational households headed by grandparents: Contexts, realities, and implications for policy. *Journal of Aging Studies, 13*(2), 199–218.

Minkler, M. (1999b). Introduction. In M. Minkler, & C. L. Estes (Eds.), *Critical gerontology: Perspectives from political and moral economy* (pp. 1–13). Amityville, NY: Baywood.

Minkler, M., & Estes, C. L. (Eds.). (1999). *Critical gerontology: Perspectives from political and moral economy.* Amityville, NY: Baywood.

Minkler, M., & Roe, K. M. (1993). *Grandmothers as caregivers: Raising children of the crack cocaine epidemic.* Newbury Park, CA: Sage.

Mireles, D. E., & Charness, N. (2002). Computational explorations of the influence of structured knowledge on age-related cognitive decline. *Psychology and Aging, 17*(2), 245–259.

Mitchell, O. S., Levine, P. B., & Pozzebon, S. (1988). Retirement differences by industry and occupation. *The Gerontologist, 28*(4), 545–551.

Moberg, D. O. (1997). Religion and aging. In K. F. Ferraro (Ed.), *Gerontology: Perspectives and issues* (2d ed.), (pp. 193–220). New York: Springer.

Moberg, D. O. (2001). The reality and centrality of spirituality. In D. O. Moberg (Ed.), *Aging and spirituality* (pp. 3–20). New York: The Haworth Press.

Mobily, K. E. (1992). Leisure, lifestyle, and life span. In M. L. Teague & R. D. MacNeil (Eds.), *Aging and leisure: Vitality in later life* (2d ed.), (pp. 179–206). Dubuque, IA: Brown & Benchmark.

Moen, P., & Erickson, M. A. (2001). Decision-making and satisfaction with a continuing care retirement community. In L. A. Pastalan & B. Schwarz (Eds.), *Housing choices and well-being of older adult: Proper fit* (pp. 53–69). New York: Haworth.

Moen, P., Erickson, W. A., Agarwal, M., Fields, V., & Todd, L. (2000). The Cornell Retirement and Well-Being Study. Ithaca, NY: Cornell University.

Molla, M. T., Madans, J. H., Wagener, D. K., & Crimmins, E. M. (2003). *Summary measures of population health: Report of findings on methodologic and data issues.* Hyattsville, MD: National Center for Health Statistics.

Mollica, R. L., & National Academy for State Health Policy (U.S.). (2002). *State assisted living policy 2002.* Portland, ME: National Academy for State Health Policy (US).

Montenegro, X. P., & AARP. Knowledge Management. National Member Research, Knowledge Networks, Inc. (2003). *Lifestyles, dating and romance: A study of midlife singles for AARP The Magazine.* Washington, DC: AARP, Knowledge Management, National Member Research.

Montgomery, A., Barber, C., & McKee, P. (2002). Phenomenological study of wisdom in later life. *International Journal of Aging and Human Development, 54*(2), 139–157.

Moody, H. R. (1976). What philosophical justification is there for educating older adults? *Educational Gerontology, 1,* 1–16.

Moody, H. R. (1988a). *Abundance of life: Human development policies for an aging society.* New York: Columbia University Press.

Moody, H. R. (1988b). Toward a critical gerontology: The contribution of the humanities to theories of aging. In J. E. Birren & V. L. Bengtson (Eds.), *Emergent theories of aging* (pp. 19–40). New York: Springer.

Moody, H. R. (1993). Overview: What is critical gerontology and why is it important? In T. R. Cole, W. A. Achenbaum, P. L. Jakobi, & R. Kastenbaum (Eds.), *Voices and visions of aging* (pp. xv–xli). New York: Springer.

Moore, A. J., & Stratton, D. C. (2002). *Resilient widowers: Older men speak for themselves.* New York: Springer.

Moore, E. G., Rosenberg, M. W., & Fitzgibbon, S. H. (1999). Activity limitations and chronic conditions in Canada's elderly, 1986–2011. *Disability and Rehabilitation, 21*(5–6), 196–210.

Moore, S. T. (1992). Housing policy and the elderly: The case for enriched senior high-rise apartments. *Journal of Housing for the Elderly, 10*(1–2), 117–124.

Morgan, L. A. (1992). Marital status and retirement plans: Do widowhood and divorce make a difference? In M. Szinovacz, D. J. Ekerdt, & B. H. Vinick (Eds.), *Families in retirement* (pp. 114–126). Newbury Park, CA: Sage.

Mori, M. (1991). *Palliative care of the elderly: An overview and annotated bibliography.* Vancouver: Gerontology Research Centre, Simon Fraser University.

Morioka-Douglas, N., & Yeo, G. (1990). *Aging and health: Asian/Pacific Island American elders.* SGEC working paper series, No. 3, Ethnogeriatric reviews. Stanford, CA: Stanford Geriatric Education Center.

Morrell, R. W., Dailey, S. R., & Rousseau, G. K. (2003). Applying research: The NIHSeniorHealth.gov Project. In N. Charness & K. W. Schaie (Eds.), *Impact of technology on successful aging* (pp. 134–161). New York: Springer.

Morrow, D. (2003). Technology as environmental support for older adults' daily activities. In N. Charness & K. W. Schaie (Eds.), *Impact of technology on successful aging* (pp. 290–305). New York: Springer.

Morse, C. K. (1993). Does variability increase with age? An archival study of cognitive measures. *Psychology and Aging, 8*(2), 156–164.

Morton, D. J., Stanford, E. P., Happersett, C. J., & Molgaard, C. A. (1992). Acculturation and functional impairment among older Chinese and Vietnamese in San Diego County, California. *Journal of Cross-Cultural Gerontology, 7,* 151–176.

Moss, M. S., & Moss, S. Z. (1984–1985). Some aspects of the elderly widow(er)'s persistent tie with the deceased spouse. *Omega, 15,* 195–206.

Mueller, K. J. (1993). *Health care policy in the United States.* Lincoln: University of Nebraska Press.

Mui, A. C., & Burnette, D. (1994). Long-term care service use by frail elders: Is ethnicity a factor? *The Gerontologist, 34,* 191–198.

Muller, C., Honig, M., Volkov, O., Oprisiu, A., & Knapp, K. (2002). *Economic status of older women.* New York: International Longevity Center. Retrieved: September 6, 2004, www.ilcusa.org/_lib/pdf/econwomen.pdf.

Murphy, P., Kreling, B., Kathryn, E., Stevens, M., Lynn, J., & Dulac, J. (2000). Description of the SUPPORT intervention. *Journal of the American Geriatrics Society, 48*(5), S154–S161.

Murray, T. M. (1996). Mechanisms of bone loss. *The Journal of Rheumatology, 23*(Suppl.45), 6–10.

Murtaugh, C. M., McCall, N., Moore, S., & Meadow, A. (2003). Trends in Medicare home health care use: 1997–2001. *Health Affairs, 22*(5), 146–156.

Mutschler, P. H. (1992, Spring). Where elders live. *Generations,* 7–14.

Myers, G. C. (1990). Demography of aging. In R. H. Binstock & L. K. George (Eds.), *Handbook of aging and the social sciences* (3d ed.), (pp. 19–44). San Diego: Academic Press.

Myers, J, International Federation on Aging. (1995). Psychological basis for empowerment. In D. Thursz (Ed.), *Empowering older people: An approach* (pp. 111–119). Westport, CT: Auburn House.

Myles, J. (1984). *Old age in the welfare state: The political economy of public pensions.* Boston: Little, Brown.

Myles, J. (1991). Postwar capitalism and the extension of Social Security into a retirement wage. In M. Minkler & C. L. Estes (Eds.), *Critical perspectives on aging: The political and moral economy of growing old* (pp. 293–309). Amityville, NY: Baywood.

Nahmiash, D., & Reis, M. (2000). Most successful intervention strategies for abused older adults. *Journal of Elder Abuse and Neglect, 12*(3–4), 53–70.

National Academy on Aging. (1995a, May). Facts on Social Security: The Old Age and Survivors Trust Fund. *Gerontology News,* 6–7.

National Academy on Aging. (1995b, October). Facts on Medicare: Hospital insurance and supplementary medical insurance. *Gerontology News,* 9–10.

National Advisory Council on Aging. (1993). *The NACA position on the image of aging.* Cat. No. H71-2/5-1993. Ottawa: Minister of Supply and Services.

National Alliance for Caregiving (NAC) & AARP (1997). *Family caregiving in the US: Findings from a national study.* Bethesda, MD: Author.

National Caucus and Center on Black Aged (US). (1998). *Health status of older African Americans.* National Caucus and Center on Black Aged, Washington, DC.

National Center for Health Statistics. (1990, March). *Health, United States, 1989* (DHHS Publication No. PHS 90-1232). Washington, DC: Department of Health and Human Services.

National Center for Health Statistics. (1990, October). Current estimates from the National Health Interview Survey, 1989. *Vital and Health Statistics,* Series 10, No. 176.

National Center for Health Statistics. (1994). *Health, United States, 1993.* Hyattsville, MD: Public Health Service.

National Center for Health Statistics. (2003). *Health, United States, 2003.* Hyattsville, Maryland: NCHS.

National Center for Health Statistics. (2004a). *Diabetes by year, state, sex, race-Hispanic origin, and age 1993–2001 BRFSS (BRD01a).* Retrieved: May 14, 2004, http://209.217.72.34/aging/eng/ReportFolders/Rfview/Explorerp.asp and http://209.217.72.34/aging/eng/TableViewer/wdsview/dispviewp.asp

National Center for Health Statistics. (2004b). *Fast facts A to Z.* Table 96. Nursing home residents 65 years of age and over, according to age, sex, and race: United States, 1973–74, 1985, 1995, and 1999. Retrieved: December 28, 2004, www.cdc.gov/nchs/data/hus/tables/2003/03hus096.pdf.

National Center for Health Statistics. (2004c). *Health, United States, 2004.* With chartbook on trends in the health of Americans. Hyattsville, MD: U.S. Government Printing Office.

National Center on Elder Abuse. (1998). *The National Elder Abuse Incidence Study.* Retrieved: January 7, 2005, www.aoa.gov/eldfam/Elder_Rights/Elder_Abuse/ABuseReport_Full.pdf.

National Committee to Preserve Social Security and Medicare. (1994). *Facts at your fingertips.* Washington, DC: Author.

National Conference of Commissioners on Uniform State Laws. (2004). *Uniform Health-Care Decisions Act.* Retrieved: December 16, 2004, www.law.upenn.edu/bll/ulc/fnact99/1990s/uhcda93.htm.

National Council on Disability. (1993). *Study on the financing of assistive technology devices and services for individuals with disabilities.* Washington, DC.

National Council on the Aging. (2000). *National study says retirement not determined by work status or age.* (May 9). Retrieved: September 18, 2004, www.ncoa.org/content.cfm?sectionID=105&detail=42

National Council on the Aging. (2004). Facts about senior centers. Retrieved: November 24, 2004, www.ncoa.org//content.cfm?sectionID=107.

National Hospice and Palliative Care Organization. (2004). Hospice facts and figures. Retrieved: December 13, 2004, www.nhpco.org/files/public/Hospice_Facts_110104.pdf.

National Institute of Population and Social Security Research (Japan). (2004). Key learning from the 2nd public opinion survey on population issues in Japan. Retrieved: March 15, 2004, www.ipss.go.jp/English/pospi_2nd/chosa.html.

National Institute of Population and Social Security Research. (2002–2003). *Social security in Japan 2002–03.* Retrieved: March 15, 2004, www.ipss.go.jp/English/Jasos2002/Jasos2002.html.

National Institute of Senior Centers & National Council on the Aging. (1993). *Making your voice heard: an advocacy manual for board members and staff of programs and services for older Americans.* Washington, DC: Author.

National Institute on Aging. (1991). *Age page: Hearing and older people.* Washington, DC: Department of Health and Human Services.

National Institute on Aging. (1993). *With the passage of time: The Baltimore Longitudinal Study of Aging.* Washington, DC: Department of Health and Human Services.

National Institute on Aging. (1994). *Age page: Sexuality in later life.* Washington, DC: National Institutes of Health.

National Institute on Aging. (2002). *Diet rich in foods with vitamin E may reduce Alzheimer's disease risk.* NIA News: AD Research Update. June 25. Retrieved May 14, 2004, www.alzheimers.org/nianews/nianews47.html.

National Institute on Aging. (2004). *Hearing loss. Age page. Health information.* Retrieved on April 25, 2004, www.niapublications.org/engagepages/hearing.asp.

National Institutes of Health. (1993). *In search of the secrets of aging.* Washington, DC: Department of Health and Human Services.

National Institutes of Health. (1999). *Vitamin D deficiency may increase risk of hip fracture in older women.* NIH news release. April 27. Retrieved: May 24, 2004, www.nia.nih.gov/news/pr/1999/04%2D27.htm.

National Institutes of Health & National Institute on Aging. (1993). *In search of the secrets of aging.* Washington, DC: Department of Health and Human Services.

National Park Service. (2004). *Golden age passport. Entrance Pass Programs.* Retrieved: November 13, 2004, www.nps.gov/fees_passes.htm.

National Resource Center on Supportive Housing and Home Modification. (2004). *Home modification.* Retrieved: October 2, 2004, www.homemods.org/.

National Senior Games Association. (2004) About the National Senior Games Association. Retrieved: November 24. 2004, www.nsga.com/Merchant2/merchant.mvc?Screen=CTGY&Store_Code=NSGA&Category_Code=AN.

Nedde, E. M. (1993). U.S. health care reform. International Monetary Fund report WP/93/93-EA. Retrieved: August 14, 2004, www.imf.org/external/pubs/cat/doctext.cfm?docno=WPIEA0931993.

Neleski, R. (1995). *A funny thing happened on the way to Elderhostel.* Elderhostel: United States and Canada catalogue, May. Boston: Elderhostel.

Nettelbeck, T., & Rabbitt, P.M.A. (1992). Aging, cognitive performance, and mental speed. *Intelligence, 16*(2), 189–205.

Netting, F. E. (1991). Older women in continuing care retirement communities. *Journal of Women and Aging, 3*(1) 23–35.

Neugarten, B. L. (1964). *Personality in middle and late life.* New York: Atherton.

Neugarten, B. L. (1980). Acting one's age: New rules for old. (Interview with Elizabeth Hall). *Psychology Today,* April, 66–80.

Neugarten, B. L. (1987). Kansas City studies of adult life. In G. L. Maddox (Ed.), *The encyclopedia of aging* (pp. 372–373). New York: Springer.

Neugarten, B. L., Havighurst, R. J., & Tobin, S. (1968). Personality and patterns of aging. In B. L. Neugarten (Ed.), *Middle age and aging.* Chicago: University of Chicago Press.

Neuharth, T. J., & Stern, S. (2000). Shared caregiving responsibilities of adult siblings with elderly parents. Retrieved: November 25, 2004, www.people.virginia.edu/~sns5r/resint/ltcstf/tennille2.pdf.

Neuman, W. L. (2003). *Social research methods: Qualitative and quantitative approaches* (5th ed.). Boston: Allyn & Bacon.

Newcomer, R. J., & Weeden, J. P. (1986). Perspectives on housing needs and the continuum of care. In R. J. Newcomer, M. P. Lawton, & T. O. Byerts (Eds.), *Housing an aging society: Issues, alternatives, and policy* (pp. 3–9). New York: Van Nostrand Reinhold.

Newman, S. (2003). Living conditions of elderly Americans. *The Gerontologist, 43*(1), 99–109.

Nizammudin, M. (2002). World Assembly on Aging adopts comprehensive plan of action. *Population 2005, 4*(2). Retrieved March 20, 2004, www.population2005.org/wopo-003.pdf.

Norris, J. E. (1998). Editorial: A psychology of aging: Who needs it? *Canadian Journal on Aging, 17*(4), i–xi.

Northcott, H. C., & Wilson, D.M. (2001). *Dying and death in Canada.* Aurora, ON: Garamond.

Novack, J. (1991, November 25). Strength from its gray roots. *Forbes,* 148, 89–94.

Novak, M. (1985). *Successful aging: The myths, realities, and future of aging in Canada.* Markham, ON: Penguin.

Novak, M. (1985–1986). Biography after the end of metaphysics. *International Journal of Aging and Human Development, 22*(3), 189–204.

Novak, M., & Chappell, N. L. (1994). Nursing assistant burnout and the cognitively impaired elderly. *International Journal of Aging and Human Development, 39,* 105–120.

Novak, M., & Guest, C. (1989). Application of a multi-dimensional caregiver burden inventory. *The Gerontologist, 29*(6), 798–803.

Novak, M., & Guest, C. (1992). A comparison of the impact of institutionalization on spouse and non-spouse caregivers. *Journal of Applied Gerontology, 11,* 379–394.

Nuttman-Shwartz, O. (2004). Like a high wave: Adjustment to retirement. *The Gerontologist, 44*(2), 229–236.

OASDI Trustees. (2004). *Overview. Highlights. The 2004 Annual Report of the Board of Trustees of the Federal Old-Age and Survivors Insurance and Disability Insurance Trust Funds.* Retrieved: September 11, 2004, www.ssa.gov/OACT/TR/TR04/II_highlights.html#wp 76460.

O'Brien, C., & Goldberg, A. (2000). Lesbians and gay men inside and outside families. In N. Mandell & A. Duffy (Eds.), *Canadian families: Diversity, conflict, and change* (pp. 115–145). Toronto: Harcourt Brace.

O'Brien, M. (1991). Never married older women: The life experience. *Social Indicators Research 24,* 301–315.

O'Brien, S. J., & Conger, P. R. (1991). No time to look back: Approaching the finish line of life's course. *International Journal of Aging and Human Development, 33*(1), 75–87.

O'Brien, S. J., & Vertinsky, P. A. (1991). Unfit survivors: Exercise as a resource for aging women. *The Gerontologist, 31,* 347–357.

O'Bryant, S. L. (1991a). Forewarning of a husband's death: Does it make a difference for older widows? *Omega: Journal of Death and Dying, 22*(3), 227–239.

O'Bryant, S. L. (1991b). Older widows and independent lifestyles. *International Journal of Aging and Human Development, 32*(1), 41–51.

O'Connor, B. P. (1995). Family and friend relationships among older and younger adults: Interaction motivation, mood, and quality. *International Journal of Aging and Human Development, 40*(1), 9–29.

O'Connor, D. (1999). Living with a memory-impaired spouse: (Re)cognizing the experience. *Canadian Journal on Aging, 18*(2), 211–35.

O'Grady, L. R. (1993). Changes in the lives of women and their families: Have old age pensions kept pace? *Generations, 17*(4), 27–31.

O'Rand, A. M. (1987). Employee Retirement Income Security Act. In G. L. Maddox (Ed.), *The encyclopedia of aging* (pp. 205–206). New York: Springer.

Older Women's League. (1993). *Room for improvement: The lack of affordable, adaptable and accessible housing for midlife and older women.* Washington, DC: Author.

Olshansky, S. J., Rudberg, M. A., Carnes, B. A., Casse, C. A., & Brody, J. A. (1991). Trading off longer life for worsening health: The expansion of morbidity hypothesis. *Journal of Aging and Health, 3,* 194–216.

On Lok SeniorHealth. (2004). *Our vision.* Retrieved: August 14, 2004, www.onlok.org/content.asp?catid=240000182&scatid=240000189.

Online Dictionary of the Social Sciences. (2004). *Social institutions.* Retrieved: December 17, 2004, http://bitbucket.icaap.org/dict.pl?action=about.

Oriol, W. (1993). Older drivers: Keep 'em rolling (safely). *Perspective on Aging, 22*(3), 4–11.

Oriol, W. E. (1987). Government programs: Federal. In G. L. Maddox (Ed.), *The encyclopedia of aging* (pp. 290–294). New York: Springer.

Orsega-Smith, E., Payne, L. L., & Godbey, G. (2003). Physical and psychosocial characteristics of older adults who participate in a community-based exercise program. *Journal of Aging and Physical Activity, 11*(4), 516–531.

Orzechowski, S., & Sepielli, P. (2003). *Net worth and asset ownership of households: 1998 and 2000. Household Economic Studies.* Washington, DC: U.S. Census Bureau. Retrieved: September 5, 2004, www.census.gov/prod/2003pubs/p70-88.pdf.

Osgood, N. J., Brant, B. A., & Lipman, A. (1991). *Suicide among the elderly in long-term care facilities.* New York: Greenwood.

Ostbye, T., & Taylor, D. H., Jr. (2004). Effect of smoking on Years of Healthy Life (YHL) lost among middle-aged and older Americans. *Health Services Research, 39*(3), 531–551.

Ostrom, C. M. (2000, May 14). The war on pain; Oregon leads the nation in push to improve quality of life for chronically ill and dying patients. *Seattle Times.* Retrieved: December 16, 2004, http://archives.seattletimes

.nwsource.com/cgi-bin/texis.cgi/web/vortex/display?slug=4021141&date=20000514&query=ostrom

Otto, J. (2000). The role of adult protective services in addressing abuse. *Generations, 24,* 33–38.

Ovrebo, B., & Minkler, M. (1993). The lives of older women: Perspectives from political economy and the humanities. In T. R. Cole, W. A. Achenbaum, P. L. Jakobi, & R. Kastenbaum (Eds.), *Voices and visions of aging: Toward a critical gerontology* (pp. 289–308). New York: Springer.

Owen, J. E., Goode, K. T., & Haley, W. E. (2001). End of life care and reactions to death in African-American and white family caregivers of relatives with Alzheimer's disease. *Omega: Journal of Death and Dying, 43*(4), 349–361.

Padgett, D. (1989). Editorial. Aging minority women: Issues in research and health policy. In L. Grau (Ed.), *Women in the later years: Health, social, and cultural perspectives* (pp. 213–225). Binghamton, NY: Haworth.

Pagan, J. (2002). Home care comes of age. *Contemporary Long Term Care, 25*(5),12.

Palmer, J. L., & Saving, T. R. (2004). *Status of the Social Security and Medicare programs. A summary of the 2004 Annual Reports.* Social Security and Medicare Boards of Trustees. Retrieved: September 11, 2004, www.ssa.gov/OACT/TRSUM/trsummary.html.

Palmore, E. B. (1977). Facts on aging: A short quiz. *The Gerontologist, 18,* 315–320.

Palmore, E. B. (1981). The facts on aging quiz: Part two. *The Gerontologist, 21,* 431–437.

Palmore, E. B. (1987). Centenarians. In G. L. Maddox (Ed.), *The encyclopedia of aging* (pp. 107–108). New York: Springer.

Palmore, E. B. (1998). *Facts on aging quiz* (2d ed.). Springer: New York.

Palmore, E. B. (2001). Ageism survey: First findings. *The Gerontologist, 41*(5), 572–575.

Pardasani, M. P. (2004). Senior centers: Increasing minority participation through diversification. *Journal of Gerontological Social Work, 43*(2-3), 41–56.

Park, D. C. (2000). The basic mechanisms accounting for age-related decline in cognitive function. In D. C. Park & N. Schwarz (Eds.), *Cognitive aging: A primer* (pp. 3–21). Philadelphia: Taylor and Francis.

Park, D. C., & Gutchess, A. H. (2000). Cognitive aging and everyday life. In D. C. Park & N. Schwarz (Eds.), *Cognitive aging: A primer* (pp. 217–232). Philadelphia: Taylor and Francis.

Parks, A. G. (1988). *Black elderly in rural America: A comprehensive study.* Bristol, IN: Wyndham Hall.

Parmelee, P. A., & Lawton, M. P. (1990). The design of special environments for the aged. In J. E. Birren & K. W. Schaie (Eds.), *Handbook of the psychology of aging* (3d ed.), (pp. 464–488). San Diego: Academic Press.

Parsons, T. (1951). *The social system.* New York: Free Press.

Passuth, P. M., & Bengtson, V. L. (1988). Sociological theories of aging: Current perspectives and future directions. In J. E. Birren & V. L. Bengtson (Eds.), *Emergent theories of aging* (pp. 334–355). New York: Springer.

Patterson, J. (1996). Participation in leisure activities by older adults after a stressful life event: The loss of a spouse. *International Journal of Aging and Human Development, 42,* 123–142.

Paxton, S. J., Browning, C. J., & O'Connell, G. (1997). Predictors of exercise program participation in older women. *Psychology and Health, 12,* 543–552.

Pearman, A., & Storandt, M. (2004). Predictors of subjective memory in older adults. *The Journals of Gerontology Series B: Psychological Sciences and Social Sciences, 59,* P4–P6.

Peck, R. C. [1955] (1968). Psychological aspects of aging. In J. E. Anderson (Ed.), *Proceedings of a conference on planning research, Bethesda, MD, April 24–27, 1955.* Washington, DC: American Psychological Association. Excerpted in Psychological developments in the second half of life, in B. L. Neugarten (Ed.), *Middle age and aging.* Chicago: University of Chicago Press, 1968.

Peek, M. K., Coward, R. T., & Peek, C. W. (2000). Race, aging, and care. *Research on Aging, 22*(2), 117–142.

Penman, S. (2000). *Honor the grandmothers.* St. Paul, MN: Minnesota Historical Society.

Penning, M., & Wasyliw, D. (1992). Homebound learning opportunities: Reaching out to older shut-ins and their caregivers. *The Gerontologist, 32,* 704–707.

Penning, M. J. (1990). Receipt of assistance by elderly people: Hierarchical selection and task specificity. *The Gerontologist, 30,* 220–227.

Penning, M. J. (1998) In the middle: Parental caregiving in the context of other roles. *Journals of Gerontology Series B, 53*(4), S188–97.

Penning, M. J. (2002). Hydra revisited: Substituting formal for self- and informal in-home care among older adults with disabilities. *The Gerontologist, 42*(1), 4–16.

Pennington, H. R., Pachana, N. A., & Coyle, S. L. (2001). Use of the Facts on Aging Quiz in New Zealand: Validation of questions, performance of a student sample, and effects of a don't know option. *Educational Gerontology 27*(5), 409–416.

Penninx, B., Leveille, S., Ferrucci, L., van Eijk, J., & Guralnik, J. (1999). Exploring the effect of depression on physical disability: Longitudinal evidence from the Established Populations for Epidemiologic Studies of the Elderly. *American Journal of Public Health, 89,* 1346–1352.

Pentland, A. (2003). Take two cell phones and call me in the morning: A glimpse into the future of health care technology. *Caring, 22*(3), 8–10.

Pepe, M. V., & Gandee, R. F. (1992). Ohio Senior Olympics: Creating the new adult image. In S. Harris, R. Harris, & W. S. Harris, (Eds.), *Physical activity, aging and sports: Practice, program and policy. Vol. II* (pp. 192–198). Albany, NY: Center for the Study of Aging.

Perfect, T. J., & Dasgupta, Z. R. R. (1997). What underlies the deficit in reported recollective experience in old Age?" *Memory and Cognition 25*(6), 849–58.

Perkins, K. (1993). Recycling poverty: From the workplace to retirement. *Journal of Women and Aging, 5*(1), 5–23.

Peters, A., & Liefbroer, A.C. (1997). Beyond marital status: Partner history and well-being in old age. *Journal of Marriage and the Family, 59*(3), 687–699.

Peterson, C. C. (1993). Adult children and their parents. In R. Kastenbaum (Ed.), *Encyclopedia of adult development* (pp. 1–6). Phoenix, AZ: Oryx.

Peterson, D. A. (1985). Employment experience of gerontology master's degree graduates. *The Gerontologist, 25*(5), 514–519.

Peterson, D. A. (1987). *Career paths in the field of aging: Professional gerontology.* Lexington, MA: Lexington Books.

Peterson, D. A. (1990). Personnel to serve the aging in the field of social work: Implications for educating professionals. *Social Work, 35*(5), 412–415.

Peterson, D. A., Wendt, P. F., & Douglass, E. B. (1991). *Determining the impact of gerontology preparation on personnel in the aging network: A national survey.* Washington, DC: Association for Gerontology in Higher Education.

Peterson, D. A., Wendt, P. F., & Douglass, E. B. (1994). *Development of gerontology, geriatrics, and aging studies programs in institutions of higher education.* Washington, DC: Association for Gerontology in Higher Education.

Phillipson, C. (1999). The social construction of retirement: Perspectives from critical theory and political economy. In M. Minkler & C. L. Estes (Eds.), *Critical gerontology: Perspectives from political and moral economy* (pp. 315–327). Amityville, NY: Baywood.

Pienta, A. M., & Hayward, M. D. (2002). Who expects to continue working after age 62? The retirement plans of couples. *The Journals of Gerontology Series B: Psychological Sciences and Social Sciences, 57,* S199–S208.

Pieper, H. G., & Petkovsek, L. A. (1991). Remarriage among the elderly: Characteristics relevant to pastoral counseling. *Journal of Religious Gerontology, 8*(2), 1–9.

Pierce, T., Lydon, J. E. & Yang, S. (2001). Enthusiasm and moral commitment: What sustains family caregivers of those with dementia. *Basic and Applied Social Psychology 23*(1), 29–41.

Pillemer, K., & Finkelhor, D. (1988). The prevalence of elder abuse: A random sample survey. *The Gerontologist, 28*(1), 51–57.

Pittaway, E., & Gallagher, E. (1995). *A guide to enhancing services for abused older Canadians.* Victoria, BC: Centre on Aging, University of Victoria.

Ploeg, J., Campbell, L. D., Denton, M., Joshi, A., & Davies, S. (2003). *Helping to build and rebuild secure lives and futures: Intergenerational financial transfers from parents to adult children and grandchildren.* SEDAP Research Paper No. 96. Hamilton, ON: McMaster University.

Plonczynski, D. J. (2003). Physical activity determinants of older women: What influences activity? *Medical Surgical Nursing, 12*(4), 213–223.

Podolsky, D. (1992, December 21). Health: Is Grandpa malnourished? *U.S. News and World Report,* 99–100.

Polacca, M. (2001). American Indian and Alaska Native elderly. In L. K. Olson (Ed.), *Age through ethnic lenses: Caring for the elderly in a multicultural society* (pp. 113–122). London: Rowman & Littlefield.

Polich, C. L. (1989). *Case management for long-term care: A review of experience and potential.* Report prepared for InterStudy. Excelsior: Minnesota.

Pollak, P. B., & Gorman, A. N. (1989). *Community-based housing for the elderly: A zoning guide for planners and municipal officials.* Chicago, IL: American Planning Association.

Poon, L. W. (1985). Differences in human memory with aging: Nature, causes, and clinical implications. In J. E. Birren & K. W. Schaie (Eds.), *Handbook of the psychology of aging* (2d ed.). New York: Van Nostrand.

Powers, E. A., & Kivett, V. R. (1992). Kin expectations and kin support among rural older adults. *Rural Sociology, 57*(2), 194–215.

Pratt, H. J. (1976). *The gray lobby.* Chicago: University of Chicago Press.

Pratt, H. J. (1983). National interest groups among the elderly: Consolidation and constraint. In W. P. Browne

& L. K. Olson (Eds.), *Aging and public policy: The politics of growing old in America* (pp. 145–179). Westport, CT: Greenwood.

Prentis, R. S. (1992). *Passages of retirement: Personal histories of struggle and success.* New York: Greenwood.

Presbyterian SeniorCare. (2004). *Alzheimer's care.* Retrieved: December, 31, 2004, www.srcare.org/pages/livingCare/alzheimerscare.cfm.

Preston, S. H. (1993). Demographic change in the United States, 1970–2050. In A. M. Rappaport & S. J. Schieber (Eds.), *Demography and retirement: The twenty-first century* (pp. 19–71). Westport, CT: Praeger.

Preston, S. H., Himes, C., & Eggers, M. (1988). Demographic conditions responsible for population aging. Paper presented at the annual meeting of the Population Association of America, New Orleans, LA.

Price, C.A. (2003). Professional women's retirement adjustment: The experience of reestablishing order. *Journal of Aging Studies, 17*(3), 341–355.

Proctor, B. D., & Dalaker, J. (2003). *U.S. Census Bureau, Current Population Reports, P60-222, Poverty in the United States: 2002.* Washington, DC: U.S. Government Printing Office. Retrieved: September 4, 2004, www.census.gov/prod/2003pubs/p60-222.pdf.

Prohaska, T., Mermelstein, R., Miller, B., & Jack, S. (1993). Functional status and living arrangements. In J. F. Van Nostrand, S. E. Furner, & R. Suzman (Eds.), *Health data on older Americans: United States, 1992* (pp. 23–39). Hyattsville, MD: National Center for Health Services.

Pruchno, R. A., & Rose, M. S. (2002). Time use by frail older people in different care settings. *Journal of Applied Gerontology, 21*(1), 5–23.

Prull, M. W., Gabrieli, J. D. E., & Bunge, S. A. (2000). Age-related changes in memory: A cognitive neuroscience perspective. In F. I. M. Craik & T. A. Salthouse (Eds.), *The handbook of aging and cognition* (2d ed.), (pp. 91–153). Mahwah, NJ: Lawrence Erlbaum.

Pumping iron keeps granny going strong: Payoff is better bones, balance. (1994). *Winnipeg Free Press,* December 28, p. A8.

Puner, M. (1979). *Vital maturity.* New York: Universe Books.

Purnell, M., & Bagby, B. H. (1993). Grandparents' rights: Implications for family specialists. *Family Relations, 42*(2), 173–178.

Pynoos, J., Hamburger, L., & Arlyne, J. (1990). Supportive relationships in shared housing. *Journal of Housing for the Elderly, 6*(1–2), 1–24.

Quadagno, J. (1991). Generational equity and the politics of the welfare state. In B. B. Hess & E. W. Markson (Eds.), *Growing old in America* (4th ed.), (pp. 341–351). New Brunswick, NJ: Transaction.

Quadagno, J., & Reid, J. (1999). The political economy perspective in aging. In V. L. Bengtson & K. W. Schaie (Eds.), *Handbook of theories of aging* (pp. 344–358). New York: Springer.

Qualls, S. J. (2002, Spring). Defining mental health in later life. *Generations,* 9–13.

Quam, J. K., & Whitford, G. S. (1992). Adaptation and age-related expectations of older gay and lesbian adults. *The Gerontologist, 32*(3), 367–374.

Quetelet, L. A. J. (1835). *Sur l'homme el le developpement de ses facultes.* Bruxelles, L. Hauman et compe., 1936.

Quinn, J. F., & Burkhauser, R. V. (1990). Work and retirement. In R. H. Binstock & L. K. George (Eds.), *Handbook of aging and the social sciences* (3d ed.), (pp. 307–327). San Diego: Academic Press.

Quinn, J. F., Burkhauser, R. V., & Myers, D. A. (1990). *Passing the torch: The influence of economic incentives on work and retirement.* Kalamazoo, MI: W. E. Upjohn Institute for Employment Research.

Quinn, J. L. (1987). Home health care. In G. L. Maddox (Ed.), *The encyclopedia of aging* (pp. 324–325). New York: Springer.

Quinn, J. F., & Kozy, M. (1996). Role of bridge jobs in the retirement transition: Gender, race, and ethnicity. *The Gerontologist, 36*(3), 363–372.

Quinn, M. J., & Tomita, S. K. (1997). *Elder abuse and neglect: Causes, diagnosis, and intervention strategies* (2d ed.). New York: Springer.

Quirk, D. A. (1991, Summer/Fall). An agenda for the nineties and beyond. *Generations,* 23–26.

Quirouette, C. C., & Pushkar, D. (1999). Views of future aging among middle-aged, university educated women. *Canadian Journal on Aging, 18*(2), 236–258.

Ragan, A. M., & Bowen, A. M. (2001). Improving attitudes regarding the elderly population: The effects of information and reinforcement for change. *The Gerontologist, 41*(4), 511–515.

Rahder, B., Farge, B., & Todres, R. (1992). Review of the Canadian and American literature on homesharing agencies with a service component. *Home Health Care Services Quarterly, 13*(1–2), 71–90.

Rajnes, D. (2002). An evolving pension system: Trends in defined benefit and defined contribution plans. *EBRI Issue Brief No. 249* (September). Washington, DC: Employee Benefit Research Institute.

Ralston, P. A. (1993). Health promotion for rural black elderly: A comprehensive review. *Journal of Gerontological Social Work, 20*(1–2), 53–78.

Ramsey-Klawsnik, H. (2004). Clinical practice: Investigating alleged victimization. *Victimization of the Elderly and Disabled, 7*(2), 17+.

Rathbone-McCuan, E. (1996). Self-neglect in the elderly: Knowing when and how to intervene. *Aging, 367,* 44–49.

Ray, R. O., & Heppe, G. (1986). Older adult happiness: The contributions of activity breadth and intensity. *Physical and Occupational Therapy in Geriatrics, 4*(4), 31–43.

Ray, R. E. (2003). Uninvited guest: Mother/daughter conflict in feminist gerontology. *Journal of Aging Studies, 17*(1), 113–128.

Rayman, P., Allshouse, K., & Allen J. (1993). Resiliency amidst inequity: Older women workers in an aging United States. In J. Allen & A. Pifer (Eds.), *Women on the front lines: Meeting the challenge of an aging America* (pp. 133–166). Washington, DC: Urban Institute Press.

Raz, N. (2000). Aging of the brain and Its impact on cognitive performance: Integration of structural and functional findings." In F. I. M. Craik & T. A. Salthouse (Eds.), *The handbook of aging and cognition* (2d ed.), (pp. 1–90). Mahwah, NJ: Lawrence Erlbaum Associates.

Reed, W. L. (1990). Health care needs and services. In Z. Harel, E. A. McKinney, & M. Williams (Eds.), *Black aged: Understanding diversity and service needs* (pp. 183–204). Newbury Park, CA: Sage.

Regnier, V. (2003). Purpose-built housing and home adaptations for older adults: The American perspective. In K. W. Schaie, H-W. Wahl, H. Mollenkopf, & F. Oswald (Eds.), *Aging independently: Living arrangements and mobility* (pp. 99–117). New York: Springer.

Regnier, V. A. (1993). Innovative concepts in assisted housing. *Ageing International,* June, 46–51.

Reker, G. T., & Wong, P. T. P. (1988). Aging as an individual process: Toward a theory of personal meaning. In J. E. Birren & V. L. Bengtson (Eds.), *Emergent theories of aging* (pp. 214–246). New York: Springer.

Rendell, P. G., & Thomson, D. M. (2002). Aging and prospective memory: Differences between naturalistic and laboratory tasks. *The Journals of Gerontology Series B: Psychological Sciences and Social Sciences, 57,* P3–P10.

Research and Policy Development. (1994, January). *Private pensions. Viewpoint.* Washington, DC: National Committee to Preserve Social Security and Medicare.

Reynolds, C. (2004). Boomers, act II. *American Demographics, 26*(8), 10–11.

Rich, M. L. (1999). PACE model: Description and impressions of a capitated model of long-term care for the elderly. *Care Management Journals, 1*(1), 62–70.

Rich, S. (1991). 900,000 could need long-term care. *Washington Post,* March 8, 2.

Richardson, H. (1990). Long-term care. In A. R. Kovner (Ed.), *Health care delivery in the United States* (4th ed.), (pp. 175–208). New York: Springer.

Richardson, N. R., & Harrington, H. C. (1993). Cost-effective self-care strategies for retirees. *Generations, 17*(3), 15–18.

Richardson, V., & Kilty, K. M. (1989). Retirement financial planning among black professionals. *The Gerontologist, 29*(1), 32–37.

Richardson, V., & Kilty, K. M. (1992). Retirement intentions among black professionals: Implications for practice with older black adults. *The Gerontologist, 32*(1), 7–16.

Richardson, V. E. (1999). Women and retirement. *Journal of Women and Aging, 11*(2/3), 49–66.

Richman, J. (1992). Rational approach to rational suicide. *Suicide and Life Threatening Behavior, 22*(1), 130–141.

Riegel, K. F. (1976). The dialectics of human development. *American Psychologist, 31,* 698–700.

Riegel, K. F. (1979). *Foundations of dialectical psychology.* New York: Academic Press.

Riley, M. W. (1971). Social gerontology and the age stratification of society. *The Gerontologist, 11,* 79–87.

Riley, M. W. (1985). Age strata in social systems. In R. H. Binstock & E. Shanas (Eds.), *Handbook of aging and the social sciences* (2d ed.), (pp. 369–411). New York: Van Nostrand.

Riley, M. W. (1987). On the significance of age in sociology. *American Sociological Review 52,* 1–14.

Riley, M. W., Foner, A., & Riley, J. W. Jr. (1999). The aging and society paradigm. In V. L. Bengtson & K. W. Schaie (Eds.), *Handbook of theories of aging* (pp. 327–343). New York: Springer.

Riley, M. W., Foner, A., & Waring, J. (1988). Sociology of age. In J. J. Smelser (Ed.), *Handbook of sociology* (pp. 243–290). Newbury Park, CA: Sage.

Riley, M. W., Johnson, M. E., & Foner, A. (Eds.). (1972). *Aging and society. Vol. III: A sociology of age stratification.* New York: Russell Sage Foundation.

Riley, M. W., & Riley, J. W., Jr. (1994). Structural lag: Past and future. In M. W. Riley, R. L. Kahn, & A. Foner

(Eds.), *Age and structural lag* (pp. 15–36). New York: John Wiley.

Rivas, E. E., & Torres-Gil, F. M. (1991). Politics, diversity, and minority aging: A delicate balance is required. *Generations, 15*(4), 47–51.

Rivlin, A. M., & Wiener, J. M. (1988). *Caring for the disabled elderly: Who will pay?* Washington, DC: Brookings Institution.

Rix, S. E. (1990). Who pays for what? Ensuring financial security in retirement. In C. L. Hayes & J. M. Deren (Eds.), *Pre-retirement planning for women: Program design and research* (pp. 5–26). New York: Springer.

Rix, S. E. (1993). Women and well-being in retirement: What role for public policy? *Journal of Women and Aging, 4*(4), 37–56.

Rix, S. E. (2002). The labor market for older workers. *Generations, 26*(2), 25–30.

Rix, S. E. (2004). *Aging and work: A view from the United States.* Washington, DC: AARP Public Policy Institute. Retrieved: September 17, 2004, http://research.aarp.org/econ/2004_02_work.pdf

Roberto, K. A., & McGraw, S. (1990). Educational programs for older adults: Course selection and motivational factors. *Gerontology and Geriatrics Education, 10,* 37–48.

Roberto, K. A., Teaster, P. B., & Duke, J. O. (2004). Older women who experience mistreatment: Circumstances and outcomes. *Journal of Women and Aging, 16*(1-2), 3–16.

Roberts, E., Takenaka, J. I., Ross, C. J., Chong, E. H., & Tulang, J. I. (1989). Hawaii Asian-American response to the Staying Healthy After Fifty program. *Health Education Quarterly, 16*(4), 509–527.

Robertson, I. (1987). *Sociology* (3d ed.). New York: Worth.

Robinson, J. P. (1991). Quitting time. *American Demographics, 13*(5), 34–36.

Robinson, R. (1993). How to age gracefully: An 89-year-old's primer. *New York Times,* February 28.

Robinson, T., Popovich, M., Gustafson, R., & Fraser, C. (2003). Older adults' perceptions of offensive senior stereotypes in magazine advertisements: Results of a Q method analysis. *Educational Gerontology, 29*(6), 503–519.

Roe, K. M., & Minkler, M. (1998). Grandparents raising grandchildren: Challenges and responses. *Generations, 22*(4), 25–32.

Roff, S. (2001). Suicide and the elderly: Issues for clinical practice. *Journal of Gerontological Social Work, 35*(2), 21–36.

Rogers, W. A., & Fisk, A. D. (2003). Technology design, usability, and aging: Human factors techniques and considerations. In N. Charness & K.W. Schaie (Eds.), *Impact of technology on successful aging* (pp. 1–14). New York: Springer.

Romore, T. I., & Blekeseaune, M. (2003). Trajectories of disability among the oldest old. *Journal of Aging and Health, 15*(3), 548–566.

Rones, P. L., & Herz, D. E. (1989). *Labor market problems of older workers.* Washington, DC: U.S. Department of Labor.

Ronkin, R. (1989). Maintaining independence and privacy through home equity conversion. *Ageing International, 16*(1), 40–42.

Rooney, E. M. (1993). Exercise for older patients: Why it's worth your effort. *Geriatrics, 48*(11), 68+.

Rose, A. M. (1965). The subculture of aging: A framework for research in social gerontology. In J. S. Quadagno (Ed.), *Aging, the individual and society* (pp. 73–86). New York: St. Martin's Press.

Rose, M. R. (1991). *Evolutionary biology of aging.* New York: Oxford University Press.

Rose, M. R. (1993). Evolutionary gerontology and critical gerontology: Let's just be friends. In T. R. Cole, W. A. Achenbaum, P. L. Jakobi, & R. Kastenbaum (Eds.), *Voices and visions of aging: Toward a critical gerontology* (pp. 64–75). New York: Springer.

Rosenbaum, W. A., & Button, J. W. (1989). Is there a gray peril? Retirement politics in Florida. *The Gerontologist, 29*(3), 300–306.

Rosenbaum, W. A., & Button, J. W. (1993). Unquiet future of intergenerational politics. *The Gerontologist, 33*(4), 481–490.

Rosenblatt, R. (1995). The WHCOA and lower expectations. *Aging Today, 16*(2), 2.

Rosenbloom, C. A., & Whittington, F. J. (1993). Effects of bereavement on eating behaviors and nutrient intakes in elderly widowed persons. *Journals of Gerontology, 48*(4), S223–S229.

Rosenmayr, L. (1987). On freedom and aging: An interpretation. *Journal of Aging Studies, 1,* 299–316.

Rosenmayr, L., & Kockeis, E. (1963). Propositions for a sociological theory of aging and the family. *International Social Science Journal, 15,* 410–426.

Rosenthal, C. J. (1994). Editorial: Long-term care reform and 'family' care: A worrisome combination. *Canadian Journal on Aging, 13*(3), 419–427.

Rosenthal, C. J., & Dawson, P. (1991). Wives of institutionalized elderly men: The first stage of the transition to quasi-widowhood. *Journal of Aging and Health, 3*(3), 315–334.

Rosenzweig, R. M. (1991). Generational conflict brewing, GSA members warned. *Gerontology News,* January.

Rosow, I. (1965). And then we were old. *Transaction, 2,* 20–26.

Rosow, W. W. (1978). *The world economy: History and prospect.* Austin: University of Texas Press.

Ross, I. (1995, May). Step aside, yuppies. Here come "opals." *Elderhostel: United States and Canada catalogue.* Boston: Elderhostel.

Ross, J. L., & Upp, M. M. (1993). Treatment of women in the U.S. Social Security system, 1970–1988. *Social Security Bulletin 56,* (Fall), 56–67.

Ross, M. M., & McDonald, B. (1994). Providing palliative care to older adults: Context and challenges. *Journal of Palliative Care, 10*(4), 5–10.

Ross, M. M., MacLean, M. J., Cain, R., Sellick, S., & Fisher, R. (2002). End of life care: The experience of seniors and informal caregivers. *Canadian Journal on Aging, 21*(1), 137–146.

Ross, M. M., Rosenthal, C. J., & Dawson, P. (1994). The continuation of caregiving following the institutionalization of elderly husbands. In National Advisory Council on Aging, *Marital disruption in Later Life,* 23–32. Cat. No. H71-3/17-1994E. Ottawa: Minister of Supply and Services.

Ross, M. M., Rosenthal, C. J., & Dawson, P. G. (1997a). Spousal caregiving in the institutional setting: Task performance. *Canadian Journal on Aging, 16*(1), 51–69.

Ross, M. M., Rosenthal, C. J., & Dawson, P. G. (1997b). Spousal caregiving in the institutional setting: Visiting. *Journal of Clinical Nursing, 6*(6), 473–483.

Rothman, M. L., Hedrick, S. C., Bulcroft, K. A., Erdly, W. W., & Nickinovich, D. G. (1993). Effects of VA adult day health care on health outcomes and satisfaction with care. *Medical Care, 31*(9, Suppl.), SS38–SS49.

Rotstein, G. (2004). A pearl for the elderly. *Pittsburgh Post-Gazette.* Retrieved: October 2, 2004, www.post-gazette.com/pg/04095/295927.stm.

Rovin, S., & Boniface, Z. (1988). Health promotion and prevention: A Medicare issue. In M. V. Pauly & W. L. Kissick (Eds.), *Lessons from the first twenty years of Medicare* (pp. 357–371). Philadelphia: University of Pennsylvania Press.

Rovner, J. (1995, June). Ending the great terror of life. *AARP Bulletin: Special Report,* 1ff.

Rowe, J. W., & Kahn, R. L. (1991). Human aging: Usual and successful. In Harold Cox (Ed.), *Aging* (7th ed.). Guilford, CT: Dushkin. [Originally published in Science 237 (1987): 143–149.]

Rowe, J. W., & Kahn, R. L. (1998). *Successful aging.* New York: Dell.

Rubinstein, R. L. (1996). Childless, legacy, and generativity. *Generations, 20*(3), 58–60.

Rudinger, G., & Jansen, E. (2003). Self-initiated compensations among older drivers. In K. W. Schaie, H-W. Wahl, H. Mollenkopf, & F. Oswald. (Eds.), *Aging independently: Living arrangements and mobility* (pp. 220–233). New York: Springer.

Ruggles, S. (2000). Living arrangements and well-being of older persons in the past. Paper presented at the Technical Meeting on Population Ageing and Living Arrangements of Older Persons: Critical issues and policy responses. Population Division, Department of Economic and Social Affairs, United Nations Secretariat, New York, February 8–10.

Ruhm, C. (1991). *Bridge employment and job stopping in the 1980s* (American Over 55 at Work Program, Background Paper Series, No. 3). New York: Commonwealth Fund.

Ruhm, C. J. (1989). Why older Americans stop working. *The Gerontologist, 29*(3), 294–299.

Rural Development Rural Housing Service. (2004). *Rural housing options for elderly people.* Retrieved: October 2, 2004, www.rurdev.usda.gov/rd/pubs/pa1662.htm.

Russell, C. (1999). Interviewing vulnerable old people: Ethical and methodological implications of imagining our subjects. *Journal of Aging Studies, 13*(4), 403–417.

Ruth, J., & Coleman, P. (1996). Personality and aging: Coping and management of the self in later life. In J. E. Birren & K.W. Schaie (Eds.), *Handbook of the psychology of aging* (4th ed.), (pp. 308–322). San Diego: Academic Press.

Ryan, A., Carter, J., Lucas, J., & Berger, J. (2002). You need not make the journey alone: Overcoming impediments to providing palliative care in a public urban teaching hospital. *American Journal of Hospice and Palliative Care, 19*(3), 171–180.

Rybarski, M. (2004). Boomers after all is said and done: A generation that rewrites all the rules takes on death. *American Demographics, 16*(5), 32–34.

Rybash, J. M., Hoyer, W. J., & Roodin, P. A. (1986). Adult cognition and aging: Developmental changes in processing, knowing and thinking. New York: Pergamon.

Ryff, C., & Keyes, C. L. (1996). The structure of psychological well-being revisited. *Journal of Personality and Social Psychology, 69,* 719–727.

Ryff, C. D., Kwan, C. M. L., & Singer, B. H. (2001). Personality and aging: Flourishing agendas and future challenges. In J. E. Birren & K. W. Schaie (Eds.), *Handbook of the psychology of aging* (5th ed.), (pp. 477–499). San Diego: Academic Press.

Ryff, C. D., Magee, W. J., Kling, K. C., & Wing, E. H. (1999). Forging macro-micro linkages in the study of psychological well-being. In C.D. Ryff & V. W. Marshall (Eds.). *The self and society in aging processes* (pp. 247–278). New York: Springer.

Sabin, E. P. (1993). Frequency of senior center use: A preliminary test of two models of senior center participation. *Journal of Gerontological Social Work, 20*(1–2), 97–114.

Salholz, E., Clift, E., Thomas, R., & Bingham, C. (1990). Blaming the voters. *Newsweek,* October 29, 36.

Salthouse, T. A., & Craik, F. I. M. (2000). Closing comments. In F. I. M. Craik & T. A. Salthouse (Eds.), *The handbook of aging and cognition* (2d ed.), (pp. 689–703). Mahwah, NJ: Lawrence Erlbaum Associates.

SAMHSA (Substance Abuse and Mental Health Services Administration). Drug and Alcohol Services Information System. (2001). *Older adults in substance abuse treatment.* The DASIS Report, December 7. Retrieved: February 11, 2005, www.samhsa.gov/oas/2k1/olderTX/olderTX.htm.

SAMHSA (Substance Abuse and Mental Health Services Administration). (2003). *Results from the 2002 National Survey on Drug Use and Health: national Findings* (Office of Applied Studies, NHSDA Series H-22, DHHS Publication No. SMA 03–3836). Rockville, MD. Retrieved: June 2, 2004, www.oas.samhsa.gov/NHSDA/2k2NSDUH/Results/2k2results.htm#toc.

San Jose Community Connections. (2004). *Housing.* Retrieved: November 6, 2004, www.sjlibrary.org/research/web/community.htm.

Sanchez, C. D. (2001). Puerto Rican elderly. In L. K. Olson (Ed.), *Age through ethnic lenses: Caring for the elderly in a multicultural society* (pp. 86–94). London: Rowman & Littlefield.

Sanders, C. M. (1980–1981). Comparison of younger and older spouses in bereavement outcome. *Omega 11,* 217–32.

Sanders, G. F., & Trygstad, D. W. (1993). Strengths in the grandparent-grandchild relationship. *Activities, Adaptation and Aging, 17*(4), 43–53.

Sands, R., & Goldberg-Glen, R. S. (2000). Factors associated with stress among grandparents raising their grandchildren. *Family Relations, 49*(1), 97–105.

Sastry, M. L. (1992). Estimating the economic impacts of elderly migration: An input-output analysis. *Growth and Change, 23*(1), 54–79.

Satariano, W. A., Haight, T. J., & Tager, I. B. (2000). Reasons given by older people for limitation or avoidance of leisure time physical activity. *Journal of the American Geriatrics Society, 48*(5), 505–512.

Saunders, C. (1984). St. Christopher's Hospice. In E. S. Shneidman (Ed.), *Death: Current perspectives* (3d ed.). Palo Alto, CA: Mayfield.

Savishinsky, J. S. (2000). *Breaking the watch: The meanings of retirement in America.* Ithaca: Cornell University Press.

Schafer, R. (1999). *Housing America's elderly population.* W99-4. Cambridge, MA: Joint Center for Housing Studies, Harvard University. Retrieved: November 7, 2004, www.jchs.harvard.edu/publications/seniors/schafer_W99-4.pdf.

Schafer, R., & Harvard University. Joint Center for Housing Studies. (2000). *Housing America's seniors.* Cambridge, MA: Joint Center for Housing Studies of Harvard University.

Schaffer, C. L. (1993). The regulatory structure of home health care in the United States. *Journal of Cross-Cultural Gerontology, 8*(4), 405–416.

Schaie, K. W. (1990a). Intellectual development in adulthood. In J. E. Birren & K. W. Schaie (Eds.), *Handbook of the psychology of aging* (3d ed.), (pp. 291–309). San Diego: Academic Press.

Schaie, K. W. (1990b). The optimization of cognitive functioning in old age: Predictions based on cohort-sequential and longitudinal data. In P. B. Baltes & M. M. Baltes (Eds.), *Successful aging: Perspectives from the behavioral sciences* (pp. 94–117). Cambridge, England: Cambridge University Press.

Schaie, K. W. (1996). Intellectual development in adulthood. In J. E. Birren & K. W. Schaie (Eds.), *Handbook of the psychology of aging* (4th ed.), (pp. 266–286). San Diego: Academic Press.

Schaie, K. W., & Hofer, S. M. (2001). Longitudinal studies in aging research. In J. E. Birren, & K. W. Schaie (Eds.), *Handbook of the psychology of aging* (5th ed.), (pp. 53–77). San Diego: Academic Press.

Schaie, K. W., & Labouvie-Vief, G. (1974). Generational versus ontogenetic components of change in adult cognitive behavior: A fourteen-year cross-sequential study. *Developmental Psychology, 10,* 305–320.

Scheibel, A. B. (1996). Structural and functional changes in the aging brain. In J. E. Birren & K. W. Schaie (Eds.), *Handbook of the psychology of aging* (4th ed.), (pp. 105–128). San Diego: Academic Press.

Scheidt, R. J., & Norris-Baker, C. (2004). The general ecological model revisited: Evolution, current status, and continuing challenges. In H-W. Wahl, R. J. Scheidt, & P. G. Windley (Eds), *Annual review of Gerontology and Geriatrics, Vol. 23, 2003, Focus on aging in context: Socio-physical environments* (pp. 34–58). New York: Springer.

Scheonberg, N. E., & Rowles, G. D. (2002). Back to the future. In G. D. Rowles & N. E. Schoenberg (Eds.), *Qualitative gerontology* (2d ed.), (pp. 3–28). New York: Springer.

Schieber, F. (2003). Human factors and aging: Identifying and compensating for age-related deficits in sensory and cognitive function. In N. Charness, & K.W. Schaie (Eds.), *Impact of technology on successful aging* (pp. 42–77). New York: Springer.

Schlesinger, B. (1996). Sexless years or sex rediscovered. *Journal of Gerontological Social Work, 26*(1-2), 117–131.

Schless, D., & Preede, K. (2000). *Seniors housing statistical digest.* Washington, DC: American Seniors Housing Association (ASHA).

Schmidt, K. F. (1993). Science and Society: Old no more. *U.S. News and World Report,* March 8, 67–73.

Schmidt, R. M. (1994, Spring). Preventive healthcare for older adults: Societal and individual services. *Generations, 19,* 33–38.

Schneider, E. L. (1992, Fall/Winter). Biological theories of aging. *Generations,* 7–10.

Schoenbom, C. A., Adams, P. F., Barnes, P. M., Vickerie, J. L., & Schiller, J. S. (2004). *Health behaviors of adults: United States, 1999–2001. Vital Health Stat 10(219).* Hyattsville, MD: National Center for Health Statistics.

Scholz, W. D. (1993). New prospects at the third stage of life: Older people at university. *Journal of Educational Gerontology, 8*(1), 33–46.

Schone, B. S., & Weinick, R. M. (1998). Health-related behaviors and the benefits of marriage for elderly persons. *The Gerontologist 38*(5), 618–627.

Schonfeld, L., & Dupree, L. W. (1990). Older problem drinkers—long-term and late-life onset abusers: What triggers their drinking? *Aging, 361,* 5–8.

Schreck, M. (1992). Factors influencing participation in Senior Olympic competition. In R. Rothschadl (Ed.), *Proceedings of the Sandra A. Modisett symposium on aging and leisure in the 1990s* (pp. 55–63). Indianapolis, IN.

Schroots, J. J. F. (1995). Psychological models of aging. *Canadian Journal on Aging, 14*(1), 44–66.

Schulmerich, S. C. (2000). Public policy and the crisis in home care. *Caring, 19*(9), 42–45.

Schulz, J. H. (1988). *The economics of aging* (4th ed.). Dover, MA: Auburn House.

Schulz, J. H. (2001). *The economics of aging* (7th ed.). Westport, CT: Auburn House.

Schulz, J. H., & Myles, J. (1990). Old age pensions: A comparative perspective. In R. H. Binstock & L. K. George (Eds.), *Handbook of aging and the social sciences* (3d ed.), (pp. 398–414). San Diego: Academic Press.

Schulz, R., & Martire, L. M. (2004). Family caregiving of persons with dementia: Prevalence, health effects, and support strategies. *American Journal of Geriatric Psychiatry, 12*(3), 240–249.

Schulz-Hipp, P. L. (2001). Do spirituality and religiosity increase with age? In D. O. Moberg (Ed.), *Aging and spirituality* (pp. 85–98). New York: The Haworth Press.

Schur, C. L., & Feldman, J. (2001). *Running in place: How job characteristics, immigrant status, and family structure keep Latinos uninsured.* New York: Commonwealth Fund.

Schutz, A. (1967). The phenomenology of the social world. [Tr. by G. Walsh & F. Lehnert.]. Evanston, IL: Northwestern University Press.

Schweitzer, M. M. (Ed.) (1999). *American Indian grandmothers: Traditions and transitions.* Albuquerque: University of New Mexico Press.

Scott, D. M., & Wishy, B. (Eds.) (1982). *America's families: A documentary history.* New York: Harper & Row.

Scott, P. A. (1997). *Growing old in the early republic: Spiritual, social, and economic issues, 1790–1830.* Garland: New York.

Scott, T., Minichiello, V., & Browning, C. (1998). Secondary school students' knowledge of and attitudes towards older people: does an education intervention programme make a difference? *Ageing and Society, 18*(2), 167–183.

Scott-Webber, L., & Koebel, T. (2001). Life-span design in the near environment. In L. A. Pastalan, & B. Schwarz (Eds.), *Housing choices and well-being of older adult: Proper fit* (pp. 97–122). New York: Haworth.

Searle, M. S. (1987). *Leisure and aging in Manitoba: Executive summary.* A report to Manitoba Culture, Heritage, and Recreation. Faculty of Physical Education and Recreation Studies, University of Manitoba.

Searle, M. S., & Mahon, M. J. (1991). Leisure education in a day hospital: The effects of selected social-psychological variables among older adults. Paper presented at the 1990 National Recreation and Park Association Leisure Research Symposium. Baltimore, MD.

Seefeldt, C. (1987). The effects of preschoolers' visits to a nursing home. *The Gerontologist, 27,* 228–232.

Semla, T. P., Schwartz, A., Koch, H., & Nelson, C. (1993). Patterns of drug prescribing. In J. F. Van Nostrand, S. E. Furner, & R. Suzman (Eds.), *Health data on older Americans: United States, 1992* (pp. 187–193). Hyattsville, MD: National Center for Health Statistics.

Senior*resource*.com. (2004). *Housing choices.* Del Mar, CA. Retrieved: October 31, 2004, www.seniorresource.com/house.htm#echo.

Sennott-Miller, L. (1994). Research on aging in Latin America: Present status and future directions. *Journal of Cross-Cultural Gerontology, 9,* 87–97.

Serafini, M. W. (2002). AARP's new direction. *National Journal, 34*(1), 28–32.

Serow, W., Sly, D. F., & Wrigley, J. M. (1990). *Population aging in the United States.* New York: Greenwood Press.

Settersten, R. A. (2003). Propositions and controversies in life-course scholarship. In R. A. Settersten (Ed.), *Invitation to the life course: Toward new understandings of later life* (pp. 15–45). Amityville, NY: Baywood.

Seufert, R. L., & Carrozza, M. A. (2002). Test of Palmore's Facts on Aging Quizzes as alternate measures. *Journal of Aging Studies, 16*(3), 279–294.

Sex by schedule. (1992). *Psychology Today,* March/April, 16–17.

Shanas, E. (1967). Family help patterns and social class in three societies. *Journal of Marriage and the Family, 29,* 257–266.

Shanas, E. (1979). The family as a social support system in old age. *The Gerontologist, 19*(2), 169–174.

Shapiro, E. (1988). Hospital use by elderly Manitobans resulting from an injury. *Canadian Journal on Aging, 8,* 125–133.

Shapiro, E., & Roos, N. P. (1986). High users of hospital days. *Canadian Journal on Aging, 5,* 165–174.

Shedletsky, R., Fisher, R., & Nadon, G. (1982). Assessment of palliative care for Dying hospitalized elderly. *Canadian Journal on Aging, 1,* 11–15.

Shedlock, D. J., & Cornelius, S. W. (2003). Psychological approaches to wisdom and its development. In J. Demick & C. Andreoletti (Eds.), *Handbook of adult development* (pp. 153–167). New York: Kluwer Academic.

Sheehan, N. W. (1992). *Successful administration of senior housing.* Newbury Park, CA: Sage.

Sheehan, N. W., & Stelle, C. (1998). Mixed-population issue in state-subsidized elderly housing: Management problems posed by nonelderly and elderly tenants. *Journal of Aging and Social Policy, 10*(2), 29–48.

Sheehy, G. (1992). *The silent passage: Menopause.* New York: Random House.

Shenk, D., & Schmid, R. M. (2002). A picture is worth . . . : The use of photography in gerontological research. In G. D. Rowles & N. E. Schoenberg (Eds.), *Qualitative gerontology* (2d ed.), (pp. 241–262). New York: Springer.

Shenk, D., Moore, L., & Davis, B. Teaching an interdisciplinary distance education gerontology course: Benefits of diversity. *Educational Gerontology, 30*(3), 219–235.

Shephard, R. J. (1990). The scientific basis of exercise prescribing for the very old. *Journal of the American Geriatric Society, 38*(1), 62–70.

Shernoff, M. (1997). *Gay widowers: Life after death of a partner.* New York: Haworth.

Shibusawa, T., Lubben, J., & Kitano, H. H. L. (2001). Japanese American elderly. In L. K. Olson (Ed.), *Age through ethnic lenses: Caring for the elderly in a multicultural society* (pp. 32–44). London: Rowman & Littlefield.

Shields, G., King, W., Fulks, S., & Fallon, L. F. (2002). Determinants of perceived safety among the elderly: An exploratory study. *Journal of Gerontological Social Work, 38*(3), 73–83.

Shneidman, E.S. (1984). Malignancy: Dialogues with life-threatening illnesses. In E. S. Shneidman (Ed.), *Death: Current perspectives* (3d ed.). Palo Alto, CA: Mayfield.

Shomaker, D. (1990). Health care, cultural expectations and frail elderly Navajo grandmothers. *Journal of Cross-Cultural Gerontology, 5,* 21–34.

Signorielli, N. (2001). Aging on television: The picture in the nineties. *Generations, 25*(3), 34–38.

Silberman, S. L., Cantave Burton, C., & AARP, Knowledge Management. (2004). *AARP 2004 South Dakota Member Survey: Volunteerism.* Washington, DC: AARP, Knowledge Management.

Silveira, M. J., DiPiero, A., Gerrity, M. S., & Feudtner, C. (2000). Patients' knowledge of options at the end of life: Ignorance in the face of death. *Journal of the American Medical Association, 284*(19), 2483–2488.

Silverstein, M., & Long, J. D. (1998). Trajectories of grandparents' perceived solidarity with adult grandchildren: A growth curve analysis over 23 years. *Journal of Marriage and the Family, 60*(4), 912–923.

Simmons, L. W. (1960). Aging in preindustrial societies. In C. Tibbitts (Ed.), *Handbook of social gerontology.* Chicago: University of Chicago Press.

Simmons, L. W. (1970 [1945]). *The role of the aged in primitive society.* New Haven, CT: Yale University.

Simons, R. L. (1983–1984). Specificity and substitution in the social networks of the elderly. *International Journal of Aging and Human Development, 18,* 121–139.

Singer, B. H., & Ryff, C. D. (1999). Hierarchies of life histories and associated health risks. In N. D. Adler, B. S. McEwen, & M. Marmot (Eds.), *Socioeconomic Status in Industrialized Countries. Annals of the New York Academy of Sciences, 896,* 96–115.

Singleton, J. F., Forbes, W. F., & Agwani, N. (1993). Stability of activity across the lifespan. *Activities, Adaptation and Aging, 18*(1), 19–27.

Sit, M. (1992). With elders in mind: A home can be made more suitable. *Generations, 19*(2), 73–74.

Sizemore, M. T., & Coover, M. O. (1993). Integrating information about Hispanic elderly into undergraduate gerontology: A pilot field placement. *Gerontology and Geriatrics Education, 14*(2), 53–62.

Ska, B., & Nespoulous, J-L. (1988). Encoding strategies and recall performance of a complex figure by normal elderly subjects. *Canadian Journal on Aging, 7,* 408–416.

Skinner, J. H. (1992, Spring). Aging in place: The experience of African American and other minority elders. *Generations,* 49–51.

Smale, B. J. A., & Dupuis, S. L. (1993). The relationship between leisure activity participation and psychological well-being across the lifespan. *Journal of Applied Recreation Research, 18*(4), 281–300.

Smith, A. D. (1996). Memory. In J. E. Birren & K. W. Schaie (Eds.), *Handbook of the psychology of aging* (4th ed.), (pp. 236–250). San Diego: Academic Press.

Smith, D. G. (1992). *Paying for Medicare: The politics of reform.* New York: Aldine De Gruyter.

Smith, D. S. (1995). The demography of widowhood in preindustrial New Hampshire. In D. I. Kertzer, & P. Laslett (Eds.), *Aging in the past: Demography, society, and old age* (pp. 249–272). Berkeley: University of California Press.

Smith, D. 2003. *U. S. Census Bureau. The Older Population in the United States: March 2002, Current Population.* P20-546. Retrieved: January 17, 2004, www.census.gov/prod/2003pubs/p20-546.pdf.

Smith, L. (1992). The tyranny of America's old. *Fortune,* January 13, 68–72.

Smith, M. D. (1979). Portrayal of elders in magazine cartoons. *The Gerontologist, 19*(4), 408–412.

Smith, V., Ramesh, R., Gifford, K., Ellis, E., Wachino, V., Kaiser Commission on Medicaid and the Uninsured, Henry J. Kaiser Family Foundation. (2003). *States respond to fiscal pressure: State Medicaid spending growth and cost containment in fiscal years 2003 and 2004: Results from a 50-state survey.* Washington, DC: Henry J. Kaiser Family Foundation.

Smith, W. (2004a). Good life in the big city. *AARP Bulletin, 45*(6), 4+.

Smith, W. (2004b). The good life in the big city: Empty nesters join older urbanites where the lights are brighter. *AARP Bulletin Online.* Retrieved: November 6, 2004, www.aarp.org/bulletin/yourlife/Articles/a2004-05-26-goodlife.html.

Sobczak, J. (2002). Staying stronger longer. *Quality in Aging, 3*(2), 6–10.

Social Security Administration. (2005). *Full retirement age is increasing. Find your retirement age.* Retrieved: June 5, 2005, www.ssa.gov/retirechartred.htm.

Social Security Administration. (2004a). *Fact sheet Social Security: Social Security basic facts.* Washington, DC: Social Security Administration. Retrieved: September 4, 2004, www.ssa.gov/pressoffice/factsheets/basicfact-alt.htm.

Social Security Administration. (2004b). *Full retirement benefits.* Washington, DC: Social Security Administration. Retrieved: September 4, 2004, www.ssa.gov/retirement/1960.html.

Social Security Administration. (2004c). *Retirement and Medicare: Qualify and apply.* Washington, DC: Social Security Administration. Retrieved: September 4, 2004, www.ssa.gov/r&m2.htm.

Social Security Administration. (2004d). *Social Security's future—FAQs.* Washington, DC: Social Security Administration. Retrieved: September 4, 2004, www.ssa.gov/qa.htm.

Social Security Administration. (2004e). *Social Security online. Benefits planner. Frequently asked questions.* Retrieved: September 11, 2004, www.ssa.gov/planners/faqs.htm.

Social Security Administration. (2003a). *Facts and figures about Social Security.* Retrieved: September 5, 2004, www.ssa.gov/policy/docs/chartbooks/fast_facts/2003/ff2003.html#agedpop.

Social Security Administration. (2003b). *Social Security online: Electronic fact sheet: Update 2003.* SSA Publication No. 05-10003. Retrieved: September 4, 2004, www.ssa.gov/pubs/10003.html.

Social Security Administration. (2003c). *Social Security online: Trust fund data: Fiscal year trust fund operations.* Retrieved: September 4, 2004, www.ssa.gov/OACT/ProgData/fyOps.html.

Social Security Administration. (1997). *Social Security programs in the United States.* Washington, DC: Office of Research, Evaluation and Statistics. SSA Publication No. 13-11758.9 Retrieved: September 4, 2004, www.ssa.gov/policy/docs/progdesc/sspus/sspus.pdf.

Social Security and Medicare Board of Trustees. (2004). *Status of the Social Security and Medicare programs. A summary of the 2004 Annual Reports.* Retrieved: December 28, 2004, www.ssa.gov/OACT/TRSUM/trsummary.html.

Sohal, S. S., & Weindruch, R. (1996). Oxidative stress, caloric restriction, and aging. *Science, 273,* 59–63.

Sokolovsky, J. (2000). Living arrangements of older persons and family support in less developed countries. Paper presented at the Technical Meeting on Population Ageing and Living Arrangements of Older persons: Critical Issues and Policy Responses. New York: United Nations Secretariat. New York, February 8–10.

Sokolovsky, J. (1993, Spring/Summer). Images of aging: A cross-cultural perspective. *Generations,* 51–54.

Sokolovsky, J. (Ed.). (1990). *The cultural context of aging: Worldwide perspectives.* New York: Bergin & Garvey.

Somers, A. R., & Spears, N. L. (1992). *The continuing care retirement community: A significant option for long-term care?* New York: Springer.

Sotomayor, M., & Applewhite, S. R. (1988a). The Hispanic elderly and the extended multigenerational family. In S. R. Applewhite (Ed.), *Hispanic elderly in transition* (pp. 121–133). New York: Greenwood.

Sotomayor, M., & Randolph, S. (1988b). A preliminary review of caregiving issues and the Hispanic family. In M. Sotomayor & H. Curiel (Eds.), *Hispanic elderly: A cultural signature* (pp. 137–160). Edinburg, TX: Pan American University Press.

Spencer, R. L, & Hutchison, K. E. (1999). Alcohol, aging, and the stress response. *Alcohol Research & Health, 23*(4), 272–283.

Spillman, B. C., & Pezzin, L. E. (2000). Potential and active family caregivers: Changing networks and the sandwich generation. *Milbank Quarterly, 78*(3). Retrieved: November 25, 2004, www.milbank.org/quarterly/7803feat.html.

Spivack, M. S. (1992). Washington politicians who favor seniors—and those who don't. *New Choices for Retirement Living, 32*(7), 26–29.

Spraggins, R. (2003). *Women and men in the United States: March 2002. Population characteristics.* P20-544. Washington, DC: U.S. Census Bureau. Retrieved: September 5, 2004, www.census.gov/prod/2003pubs/p20-544.pdf.

Sprott, R. L., & Roth, G. S. (1992, Fall/Winter). Biomarkers of aging: Can we predict individual life span? *Generations,* 11–14.

St. Hill, H., & Edwards, N. Interndisciplinary gerontology education online: A developmental process model. *Gerontology and Geriatrics Education, 24*(4), 23–44.

St. John, P., & Man-Son-Hing, M. (2002). Requests for physician-assisted suicide in older persons: An approach. *Geriatrics Today, 5*(2), 81–83.

Stack, S., & Eshleman, J. R. (1998). Marital status and happiness: A 17-nation study. *Journal of Marriage and the Family, 60,* 527–536.

Stanford, E. P. (1990). Diverse African American aged. In Z. Harel, E. A. McKinney, & M. Williams (Eds.), *African American aged: Understanding diversity and service needs* (pp. 33–49). Newbury Park, CA: Sage.

Stanford, P. E., Happersett, C. J., Morton, D. J., Molgaard, C. A., & Peddecord, K. M. (1991). Early retirement and functional impairment from a multi-ethnic perspective. *Research on Aging, 13*(1), 5–38.

Staplin, L., Lococo. K. H., Stewart, J., & Decina, L. E. (1998). *Safe mobility for older people notebook.* Report No. DTNH22-96-C-05140. Washington, DC: U.S. Department of Transportation, National Highway Traffic Safety Administration.

Starr, B. D., & Weiner, M. B. (1981). *The Starr-Weiner report on sex & sexuality in the mature years.* New York: Stain and Day.

Statewide Resources Consultant. (2002). *California Caregiver Resource Centers' Uniform Database, 2001.* San Francisco, CA: Family Caregiver Alliance.

Statistics Canada. (2000a). Stress and well-being. *Health Reports,* 12(3). Catalogue No. 82-003. Retrieved: May 27, 2005, www.statcan.ca/english/freepub/82-003-XIE/art2.pdf.

Statistics Canada. (2000b). Stress and well-being. *Health Reports 12*(3). 21–32. Cat. No. 82-003-XIE Retrieved: November 23, 2003, www.statcan.ca/english/freepub/82-003-XIE/art1.pdf.

Stearns, S. C., & Partridge, L. (2001). The genetics of aging in Drosophila. In E. J. Masoro & S. N. Austad (Eds.), *Handbook of the biology of aging* (5th ed.), (pp. 353–368). San Diego: Academic Press.

Stern, L. (1993, February–March). Nothing ventured. *Modern Maturity,* 52–83.

Stevens-Long, J., & Michaud, G. (2003). Theory in adult development. In J. Demick & C. Andreoletti (Eds.), *Handbook of adult development* (pp. 3–22). New York: Kluwer Academic/Plenum.

Stich, S. (2000). Room for a housemate? *New Choices: Living Even Better After 50, 40*(8), 51–53.

Stoller, E. P., & Gibson, R. C. (1997). *Worlds of difference: Inequality in the aging experience* (2d ed.). Thousand Oaks, CA: Pine Forge Press.

Stoller, E. P., & Gibson, R. C. (2000). *Worlds of difference: Inequality in the aging experience* (3d ed.). Thousand Oaks, CA: Pine Forge Press.

Stone, L. O., Rosenthal, C. J., & Connidis, I. A. (1998). *Parent–child exchanges of supports and intergenerational equity.* Cat. No. 89-557-XPE. Ottawa: Ministry of Industry.

Stone, R. (1989). The feminization of poverty among the elderly. *Women's Studies Quarterly, 17*(1-2), 20–34.

Stone, R. (1995). Foreword. In R. A. Kane & J. D. Penrod (Eds.), *Family caregiving in an aging society* (pp. vii–ix). Thousand Oaks, CA: Sage.

Stone, R., Cafferata, G., & Sangl, J. (1987). Caregivers of the frail elderly: A national profile. *The Gerontologist, 27*(5), 612–626.

Strahan, G. W. (1994). *An overview of home health and hospice care patients: Preliminary data from the 1993 National Home and Hospice Care Survey.* Advance data from vital and health statistics, No. 256. Hyattsville, MD: National Center for Health Statistics.

Strain, L. A., & Blandford, A. A. (2003). Caregiving networks in later life: Does cognitive status make a difference? *Canadian Journal on Aging, 22*(3), 261–273.

Strain, L. A., Grabusic, C. C., Searle, M. S., & Dunn, N. J. (2002). Continuing and ceasing leisure activities in later life: a longitudinal study. *The Gerontologist, 42*(2), 217–223.

Strehler, B. (1977). *Time, cells and aging* (2d ed.). New York: Academic Press.

Streib, G. F. (1987). Retirement communities. In G. L. Maddox (Ed.), *The encyclopedia of aging* (pp. 581–583). New York: Springer.

Streisand, B. (1992, June 8). Never too old for games. *U.S. News and World Report,* 68–72.

Stuart-Hamilton, I., & Mahoney, B. (2003). Effect of aging awareness training on knowledge of and attitudes towards older adults. *Educational Gerontology, 29*(3), 251–260.

Stutts, J. C. (2003). The safety of older drivers: The U.S. perspective. In K. W. Schaie, H-W. Wahl, H. Mollenkopf, & F. Oswald, F. (Eds.), *Aging independently: Living arrangements and mobility* (pp. 192–204). New York: Springer.

Subcommittee on Institutional Program Guidelines. (1989). *Palliative care services. Health and Welfare Canada.* Cat. No. H39-32/1989E. Ottawa: Minister of Supply and Services.

Sung, K. (2000). Respect for elders: Myths and realities of East Asia. *Journal of Aging and Identity, 5*(4), 231–239.

Swedburg, R. B. (1992). Elderhostel: Lifelong learning and leisure education. In R. Rothschadl (Ed.), *Proceedings of the Sandra A. Modisett symposium on aging and leisure in the 1990s* (pp. 15–22). Indianapolis, IN.

Swinburn, B., & Sager, R. (2003). Promotion of exercise prescriptions in general practice for older populations. *Geriatrics and Aging, 6*(7), 20–23.

Szanto, K., Gildengers, A., Mulsant, B. H., Brown, G., Alexopoulos, G. S., & Grynolds, C. F. III. (2002). Identification of suicidal ideation and prevention of suicidal behaviour in the elderly. *Drugs and Aging, 19*(1), 11–24.

Szinovacz, M. (1982). Research on women's retirement. In M. Szinovacz (Ed.), *Women's retirement: Policy implications for recent research* (pp. 13–21). Newbury Park, CA: Sage.

Szinovacz, M. (1983). Beyond the hearth: Older women and retirement. In E. W. Markson (Ed.), *Older women: Issues and prospects.* Lexington, MA: D. C. Heath.

Szinovacz, M. E. (2003). Contexts and pathways: Retirement as institution, process, and experience. In G. A. Adams & T. A. Beehr (Eds.), *Retirement: Reasons, processes, and results* (pp. 6–52). New York: Springer.

Takamura, J. (2002). Social policy issues and concerns in a diverse aging society: Implication of increasing diversity. *Generations 26*(3), 33–38.

Talbott, M. M. (1998). Older widows' attitudes towards men and remarriage. *Journal of Aging Studies, 12*(4), 429–449.

Tammeveski, P. (2003). Making of national identity among older Estonians in the United States. *Journal of Aging Studies, 17*(4), 399–414.

Taylor, H. (1999, October 27). 3.7 million people over 55 not working now are ready, willing and able to work. *The Harris Poll #62.* Retrieved: February 12, 2005, www.harrisinteractive.com/harris_poll/index.asp?PID=19.

Taylor, M. A., & Doverspike, D. (2003). Retirement planning and preparation. In G. A. Adams & T. A. Beehr (Eds.), *Retirement: Reasons, processes, and results* (pp. 53–82). New York: Springer.

Taylor, R. J. (1993). Religion and religious observances. In J. S. Jackson, L. M. Chatters, & R. J. Taylor (Eds.), *Aging in African American America* (pp. 101–123). Newbury Park, CA: Sage.

Taylor, R. J., Keith, V. M., & Tucker, M. B. (1993). Gender, marital, familial, and friendship roles. In J. S.

Jackson, L. M. Chatters, & R. J. Taylor (Eds.), *Aging in African American America* (pp. 49–68). Newbury Park, CA: Sage.

Teague, M. L., & MacNeil, R. D. (1992). Delivery of leisure services to community-based older adults. In M. L. Teague & R. D. MacNeil (Eds.), *Aging and leisure: Vitality in later life* (2d ed.), (pp. 253–295). Dubuque, IA: Brown & Benchmark.

Thau, R., & Roszak, T. (2001). Are we heading for intergenerational war? *Across the Board, 38*(4), 70–78.

Theroux, P. (2003). *Dark star safari: Overland from Cairo to Capetown.* Boston: Houghton Mifflin.

Thomas, J. L., Sperry, L., & Yarbrough, M. S. (2000). Grandparents as parents: Research findings and policy recommendations. *Child Psychiatry and Human Development, 31*(1), 3–22.

Thomas, W. I., & Thomas, D. S. (1928). *The child in America: Behavior problems and programs.* New York: Knopf.

Thompson, M. E., & Forbes, W. F. (1990). The various definitions of biological aging. *Canadian Journal on Aging, 9,* 91–94.

Thomson, E. F., Minkler, M., & Driver, D. (2000). A profile of grandparents raising grandchildren In the United States. In C. B. Cox (Ed.), *To grandmother's house we go and stay* (pp. 20–33). New York: Springer.

Thornton, K. A., & Tuck, I. (2000). Promoting the mental health of elderly African Americans: A case illustration. *Archives of Psychiatric Nursing, 14*(4), 191–198.

Tierney, M. C., & Charles, J. (2002). The care and treatment of people with dementia and cognitive impairment: An update, in *Writings in gerontology: Mental health and aging* (pp. 97–112). Ottawa: National Advisory Council on Aging.

Tomita, S. K. (1994). The consideration of cultural factors in the research of elder mistreatment with an in-depth look at the Japanese. *Journal of Cross-Cultural Gerontology, 9,* 39–52.

Tornstam, L. (1999). Late-life transcendence: A new developmental perspective on aging. In L. E. Thomas & S. A. Eisenhandler (Eds.), *Religion, belief, and spirituality in late life* (pp. 178–202). New York: Springer.

Torres-Gil, F. (1990). Seniors react to the Medicare Catastrophic bill: Equity or selfishness? *Journal of Aging and Social Policy, 2*(1), 1–8.

Torres-Gil, F. M. (1987). Ethnic associations. In G. L. Maddox (Ed.), *The encyclopedia of aging* (pp. 227–229). New York: Springer.

Torres-Gil, F. M. (1992). *The new aging: Politics and change in America.* New York: Auburn House.

Tournier, P. (1972). *Learning to grow old.* London: SCM Press.

Townson, M. (1994). The social contract and seniors: Preparing for the 21st century. Ottawa: National Advisory Council on Aging.

Tran, T. V., Wright, R., & Chatters, L. (1991). Health, stress, psychological resources, and subjective well-being among older blacks. *Psychology and Aging, 6*(1), 100–108.

Tran, T. V., Ngo, D., & Sung, T.H. (2001). Caring for elderly Vietnamese Americans. In L. K. Olson (Ed.), *Age through ethnic lenses: Caring for the elderly in a multicultural society* (pp. 59–70). London: Rowman & Littlefield.

Troll, L. E., & Bengtson, V. L. (1992, Summer). The oldest-old in families: An intergenerational perspective. *Generations,* 39–44.

Trombley, J., Thomas, B., & Mosher-Ashley, P. (2003). Massage therapy for elder residents. *Nursing Homes Long Term Care Management, 52*(10), 92+.

Tsiantar, D., & Miller, A. (1991). Dipping into granny's wallet: Marketers woo seniors. *Newsweek,* April 1, 43.

Turnbull, C. (1962). *The forest people.* New York: Simon & Schuster.

Turvey, C. L., Conwell, Y., Jones, M. P., Phillips, C., Simonsick, E., Pearson, J. L., & Wallace. R. (2002). Risk factors for late-life suicide: A prospective, community-based study. *American Journal of Geriatric Psychiatry, 10*(4), 398–406.

U.S. Census Bureau. (1989). *Voting and registration in the election of November 1988.* Current Population Reports, Series P-20, No. 440. Washington, DC: U.S. Government Printing Office.

U.S. Census Bureau. (1991). *Statistical abstract of the United States, 1991.* Washington, DC: U.S. Government Printing Office.

U.S. Census Bureau. (1994). *Statistical abstract of the United States: 1994* (114th ed.). Washington, DC: U.S. Government Printing Office.

U.S. Census Bureau. (1995). *Population profile of the United States: 1995.* Current Population Reports, Series P23-189. Washington, DC: U.S. Government Printing Office.

U.S. Census Bureau. (1996). *65+ in the United States.* Current Population Reports, Special Studies, P23-190. Washington, DC: U.S. Government Printing Office. Retrieved: March 21, 2004, www.census.gov/prod/1/pop/p23-190/p23-190.html.

U.S. Census Bureau (2000a). *Census 2000 summary file 1; Population 65 years and over by age: 1990 and 2000; 1990 Census of population, general population characteristics, United States (1990 CP-1-1).* Retrieved: January 17, 2004, www.census.gov/prod/2001pubs/c2kbr01-10.pdf.

U.S. Census Bureau. (2000b). *DP-1. Profile of general demographic characteristics: 2000.* Data Set: Census 2000 Summary File 2 (SF 2) 100-Percent Data. Geographic Area: United States. Retrieved: January 19, 2004, http://factfinder.census.gov/servlet/QTTable?_bm=y&-geo_id=D&-qr_name=DEC_2000_SF2_U_DP1&-ds_name=D&-_lang=en.

U.S. Census Bureau. (2000c). *Social insurance and human services. Statistical abstract of the United States: 2000.* Washington, DC: U.S. Census Bureau. Retrieved: September 11, 2004, www.census.gov/prod/2001pubs/statab/sec12.pdf.

U.S. Census Bureau. (2000d). *Voting and registration in the election of November 1998.* Detailed tables for current population report, P20-523. Washington, DC: U.S. Census Bureau. Retrieved: December 6, 2004, www.census.gov/population/socdemo/voting/cps1998/tab01.txt; www.census.gov/population/socdemo/voting/cps1998/tab02.txt; www.census.gov/population/socdemo/voting/cps1998/tab05.txt.

U.S. Census Bureau. (2001). *Poverty in the United States: 2000.* Retrieved: June 10, 2002, www.census.gov/prod/2001pubs/p60-214.pdf.

U.S. Census Bureau. (2002a). *Statistical abstract of the United States: 2002.* Retrieved: April 26, 2004, www.census.gov/prod/2004pubs/03statab/pop.pdf.

U.S. Census Bureau. (2002b). *Statistical abstract of the United States.* Washington, DC: U.S. Government Printing Office. Retrieved: March 21, 2004, www.census.gov/prod/www/statistical-abstract-02.html.

U.S. Census Bureau. (2003a). *America's families and living arrangements: 2003. Marital status of people 15 years and over, by age, sex, personal earnings, race, and Hispanic origin, 2003.* Retrieved: October 2, 2004, www.census.gov/population/www/socdemo/hh-fam/cps2003.html.

U.S. Census Bureau. (2003b). *Participation in adult education: 1994–1995 and 1998–1999. Statistical abstract of the United States.* Retrieved: November 24, 2004, www.census.gov/prod/2004pubs/03statab/educ.pdf.

U.S. Census Bureau. (2003c). *Population reports, P20-548.* Retrieved: March 27, 2004, www.census.gov/prod/2003pubs/p20-548.pdf.

U.S. Census Bureau. (2003d). *Statistical abstract of the United States. Income, expenditures, and wealth.* No.697. Retrieved: July 13, 2004, www.census.gov/prod/2004pubs/03statab/income.pdf.

U.S. Census Bureau. (2003e). *Statistical abstract of the United States.* Population. No. 13. Retrieved: July 13, 2004, www.census.gov/prod/2004pubs/03statab/pop.pdf.

U.S. Census Bureau. (2003f). *Statistical abstract of the United States: 2003.* Retrieved: January 2, 2005, www.census.gov/prod/2004pubs/03statab/educ.pdf.

U.S. Census Bureau. (2004a). *National population projections.* Summary files. (NP-T4) projections of the total resident population by 5-year age groups, race, and Latino origin with special age categories: Middle series, 1999 to 2100. Retrieved: July 13, 2004, www.census.gov/population/www/projections/natsum-T3.html.

U.S. Census Bureau. (2004b). *Statistical abstract of the United States.* Table 37. Persons 65 years old and over—characteristics by sex: 1990 to 2002.

U.S. Department of Health and Human Services, National Institute on Aging (NIA). (1993) (June 17). *Health and retirement study.* Press release. Washington, DC: NIA.

U.S. Department of Health and Human Services. (1994). *The Medicare 1994 Handbook.* Baltimore, MD: Author.

U.S. Department of Health and Human Services. (2003). *Summary health statistics for the U.S. population: National health interveiw survey, 2001.* Vital and health statistics. Series 10, Number 217.

U.S. Department of Health and Human Services, Centers for Disease Control and Prevention. (2004). *The burden of chronic diseases and their risk factors: National and state perspectives.* Washington, DC: U.S. Government Printing Office.

U.S. Department of Health and Human Services, Social Security Administration, Office of Research and Statistics. (1993). Social security programs in the United States. *Social Security Bulletin, 56*(4). Washington, DC: U.S. Government Printing Office.

U.S. Department of Health and Human Services, Social Security Administration, Office of Research and Statistics. (1994). *Fast facts and figures about Social Security.* Washington, DC: U.S. Government Printing Office.

U.S. Department of Labor. (2000, November 14). Working group report on phased retirement. Retrieved: February 11, 2005, www.dol.gov/pwba/adcoun/phasedr1.htm.

U.S. Department of Labor. (2004). *Women and retirement savings.* Washington, DC: U.S. Printing Government Office.

U.S. Department of Labor Women's Bureau. (2004). *Statistics and data.* Washington, DC. Retrieved: September 17, 2004, www.dol.gov/wb/stats/main.htm.

U.S. Department of Labor, Bureau of Labor Statistics. (1982). *The female/male earnings gap: A review of employment and earnings issues* (Report No. 673). Washington, DC: Author.

U.S. Department of Labor, Bureau of Labor Statistics. (1995, January). *Employment and Earnings 42(1).* Washington, DC: U.S. Government Printing Office.

U.S. Department of Labor, Bureau of Labor Statistics. (2002, August). *Worker displacement, 1999–2001.* News, USDL 02-483. Washington, DC: U.S. Government Printing Office.

U. S. Department of Labor Employee Benefits Security Administration. (2004). Retrieved: September 17, 2004, www.dol.gov/ebsa/publications/women.html.

U.S. General Accounting Office. (1994). *Long-term care reform: States' views on key elements of well-designed programs for the elderly* (Report GAO/HEHS-94-227). Washington, DC: Author.

U.S. Senate Special Committee on Aging. (1986). *Aging America: Trends and projections* (1985–1986 ed.). Washington, DC: U.S. Government Printing Office.

U.S. Senate Special Committee on Aging, the American Association of Retired Persons, the Federal Council on the Aging, & the U.S. Administration on Aging. (1991). *Aging America: Trends and projections.* Washington, DC: Author.

United Nations. (2002a). *World population aging 1950–2050.* Retrieved: January 19, 2004, www.un.org/esa/population/publications/worldageing19502050/pdf/002mored.pdf.*

United Nations. (2002b). *World population aging: 1950–2050.* Department of Economic and Social Affairs. Population Division. Retrieved: December 23, 2004, www.un.org/esa/population/publications/worldageing19502050/index.htm.

United Seniors Health Cooperative. (1991). *Long-term care: A dollar and sense guide.* Washington, DC: Author.

United Seniors Health Council (A Program of the National Council on the Aging). (2004). *Private long-term care insurance: To buy or not to buy?* Retrieved: October 3, 2004, www.ncoa.org/attachments/LTC.pdf.

University of North Dakota. School of Medicine and Health Sciences. Center for Rural Health. (2003). *National family caregiver support program: North Dakota's American Indian caregivers.* Grand Forks, ND: Center for Rural Health, University of North Dakota, School of Medicine and Health Sciences.

Unreported crime: The secret shame of the very old. (1994, July/August). *Aging Today,* 4.

Valdez, C. A. (2000). *A profile of Latino elders.* HORIZONS Project.

van den Hoonaard, D. K. (1994). Paradise lost: Widowhood in a Florida retirement community. *Journal of Aging Studies, 8*(2), 121–132.

van den Hoonaard, D. K. (1997). Identity foreclosure: Women's experiences of widowhood as expressed in autobiographical accounts. *Ageing and Society 17*(5), 533–551.

van den Hoonaard, D. K. (1999). No regrets: Widows' stories about the last days of their husbands' lives. *Journal of Aging Studies, 13*(1), 59–72.

Van der Veen, R. (1990). Third age or inter-age universities? *Journal of Educational Gerontology, 5*(2), 96–105.

Van Ellett, T. (1993). Social health maintenance organizations: An American experiment. *Aging International, 20*(2), 39–41.

Vesperi, M. D. (2002). Seeing the unseen: Literary interpretation in qualitative gerontology. In G. D. Rowles & N. E. Schoenberg (Eds.), *Qualitative gerontology* (2d ed.), (pp. 263–278). New York: Springer.

Vierck, E. (2002). *Growing old in America.* Farmington, MI: Gale Group, Thomson Learning.

Vijg, J. (2000). Somatic mutations and aging: A re-evaluation. *Mutation Research, 447,* 117–135.

Villa, V. M., & Aranda, M. P. (2000). Demographic, economic, and health profile of older Latinos: Implications for health and long-term care policy and the Latino family. *Journal of Health and Human Services Administration, 23*(2), 161–180.

Vinick, B. H., & Ekerdt, D. J. (1992). Couples view retirement activities: Expectation versus experience. In M. Szinovacz, D. J. Ekerdt, & B. H. Vinick (Eds.), *Families in retirement* (pp. 129–144). Newbury Park, CA: Sage.

Vintners, H. V. (2001). Aging and the human nervous system. In J. E. Birren & K. W. Schaie (Eds.), *Handbook of the psychology of aging* (5th ed.), (pp. 135–160). San Diego: Academic Press.

Vinton, L. (1992). Battered women's shelters and older women: The Florida experience. *Journal of Family Violence, 7*(1), 63–72.

Vinton, L. (1999). Working with abused older women from a feminist perspective. *Journal of Women and Aging, 11*(2-3), 85–100.

Vita, A. J., Terry, R. B., Hubert, H. B., & Fries, J. F. (1998). Aging, health risks, and cumulative disability. *New England Journal of Medicine, 338,* 1035–1041.

von Zglinicki, T., Nilsson, E., Docke, W. D., & Brunk, T. T. (1995). Lipofuscin accumulation and aging of fibroblasts. *Gerontology, 41*(Suppl.2), 95–108.

Wagenaar, D. B., Mickus, M. A., & Wilson, J. (2001). Alcoholism in late life: Challenges and complexities. *Psychiatric Annals, 31*(11), 665–672.

Wagner, D. L. (1991). Eldercare: A workplace issue. In B. B. Hess & E. W. Markson (Eds.), *Growing old in America* (4th ed.), (pp. 377–387). New Brunswick, NJ: Transaction.

Wagner, D. L. (1995). Senior Center research in America: An overview of what we know. In D. Shollenberger (Ed.), *Senior centers in America: A blueprint for the future.* Washington, DC: National Council on the Aging and National Eldercare Institute on Multipurpose Senior Centers and Community Focal Points.

Wagner, D. L. (2003). *Workplace programs for family caregivers: Good business and good practice.* Retrieved: November 25, 2004, www.caregiver.org/caregiver/jsp/content/pdfs/op_2003_workplace_programs.pdf.

Wagner, L. S., & Wagner, T. H. (2003). Effect of age on the use of health and self-care information: Confronting the stereotype. *The Gerontologist 43*(3), 318–324.

Wagnild, G. (2001). Growing old at home. In L. A. Pastalan & B. Schwarz (Eds.), *Housing choices and well-being of older adult: Proper fit* (pp. 71–84). New York: Haworth.

Waldrop, D. P., & Weber, J. A. (2001). From grandparent to caregiver: The stress and satisfaction of raising grandchildren. *Families in Society 82*(5), 361–472.

Walford, R. L. (1983). *Maximum life span.* New York: W. W. Norton.

Walker, A. (1991). The relationship between the family and the state in the care of older people. *Canadian Journal on Aging, 10,* 94–112.

Walker, A. (1996). Intergenerational relations and the provision of welfare. In A. Walker (Ed.), *The new generational contract: Intergenerational relations, old age and welfare* (pp. 10–36). London: UCL Press.

Walker, B. L., & Ephross, P. H. (1999). Knowledge and attitudes toward sexuality of a group of elderly. *Journal of Gerontological Social Work, 31*(1-2), 85–107.

Walker, E. (2002). *The needs of Indian elders: A hearing by the Senate Committee on Indian Affairs.* Retrieved: July 6, 2004, www.nicoa.org/policy_walker.html.

Wallace, S. P. (1990a). The no-care zone: Availability, accessibility, and acceptability in community-based long-term care. *The Gerontologist, 30*(2), 254–261.

Wallace, S. P. (1990b). Political economy of health care for elderly blacks. *International Journal of Health Services, 20*(4), 664–680.

Wallace, S. P., & Williamson, J. B. (1992). *Senior movement: Reference and resources.* New York: G. K. Hall and Maxwell Macmillan.

Wallace, S. P., Williamson, J. B., Lung, R. G., & Powell, L. A. (1991). A lamb in wolf's clothing? The reality of senior power and social policy. In M. Minkler & C. L. Estes (Eds.), *Critical perspectives on aging: The political and moral economy of growing old* (pp. 95–114). Amityville, NY: Baywood.

Wallerstein, I. (1979). *The capitalist world-economy.* Cambridge, England: Cambridge University Press.

Walls, C. T. (1992, Summer). The role of church and family support in the lives of older African Americans. *Generations,* 33–36.

Walters, W. H. (2002). Place characteristics and later-life migration. *Research on Aging, 24*(2), 243–277.

Walton, D. N., & Fleming, W. H. (1980). Responsibility for the discontinuation of treatment. *Essence 4,* 57–61.

Wang, D. (2004). Service delivery and research considerations for the 85+ population. *Journal of Gerontological Social Work, 43*(1), 5–17.

Wang, E., Autexier, C., & Chen, E. (2001). Apoptosis and aging. In E. J. Masoro & S. N. Austad (Eds.), *Handbook of the biology of aging* (5th ed.), (pp. 246–266). San Diego: Academic Press.

Wapner, S., & Demick, J. (2003). Adult development. In J. Demick & C. Andreotti (Eds), *Handbook of adult development* (pp. 63–83). New York: Kluwer.

Ward-Griffin, C. (2002). Boundaries and connections between formal and informal caregivers. *Canadian Journal on Aging, 21*(2), 205–16.

Warren, C. A. B. (2002). Aging and identity in premodern times. In D. L. Infeld (Ed.), *Disciplinary approaches to aging, Vol. 4, Anthropology of aging* (pp. 73–97). New York: Routledge.

Warshaw, G. A., & Bragg, E. J. (2003). Training of geriatricians in the United States: Three decades of progress. *Journal of the American Geriatrics Society, 51*(7, Suppl.), S338–S345.

Watson, C., & Hall, S. E. (2001). Older people and the social determinants of health. *Australian Journal on Ageing, 20*(3), 23–26.

Watson, W. H., & Maxwell, R. J. (Eds.). (1977). *Human aging and dying: A study in sociocultural gerontology.* New York: St. Martin's Press.

Wayne State University. (1994). Survey results. *Chinishnaabe Mzinhigan (Elder's paper),* 1, 4–6.

Weaver, D. A. (1994). Work and retirement decisions of older women: A literature review. *Social Security Bulletin, 57*(1), 3–24.

Weber, M. (1905/1955). *The Protestant ethic and the spirit of capitalism.* New York: Charles Scribner's Sons.

Weeks, D. J. (1994). Review of loneliness concepts, with particular reference to old age. *International Journal of Geriatric Psychiatry, 9,* 345–355.

Weg, R. B. (1983a). Introduction: Beyond intercourse and orgasm. In R. B. Weg (Ed.), *Sexuality in the later years: Roles and behavior* (pp. 1–10). New York: Academic Press.

Weg, R. B. (1983b). The physiological perspective. In R. B. Weg (Ed.), *Sexuality in the later years: Roles and behavior* (pp. 39–80). New York: Academic Press.

Weibel-Orlando, J. (1990). Grandparenting styles: Native American perspectives. In J. Sokolovsky (Ed.), *The cultural context of aging: Worldwide perspectives* (pp. 109–125). New York: Bergin & Garvey.

Weindruch, R., & Walford, R. L. (1988). *The retardation of aging and disease by dietary restriction.* Springfield, IL: Charles C. Thompson.

Weinreich, D. M. (2004). Interdisciplinary teams, mentorship and intergenerational service-learning. *Educational Gerontology, 30*(2), 143–157.

Weinstein, M. H. (1988). Changing picture in retiree economics. *Statistical Bulletin, 69*(3), 2–7.

Weiss, R. S. (Ed.). (1973). *Loneliness: The experience of emotional and social isolation.* Cambridge, MA: MIT Press.

Weissert, W. G., & Hedrick, S. C. (1994). Lessons learned from research on effects of community-based long-term care. *Journal of the American Geriatrics Society, 42*(3), 348–353.

Weitzen, S., Teno, J. M., Fennell, M., & Mor, V. (2003). Factors associated with site of death: A national study of where people die. *Medical Care, 41*(2), 323–335.

Welford, A. T. (1993). Work capacity across the adult years. In R. Kastenbaum (Ed.), *Encyclopedia of adult development* (pp. 541–553). Phoenix, AZ: Oryx.

Wendt, P. F., & Peterson, D. A. (1992). Transition in use of human resources in the field of aging. *Journal of Aging and Social Policy, 4*(1–2), 107–123.

Wenger, N. S., Phillips, R. S., Teno, J. M., Oye, R. K., Dawson, N. V., Liu, H., Califf, R., Layde, P., Hakin, R., & Lynn, J. (2000). Physician understanding of patient resuscitation preferences: insights and clinical implications. *Journal of the American Geriatrics Society, 48*(5, Suppl.), S44–S51.

Wetle, T. (1993). Mental health and managed care for the elderly: Issues and options. *Generations, 17*(1), 69–72.

Wheeler, J. R. C. (2003). Can a disease self-management program reduce health care costs? The case of older women with heart disease. *Medical Care, 41*(6), 706–715.

White, K. (1993). How the mind ages. *Psychology Today, 26*(6), 38–42, 80.

White, M. (1987). Case management. In G. L. Maddox (Ed.), *The encyclopedia of aging* (pp. 92–96). New York: Springer.

Whitehouse, P. J., Bendezu, E., Fallcreek, S., & Whitehouse, C. (2000). Intergenerational community schools: a new practice for a new time. *Educational Gerontology, 26*(8), 761–770.

White-Means, S. I. (1993). Informal home care for frail black elderly. *Journal of Applied Gerontology, 12*(1), 18–33.

Whitfield, C. (2001). Benign or malign? Media stereotyping. *Nursing Older People, 13*(6), 10–13

Wiener, J. M., & Harris, K. M. (1990, Fall). Myths & realities: Why most of what everybody knows about long-term care is wrong. *The Brookings Review,* 29–34.

Wilbur, K. H. (2004). *Future shock: The effects of the demographic imperative for jobs in aging.* Retrieved: December 11, 2004, www.asaging.org/am/cia2/jobs.html.

Wilcox, S. (2002). Physical activity in older women of color. *Topics in Geriatric Rehabilitation, 18*(1), 21–33.

Wilcox, S., & King, A. C. (2004). Effects of life events and interpersonal loss on exercise adherence in older adults. *Journal of Aging and Physical Activity, 12*(2), 117–130.

Williams, C. D., Lewis-Jack, O., Johnson, K., & Adams-Campbell, L, (2001). Environmental influences, employment status, and religious activity predict current cigarette smoking in the elderly. *Addictive Behaviors, 26*(2), 297–301.

Williams, D. R., & Wilson, C. M. (2001). Race, ethnicity, and aging. In R. H. Binstock & L. K. George (Eds.), *Handbook of aging and the social sciences* (pp. 160–178). San Diego: Academic Press.

Williams, E. (2003). *Opportunities in gerontology and aging services careers.* (Rev. ed). Chicago: VGM Career Books.

Williams, T. F. (1992, Fall/Winter). Aging versus disease. Which changes seen with age are the result of "biological aging"? *Generations,* 21–25.

Williamson, J. B., Evans, L., Powell, L. A., & Hesse-Biber, S. (1982). *The politics of aging: Power and policy.* Springfield, IL: Charles C. Thomas.

Willis, S. L. (1996). Everyday problem solving. In J. E. Birren & K. W. Schaie (Eds.), *Handbook of the psychology of aging* (4th ed.), (pp. 287–307). San Diego: Academic Press.

Wilmoth, J. M. (2001). Living arrangements among older immigrants in the United States. *The Gerontologist, 41*(2), 228–238.

Wilson, L. B., Nippes, J. K., Simson, S., & Mahovich, P. (1993). Status of employee caregiver benefits. *Employee Benefits Journal, 18*(1), 10–12.

Winkler, M. G. (1992). Walking to the stars. In T. R. Cole, D. D. Van Tassel, & R. Kastenbaum (Eds.), *Handbook of the humanities and aging* (pp. 258–284). New York: Springer.

Wiseman, R. R., & Roseman, C. C. (1979). A typology of elderly migration based on the decision-making process. *Economic Geography, 55,* 324–337.

Wisensale, S. K. (1993). Generational equity. In R. Kastenbaum (Ed.), *Encyclopedia of adult development* (pp. 175–180). Phoenix, AZ: Oryx.

Wister, A. V., & Strain, L. A. (1986). Social support and well-being: A comparison of older widows and widowers. Paper presented at the 21st annual meeting of the Canadian Sociology and Anthropology Association, Winnipeg, Manitoba.

Wolf, R. S. (2001). Support groups for older victims of domestic violence. *Journal of Women and Aging, 13*(4), 71–83.

Wolf, R. S., & Pillemer, K. A. (1989). *Helping elderly victims: The reality of elder abuse.* New York: Columbia University Press.

Women's Institute for a Secure Retirement (WISER). (2000). *Instead of golden years, America's minority women face bleak retirement in poverty, new report finds.* Retrieved: September 11, 2004, www.wiser.heinz.org/prminorityretirement.html.

Wong, R. (2002). *Migration and socioeconomic conditions of older adults.* Demos: carta demografica sobre Mexico (DEMOS: A demographic letter concerning Mexico), 14. Retrieved: September 18, 2004, www.ssc.upenn.edu/mbas/Papers/3.pdf.

Wood, J. B., & Estes, C. L. (1990). Impact of DRGs on community-based service providers: Implications for the elderly. *American Journal of Public Health, 80*(7), 840–843.

Woodruff, D. S., & Birren, J. E. (Eds.). (1975). *Aging: Scientific perspectives and social issues.* New York: Van Nostrand.

Woodruff-Pak, D. S. (1989). Aging and intelligence: Changing perspectives in the twentieth century. *Journal of Aging Studies, 3,* 91–118.

World Health Organization/International Network for the Prevention of Elder Abuse. (2002). *Missing voices: Views of older persons on elder abuse.* Geneva, Switzerland: World Health Organization.

Wortman, C. B., & Silver, R. C. (1990). Successful mastery of bereavement and widowhood: A life-course perspective. In P. B. Baltes (Ed.), *Successful aging: Perspectives from the behavioral sciences* (pp. 225–264). Cambridge, England: Cambridge University Press.

Wu, K. (2003). *Income and poverty of older Americans in 2001: A chartbook.* Washington, DC: American Association of Retired Persons. Retrieved: September 6, 2004, http://research.aarp.org/econ/ip_cb2001.pdf.

Wu, M-T. (2000). Factors that influence the participation of senior citizens in recreational and leisure activities. Ann Arbor, MI: UMI Dissertation Services, ProQuest Information and Learning.

Wu, Z. (1995). Remarriage after widowhood: A marital history study of older Canadians. *Canadian Journal on Aging, 14*(4), 719–36.

Wykle, M., & Kaskel, B. (1994). Increasing the longevity of minority older adults through improved health status. In *Minority elders: Five goals toward building a public policy base* (2d ed.), (pp. 32–39). Washington, DC: Gerontological Society of America.

Yahnke, R. E. (2000). Intergeneration and regeneration: The meaning of old age in films and videos. In T. R. Cole, R. Kastenbaum, & R. E. Ray (Eds.), *Handbook of the humanities and aging* (2d ed.), (pp. 293–323). New York: Springer.

Yankelovich, D., & Vance, C. R. (2001). Final request. *American Demographics, 23*(4), 22.

Yee, D. L. (1999). Preventing chronic illness and disability: Asian Americans. In M. L. Wykle & A. B. Ford (Eds.), *Serving minority elders in the 21st century* (pp. 37–50). New York: Springer.

Yeo, G. (1991). Ethnogeriatric education: Need and content. *Journal of Cross-Cultural Gerontology, 6,* 229–241.

Young, R. F. (1994, Spring). Older people as consumers of health promotion recommendations. *Generations, 19,* 69–73.

Yu, B. P., Masoro, E. J., & McMahan, A. (1985). Nutritional influences on aging of Fischer 344 rats: I. Physical, metabolic, and longevity characteristics. *Journal of Gerontology, 40,* 657–670.

Zacks, R. T., Hasher, L., & Li, K. Z. H. (2000). Human memory. In F. I. M. Craik & T. A. Salthouse (Eds.), *The handbook of aging and cognition,* (2d ed.), (pp. 293–357). Mahwah, NJ: Lawrence Erlbaum Associates.

Zarit, S. H., Femia, E. E., Watson, J., Rice-Oeschger, L., & Kakos, B. (2004). Memory club: A group intervention for people with early-stage dementia and their care partners. *The Gerontologist, 44*(2), 262–269.

Zawadski, R. T., & Eng, C. (1988). Case management in capitated long term care. *Health Care Financing Review,* Annual Supplement: 75–81.

Zedlewski, S. R., Barnes, R. O., Burt, M. R., McBride, T. D., & Meyer, J. A. (1990). *The needs of the elderly in the 21st century.* Washington, DC: Urban Institute.

Zeiss, A., & Kasl-Godley, J. (2001). Sexuality in older adults' relationships. *Generations, 25*(2), 18–25.

Zhang, A. (2001). China faces the challenge of an aging society. *Beijing Review,* July 19, 12–15.

Zimmerman, L., Mitchell, B., Wister, A., & Gutman, G. (2000). Unanticipated consequences: A comparison of expected and actual retirement timing among older women. *Journal of Women and Aging, 12*(1-2), 109–128.

Zisook, S., & Schuchter, S. R. (1991a). Depression through the first year after the death of a spouse. *American Journal of Psychiatry, 148*(10), 1346–1352.

Zisook, S., & Schuchter, S. R. (1991b). Early psychological reaction to the stress of widowhood. *Psychiatry, 54*(4), 320–333.

Zopf, P. E. (1986). *America's older population.* Houston, TX: Cap and Gown Press.

Zsembik, B. A., & Singer, A. (1990). The problem of defining retirement among minorities: The Mexican Americans. *The Gerontologist, 30*(6), 749–757.

INDEX

D

I

PHOTO CREDITS

Page 1: Alon ReiningerWoodfin Camp & Associates; p. 8L: Bruce Byers; p. 25: Bob Daemmrich/Stock Boston; p. 33: © Deidre Scherer, 1996; p. 52: Taxi/Getty Images; p. 63: Courtesy Elias S. Cohen; p. 72: James T. Sykes; p. 76: Taxi/Getty Images; p. 89: © Paul Kleyman/Aging Today; p. 94: Will Van Overbeek; p. 98: AP/Wide World Photos; p. 123: © 2001 Don Frazier; p. 127: Frank Fournier/Contact Press; p. 128: Photodisc/Getty Images; p. 131: Stockbyte; p. 144: Copyright Jeffrey M. Levine 2004; p. 149: Sally Trussler, Brunel University; p. 163: David Young-Wolff/PhotoEdit, Inc.; p. 181: Steve Zorc; p. 186: Michael Newman/PhotoEdit, Inc.; p. 196: Spike & Ethel/Index Stock Imagery; p. 216: Rosalie Winard; p. 220: David Wells/The Image Works; p. 227: Taxi/Getty Images; p. 240: Mitch Wajanarowicz/The Image Works; p. 242: Bob Walmmrich/The Image Works; p. 255: Stockbyte; p. 260: Courtesy of Dr. Edith Irby Jones; p. 282: Stone Allstock/Getty Images; p. 287: Marianne Gontarz York; p. 299: Voisin/Photo Researchers, Inc.; pp. 314, 322BL, 338, 356, 366, and 377: Marianne Gontarz York; pp. 392, 397: AP/Wide World Photos; p. 398: Susan Lapides/Design Conceptions; p. 413: AP/Wide World Photos; p. 419: UPI/Bettman/Corbis; p. 424: Marianne Gontarz York; p. 429: Joel Gordon; p. 432: Taxi/Getty Images.